MAKING NORMAL
social regulation in canada

Edited by
DEBORAH BROCK

Australia   Canada   Mexico   Singapore   Spain   United Kingdom   United States

Making Normal:
Social Regulation in Canada
Deborah Brock

Editorial Director and Publisher:
Evelyn Veitch

Executive Editor:
Joanna Cotton

Acquisitions Editor:
Brad Lambertus

Marketing Manager:
Lenore Taylor

Developmental Editor:
Glen Herbert

Production Editor:
Carrie Withers

Production Coordinator:
Helen Locsin

Copy Editor and Proofreader:
Karen Hunter

Creative Director:
Angela Cluer

Interior Design Modifications:
Brenda Barrett

Cover Image and Design:
Faith

Compositor:
Brenda Prangley

Indexer:
Belle Wong

Printer:
Transcontinental

COPYRIGHT © 2003 by Nelson Thomson Learning, a division of Thomson Canada Limited. Nelson Thomson Learning is a registered trademark used herein under license.

Printed and bound in Canada
1 2 3 4 06 05 04 03

For more information contact Nelson, 1120 Birchmount Road, Scarborough, Ontario, M1K 5G4. Or you can visit our internet site at http//www.nelson.com

ALL RIGHTS RESERVED. No part of this work covered by the copyright hereon may be reproduced, transcribed, or used in any form or by any means—graphic, electronic, or mechanical, including photocopying, recording, taping, web distribution or information storage or retrieval systems—without the written permission of the publisher.

For permission to use material from this text or product, contact us by
Tel 1-100-730-2214
Fax 1-800-730-2215
www.thomsonrights.com

Every effort has been made to trace ownership of all copyrighted material and to secure permission from copyright holders. In the event of any question arising as to the use of any material, we will be pleased to make the necessary corrections in future printings.

National Library of Canada Cataloguing in Publication Data

Making normal: social regulation in Canada/edited by Deborah Brock

Includes bibliographical references and index.
ISBN: 0-7747-3740-9

1. Social control—Canada.
2. Deviant behavior—Canada.
3. Canada—Social policy—Moral and ethical aspects.
4. Canada—Moral conditions.
 I. Brock, Deborah R. (Deborah Rose), 1956–

HM811.M34 2003   303.3'3'0971
C2002-904592-4

For Philip Corrigan
Teacher, Scholar

Table of Contents

Preface vii

Introduction ix

Part 1: Doing Historical Sociology 1

1. Moral Reform, Discipline, and Normalization: Juvenile Delinquency and
   Rehabilitation in Ontario *Paula Maurutto, University of Toronto* 4
2. An Important Archive of Usefulness: Regulating "the Parent" at School
   Kari Dehli, OISE, University of Toronto 18
3. Towards Theorising the Connections Between Governmentality, Imperialism, Race,
   and Citizenship: Indian Migrants and Racialisation of Canadian Citizenship
   Enkashi Dua, York University 40
4. Regulating (Ab)Normal Sex: Anti-VD Strategies in British Columbia 1918–1945
   Dorothy E. Chunn, Simon Fraser University 63

Part 2: The Consolidation of "Normal" 87

5. Excerpts from "The Trouble with Normal": Postwar Youth and the Construction of
   Heterosexuality *Mary Louise Adams, Queen's University* 90
6. Constructing "Normal": Psychology and the Canadian Family, 1945–1960
   Mona Gleason, University of British Columbia 104
7. National Security as Moral Regulation: Making the Normal and the Deviant
   in the Security Campaigns Against Gay Men and Lesbians
   Gary Kinsman, Laurentian University 121
8. Striptease on the Line: Investigating Trends in Female Erotic Entertainment
   Becki L. Ross, University of British Columbia 146

Part 3: Bad Mothers and Endangered Children 179

9. Vengeance for the Innocents: The New Medico-Legal Designation of "Infanticide"
   as "Child Abuse Homicide" *Kirsten Johnson Kramar, Brock University* 182
10. Constituting "Dangerous Parents" Through the Spectre of Child Death:
    A Critique of Child Protection Restructuring in Ontario
    Xiaobei Chen, University of Victoria 209

11. The Leaner, Meaner Welfare Machine: The Ontario Conservative Government's Ideological and Material Attack on Single Mothers
   Margaret Hillyard Little, Queen's University 235

PART 4: CONTEMPORARY CONTROVERSIES 259

12. Queerness is Not in Our Genes: Biological Determinism Versus Social Liberation *Gary Kinsman, Laurentian University* 262
13. Moral Panic and Child Pornography: The Case of Robin Sharpe
   Kegan Doyle, University of British Columbia and Dany Lacombe, Simon Fraser University.. 285
14. Party Girls and Predators: "Date Rape Drugs" and Chronotopes of Gendered Risk *Dawn Moore and Mariana Valverde, University of Toronto*.............. 306

GLOSSARY 329

AUTHOR PROFILES 337

REFERENCES 339

CREDITS 362

INDEX 363

Preface

Over several years of teaching regulation studies to undergraduate students in sociology, I was becoming increasingly frustrated with the lack of written material directed toward and accessible to an undergraduate student audience. Moreover, while reading packages allow faculty to tailor a course to our own pedagogical interests and produce what we hope are unique and interesting courses, we also realize that students appreciate the continuity and integration of a text. The solution for me (and I hope for you too), was to produce a text which would satisfy these pedagogical interests. I solicited the assistance of a number of wonderful scholars, and was rewarded by their enthusiasm and support for this project. Their work represents a range of approaches to the study of regulation. It does not shy away from controversy, and will engage and challenge students analytically and often personally. We trust that our efforts will be met with students willing to take on these challenges.

The title for *Making Normal* was inspired by Mary Louise Adam's 1997 book *The Trouble with Normal: Postwar Youth and the Making of Heterosexuality*. Mary Louise was inspired by the title of a Bruce Cockburn song, which declares that "the trouble with normal is that it always gets worse." I am grateful to Mary Louise for making the selection of the first part of my book title so easy. The second part of the title was more difficult. Most of the contributors to the collection have conducted their research in British Columbia and Ontario, and I was concerned about providing a title that might appear to claim a pan-Canadian character. In the end though, I decided to stay with *Making Normal: Social Regulation in Canada*, because so much of the social and legal policy content and issues do indeed have a pan-Canadian character, and will be of interest to students across the country.

I would like to thank all of the contributors for the work that they have done for this collection. I would particularly like to thank Gary Kinsman for his thorough read and critique of the introductory chapter. While I was not able to address all of his comments and suggestions, I know that the analysis presented here is much improved as a result of his assistance. I would also like to give special thanks to all of the contributors who not only produced book chapters, but also produced new people during the time that we worked on this collection. Dany Lacombe and Kegan Doyle brought Mina Doyle into the world on February 8, 2001. Mona Gleason gave birth to Will Bragg on April 10, 2002. Paula Maurutto gave birth to Cailan Maurutto-Robinson on May 13, 2002. And Kirsten Johnson Kramar gave birth to Mieka Lee Kramar on June 27, 2002. I am in awe of all of them for their ability to simultaneously care for newborns and engage in scholarly work.

Some final acknowledgements are in order. Thanks to the staff at Thompson Nelson for their support of this project. Thanks once again to Andie Noack for her editing assistance with the introduction to the collection. My partner, Jennifer McNenly, deserves sustained applause for enduring the two years of planning, writing, and fretting that were part of the production of this book. And finally, I would like to thank Philip Corrigan, to whom this book is dedicated, for bringing studies of moral regulation to Canada. His influence is everywhere in this book.

Deborah Brock
Toronto
August 2002

Introduction

Moving Beyond Deviance: Power, Regulation, and Governmentality

by Deborah Brock

The purpose of this collection of essays is to introduce undergraduate students to studies of social regulation in Canada, although we expect that it will have much to offer researchers and educators also. The collection contains reprints, revised material, and newly published writings by an impressive gathering of scholars working in the areas of sociology, criminology, women's studies, political studies, and social work. While the theoretical terrain that we will explore can be at times challenging, we have attempted to avoid the use of language that is specific to any one discipline, in order to produce an inter-disciplinary text. In this introduction, I establish the groundwork for the essays that follow. These essays focus on how, what our contributors refer to as social regulation, moral regulation, and governance, shape the making of "normal." The collection also examines questions of power, so that readers will better understand why the contributors have such different starting points in their analyses, as approaches to power are linked to the theoretical assumptions that inform one's analysis. In this collection, some contributors work with materialist-based analyses and others with post-modern or post-structuralist analyses, which will be explained in due course.

Why a focus on normal? A first response might be to think about what happens to people when they are considered not to be normal. However, the intellectual work needed here is far more complicated than that. It is important that we explore the making of normal through the discourses and practices of **normalization**, and their contingent and provisional successes. This requires that we move beyond studies of deviance and problematize practices of power.

MOVING BEYOND "DEVIANCE"

Deviance refers to any behaviour or appearance that violates social norms, rules, or laws. The determination of deviance is clearly about defining and regulating differences, particularly moral differences. Beyond that, it is a pretty ambiguous concept.

Deviance is not outside of us; it is something in which we are all implicated. It would probably not take us too long to come up with a list of acts of deviance in which we have participated, most of them likely pretty inconsequential acts in the larger scheme of things. For example, jaywalking is a common rule violation, so common that it seems incongruous with the potential implications of a word like deviance. Deviance is clearly a label that people resist (at least in some contexts), by trivializing the concerns of those who label an action deviant. As well, people may attempt to minimize the impact of the label because of its profound ability to affect self-identification and how others identify us. Often we resist the label because we regard the labelling of particular actions as deviant as excessive attempts to regulate our lives. In other ways, however, we may be full participants in the process.

To label a belief or behaviour as deviant can be powerfully proscriptive. It can be a means of shaming or ridiculing. We participate in this process when we refer to people as weird or sick or strange. We are all implicated in the social relations of deviance when we mark people as different and then speak of them in a pejorative manner. Yet clearly, a deviant designation is at its most powerful when it implicates our own selves. This is demonstrated when the labelling of our actions as deviant invokes feelings of shame. Sometimes this involves our sexuality. Why does sexuality still have the ability to invoke feelings of shame, even in these sexually knowledgeable and relatively permissive times? This is a question that we will explore later in the text.

It should be clear that not all behaviours labelled deviant are of the same importance and impact. For example, skipping classes or serial murder is simply not in the same league. Whether or not a deviant designation is backed up by legal proscription is one way in which the seriousness of a breach can be gauged. Nor does one form of deviance necessarily lead to other forms, although some would argue that there is a slippery slope or domino effect, and that people who flout one significant social norm are likely to challenge others as well. It is also the case that deviance may sometimes have a positive character, for example, in breaking unjust laws. As Nelson Mandela, who spent twenty-five years in a South African prison for his role in the leadership of the anti-apartheid African National Congress, demonstrates so ably, sometimes it is necessary to break the rules in order to achieve social justice.

The labelling of a behaviour or appearance as deviant will change over time, and will vary by place, revealing its social and historical construction. For example, smoking cigarettes is increasingly regarded as a socially harmful activity, after enjoying decades as a sign of conformity and acceptance. Facial piercings on North American youth are now quite common, although as recently as a decade ago they were unusual and even considered freakish.

Deviant behaviours are not necessarily uncommon. For example, a married person having an extramarital affair is a quite common occurrence, yet it is considered to be a deviant behaviour because it violates social values; it transgresses what is considered to be normal and appropriate conduct. Just because many people, even the majority of people, act in a particular way does not make it socially acceptable. This also makes it clear that labelling behaviour as deviant will not necessarily prevent that behaviour, although it may cause the participants to feel badly about themselves.

Nineteenth-century theorist, Émile Durkheim, regarded as one of the founding fathers of sociology, believed that it is only as a result of the creation of norms that the possibility of violating those norms exists. "Good" behaviour reminds us of what is "bad" and "bad" behaviour reminds us of what is "good." The definition and regulation of so-called bad behaviour helps to keep socially desired rules in place by setting boundaries, successfully regulating the conformists even more than the non-conformists. Functionalist theorists like Durkheim would say that this helps to preserve social cohesion, as it keeps societies stable and that a consequence of this regulation is that conflict and change can be perceived as destabilizing. When you think about Durkheim's approach, you can see that he makes an interesting point regarding the relation between goodness and badness. Yet we can also see how a functionalist analysis is inherently conservative. Functionalism examines society as a whole system, where each part of the society has a place in maintaining the whole. However, rather than accepting a normative order, some critics of functionalism contend that we need to question who is making the rules, and for whom. Why is a static society desirable and change threatening? What if conflict happens because the people who don't make the rules get a little tired of their subordinate position?

As an example, what is implied by the term, **slut**? Who is most likely to be called a slut? What are the implications of calling someone a slut? Perhaps the greatest role that the slut designation has in our society is the symbolic. The slut can be said to function as a symbol in a way that warns all girls to be "good" even more than it serves as a warning to bad girls to change their ways or suffer the consequences.

However, functionalist analysis has rightly been accused of being **teleological**; it assumes that "things happen the way that they do because they serve some ultimate purpose or contribute to some ultimate goal or end point" (Blackwell Dictionary, 295). We can look at the work of Talcott Parsons, who was the most well known functionalist theorist in North America in the 1950s, for an example of how teleological analysis works. Parsons believed that gender inequality is functionally necessary for family and social stability. He believed that women and men should have separate roles, and while those roles allow men greater social power than women, this is functionally necessary for the maintenance of a society. We can see how the labelling of some women as sluts could be closely tied to prescribing sexual relations for women only with their husbands within a patriarchal, nuclear family. So while labelling women as sluts can be said to perform a social function, it is a function which precludes other visions and possibilities for women.

One of the tasks of alternative critical social theories is to not only to identify but also to challenge the social relations through which notions of normativity and deviance are created. For example, feminism, which at its minimum is a theory and a politics that promotes equality between women and men, encourages women to resist any sexual policing of their behaviour that would curtail women's attempts to enjoy their own sexuality, on their own terms. After first ensuring their own safety and comfort in any given situation, women should be free to resist the double standard of sexual behaviour for women and men.

Research in the sociology of deviancy has had a double-edged character. On one hand, some deviancy theorists have undertaken this research in the hopes of rendering people considered to be deviant less "strange"; in other words, to chip away at some of the marginality of out groups. Sociologists working at the University of Chicago in the late 1950s began questioning the ways in which people like jazz musicians, marijuana users, the mentally ill, homosexuals, prostitutes, members of the street culture, and so on had been pathologized. Sociologists such as Howard S. Becker and Erving Goffman believed that deviancy could only be understood within the context of societal relations that named deviant behaviours as such. They asserted that there is no deviance unless a particular behaviour is labelled as deviant and they directed attention to the ways in which a particular social phenomenon acquired a deviant status or designation (Chauncey, 2000). This observation was to have a profound impact on the ways in which deviance and normalization were understood and studied by future researchers, working within a range of theoretical approaches, including the approaches represented in this text.

However, as early as 1972, Alexander Liazos raised concerns about the directions of deviancy theory in his article, *The Poverty of the Sociology of Deviance: Nuts, Sluts, and Preverts*. Liazos was an American scholar whose approach to sociology, like much of his generation, was deeply influenced by the social movements of the 1960s, including the opposition to the war in Vietnam. He noted that from the late 1940s the field of deviance gradually supplanted the social problems orientation which characterized much sociological work, because early social problems analyses tended to be moralistic in approach, and avoided situating these analyses within a larger political, historical, and social context. More recent scholarship on social problems focuses on how social problems come to be made, however.[1] Moreover, social problems analyses of the period were not sufficiently systematically and theoretically grounded. Deviancy studies promised to avoid moralism and to approach social issues objectively, in order to develop a more sustained and detailed theoretical orientation in research projects, and to connect this theoretical work to larger theories and issues in sociology. However, the end result Liaszos found, was that,

---

[1] See, for example, my book (1998) *Making Work: Making Trouble: Prostitution as a Social Problem.* Toronto: University of Toronto Press. Joseph Gusfield's work has been very influential in establishing new directions in social problems research. See, for example, his (1981) *The Culture of Public Problems.* Chicago: University of Chicago Press.

> The "deviant" has been humanized; the moralistic tone is no longer ever-present (although it still lurks beneath the explicit disavowals); and theoretical perspectives have been developed. Nevertheless, all is not well with the field of "deviance." Close examination reveals that writers of this field still do not try to relate the phenomena of "deviance" to larger social, historical, political, and economic contexts. The emphasis is still on the "deviant" and the "problems" he (sic) presents to himself and others, not on the society within which he emerges and operates. (Liazos, p. 117)

Moreover, Liazos points out that it is marginalized populations whose actions continue to be explored, rather than the actions of people in positions of authority and control. My own research on prostitution and on same-sex sexuality leads me to state that even now, several decades after he wrote this reflection, his more cynical observations remain valid. I cannot, however, share Liazo's more optimististic assertions. The deviants, characteristically, the "nuts (mentally ill), sluts (prostitutes), and perverts (homosexuals)" referred to in his title, have been studied repeatedly by deviancy theorists reconfirming their status as "other"; as "not like most people." This is precisely because, as Liazos points out, the focus remains on the deviant and the problems that the deviant represents.

There is little escape from the value-laden character of the concept of deviancy. This is because "deviancy" assumes a state of normalcy against which difference and rule breakers must be judged. Indeed, the deviant designation can be used to suppress, contain, and stigmatize difference. It does not tell us how rules come to be made and who gets to be "normal," how certain individuals and populations come to be rule makers, and why they make the rules that they do. It does not address the question of **power**. That is why theorists who are interested in these kinds of "big questions" often find deviancy research a dead end for social analysis, not to mention social justice. They have begun to shift the focus from the margins to the centre and to unpack the centre in order to develop a better understanding of how social relations are organized. By analogy, this is undertaken in much the same way as a person will take apart a piece of mechanical equipment and then reassemble it, in order to find out how it works. Moreover, when we focus on that which has been marginalized while not interrogating the centre, we unknowingly reproduce a set of normative relations, which defines the margins as the location of **the problem**. Here are two examples of how this might happen.

Some recent research asks us to investigate the social construction of *heterosexuality* for a change (Katz, as well as chapters by Adams and Kinsman in this volume). When we focus on homosexuality at the expense of heterosexuality, we continue to name homosexuality as *the problem*, even though our objective may be to explain why homosexuality should not be a problem. Heterosexuality is located as the normal, taken for granted, indeed even the natural form of sexual expression. There is little awareness of how our contemporary understanding of heterosexuality is itself of recent origin, and how the two identities have been constructed in relation to one another. Moreover, if heterosexuality is so natural and normal, why has such an enormous range of social resources been devoted to producing the proper heterosexual, as Mary Louise Adams notes in her contribution to this volume? Why are the causes of heterosexuality not investigated? Once we open the door to this kind of analysis, we can then begin to question the binary model of sexuality, where one must identify as straight or gay, save for some reputedly confused people (bisexuals) in the middle. This is a task that Gary Kinsman takes on in his second contribution to this volume.

Think about a parallel situation to the location of heterosexuality as the centre. Think about why we overwhelmingly focus on the impact of racism on people of colour, and ignore the social construction of *whiteness*, which, when you think about it, is the real source of the problem. Whiteness is a social location that brings with it privileges and entitlements to white people even where we lack privileges and entitlements in other areas of our lives. This is something that white people generally ignore. We can then more easily locate the racial structuring of our society as something that takes place external to us, instead of seeing how we are all implicated in this systemic organization of power, and how it shapes the lives of white people. We can remain blinkered about the ways in which we might unwittingly participate in reproducing systemic racism, even while we wear our "Let's End Racism" buttons. At the same time, we must keep in mind the question that black scholar and activist W.E.B. Dubois posed in his landmark work, *The Souls of Black Folk*; "How does it feel to be a problem?" (Gilroy, 1987, p. 11)

POWER

So who or what shapes the norms and makes the rules? What are the processes at work? The answers that you get will depend on whom you ask. From a conservative Christian perspective, God makes the rules, and the state backs him up. If you decide to seek your answer in liberal political theory, you will be told that we all do, as citizens in a participatory democracy. One critical perspective that informs some of the contributions to this collection, is that what gets defined as deviance and what does not largely reflects the interests of ruling groups. Another critical perspective found in this collection is that normalization and its opposites are produced through the deployment of discourses. Both critical perspectives emphasize the importance of historical investigation to social analysis. All of these perspectives regard power relations as central. However, they all take different approaches to the study of power. Power is being exercised when we are so located within a particular vision or way of seeing that we cannot imagine alternatives to it; it shapes our thoughts, preferences, and acceptance of ourselves within the existing order of things. We may think that this "way" has been designed by God or by the natural order, and is thus unchangeable.

While an exploration of power *per se* is not the central focus of this collection, it does inform the work that we do. The contributions to this collection implicitly ask us to take a look at the ways in which power shapes our lives, and the lives of others, past and present. We are always inside of power. To speak about power is to signal the existence of an enormous range of social beliefs, discourses, and practices, some of, which, it might be argued, are more influential than others. These are often invisible to us, as we are so much inside of them, and we take them so much for granted, as if they were a part of a natural order. Usually, power is only visible to us when it involves coercion. It is our task here to try to make power more visible.

A common sense approach to power is that it entails one person making another person do something that this other person would not normally do. Force or manipulation is always involved. However, McConnell, McDowell, and Sharp find that the operation of power is usually more complex than this. First, even a basic definition of power reveals that power usually involves, a) the ability of a person, group, organization, discourse, etc., to put into place a **definition of a situation**, b) the establishment of the terms through which events will be **understood**, c) the establishment of the terms through which one can discuss the issues at hand. In other words, how we come to understand what is going on and why it is going on. Second, power also involves the formulation of **ideals** which people and organizations should strive to achieve. Third, power entails the ability to define **morality**, as we will see repeatedly in this volume (McConnell, 1987, McDowell & Sharp, 1999). For now, let us turn our attention to the first of the points raised. An example of this is the power of medical discourses to define illness and therefore also wellness. Physicians and scientists don't simply discover and name diseases that are present in human and animal life; they also make judgements about what it means to be sick or healthy, with profound social implications. Populations of people (for instance, HIV positive people, lepers, prostitutes) become associated with contagion, regardless of an individual's likelihood to transmit disease. They become a source of public anxiety and subject to social rejection and isolation. Another example of the operation of power is the way in which discussions of "the market" dominate the public agenda, as if it were a life force of its own. This signals the values that are most important in our society at this time. When I turn on CBC radio and hear from the "market watchers" it reminds me of the daily radio announcements of body counts during the war in Vietnam ("our" side versus "their" side), a war that was the focus of political debate in the U.S. in the 1960s and early 1970s, and re-shaped Canadian political discussion as well. However, at that time, political debate about the meaning of democracy pervaded North America. Now, we wait for the "experts" to inform us about what steps they consider to be necessary in order to massage the market into favouring rather than harming us.

We will now explore several general approaches to power. The first approach, power in liberal political theory, is not taken up by authors in this collection.

The second approach, explores power in theories of social inequality like Marxist theory, the many approaches to feminist and anti-racist theory, as well as in materialist approaches to queer theory. Third, we will explore how power is taken up in the governmentality literature, which has been inspired by the writings of Michel Foucault.

Liberal political theory is the approach that informs Canadian economic and legal systems. In a nutshell, liberal political thought developed along with the growth of the capitalism in Europe. As the transition from the feudal order to capitalism occurred, some people who were not part of the aristocracy began to accumulate private property and wealth through trade. While the aristocracy claimed a right to land title and to wealth as a result of God's favour, this growing group of non-aristocratic property owners began to claim that they too had the right to be involved in political decision making. Parliamentary systems were formed in countries like England and France, comprised of elected public representatives. Initially, only people who owned property of some significance could participate in this system, but this was gradually extended to non-property-owning white men, to women, and to aboriginal peoples and non-white people.

In liberal political thought, all citizens who reside within a nation now have the right to political participation, and to accumulate private property to the extent of their abilities to do so. However, as indicated in my last comment full citizenship rights only gradually expanded to include a comprehensive range of actual people, so that now liberalism therefore extends formal legal equality to all citizens. This does not mean that power is equally shared among all people. Rather, people who accumulate wealth, prestige, and authority, who attain power, do so largely because of their ability to maximize the social opportunities made available to them by a competitive capitalist economy. An objective of liberal democratic societies is to establish the conditions for competitive individualism, which characterizes capitalist systems. As Dennis Forcese states, capitalist societies like Canada are conceptualized as systems which provide people "equal opportunity to compete for unequal rewards" (Forcese, 1986 p. 72). In Social Darwinist terms, capitalism is predicated on the "survival of the fittest." Herbert Spencer (1820–1903) first applied Darwin's conceptualization of "survival of the fittest" to human social life. **Social Darwinists** like Spencer applied the concept in order to attempt to explain differences among human groups. He and his contemporaries believed that there existed a hierarchy of superiority and inferiority among human groups. Of course, they held their own group, white Europeans, to be the most highly evolved, and white Europeans of their own class to be the most highly evolved of all. We can see how **ethnocentrism** (the belief that one's own nation and culture are superior to those of others, and the judgement of other nations and cultures against the presumed superiority of one's own) is at work here. We can also see how this approach can be used to justify social inequality, as if it is a part of the natural order of things.

In this formulation, power is something that is possessed by individuals seeking to maximize their own opportunities and rewards. From this perspective (which is important for us to examine, because it is the dominant one in our society), although some people may gain more power than others, the state functions as a neutral arbitrator between competing interest groups. It is a **pluralist** state and the state remains the ultimate authority. Power, therefore, is also conceptualized as authority. While power can entail domination, generally power is available to those who seek to achieve it, and is widely enough shared so that everyone in a democratic society can have their interests addressed. From this perspective, we can see that **power is regarded as something that can be possessed; that is, power is the property of individuals**.

Let's compare this to the perspective on power that is advanced in Marxist political theory. Here too, power is something that can be possessed. It is the property of groups, and accrues to individuals by virtue of their membership in privileged classes (although as we will see, most contemporary Marxists do not limit their analysis of privileged groups to class position). However, the Marxist tradition takes a rather different view of power in capitalism than the liberal tradition. In Marxist thought, the transition from feudalism to capitalism merely replaced one system of domination with another. Capitalism, like feudalism before it, is a **mode of production** of material life: it is a social, political, and economic system in which people go about meeting needs like acquiring food and shelter in particular kinds of ways. (Marx insisted that any analysis of power and social change must be grounded in what happens in the material world.) A key feature of the economics of capitalism is that the vast majority of the labour force provides their labour power to the owners and managers of capital in exchange for a wage while these same owners and managers accumulate profits from the labour that others provide. Integral to capitalism is the division of people into classes. The two fundamental classes are the ruling class (bourgeoisie), who own and control the means of production, and the working class (proletariat), who must sell their labour power for a wage. While a middle class was only beginning to emerge in Marx's time (1818–1883) and was therefore subject to limited analysis by the man himself, subsequent analysis by Marxists have found that the middle class tends to have more autonomy and control over their working conditions than the working class. They may own their own businesses or be professionals, for example. As well, they have almost certainly placed their faith in the economic system by investing their savings in stocks, bonds, and RRSPs. However, they lack the access to decision-making power enjoyed by the ruling class. They do not run corporations or hold controlling shares in stocks, nor will they ever be chosen to accompany Canadian prime ministers on the head of state's "Team Canada" visits to other nations, promoting Canadian business.

From this formulation, power equals top-down domination and control, over land, labour, and capital. Power rests heavily in the accumulation and possession of economic resources. Having power means having the ability to organize social life as one, or rather one's class, sees fit. For example, when we turn on the TV or read the newspaper, we invariably hear business leaders stating that what is good for the corporation is good for the people who work for the corporation; indeed, is good for the well being of everyone in a capitalist society.

Unlike liberal democratic theory, theorists who are influenced by Marx's work insist that the state is not neutral. It secures and preserves the interests of the ruling groups. For example, there are close ties between people in positions of political power and people in positions of economic power because they generally share the same class background, and/or have a strong economic investment in the profit system. In this example, the Canadian state is a capitalist state, because the work that it does helps to sustain the capitalist economic system and the social inequalities which are found in this kind of a system.

That said, many of us who are deeply influenced by Marx's analysis do not reduce the reproduction of social life to economic determinants alone, and are quite critical of those who interpret Marx's work in this way. To describe contemporary capitalism as merely an economic system ignores the diversity and complexity of social life, including social inequalities. A richer interpretation of Marx's work is that **all** social relations are also material relations because they are lived in and through the body. A materialist analysis must include the actual activities that we engage in as we go about our lives. This includes everything from how one earns a living, to the writing of poetry, or the romantic or gritty realization of our sexual desire. So culture, and people's every day activities, are also part of what makes capitalism what it is and what it will be.

When undertaking this kind of materialist analysis, we must account for social relations that are hierarchically organized through the process of racialization, through gender power relations, through sexuality, through nation building, and so on. Race, gender, and sexuality are as fundamental to social organization as is class. For example, the white European descent of the overwhelming number of political, legal, and economic decision-makers has influenced the crafting of immigration laws. These laws have made it more difficult for non-white people to gain Canadian citizenship and have kept aboriginal peoples at the bottom of the social hierarchy, as Dua demonstrates in this volume. Not surprisingly, the theoretical debates about what Marx really said, where his work is still relevant, and where we need to go beyond it, are quite intense. We don't need to elaborate on them here. What we do have to keep in mind, however, is that this kind of analysis has profound implications for who has power and how they came to possess it.

The Marxist definition of power should now be evident. Power in capitalism has largely been conceptualized as the exercise of social control by the ruling class. Many of the contributors to this volume, however, support Marx's analysis of capital, but find a focus on economic relations too restrictive, so choose to look at the numerous forms that ruling relations take.[2] In this analysis, power (or lack of power) accrues to individuals as a result of the social location into which they are born. Power is largely exercised through a process that the Italian Marxist, Antonio Gramsci (1891–1937), named **hegemony**, in which domination is secured through the organization of consent. The values and interests of ruling groups are more or less successfully promulgated as the values and interests of all, although resistance to this domination demonstrates that hegemony is always tenuous and struggled over. In countries that declare themselves to be liberal democracies, coercion, these days, is less often resorted to for the control of one's own citizens, given that producing consent does a far better job, and is much less bloody. However, we see the coercive power of the state in the army, the police, and the judicial and corrections systems. They are not in place merely to prevent the possibility of foreign invasion or the spread of a criminal underclass. We see these powers increasingly used against social protest movements, particularly against people involved in anti-globalization protests. Indeed, police considered public protest a serious enough threat to the prevailing economic and social order that an international "Conference to Combat Activism" was held in Holland in October, 2001. In Canada, police are demanding the legal tools to increase the surveillance and detention of activists involved in a broad range of issues, from every walk of life.

Domination is much more stable and secure, though, where those who are ruled come to regard their interests as being the same as those who rule. It involves maintaining the means to convince the population that reasonable and fair mechanisms are in place, and that some inequality is inevitable and normal. Indeed, inequality is justified through a broad range of social institutions such as religion, schooling, family organization, and the work place, where inequality is so pervasive that it appears to be natural. Let's for a moment try to imagine a mainstream media that presented news from the standpoint of labour, rather than the standpoint of capital. How different would the reporting be? How would this influence the way that people think about the society in which they live? This re-visioning should inspire us to question who the "we" is that owners of capital are referring to when they discuss means to improve the economy. Why is it that the "improvements" of neo-liberalism have lead to a widening gap between rich and poor in Canada and globally?

This should also help us to question what people are referring to when they speak of society as if it represented a singular voice or perspective. We continually hear people state that "society says" as if societies were sentient beings. In other words, they reify society. **Reification** occurs when a society is presented as if it has needs and intentions. Instead of speaking or writing in this way, it is important to always specify

---

[2] "Ruling relations" is a concept developed by Dorothy E. Smith. See, for example, Dorothy E. Smith (1990) *The Conceptual Practices of Power, A Feminist Sociology of Knowledge*. Toronto: University of Toronto Press.

concretely the social relations to which one is referring in order to make them visible. Think about whose interests are being represented when you hear statements like, "Society says that we have to be competitive in order to get ahead," or "Society says that homosexuality is wrong." Otherwise, you close off the possibility of comprehending power.

From this perspective, where there is power, there is also resistance to power. This is evident in the plethora of social movements that have developed to contest power; for example, class struggles, union organizing, the women's movement, anti-racist organizing, queer politics, indigenous people's organizing, and national liberation movements. It should be evident that Marxism is not the only critical theory which approaches power as domination and social control. Many feminist and anti-racist analyses also take this approach and much contemporary theoretical and empirical work explores the intersections of power relations organized by race, gender, sexualities, class, and nation. However, one can also find feminist and anti-racist theory situated within the framework of both liberal democratic theory and post-modernism.

Now we can address the third approach to power, which was developed by Michel Foucault (1926–1984). While Foucault's work can at times be difficult to categorize, he is considered to be a key contributor to post-modern analysis. This analysis of power will take a little longer, because it takes us on to unfamiliar and sometimes difficult terrain. First, however, we need to explain what is meant by post-modernism, which in turn first requires an explanation of what it is post of: modernism. Enlightenment thought was under way in Europe in the 17th and 18th centuries. It posed that we could use human reason to shape history. It was not up to God or to the devil to shape human action. In other words, science supplanted religion. Through scientific exploration, one could measure and understand not only the natural environment, but also human behaviour, and use these as tools for social progress. These principles formed the basis for what became known as modernist thought. Modernist thought informed virtually all social analysis until the development of post-modern theory in the 1970's. Post-modernism challenged the belief that there is an underlying reality that can be discovered and controlled through the application of scientific practices. Post-modern theorists reject the belief that through scientific exploration, one can measure and understand not only the natural environment, but also human behaviour, and that history and time could be shaped through human intervention, in order to create progress. They reject the belief that there is any essential meaning to being human, thereby challenging **humanist** thought. The belief that we share a common nature as humans is an important ingredient of modernism. Post-modernists reject **master narratives** (universalizing explanations of social life and historical change), and instead approach social life and history as fragmented and discontinuous. Beyond this, post-modernism has a diversity of meanings, which are specific to the areas of art, culture, and theory to which it is applied. Moreover, post-modernism is also used as a term to describe the present condition of what were formerly modern capitalist societies. It expresses a social condition of fragmentation and incoherence, which make it impossible to attribute larger meaning and purpose to social life (Seidman & Alexander, 2001).

Post-modernism is strongly connected with **post-structuralism**. Post-structuralists reject the structuralist belief that there are underlying "structures" shaping social life and shaping language, and which can be studied in an objective, scientific manner. The reference to "structures" is made to signal the belief that there are underlying features or elements to a particular phenomena (such as systems of language, or class) that are linked together in a way that produces that particular phenomenon. Once these elements are discovered, one can then undertake a full explanation of the phenomenon (Payne, 1996, p. 513). Post-structuralists believe that structuralism does not allow for human agency or for open-ended social processes, in other words, the structures determine what people will do. They argue that meaning is always unstable and plural, and that people occupy a number of **subject positions**, situating them so as to have conflicting interests and alliances. What does this mean for a post-modern or post-structuralist analyses of power?

For Foucault, there is more to power than domination, repression, and inequality. Power is not simply about the domination of one individual over others or one group over others. It is not simply about the repression of a person's true feelings or interests. Foucault is not concerned with who has power, because for him it is not something that anyone can possess and exercise over others. Rather, it is "a multiplicity of force relations" (Foucault, 1980, p. 92) which operates not through the consolidation of power as if it were an iron fist, but which is produced from moment to moment, point to point. "Power is everywhere; not because it embraces everything, but because it comes from everywhere…power is not an institution, and not a structure; neither is it a certain strength that we are endowed with; it is the name that one attributes to a complex strategical situation in a particular society." (p. 93) The state, the law, and social classes, are not sources of power, but rather "the terminal forms power takes." (p. 92) In other words, they are produced through the operation of power. So while power is not tangible, it does have material effects. The effect might also be the making of a particular kind of **subject**, acting in particular ways. Power, therefore is relational, rather than having a fixed character. It is always produced anew. Foucault wants to direct us away from the notion that power is intrinsically bad, or good as it is much more complex than that. Yet we must also be aware that power can indeed be dangerous, because techniques of power can appear to be neutral, and the political ramifications invisible (Fabion, 2000, p. xv).

For Foucault, knowledge cannot be neutral. He also rejects the popular formulation that "knowledge is power." Rather, Foucault believes that power and knowledge exist in a circular relationship. Power produces knowledge and knowledge produces power. As Foucault comments, "the exercise of power creates and causes to emerge new objects of knowledge and accumulates new bodies of information....The exercise of power perpetually creates knowledge and, conversely, knowledge constantly induces effects of power" (cited in Fabion, 2000, p. xv-xvi). Knowledge is comprised of truths by which we live. So for Foucault, truth is produced through power and there can be no exercise of power except through the production of truth. Moreover, the production of the truths, and of power-knowledge relations, can only occur through the production and circulation of discourses.

What, then, is **discourse**? Fabion refers to discourses as "identifiable collections of utterances governed by rules of construction and evaluation which determine within some thematic area what may be said, by whom, in what context, and with what effect" (Fabion, 2000, p. xvi). I prefer the simpler definition that Mary Louise Adams offers in this volume, as she refers to discourse as "Organized systems of knowledge that make possible what can be spoken about, and how one can speak about it."

One cannot, however, assess these systems of knowledge to determine the degree of truth that they offer. In his work, Foucault avoids making universal claims, for example, that there is such a thing as "truth" or "human nature." Instead, he undertakes an analysis of how we come to believe in universal claims, seeking to discover how particular discourses come to be regarded as "truth."

Let's briefly compare this approach to Marxist theory. Most of Marx's life's work focused on the study of capitalism. He considered his work to be a scientific study, in which he pursued the truth about capitalism. He wanted the facts to be known, and he believed these facts would become increasingly evident as capitalism began to outstrip its capacities to sustain itself (for example, as class tensions mounted, and finite resources were depleted). Marx believed that in time, capitalism would be rejected and more equitable socialist societies would replace them. While Foucault could be said to be sympathetic to certain aspects of Marx's project (he too believed that people needed to liberate themselves from oppression), he also believed that Marxist theory was another example of modernist discourse which claimed to be scientific, in that it claimed to discover an underlying factual condition, and which formulated a master narrative said to be a true history of societies.

This is one reason why Foucault's use of discourse is so different from Marxist influenced approaches to ideology. In Foucault's use of the term, discourses do not represent truth or falsity; they are about how particular social phenomenon are represented and understood. Again, this gets us away from the modernist belief that there is an underlying truth that can be discovered. In Marxist theory, ideology is the false representation of the real. Ideology exists to serve the interests of the ruling groups, through falsely representing the world to subordinate groups. It creates false consciousness. As always, however, the division between discourse and ideology is not always that simple or clear. Many theorists use the concept of discourse in a variety of ways. Some who hold to a materialist standpoint will also make reference to "discourses" as if they are ideological. Since no one owns the concept, it is up to the reader to interpret how a particular writer or speaker is making use of the concept of discourse.

So does that mean that everything is discursive? Stuart Hall clarifies this for us when he asserts that it is **not** the case that "nothing exists outside of discourse." There is indeed a natural world; there are indeed material objects. However, it **is** the case that "nothing meaningful exists outside of discourse." Discourses provide the framework for understanding and interpreting the world around us, in all of its forms and expressions (Hall, 1999). Gary Kinsman (in this volume) is critical of this kind of claim. He believes that this amount of emphasis on discourse gives agency to discourses, but not to people. An example of what he means by this will be provided further down the page but first, more from Foucault.

Here is an example of Foucault's approach, from volume one of his *History of Sexuality*. Foucault's work shows that sexuality is a **social and historical construction**, rather than simply something that is given by nature. In this way, he challenges **essentialist** interpretations of sexuality, which locate it as a natural force or drive, whose predilections are determined by genetics and so on. Foucault is of course not the first person to think about sexuality in this way; however, his focus on power-knowledge relations and discourses about sexuality in the Victorian period have transformed the way in which research about sexuality has been pursued. Foucault found that a range of sexualities and sexual identities were being created in Europe from the late 19th century, through the development of a scientific approach to sexuality. For Foucault, this approach was a discursive one, while for the scientists involved, it entailed the discovery of incontrovertible facts. The belief that one could explore sexuality scientifically, just as one could explore other aspects of social and physical life scientifically, was very new. This scientific approach, "claiming to speak the truth…stirred up people's fears" (Foucault, 1980, p. 53). For example, prior to this period, there was no such thing as the homosexual *per se*. One could commit specific sexual acts like buggery (anal intercourse), which were considered to be sins against God. However, not until the development of a scientia sexualis were these acts connected to a specific identity. Peripheral sexualities became known as perversions, and their practitioners acquired distinct *sexual identities*. Thus, "the nineteenth-century homosexual became a personage" (p. 45) and no aspect of his (and later her too) behaviour could be considered separate from his sexuality. This is just one example of a range of new orders of knowledge developed through this new scientific approach. It was believed that sexuality not only spoke the truth about individuals, but it came to be regarded as causing a growing range of maladies affecting the human condition. This gives us some indication of why Foucault challenged "the repressive hypothesis" about Victorian sexuality. He found that while sexual repression did indeed occur, it was part of a larger dynamic of an incitement to discourses about sexuality (Foucault, 1980). The history of sexuality since the 19th century at least, must therefore be understood as a history of discourses. These include "reverse discourses" such as those evident in forms of resistance like the lesbian and gay liberation movement, for once it became a distinct identity, "homosexuality began to speak on its own behalf" (Foucault, 1980, p. 101). So we find power too, in practices of freedom. We can explore these discourses, and in doing so make power relations visible. For Foucault, "It is in discourse that power and knowledge are joined together" (p. 100).

Now for the example of why Gary Kinsman believes that Foucault places too much emphasis on discourses. In his research on the emergence of gay identities, Kinsman has found that the growth of capitalism opened up social spaces in which a gay identity could begin to be consolidated. The growth of large urban spaces and emergence of commercial culture created the possibility for people who experienced same gender desire to meet and to develop their own communities, which was fundamental to the creation of lesbian and gay identity. It also led to new forms of regulation. The policing of these spaces clearly reinforced the notions of lesbians and gay men as deviant, while simultaneously demonstrating what it meant to be normal.[3] For Kinsman and others, one needs to locate the development of discourses about sexuality within changing material relations. This entails a very different understanding of power.

Foucault's writing about the history of sexuality provides an example of how, from his perspective, power produces truths, as well as new social relations. It produces reality as we come to understand it. That is why for Foucault, power is also **productive and creative**. It is also **technical**. In other words, we need to explore the **techniques of power**. We can find these in the administration of life; for example in discourses about mental illness, disease, sexuality, penology, immigration, and so on. In his many books, Foucault explores the production of new areas of knowledge like medicine, criminology, epidemiology, statistics, and psychology. These areas of knowledge produce the disciplinary society, with new techniques for the surveillance and regulation of populations.

For Foucault, therefore, power is most effective through the **normalization** of particular ideas and practices. He did recognize that coercion and social control exist through the exercise of what he referred to as **juridicial power**, for example, the power of law (Smart, 1989), but he believed that these were less effective than the normalization of discourses and their disciplinary practices. Foucault believed that new means of disciplining populations and a moral impetus had to be in place in order for people to participate in the beliefs and practices that would make capitalism work. In contrast, Marxism emphasizes people being deprived of other means to make a living, through being forced off of the land (for example, through a series of Land Enclosures Acts in 18th century England), and compelled to find employment as wage labourers through laws punishing wageless people as vagrants and vagabonds.

---

[3] Gary Kinsman. (1996). *The Regulation of Desire: Homo and Hetero Sexualities, Second Edition*. Montreal: Black Rose.

In conclusion, much of Foucault's work explores the production of techniques for the management, discipline, and surveillance of populations. He explored how new areas of knowledge were produced as means of administering to bodies and governing populations. Again, these techniques often appear to be neutral, and their political implications hidden, yet they are techniques of power that can be dangerous. It is this approach in Foucault's work, which has led some readers to mistake his analyses as studies of social control. Our brief discussion of Foucault on power should indicate that his analysis demands more than this.

We have now reviewed three main approaches to power; 1) the approach found in liberal theory; 2) the approach found in critical theories such as Marxism, which explores the reasons for social inequality; and 3) the unique approach to power developed by Foucault. The contributors to this collection are very much concerned with issues of power. Their analyses take us beyond the study of deviance and toward a specification of the concrete power relations that shape the events that they describe. Power, however, is rarely explicitly discussed. What **is** the focus of contributors' work is research into what they variously refer to as social regulation, moral regulation, and governance. While not losing track of what happens when people are regulated or governed, this work shifts our attention from the margins to the centre.

UNPACKING "THE CENTRE": MORAL REGULATION AND GOVERNANCE

SOCIAL REGULATION

Social regulation occurs in many forms, in complex relationships and dynamics. By social regulation, I refer to the ways in which the beliefs and practices of people, individually and as members of specific populations, are infused with power relations which shape our will, our interests…in a word, our subjectivity, as well as our actions. Most often, when we think about regulation at all, we think of it as something that happens in the sphere of economics or the sphere of politics. Indeed, as Valverde and Weir remind us, the formation of economic subjectivity and the formation of political subjectivity were two significant regulatory projects of the 19th century in countries such as Britain and Canada. They were, however, accompanied by and permeated with the moral (Valverde & Weir, 1988). It is to the formation of moral subjectivity since this time that the contributors to this volume largely orient their work. As we will see, some work with the concept of moral regulation, while others find the concept of governance more useful for their purposes. In the subtitle to this book, I have made references to "social regulation" as an umbrella term to encompass both of these directions, as well as to encompass the work of contributors who do not employ either concept, but who work with a more general reference to "regulation."

Moral Regulation

Try to think of a society without a moral landscape. In other words, without pervasive general ideas about what is normative character or behaviour for the people who comprise a society. To imagine a society without a moral landscape is to imagine a society without beliefs about what is right or wrong, appropriate or inappropriate, good or evil. This moral landscape finds more specific expression in what we know as morality. Morality informs specific principles, rules, and judgements about how we are expected to conduct ourselves. It is a cornerstone of religious beliefs, as the Ten Commandments are to the Christian Bible. It informs laws, which govern societies, such as the Canadian Criminal Code.

Try to go through a day without using the word, **normal**. Once you realize the difficulty of this exercise, record what you mean by it, every time you use it. What assumptions are you making about what is normal? Where do you think that your ideas come from? Are you aware of any perspectives that challenge the way that you use the word? How often do you think the normal also implies the moral?

If the activities that people engage in are labelled as deviant, indeed if this identification becomes integrated into the way that people are identified and identify themselves, and if people are subject to a range of negative sanctions as a result, then moral regulation must be taking place. Building on a critical analysis of the work of both Émile Durkheim and Basil Bernstein, Philip Corrigan adapted the term, moral regulation from Durkeim's 1897 book, *Suicide* (Corrigan, 1980). He was able to elaborate further on the concept in his 1985 book, written with Derek Sayer, *The Great Arch*. First, moral regulation establishes what is right and proper. Second, it encourages certain forms of conduct and expression, while discouraging others. Third, it establishes disciplinary regimes, including a system of rewards and punishments, at the symbolic and institutional levels (Corrigan, 1980). As Rousmaniere, Dehli, and de Coninck-Smith find, "Such forms of discipline have as their object the production of self-disciplined individuals who adhere to explicit and implicit rules of conduct and norms of conscience as if they were their own…we refer to such normative practices as moral regulation" (Rousmaniere, Dehli, & de Coninck-Smith, 1997, p. 3). Moral regulation need not entail coercive measures such as the use of direct physical contact or threats, nor the use of authority. Rather, moral regulation is part of what makes the person who she or he is; what he believes to be true; how she conducts herself. It shapes our identities, our conduct, and our conscience "through self-appropriation of morals and beliefs about what is right and wrong, possible and impossible, normal and pathological" (Rousmaniere et al. 1997, p. 3). Yet the subject who is produced through these processes is very much a post-structuralist subject, as Valverde and Weir comment in their assessment of this work, because moral regulation produces a subject which is multiple and contradictory" (Valverde & Weir, 1988, p. 31). In other words, the kinds of people, or subjects, who are made through these processes cannot be reduced to one dimensional people whose entire lives and identities are pre-packaged for them. Differences of class, race, gender, age, sexuality, and geographical location, mean that we remain complex and thinking subjects. This should indicate to us that no theory is pure, that is, theorists across a range of approaches critique and learn from one another. Corrigan manages to incorporate elements of post-structuralism while maintaining a commitment to a materialist analysis that emphasizes the centrality of the development of capitalism in creating a revolution in social life over the past two centuries. Numerous contributors to *Making Normal* (Kari Dehli, Gary Kinsman, Becki Ross, and I, Deborah Brock) were extremely fortunate to be able to study with Philip Corrigan at the Ontario Institute for Studies in Education in Toronto, where he taught courses in state formation and moral regulation during the 1980s. Corrigan's research and teaching has an abiding influence on the work that we do.

Moral regulation is often an invisible disciplinary process, which curtails difference as it homogenizes behaviour. It is never, however, completely successful. Strange and Loo liken the concept of regulation to "a net—restrictive, yet full of holes" (1991, p. 5). Rousmaniere, Dehli, and de Coninck-Smith find that "wherever there is moral regulation, there is resistance" (1997, p. 5). Most studies also reveal how the making and meaning of moral regulation is always contested, struggled over, and re-fashioned. Successful resistance does not necessarily mean that moral regulation disappears in a given area; it is possible that new forms of regulation supplant the old. We will find examples of resistance throughout the chapters that follow.

For Corrigan and Sayer, moral regulation sets the boundaries of what comes to be considered normal and appropriate behaviour; that which is considered to be good, not so good or downright bad. Some key questions to keep in mind are, if moral regulation is occurring, whose morals are being regulated, by whom or through what social relations, for what purpose? How is this kind of power conferred on some social groups and institutions and not others? For example, in this volume, Margaret Little identifies the place of class and gender in the regulation of mothers. Gary Kinsman provides examples of the regulation of gays and lesbians through a process of **heterosexual hegemony**, which he defines as the social practices, discourses, and ideologies constructing heterosexuality as the only "natural," and "normal" sexuality (this volume). Ena Dua locates the process of racialization at work in the determination of who is fit to be a citizen of Canada. One key way in which moral regulation takes place is through state power. An example is the creation of thousands of laws that govern our actions. Another example is the expansion of record keeping and public administration, beginning with the expansion of the 18th century British state. The emergence of the idea of the **fact**, wherein all could be objectively and scientifically known, led to new means of social investigation by state and nonstate organizations (Valverde & Weir, 1980). In their work, Corrigan and Sayer always tie moral regulation closely to the process of state formation (with an emphasis on "formation" because this is a process which is always ongoing, and never static). Although they recognized that there were other means, such as organized religion, through which moral regulation occurred, they privileged the role of the state, given that moral regulation has been considered a key ingredient in the making of good citizens and strong nations (Corrigan, 1981, p. 313). We find moral regulation at work in virtually every area of state activity, from less obvious areas such as finance and taxation (what models of family are assumed in those seemingly benign documents which we must complete each year?) to citizenship (who gets in?) to (more obviously) the judicial system. The creation of the modern state entailed a process of deepening involvement in virtually every aspect of social life, from schooling, to voting, to policing, to immigration, to social welfare (practices which it should be noted only became knowable and doable through the very work of state agencies and agents), and so on. The pervasiveness of state power is such that they determined that "state formation itself is cultural revolution" as there was virtually no place, belief, or practice which was not somehow affected (Corrigan & Sayer, 1985, p. 3). The late Philip Abrams, whose work was of enormous influence on Corrigan and Sayer, preferred to conceptualize the state as "politically organized subjection" because of its amorphous yet powerful character (Corrigan & Sayer, 1985, p. 7).

Far from having a neutral character, Corrigan and Sayer find that the state uses moral discipline in order to enforce rule, fulfilling bourgeois interests in a fundamentally unequal capitalist society. Their research located studies of moral regulation in "an understanding of the broad ethos and concrete practices of representation that are specific to capitalism and modern forms of regulation and rule" (Rousmaniere, Dehli, & de Coninck-Smith, 1997, pp. 5–6). In other words, for Corrigan and Sayer state formation and moral regulation were tied directly to the emergence of a particular historical and social order: capitalism. While all of the contributors to this collection locate their studies implicitly or explicitly within the context of a capitalist society, you will find, however, that they do not attribute to capitalism equal importance for their research.

While Corrigan and Sayer suggest that moral regulation is not confined to the realm of the state (Corrigan & Sayer, 1985, p. 5), the state remained the focus of their work. Valverde & Weir suggested in their own 1988 work that the role of the state was indeed over determined, and that we need to begin to undertake projects which will enrich moral regulation studies by taking our analysis beyond the exercise of state power (Valverde & Weir, 1988). Powerful discourses such as those of the medical profession, of professional and popular psychology and those of social reform movements, also have significant impact in shaping subjectivity. For example, we can think about how new discourses arise that deploy power in new ways, normalizing particular ideas and practices. Hunt uses the example of the moral regulation of the consumption of alcohol and tobacco. While there is a long history of the moral regulation of these products, recently a new discourse of health and prevention of illness has shaped the moral regulation of tobacco and alcohol. This link now appears to be common sense to us, but it is new, the product of discourse. It provides a new way of thinking about the need for self-discipline and for the regulation of others. Mona Gleason and Mary Louise Adams provide further examples that draw attention to the influence of psychology in this volume.

Alan Hunt finds that moral regulation projects are first, often initiated "from below" that is to say, with people who do not occupy positions of institutional power. This includes practices like the public shaming of rule breakers. Second, he finds them initiated from the middle. The middle class, particularly middle-class women, has had a significant role in moral reform projects since the late 19th century. Finally, he finds moral regulation coming from the top; from state institutions and official/mainstream politics. Recent campaigns like the "war on drugs" are an example of this. So are campaigns like the national security campaign, which Gary Kinsman discusses in this volume. However, the success of participants in these campaigns does depend on their social positions and social resources. Numerous contributors to this volume (for example, Kinsman, Little, Dehli, & Chunn) would take this as evidence that we cannot abandon materialist analysis. One's access to social resources is indeed shaped by the social and economic position into which one is born. For example, even if one were to accept the idea that class is produced through discourse, once class differentiation is in place, it takes on a material character and has significant consequences. Much of the current research on moral regulation, however, ruptures the link between moral regulation and the materialist analysis of history and society, which shaped Corrigan's original offering of the concept.

While Philip Corrigan in particular deeply influenced a number of the contributors to this volume (Dehli, Adams, Kinsman, Ross, Little, Valverde, and me), we have subsequently broadened our investigations of moral regulation to include state and nonstate processes. We agree with Hunt that moral regulation is a discursive and a political practice that is found everywhere in contemporary life (Hunt, 1999). This broadening of the analytic terrain was indeed welcomed by Corrigan early in these interventions, (Corrigan, 1994). Moreover, in their contributions to this volume, both Dorothy Chunn and Becki Ross find that it is often difficult to make clear distinctions between state and nonstate regulation. Finally, we can see how powerful professional discourses shape state practices like legal regulation, and are in turn reinforced through these same regulatory practices. For example, see Kirsten Johnson Kramar's analysis of the medico-legal construction of child abuse homicide, and Ena Dua's analysis of the impact of racialization on the determination of citizenship, both in this volume. The sample of work presented here forms a small part of the field, which includes contributions such as Mitchell Dean's work on the English poor laws (Dean, 1991), Mariana Valverde's work on the regulation of alcohol (Valverde, 1998), and Alan Hunt's work on social reform movements (Hunt, 1999).

Governmentality

There is another concept which has been used in ways that overlap with moral regulation, and which influences numerous contributions to this collection. That is **governmentality**. Just as there is no singular meaning of the concept, moral regulation, governmentality too is a concept that defies singular definition. It represents a relatively new body of literature, which has experienced enormous growth and a broad range of applications in a short period of time (O'Malley, Weir, & Shearing, 1997). Michel Foucault introduced the concept late in his life's work, and he was unable to provide the more elaborate study that he had intended before his premature death in 1984.

The governmentality approach rejects the idea that government is synonymous with the state (O'Malley, Weir, & Shearing, 1997). Indeed, Foucault believed that what was important was not the "etatisation of society" (state domination of society) but "the governmentalization of the state" (Foucault, in Burchell, Gordon, & Miller, 1991, p. 103). Burchell, Gordon, and Miller suggest that Foucault "proposed a definition of the term 'government' in general as meaning 'the conduct of conduct': that is to say, a form of activity aiming to shape, guide or affect the conduct of some person or persons…Government as an activity could concern the relation between self and self, private interpersonal relations involving some form of control or guidance, relations within social institutions and communities and, finally, relations concerned with the exercise of political sovereignty." So there are a variety of often interconnecting forms and meanings through which one can approach governance (Burchell, Gordon, & Miller, 1991, pp. 2–3).

We can see that one objective of governmentality research is to look at government within micro-settings including within subjects themselves (O'Malley, Weir & Shearing, 1997, p. 501). As well, governmentality research explores how governance occurs through discourses, which manage and administer individuals and populations. For example, in this volume, Xiaobei Chen looks at how "mothers at the margins are made into a particular type of subject to be regulated by risk management and supplementary criminal punishment" (Chen, this volume). She focuses her work on how governmental activities might occur through **political rationalities** which govern action (for example, through the naming of objectives, application of theories, and invention of categories), as well as how **governing technologies** (the programmes, techniques and procedures of government) provide the means to turn ideas into practices. Chen addresses the management of **risk** through governance, in cases where mothers are seen as "bundles of risk." Chen's work provides a good example of one of the ways that the governmentalization of the state occurs. However, Doyle and Lacombe's contribution to this volume examines the making of "the risk society" through **moral panics** about and the moral regulation of pedophilia (Doyle and Lacombe, this volume). Moore and Valverde discuss the regulation of different kinds of spaces in order to minimize some forms of risk (i.e., rape) in an analysis that locates moral regulation within broader relations of governance (Moore & Valverde, this volume).

So what is the relation between moral regulation and governance? Alan Hunt's work more explicitly links the work of Foucault to the concept of moral regulation. Foucault himself never used the concept; he only spoke of governing. However, Hunt and others believe that **moral regulation is a practice of governing**. As he comments, "The powerful claim at the heart of the sociology of governance is that a wide range of social agents are involved in the practices of governing directed at diverse targets" (Hunt, 1999, p. 5). Governance, however, is broader in that it can occur in ways that are not linked to moral regulation, as Dawn Moore and Mariana Valverde suggest in this volume. Moreover, since writing her contribution to this collection, Mariana Valverde has decided to stop using the concept of moral regulation because it is too often used as synonymous with social control. She finds that the concept of governmentality can accomplish the same purposes, without being burdened with the range of uses associated with the concept of moral regulation.

Like every living idea, moral regulation is continually in a process of revision. Studies in moral regulation are not about to be eclipsed by newer approaches, however. It is an area that has found a home in numerous universities across the country, where courses have been launched in order to provide forums for the generation of new scholarship.

CONCLUSIONS AND BEGINNINGS

As you read the contributions to this collection, think about how the authors integrate an analysis of social regulation, particularly moral regulation and governance, into their research. How do they believe that regulation or governance is occurring? Who or what can be said to be initiating these processes? What are the results? How do these approaches lead you to think about the social differently? Can you see the benefits of taking one particular approach over another? Some scholars of social theory insist that we must make this kind of a choice, and work with it consistently in order to maintain the integrity and intentions of a particular underlying theoretical approach. However, many of us are finding that this is not so easy to do. Very different theories can offer rich insights into the making of the social, and provide compelling directions for social analysis. Moreover, they do not exist as if in parallel universes. For example, post-structuralist approaches have pushed contributors to this collection who are committed to a materialist analysis to develop more complex analyses of social, political, and economic interrelationships. Materialist analyses have pressured contributors to this collection who undertake post-structuralist analyses not to abandon politics and become completely relativist. As you will see, numerous contributors to this volume find that there are elements of both approaches that are useful for their research.[4] It is our hope that some of the readers of this collection will one day offer fresh insights and directions for studies in regulation and governance.

---

[4] For more on this discussion, see the Introduction to Part One, Doing Historical Sociology.

Part One

Doing Historical Sociology

This book places a lot of emphasis on history. As you read through these chapters, think about why and how the past is also part of the present. We believe that it is essential for students to develop an understanding and appreciation of times, places, and peoples who are not directly related to the student's own life. And finally (although by no means exhaustively), we believe that this breadth of knowledge is essential for one to contribute in a meaningful way to social critique and politics in one's own time and place.

The most basic premise of historical sociology is that in order to understand how social life works one must understand it from an historical perspective. One may focus more on general theories about how societies work, or be more interested in exploring the events and issues of a particular time and place. Many who contributed to the growth of historical sociology as a discipline (most notably, Philip Abrams) believed that even more than this could be accomplished through studying historical sociology. One could explore not only how societies work, but also how and why they change (Allen, 1995, p. 131).

More recently, the work of Michel Foucault has had an enormous influence on how people across a range of disciplines conduct historical research. He believed that rather than taking the present for granted, we should ask how present social arrangements and ways of thinking about the social world came about. Calling his approach the **History of the Present,** Foucault challenged the belief that history can be understood and documented as a process of steady advancement toward the present. Rather, he found that history is discontinuous and fractured, and that it is the stories that we tell about history which make it appear to be otherwise. Foucault proposed that we explore particular "regimes of truth." These regimes create the ways of knowing that characterize specific historical circumstances and influence how we understand these circumstances now. He argued that knowledge is always linked to power because knowing something is always about organizing and ordering it. Therefore, we need to explore power-knowledge relations by investigating how these regimes of truth are produced, circulated, and used. Foucault did not propose a general theory of history and society; rather his research encountered a focus on specific, localized projects and events. He described his approach as **genealogy**. To summarize, Foucault's genealogical approach was to uncover histories of discourses and knowledge; to generate specific histories of power and their effects. He was not concerned with mapping an underlying reality and continuous history, but rather with how what is understood as truth is produced—and challenged—in particular times and places.

In the introduction to this collection, I noted that bodies of theory are not "pure" but rather are constantly re-thought and revised as they are subject to the challenges of alternative theoretical approaches. In order to draw attention to the distinctiveness of their contributions I, at times, present the ideas of Marx and Foucault in a binary model. This does not mean, however, that their work is always positioned in opposition to one another as contemporary scholars undertake the exploratory tasks of research and writing. Throughout this collection, we will see authors drawing on elements of a range of theoretical approaches in order to attempt to create new directions for theory and research. This may appear to be confusing at times, but it is the reality of intellectual creativity and the only way in which new directions in thinking about social organization and social life can emerge.

The chapters in this first section cover four important and fascinating areas of historical investigation. Paula Maurutto explores the moral regulation of juvenile delinquency. Kari Dehli takes a different approach than usual to studies of schooling as she explores the moral regulation of parents in relation to schooling, rather than of young people. Both Dehli and Maurutto draw our attention to important processes in the development of the **disciplinary society**. As Maurutto points out, for Foucault **discipline** is the "art of correct training." It produces citizens: citizens who are obedient, law-abiding, industrious, and hard working. This requires exploring the micro-relations of the circulation of power. As Dehli finds, disciplinary techniques and practices are practices of moral regulation, including how individuals and groups regulate themselves. When we undertake these kinds of investigations, we find that what we assume to be normal, reasonable, and natural are really the products of history, and inseparable from power. Moreover, we see that the making of normal is a product of conflict, struggle, and resistance.

In her chapter, Ena Dua explores the racialization of immigration and Canadian citizenship through practices of governing (for information about the relationship between moral regulation and governance, see the introduction to this book). She investigates "the historical emergence of citizenship as a technology of governance." That is, she is interested in the production of citizenship (i.e., who could be a citizen; what was required to be a citizen; on what bases one could be excluded) as a governing practice, administered by the Canadian state. She is particularly interested in how the production of citizenship has relied on discourses about race and ethnicity. Dorothy Chunn's research explores the regulation of sexuality, particularly what has been considered abnormal sex. She finds that early to mid 20th century anti-venereal disease strategies were not merely a means of administering to public health, but that medical and scientific discourses were highly dependent on morals discourses about appropriate and inappropriate forms of sex. She draws our attention to the normalization of these medical-moral discourses, such that it is now often hard to distinguish where self-regulation ends and external compulsion or coercion begins. Indeed, she finds that these are usually intertwined.

This kind of thinking may seem abstract and even arcane to you. However, it has everything to do with people, what happens in our lives and the ways in which we come to know ourselves and others. People are, after all, the subjects of the discourses and the practices that are being investigated. Thus, these authors ask how categories of identity and identification—juvenile delinquent, citizen, immigrant, parent and so on—were produced, and how they were understood by (some of) those who were named by them. We will see how the **subject** is actively constructed through regulatory practices, practices which discipline populations and the individuals who comprise those populations. After reading these chapters, we urge you to consider how the research presented in these chapters continues to have relevance for today.

CHAPTER 1

MORAL REFORM, DISCIPLINE, AND NORMALIZATION: JUVENILE DELINQUENCY AND REHABILITATION IN ONTARIO

BY PAULA MAURUTTO

The 1890s marked a radical shift in the punishment and regulation of juvenile delinquents in Canada. The use of harsh corporal methods of punishment in juvenile detention centres was slowly replaced with disciplinary practices that focused on proper training and spiritual and moral development. No longer were young offenders thought to be hardened criminals to be punished for violating the law; they were now seen as misguided youths in need of understanding and rehabilitation. Incarceration in reformatories or prisons was condemned by a number of social reform groups, such as the Child Savers Movement, and the Protestant and Catholic Children's Aid Societies, which characterised such institutions as breeding grounds for criminals. By the 1880s, many new crime control strategies were implemented to rehabilitate and reform delinquent youth. Among these strategies were the development of industrial schools and parole and probationary programmes.[1] These innovations were designed to remake young offenders, turning them into productive, law-abiding citizens.

UNDERSTANDING MORAL REGULATION AND DISCIPLINE

The following section examines the transition and development of these new initiatives in Ontario. The primary focus of this section is to explore how these developments formed part of a moral reform campaign to rehabilitate or "correct" juvenile delinquents. Here moral regulation is understood as the production of ethical and moral subjectivities such that young offenders not only exhibited desired behaviour but internalized and came to support the dominant values and beliefs of society. Moral regulation

---

[1] In the 1930s, industrial schools were replaced with training schools. Some industrial schools were closed while others merely changed their name to training schools.

is understood as practices that seek to reshape and mould behaviour and inner beliefs through normalizing discourses and techniques. To this end, the paper examines how moral reform and normalization was enforced in industrial school through training programmes, casework practices, and employees of the school. It then examines how parole and probation extended this moral reform effort into the community, where similar techniques continued to work on the subjectivities of adolescents.

Michel Foucault's work on the disciplinary society is used to make sense of and critically analyze the shift in Ontario's juvenile justice practices and legislation. In *Discipline and Punish: The Birth of the Prison* (1977), Foucault examines the rise of disciplinary practices beginning in the nineteenth century and how they came to replace corporal forms of punishment. Although, repressive forms of punishment were not eliminated, modern penal systems became more consumed with correcting and normalizing behaviour than with dispensing corporal punishment. The focus shifted from repression to discipline, which reflected a new approach concerned with *knowing the criminal* and rehabilitating behaviour. Juvenile delinquents were inscribed not as inherently evil felons but rather as irresponsible children marred by family dislocation and improper socialization. Mere corporal punishment was deemed ineffective, as it did not result in moral and social re-development. Physical punishment of the body gave way to new techniques and practices designed to reform the very soul of young offenders, which included instruction in moral and religious education, proper grooming habits, vocational training, and accepted recreational pastimes. Casework practices designed to diagnose and classify types of abnormalities were introduced. These techniques were to be used to rehabilitate not only behaviour but also the actual beliefs and inner souls of young offenders. They were designed to produce "docile bodies' for a disciplined society.

Discipline, as Foucault claims, is an "art of correct training," it "makes individuals," it produces obedient, law-abiding, industrious, and hard-working citizens, thus meeting the objective of industrial schools (Foucault, 1977, p. 170).

Regulating Destitute and Working-Class Youth

These new disciplinary institutions were deemed constructive not only for those youths who broke the law, but for any child displaying a potential for criminal behaviour, and in particular, for the neglected and wayward children of working-class parents. The 1874 Ontario Industrial School Act empowered the courts to incarcerate juveniles, not only on the basis of criminal transgressions, but also on the perceived delinquent potential of a child. The Act allowed for any child under the age of 14 to be brought before the courts if they were,

> found begging or receiving alms, found wandering in the streets and had no settled place of abode, who were found deserted or whose parents were in jail, whose parents or guardians claimed they were unable to control the child or who, owing to

the vice of the parents, was growing up without salutary parental control. (Ontario Department of Public Welfare, 1957, p. 31)

Later, other behaviours such as truancy and sexual immorality were added to the list. In effect, the act legislated the courts to make assessments based not exclusively on criminality but also on "normality;" that is, the extent to which children fit within societal norms. The courts thereby wielded a tremendous power over the regulation of working-class and dependent families, whose children could be labelled neglected and thus incarcerated (Chunn, 1992; Garland, 1985; Rothman, 1980; Schlossman, 1998). Increasingly, neglected, abandoned, and working-class children became governed as potential criminals.[2] Boys were two to three times more likely to be institutionalized than girls.[3]

Children in industrial schools ranged between the ages of eight and sixteen. Legislation prohibited younger children from being placed in industrial schools; they were typically sent to orphanages or foster homes. As of 1900, children could be detained for a maximum of three years, but they remained under the supervision of the schools until the age of 21. In a few cases, when release to parents or foster homes could not be arranged, they were detained for a longer period. In one case, for example, a child was institutionalized for nine years (Ontario Department of Provincial Secretary, St. Mary's Industrial School papers, 1917, 1918, 1919; Department of Provincial Secretary, J.J. Kelso personal communication). In general, most children were committed for stealing or incorrigibility. The latter category encompassed anyone who had not actually committed a crime, but was thought to be at "moral risk". The following statistics on the general industrial school population from 1929 to 1933 provide some indication of the frequency of offenses. Boys were more likely to be incarcerated for stealing (49%), breaking and entering (18%), truancy (14%) and incorrigibility (12%). Girls, on the other hand, were most often detained for moral misconduct including incorrigibility (28%), uncontrollability (22%) and immorality (22%). The frequency with which girls were institutionalized for minor offenses reflects the general moral panic and association of female misconduct with sexual promiscuity. Many were committed for being found in a "house of bad repute" or for failing to inform their parents of their whereabouts (Strange, 1995).

INDUSTRIAL SCHOOLS

Ontario's first two industrial schools, the Victoria Industrial School for boys, and the Alexandra Industrial School for girls, built in 1887 and 1891 respectively,

---

[2] These types of status offences remained in effect until the enactment of the 1984 Young Offenders Act.
[3] The figures for the girls sent to the Good Shepherd Refuge and the few Catholic boys who were placed in Protestant institutions do not exist, and as such the data are approximate numbers only.

were administered by the Protestant Churches. Tensions over the education of Catholic youth in Protestant schools led to the formation of separate Catholic institutions. The Christian Brothers opened St. John's Industrial School in 1895 and soon after, the Sisters of the Good Shepherd took on the administration of St. Mary's Industrial School in 1900.[4] Children in the Industrial Schools were offered a daily regime of academic, vocational, physical, and, religious training. Adherence to a rigid schedule enabled social reformers to represent these schools more as private boarding schools than detention centres, schools in which every minute of the student's day was filled with productive re-education. Disciplined education was said to be essentially corrective and productive: it sought to repair the behavioural problems of children, and was a "means of developing personality and encouraging self-expression" (Reeves, 1929, pp. 337–338). Activities and courses were carefully chosen to maximize character building and to instill industrious work habits that would turn inmates into useful, self-sufficient members of society. Each task was designed to mould juveniles into compliant, obedient citizens who would govern their behaviour according to normative social and moral rules. Hence, coercive methods of control were only to be used as a last resort (*"Proper function of Correctional Institutions"*, 1929 December 6; Schlossman, 1998; Valverde, 1995).

A typical daily routine at one of the boy's industrial school—the St. John's school—involved three hours of academic training and four hours of vocational work. A full academic curriculum was offered, as well as an "Opportunity Class" for the alleged "backward" boys, approximately 20 percent of the school's population, who were thought to be in need of remedial education. Vocational instruction in a range of trades was designed to instill "habits of industry" and personal "satisfaction of accomplishment." Vocational training was offered in, baking, tailoring, printing, shoemaking, barbering, and gardening—trades deemed appropriate for working-class children. Recreational activities were highly valued for their contribution to physical health, self-esteem, and teamwork experience and were seen as a way of instilling acceptable leisure pastimes that could be pursued once the boys were discharged. School administrators believed that one of the greatest deterrents to juvenile delinquency was the provision of recreational pastimes. Hence, the

---

[4] In 1939, when industrial schools were no longer popular and training schools were promoted as the innovation in juvenile corrections, both schools took on the designation of training schools for juvenile delinquents. Later, with the passage of the Young Offenders Act, training schools became referred to as Youth Detention Centres. Bennett, Paul W. (1988, May). Taming "Bad Boys" of the "Dangerous Class": Child Rescue and Restraint at the Victoria Industrial School 1887–1935, *Social History*, 21, p. 86; Griffiths, Curt T. and Verdun-Jones, Simon, N. (1994). *Canadian Criminal Justice* (pp. 600–601). Toronto: Harcourt Brace; Archives of Ontario (AO), Ministry of Correctional Service, (1935). RG 20, J 2, Vol 22, *Report of the Committee Appointed to Investigate the Present Juvenile Reformatory School System of Ontario*, p. 37.

school sponsored a variety of outdoor programmes, such as swimming, track and field, rugby, lacrosse, baseball, and hockey which were supplemented with indoor activities, such as table games, hobby work, and music (Ontario Department of Public Welfare, 1932/33, 1933/34, 1934/35, 1936/37). Religious and moral guidance were of paramount importance in the rehabilitation process. According to Brother Cyril, Superintendent of the School,

> by means of prayer, Mass, formal instruction, private interviews, selected readings, annual spiritual retreats and frequent opportunities for the reception of the Sacraments, we have endeavoured to build up desirable moral habits, to give the boys a real understanding of their obligations to God and to society and to convince them that their religion is a life to be lived. (Ontario Department of Public Welfare, 1936/37, p. 28)

Industrial school training at St. Mary's reinforced gendered stereotypes and traditional feminine skills. The girls were provided with some scholastic instruction, but the Sisters were ill-equipped to provide a full range of academic courses. Hence, few of the girls gained entrance into high school. Likewise, the vocational programme was limited to little other than household management. The girls were schooled in,

> personal cleanliness [as] the first study....They are instructed in the care of a household, and this comprises sleeping apartments, drawing room, living rooms, dining room, sewing rooms, kitchen, and store rooms. The linen assigned to each of these must be made, marked, mended, sorted, and kept in good order. They are taught dress-making, hand sewing, machine sewing, power machines, and other, knitting, darning, embroidery, lace-making, mending, repairing and making over wearing apparel....They are trained to a solid knowledge of the fundamentals with cleanliness and economy stressed. (Ontario Department of Public Welfare, 1936/37, p. 26)

Particular attention was paid to educating the girls in modern household techniques such as the proper "care of hardwood floors and good linoleum" (Annual Report, 1933/34, p. 31). Such training prepared the girls for little else than a career in domestic service or motherhood. The future roles envisioned for these girls were also evident in the importance placed on grooming and hair dressing. The girls were encouraged "in everything which contributes towards personal attractiveness and daintiness" (Ontario Department of Public Welfare, 1934/35, p. 17). Kelly Hannah-Moffat, in her study of female prisoners, describes how "emphasizing a woman's appearance became a wider strategy to morally regulate her by creating "a marriageable woman" (Hannah-Moffat, 1997). In essence, the Sisters were participating in state formation by preparing these girls for their future roles as mothers of the nation.

The Role of Experts in the Governance of Delinquents

The enforcement of corrective rehabilitation and disciplinary powers was intimately tied to the rise of an expert class of professionals, including doctors, psychologists, psychiatrists, and social workers. By the 1920s, industrial schools in Ontario increasingly began to employ professionally trained workers. Volunteers and religious orders continued to play a role in the administration of industrial schools, but increasingly, workers were expected to be professionally trained. This new group of experts introduced a range of scientific and technical knowledges that were deployed to regulate offenders. They elaborated a new set of practices to diagnose, classify, record, and reshape behaviour. These practices, first made popular in the field of medicine and social welfare, were brought to bear on juvenile reform such that the result was a blending of social welfare and juvenile justice.[5]

By the 1920s, social workers had promoted casework as the key mechanism in the reform of young offenders. Social casework was designed to probe beneath the symptoms of deviant behaviour to diagnose underlying causes. It enabled experts to delve "behind the crime" to uproot the causes of delinquent behaviour which could then be measured, diagnosed, treated, and normalized. The causes of delinquency were then to be detailed in extensive social case records that could be circulated within institutions and between agencies. Standardized forms were introduced to record information on the child's physical and emotional state, educational and moral progress, and family background. The causes of delinquency were often traced back to the home environment. Family interactions and practices were documented and parents and siblings were often interviewed. Thus, experts brought not only the offending child but also whole families under the gaze of professional scrutiny.

Two such standardized reports produced by the Ontario government in the 1920s included the "Committal Report" and the "School Attendance Report" (St. Mary's and St. John's Training School Files, 1919–1939). The Committal Report was completed by the Children's Aid Societies prior to the sentencing of a young offender. It included details on the offence and background information to be used during the trial. The School Attendance Report, administered on a quarterly basis by the school supervisor, monitored the progress of the child within the institution. Once completed, copies of both records were submitted to the Department of the Provincial Secretary, and after 1930, to the Ontario Department of Public Welfare.

---

[5] This phenomenon, identified by Foucault, has also been referred to as the "tutelary complex" by Donzelot, the "psy" complex by Nikolas Rose, and part of socialized justice by Chunn. Foucault, Michel (1979) *Discipline and Punish*. New York: Pantheon; Donzelot, Jacques (1979). *The Policing of Families*. New York: Pantheon Books; Rose, Nikolas (1985). *The Psychological Complex: Psychology, Politics and Society in England, 1869–1939*. London: Routledge and Kegan Paul; Chunn Dorothy E., *From Punishment to Doing Good*. Toronto: University of Toronto Press.

The reports included socio-biographical information on age, reason for committal, previous infractions, and scholastic standing, in addition to medical and psychological diagnoses (Ibid.). A detailed family history profiling the child's upbringing was also contained in the committal report. As the root causes of juvenile delinquency was said to be located in the family, this section formed a significant part of the assessment. Information was compiled on parent and sibling occupation, general behaviour and appearance, church attendance, infractions of the law, the amounts of social assistance received and the prevalence of such vices as alcoholism or gambling. Inspection of the home was mandatory and evidence of uncleanliness, lack of furnishings or bedrooms for children, poor neighbourhoods, and other structural conditions were documented. The character of the mother was of particular importance, and much of the analysis was devoted to a detailed description of her activities. Working mothers were often reproached for leaving their children alone for the better part of the day (Ibid.).

Medical and psychiatric exams were a requirement for each child. The general health of the child was noted, including the condition of the heart, tonsils, eyes, teeth, weight, skin conditions, and any habits such as nail biting. Every attempt was made to correct any abnormality, for administrators believed that poor physical health was directly related to the propensity for delinquent behaviour. As the Industrial School Advisory Board noted in 1932,

> the physical state of the child, such as diseased tonsils, decayed teeth and undernourishment, has also contributed to delinquency and the medical reports have been of great assistance to us in recommending immediate treatment. We have found in a number of cases that the elimination of these defects has, in as short a period of six months, raised the mentality of certain inmates so as to admit of definitely higher standards of training. (Ontario Department of Public Welfare, 1931/32 p. 39)

In addition to physical health, evidence of sexual impropriety was closely monitored, particularly among girls, and any indication of venereal disease was accepted as proof of delinquency. Such close scrutiny was particularly evident in one report which identified how "the hymen was partially ruptured, intromit admitting one finger" (St. Mary's Training School Files, 1937, March 8). Gonorrhea and syphilis tests were commonly performed on the girls, but were rarely reported in boys' case files. The concern with detecting venereal disease reflected prevailing fears that such illnesses could spread immorality as well as disease. Concerted efforts were made to transfer those infected out of the schools to local hospitals. As one government report stated in 1934, "the Girls' schools are not equipped to deal adequately with this problem; and we fear that by attempting to do so, the main purpose of the schools may be endangered, and that the health, morals, and general training of the younger girls may suffer" (Ontario Department of Public Welfare, 1933/34, p. 33).

Medical examinations were not only used to identify actual health risks, but were laden with moral judgements.

Ontario was one of the first provinces to introduce psychiatric examinations of juvenile delinquents. IQ and other psychometric tests were regularly administered for the purpose of isolating "mental defectives" and the "feeble-minded." That 25 percent of the industrial school population in Ontario in the 1930s was designated "mentally deficient" testifies to the indiscriminate use of such labels. This figure does not include the large number of children identified as "dull normal" (Ibid.). Apart from the use of such questionable methods to measure intelligence, Bennett also suggests that "little distinction was made between illiteracy and mental incapacity" (Bennett, 1988, p. 82). Illiterate or foreign-born children, for example, were frequently labelled as "feeble-minded" and attempts were made to transfer them to the Orillia Hospital for the mentally defective. However, lack of funding meant that the majority remained in the industrial schools. Psychiatrists and psychologists did not provide much in the way of treatment, and the schools lacked the resources to implement adequate remedial programmes.[6] The assessments did, however, have an impact on decisions for release and aftercare.

The primary effect of such assessments was to induce normalization. The documents were used to identify problems, abnormalities, and deficiencies that, it was believed, could be reformed. The nature of assessments presupposed normal versus abnormal categories that could be detected and distinguished. Those who failed to conform to prescribed norms could be identified, isolated, and their progress could be monitored over time. The more that was known about the juveniles the more controllable they became. Case records legalized and normalized the intrusions of experts and private social work agents into the lives of children and their families. These assessments, however, were never simply neutral judgements, but reflected class, gender, and racial biases. The assessments were advanced as objective scientific procedures, but attempts at classification, categorization, and assessment are always shaped by official discourses and "competing truth claims" (Iacovetta & Mitchinson, in press, p. 21).

THE REGULATORY PROCESSES OF PAROLE

Parole emerged as a post-institutional practice designed to assist children who were re-adjusting to community life while also monitoring their behaviour and activities. Parole supervision was to ensure both the proper conduct of juveniles and the

---

[6] Ontario Department of Public Welfare, 1932/33, p. 38. Similar issues are discussed in Bennett, Taming 'Bad Boys,' p. 82; Rothman, *Conscience and Convenience*, pp. 245, 275; Reeves, *Training Schools*, pp. 248–249; Chunn, *From Punishment to Doing Good*, p. 19; Valverde, Building Anti-Delinquent Communities, p. 32–33.

detection of any breach of social norms and responsibilities. In effect, parole extended the powers of the juvenile justice system into the community, as knowledge of the released child's habits, character, and daily activities continued to be made available. It furthered the ability of government to regulate and reform young offenders and their families. It was a regulatory practice that brought whole families into the web of moral regulation.

The Ontario Industrial School Advisory Board was formed in 1931 to oversee the supervision of industrial schools and also the terms for releasing children to the community. Each eligible case for parole was forwarded to the Board which determined which children would be returned to their parents, placed in foster care, or employed (Report of the Committee, 1935). A progress report on each child released to the community was to be conducted by the Children's Aid Society and submitted to the Industrial School Advisory Board every three months. The "Placement Officer's Report," as it was known, included information on living conditions, general health, employment, and educational achievement. Leisure activities were closely monitored and any sport, special interest, or church affiliations were recorded. Interviews were regularly conducted with family members, employers, educators, priests, social workers, and probation officers. Many aspects of the child's life were monitored, and any indication of potential delinquency could result in peremptory re-committal.

This system enabled the authorities to wield tremendous power over the future of young offenders and their families. For instance, before children could be returned to their parents, the Board insisted on a detailed examination of families and neighbourhood conditions. Members of the Children's Aid Societies were licenced to enter the homes of families and inspect every aspect of their lives. They questioned neighbours, local priests, and agency workers about the parents' character, habits, and values. Even parents who themselves had laid charges against their children came under the intrusive inspection of authorities. The decision to place their children in industrial schools opened the door to government and private agency regulation.[7] In effect, it displaced parental rights with those of bureaucratic administration. This was a serious concern during the Depression when many working-class and destitute homes were deemed unsuitable for the upbringing of children by middle-class social reformers (St. Mary's and St. John's Training School Files, 1919–1939). Moreover, by licensing voluntary organizations to police and regulate children through parole, the state extended its scope, range, and penetration of legal control. These methods worked to intensify the state's ability to "govern at a distance" (Ibid.).

---

[7] For similar arguments in the post-World War Two era see Iacovetta, Franca. (1996, June). *The Making of a Delinquent Girl: "Truth," "Fiction", and "Expert," Opinion in Family Court Cases, 1940s–1960s.* Paper presented at the Canadian Historical Association Annual Meeting, Brock University.

PROBATION: EXTENDING MORAL REGULATION INTO THE COMMUNITY

This final section examines the rise of probation as a new twentieth-century technology of governance. Probation emerged as a form of community-based corrections that ensured supervision and rehabilitation without removing deviant children from their homes. Rather than institutionalizing youth, probationary programmes allowed the police and courts to remand an adolescent into the care of a probation officer who would be responsible for monitoring youth rehabilitation in the community. The Ontario 1892 Act for the Prevention of Cruelty to, and Better Protection of Children, and the subsequent federal Youthful Offenders Act passed in 1894, and the 1908 Juvenile Delinquents Act entrusted guardianship over all children whether they be in industrial schools, reformatories, foster homes, or under parole or probation to the Children's Aid Societies. The police and the Children's Aid Societies were given the authority to determine whether a neglected or delinquent child would be brought before the courts, released, or placed under probationary supervision. Probation was identified as a strategy that reinforced prevailing conceptions of juvenile delinquency as not simply a criminal activity, but a problem of socialization that necessitated the intervention of philanthropic agencies to ensure proper moral reform. Philanthropic agencies, in particular the Protestant and Catholic Children's Aid Societies and later the Big Brothers and Big Sisters comprised the major support base of probation's emergence. The courts typically placed juveniles under probation, but a variety of social welfare agencies and businesses could also recommend a youth for probationary supervision. For instance, the Canadian railway companies, which often picked up juveniles for minor misdemeanours would refer children to probationary programmes. Some children, attracted to the recreational activities, appeared voluntarily; others were sent by parents who believed that their child was in need of reform.

The goal of probation was to reshape the moral character of not only the children placed under their care, but of entire families. "Lack of judicious home training" was identified as the root cause of "lawless behaviour." As such, unless the family as a whole was treated, rehabilitative efforts would be ineffective since children would be returned to the depraved moral environment that produced their moral turpitude (Archbishop Neil McNeil Papers, 1925, September). J. J. Kelso himself voiced such sentiments when he claimed that,

> the modern conception of a probation officer is not that he should exercise constabulary powers, but that he should be the friend of the parent equally with the child....It is not his duty to size a child...but by friendly tactics to bring about the cordial cooperation of the parents in securing the child's best welfare and its continuance in the home, which is its birthright. (*Globe*, 1905 April, p. 116)

Probation officers were to gain the confidence not only of the child, but of the entire family, for "the home is the workshop in which the character and personality…[are] moulded" (Catholic Big Brothers, 1930, December 25).

The specific target of this rehabilitation project was the reform of "habit." Probation did not typically involve the accumulation of extensive case files that documented a youth's life history and behaviour. Rather, probation typically operated through the reform of everyday behaviour. In Mariana Valverde's study of the regulation of habit, she discusses how habit is an everyday behaviour that is not governed through expert-based or scientific knowledges—such as diagnostic categories produced by psychologists—rather it is regulated through commonsensical, normative assumptions. Vice and habits, for example, are not discussed in terms of personality disorders, but as reflections of a lack of self-control, as in smoking. Habit, as described by the Catholic Big Brothers,

> is such a common, everyday sort of term, with which everyone is more or less familiar, that it hardly seems necessary to discuss it at all. However, it is in this very fact—that habits are so commonplace and ordinary in the minds of the great mass of individuals—that the danger lies. All too frequently the fundamental importance of forming right habits in early life is minimized or overlooked altogether. (Ibid.)

Reformers in the 1930s typically described their work as the reforming of habits.

Probationary programmes sought to instruct parents on how to produce desirable habits among their children, and on strategies for breaking deep-rooted "bad habits." Parents were warned of the grave danger in "babying" children for this fostered "habits of dependency" (Catholic Big Brothers, 1931, March 19). When children displayed "slovenly habits," parents were advised not to scold or "nag" children. "Nagging will not improve him. He must be made to return to his room and wash or comb his hair, or adjust his clothing when he has neglected to do so. Praise, when he is properly groomed, is also quite effective" (Catholic Big Brothers, 1930, June 5). Parents were told that if their "child has habits of sulking and pouting, break them at once. Do not argue, or punish, or scold, or try to divert his attention through bribery. Such tactics increase the condition of making him an object of special attention…Ignore him completely and absolutely till he snaps out of it" (Catholic Big Brothers, 1930, June 3).

Particular emphasis was placed on the importance of good grooming, reading, and posture (Catholic Big Brothers, 1929, November 7 & 1932, June 12; Catholic Welfare Bureau, 1928, April 5 & 1929, November 14).

Children were encouraged in a range of recreational activities, including sports for boys, sewing for girls, and dual-sex pastimes like reading and music. Those with academic interests were provided with scholarships and bursaries to pursue high school and technical or college education. Church attendance was an important convention that all children were encouraged to observe. Employment opportunities, primarily in blue-collar positions, were also provided and children were taught the value of saving their earnings for future endeavours. Big Brothers also worked to condition their "little" friends to proper grooming practices such as the "use of a toothbrush" which was said to be "an article entirely foreign to many of [the] boys." Habit training pledged to transform dependent, wayward, vagrant, and misbehaving juveniles into self-sufficient, productive, and contributing members of society. It also sought to ensure that immigrant and working-class children adopted dominant middle-class standards and customs.

CONCLUSION

Industrial schools, parole, and probationary programmes were designed to re-moralize juvenile "deviants." The rise of a disciplinary ethos championed moral and spiritual reform through education and socialization rather than corporal measures. Corporal measures might reduce immediate offending behaviour by instilling fear, but they could never effect a change in the actual beliefs and soul of youths. Rather, reform of habit and family life through proper instruction and the detection and normalization of abnormalities through social casework were identified as the key to long-term reform. Such reform could not be provided by prison guards trained in the deployment of corporal methods. Rather, this project necessitated the involvement of a wide array of voluntary agencies and trained experts in the fields of medicine and social science.

The specifically Foucaultian approach used to understand moral regulation draws attention to the multiple and competing practices and institutions involved in the production of subjectivities. The rise of disciplinary ethos manifested in the formation of industrial schools, parole, and probation worked to decentre the role of the state in juvenile justice. Juvenile justice was no longer solely the purview of the state. Rather, a number of voluntary organizations and professionals come to play an increasing role, thereby blurring the lines between the public and private. As Mariana Valverde and Lorna Weir contend, non-governmental organizations "cannot be seen as mere pawns of the state engaged in doing its dirty ideological work in puppet-like fashion; voluntary organizations usually have their own agendas and are in some ways in opposition to the state even when they receive their funding from it" (1988, p. 32). Valverde uses the concept of the mixed social economy to deconstruct the dichotomy between public/private and state/civil society, by highlighting the "complex web of relationships" involved in the operation of moral reform (1995, Summer, pp. 33–60). The mixed social economy refers to a process in which regulation is achieved not simply as the product of state or economic interests, but is rather a complex negotiated outcome that is also affected by those operating within the social sector, in this case by such actors as the churches, voluntary organizations, social workers, and other professionals.

While Valverde and others mostly confine their analyses of the mixed social economy to the charity sector, the concept is used here to highlight how the juvenile justice system operated as a mixed economy. This analysis redefines law enforcement as not the exclusive domain of the state but rather as an interplay between public and private institutions involved in the surveillance of families and the regulation of juvenile delinquents.

While the state did enact legislation and license professional workers, it was social reformers and professionals who where involved in devising regulatory techniques and practices, and it is they who lobbied governments to introduce policies and laws that would facilitate their endeavours. Their involvement in the youth criminal justice system served to accredit their knowledges and legitimate their work, thereby enabling them to expand their services and practices of intervention.

The result of this interrelation is that it furthered the intrusions into community and family life through community correctional strategies like parole and probation. These extended the power of both state and extra state organizations beyond criminal justice institutions and into communities, thereby allowing for more effective policing, disciplining and regulation of young offenders and their primarily working-class families.

CRITICAL THINKING QUESTIONS

1. Describe how modern forms of punishment reflect a shift from corporal to disciplinary practices.
2. What is the connection between moral regulation and Foucault's notion of discipline?
3. What was the purpose of industrial schools?
4. How did gender affect the moral regulation of juvenile delinquents?
5. What was the purpose of social casework? How did it impact on the moral reform of juvenile delinquents?
6. How were parole and probation programmes designed to re-moralize juvenile delinquents and their families?
7. How did probation extend the regulatory powers of the government into the community?

SUGGESTED READINGS

Bell, Sandra J. (1999). Creating a Juvenile Justice System: Then and *Now. Young Offenders and Juvenile Justice: A Century after the Fact*. Toronto: ITP Nelson.
   Includes a general overview of the Canadian juvenile justice system from its origins in the nineteenth century to the present.

Carrigan, Owen, D. (1991). The Treatment of Juvenile Delinquents. *Crime and Punishment in Canada: A History*. Toronto: McClelland and Stewart.
> Provides a general historical overview of legislation and the treatment of juvenile delinquents in Canada.

Garland, David (1990). Punishment and the Technologies of Power: The Work of Michel Foucault. *Punishment and Modern Society: A Study in Social Theory*. Chicago: The University of Chicago Press.
> Provides an excellent overview of Foucault's book *Discipline and Punish*. It reviews Foucault's understanding of modern penal systems, the birth of the prison, and his concept of discipline.

Houston, Susan E. (1972, Fall). Victorian Origins of Juvenile Delinquency: A Canadian Experience, *History of Education Quarterly, 12*, 254-280.
> Examines how the concept of juvenile delinquency took hold in Canada and how it affected the regulation of youth.

Iacovetta, Franca (1998). Parents, Daughters, and Family Court Intrusions into Working-Class Life. In Franca Iacovetta and Wendy Mitchinson (Eds.), *On the Case: Explorations in Social History*. Toronto: University of Toronto Press.
> The article explores the themes of delinquency, parental responses, and court intrusions involving female juvenile delinquents who appeared before the York County Family and Juvenile Court between 1945 to 1956.

Sangster, Joan (2000). Girls in Conflict with the Law: Exploring the Construction of Female "Delinquency" in Ontario, 1940-1960. *Canadian Journal of Women and the Law, 12:1*, 3-31.
> The article examines the social construction of female juvenile "delinquency" in the 1940s and 1950s. It questions the dominant theoretical paradigms that are used to understand the history of criminality.

Schlossman, Steven (1998). Delinquent Children: the Juvenile Reform School. In Norval Morris and David J. Rothman (Eds.), *The Oxford History of the Prison: The Practice of Punishment in Western Society*. New York: Oxford University Press.
> This chapter traces the history of the reform school in the United States and address the following questions: What is a "reform school"? What is a "juvenile delinquent"? What is "rehabilitation"?

WEB LINKS

www.canada.justice.gc.ca/en/dept/pub/ycja/youth.html
> <http://www.canada.justice.gc.ca/en/dept/pub/ycja/youth.html>
> Canada's new Youth Criminal Justice Act.

www.lfcc.on.ca/index.htm <http://www.lfcc.on.ca/index.htm>
> The web site for The Centre for Children and Families in the Justice System located in London, Ontario includes publications about and services for young offenders.

www.johnhoward.ab.ca/res-pub.htm#cc <http://www.johnhoward.ab.ca/res-pub.htm#cc>
> Web site for The John Howard Society of Alberta which includes a number of critical resource papers on young offenders.

CHAPTER 2

An Important Archive of Usefulness: Regulating "the Parent" at School[1]

by Kari Dehli

In today's school system we often hear calls for parents to become more involved in their children's education, for local communities to join in "partnerships" with schools, and for schools, in turn, to become more accountable to their most immediate public, parents. The claim that "parents are their children's first and most important teacher" is often repeated in policy-documents, speeches, and everyday conversations and there are numerous programs that teach parents how to support children's learning at home: by reading together, creating time and space for homework, and taking a general interest in what children experience at school. Parents are also recruited into school governance, and provincial governments across Canada, and governments elsewhere, have introduced policies that require schools to establish advisory councils or governing committees with a majority of its membership drawn from parents (Levin, 2001).

Paradoxically, these policies, practices, and sentiments are discussed as if they are both obvious and normal, what every reasonable parent and every good school should do, while there is also a sense that the benefits of such "involvement" have only recently been discovered by educators, researchers, and parents themselves. There are cautionary strands in these discussions, which suggest that some forms of involvement may not be desirable, and that some parents invest "too much" in their children's schooling. At the same time, educators lament that many parents "fail" to assume their responsibilities in relation to the school. Thus, relations between "the parent" that appears in policy documents, political speeches, notices about homework and fieldtrips, and invitations to attend parent-teacher night, on the one hand, and actual parents who encounter this

---

[1] This chapter is a substantially revised version of a previously published paper, "Loyally Confer through Regular Channels. In Rousmaniere, Dehli, & de Coninck-Smith (Eds.), *Discipline, Moral Regulation, and Schooling*. New York: Garland. I am grateful to the publisher and co-editors for granting permission to use this work here.

category, on the other, are neither easy nor natural. I argue in this chapter that, as a category in talk and text about education, "the parent" operates both to suggest what is good and proper—its moral and normative dimension—as well as what is natural and obvious—its truth dimension. Giving content and meaning to this category, realizing it in practice, is a social and political matter, the product of a great deal of effort and, at times, of conflict.

To make these rather abstract ideas more concrete, I am interested in how we can trace the histories of "the parent" and *her* "involvement" in schools? We need to go back to an earlier period to ask how and why it is that the truth of "parental involvement" is being promoted now by policy makers and educators, as well as by some parents. What does all this promotion of parents and their involvement in education accomplish? To challenge the obviousness and the moral force of this category, I suggest that "the parent" is a social accomplishment; it is a category that has a history, or rather several histories, in relation to "the school." Moreover, in contrast to what official histories of schooling may suggest, this is not a story of harmony and progressive unfolding of nature or commonsense. Rather, relations between schools and families, and the language used to describe and organize those relations, were complicated from the start. Schools demanded a regularity of children's participation that encroached on families' labour and time. At the same time, school learning required forms of conduct and forms of discipline that were often at odds with relations within families and parental authority in particular. Today's "normal" ideas about what a family is, how families should be organized, and how parents should deal with children, are all intertwined with the history of schooling and its expectations of discipline and obedience. Indeed, as Bruce Curtis has argued, the organization of formal, state-regulated schooling sought to create "parents" and "children" as "categories of persons," who "collectively were to constitute 'families'" (Curtis, 1988, p. 145).

As in the present, many "families" did not live up to the school's expectations and failed to organize themselves in ways that would prepare "children" to be attentive and obedient "students." Soon after the introduction of state schooling in the middle of the nineteenth century, educators began complaining about fathers and (particularly) mothers who caused problems for teachers by failing to instill a positive attitude towards schooling, to discipline their children, or to reinforce the teacher's lessons at home (Donzelot, 1979). The supposedly "indifferent" dispositions and "ignorance" of many mothers became a particular concern in these complaints, as mothers were increasingly targeted as the source of social ills and educational failure, while they were also seen as the vehicle through which families could be "policed" and transformed. In order to enlist more reliable and organized cooperation and support from mothers, nineteenth—century teachers, particularly those teaching younger children, began to organize meetings of mothers after school (Dehli, 1993). Most of these organizations were, as they are today, initiated by teachers or administrators, and the parent most often recruited to participate in them was the mother. Yet, it would be a mistake to read this early history as if it were a simple matter of lining up mothers to take up their new tasks or that all women enrolled in these new organizations with enthusiasm. In spite of lofty rhetorical claims by their promoters, only a minority of mothers attended school club events, and an even smaller group became "involved." To complicate matters further, some of those who did accept the invitation to participate in this domain did so in ways that offended contemporary sensibilities for proper conduct by women in public spaces: they spoke "out of turn" to claim unreasonable privileges, or they spoke the wrong language altogether. In other words, they crossed boundaries of respectable and reasonable feminine behaviour in public spaces such as the school, causing education authorities to make explicit in written rules what had previously been implicit expectations of "parents" while at school.

In this chapter I discuss three "incidents" when groups of women crossed borders of proper conduct in relation to schools and teachers. They are drawn from the early history of an organization called the Toronto Home and School Council. Formed in 1916, the Council was a federation of clubs in local city schools. I piece together stories of these incidents from old letters, minute-books, newspaper clippings, organizational histories, and so on from the collection of the Toronto Board of Education's Archives. The incidents are fascinating in themselves. There is conflict, drama, politics, and accusations, the stuff that historians love to write about. But while all this is intriguing, I am reading these moments through a frame of moral regulation. I do that to show how women in the Home and School Council were caught up in efforts to define and discipline their own members, and mothers more generally, so as to avoid precisely these kinds of conflicts. In these ways, I argue, they not only sought to regulate and define others; they also regulated and defined themselves. In other words, they helped to shape the social category of "parent" in relation to schools, thus enabling norms to be specified and judgements to be made about the conduct and attitudes of individuals and groups.

It was a central premise of Home and School clubs that mothers and teachers were naturally positioned to share an interest in the future of children, that together they could become a powerful movement, "an important archive of usefulness in the co-operation of home and school and state matters" (Toronto Home and School Council, 1916, February 12, p. 375). Yet, as the "incidents" in this chapter will illustrate, no matter how "natural" or desirable their shared interests might be, collaboration and understanding could only be achieved through instruction and effort, and sometimes by ruling some activities as inappropriate. Mothers, in particular, had to learn to recognize their position and to conduct themselves properly in order to be recognized by teachers and school officials. And when their organizations were accepted as "insiders," the position accorded to Home and School clubs was a subordinate one. Moreover, even a subordinate "insider" position was precarious, not something that could be secured for Home and School members once and for all; nor was it possible for every mother to claim a legitimate identification of "parent" in the domain of schooling. The incidents that I discuss here were moments when these definitions and expectations were challenged. Indeed, it was in response to these, and similar, acts of transgressions that expectations that had been implicit had to be codified and written into rules and regulation. Who could speak about what, how, and in what language were central in each of the three stories I will tell: one group's offence was to speak in a "foreign" language, another claimed the unreasonable privilege of running French classes after school in a classroom, and members of the third dared to challenge the authority and qualification of a school principal by suggesting she be fired.

Before getting into the stories themselves I want to make a short detour to discuss how a focus on moral regulation is helpful for understanding what is at sake in these kinds of issues. In a 1981 article, Philip Corrigan suggested that investigations of moral regulation can direct our attention to the ways in which formation of social individuality or subjectivity is constrained *and* constructed in and through social relations and through the disciplinary powers and practices of the state (Corrigan, 1981 pp. 313–335). Moral regulation is about organized, repetitive, and often mundane practices and relations which privilege certain forms of expression and behaviour, all the while rendering other forms as marginal, contained, illegitimate, or immoral. For Corrigan moral regulation involves something like a "repertoire" of historically shaped and valued forms of speech and conduct, or "proper forms of expression." These forms, he argues, are particularly important in the ways they establish terms of social identity, the categories through which we are identified by others, and identify ourselves as particular kinds of persons.

In the domain of schools, we can see how moral regulation shape categories of identity such as student, teacher, and principal. Such categories, and the relations and practices they facilitate, are integral to implicit and explicit rules of conduct and discipline, announcing who someone must be and how they must behave in order to belong in that space. It is a bit more complicated to understand how the individuals named by these categories are allocated to, and come to know their place in, the social order of the school and its relations of authority, or how they might ignore or challenge them. The category of "parent" sits on the edge of the school's domain, and those who deal with schools as parent are caught up in ambivalent relations to it: in some senses they are invited to be part of it, in other ways they are excluded, subordinated, or ignored. And some are clearly more welcome than others. In spite of much recent talk of parental choice and rights, it seems that many parents are ill at ease at school. Even when called on to "involve" themselves and "participate," they do so on terms that are largely defined by teachers and administrators. To do otherwise is to risk being seen as difficult or intrusive, or too political. To avoid responding to schools' invitations, however, could earn the reputation of being apathetic and irresponsible. Finally, there are vast differences between parents and the material and "cultural capital" they can draw on to meet the school's expectations, and realize their own hopes for their children (Lareau, 1989).

While the history of "parent" organizations is filled with stories of mothers volunteering for the bake sale, cheerfully escorting children on field trips, and making sure that Mary or Tony do their homework, I trace more ambivalent stories. They are stories that show how what is now taken as natural and normal about this social category and role is the outcome of a great deal work, argument, conflict, and exclusion. As other authors in this book would argue, it is important to trace the history of those figures and relationships that we take most for granted. By doing so we can begin to see how even conduct that seems quite ordinary, and ideas that appear both reasonable and normal, have been shaped through histories that are inseparable from relations of power. Two arguments run through this chapter: that the norms, expectations and differences attached to "the parent" have been generated though histories of conflict, and that these norms are shaped by, and argued through, changing relations of gender, class, race, ethnicity, and sexuality. By examining moments when norms were challenged through deliberate or accidental trespass, I hope to make visible some of what and who have been excluded and silenced in order to fashion "the good parent" and "the good mother."

"AN IMPORTANT ARCHIVE OF USEFULNESS…": THE MAKING OF "HOME AND SCHOOL"

The Toronto Home and School Council was formed in 1916 as a federation of local home and school or mothers' clubs (Burgoyne, 1935, p. 2). The Council's first president and advocate was Ada Courtice, an active participant in several Toronto social and education reform groups, including the Local Council of Women (Crowley, 1980). Membership in the new Council grew rapidly. By 1921 thirty-three associations had joined, ten years later there were seventy member clubs, and in 1935, eighty Home and School clubs made up the membership, most of these were in elementary schools (THSC, 1936, pp. 44–46). With few exceptions, the leadership of the Home and School Council were part of the city's growing "British," professional and middle classes: they were white, most were full-time mothers and homemakers, they were married and had children in school. A small number of single, professional women were also active in the Council's affairs. Over the years, however, most of the leaders of this group were married women, wives of business men or professionals, such as school principals, university professors, physicians, engineers, civil servants and the like. As we will see below, the Council had very mixed success in its attempts to organize Home and School Clubs in poor and working-class neighbourhoods, particularly ones with substantial "foreign" populations. The goal of involving fathers as well as mothers was also largely unrealized except when, as I will discuss, fathers were mobilized as husbands to settle conflicts among their wives.

Local clubs were organized by teachers to provide a way for them to meet with mothers of the children they taught. From teachers' point of view, the clubs' purpose was primarily educational; to enable mothers to better support teachers' work. Accounts of the early years of individual clubs, however, emphasize their social functions as much as their educational benefits. Annual reports of these clubs provide glimpses of groups of women—twenty to sixty members was standard—getting together for fundraising efforts, afternoon entertainment and teas, meet-the-teacher nights, and lectures for educational and "social uplift" (See Evans, 1922, December, pp. 262–263). Most clubs reported that their working meetings were held in the afternoon, usually after the end of the school day, between two and four o'clock. Public events were also held during the daytime, and on occasion in the evening. Organizational activity during the afternoon might suit the participation of school principals, and it presumed that mothers of school children could attend meetings during the day. This practice excluded men and women who were engaged in wage labour, while also placing pressure on teachers to "stay after school." For women with small children it would also be difficult to attend such meetings. There is no indication in the Council records that childcare was provided, or that children were brought along, unless they were providing entertainment or serving tea with their mothers. Daytime gatherings assumed a gender division of household and childrearing labour, where women were expected to be full-time mothers and homemakers. It also presumed that teachers had no domestic responsibilities requiring their attention at the end of the workday.

Home and School clubs served both pastoral and pedagogical functions for those who were able to attend; they provided social spaces for shaping a sense of community around local schools, as well as recruiting mothers into the relatively novel role as auxiliary teachers. The founders of the Home and School Council had more ambitious goals. Their vision was a social movement emerging out of the network of local clubs that could be mobilized for social reform and national improvement. The idea that collaboration between family and school would benefit the individual and the nation and state, was made explicit from the start. In a speech to the Elementary Teachers' section of the Ontario Education Association in 1918 Ada Courtice pleaded with teachers,

> If we want a democratic country the best type of democracy will come from a chain of democratic groups of neighbourhoods....In order that the process of education

should have its cultural and practical results, parents and teachers must naturally think and work together and must have a common meeting-place from which to send out their vision and their effort. (Courtice, 1918, p. 166)

The historical context is important to understand some of the fervour of these arguments. Founded during World War I, the Toronto Home and School Council was one of several likeminded social reform groups in Toronto and elsewhere in Canada and North America. This was a time of great change and growth in North American cities. Thousands of men had joined the war effort, and patriotism for Canada and Britain saturated public discourse. For the first time since Canada was colonized and made part of the British Empire, significant numbers of migrants made their way to North America from southern and eastern Europe. Toronto was an important terminus on the recently built railways linking Eastern Canada to the West Coast, and the city was rapidly becoming a centre of factory production and commerce. Housing construction was booming in new suburbs to accommodate workers and their families. Lagging behind, schools were built to receive growing numbers of students, a growing number of whom were not "of British stock."

This period was also one when social movements challenged traditional arrangements of authority in workplaces, households, and politics. Groups of women fought for the right to vote, while workers organized themselves into labour unions. At the same time, there was a proliferation of groups, among them the Home and School Council, who joined in social reform. Their favoured approach was to make use of knowledge and techniques from emerging social sciences—surveys, questionnaires, statistics, and maps—to identify social problems, and to propose government or voluntary intervention (Delhi, 1996, pp. 207–228). While on the one hand arguing for increased public expenditures on social services, health, and education, the Council joined other middle-class reform groups to demand greater efficiency from local governments, and to hold them accountable for how property taxes were spent. The Council joined with other organizations, including the Big Sisters' and Big Brothers' Associations, the Board of Trade, the Bureau of Municipal Research, as well as the Toronto Trades and Labour Council, to influence the Board of Education and municipal and provincial governments. Alone or in collaboration, they advocated for child welfare and health-care provision, water purification and sanitation and, especially, for better and more "progressive" schooling. One of their objectives, therefore, was to "reform" government at all levels, to organize its procedures and management around scientific knowledge, rather than personal relationships and inclinations. This, they believed, much like contemporary "reformers" claim, would make government more efficient, systematic, and fair.

Making Good Mothers, Making Good Canadians

Most of Toronto's Home and School clubs were formed in Anglo-Canadian and middle-class neighbourhoods, yet the Council's records detail much concern with schools in "foreign" and working-class districts. One such school was Elizabeth Street School, later named Hester How School. The school was located in "the Ward," a downtown area comprised of busy streets, shops, and small rental flats. The area provided the cheapest lodgings in the city and many immigrants found housing there when they first arrived in Toronto. Among middle-class observers in the early twentieth century, the area had a reputation as morally dangerous and physically unsanitary, and it was described by one observer as "the festery sore of our city life" (Magee, 1979 p. 126; Jones, 1982, June 12, F14). Ida Siegel, an activist and social reformer in Toronto's Jewish community, helped teachers organize a Mothers' Club at this school as early as 1912.[2] Among the Home and School Council's largely Protestant and Anglo-Saxon leadership, Siegel was identified and identified herself as Jewish. She was remarkable in other ways as well. With the aid of the Council and other social reform groups, she was elected as a school trustee in the late 1920s and 1930s. Before gaining that position, however, she became embroiled in an intense controversy surrounding the Mothers' Club at Elizabeth Street/Hester Howe school (Pennacchio, 1985 Spring, pp. 41–60).

The purposes of the club were two-fold: to foster closer co-operation between mothers and teachers, and to build citizenship and patriotism among "foreign" families. Hester How School was designated by the Board of Education as a school where special efforts should be made to make "good Canadians" out of "newcomers" (Weaver, 1979). The club extended this work to families, and particularly to mothers. As part of their English curriculum, children prepared invitations—in English—for their mothers to attend club meetings. Children also accompanied and acted as their mothers' interpreters. Most of the women who attended the club were either Italian or Jewish, recent immigrants to Canada. The club was used to instruct mothers in English and introduce them to a "Canadian way of life" (Pennacchio, 1985, Spring, pp. 41–60). Through talks (in English) on topics such as childcare, hygiene and nutrition, school nurses, teachers and Home and School Council members attempted to transmit "Canadian values" to the women members (THSC, 1917, June 11 & 1919, November 17). We can see here how "foreign" women were recruited into wartime programs of nation-building and citizenship, and how the Mothers' Club was used to this end. In this case, however, women themselves appear to have had different ideas about what they

---

[2] Ida Siegel, Taped Interview by Don Nethery, 31 May 1976, TBEA, Vertical Files, Biographies, Siegel; THSC, *The Story* (1935), p. 44; Shmuel Shamai (1986). *Ethnic National Identity among Jewish Students in Toronto*. Doctoral dissertation, University of Toronto (OISE), 1986.

wanted from this space, and also about how to conduct themselves there. Language, it turned out, became a key point of contention between them and the school's teachers.

As president of the Club, Ida Siegel recollected later that she did not object to the goals of promoting co-operation, citizenship, and patriotism among women. She disagreed about strategies and methods. Her approach to the work of citizenship was unconventional and quite radical at the time. First of all, she was able to change the practice of writing invitations to mothers and conducting meetings entirely in English. Invited speakers would occasionally address the Mothers' Club in Yiddish or Italian, or Ida Siegel or an Italian mother would interpret from English. Second, she encouraged the mothers to speak among themselves in their own language during the social portion of the meetings. Thus, it seems that teachers and the school's principal felt positioned on the margins of a space which they presumed entitled to dominate, as the mothers, with Siegel's assistance, gained some control of how the meetings were conducted, what should be discussed and, particularly, the languages that were spoken.

At the end of 1918 the teachers and school nurse resigned from the club. In a letter to Chief Inspector of Schools Robert Cowley, they accused Ida Siegel, their former ally and collaborator, of being a "non-Ward resident." Therefore, they argued, she was an outsider with no legitimate claim to take part in the club's activities. What angered them was that she had relegated them, the club's "legitimate" leadership, to a secondary role. Finally they charged that the use of Yiddish and Italian on school property was unpatriotic and ought not to be permitted (Toronto Board of Education, 1918, December 19 p. 246; "Must Use English," 1918). Inspector Cowley and the majority of Board trustees concurred. One trustee even argued that Siegel's and the mothers' conduct was tantamount to "Bolshevism" ("Bolshevism in Schools?" 1919). To prevent such unpatriotic behaviour in Toronto schools in the future, the School Board passed a motion that only the English language could be used during events held in city schools ("Bolshevism," 1919; TBE, 1919, January 8). This rule remained in force until the 1960s, and became the centre of numerous controversies between the School Board and community groups wanting to use school facilities for educational and cultural activities.[3]

How did a small group of women meeting and speaking together in Yiddish and Italian about cooking, childrearing, and health, come to be seen as a threat to the social order and to the Canadian nation? Remembering these events in an

---

[3] It might be that, unwittingly, this exclusionary practice helped to strengthen the independence of some immigrant organizations. See for example Polyzoi, Eleoussa (1986). Greek Immigrant Women from Asia Minor in Prewar Toronto: the Formative Years. In Jean Burnet (Eds.), *Looking Into My Sister's Eyes: An Exploration of Women's History* (pp. 107–124). Toronto: the Multicultural History Society of Ontario.

interview taped in 1976, Ida Siegel described how she had no "political" intentions in her work with the Hester How Mothers' Club. She talked about how the racist accusations levelled against her and about how she could not understand how the mundane activities of the Hester Howe Mothers' Club could cause such hysteria. She also recalled that hostility against Jews was not an uncommon experience in Toronto during this period, nor in later years.

In retrospect, Siegel fondly recounted the Toronto Home and School Council and the small number of women trustees among the few who publicly supported her in her battle to be "exonerated" in the aftermath of this affair (Siegel interview, 1976). Searching in the records of the Council, however, I could find no trace of their support. The minutes books make no reference to the issue, there are no letters, and while Council leaders may have supported Ida Siegel as an individual, there is no indication that they intervened on behalf of mothers at Hester How School when the Board made the decision to bar their meetings. In June 1917 a committee had been established "to study the question of interesting the Non-English speaking parents in H. & S. Work" (THSC Minutes, 1917, June 11). Nothing further was reported from this committee until November 1919, several months after the Board had passed its English-only motion.

Ada Courtice was a school trustee at this time. She not only supported Ida Siegel, she also voted against the English-only motion in the Board meeting. Much like Siegel herself, she was not in disagreement about the overall project of making good citizens of "foreign" mothers, nor that Mothers' Clubs should not be used to achieve this end. But she, too, doubted the School Board's restrictive language policy. English-only, she argued, was "not the way to assimilate them as Canadians" ("English Only," 1919). A more moderate, today we might call it a more inclusive and progressive, approach would be more successful in the long run. The friendly, neighbourly, woman-to-woman contact established through Home and School Clubs would, she believed, foster a stronger, more enduring patriotism, citizenship, and democracy. While learning English was an important goal and component of citizenship, permitting the mother tongue, so to speak, was a good practice, if only as a way of making the school a more welcoming space where "foreign" women would be able to benefit from the advice of teachers and other education and childrearing "experts." At the same time, as recognized participants in the education of children, mothers might more easily see the advantages of conducting their childrearing, domestic labour, and familial relations according to the norms privileged by the school. In this sense, Siegel and Courtice shared a more forward-looking and progressive approach to moral regulation than the teachers of the school and the School Board's majority.

It was unusual that contradictions between the Home and School "idea" and working class and immigrant life would come to the attention of the School Board in this way. Nevertheless, the events at Hester Howe School and the Mothers'

Club in 1919 were by not isolated ones. It seems that the Council encountered a great deal of difficulty in creating and sustaining clubs in working class and "foreign" districts, even though school officials and Council leaders alike agreed that it was in these schools that Home and School would be of the greatest benefit. For the few clubs which were established, only scattered records are available. Some appear to have lasted for short periods only. Minutes of Council meetings indicate that schools such as Sackville, York, Duke, Park, Niagara, and Ryerson either did not have a club at all, had one for only a short period, and/or were consistently "represented" at Council meetings through school principals.

In an investigative report on another school located in "the Ward" (York Street School), written in March 1920, the Bureau of Municipal Research proposed that parent's associations in "finer districts" adopt downtown schools and donate works of art so that "prevailingly foreign" children could be exposed to proper Canadian culture (Bureau of Municipal Research, 1920). Some efforts were made by the Council in this direction, but with hesitation. A report of the work of the Council's Extension Committee in 1928 explained that its duties were "to visit schools where there are difficulties in the way of forming a Home and School Association, and with the co-operation of the principal and teachers to arrange a meeting."[4] The report goes on to describe how Dewson and Howard Home and School Clubs in the city's west end, organized meetings and social gatherings in Edith L. Groves and St. Clair Avenue schools, where a "short address on some pertinent topic is combined with a programme of music and reading, followed by refreshments. The latter are always much appreciated." Edith L. Groves was a so-called auxiliary senior school for girls classified in some way as "defective," while St. Clair School was located in an industrial district (dominated by slaughter houses and meat-packing plants) to the north-west of the city. While the report mentioned the desire of principals to have such meetings, nothing is said about the mothers who attended, aside from the reference to appreciation of refreshments.

A few associations were apparently formed as a result of this committee's work, although its purpose was only to "bring the aims and ideals" of Home and School before parents and teachers, it was "not meant for organization purposes" (THSC, 1936). Another account of the "extension" work reported on "programmes put on in downtown schools, where it seemed impossible or inadvisable to have Associations" (Ibid.). This appears to be a clear indication that Home and School clubs, in spite of Council rhetoric, were better suited to the realities of middle-class mothers, and were not intended or successful as organizations of and for working-class and "foreign" women.

[4] Jean E. Tedman, (1928 December) "Extension Committee," *Home and School* 1, no. 1: 11. Edith L. Groves School (later renamed Heyden Park Secondary School) was established in 1926 and named after a trustee who was closely associated with the Council and other Toronto women's organization.

One further reference hint at the problems of establishing clubs in working class schools. The Council agreed in April 1917, to "look into the difficulties of Duke St. Home and School Club" (THSC Minutes, 1917, April 10). This club had been formed by one of the kindergarten teachers in 1912. Duke Street School, much like Elizabeth Street/Hester Howe, was a school that was repeatedly identified as a "problem" school in Council and Toronto Board of Education records.[5] We can only guess what the substance of the club's problems might have been; there is no indication in Council records that mothers of children at Duke Street School ever attended a Council meeting to speak about their situation. Rather, the principal and teachers report on "problems." Again in 1925, this school was on a list to be assisted by a committee established "to visit schools where there are difficulties in the way of forming a Home and School Association."[6] These efforts, too, appear to have been in vain, and the club at Duke disappeared from Council records in the late 1920s. In a 1926 report, the convenor of the Extension Committee referred to Duke Street School as "unorganized."[7] In 1928, the school was discussed again, this time it was reported at Council that twenty-five home visits had been made by school nurses and members of the extension committee in connection with "pre-school work" (THSC Minutes, 1928, September 19). The "pre-school" work was a relatively new creation, urged by the University's Institute for Child Study and the Department of Public Health, to ensure that mothers would seek regular medical advice on childrearing during the "critical," but hitherto unsupervised years between infancy and the first year of schooling.

Fussing, Feathering, and French

In 1921 members of Brown Home and School Club, in one of Toronto's "better" neighbourhoods, wanted their children to learn French. French was not included as a subject in the elementary school curriculum and some of the parents hired one of the school's teachers to instruct the children after regular school hours. In order to pay for the teacher's services, the club charged a fee from those parents

---

[5] See several TBE, *Annual Reports*, and also Bureau of Municipal Research, *Biographies of Individual Schools under the Toronto Board of Education, 3, Duke Street School* Toronto: Bureau of Municipal Research, 1921.

[6] THSC, *Minutes*, 20 May 1925; "Extension Committee," *Home and School* 1, no. 1 (December 1928): 11. Other references in Council records suggest that the preferred activities of this committee consisted of educational lectures, a social tea, and encouragement of discipline and thrift among poor and "foreign" mothers and children. All of these suggest that the Home and School Council participated in a "civilizing mission" whereby "newcomers" would be made into "Canadians" and into "citizens."

[7] THSC, *Minutes*, 17 March 1926. The announcements for this meeting invited "The Mothers of Toronto" to discuss "salvaging the human derelict." Edith L. Groves was among the featured speakers.

whose children participated. A permit was needed to use a classroom for such a purpose, and it was first obtained without incident in September 1921. It was when the club approached the Board's Management Committee in January 1922 to renew the permit that problems arose. After a bitterly fought election, the new Board was for the second year in a row dominated by opponents of "fads and frills," several of whom owed their political fortunes to the city's business community and the Orange Lodges. Rather than treat Brown Home and School Club's application as a routine request, some trustees seized upon the issue as an unpatriotic "threat" to the "Britishness" of Toronto. Here, too, arguments were framed around loyalty, language, and race. One of the trustees charged that the Brown Home and School Club was stirring up a "racial" issue,

> The attempt to develop a racial issue is unpatriotic, un-British and calls for the condemnation of all true citizens. If French is granted in these primary schools, what is to be done if classes are requested also in Italian, Hebrew, Finnish and Bulgarian and where is the money to come from? This is an English-speaking city and provision must first be made for Anglo-Saxons. ("Home and School Club," 1922)

It was, in his opinion, an unfortunate oversight that the first permit had been issued. The Management Committee would ensure that it would not happen again.

Looking from the vantage point of present-day Canada, it may seem odd that using a classroom to teach French after school would be construed as a threat and as an issue of "race." Moreover, the parents of Brown school children were members of a French-speaking minority, claiming language rights. There were, however, hotly contested debates at the time about the position of English and French language in Ontario schools, and one of Brown School Club's supporters, Professor C. B. Sissons of the University of Toronto, argued that the public schools had a responsibility to foster understanding between the English and French in Canada, and that learning French was one way to achieve this. However, this was not the main concern of the parents involved (Sissons, 1922). Trustee McClelland, who also spoke in favour of the Home and School Club, explained their more pragmatic concerns,

> The boys and girls who wanted to go higher did not like to take the fourth form in that school because they could not get the languages. Then when they went on to U.C.C. and St. Andrew's, they had to step back a full year. It was to remedy this situation and build up the fourth form that it was decided to hold special classes.[8]

---

[8] "Trustees Vote 9 to 7 Against French Class," *Toronto Daily Star*, February 3, 1922. U.C.C. refers to Upper Canada College, which along with St. Andrew's was, and still is, among the most exclusive private schools for boys in Canada.

Thus, learning French would enable public school students at Brown School to compete in the private, secondary schools their parents intended for them. One trustee characterized the parents as a "highbrow" group, who sought to take advantage of the public schools in order to provide their children with special privileges, which he contrasted with the "poorer schools like York Street" ("Trustees Vote 9 to 7," 1922). The controversy, therefore, was not simply about language: it had as much to do with class and race relations and with conflicts over the purpose of public schools. It was also a contest over who could claim to represent "the people" and "the parents" in educational matters, and over how such representatives should conduct themselves.

In contrast to the Mothers Club at Hester Howe, the Brown Home and School group did obtain strong and public support from the Home and School Council, which helped to mobilize an impressive and influential range of groups and individuals to make deputations to the Board of Education. They included the Collegeview Heights Ratepayers (from the area surrounding Upper Canada College), several university professors, school principals, and even the Chief Inspector of Schools, Robert Cowley. This was an instance where Toronto's white, middle-class and professional educational reform "intelligentsia" confronted "ward politicians," who in this instance claimed to speak on behalf of ordinary parents and taxpayers.[9] Some trustees ridiculed the Home and School representatives and their supporters when they said they spoke in the interest of all Toronto children and on behalf of the women of Toronto. To this the trustees retorted angrily that only elected trustees were the legitimate representatives of "the people,"

> These women arrogate to themselves the right to sit in judgement on the qualifications of the trustees, to formulate and direct the educational policy of Toronto, overlooking or forgetting the fact that the board…represents the concentrated selection of citizens and is made up of medical men, business men, lawyers, clergymen, contractors and educationists….The board will not allow any group to usurp its prerogatives by any amount of fussing and feathering, but will be at all times willing to give a courteous hearing to any group of citizens who loyally confer through the regular channels. ("Home and School Club," 1922)

While several men had joined the Home and School Council on this occasion, it was the presence and presentations of women which angered this and other trustees. "Fussing and feathering" are hardly terms that could be applied to men.

---

[9] For a detailed history of urban reformers and ward politicians on Toronto's City Council, see Weaver (1979). The Modern City Realized: Toronto Civic Affairs, 1880–1915. In Alan F. Artbise & Gilbert A. Shelter (Eds.), *Planning and Politics in the Modern Canadian City* (pp. 39–73). Toronto: MacMillan,

The second request for a permit to teach French at Brown School was denied ("No French in Brown School," 1922).

This dispute brought out contradictions between the "political" and "educational" arms of the Board of Education, and between the "political" and auxiliary or servicing features of the Toronto Home and School Council. As well, the events illustrated the pervasive sexism of the School Board, and how middle-class women entering public and political spaces faced particular scrutiny and even ridicule. Such strategies were applied to women, such as those from Brown Home and School Club, with access to substantial material resources, an impressive social network of supporters, and a high degree of knowledge of and competence in educational and local, political affairs. It is interesting to notice that Ida Siegel and the mothers of Hester Howe Club were also accused of subversive and unpatriotic conduct, yet their exclusion from the school's space was far more decisive than the denied after school permit for Brown members. While the former were denied the right to speak their own language at school, the latter were inconvenienced by having to find another space to offer their children a social and educational advantage in the elite educational marketplace. Similar issues were at stake in the third story.

MOTHERS VERSUS THE LADY PRINCIPAL

In 1921 a conflict between a Home and School Club and a school principal made newspaper headlines in Toronto for several weeks. The president of the club at John Ross Robertson School in upper middle-class north Toronto wrote a letter to the Board of Education asking for the principal, Miss Cullen,'s resignation.[10] The club members complained that Miss Cullen had blocked their access to school space for its events, and their letter referred to "a series of unpleasant situations existing between the club and the principal" ("Ask Principal's Removal," 1921, October 28). According to newspaper accounts, the divisions were so deep that the principal had convened her own, competing mothers' club, of which she herself was president ("Knock Insane Ideas," 1921). Toronto papers delighted in detailing every bit of tension and accusation between "the Lady Principal" and warring factions of "North Toronto Mothers." In midst of the controversy a school trustee called a meeting of fathers, which sixty men attended. According to the newspapers they resolved to apologize "to the Board of Education for the annoyance caused the trustees," ("Fathers Settle It," 1921) by their wives. On their part, male school trustees proclaimed their outrage that a group of women would dare to request that a principal resign. As we shall see, this public expression of outrage

---

[10] *Telegram*, 28 and 29 October, 4 and 24 November and 8 December 1921; *Toronto Daily Star*, 28 October, 1 and 2 November, 16 and 17 December 1921, 24 January 1922; *Mail and Empire*, 6 December 1921.

did not prevent the same trustees from launching an inquiry into the "disciplinarian and academic qualifications of female principals" ("Come to Defence," 1916–1921).

This was a difficult matter for the Home and School Council. Although one of its member clubs was a key protagonist, there were several complications. First, members of the Home and School Club at John Ross Robertson were not among the most active in Council affairs; second, some of the Club's members were not mothers of children attending the school; third, the controversy might have long term consequences for Home and School clubs' access to school space; and finally, the School Board used the occasion to question the ability of women principals to handle their jobs. The Home and School Council were strong supporters of women teachers and principals.

As the story was told in the newspaper, it turned out that several of the most vocal members of the Home and School Club of John Ross Robertson School did not, in fact, send their children to John Ross Robertson School. Instead they were students in private schools in the area. The question was therefore raised, initially by Miss Cullen and the school's teachers, and later by members of the rival club that she organized, as to the legitimacy of the first club. On what basis could the claim to be this school's home and school club? Moreover, and perhaps more important, it seems that the first club had exceeded the boundaries of proper conduct for Home and School clubs by getting into conflicts with the school's staff. An executive member of the "rival" club stated to the Board of Education,

> We represent the parents whose children attend the school. The Home and School Club do [sic] not represent the parents. We are the stronger league and have made more money for the school than the other side. We have no feelings against the Home and School, but we are all mothers of children attending the school and are consequently very busy looking after their welfare. Our efforts are confined to this particular school whereas the work of the Home and School Club affects various schools....Parents are beginning to ask if it is right for outsiders to come in and demand the resignation of a teacher,...we have never attempted to dictate,...we have never had the slightest friction. ("Jealously the Cause," 1921)

One consequence of this dispute was to circumscribe the claim of Home and School groups to represent all parents. School trustees would not accept any challenge—perceived or real—to their representative authority. Moreover, this incident suggested that "parents" may not be a unitary category, indeed parents could and did disagree. Perhaps, more importantly in the long run, this dispute brought into view the hierarchical relationship between "school" and "home." In this sense, it was a moment when mothers publicly stepped over a line dividing professionals and "lay" roles in the school system. Even though well-to-do parents such as those involved in this conflict were (and are) better able to influence teachers and public schools than others, such influence is more often exercised informally and out of the public view. The greatest "mistake" of mothers at John Ross Robertson School, therefore, might be that they made their criticism of the school principal in a highly public manner.

Ada Courtice, who was then the organizing secretary for the Ontario Federation of Home and School Associations, declined to support either club at John Ross Robertson School. When the Toronto Home and School Council discussed the dispute in January 1922, the Executive decided not to take any action until the School Board had met to review its policies regarding use of school space. One rationale for not intervening was that "the Council is hopeful that the Board would recognize H. & S. Clubs as 'Inside Organizations' and this in a great measure would solve the difficulty of permits and fees" (THSC Minutes, 1922). As an "inside organization" the Council and clubs would not be required to obtain individual permits for use of school space, nor pay fees for each event they wished to organize in a school building. This would save substantial work, money and time. Siding with an assertive group of mothers, whose claim to represent parents in the local school was in doubt, could jeopardize the Council's chances of achieving the coveted status.

The final difficulty was that the school principal in question was a woman, of whom only a few were employed at the time. When the Board of Education decide to launch an inquiry into the qualification of female principals in the aftermath of this affair, the president of Toronto Home and School Council was outraged at the attempt to judge "women in general…based on one local incident." She added that she was certain that women had made "great successes as school principals" ("Come to Defence," 1921). With this added dimension to the conflict, and the persistent attempts to block and undermine women's opportunities for advancement within the schooling hierarchy, it becomes clearer why the Council was reluctant to offer one of its member clubs any public support in this instance. Indeed, some of the few women who did manage to attain positions as principals, were active members of the organization and relied on it for support.[11] It is worth remembering, moreover, that this issue developed in an affluent area of the city, where mothers—or women deciding to become involved in an organization such as Home and School—likely considered themselves superior to women teachers and principals, in terms of social status and class. It may not be too far fetched to speculate that women in such neighbourhoods expected teachers of

---

[11] Aletta Marty, Toronto's first female public school inspector, for example, sought and received active endorsation from the Home and School Council, as well as from women trustees. Marty became president of the Ontario Federation of Home and School Associations. Margaret Pettigrew, the Board's first female chief attendance officer also received support from the Council in her bid to obtain this position.

their children to comply with their wishes, and were frustrated to find school staff who instead considered their involvement in Home and School as rather meddlesome interference (Prentice, 1985).

CONCLUSION

Even more than classroom teachers, most mothers have little control over how decisions about schools and schooling were made. However, while making that assertion, it is important to take apart the social category of "mother". Disparate groups of mothers fared quite differently in their attempts to influence programs and personnel in the schools their children attended. The Jewish and Italian women of Hester How Mothers' Club were viciously attacked for wanting to speak their own language among themselves, and while they received some support from individual Home and School leaders, their cause was never championed with the vigour that benefited Brown Home and School Club's campaign for French courses. On the other hand, the affluent and Anglo-Saxon members of John Ross Robertson Home and School Club received even less support from the Council. But, as we have seen, this particular case touched on much broader issues and relations in which the Council was engaged, specifically the use of school space, the position of women principals, and more generally, a definition of boundaries of Home and School activities in relation to schools and the School Board.

As a result of the controversies I have discussed, both trustees and Home and School leaders agreed that the School Board ought to chart a clear map to better organize relations between community groups, administration, and trustees in order to define how, by whom, and for what purposes school buildings could, or could not, be used. This work had already begun in December 1921. To help define "regular channels," the School Board established detailed guidelines. According to a lengthy article in *The Daily Star*, these guidelines permitted discussion of "civic and educational" topics, but without "partisanship" and with safeguards as to "the loyal nature of any meeting held in the schools." "Political and religious" activities were explicitly prohibited, and regulation number one stated that: "Any utterance of a seditious or disloyal nature will automatically revoke this permit, and will disqualify the parties from holding any further meetings in school buildings" ("Rigid Rules to Govern," 1921). The article went on to assure "the public that no revolution-breeding gatherings will be countenanced,…one of the significant rules of the board is that lectures, addresses, etc. are to be given only in the English language. No bilingualism for Toronto trustees" (Ibid.).

Moreover, persons signing the permit had to be British subjects and "bona fide ratepayers." Edith L. Groves, who was very active within the Home and School Council, and who was first elected to the Board of Education in 1920 with enthusiastic Council support, chaired the committee which drew up these regulations.

Subsequent records of the Toronto Home and School Council and the Board of Education indicate that the Council worked quite hard to ensure that its members and member clubs adhered to these rules.

Whether they were elected as trustees or organizing women to express their view to the School Board or City Council, women were constantly and critically watched, their behaviour being the subject of comments by male colleagues on the School Board as well as pundits in Toronto newspapers. When they supported women teachers' campaigns for equal pay and access to promotions, for example, they were accused of bringing "sex politics" into the School Board. An editorial in *The Telegram* charged in 1925 that "The game of sex politics is already played out in the educational civic affairs of this city….The women of Toronto are not represented or controlled by the busybody organizations that represent nobody outside of the ranks of an extremely limited membership" (*Telegram* Editorial, 1925). The chairman of the Board, on his part, charged that: "The only time politics is introduced is when a lot of women's organizations start interfering and try to control the board" (McBrien, 1925).

Through constant negotiations over such boundaries women in Home and School associations became important supporters of the day-to-day running of many schools, through fundraising events and organization of trips, theatre nights and meet-the-teacher events. Criticism and "political" activities were explicitly discouraged, while schools assumed and came to rely on the unpaid support and caring labour of women in the family and in local clubs and organizations such as the Toronto Home and School Council. All this is not to suggest that the Home and School "failed" as an organization. While visible political achievements may be few, the long-term relations which Home and School associations facilitated between middle-class women and schools in Toronto are, in my view, far more significant. Through these relations, middle-class women not only shaped school practices which were advantageous to their own children, but helped to develop programs which aimed to re-structure the relations of other women and children to schools and schooling as well.

The moral regulation of mothers in relation to schooling centred on how to behave, how to speak, and how to take up one's place in a gendered hierarchy of position and labour. But as I have sought to show in this chapter, notions of the good mother and the good parent are also organized through class and race. Successful claims to "goodness" and "intelligence" relied on self-regulation—proper conduct, visible displays of knowing and following rules of public, political interaction. At the same time, not everyone who sought to conduct themselves well were welcomed as "reasonable subjects" in the Home and School or the School Board's affairs. The specific aims that the Home and School movement sought to achieve centred on Christian notions of femininity and masculinity, and Ada Courtice argued that parents and teachers shared the objective of educating children and in "building strong, good character, and a healthy body, training the mental faculties, and cultivating the virtues that constitute Christian manliness and womanliness" (Courtice, 1918). These notions were integral to dominant Anglo-Canadian discourses of citizenship and nation-building, made even more explicit in the conflicts over language and proper conduct that I have examined here.

A handbook circulated by the Council to member clubs in 1927 or 1928, a little more than ten years after its formation, illustrates how quickly such sentiments were embedded in organizational practices. The handbook made clear distinctions between acceptable and unacceptable purposes and activities of Home and School clubs

The guiding principles of the association are the embodiment of social service, civic virtue and patriotism, maintaining, as it does, that it is not "a means of entertainment, or charity or criticism of school authority, but a co-operative, non-political, non-sectarian, non-commercial effort to produce Canadian citizens who shall be capable of perpetuating the best which has been developed in our national life."

Within just a few years, then, the Council found it necessary and useful to generate a detailed set of rules of conduct, rules that had to be made explicit to regulate the behaviour of its members, and of "parents" who ventured into the space of schooling. In the process of working out such regulations, I have argued, the Home and School Council participated in shaping the categories of "parent," and "mother" as normative categories by which the Council's members would scrutinize and discipline themselves, while also marking their difference from "other" women and "other" families. Indeed, while the Council often claimed to speak on behalf of all parents in school affairs, not everyone could be included in that representation.

CRITICAL THINKING QUESTIONS

1. If moral regulation works in ordinary places and everyday situations such as schools, try to identify two cases or types of moral regulation from your own elementary or secondary school experience.

2. How does moral regulation work in schools, and by what methods is it exercised? How are teachers and parents, as well as students, regulated through schooling?

3. Can you think of strategies that students use to evade, subvert of resist moral regulation in schools?

4. In this chapter it is argued that power is both constructive and constraining. Think about what this means (use examples) and whether you agree. Can you think of two examples of constructive forms of power?

5. It is suggested here that knowledge has productive effects and that knowledge participates in "making" us into who we are and how we are seen by others. Yet, we also work with and shape knowledge and ourselves. Discuss some of the strategies used by members of the Toronto Home and School Council to "take up" and extend contemporary knowledge about women. How did class, ethnicity and race, as well as gender, shape their strategies and the effects of their organizing?

6. Discuss the links that Home and School members made between goodness and intelligence. Can you think of examples (historical or current) when the link between goodness and intelligence has been challenged or eroded? What kinds of links have been made, in the past and in the present, between these terms and notions of femininity, class, race and culture?

7. Today school authorities in several countries, including Canada, are calling for "parents" and "communities" to involve themselves in the work and decision-making of schools. Think about some of the continuities and differences between the 1920s and the present. Have the "regular channels" changed, and if so how and how much?

SUGGESTED READINGS

Brehony, Kevin, Deem, Rosemary & Heath, Sue (1995). *Active Citizenship and the Governing of Schools*. Buckingham: Open University Press.
    This is a contemporary analysis from England, which draws on ethnographic case studies and reading of policy to question, the idea of "lay" participation and "active citizenship" in school government.

Butler, Judith, & Scott, Joan W. (Eds.) (1992). *Feminists Theorize the Political*. (pp. 3–21). New York: Routledge.
    This collection includes several papers that question taken for granted categories in history and social science, as well as in feminist movement politics. The authors challenge the idea that feminist politics "needs" a set of foundational grounds, normative frameworks, and a stable subject "woman," and then explore the effects of assuming that we do. A few of the papers begin to outline alternatives to "foundational" feminist politics.

de Conick-Smith, Ning, Dehli, Kari & Rousmaniere, Kate (Eds.) (1997). *Discipline, Moral Regulation and Schooling: A Social History*. New York: Garland.
    All of the chapters in this edited collection deal with moral regulation in some way, considering curriculum, teachers, students, parents, and policy.

Curtis, Bruce (1988). *Building the Educational State: Canada West, 1836–1871*. London: Althouse Press.
    This book offers a detailed historical account of the first forty years of formal, state schooling in Ontario. Curtis' theoretical approach makes use of moral regulation as a concept to analyze how

relations between state forms and practices, on the one hand, and organization of civil society and citizenship, on the other.

Foucault, Michel (1980). *The History of Sexuality, Volume 1.* New York: Vintage.
   Marking something of a transition point in Foucault's work, the first volume of the History of Sexuality provides an introduction to thinking about regulatory forms of power—what they are, how and where they work, what forms they take, and the effects they have. While Foucault's "early" work on archaeology of knowledge and disciplinary institutions considered how power operated within specific forms of knowledge (penology, psychology, medicine), or within highly organized and confined spaces (such as prisons, asylums and hospitals), the History of Sexuality explores more dispersed and general forms of power that name and regulate the population as well as the individual.

Steedman, Carolyn (1985). The Mother Made Conscious: The Historical Development of a Primary School Pedagogy. *History Workshop 20*, Autumn: 149–163.
   Although she does not make use of moral regulation as a concept, this article—along with her paper on women teachers in "Prisonhouses" (*Feminist Review* 20, Autumn 1985: 7–21)—provide good example of how moral regulation works. Steedman shows how relations with children and skills in childrearing were considered "naturally" feminine, while, at the same time, pedagogical knowledge of childhood was viewed as a masculine domain of reason and administration.

WEB LINKS

www.oise.utoronto.ca/~mpress/eduweb/eduweb/
   An excellent resource for research in/about Canadian education.

www.peopleforeducation.com
   One contemporary organization that tries to turn "parents/home and school" into a political force is People for Education.

www.qut.edu.au/edu/cpol/foucault/
www.synaptic.bc.ca/ejournal/foucault
   There are several Web sites devoted to Foucault which are very dense and difficult to navigate, these two are quite easy to use, and have several resources along the lines of "Foucault for Beginners."

CHAPTER 3

TOWARDS THEORISING THE CONNECTIONS BETWEEN GOVERNMENTALITY, IMPERIALISM, RACE, AND CITIZENSHIP: INDIAN MIGRANTS AND RACIALISATION OF CANADIAN CITIZENSHIP

BY ENKASHI DUA

In 1914, Gurdit Singh, an Indian anti-colonial activist, chartered a steamship, the *Komagata Maru*, to bring more than 300 potential Indian migrants to Canada. Upon arriving in Canadian waters, the *Komagata Maru* was prevented from landing and those Indians who had not previously entered Canada were denied entry. With the assistance of Indian residents in Canada, those aboard the ship filed a court case that questioned whether the Canadian government had the power to deny entry to migrants from India.[1] This case questioned whether the Canadian state had the power to control the movement of people, to regulate immigration, and to define the qualifications for Canadian citizenship. As government policies and legal practice at that time allowed those who were British subjects the right to move throughout the empire, Indian migrants pointed out that access to citizenship in white settler formations was located in the rights of British subjects. Moreover, they pointed out that, as British subjects, those from India possessed the same rights as white subjects to move throughout the empire and to qualify for Canadian citizenship.

The British Columbia Court of Appeal disagreed. This decision had a significant effect on Canadian citizenship practices. First, it altered the existing legal practice with regard to the relationship between British subjects and Canadian citizens. Until that time, most British subjects were considered Canadian citizens, and did not have to

---

[1] While the purpose of this article is to illustrate that racial and national categories are socially constructed, ironically due to the limitations in our linguistic resources it is difficult to avoid using such categories for analytical purposes (for a further discussion of this issue see Miles, 1989, pp. 69–77). In this article, the term "Canadian" refers to those who were legally defined as Canadian. This includes white immigrants and their descendants. As in this period, indigenous peoples as well as those who migrated from Asia were denied rights associated with citizenship, my use of "Canadian" excludes these groups. I use the terms First Nations, indigenous, Métis, Asian, Chinese, Indian, and Japanese to refer to these residents.

apply for naturalisation.[2] Second, the Court of Appeal asserted that the Canadian federal government had ultimate authority and autonomy to determine who was a Canadian citizen. This ended the ambiguity in Imperial policies over who had power to define citizenship in white settler societies—the British government or local authorities. Third, the decision set an important legal precedent for the racialisation of citizenship in Canada, as the court rejected the claim that as British subjects, Indians had the right to enter Canada and legally defined Indian migrants as aliens.

This article explores the history through which citizenship and its associated rights were racialised in Canada. In particular, I point to the importance of an often forgotten aspect of citizenship rights—the right to enter and reside in a country in racialising citizenship practices. The right of a state in international and national law to control the entry and residence of individuals within its borders is today taken as one of the essential conditions of sovereignty. States closely protect the right to determine who holds and who does not hold nationality. The development of this right marked a break in the legal tradition of how subjects and citizens were defined, a break brought about by the tensions around the racial composition of Canada. It also marked the formalization of the ability of the state to regulate Canadian populations.

Brock (2003) has discussed how governance occurs through discourses which manage and administer individuals and populations, as well as governing technologies that provide the means to turn ideas into practices (the programmes, techniques and procedures of government). In this article, I explore the historical emergence of citizenship as a technology of governance—a governing technology that enabled the Canadian state to administer membership to Canada. I point out that such a regime of regulation was intimately premised on a discursive understanding of "race," nation, and citizenship.[3] Finally, I illustrate that the realization of this form

---

[2] While most British subjects were automatically considered citizens, Canadian citizenship practice had established two notable exceptions. First Nation peoples and Chinese residents regardless of being British subjects were denied access to citizenship rights.

[3] It is important to note that, in complex and contradictory ways, citizenship as a technology of governance was premised on gender/gender relations. First, in this period, while "white" women had citizenship in Canada, the rights associated with citizenship were gendered, as it did not include the right to vote and hold office. Such gendering of citizenship rights had contradictory effects for "white" women. On one hand, it led to state and moral regulation that channelled their labour into reproduction and motherhood, and thus relegated these (and other) women to a gendered position within the nation-state. On the other hand, such regulation empowered middle class women as it made them responsible for the moral health of the nation, and thus privileged them vis a vis working class and colonised women. Second, this was also a period in which Canadian feminists were making the claim for the franchise. As Valverde (1991) and Dua (2000) illustrated, claims for gender equality were often premised on the project of making Canada 'white.' At the same time, the claim for citizenship rights made South Asian anti-colonial activists was also premised on a masculinist project of citizenship, as these activists advocated that South Asian women be included in Canada as their wives, not as independent migrants (see Dua, 1999).

of regulation hinged on the development of Canadian state legal and administrative apparatuses to determine who could be a member of the Canadian nation.

CITIZENSHIP, MIGRATION, AND RACE

Recently there has been considerable interest in state control of migration, and the implications for how immigrants experience the nation-state. Much of this interest has been inspired by the recent phase of globalization in which, on one hand, nation-states appear to have less control over the movement of money, credit, investment, goods, services, ideas, and information, but, on the other hand, still impose considerable control over the transborder movement of people (Featherstone, 1990; Robertson, 1994; Waters, 1995). While this body of research is rich in demonstrating the ways in which migrants experience citizenship rights in European and North American contexts, it takes for granted that modern states have always had the right and ability to regulate borders. Despite this limitation, this literature offers important insights for understanding the implications of such regulatory powers for the social construction of racism.

Several scholars have pointed out that modern practice of citizenship has always implied the exclusion of non-members. Much of this literature has pointed to the ways in which practices of citizenship in modern western countries have shaped practices of racial and ethnic exclusion (Bader, 1997; Kymlica, 1997; Spinner, 1994). This work has pointed out that citizenship is not simply a legal concept but also a cultural concept, and explored the implications of such cultural underpinnings for racial and ethnic minority members of nation-states (in Canada, see Juteau, 1996, 1997). These writers have noted that cultural notions attached to citizenship translate into differences in power for racial and ethnic groups (Juteau, 1997). However, these writers do not explore the history through which citizenship has taken on cultural meanings. Despite the richness of work in the area of migration and citizenship, an investigation of how practices of citizenship became culturally tied to notions of race is missing.

In this context, recent studies on nations and nationalisms are informative, as they point to the process by which nineteenth-century ideas of citizenship became tied to the discourse of race. Two ideas from this work are particularly relevant for our understanding of regulation, citizenship, and race. First, that citizenship is based on the notion of a natural community—a notion that lends itself to racialisation (see Balibar, 1991; Miles, 1989). Inspired by the work of Gellner (1983) and Anderson (1983), scholars have demonstrated how the process of nineteenth-century European and North American nation-building naturalised notions of nationality or state-membership. Davidson (1997) shows that in the context of projects of nation-building, the concept of a citizen became synonymous with the notion of a people. Stolcke (1997) argued that this convergence led to an inherent contradiction for the practice of citizenship. On the one hand, liberals advocated a universalistic, voluntaristic idea of citizenship and on the other hand, states closely regulated who gained access to membership, particularly through criteria such as race and language (see also Anderson, 1983; Balibar, 1991). This work suggests that the regulation of borders was tied to the imperatives of nation-building.

Second, nineteenth-century practices of citizenship were not simply based on notions of exclusion, but notions of exclusion that were tied to the discourse of race. Haney-Lopez's (1996) excellent study on the legal construction of race through law in the United States illustrates that nineteenth-century laws of citizenship betray a dismal record of racial exclusion. From that country's inception the laws regulating who could or could not become a citizen were based on racial membership. Those of African and Asian descent were denied access to citizenship rights. Moreover, Haney-Lopez (1996) suggests that exclusionary immigration policies were tied to the struggle to protect the racial criteria for citizenship. Exclusionary entry (immigration) policies were justified through the discourse of citizenship—the understanding that colonized peoples were not capable of participating in democratic citizenship.

This diverse body of research has been important in demonstrating that modern practices of citizenship not only organize the marginalization of minority groups but also have been based on the notion that certain races were not qualified for citizenship rights. However, it is missing an understanding of how the development of border regulations have historically been tied to keeping colonised peoples out of Europe and white settler societies. Also this literature fails to note that the development of such controls altered the practice of citizenship within the British Empire. Next, I investigate the historical process through which the Canadian state developed the legal power to control who enters into its territories, and the implications of these controls for the practice of citizenship.

NOTIONS OF SUBJECT AND CITIZEN UNDERLYING CANADIAN CITIZENSHIP AND NATURALISATION LAWS IN CANADA

The development of Canadian citizenship and naturalisation laws reflect the legacy of British legal tradition of the subject, British imperial policies and the imperatives of a white settler formation. In both British and Canadian legal tradition, citizenship rights were juxtaposed on pre-existing feudal notions of the subject and alien. A subject was simply someone who owed allegiance to the Crown. Initially, one obtained the status of a subject if born under the monarch's protection. This has been referred to as the principle of *ius suli*. The problem of defining a subject became more complex when England and Scotland were united. Given that subjects were governed under the laws of the monarch, particularly laws governing property and inheritance, it was essential to establish whether those who resided in Scotland were subjects of the Crown. Beginning with the Calvin case

(1608), the British courts established that someone who resided or was born on British soil—in those territories obtained either by conquest, by treaty, by taking possession of, and peopling when found uninhabited was also a subject of the Crown (Chitty, 1968, p. 25).

British legal practice also established who was an alien, as someone who resided in the King's territories but owed allegiance to another monarch. When an alien gave birth to a child in the King's territories, that was not sufficient for the child to become a subject, as he was not born under the King's obedience and protection (Chitty, 1968, p. 12). However, Britain allowed aliens to become naturalised. Through various acts of Parliament, particularly, an alien could apply for a denizen, which would confer the right to purchase land and be subject to the monarch's laws of inheritance. Thus, a third way someone could become a subject was through an application to an agent of the monarch.

Vincenzi (1998) has pointed out that the powers of the Crown and the rights of subjects that derive from these relationships are unclear. "The word right is not capable of a comprehensive and exact definition in English law" (1998, p. 91) particularly when it came to the right of residence, and the power to control entry. The Crown never had the prerogative to prevent its own subjects from entering the kingdom, or to expel them from it. Also, the power of the Crown to do this was limited by the Magna Carta, which provided that anyone may leave the kingdom and return at will (Vincenzi, 1998, p. 93). In other words, while subjects had the right to reside in Crown's territories, according to the Magna Carta, aliens also the right to enter England (Vincenzi, 1998, p. 97). The Crown had no general power to detain either British subjects or aliens. As Vincenzi has noted (1998, p. 96), it was not clear in British law whether the right of entry gave rights of residence. As we shall see, the legal ambiguity in the Crown's powers to control entry became the point of struggle in Britain and several white settler formations, including Canada.

In Canada, definitions of citizen and alien were based on these pre-existing notions of subjects and aliens. The British North America Act (1867) gave the federal government the power to control aliens and naturalisation, while provinces were allocated the responsibility of defining civil rights. According to the British North America Act, a citizen was someone who was a "male British subject, aged Twenty-one Years or upwards, being a householder" (1867, p. 8), in other words, someone born in either Canadian or British territories, or naturalised in one of these territories. Thus, someone born not in Canada, but in British territories was automatically considered a citizen (Canada, *Acts and Statutes*, 1881). The first Naturalisation Act (1881) stipulated who was not qualified for citizenship; "Disability means the status of being an infant, lunatic, idiot, or married woman" (1881, p. 78). The definition of an alien continued to be based on the earlier definition—a person born outside of "Her Majesty's Dominions," who owed allegiance to another sovereign or country. While this excluded all British subjects, as we shall see, the question of whether certain subjects could be legally defined as aliens was an issue that several governments would struggle with by the end of the nineteenth century.

The Canadian state allowed aliens or immigrants to become naturalised. According to the 1886 Immigration Act, an immigrant "referred to someone about to leave Europe for Canada" (Canada, *Revised Statutes*, 1886, p. 969). The first Naturalisation Act of 1881 was shaped by consideration of settlement policies. As a country founded through migration, Canada allowed the waves of European immigrants easy access to citizens' rights. As the Act stated, "this law embodies the principle that it should be free to every one to expatriate and denationalize himself, and to transfer his allegiance to another country (Canada, *Revised Statutes*, 1886, p. 56). Constitutional expert, Alfred Howell, in *Naturalisation and Nationality in Canada* (1884) explained who the Act was intended for and the motivation underlying the Act,

> …the decennial census, 1881, showed the population of foreign nationalities resident…has been increased by many thousands…unlike those who come from the British Islands, and other British possessions, who are our fellow subjects, they are the subjects or citizens of foreign powers, and not entitled to the privileges of British subjects in this country unless they become such by naturalisation. (1886, p. i)

As Howell noted, there were two important reasons for providing aliens with access to citizenship rights. First, to confer the same capacities regarding property to aliens that are enjoyed by British subjects (1886, p. 1). Second, to ensure uniformity of law throughout the Empire (1886, p. 3). As John A. Macdonald stated to the House of Commons, the Naturalisation Act "is framed very much on the model of the Imperial Act with such modifications as suit the circumstances of this country." (Canada, *Commons Debates*, March 11, 1880, p. 1340)

THE RACIALISATION OF CITIZENSHIP RIGHTS

The first immigration and naturalisation laws allowed Europeans easy entry into Canada, and easy access to citizenship. However, this is only half the story. The other half was the application of differential rights to those subjects; citizens and aliens who were colonised subjects—the racialisation of subject and citizenship rights. As Canada developed its citizenship practices, First Nation peoples were deliberately treated as if they were incoming migrants moving on to uninhabited soil already occupied by British settlers. As such, they were not defined as British subjects, they did not have rights that were recognised by British law, and their legal system was seen as irrelevant. The Indian Act of 1876 specified both the conditions under which Indians could become citizens of Canada or members of an Indian band.

According to the Indian Act (Canada, *Acts and Statutes*, 1876) there were two ways for an aboriginal man to become enfranchised. First, was to obtain a university degree, particularly in medicine or law. The second was to apply for enfranchisement. In this case, the "Indian" was required to have consent of the band of which he was a member, an allotment of band land, and had to make an application to the Superintendent-General, which proved "the degree of civilization to which he or she has attained, and the character of integrity, morality and sobriety which he or she bears, appears to be qualified to become a proprietor of land" (1876, p. 69). Upon making such an application, the applicant (unlike the immigrant) is placed on probation for three years during which he, his spouse, and his children must act with sobriety. After the probationary period, the applicant was required to make a declaration to the Superintendent-General as to the name and surname he or she would hold in the future. Only at this point shall "any act or law making any distinctions between the legal rights, privileges, disabilities and liabilities of Indians and those of Her Majesty's other subjects shall cease to apply to any Indian, or to the wife or minor unmarried children of any Indians aforesaid" (1876, p. 70).

For all other First Nation peoples, the Indian Act also specified whether or not they could hold the legal status of "Indian," hold legal membership in a band, vote in band elections, and hold band property. Indians could not freely elect their own chiefs and band councils, as the Indian Act specified that those elected could be disposed of by the Superintendent-General, if they were "intemperate, immoral, dishonest or incompetent" (Canada, 1876, p. 56). Other rights were also restricted. The Act specified the conditions under which Indians or half-Indians could purchase and sell land. Until 1920, First Nations people were not allowed to participate in federal, provincial, or municipal elections. Clearly an Indian was a different kind of subject and citizen.

Asian migrants, irrespective of whether they were British subjects or aliens, were also denied access to Canadian citizenship. As noted earlier, the British North America Act gave the federal government the power to control aliens and naturalisation, while provinces were allocated the responsibility of defining civil rights. This constitutional division of power led to considerable tensions between the federal and the British Columbian provincial government over issues of race, migration, and citizenship. When British Columbia became a province in 1871, Chinese residents had the right to enter, reside, and to vote in some districts. But in the first session of the provincial legislature, An Act to Amend the Qualification and Registration of Voters Act (1875) was passed which precluded Chinese and First Nations from voting. Notably, the Act stated that this held even if they were British subjects.

As it made all Chinese residents into aliens, including those who were subjects of the British Crown, this act officially altered existing practices toward British subjects, Canadian citizens, and aliens. It marked the beginning of the process of racialising Canadian citizenship and naturalisation laws, as it allowed for further closure. In 1878, the Provincial legislature attempted to prohibit Chinese residents from employment on provincial and federal works. This was followed by the Chinese Tax Act, the imposition of a quarterly licence in the form of a $10 levy on employers for every Chinese worker in their employ.

However, when his goods were seized for default of taxes, Tai Sing filed a court case that the Chinese Tax Act was *ultra vires* provincial jurisdiction. According to the British North America Act, the authority for establishing the privileges and disabilities of aliens in Canada was vested in the federal government. In response to the demands of the British Columbia provincial government, the federal government appointed the Royal Commission on Chinese Immigration. In 1885, on the recommendation of this commission, the federal government passed the Bill to Restrict and Regulate Chinese Immigration to the Dominion of Canada (Canada, *Acts and Statutes,* 1885).

This Act further redefined Canadian citizenship practices. In order to restrict the entry of Chinese migrants, the Bill imposed a $50.00 levy on all those of the "Chinese race" who entered Canada. It also denied those Chinese residents in Canada the right to permanent residence. In addition, through parliamentary debates, Chinese residents were defined as racially incapable of holding citizenship rights. In doing so, politicians discursively redefined a British subject as someone who was white.[4] As Chapleau stated, "Is it not the natural and well-founded desire of British **subjects, of the white population** of the Dominion, who come from either British or other European states, that their country should be inhabited by a vigorous, energetic and white race of people?" (Canada, *House of Commons Debates,* 1883, p. 3010).

Subsequently, attempts were made to deny Japanese residents and Canadian-born Chinese residents the right to naturalise. In 1895, the British Columbia provincial government moved to deny the franchise to naturalised and Canadian-born subjects of Chinese and Japanese origins. This legislation attempted to take away the right of *ius suli*, the right to citizenship due to birth. In addition, the British Columbia legislature proposed an amendment to the federal naturalisation laws that would require a residency requirement of 10 years prior to naturalisation. However, as these attempts violated existing treaties between Britain, Japan, and China, the federal government stepped in and declared both pieces of legisla-

---

[4] In Canada, there has not been a direct investigation of how notions of citizenship were racialised. However, Anderson (1991) provides insights into the relationship between citizenship and the discourse of race.

tion unconstitutional.[5] Over the next ten years, the British Columbian government attempted to pass several other bills that would restrict the rights of Chinese and Japanese residents and migrants, only to have the federal government declare these attempts *ultra vires*. Finally, in 1910, the federal government passed an Immigration Act that restricted the entry of those of the "Asiatic race," again irrespective of whether they were British subjects.

The situation of Indian migrants was different from that of those from China and Japan. As India was part of the British Empire, in their case, they were subjects of same sovereign, and therefore technically regulated by the same laws as other subjects. The Canadian government needed to be careful in how they prevented Indians from entering and residing in Canada. Moreover, the issue of whether Indians had the right to move freely throughout the Empire was an issue that had been discussed at length in other white settler colonies. When Australia and South Africa were granted self-government, their administrations were reluctant to treat Indian subjects in the same way as other subjects. The issue of Indian migration created considerable dilemmas and tensions in British Imperial policies, tensions that were eventually resolved by imposing differential rights for Indian subjects of the Crown.

INDIAN MIGRANTS, FROM BRITISH TO COLONIAL SUBJECTS

The nineteenth century witnessed one of the largest movements of peoples in history, as free, indentured, and slave labour was transported throughout the world. As colonial formations incorporated different kinds of labour, the issue of whether all subjects of the Crown had the same rights echoed throughout the colonial world.[6] In addition, in Canada, Australia, New Zealand, and South Africa—the commitment to the project of white settlement, meant that colonial administrators were reluctant to treat Chinese, Japanese, and Indian migrants the same as "white" migrants. The tension between incorporating different kinds of labour with projects of white settlement began a process through which institutional and legal differentiation between subjects began to take place. Given the position of

---

[5] The treaty of Nanking (1842) had stipulated that the subjects of Great Britain and China would enjoy full security and protection of their persons and property within the dominions of the two powers (Huttenback, 1976, p. 75). In 1880, the Convention of Friendship between Great Britain and China reassert these principles. In case of Japan, the Anglo-Japanese treaty assured that the subjects of both Great Britain and Japan respectively "full liberty to enter, travel or reside in any part of the dominions and possessions of the other contracting party" (Huttenback, 1976, p. 157). However, an article specified that the treaty did not apply to British self-governing Dominions. This led several Dominions, including Canada, to arrange for their own treaties.

[6] For examples see Backhouse, 2000; Chomsky, 1996; Kelly, 1991.

Indians as subjects of the Crown, much of the differentiation took place through the issue of Indian migration.

Beginning in 1842, migrants from India had moved throughout the colonial world. After the British government abolished slavery in 1833, colonial administrators began to look for alternative sources of unfree labour (see Huttenback, 1976; Tinker, 1976). The first proposal to export indentured labour from India was put forward by colonial officials in New South Wales in 1836 (Huttenback, 1976, p. 28). From the outset, the Colonial Office was not in favour of the introduction of Indian indentured labour. Lord Glenieg, the Secretary of State for the Colonies, argued that the introduction of Indian labour would have an adverse effect on the colony, as it would discourage emigration from England. As importantly, Glenieg pointed out that the presence of Indian indentured labour raised the question of the status of such labour—their legal rights to settlement—a question the Colonial Office felt it wise to avoid (Colonial Office, 13/24, no. 21 and no. 50, February 22 and August 23, 1842).

While the Colonial Office would continue to oppose the introduction of indentured labour in colonies of white settlement, there was very little it could do to prevent it as long as emigration was handled through private agents. In the following 50 years, indentured labour from India was imported into Australia, Fiji, Singapore, Hong Kong, Malaysia, South Africa, Kenya, Mauritius, and British Guyana. Huttenback has noted that in this period, colonial administrators did not see Indian indentured workers as a threat—they were members of a British dependency, and thus were thought to be disinclined to settle (1976, p. 32). However, emerging difficulties with indentured labour—racist sentiments, high rates of mortality and suicide, extreme brutality, and violation of contracts—meant that by 1880 colonial administrators also began to question the desirability of indentured labour. In particular, as a generation of indentured workers finished their contracts, but did not return to India, the question of their status became contentious issue. As free workers, Indians began to press for the right to own property, to vote, to enter into restricted occupations, and for family reunification. They began to ask for the rights given to other subjects of the Crown (see Huttenback, 1976; Tinker, 1976).

Colonial officials began to rethink the status of indentured labour. In 1885, the Governor of Australia, Musgrove, argued that the labour question was an imperial responsibility (Colonial Office, 234/44, Q.6961, 1885). The Colonial Office agreed, but felt that it could not interfere in the internal affairs of a colony that had been given the privileges of responsible government (Colonial Office, 234/44, Q.6961, 1885). The colonies of white settlement responded in different ways. Later that year, Australia passed legislation that required employers to support workers whose contracts had expired until they re-indentured or were returned to their native lands (Huttenback, 1976, p. 98). In Natal, most Indians who arrived as indentured workers did not return to India but purchased small plots of land.

The Governor of the Colony stated that they were welcome as long as they stayed in their place and did not aspire to such rights as the franchise, which he felt should be reserved for white men (Huttenback, 1976, p. 101).

After 1880, free Indian labour began to move throughout the Empire. The entry of free Indians into white settler colonies exacerbated the situation. These free migrants were financially independent, and again raised the issue of rights to settle, own property, and to vote in elections. White workers and colonial governments began to demand that the Colonial Office provide legislation that restricted the free movement of Indians. However, the legal structure of the Empire placed no impediments on immigration within the Empire or from abroad. The Colonial Office felt compelled to demonstrate an official commitment to the principle of the rights of British subjects, and their responsibility to all subjects. The Colonial Office responded that their hands were tied (Colonial Office, 311/159, 1885).

Australia and South Africa began to contemplate restricting Chinese, Japanese, and Indian migration. Australia, in 1887, passed a law to disenfranchise Indians. Acting on behalf of the Colonial Office, the Governor of Australia opposed the law, on the grounds that denying British subjects the right to vote exceeded the powers of the Australian government. The legislation raised the issue of the respective powers of the Dominion and Imperial governments with respect to citizenship rights. The British Government had the power to disallow all legislation passed by British colonies, but in practice, after a colony attained responsible government, the Colonial Office interfered only in matters of imperial concern. But Indians were British subjects. The Colonial Office agreed with the Governor of Australia. They responded that the bill was imperial by nature and fell to the Imperial Government under the Australian constitution (Colonial Office 234/37, 1887). The situation placed the British government in an awkward position. The Colonial Office moved to disallow the bill (Colonial Office 234/37, 1887).

The Colonial Office warned that direct measures to exclude or disenfranchise Indians would not only pose difficulties for the British Government, it would also violate the policies of the Imperial Government with regard to subjects. Thus attempts were made to exclude Indians indirectly, especially by passing restrictions that appeared to be neutral and avoided racial language. In 1897, the Natal Government enacted legislation that excluded Indians through qualifications based on property and knowledge of a European language, with the judgement of language skills to be at the discretion of the immigration officer. The education test became known as the Natal formula (see Huttenback, 1976).

The Colonial Office was much more comfortable with this solution. Chamberlain, at the Imperial Conference in 1897, argued that the Natal formula allowed colonial governments to restrict Indian emigration and at the same time preserve the notion of a British subject. "The Colony of Natal has arrived at an arrangement which is absolutely satisfactory to them…(and) arranged a form of words which will avoid hurting the feelings of her Majesty's subjects" (Proceedings of a Conference between the Secretary of State for the Colonies and the Premiers of Self-Governing Colonies, 1897, p. 51). As Chamberlain pointed out, the important issue was to maintain the idea that the status of non-white British subjects within the Empire was protected by the Crown. However, as Huttenback notes (1976, p. 167), once the Natal formula was accepted, Colonial Office as *quid pro quo* abandoned its previously consistent stand—that the rights of British subjects receive at least pro forma recognition. While not overtly, in practice they had accepted that "white" British subjects had rights not enjoyed by "coloured" British subjects.

Indians, throughout the Empire, attacked colonial and British governments for differential treatment of themselves as subjects. They pointed out that their status as British subjects allowed them the right to enter white settler colonies, and, upon entry, to the same status as other residents. For example, after the Natal formula was adopted, 46 Sikh men in Australia claimed that they had risked their lives to protect the British flag, believing that all British subjects were equal before the law. They pointed out that once they emigrated to her Majesty's Dominions, they were to their surprise treated as aliens along with "enemies of her Imperial Majesty" (*The Hindustanee*, 1910, January 1). In 1906, the Indian National Congress, under Gandhi, began to challenge the discriminatory policies towards coloured British subjects in Natal. Threats of exclusion became an issue among nationalists in India. On October 11, 1897, Dadabhai Naoroji, remarked in a letter to Chamberlain "we are repeatedly told that we are British subjects, quite as much as the Queen's subjects in this country, and not slaves and I always look forward with hope to a fulfilment of these pledges and Proclamations…and pray it maybe a reality and not remain a romance" (NA, Ind. Coll, no 102, Naoroji to Chamberlain, 1897, October 11).

Despite the Imperial philosophy of equality before the law, it was clear that the status of a British subject and the rights supposedly inherent in that status were not common to all subjects of the Crown in the dominions. A compromise was posed—the racialisation of subject rights. *The Times* (London) reflected this compromise when it stated; "The principles by which we must be guided are clear. In the past we have conceived of British citizenship as conferring in the same way as Roman citizenship of old, an equal status in all parts of the King-Emperor's Dominions. But this is not a principle the colonies will accept. Consequently, we must strive to make our Indian fellow-subjects realize that…inequality is inevitable…not due to inferior status but to facts of race" (1910, September 12).

FROM COLONIAL SUBJECTS TO ALIENS: THE MUNSHI SINGH CASE

As we have seen, from Canadian Confederation, First Nation and Chinese residents had been stripped of their rights as British subjects, and legally redefined as aliens. The next step in this process of redefining subjects, citizens and aliens would take place through the issue of Indian migration. The compromise of the British Government did not sit well with Indians. Indians continued pointing out that they were British subjects, and not aliens under Imperial and national citizenship practices. In Canada, Indian residents began to organize a series of challenges to the racial inequities embodied in these regulations. This meant organising immigration from India, and upon being denied entry, launching legal challenges to these regulations. In the courts they fought to have the racially differential practices towards entry, residence, and rights overturned.

In the beginning of the twentieth century Indians began to arrive in Canada. As the numbers increased, Canadians began to protest the inclusion of Indians, especially in British Columbia. The federal government attempted to find a mechanism which would prevent the entry of Indians while avoiding to inflame the claims of racism that were being made throughout the Empire. In 1908, the federal government appointed Mackenzie King to investigate the issue. He suggested that one resolution was to require that all immigrants possess a large amount of money, as this would act as a disincentive. Mackenzie King also suggested the requirement of what was called the continuous journey stipulation, a stipulation in immigration regulations that required an immigrant to come directly from his place of origin. The only company that provided a continuous journey from India was the CPR. The Government of Canada then issued directives that prohibited the CPR from selling any through tickets from India to Canada (Bolaria and Li, 1988, p. 170; Walker, 1997, pp. 225–226). As King noted in his report, this regulation would avoid overtly distinguishing between British subjects, but at the same time, allow Canada to prevent the entry of Indians (Canada, *Reports,* 1908).

As a result, later that year, the Canadian government passed two order-in-councils. The first, PC 926, stated that "no immigrant of Asiatic origin shall be permitted to enter Canada unless in actual and personal possession in his or her own right of two hundred dollars." The second, PC 920, stated that "the landing in Canada shall be and the same is hereby prohibited, of any immigrants who have come to Canada otherwise than by a continuous journey from the country of which they are natives or citizens, and upon through tickets purchased or prepaid in Canada" (*British Columbia Law Reports*, V. XX, pp. 244–245). In addition, in 1910, the Canadian government revised the Immigration Act to give it the power to impose these stipulations (Canada, *Revised Statutes*, 1910). These regulations did not fool anyone. Indians, in Canada and throughout the Empire, saw this as another attempt to deny them their rights of movement as British subjects. They launched a series of legal challenges to the regulations. Three cases were filed, each challenging the powers of the Canadian government to control the entry of Indians, culminating in the Munshi Singh case.

In 1910, Rahim, an Indian anti-colonial revolutionary, entered Canada as a tourist. He was arrested 10 months later, and ordered deported (for more details see Johnson, 1989, p. 9). Rahim went to court to challenge the validity of his deportation order. His lawyers argued that the 1910 Immigration Act did not apply to someone who entered Canada before the passage of the Act, therefore the order-in-council passed since that Act did not apply to Rahim (*British Columbia Reports*, 16, p. 472). The judge, Morrison, agreed. He stated, "It seems clear that Parliament was dealing with those persons who after the passing of the Act entered Canada" (*British Columbia Reports,* 16, p. 472). In addition, Morrison noted that the orders-in-council may be problematic, stating; "Nor do I think there is a valid order in council, pursuant to section 38 of the Act. Doubtless, the limitations which the word 'naturalised' has been placed upon the word 'citizen'" (*British Columbia Reports*, 16, p. 472).

The Immigration Department appealed. They argued that Rahim, as an alien, did not have the right to appeal an order discharging an accused person on a writ of habeas corpus. In 1912, in the Courts of Appeal, the judges, Macdonald, Martin, and Galliher (with Judge Irving dissenting), upheld the lower courts decision. They held that under the previous law Rahim had been legally landed. However, the judges did not deal with the issue of Rahim's status as an alien, and whether the Canadian government had the power to deport him under a writ of the habeas corpus, leaving the ability of Canadian government powers to control entry ambiguous.

The next legal challenge came when, on October 17, 1913, fifty-six Indians arrived in Victoria. Those who had previously established residence were allowed to re-enter, but 39 were ordered deported under the new regulations. With the assistance of Indian residents, the new arrivals filed a court challenge (see Walker, 1997, p. 257). This time they challenged the legality of the orders-in-council directly. The lawyer, J. Edward Bird, argued that the continuous stipulation was a subvert way of imposing racial discriminatory immigration rules, and should be overturned (*Western Weekly Reports*, 5, p. 686). In his judgement, Justice Hunter disagreed, holding that the court's responsibility was only to interpret the Acts, not to judge them, stating,

> At the outset Mr. Bird vehemently urged that Parliament knew that it was impossible for Hindoos to come to a Canadian port by a continuous journey and that it had employed a subterfuge to place a ban on Hindus as a race, and that therefore the court ought to be astute, if possible, to defeat the alleged injustice. (*Western Weekly Reports*, 5, pp. 686–87)

However, like the courts before him, Judge Hunter raised questions about the wording of the orders-in-council. He suggested that as these orders employed the word "Asiatic origin" they were problematic, as this wording did not differentiate between those of the British race born in India and those of the Indian "race."

> It is obvious that the word "origin" included more than the word "race". A person born in India of British parents domiciled there would be Asiatic origin, but not race. The prohibition therefore, exceeds that contained in the statute itself and is accordingly *ultra vires*…has already been decided invalid by Mr. Justice Morrison in the Rahim's case…on the grounds that it omitted the qualifying word "naturalised" before the words "citizen"…the difficulty is that the word "native" is used as a noun in the Order-in-Council and would therefore include persons of British race born in India, which it is difficult to suppose Parliament intended. (*Western Weekly Reports*, 5, p. 687)

Thus, the court's concern was that the wording on the orders-in council could be used for contrary purposes—to exclude those of the British race who had the right to enter Canada.

Finally, Judge Hunter referred to the issue of whether those deported had access to the Canadian court, and the right to question the power of the Canadian government to deport subjects or aliens; "Reference is made to s. 23 which purports to limit the jurisdiction of the court to interfere with deportation proceedings…it would be strange to find the doors of the court were shut against any person of any nationality no matter what the Act complained of might be" (*Western Weekly Reports*, 5, p. 688). Given these concerns, he allowed those who had come to Canada to stay, and threw into question the validity of the regulations.

This set up the next crucial challenge. Indians felt that the Hunter decision meant that the orders-in-councils were overturned, and began to organize immigration from India. In India, Gurdit Singh began to raise funds to charter a steamship to bring Indian migrants to Canada (see Johnson, 1989). In the meantime, the Canadian government quickly responded to the two court decisions. One week after the Hunter decision, the Government passed an order that barred all artisans and labourers from landing in British Columbia ports. New orders P.C. 23 and 24, were issued on January 7, 1914 that dealt with the objections of the courts (Johnson, 1989, pp. 26–27).

Meanwhile, Gurdit Singh had recruited 376 people. Gurdit Singh was informed of the legal changes, and was well aware that his arrival would bring about another court challenge. He stated he would fight in the Supreme Court of Canada "for a decision in our favour for ever" and go on to organize further immigration (Johnson, 1989, p. 28). In an interview, Gurdit Singh reiterated the claim to British status, stating that the voyage was taken to test the justice of the British towards all of their people (Johnson, 1989, p. 30). The ship left Hong Kong on April 6, 1914. The Governor of Hong Kong sent a telegram to the federal government that the ship was on its way. The Canadian government, alerted, was waiting for the ship's arrival. The ship arrived on May 23 at Burrard Inlet, to be met by a party of immigration officers, and denied entry. Upon arrival, Gurdit Singh again declared to the Canadian press, that he was attempting to gain the rights conferred through being a subject; "We are British citizens and we consider we have a right to visit any part of the Empire. We are determined to make this a test case and if we are refused entrance into your country, the matter will not end here" (quoted in Johnson, 1988, p. 38).

The case was indeed a test case, one that would prove to be instrumental in resolving who would be a Canadian citizen, an immigrant, and an alien. In addition, it would determine that the Canadian federal government, not British law nor the provincial government, had ultimate authority to define citizenship. After considerable negotiation, the Indians aboard the steamship and the Canadian authorities agreed to a single test case. The lawyers chose Munshi Singh. The lawyers, Bird and Cassidy, put forward several arguments, but most importantly they directly raised the issue that as British subjects, Indians should have equal rights within the Empire. They pointed out that this meant Indians were not aliens and had the right to enter Canada. Finally, the lawyers challenged the constitutionality of the 1910 Immigration Act, pointing out that under the British North America Act, the federal government had control over aliens, but not over British subjects. Cassidy argued,

> We contend that Parliament has not the power to authorize the detention and deportation of a British subject who presents himself at a port in Canada claiming the right to enter Canada as an immigrant. (*British Columbia Law Reports*, 20, p. 251)

Bird and Cassidy argued that the Immigration Act was *ultra vires* and violated the "civil rights" of Munshi Singh, exceeding the authority delegated to the Dominion Government by the British North America Act.

A law for the detention and deportation of a person rejected as an immigrant is certainly an interference with "civil rights within the Province" which all immigrants possess from the moment they enter the Province…we submit this authorization is in excess of the Dominion legislative powers in relation to "immigration" and an unwarranted trenching on the appellant's "civil rights within the Province"….The Dominion government has power to imprison and deport rejected immigrants being aliens…but we submit it has no such power over rejected immigrants being British subjects (*British Columbia Law Reports*, 20, p. 251).

Bird and Cassidy concluded by pointing out that such use of unwarranted powers raised important implications for the racialisation of citizenship within the Empire.

> The discrimination we refer to are not trifling, but of great and far-reaching consequence….Nothing had occasioned so much international jealousy, friction, and ill-feeling, as laws discriminating against a particular race or nation in the matter of immigration. (British Columbia Law Reports, 20, p. 251)

All of the judges overruled the arguments, holding that the Canadian government did have the power to define subjects, citizens, and aliens according to their own criteria. In doing so, the court also dealt with the question of who was subject, citizen, and alien, and the relationship between the three. The court made three crucial decisions that would have profound effect on the practice of citizenship in Canada.

First, their interpretation the British North America Act provided the Canadian government with ultimate sovereignty with all matters in Canada, including citizenship and immigration. Judge Macdonald reflected the opinion of Irving, Martin, and McPhillips stating;

> On the threshold of the case is the question of the constitutionality of the Immigration Act. That the king, with the advice and consent of the Imperial Parliament, had the power to make laws for the exclusion from British possessions of immigrants, whether British subjects or not, has not been questioned, as indeed, it could not be doubted. By the terms of the British North America Act the Parliament of Canada is clothed with sovereign power in matters relating to immigration into any part of the Dominion…and hence…Canada's authority to admit immigrants of any or every race or nationality, on any terms she pleases, is complete. (British Columbia Law Reports, 20, pp. 255–256)

Judges Ritchie and Ladner went further, stating that the British North America Act gave the Canadian government the equivalence of "sovereign" power in Canada (British Columbia Law Reports, 20, p. 261). Making this decision, the courts asserted that the Canadian state had the power to control the entry of anyone who was not legally a citizen. Judge McPhillips stated: "It is irresistible that self-government and national status must attach itself to this power. It is a power of preservation of the nation" (British Columbia Law Reports, 20, p. 287).

Second, the Canadian government could define an alien according to its own criteria. Judge Irving stated: "By section 95 of the British North America Act, passed by the Imperial government….Parliament of Canada was authorised to deal with all matters coming within the class of subjects embraced within the words 'naturalisation and aliens'" (259). This power, according to Judge McPhillips, gave the Canadian government the right to define an alien according to racial criteria,

> The Parliament of Canada—the nation's Parliament—may be well said to be safeguarding the people of Canada from an influx which is no chimera to conjure up might annihilate the nation and change its whole potential complexity, introduce Oriental ways as against European ways, eastern civilization for western civilization, and all of the dire results that would naturally flow there from….In that our fellow British subjects of the Asiatic race are of different instincts to those of the European race—and consistent there with, their family life, rules of society and laws are of a

very different character—in their own interests, their proper place or residence is within the confines of their respective countries in the continent of Asia, not in Canada. (*British Columbia Law Reports*, 20, pp. 291–292)

Finally, as Judge Martin noted, this power was consistent with legislation regarding First Nations people, who also had an "alien" status,

That prohibition covers not only British subjects residing in other parts of the Empire, but also in Canada itself…even a native Canadian Indian, a British subject and labourer who attempted to cross the boundary into this Province and work in a salmon cannery would be turned back. That would indeed, be a strange perversion of British citizenship which would give to others greater rights and privileges in Canada than are therein possessed and enjoyed by Canadians themselves." (*British Columbia Law Reports*, 20, p. 276)

The court agreed that the Canadian Government possessed both the powers as well as was justified on "cultural" grounds to racialize the qualifications for citizenship.

Finally, being a British subject did not automatically give one the right to Canadian citizenship, including the right to enter and reside in Canada. The two were exclusive. As Judge Macdonald stated, "The appellant's suggestion is that a British subject born in one part of the King's possessions is a native citizen of every other part. This, I am confident, was not the meaning attached to the term 'native citizen' by Parliament" (*British Columbia Law Reports*, 20, p. 257). Similarly, Judge Irving stated "That Parliament has distinguished between the rights of those who are citizens of Canada and those who are not, gives point to the argument that the Act itself, subject matter and language together, contemplates all matters relating to the detention and deportation of any rejected immigrant" (*British Columbia Law Reports*, 20, p. 291). In this way the court ended the legal ambiguity between British citizenship and Canadian citizenship.

In Canada, this case set into motion a legal reformulation of the practices and policies towards citizenship and naturalisation in Canada. Underlying this reformulation was the project of a racialised citizenship. As we have seen, at this point in history Canada broke with existing British notions of the rights associated with being a subject. The courts proclaimed that the status British subject did not translate into the status of Canadian citizenship. Importantly, it was in order to prevent the entry of Asian British subjects that the courts asserted national autonomy over citizenship, naturalisation, and immigration. As McPhillips claimed in his judgement: "it may also now be stated to be settled law that the Parliament of Canada, acting under the power conferred by section 91 of the British North America Act, in the making of laws for the peace, order and good government of Canada, is paramount in legislating in respect to all matters coming with the section 91 of the Act, and the legislation of the Parliament of Canada is to prevail" (p. 283).

TOWARDS THEORISING THE CONNECTIONS BETWEEN GOVERNMENTALITY, IMPERIALISM, CITIZENSHIP, AND RACE

Recently several scholars have attempted to theorise the relationship between race, migration, and citizenship practices in Western societies. This work has been instrumental in demonstrating that despite liberal notions of citizenship as universal, people of colour's access to citizenship in Western societies has been strictly controlled. In the nineteenth century this took place through differential citizenship practices (Davidson, 1997; Haney-Lopez, 1996) and in the post-war period this has taken place through the control of migration (Joppke, 1998; Sassen, 1996). However, these writers fail to examine the connections between nineteenth century practices of citizenship and post-war border controls. In addition, as many writers have located the racialisation of citizenship in the imperatives of nineteenth century nationalism (Anderson, 1983; Balibar, 1991; Davidson, 1997; Miles, 1989; Stolke, 1997), they fail to adequately explain why nationalist projects take on such exclusionary forms. In such a framework, exclusionary practices appear as a functional consequence of nationalism—a consequence of the projects of creating imagined communities. As a result, the ability of the state to regulate citizenship appears as the natural prerogative of state. In this context, my study of the racialization of citizenship in Canada provides several insights for our understanding of state regulation and governmentality.

First, it extends our understanding of state regulation. Foucault (1991) has argued that the development of modern state power needs to be placed in the context of governmentality—the process by which states have come to administer and regulate populations. (See also Burchell, Gordon, and Miller, 1991). In the Canadian context, Valverde (1991) has illustrated how the governance of the Canadian population; the regulation of the entry of British and European immigrants led to the growth of the state apparatus. As I illustrate in this article, it was in order to prevent the entry of people of colour that the Canadian state gained the legal power to define whether all male subjects would have access to citizenship. It is notable that the formalization of the state's power to construct a population took place though the desire to exclude people of colour. This points to the importance of integrating a racialized landscape into our explorations of contemporary state powers.

As such, my study extends our understanding of governmentality. Much of the scholarship on governmentality has not explored the ways in which discursive regimes of power and technologies of governance have been have been situated on a racialized (and imperial) landscape. As Stoler (1995) has pointed out, in part, this omission is reminiscent of Foucault's own framing of the bourgeois order, which systematically excludes or subsumes the fact of colonialism. In her study of sexuality, she explores what would happen to Foucault's chronologies when the technologies of sexuality are refigured in a racialised field. She illustrates that in the nineteenth century the figures of the bourgeois family, such as the "hysterical" woman and the perverse adult, all existed as objects of knowledge and discourse through an erotically charged counterpoint. This counterpoint was the perverse libidinal energies of the colonized, which provided crucial reference to points of difference. Similarly, I illustrate the ways in which the discourse of citizenship and nation was premised on a charged counterpoint—the exclusion of people from citizenship rights and white settler societies.

Third, my study suggests that the development of governing technologies needs to be placed in the context of imperial labour, settlement, and movement policies, and the position of different colonies within the British empire. As I illustrated, the development of Canadian state ability to regulate citizenship was profoundly influenced by tensions within British imperialism. Notably, British imperialism affected Canadian citizenship practices in different and contradictory ways. On one hand, Canadian citizenship laws drew on British law and were tied to British imperial policies, especially those related to settlement and naturalization. On the other hand, the global politics over the racial composition of white settler societies played itself out in the national scale, as Canadian authorities moved to insure that Canada remained a white settler formation. The influence of British imperialism on Canadian citizenship practices suggests that the exclusionary practices of white settler nation-states need to be placed in the context of imperial projects. However, Canada, and other white settler societies, are only part of the story in the history of governmentality. Notably, it was as white settler formations (Canada, Australia, New Zealand, and Australia) were given the right to self-government, and within these formations white residents given the right to citizenship, that the issue of the rights of colonised subjects of the Crown reverberated throughout the Empire. Thus, another part of the story of the emergence of governmentality has to do with the ways in which early twentieth century British imperial policies granted certain colonialised nation-states "the privilege of self-government" and denied others.

While I begin to investigate the relationship between governmentality, imperialism, race, and citizenship, a number of questions still remain. As underlying the racialisation of the citizenship was the discursive construction of certain races as unfit for citizenship, we need to more thoroughly investigate the relationship between nineteenth century discourse of race and Canadian citizenship practices. The impact of American tensions over race and citizenship on Canadian and Imperial policies remains to be investigated. As importantly, to thoroughly understand the racialisation of citizenship practices we need further research on how other groups, such as First Nations, Chinese, Japanese, Afro-American, Afro-Caribbean, and Middle-Eastern, were excluded from Canadian citizenship.

In addition, my study raises the importance of further investigating how imperialism shaped the both the emergence of governing technologies in the context of other British post-colonial formations, both white settlement and others. As I suggested above, we need to investigate how the discursive understanding of race and citizenship was deployed within the British Empire to grant self-government to the white Dominions while other colonies (peoples) were denied democratic rights. My study also raises the question of whether racialised tensions over citizenship was deployed in similar ways in French, Dutch, German, Spanish settler formations, and on the ways in which these imperial projects shaped practices of citizenship. In the Canadian context, the ways in which citizenship was racialised in France, and the legacy of this for Quebec and Canada remains to be investigated.

CRITICAL THINKING QUESTIONS

1. In his judgement, Judge McPhillips claimed that "In that our fellow British subjects of the Asiatic race are of different instincts to those of the European race—and consistent there with, their family life, rules of society and laws are of a very different character—in their own interests, their proper place or residence is within the confines of their respective countries in the continent of Asia, not in Canada." Discuss the ways in which this statement is based on notions of difference. Discuss the way in which this statement constructs the idea of "race." Do similar attitudes exist today?

2. Make a list of five symbols that are commonly used to represent Canada. Can you discover how they were produced? Can you see how these symbols could be used to exclude people of colour? Can you see how these symbols could be used to marginalize aboriginal peoples? Discuss the ways in which national symbols shape current practices of racial and ethnic exclusion.

3. In the past decade, aboriginal activists have been arguing that aboriginal people have an inherent right to self-determination. Discuss the ways in which this claim is tied to Canadian and imperial history of race and citizenship.

4. Outline the current rules that are employed for determining who gets immigration status today. Who is allowed in? Who is kept out? What does this tell us about how national borders are employed today? How is this tied to Canada's history as a white settler nation?

5. What kind of powers do these immigration regulations give to Canadian state officials? Discuss how these rules allow the Canadian state to regulate the population of Canada. How are these powers tied to the concept of govermentality?

6. If national borders are invented, and tied to projects of racial exclusion, what role do they play in a globalizing world?

SUGGESTED READINGS

Anderson, Benidict (1983). *Imagined Communities: Reflections on The Origins and Spread of Nationalism*. London: Verso.
> This classic text was crucial in illustrating the way in which nations are socially constructed. Anderson argues nineteenth-century nations are neither the products of an august past, nor of territorial states. Rather, he illustrates that nations were the result of nineteenth and early twentieth century political and social projects of nation-building, in which nationalists employed social invention and social engineering to construct nations. Anderson (1983, p.7) points out that such social invention relied on the creation of an imagined community, in which members of a nation-state acquired a sense of "fraternity."

Bannerji, Himani (2000). *The Dark Side of the Nation: Essays on Multiculturalism, Nationalism and Gender*. Toronto: Canadian Scholars Press.
> Bannerji illustrates the ways in which the discourse of race shapes contemporary politics of state, nation and citizenship. Bannerji explores the ways in which contemporary multicultural policies work to construct a politics of diversity that inscribes those as "white" as insiders, and all others, including aboriginal people, as outsiders. Her book provides an excellent example of the way in which the idea of "race" is fluid, and is produced and reproduced in the current context.

Haney-Lopez, Ian (1996). *White by Law: The Legal Construction of Race*. New York: New York University Press.
> Haney-Lopez's study explores the ways in which a discourse of "race" shaped the practice of citizenship in the United States, and in turn, the way in which the practice of citizenship shaped the discourse of "race." As he shows, in its first words on the subject of citizenship, the Congress restricted naturalisation to "white" persons. He points out that this put into place an on-going legal search for who was "white" and who was not. He illustrates that through this search, the courts came to social construct racial categories, such as "White," "Asiatic," "Negro," "Indian."

Loomba, Ania (1998). *Colonialism/Post-colonialism*. London: Routledge Press.
> A thorough and accessible introduction to post-colonialism, and post-colonial theories. Loomba begins by defining post-colonialism, discussing the strengths and limitations of the concept. She provides a thorough introduction to the major debates located within post-colonial theories; debates around colonialism, imperialism, nationalism, national representation, gender, post-colonial, and diasporic identities. A strength of the text is that it places the writing of the major post-colonial writers, such as Said, Fanon, Bhabha, Spivak, McClintock, within the context of ongoing debates.

Monture-Angus, Patricia (1995). *Thunder In My Soul: A Mohawk Woman Speaks*. Halifax: Fernwood Publishing.
> Monture-Angus explores the meaning of Canadian nation and law for aboriginal people in Canada. She argues that colonialism has not ended for aboriginal people, and demonstrates the ways in which the Canadian nation, its legal system, and its educational system are the mechanism by which colonial relationships are continually reproduced. She suggests that the only way for aboriginal peoples to end colonial relations is to become self-determining. Moreover, she argues that it is not possible for aboriginal people to achieve self-determination through changing the laws, particularly through the courts, as these institutions are embedded in the relations of colonization. Rather, she advocates for independent aboriginal nations.

Stepan, Nancy (1991). *The Hours of Eugenics: Race, Gender and Nation in Latin America*. Ithaca: Cornell University Press.
> Stepan examines the ways in which the idea of "race" was coded through science. She documents the emergence of eugenics, a science of genes and evolution, in the mid-nineteenth century. She explores the way in which eugenics shaped a discursive view of social life, where all aspects of social life was linked to biology and biological laws. She also illustrates the way in which the discourse of biology (race) was linked to defining social groups such as the poor, the working class, prostitutes. She documents that eugenics became a social movement, which influenced state policies, ranging from immigration, citizenship, family, sexuality, adolescence.

Yuval-Davis, Nira and Floya Anthias (Eds.) (1989). *Women-Nation-State*. London: MacMillian Press.
> In this classic text, Yuval-Davis and Anthias explore the meaning of nationalist projects for women's experiences with race and gender. Yuval-Davis and Anthias point out that women are central to nationalist projects in multifaceted ways. First, women physically reproduce the nation. Second, women often are the boundary markers of nationalist projects. Third, women participate in consolidating nationalist projects. Such positioning has had contradictory effects for these women. On one hand, during the nationalist period, gender became reorganised such that some women—in the case of the West, white bourgeois women—came to be seen as exalted breeders of a virile race of nation and empire-builders, as "mothers of the nation." This led to state and moral regulation that channelled these women's labour into reproduction and motherhood, and thus relegated these (and other) women to a gendered position within the nation-state. On the other hand, such regulation empowered middle class women as it made them responsible for the moral health of the nation, and thus privileged them vis a vis working-class and colonised women in complex ways.

WEB LINKS

www.opentheborders.org
> This Web site provides references to recent debates on the movement of peoples across borders.

www.saxakali.com
> This Web site provides references and material on racism in Canada.

www.uwm.eduwhiteness
> This Web site provides references to recent scholarship on whiteness.

Chapter 4

Regulating (Ab)Normal Sex: Anti-VD Strategies in British Columbia/Canada, 1918-1945[1]

by Dorothy E. Chunn

> Of all sources of venereal infection, that found in commercialized prostitution is most obvious to health departments and yet it has consistently evaded the effective deterrent attention of both health department and legal authority. This illegal commerce has continued to reap its monetary gain at the expense of the degradation of young women and the public health. Public prudery is rapidly breaking down, and a healthier public attitude will no longer permit this disease-riddled business to continue. The health departments of Canada cannot evade the issue. (Williams, 1943, p. 461)

This chapter outlines the transformation of ideas and practices related to the regulation of venereal disease in the developing Canadian welfare state. Specifically, I examine the changes in the regulation of sex, sexuality, and reproduction through an analysis of post-World War I efforts to eradicate sexually transmitted diseases in British Columbia. I focus primarily on the use of educational and legal strategies toward women over the decade from 1935 to 1945.[2]

I begin with a brief overview of the movement from social/sexual purity to social hygiene in the regulation of sex, VD, and reproduction during the late 19th and early 20th centuries in Canada and elsewhere. Following this contextualization of the issues, a number of educational and legal initiatives that addressed the issue of sex, sexuality,

---

[1] This is a revised, updated version of a chapter in Susan B. Boyd, (Ed.). (1997). *Challenging the Public/Private Divide: Feminism, Law, and Public Policy*. Toronto: University of Toronto Press. I am grateful to SSHRC for the Postdoctoral Fellowship (1989/90) that enabled me to begin the research for this paper and the Standard Research Grant that allowed me to continue it. Thanks to Deborah Brock for her helpful editorial comments and suggestions and to the anonymous reviewers for their input on the chapter.

[2] This paper is not a comprehensive account of the struggles against venereal disease in British Columbia/Canada. The analysis of selected anti-VD initiatives is intended to illustrate the reconceptualization of sex, sexuality, and reproduction that occurred in emergent welfare states.

and VD among heterosexual women in British Columbia are examined. First, legislation and policies that ostensibly were aimed at all women but which in practice were intended to encourage self-regulation of sexuality and sexual relations among "deserving" middle- and working-class women; the "mothers of the race". Second, the explicitly coercive measures that were directed at the containment and control of "undeserving" or incorrigible women; the sexual "others", whose sexual deviance was considered to be either willful or untreatable. I conclude with some observations on the relevance of this historical retrospective to a critical, feminist analysis of regulation in the current period of state (re)formation.

This historical case study has more general significance for research on social regulation. Most writers agree that people are both compelled to regulate their conduct through laws and policies and to learn to be self-regulating so that external compulsion is less in evidence. However, there is ongoing debate about whether regulation stems primarily from state or non-state sources (Foucault, 1991; Hall, 1980; Hunt, 1999; Hunt & Wickham, 1994; Loo & Strange, 1997; Valverde, 1991). This chapter is based on the assumption that self-regulation and compulsion are always intertwined and it is impossible to draw a clear line between state and non-state regulation.

It is also assumed that modes of regulation are neither universal nor immutable. While there are many reasons for changes in modes of regulation, an extremely important one in liberal societies has been the shifting and contested relationship between private and public spheres (Corrigan & Sayer, 1985; Hall, 1980; Hunt, 1993). Historically, the public/private distinction has been conceptualized in three ways. First as the separation between state regulation (government activity) and private economic activity (the market). Second, as the divide between the (public) market and the (private) family. Third, as the connection between state regulation and family relations (Boyd, 1997 pp. 8–10). Examining this relationship over time seems more important to me than the debate about whether state or non-state forces are most responsible for social regulation.

The public/private distinction is important because it sets out areas of social life that ought to be unregulated and free of state intervention. Forms of state change, and not surprisingly, these changes are connected to changing modes of regulation. In Canada and other western countries, we can identify three distinct types of liberal state, each of which is premised on a different conception of the relationship between public and private spheres which, in turn, produces modes of regulation that are based on a different relationship between compulsion and self-regulation. The 19th-century "laissez-faire" state was based on a strict separation between public and private areas of social life. In contrast, the 20th century welfare state allowed increased intervention in and regulation of the market and the family. With twin emphases on deregulation and privatization, the current neo-liberal state is reminiscent of the "laissez-faire" state with its sharp separation of public and private spheres (Brodie, 1995).

As critics have argued, however, the division between private and public is more ideological than real since what is designated as "off limits" for state intervention has changed historically and, more importantly, because liberal states have always regulated the so-called "private" sphere (Garland, 1985; Pateman, 1989). Therefore, it is not a matter of whether state intervention exists but rather the form and degree of such intervention (Chunn, 1992; Donzelot,1980; Sears, 1995; Smart, 1982). Arguably, then, an examination of initiatives aimed at regulating sex and reproduction that were advocated or implemented from the 1880s to the 1940s can tell us much about how the dominant modes of regulation in laissez-faire states were transformed in welfare states and also provide a basis for assessing the regulatory modes in contemporary neo-liberal states. An analysis of shifting approaches to venereal disease (hereafter VD) is particularly instructive in this regard.[3]

The regulation of sex, sexuality, and reproduction was an increasing concern in Canada and other western countries during the late 19th and early 20th centuries as industrialization, urbanization, immigration, and "universal" suffrage began to transform laissez-faire states into mass (welfare) societies.[4] In the context of perceived social deconstruction, reformers linked "sexual anarchy" to potential "race suicide" and seized on the (white) nuclear family as the basis for the reconstruction and reintegration of society (Showalter, 1990). A major ideological underpinning of the nuclear family model is a repressive conceptualization of sex; sex is "bad" unless stringently controlled and the control is heterosexual marriage. Therefore, the only legitimate sexual relations are implicitly intra-racial ones between a wife and husband for the purpose of procreation; uncommitted sex for pleasure—pre- and extra-marital, homosexual—is "deviant," dangerous, and must be prevented or contained to safeguard "the family" and ensure social continuity (Foucault, 1980; Showalter, 1990; Weeks, 1981, 1986; Young, 1995).

The question was: How could sex, sexuality, and reproduction be regulated effectively in a mass society? Reformers concluded that greater state involvement and different forms of intervention were needed. Not surprisingly, (re)producing the "middle-class family" became a major focus of reform initiatives (Chunn, 1992; Donzelot, 1980; Finch, 1993; Ursel, 1992) and regulating sex became synonymous with the national interest in emergent welfare states such as Canada, the United States, and Britain (Bacchi, 1983; Bland, 1995; Hunt, 1999; McLaren, 1988; Showalter, 1990; Snitow, et al. 1983; Strange, 1995; Valverde, 1991; Weeks, 1981). Increased state involvement in the regulation of reproduction from the late 19th century onward occurred in the context of what has been described as a

---

[3] The "classic" sexually transmitted diseases were chancroid, gonorrhea, and syphilis (Cassel, 1987, p. 12).

[4] The racist basis of suffrage should be noted. In 1920, universal suffrage meant that most white, adult Canadians could vote in federal elections, but most aboriginal persons and persons of colour could not (Bacchi, 1983; Barman, 1991).

movement from sexual or social purity to social hygiene (Hunt, 1999; see also Dickinson, 1993; Menzies, 2002). Purity advocates included first wave feminists and other lay reformers who were particularly influential until the early 1920s. They sought, and often received, state assistance in the form of legislation and policies designed to induce adherence to the norms governing the nuclear family and thereby guarantee the moral, mental, and physical fitness of the population. An emphasis on social hygiene emerged after WWI, when medical, social work, and other experts/professionals assumed leadership roles, inside as well as outside the state, in the advocacy of "scientific" approaches to sex, sexuality and reproduction. As "mothers of the race," women were particular targets of late 19th and early 20th century campaigns to confine sex to marriage, to monitor sexuality before and after marriage, and to oversee reproduction (Arnup, 1994; Snell, 1983; Snell & Abeele, 1988).

Increasing state intervention in the "private" sphere was reflected in a shift from an exclusive focus on target populations such as prostitutes and military men to an inclusive focus on the sexual health of the general population and the need to guarantee the reproduction of healthy citizens. Canada and other western countries implemented a two-pronged approach to VD control: initiatives based on education and voluntary compliance with non-criminal laws aimed at inducing self-regulation among "deserving" populations; and medico-legal repression of the recalcitrant, "undeserving others."

SEX, VD, AND REPRODUCTION

Social hygiene is at once more radical and more scientific than the old conception of social reform. "It is the inevitable method by which at a certain stage civilization is compelled to continue its own course, and to preserve, perhaps to elevate the race" (Ellis, 1912, pp. 1–2).

Sex, VD, and reproduction among women did not become public concerns for the first time during the 1880s. The regulation of these "private" matters was an item on the political agenda of reformers throughout the 19th century in Canada and other capitalist liberal states. But the period from the 1880s to the 1940s, especially the interwar years, was marked by a rationalization of the process through which "social problems" were defined, analyzed, and treated. Positivism, which reflected the explosion of the "value-free" natural, physical, and social sciences, provided the philosophical rationale for the emergent technocratic, interventionist state where "social problems" are stripped of their political content and transformed into technical ones to be diagnosed and resolved on an individualized basis using professional expertise. Thus, the interwar period in particular was characterized by two related developments that distinguished it from the pre-war era: the decline of the overt moralism that had defined pre-war responses to "deviant" sex and the ascendancy of "scientific" approaches; and, a blurring of the public/private distinction so central to laissez-faire ideology (Chunn, 1992; Weeks, 1981).

In regard to issues related to sex and sexuality, the medical doctor, the sexologist, and, to a lesser extent, the social worker emerged as state-sanctioned "experts" who could disseminate authoritative knowledge on such matters. Especially interesting is how sex and sexuality came together in relation to "scientific" pronouncements on VD and reproduction during the 1920s and 1930s. The increasingly authoritative voices of doctors translated into a growing monopoly over pregnancy and birthing practices— evidenced by their control over pre- and post-natal care and hospital births—that coalesced around anti-VD campaigns from the First World War onward (Arnup, Levesque, & Pierson 1990; Cassel, 1987; Dickinson, 1993). By 1945, the dominance of professionals (and the foundations of the welfare state) was secured. However, it is important to emphasize that in Canada generally, and British Columbia specifically, the "experts" did not displace the traditional moral and social reform constituencies. Rather, they subsumed them and in the process gained considerable control over the definition, explanation, and response to "'sexual problems."

Shifting perspectives on VD mirrored the more general reconceptualization of sex, sexuality, and reproduction in developing welfare states from the 1880s to the 1940s. During the late 19th century in Canada and other liberal states, VD crystallized fears about the decline of civilization that are "typical of the fin de siecle" (Showalter, 1990, p. 4). Syphilis became a graphic illustration of the consequences of "sexual anarchy." In the context of uncertainty generated by rapid social change, it posed a triple threat to the moral, physical, and mental health of the nation. It also triggered a pervasive anxiety among the middle classes about sexual epidemic that intensified after the turn of the century, reaching a crescendo during World War I and erupting periodically ever since (McGinnis, 1990; Showalter, 1990; Singer, 1993). As sexual and social purity metamorphosed into social hygiene after the First World War, both the form and degree of state involvement in the regulation of sexually transmitted diseases were transformed. Increasingly, secular professionals, such as doctors, became the primary definers of VD as a public health and a social problem. They attained growing power to influence state intervention around VD, reproduction through the disqualification of lay knowledge as quackery and/or unscientific, uninformed moralism (Brandt, 1985; Cassel, 1987; Weeks, 1981). The "leprosies of lust" were reconstructed as a public health problem that could be solved only by experts, especially doctors, and with strong state support (Brandt, 1985; Buckley & McGinnis, 1982; Cassel, 1987; McGinnis, 1988, 1990; Weeks, 1981). Therefore, proactive and expanded intervention in the private realm not only was necessary but also had a "scientific" basis.

The professionals in the forefront of the social hygiene movement gained dominance only with support from the pre-war social purity reformers and their successors who began to interweave the "scientific" discourses of the experts with older religious, moral discourses. Far from disappearing, then, the discourses of overt religious moralism that informed pre-World War I discussions of VD meshed with and ultimately were submerged by the discourses of "science". Thus, the 19th-century distinction between the blameless and the blameworthy among the infected was not erased (Showalter, 1990; Walkowitz, 1980, 1992). Rather, it was obscured through a process of "scientification" whereby experts claimed a monopoly on the technical knowledge necessary to differentiate among, and tailor responses to, distinct categories of women (and of men). These categories included the potentially deviant who required protection from and education about the dangers of uncontrolled and unsafe sex; the deviant but salvageable who were "deserving" of timely intervention that would help them to comply with sexual norms; and the incorrigible, "undeserving" deviants such as prostitutes who were the appropriate candidates for coercive state control (Brandt, 1985; Cassel, 1987; McGinnis, 1988). Clearly, the "scientific" categorization of the population was laced with class-based, gendered, racialized, and heterosexist assumptions about health and disease.

The degree of state intervention with respect to VD also changed dramatically from the 1880s to the 1940s. While a focus on the (nuclear) family as the bulwark against social disintegration runs through the entire period, the state showed increasing willingness to regulate the most intimate aspect of social life—sexual relations—to combat VD. During and after the First World War, Ottawa and most provincial states in Canada enacted legislation and policies and provided funding for initiatives aimed at eradicating the scourge of VD; including the creation of government venereal disease control units and public clinics, educational programs, the distribution of free drugs to private physicians, and so on (Cassel, 1987, pp.145, 149).[5] In addition, the growing emphasis on proactive rather than reactive approaches to sexually transmitted diseases, on prevention rather than treatment after the fact, greatly expanded the scope of anti-VD campaigns and activities. Now the entire population was potentially at risk and VD became a question of public health like any other communicable disease and linked to the general good. As a result, the line between public and private life that defined the laissez-faire state was rendered increasingly invisible in the developing welfare state, particularly during the interwar years (Buckley & McGinnis, 1982; Cassel, 1987; Mawani, 2002).

[5] In Canada, one of the first conditional federal grants to the provinces was for anti-VD initiatives and when Ottawa eliminated this funding during the 1930s Depression, most provinces continued their efforts at VD control "despite serious financial difficulties" (Cassel, 1987, pp. 145, 199).

Thus, the sin/disease model of venereal disease associated with a distinct group of women—prostitutes—who infected foolish men, particularly military men, was transformed into a scientific/medical model that targeted the civilian population as much as the military (Walkowitz, 1980). This model differentiated between women (prostitutes and "casuals"), who through willfulness or negligence infected foolish men, and innocent victims (married and single-working women) of foolish or predatory men who, in turn, constituted actual or potential threats to new life (fetuses). Consequently, all women were active, passive, or possible sources of danger to men, fetuses, and the "race" through the transmission of VD, especially syphilis. However, the criteria (i.e., race, ethnicity, class) for separating the guilty from the innocent, the deserving from the undeserving, remained consistent over time. Redefining VD as a preventable plague that put entire nations at risk also entailed rethinking the traditional responses to it. During the 19th century, when VD was identified almost entirely with particular marginalized groups, such as prostitutes, laissez-faire states relied on criminalization, detention of prostitutes under the Contagious Diseases Acts (enacted but never proclaimed in Canada), and/or private medical practitioners to stem the "leprosies of lust" (Backhouse, 1985; McGinnis, 1990; Walkowitz, 1980). Therefore, responses to VD were privatized (individual or non-state) for most of the population while public concern was focused on prostitutes and their hapless male "victims."

After World War I, state-sanctioned responses such as government-operated VD divisions working in conjunction with non-governmental organizations concerned about VD, became more dominant in liberal societies. There was a growing emphasis on the promotion of strategies that would encourage self-regulation: mass education (often sex-specific) through the dissemination of advice literature, films, radio broadcasts, poster campaigns, and public lectures (Brandt, 1985; Cassel, 1987; Kuhn, 1988; Mawani, 2002); and voluntary, mass testing (pre-marital and pre-natal) of the population of "deserving" women (and men) under the direction of medical authorities and other experts. Publicly funded clinics were established to serve the poor—both "deserving" and "undeserving"—while the more affluent continued to rely on private treatment by family physicians.

The gendered nature of anti-VD educational initiatives is noteworthy. Educational materials for men focused mainly on the dire consequences for them of consorting with "bad" women and medical quacks whereas those directed at women centred largely on the threat they posed to biological and social reproduction if they contracted VD (Cassel, 1987, p. 9; Mawani, 2002). The onus also was placed on women to assume general responsibility for the prevention of VD, not least by educating their own children that VD is "an illness to be cured" not a "disgrace,"

> It is the solemn duty of every generation of women to make better the world for the generation that follows. Here is an opportunity…that ought to be taken up by

every woman's club, by every individual woman who is smart enough to read statistics, and wise enough to know that sin and danger can not be lessened simply by shutting one's eyes, and wishing fervently that all boys would be good, all women pure, and all human appetites and impulses controlled by decency and the law. (Norris, 1938)

The legal structures aimed at eradicating VD and (ab)normal sex among the "undeserving" through compulsion also expanded in the aftermath of World War I. In Canada, most provinces enacted quasi-criminal legislation for the suppression of venereal diseases that was under the control of doctors (Cassel, 1987). Such statutes could be used in tandem with the criminal law to deal with infected prostitutes but more importantly to regulate the wider population of so-called "casuals" or "pick-ups"—usually young, single women—who threatened public health through their allegedly indiscriminate sex lives (Freund, 2002; see also Brock, 2000). Deportation was a last resort for the incorrigible, non-citizen (Roberts, 1988).

Overall, the belief that venereal diseases could be eradicated through the "magic bullet" (Brandt, 1985) of scientific knowledge and technique provided the rationale for a greatly expanded state role in dealing with them. Concern about VD always has centred on syphilis, presumably because it was more debilitating and therefore more feared than gonorrhea, although the latter disease was far more prevalent (Brandt, 1985, p. 154; McGinnis, 1988, p. 126). Thus, the detection and treatment of syphilis were the primary objectives of all attacks on sexually transmitted diseases, regardless of the target populations. The scientification of approaches to syphilis after the turn of the century that allowed its redefinition as a public health problem is easily tracked: the identification of the causal organism of syphilis—the spirochete—in 1905; the development of the Wassermann Test in 1906; the discovery of salvarsan or "606," an effective, albeit risky, treatment in 1909; the development of the Kahn test in 1924 (used initially in Canada to corroborate results from the Wassermann Test, which was difficult to perform and unreliable, and ultimately replacing it); and the introduction of penicillin during the Second World War (Brandt, 1985; Cassel, 1987; McGinnis, 1988). It also is important to emphasize that public concern about syphilis (and VD in general) may have been exacerbated by, but was not simply a product of, wartime conditions. British Columbia is a case in point.

COMBATTING VENEREAL DISEASE IN BRITISH COLUMBIA

It is unfortunate that syphilis and gonorrhea have been confused with sin. The rational approach is to deal with these diseases as problems in public health and to attempt to bring them under control in much the same way that tuberculosis is being brought under control. The methods, tested and found sound, are three: (1)

good medical treatment freely available (2) honest and fearless law enforcement; and (3) popular education to make the simple facts known to everyone. (Brown & Williams, 1941, p. 5)

During the period from 1919 to 1945, British Columbia emerged as a recognized leader in the field of VD regulation and control. Thus, while governmental and non-governmental agencies were influenced strongly by ideas and developments within and outside Canada, they were influential, innovative, and progressive forces in their own right in the battle against sexually transmitted diseases ("British Columbia Leads," 1942, p. 8). The Provincial Board of Health launched the first organized anti-VD effort in 1919 after the enactment of the Venereal Diseases Suppression Act (SBC 1919, p. 88). By 1920 a new program was in place that consisted of public clinics in Vancouver and Victoria; distribution of free medication to doctors; payment to doctors who served indigent patients in rural areas; and a system of notification of VD (British Columbia Provincial Board of Health, 1946).

In the mid-1930s, a perception that the incidence of disease was rising prompted the Liberal government of Premier Duff Pattullo to expand the VD program. In October 1936, the Division of Venereal Disease Control was created as a separate unit of the Provincial Board of Health, analogous to the previously established Division of Tuberculosis Control; (British Columbia Board, 1937) and the following year, the provincial government initiated a "five year plan" that provided "a substantial increase in the amounts allotted for VD control" (Cassel, 1987, p. 200). Greater financial resources enabled the establishment of more public clinics for the testing, either voluntary or compulsory, of people without the means to consult a private physician. By the end of 1938, clinics were operating in Vancouver, Victoria, New Westminster, Nanaimo, Trail, and the Oakalla Prison Farm and a Rural Consultative Travelling Service had been established (B.C. Provincial Board of Health, 1939).

The reconceptualization of VD and the transformation of the form and degree of state intervention to control sexually transmitted diseases in developing welfare states, discussed above, were evident in the B.C. context. VD was redefined as a communicable disease like TB that threatened public health and required vigilance and proactive, state-sanctioned interventions by experts that targeted the civilian population as well as the military and prostitutes. By the mid-1930s, medical authorities and other experts had assumed the leading role in British Columbia's battle against VD. However, they actively cultivated and mobilized support among long-established reform constituencies, including churches, women's organizations, and social welfare agencies, as well as community groups concerned specifically with public health such as the Greater Vancouver Health League and the medical profession itself ("International Society Hygiene Day," 1939; "University

Health Week," 1939). The close links between governmental and non-governmental organizations became even tighter when the Director of the provincial Division of VD Control, Dr. Donald Williams, was elected President of the Greater Vancouver Health League in 1941 ("Health League Hits," 1941).

Indeed, Dr. Williams' approach to VD control was an interesting amalgam of the old sexual and social purity moralism and the "science" of social hygiene. On one hand, he viewed prostitutes as "the main root and source of venereal disease in B.C." and the suppression of "organized prostitution in the form of bawdy houses" as pivotal to the eradication of VD ("Veneral Disease Cases," 1939). On the other hand, he placed great emphasis on the centrality of anti-VD education and the role of "science" in eliminating this modern plague "The public must be given the facts of modern medical science and not the timeworn fallacies of mediaeval hearsay and irrational thinking" (Williams, 1940).

Women—and in particular the sex lives of single, young female workers and of married, working-class women—were a major focus of anti-VD campaigns during the interwar years. In British Columbia as elsewhere, initiatives tailored to the "deserving" emphasized self-regulation, prevention through education and voluntary testing. At the same time, the older association of VD with vice remained strong and underpinned both provincial legislation[6] that mandated compulsory treatment for identified carriers and the federal criminal law provisions aimed at suppressing (as opposed to segregating) prostitution and other "undeserving" women.[7] The growing emphasis on distinguishing between "deserving" and "undeserving" women in dealing with VD was clear in a 1936 evaluation report on the B.C. situation prepared by Harry Cassidy, Director of Social Welfare, for the Division of Health and Welfare Services (Cassidy, 1936). In his confidential assessment, Cassidy noted that, among other things, the Vancouver Clinic had been critiqued for failing to adopt individualized approaches in diagnosing and treating VD:

> Wholesale methods are employed at the clinic, with lack of segregation of different classes of patients (e.g., inadequate provision to keep respectable women apart from prostitutes), lack of consideration for the sensibilities of individuals, routine methods of dealing with all patients on exactly the same basis, etc. It is argued that

---

[6] British Columbia was in keeping with many provinces that enacted anti-VD legislation after the First World War (Cassel, 1987, pp. 160–64).

[7] While systematic data are lacking, I am assuming that in British Columbia the "deserving" tended to be white, anglo, Protestant, middle or respectable working-class, whereas the "undeserving" included disproportionate numbers of working and dependent poor from ethnic (e.g., continental European), racial (e.g., Asian and aboriginal), and religious (e.g. Catholics, Doukhobors) minorities (Barman 1991, p. 363).

such methods are bad socially and that they do not inspire confidence or cooperation in patients. (Ibid., p.19)

This categorization of women and, more specifically, a concern with the sexual threat to health posed by young, working-class women also are reflected in Cassidy's emphasis on the need for follow-up by the clinic "Women put under treatment often live in rooming houses and are a source of infection to other persons. Likewise, domestic servants who are infected may be living in homes where there are children and may constitute a menace to these children" (Ibid., p. 18). Clearly, legislation and policies aimed at regulating sex, VD and reproduction among "deserving" women in British Columbia would not be suitable for the "undeserving."

Regulating Sex Among the "Mothers of the Race"

My research suggests that in post-1918 British Columbia, medical authorities, social workers, politicians, and reformers were equally concerned about the sex lives of married and single women because of their shared capability to reproduce the species. To guarantee the future of the (white) race, the reproductive health of certain women had to be protected against the dire consequences of disease. Like other jurisdictions during the interwar years, British Columbia emphasized two types of anti-VD initiatives, presumably universal in scope but in reality aimed at forestalling or counteracting sexual deviance and disease among "deserving" women who were deemed to be at risk through ignorance or abuse. The first initiative focused on self-regulation in sexual matters through public education about congenital syphilis that would encourage voluntary pre-marital and pre-natal blood tests. The second initiative focused on "soft" compulsion in the form of non-criminal legislation and policy that mandated such tests. Thus, British Columbia followed the post-World War I trend in liberal democracies to make mass education a central focus of anti-VD programs. Indeed, by 1936 the government had apparently smuggled sex education into the schools ("Sex Education in B.C. Schools," 1939). By 1940, the educational initiative of the Division of VD Control had expanded to the point that a fulltime Educational Supervisor was appointed and a program aimed at both professionals and lay citizens was developed: disseminate information about venereal disease; make provincial facilities for diagnosis, treatment, epidemiology and education available; emphasize the need for prenatal and premarital blood tests; eradicate quackery; and suppression of commercialized prostitution (Williams, 1940).

A very public and central focus of educational work aimed at VD control was the prevention of congenital syphilis, which was viewed as a leading cause of blindness and death in many infants. In the late 1930s, the Provincial Health Officer, Dr. Gordon Amyot, and the Director of the VD Control Division,

Dr. Donald Williams launched a concerted effort to link education with voluntary pre-natal testing of pregnant women. Even the Division stationery was used to publicize the issue, *Prevent Prenatal Syphilis in Children—A Blood Test for Every Expectant Mother*. In their educational work throughout the province, Division personnel put special emphasis on the threat to marriage and the "race" posed by pre-natal syphilis and the need for pre-natal blood tests,

> Syphilis can invade marriage along two paths. First, syphilis may be transferred from one partner to the other. Women are more frequently the innocent victims of the disease, contracted from their infected husbands. Secondly, syphilis may be carried on to the off-spring of a marriage. Where syphilis is transferred in marriage we now have two or more individuals, instead of one, whose problem may later prove of considerable significance in our social structure. We must endeavor to have every woman expecting a baby to undergo examination [that] includes above all else a blood test. (Leroux, 1939)

In 1942 the Division went even further and developed a special educational program on the prevention of prenatal syphilis that targeted both professionals and the public. The assumption that "science" could easily prevent women from unwittingly causing harm to their babies was clearly one that resonated across a broad spectrum of individuals and organizations, and garnered strong support for the Division's campaign around pre-natal blood testing. Dr. Amyot informed Provincial Secretary Pearson that the B.C. Medical Association's Committee on Maternal Welfare had sent letters "to every physician in British Columbia advising them of the importance of taking blood tests for syphilis in every expectant mother;" local health departments, public health nurses, and welfare workers were all participating through the Provincial Board of Health; the National Council of Women of Canada, which included approximately 150 B.C. women's groups, "endorsed and supported" the campaign; and the media—radio, newspapers, and "prominent store windows"—were enlisted to publicize "this important health problem." In addition, the Mayors of Vancouver, New Westminster, and Victoria were going to proclaim a "Prevention of Prenatal Syphilis Week," February 1 to 7, 1942, to mark National Hygiene Day in Canada and the United States, and Amyot felt that an endorsement from the Lt. Governor also "would be highly advantageous" (British Columbia Provincial Secretary, 1942, January 27).

In a letter that reveals a wholly uncritical acceptance of Amyot's definition of the problem, the Provincial Secretary apprised the Lieutenant Governor about the upcoming event and requested his endorsement. Pearson cited the Provincial Board of Health's concern over "the preventable tragedy of children born in our Province with Syphilis;" and emphasized that it is a health problem "most easily solved" by "providing our citizens with knowledge regarding the simple fact that the discovery of infection in an expectant mother, followed by treatment, will give the new born baby an almost certain chance of being perfectly normal and healthy" (British Columbia Provincial Secretary, 1942, January 28). The Lieutenant Governor was quick to oblige. His endorsement, and the mayoral proclamations, of the "Prevention of Pre-Natal Syphilis Week" were virtual replicas of Pearson's letter: "The heritage of health is the birthright of every child;" "healthy children, the citizens of tomorrow, are our greatest civic asset;" "modern medical science has one by one, removed the health hazards to our lives" and it can easily prevent syphilis which "still robs some children of their heritage;" the efforts of the Provincial Board of Health to co-ordinate the work of "citizens, physicians and health departments" in B.C. "against this menace to our children…deserve support" ("Woodward Backs Prevention Week," 1942; "Drive Launched Against," 1942; "Mayor Endorses," 1942). In his annual report for 1942, the Acting Director of the VD Control Division was obviously pleased with the results of the educational campaign for pre-natal testing; noting that: "Its success can be partially judged by the fact that several States and Provinces have already written us requesting complete details" (Cleveland, 1942, CC 59).

The second type of initiative aimed at preventing or pre-empting the effects of sexual deviance among "deserving" women (and men) was the implementation of non-criminal legislation and policies requiring pre-natal and pre-marital blood tests. Proponents of such "soft" compulsion often were concerned that "innocent" (women) or "foolish" (men) VD carriers would not think of themselves as appropriate candidates for voluntary testing. Calls for statutes to compel VD testing before a marriage licence was issued and during pregnancy predated World War I in some jurisdictions. However, organized campaigns for such tests arose out of the more general movement to regulate heterosexual marriage and shore up the nuclear family during the interwar period (Arnup, 1994; Chunn, 1992; Snell & Abeele, 1988). These campaigns increasingly were driven by a concern with eugenics or "scientific breeding" that would encourage the "fit" to reproduce and prevent the "unfit" from doing so (Brandt, 1985; McLaren, 1990; Stephen, 1995).

In British Columbia as in many other jurisdictions, the campaigns to implement compulsory pre-natal and pre-marital blood testing ultimately failed. With respect to the former, the province seems to have done very little to mandate such tests. In January 1942, presumably as part of the anti-congential syphilis drive, Dr. Amyot approached the Provincial Secretary, George Pearson, with a proposal for an organized six-month program that would require physicians to state on each Birth Notice Form "whether the mother was examined for syphilis by a blood test."[8] It is not

---

[8] In January 1942, Dr. Amyot approached the Provincial Secretary, George Pearson, with a proposal for an organized six month program that would require physicians to state on each Birth Notice Form "whether the mother was examined for syphilis by a blood test, Ibid., Box 37, File 1, Amyot to Pearson, 1942, January 27.

clear that such a program was introduced. However, the campaign for mandatory, pre-marital testing was more sustained during the interwar period. The perception that the spread of VD was threatening the reproductive health of the province's most valuable women fuelled recurrent demands that the province follow the example of some American states (Brandt, 1985) and amend the Marriage Act to require compulsory pre-marital tests for venereal disease, mental defectiveness, and tuberculosis.

Through the 1930s, individual Liberal and opposition Cooperative Commonwealth Federation (CCF) politicians, with support from churches, women's organizations, and doctors, among others, tried and failed in attempts to obtain such an amendment.[9] In 1937, however, the Liberal government pre-empted the latest attempt of Ernest Winch, leader of the CCF opposition, to introduce a Bill mandating pre-marital tests by establishing a committee to review the entire Marriage Act and make recommendations for change (Baber, 1937). Chaired by the Provincial Health Officer and with broad representation, including women's organizations, ministerial associations, departmental officials, and Winch himself, the committee reported in March 1938 and the Marriage Act was amended later that year (SBC 1938, chap. 33) to require that: a standard lab test for syphilis be performed in an approved facility; the test be conducted by a medical practitioner 20 days before marriage; and the result of the test be communicated to both parties to the intended marriage. However, the amended Act did not follow American precedent by making positive test outcomes an absolute bar to marriage (Brandt, 1985, pp. 147–148). More importantly, the amendment was not proclaimed and thus remained unenforceable.

Even wartime anxiety about VD did not persuade the then Coalition government (Liberal-Conservative) to proclaim the 1938 Marriage Act amendment. Letters and resolutions urging the government to implement pre-marital VD testing—and in some cases pre-natal blood tests—streamed into the Premier's office from various organizations throughout the province, including women's groups, church associations, and social agencies, in what clearly was a coordinated campaign. Eight months after the educational "Prevention of Pre-Natal Syphilis Week" in February 1942, the Vancouver Local Council of Women raised the issue of compulsory pre-natal testing for syphilis as part of the general wartime campaign against VD that had been launched under the auspices of the federal government.

---

[9] For example, in 1930 a Liberal MLA, A.M. Manson, garnered support for a proposal that all people be required to obtain a medical bill of health before receiving a marriage licence, but the ruling Conservative party argued against hasty action in the interests of national uniformity of legislation. See "Uniform Eugenic Laws," VP, 22 Feb. 1930, p.14; in 1936 Ernest Winch, leader of the CCF party, introduced the Marriage Act Amendment Act that would have required doctors to test all prospective brides and grooms for VD and inform them of the results. PABC, Provincial Secretary, GR496 Box 50, File 16.

A resolution forwarded to Premier Hart in October 1942 urged the provincial government to "build the New Laboratories at the University which were planned sometime ago" because "the present lab facilities are completely inadequate" to assist the campaign against VD "which otherwise is likely to increase in Wartime." The resolution then explicitly emphasized that "one part of that Campaign is an effort to have pregnant women daignosed [sic] for venereal disease and treated if found infected so that congenital venereal disease may be checked…" (British Columbia Premier, 1942, October 7).

On the subject of compulsory pre-marital blood tests, the Cobble Hill Women's Institute forwarded a "typical" resolution to Premier Hart in December 1943. It noted the "grave prevalence" of social diseases in Canada and urged that any existing legislation "and especially legislation requiring Pre-Marital Health Certificates be immediately [made operational and] enforced" (British Columbia Premier, 1943, December 22). Subsequently, Hart received almost identical letters from the Women's Institutes in other areas, as well as a follow-up from Cobble Hill (British Columbia Premier, 1944, January 14; 1944, January 17; 1944, January 28). Women's religious associations also joined the chorus of voices urging the government to proclaim and enforce the provincial legislation "providing for pre-marital blood tests" (British Columbia Premier, 1944, April 27; 1944, May 12; 1944, June 6; 1944, April 27).

By 1944, the Councils of Social Agencies in Victoria and Vancouver also were pressuring the Premier to put teeth in the Marriage Act. The CSA of Greater Victoria attributed the government's inaction to "the scarcity of accommodation for laboratory tests," but argued "that it would be in the best interests of all concerned for this act to be made effective and that the cost of providing lab service would be saved many times over and the future generation protected from congenital venereal disease" (British Columbia Premier, 1944, March 6). A month later, the Vancouver Council of Social Agencies urged the government "to consider at this time the advisability of proclaiming and enforcing the existing legislation in respect to blood tests for those contemplating marriage" (British Columbia Premier, 1944, April 4). Despite the concerted campaigns, the B.C. government did not implement mandatory pre-marital and pre-natal testing. On the surface, the issue was the lack of testing facilities. In April 1944, the Provincial Health Officer, informed the Premier that the existing laboratory facilities could not cope with "this added burden," but "if and when suitable accommodation for the laboratory can be made available, we shall be pleased to undertake the examination of pre-marital blood specimens" (British Columbia Premier, 1944, April 17). The government was quick to use the rationalization of fiscal restraint for its own ends. Official responses to the letters and resolutions demanding compulsory blood tests stressed that it was "impossible…to get material and labour to have the [new] building erected" (British Columbia Premier, 1942, October 14). They added that:

"owing to the exigencies of war and the increased demand on our laboratory facilities, it has not been possible for the Government to consider the enforcement of the legislation it enacted in this respect. Until such time as the demands upon the laboratories relax, or we are in a position to obtain the necessary equipment, this matter will have to stand in abeyance" (British Columbia Premier, 1944, April 18).

Political decisions to spend or not spend public monies always rest on a cost-benefit analysis, however. The fact that the wartime Coalition government in British Columbia declined to provide funding to implement mandatory blood testing for VD may well have reflected the lack of agreement among its members on the issue.[10] The same disunity, and even resistance to, compulsory blood tests were evident among important segments of the voting public. For instance, while medical authorities involved in VD control supported the idea of compulsory pre-marital blood tests, at least in principle, the medical profession itself apparently favoured voluntary rather than mandatory testing (Vancouver Medical Association, 1942). Although Protestant churches supported mandatory pre-marital testing, the Catholic Church had strongly opposed it: ("Cleric Urges," 1939) "The state has no power to institute impediments to marriage between baptised persons. This right was left by Christ to the Church and it has always exercised it in every country" ("Archbishop Denounces," 1939). Thus, the 1938 Marriage Act Amendment may have been more an attempt to appease the moralist pressure for action emanating from individuals and groups inside and outside government than a serious attempt to compel "deserving" women (and men) to undergo testing. Underlying unease with the idea of using coercion to regulate the "private" sex lives of "deserving" women (and men) perhaps reflected an assumption that the 'better' classes would meet their obligations to family and the nation without compulsion.

REGULATING SEX AMONG "UNDESERVING" WOMEN

In contrast to the velvet glove approach accorded "deserving" women, political, medical, and legal authorities had no qualms about using direct legal coercion against "undeserving" women who were identified as potential or actual carriers of venereal disease because they were viewed as "sexual others" and as inherently or irredeemably deviant. Again "science," often in the form of IQ and VD tests, was increasingly important in identifying these sources of contagion so that they could be segregated in the interests of social defence. However, legal strategies directed at the containment of women who were labelled by experts as "incorrigibles" must be viewed within the more general context of class and race-driven attempts during the interwar years, including the use of sterilization, to prevent "defective" women

---

[10] For instance, Pat Maitland, Conservative Party leader and Attorney General in British Columbia's wartime coalition government, had always opposed unilateral implementation of such tests by the province. "Seek Uniform Eugenic Laws," VP, 22 Feb. 1930, p. 14.

from reproducing (Chapman. 1977; McLaren, 1990; Stephen, 1995). In other words, many of the women who were identified "scientifically" as likely sources of contagion also were women deemed to be potentially or demonstrably incapable of being "good" mothers.

As discussed earlier, the major pieces of Canadian legislation used to contain "undeserving" women who were suspected or known carriers of VD were the federal Criminal Code and the anti-VD statutes enacted by various provinces. The Code was used almost exclusively against prostitutes who were historically perceived as a major repository of social diseases. The provincial laws were applied much more broadly to anyone suspected of having VD, including prostitutes. In British Columbia, the Venereal Diseases Suppression Act (SBC 1919, c.88) played a key role in the organized efforts to eradicate VD from the 1920s to the 1940s. Like most of the provinces, BC modelled its law after the pioneer Ontario statute (SO 1918, c.42). Viewed retrospectively, the legislation is significant for two reasons. First, it contained extremely sweeping provisions that allowed extensive state-sanctioned intervention into peoples' private lives. Second, it created a medical and public health monopoly over the application of the Act (Cassel, 1987 p. 161–164).

Among other things, the B.C. legislation stipulated that any person incarcerated for a Criminal Code or provincial offence was to be tested for VD at the time of admission to the penal institution. Doctors and heads of public institutions also were to keep a record of all infected persons under their care or supervision and report all cases to the Provincial Health Officer. However, the VD Suppression Act did not specifically mandate the routine testing of admissions to non-penal institutions, nor did it stipulate the testing of young offenders incarcerated for status offences under the Juvenile Delinquents Act (SC 1929, c.36). Nonetheless, the growing influence of the medical profession on the government response to VD during the 1930s became evident in 1937 when the Director of Venereal Disease Control, Dr. S.C. Peterson, persuaded the Provincial Secretary that all persons admitted to any institution should be tested for syphilis. Subsequently, the respective heads of the Provincial Gaol, School for the Deaf and the Blind, Provincial Mental Hospital, Provincial Industrial Home for Girls, Provincial Industrial School for Boys, and Provincial Home for Incurables, received a letter with instructions "to make a routine blood test for syphilis of all the patients under your care" and to submit statistics to the Ministry if the test already was a "regular practice" (British Columbia Premier, Provincial Secretary, 1937, March 2).

Responses revealed contradictory institutional practices. On one hand, the Warden at the Oakalla Prison Farm for men, who ostensibly was required by law to test all new admissions for VD, reported that only those inmates suspected of having syphilis—either on admission or later—actually were tested. Moreover, to test the 420 inmates currently in the prison all at once "would lead to misunderstanding and friction" (British Columbia Provincial Secretary, 1937, March 24;

Warden, Oakalla, 1937 March 24; Inspector of Gaols, 1937 March 8). On the other hand, the Superintendent of the Industrial Home for Girls, who was not required by law to test all admissions, reported that it was "a routine procedure for every girl upon admission to have a blood test;" and only 12 positive cases had been identified during an eight-year period from 1929 to 1937 (British Columbia Provincial Secretary, 1937, March 8). In contrast, Matters (1984, p. 270) found that from one-third to two-thirds of young women incarcerated in any given year between 1914 and 1936 were "suffering from either syphilis or gonorrhea." But she also noted that, while the vast majority of young women admitted to the Home had been convicted of status offences, such as sexual immorality, and were sexually active prior to admission, many inmates had been "sexually active only with a single partner"; "several had asked permission to marry the men with whom they were involved"; and several "were already married at the time of committal" (Ibid. p. 270).

Thus, it is difficult to avoid the conclusion that assumptions about the sexual threat posed by "promiscuous" women and the need for social defence against this danger, which underpin the sexual double standard, were operating against young women committed to the Industrial Home. Authorities relied on IQ testing by the provincial Child Guidance Clinic that consistently revealed the subnormal mental abilities of a large number of the inmates and confirmed links between low intelligence and sexual deviance. Ironically, the belief that so many incarcerated women were mentally subnormal justified training and placing the great majority of them in situations of high sexual risk as domestics (Ibid, p. 272). As "undeserving" women, they also were prime candidates for sterilization (McLaren, 1990).

After Dr. Donald Williams became the Director of the Division of VD Control in April 1938, there was increasing emphasis on the legal suppression of venereal disease and the weakness of the existing provincial legislation. The Vancouver City Prosecutor and Chief Constable informed Williams that "their efforts to cooperate with the Division were hampered by the fact that the Act did not provide the power to examine individuals when in custody or under arrest, but only after commitment for an offense" (B.C. Provincial Board of Health, 1939). Following a recommendation from Williams for a review of the "present efficacy" of the Venereal Diseases Suppression Act "in light of recent changes in the VD problem," (B.C. Provincial Board of Health, 1938) the government amended the law (SBC 1938, c.63) to further facilitate its use against the historical targets of anti-VD campaigns—prostitutes. The amendments shifted initial control over the administration of the legislation from local medical health officers to the provincial health officer, thereby centralizing state power in the hands of a doctor; and the PHO was empowered to order VD testing of any person in police custody and to deal with persons with VD who refused treatment. The revised statute, together with the Criminal Code, underpinned a sweeping drive against "commercialized prostitution" (and VD) in

Vancouver that was launched in January 1939 and continued throughout the Second World War ("Drastic Drive," 1939). No less than the eradication of the "social evil" would do. Therefore, traditional tolerance of prostitution in segregated areas was no longer acceptable and law enforcers were expected to clean up the streets and the brothels (Freund, 1995).

The moral impetus for the suppression of prostitution campaign was unmistakable. Longstanding conceptions of prostitutes as reservoirs of disease who infected unsuspecting men, clearly remained engrained in the public culture. Notwithstanding his talk of medical science and public health, the B.C. Director of VD Control sounded more like an old-fashioned social purity reformer than a "modern," social hygienist in his pronouncements on the need to eradicate commercialized vice, "The day has come when this illegal and unsavory provincial BUSINESS can no longer be tolerated…" (Williams D.H., 1941, June 10) Moreover, Dr. Williams proactively and successfully recruited assistance for his anti-vice crusade from churches and other social reform constituencies; the media; the B.C. Medical Association; and government ministers, including the Provincial Secretary (Dobson Papers, 1941, May; Dobson, 1943, September 2; "Victorians Support Anti-Vice Drive," 1941, May 15; "Public Information," 1941, June 14; Vancouver Medical Assn., 1941, July). As the latter explained to the Mayor of Tacoma, Washington in 1941 "Despite all the insidious attacks that have been made upon Dr. Williams and myself…we are…actively committed to a policy of suppression…and so long as I am actively charged with responsibility for administering the health services of the province I propose to continue the policy upon which we are now embarked" (British Columbia Provincial Secretary, 1941, August 19).

Despite challenges from critics of the suppression policy, Williams and his supporters were able to point to a marked decline in VD cases as evidence that the anti-vice campaign had been successful ("Vancouver Leads," 1941). Clearly, Tacoma's mayor was impressed because he launched his own apparently successful drive against prostitution after consultation with Dr. Williams ("Tacoma's Mayor," 1941).

But one of the biggest problems for those who argued that prostitutes on the street and in bawdy houses were the main source of VD was that women who did not receive payment for sex were more and more likely to be named by infected men as sources of disease. Undeterred, the anti-prostitution forces expanded the definition of prostitute to include "pick-ups," "very promiscuous young girls" who "though no payment of money was admitted, sold their services for liquor, entertainment, board, and lodging, etc." (B.C. Provincial Board of Health, 1941, pp. 20–21). Their numbers increased "as suppression of bawdy houses led to less gonorrhea from bawdy house inmates" (Ibid., pp. 22–23). Since "pick-ups" frequented commercialized entertainment sites such as beer parlours and dance halls that acted as "facilitation centres" for dangerous sex intensified policing and supervision of these public places was "clearly needed" (Ibid., pp. 22–23). In the end, social hygiene still required the targeting of "undeserving" women—"Hitler's Girlfriends."[11] This was the old moralism in not-so-technocratic guise.

CONCLUSIONS

"I myself have never been able to find out precisely what feminism is: I only know that people call me a feminist whenever I express sentiments that differentiate me from a doormat" (West, 1913 in Kramarae & Treichler, 1985, p. 160).

Virtually every contentious issue today, including sexual epidemic, safe sex, and separating the "fit" from the "unfit," also was the subject of debate during the late 19th and early 20th centuries (see, e.g., Brock, 1998; Walkowitz, 1980). Thus, the foregoing analysis arguably has much relevance in the contemporary world. In conclusion, then, I want to discuss the implications of my research on the historical regulation of VD in British Columbia. I suggest that the study is important for four reasons: (1) understanding social regulation; (2) looking at how social regulation shapes policy; (3) seeing how this in turn impacts upon the lives of women in particular; and (4) demonstrating the importance of feminist analysis, critique, and politics.

First, the B.C. study contributes to an understanding of social regulation by illustrating that the form and degree of state regulation of the "private" are never preordained. The historical context limits the possible regulatory options at a given moment but it does not determine which of them will be pursued and/or implemented. Different approaches between (and within) countries are obvious. For instance, anti-VD initiatives in Canada were much more explicitly state-directed with respect to funding and collaboration between governmental and non-governmental groups than they were in the United States and Britain. However, mandatory pre-natal and pre-marital VD testing was enforced in many U.S. states but not in B.C./Canada and so on.

Second, the B.C. case study demonstrates that social regulation does not shape policy in a unidirectional top-down manner. Historical constructions of, and reactions to, "social problems" are the outcome of struggle, resistance and even chance. Competing ideologies and discourses underpin contradictory motivations and practices among and between the regulators as well as the regulated. On one hand, during the interwar years in British Columbia a diversity of individuals and groups—lay reformers, doctors and other non-legal experts, legal agents, pharmaceutical companies, and government officials—agreed that VD was "bad" and ought to be eradicated.

---

[11] This was the theme of anti-prostitution propaganda aimed at allied military personnel during the Second World War (Brandt, 1985).

On the other hand, there were intra- and inter-group conflicts related to the explanation of, and solution to, the problem. These disagreements obviously mitigated the impact of any measures that were implemented. For example, notwithstanding their legal obligation to do so, many doctors in private practice failed to report cases to the B.C. Division of VD Control, perhaps out of a class-based desire to protect a clientele that could afford their services in a pre-medicare era. The limits of state commitment to anti-VD initiatives also were demonstrated by a chronic under-funding of public clinics. In addition, the targets of VD regulation themselves—both public clinic and private patients—undermined enforcement efforts by using false names, lying about or not providing the names of their contacts, failing to return for follow-up treatment and/or resorting to quacks.

Third, the B.C. study illuminates the impact of regulation and, in particular, the effects of regulation on the lives of women, by revealing the falseness of the persistent dichotomy between moralism and science in liberal states. Doctors and other experts who differentiated themselves so carefully from religious, "non-scientific" moralists during the interwar campaigns against VD often shared the same approach-avoidance attitude toward sex. Ostensibly focused on the scientific tip of the iceberg above water, they foundered on the pervasive moralism that was submerged. They too harboured class, racialized, and gender-based assumptions about who was blameless and who blameworthy in the spread of VD. Respectable (white) working-class and affluent women deserved protection and assistance, not as individuals but as the reproductive insurance of the nation. All others were "undeserving" and legitimate targets of coercion to protect society from their irresponsibility.

Finally, the historical study of anti-VD campaigns in British Columbia shows the relevance of feminist analysis and politics. Feminist analyses of state-family relations in particular have revealed the ideological resonance, malleability, and differential application of the public/private distinction in liberal states over time (MacKinnon, 1983; O'Donovan, 1985; Pateman, 1989; Boyd, 1997). While it can be a "haven in a heartless world", against racism for example (hooks, 1990), the family has never been a completely privatized institution in liberal states. Moreover the variability and inconsistency of state interventions into the domestic realm—especially with respect to reproduction and violence against women and children—reveal the malleability of the ideology of privacy (see, e.g., Arnup, 1994; Brodie, Gavigan, & Jenson, 1992; Dobash & Dobash, 1979; Gordon, 1977, 1988; McLaren, 1990; McLaren & McLaren, 1997). Additionally, the ways in which intertwined assumptions about gender, class, race, ethnicity, and sexual orientation either exacerbate or minimize state regulation of family life further illustrate the elasticity of the "separate spheres" ideology. In general, the more closely men, women, and children adhere to the norms governing their respective roles in the "white," middle class, nuclear family the more freedom from overt state surveillance they will enjoy (Arnup, 1994; Barrett & McIntosh, 1990; Boyd, 1989; Chunn, 1992; Donzelot, 1980; Gavigan, 1993; Roberts, 1993).

Feminist analysis is thus important in the current context. It can help us to identify, analyze, and exploit the contradictions, within and outside state institutions, which create spaces for struggle and change. The same lack of homogeneity that exists among women also characterizes those who make decisions about if and how particular women should be regulated. As the historical response to VD tells us, regulators or would-be-regulators—whether they are in government bureaucracies or non-governmental agencies, legal or non-legal experts—are rarely of one mind on an issue. But perhaps most importantly, feminist analysis can help us to think beyond "what is" to consider "what could be;" in short, to move beyond the parameters of debate and struggle which are set by and reflect the limits of liberalism and the public/private distinction which is the defining characteristic of liberal states and regulatory modes.

CRITICAL THINKING QUESTIONS

1. Today, many people in Canada and elsewhere assert that "history is dead." Outline and assess the arguments for and against this assertion that history is irrelevant to the present using the example of sexually transmitted diseases.

2. Compare the historical construction(s) of VD as a social problem in Canada and other western countries.

3. What does it mean to say that science is constructed? What are the uses of the "science construct" for regulatory practices related to sex and sexuality in liberal societies?

4. Compare the historical response to VD and the contemporary response to AIDS with respect to the regulation of sex and sexuality.

5. What is the relationship between compulsion and self-regulation in your life? How, if at all, would the relationship change if you were situated differently in terms of gender, race, class, age, (dis)ability, sexual orientation, etc., and/or if you were living in the early 20th century?

6. Assess the possibilities for feminists and members of similar social movements to influence and shape regulatory modes in Canada and other liberal democracies in ways that will help mitigate and perhaps ultimately eliminate existing inequalities among individuals and/or groups.

SUGGESTED READINGS

Adams, Mary Louise. (1997). *The Trouble with Normal: Postwar Youth and the Making of Heterosexuality.* Toronto: University of Toronto Press.

The author examines various discourses about youth in post-World War II Canada; specifically, how they were used in debates about juvenile delinquency, sex education, and indecent literature, and how they constituted and reconstituted heterosexual norms. She argues that the pervasive assumption that being "normal" was being heterosexual restricted the sexual possibilities for both youth and adults.

Bland, Lucy (1995). *Banishing the Beast: English Feminism and Sexual Morality 1885–1914.* London: Penguin Books.

This book examines sexual politics in England at the turn of the 20th century. The author focuses, in particular on feminists' contributions to campaigns and struggles to resolve issues related to marriage, prostitution, birth control, and sex.

Hunt, Alan (1999). *Governing Morals: A Social History of Moral Regulation.* Cambridge: Cambridge University Press.

This is a comparative, historical study of moral regulation in Britain and the United States since the 17th century. The author argues that an important aspect of moral regulation movements is that the impetus for such projects often comes from the middle class individuals and groups who are outside conventional politics and positions of institutional power.

Chunn, Dorothy E., McLaren, John P. S., & Menzies, Robert, (Eds.) (2002). *Regulating Lives: Historical Essays on the State, Society, the Individual and the Law.* Vancouver: UBC Press.

This collection of essays chronicles diverse experiences of social control, moral regulation, and governmentality in British Columbia and Canada during the late 19th and early 20th centuries. The regulation of lives ranges from aboriginal-settler intermarriage to incest in the criminal courts to public health initiatives around venereal disease to the politics of prostitution control.

McClintock, Anne (1995). *Imperial Leather: Race, Gender, and Sexuality in the Colonial Context.* London: Routledge.

This book is a study of the complex and sometimes contradictory relationships between race, gender, class, and sexuality that shaped British imperialism from its zenith in the Victorian era to its decline after World War II. She argues that an understanding of these categories of social power and identity is key to understanding imperialism and anti-imperialist resistance.

Sangster, Joan (2001). *Regulating Girls and Women: Sexuality, Family, and the Law in Ontario, 1920–1960.* Toronto: Oxford University Press.

This book traces the role of law in regulating girls and women over four decades of dramatic social change in Canada. The author highlights the differential treatment of females vis-à-vis males with respect to sexuality, family matters and related issues.

Smart, Carol (Ed.) (1992). *Regulating Womanhood: Historical Essays on Marriage, Motherhood and Sexuality.* London: Routledge.

This collection explores how the category "woman" has been constructed historically as a specific object of legal and social regulation in a number of western societies. The authors demonstrate that modes of regulation are not fixed and that women's resistance contributes to regulatory change.

WEB LINKS

www.sfu.ca/~fisls

Feminist Institute for Studies on Law and Society. The Web site states that "the Feminist Institute was established at Simon Fraser University in the spring of 1990 to facilitate and continue the development of feminist socio-legal analyses. It is designed to provide an environment for creative interaction among scholars and community representatives who are involved in this work locally, nationally and internationally, and to bridge gaps between legal and social science research."

www.archives.ca

The National Archives Web site provides access to records and databases, which cover a wide range of topics and interests.

www.bcarchives.gov.bc.ca

The B.C. Archives Web site states that it "contains an extensive library of publications with a strong emphasis on the social and political history of British Columbia and the Pacific Northwest."

Part Two

The Consolidation of "Normal"

When we think about the post-World War II period in Canada, the first thing that usually comes to mind is that it was a time of unrelenting homogeneity and conformity, in other words, everyone really wanted to be "normal" and worked diligently toward this end. The chapters in this section certainly emphasize the ways in which the post war period was one is which "normal" was consolidated as a powerful discursive tool for the regulation of self and others. However, we also see how the pressure toward normalization was resisted by unable or unwilling subjects. Gary Kinsman discusses the attempts by gay men and lesbians of the period to avoid the suppression of their sexuality. Becki Ross documents the enormous popularity of striptease, a form of sexual entertainment that flew in the face of social mores, and which women performed despite the attendant stigma. However, rather than positioning these women as either stigmatized deviants or the passive victims of male customers, corrupt politicians and police, Ross locates them at the centre of her inquiry, as active agents attempting to assert control over their own lives. Not all resistance occurs in as conscious and deliberate way as implied by these examples, though. Privately masturbating despite sex advice that cautioned against it, publicly presenting oneself as a "sissy boy" or butch girl, or dismembering one's Barbie doll are some of the numerous ways in which young people might engage in resistance without every consciously thinking about their actions as such and then carrying out their actions with deliberation.

This resistance helps us to keep in mind the agency of subjects: that people and social groups retain the capacity to make decisions and to act, as we consciously or unconsciously negotiate the range of competing and often contradictory discourses which give meaning to our social worlds. Moreover, the constitution of subjects (which might also be referred to as "making up the person") through influential discourses like psychology are not simply externally imposed, like an iron fist of social control. Mona Gleason finds that people actively sought out psychological knowledge hoping for the betterment of themselves. Mary Louise Adams finds that the constitution of knowledge (i.e. what is a good family, what creates juvenile delinquency, what is unhealthy sex) develops through the process of its application. For example, she finds that postwar young people were not only the targets of sexual knowledge, they were important to the very construction of that knowledge, and moreover, at the centre of the construction of sexual knowledge in the period. The perceived needs of young people (for example, their need for protection from harm) shaped how sexuality was understood (carrying on with the same example, that sexuality was potentially dangerous).

Dorothy Smith teaches us that **the social** only exists through people's activities, and how we coordinate those activities with one another. While social organization is mediated by discourses, this is different than claiming that social organization is determined by discourses. (For example, see Dorothy E. Smith *Writing the Social: Critique, Theory and Investigations.* Toronto: University of Toronto Press, 1999.) Numerous contributors to this collection support this kind of assertion in order to avoid what Gary Kinsman and others perceive as "discourse determinism."

While we may be accustomed to thinking about sexuality as a natural impulse or drive, we will see that sexuality indeed has a history, and that this history reveals its **social construction**. A significant project over the past twenty-five years of scholarship has been to explore that history. This investigation has largely been spurred on by two of the most successful social movements of the twentieth century: the women's liberation movement and the lesbian and gay liberation movement. Feminist, lesbian, and gay theorists in particular were interested in exploring the ways in which social regulation occurred through sexuality, and how a particular model of sexuality: monogamous, married heterosexual activity within the context of a patriarchal nuclear family, came to be elevated to the status of normal, while other forms of sexual expression were subordinated or prohibited in law. However, as Adams makes clear, we cannot limit ourselves to researching the history of subordinated forms of sexuality like homosexuality, for while this may help to legitimate same gender sexuality, it does not actually challenge the assumption that heterosexuality is the natural form of sexual expression, and therefore beyond need of investigation. As Adams states, homosexuality and heterosexuality cannot exist without one another. She overviews the historical creation of this binary model of sexuality, and asks how this model came to be so important. Moreover, she asks why, if heterosexuality is so natural, such a tremendous effort has gone in to producing the proper heterosexual. Her research reveals the active constitution of normality during the postwar period as teens were inundated with an endless stream of guidance and advice. This period was important in consolidating a particular model of normative heterosexuality, which is today treated as commonsensical. Indeed, her work directs us to understand just how important the category of normal was in classifying people during the postwar period. Given that only brief excerpts from her book, *The Trouble with Normal*, are available here, we encourage you to go to the original source for a more complete account.

It is to psychology's construction of the model of the "ideal family" that Mona Gleason directs our attention. This was an ideal that only some could live up to, whatever their hopes might be. Nonetheless, the model of the ideal family continues to remain popular (with some modifications in the contemporary period in order to accommodate the mass participation of women in the paid labour force), even as the very institution of marriage is challenged by high divorce rates. Why is re-marriage so popular, despite past failures? I suggest that the answer to this lies with the very success of discourses about family, discourses which reproduce the notion that the ideal family is at the heart of a normal life. The contemporary call for recognition of same gender/sex marriages is not just about a demand for inclusion through the provisions equal civil rights, but a demand to be considered normal. This means that the demand for same sex marriages is simultaneously a radical act of resistance to heterosexual hegemony, and a willing embracement of conformity and previously inaccessible forms of legal regulation. As Gary Kinsman's chapter reveals, to even think of launching such a demand would have seemed preposterous scant decades ago, when the borders of normal were not only consolidated, but also tightly policed.

CHAPTER 5

Excerpts from The Trouble with Normal: Postwar Youth and the Construction of Heterosexuality

BY MARY LOUISE ADAMS

This chapter is composed of excerpts from Mary Louise Adams' book, The Trouble with Normal: Postwar Youth and the Construction of Heterosexuality [1] *(1997). Toronto: University of Toronto Press.*

> Pause of a moment to consider what the boy or girl of today is confronted with: countless novels filled with immortality, profanity, and a profound belief in nothing—most of them, hailed as masterpieces by reviewers who don't know a sentence from a group of words; radio programs that in the main get laughs by scoffing at what were once considered sterling virtues; movies that glorify rudeness, riches, power, animal passion, and drinking; a world that cheerfully squanders billions on liquor, cars, tobacco, gambling, sports, chewing gum, and sleeping tablets[…]

This postwar version of "the world's going to hell in a handbasket" was penned by the principal of Toronto's Palmerston Avenue Public School in 1948.…[yet] Present-day sexual conservatives like to remember the 1950s as a lost era of family values and solid, "traditional" morals. In contemporary sexual politics, the 1950s are the standard against which some conservatives measure changes in the organization of sexuality. The mores of that decade sit as a kind of benchmark, a symbol of how far North Americans have travelled since morality was "as it should be," with clear gender roles in every household and heterosexual conjugal monogamy as the primary form of sexual partnership.[2] That this portrait is an idealized version of fifties norms does not decrease its effectiveness in contributing to present-day anxieties about changing sexual behaviours and identities. A

---

[1] *The Trouble with Normal* appears on Bruce Cockburn's album of the same name, True North Records, 1983 (title used with permission). Cockburn's lyrics decry the "normalness" of a pervasive neocolonial capitalism.

[2] Stephanie Coontz gives an excellent account of this kind of "nostalgia" in her book, *The Way We Never Were*.

study of the late 1940s and 1950s makes apparent the ideological underpinnings of the nostalgia that currently runs counter to the gains made by feminists, gay men, and lesbians over the past two decades[....]

During the postwar years, young people were the targets of a range of formal and informal sex-education materials through which mainstream sexual norms were both reproduced and constituted. But the importance of young people to sexual discourses did not lie solely in their position as targets of knowledge; they were also important to the construction of that knowledge. Assumptions about the corruptibility of young people, about their need for protection from moral harm, and about their role as representatives of the future helped to set boundaries for how sexuality in a general sense, could be understood[....]

The notion of discourse I use here is a Foucauldian one and refers to organized systems of knowledge that make possible what can be spoken about and how one may speak about it. At their most fundamental level, these "systems" are about the production of meaning, a process that is not without its material effects. Discourses, according to Foucault, "crystallize into institutions, they inform individual behaviour, they act as grids for the perception and evaluation of things."[3] They are not, as some have suggested, unrelated to the material aspects of our world. Indeed, material factors—printing presses, institutional resources, money—are what allow certain discourses to become more powerful than others. The task of discourse analysis is to determine which discourses are operating when and how and in what configurations. What possibilities for the construction of meaning arise through their circulation? In analyzing discourses one investigates the various processes—language and social practices—which make possible the statement of the "truths" that order our social world—for instance, the claim that heterosexuality is the most (or, in some versions the only) natural form of sexual expression. The intent is not to prove the veracity of such claims or their alternatives, but to understand how it is that they have come to be made.

HETEROSEXUALITY AS SUBJECT OF INVESTIGATION

Heterosexuality is not natural, just common
—T-shirt slogan, 1993

In the late 1800s, sexologists across Europe and North America compiled vast lists of strange and unusual sexual "types" and sexual behaviours. These ranged

---

[3] For discussions of discourse, see the following by Foucault: *Power/Knowledge; The History of Sexuality; Questions of Method;* and *The Subject and Power.* The following texts have also been useful: Belsey, *Critical practice;* Weedon, *Feminist Practice and Postindustrialist Theory;* Henriques et al., *Changing the Subject.*

from various forms of bestiality and sado-masochism to auto-eroticism, fetishism, and a wide array of what were assumed to be neurotic distortions of the "sex instinct." Given this history, it is interesting that out of all these possibilities, the most profound sexual-social division in present-day western culture is the one between straight and gay, although the divide between homo- and heterosexualities is perhaps more a linguistic construction than a reflection of the sociosexual landscape. Clunky and inefficient in an analytic sense, this divide works politically to obscure the diversity of experience and allegiance among those who participate in same-sex sexual activity—a diversity that makes it impossible to construct a firm boundary around the proper subject matter of specifically lesbian and gay or specifically heterosexual research. As long as homosexualities and heterosexualities are dichotomized, it is difficult to understand either side of the dichotomy without also considering its so-called opposite. As an analytic category, sexuality—like race, like gender, like class—is relational. There can be no homosexuality without a heterosexuality from which to differentiate it. Thus, it makes sense for those of us interested in the social meanings of the former to engage in research on the latter.

As a means of categorizing and regulating particular types of behaviour and people, both homo- and heterosexuality are relative latecomers to everyday discourse. The term "homosexuality" was coined in 1868 by German sodomy-law reformer Karl Maria Kertbeny. In his usage, the term referred not to sexual object choice, as it does now, but to gender inversion, that is to effeminacy exhibited by men and masculine demeanour exhibited by women.[4] According to gay historian Jonathan Ned Katz, in his important book *The Invention of Heterosexuality*, this new category of homosexuality was initially counterposed not to heterosexuality, which did not yet exist as either a word or a concept, but to a narrowly defined reproductive sexuality. Katz says that it wasn't until 1880 that Kertbeny's new word "heterosexuality" went public—in a published defence of homosexuality (Katz, 1990, p. 54). Twelve years later, an American doctor named James Kiernan used the new term to refer to those who were sexually inclined towards both sexes (p. 19). A 1901 medical dictionary, cited by Katz, gave a more narrow definition: "Abnormal or perverted appetite toward the opposite sex" (p. 85).

The equation of heterosexuality with perversion reflected the centrality of reproduction to pre-twentieth-century sexual systems. It was not until the beginning of this century that the criteria for classifying sexual behaviours shifted from their reproductive to their erotic possibilities. Katz argues that the emergence of the homosexual/heterosexual opposition was part of this shift away from repro-

---

[4] For discussions of the linguistic and political emergence of the homosexual, see: Weeks, *Coming Out: Homosexual Politics in Britain, from the Nineteenth Century to the Present;* Foucault, *The History of Sexuality,* vol. 1; and Jonathan Ned Katz, *Gay/Lesbian Almanac.*

ductive norms and towards what he calls a "different-sex erotic norm" (p. 81). The work of Viennese sexologist Richard von Krafft-Ebing helped to crystallize this binary as well as the notion of heterosexuality as a non-pathological predisposition to different-sex erotic feelings and behaviour. In his book *Psychopathia Sexualis*, which first appeared in English in 1893, the erotically normal heterosexual is counterposed to the abnormal homosexual, thus setting the groundwork for the hierarchical organization of sexuality that we continue to face today.[5]

It took some time, however, for the homosexual/heterosexual binarism to be widely adopted as a form of classifying erotic attraction. George Chauncey argues that in male working-class communities in New York City, for instance, "homosexual behaviour *per se* became the primary basis for the labelling and self-identification of men as 'queer' only around the middle of the twentieth century." Prior to that time, "queerness" had been attributed to a man's inability to fit into normative gender roles, not to the sex of the people he chose to have sex with. Thus, masculine men who had sex with effeminate men—"fairies"—had not been considered to be abnormal or homosexual. It wasn't until the 1930s, 1940s, and 1950s, says Chauncey, that "the now-conventional division of men into 'homosexuals' and 'heterosexuals,' based on the sex of their sexual partners, replace[d] the division of men into 'fairies' and 'normal men,'" a distinction that had been based on their display of accepted gender attributes. For white, middle-class men in New York, the importance of erotic inclination and the division between homo- and heterosexuality had become a way of normality two generations earlier (Chauncey, 1994, p. 13).

Chauncey says that the increasing importance of heterosexuality to the middle class reflected the reorganization of gender relations in the early part of the twentieth century. New corporate forms of work, the growing participation of women in the public sphere, and perceptions that modern life was "softening" the male character had led to a crisis of middle-class masculinity. Widespread fear of effeminacy—crystallized around the public image of the fairy—translated into a fear of homosexuality, thereby making heterosexuality a route for the demonstration of manliness. Exclusive erotic desire for women came to be a mark of being a man, while gender identify and sexual identity came to be an inseparable pair (pp. 111–127; see also White, 1993).

This coupling of gender and sexual identities helped to transform the place of sex in North American cultures. Victorian discourses about the need for sexual control and about women's sexual passivity and passionlessness were, increasingly, being questioned by young women and men and by political and sexual radicals. Christina Simmons says that by the 1920s in the United States, the "predominant tone" about sex was one of "liberal reform" (Simmons, 1989, p. 160). Simmons

---

[5] Krafft-Ebing, *Psychopathia Sexualis* (numerous editions; English translations are generally of the 12th, revised edition, originally published in the United States in 1906).

writes that the "new" thinkers argued for less distance between husband and wife, especially in terms of sex. They claimed that "denying sexual urges made marriage itself less stable"; hence they argued for companionate marriages based on emotional intimacy and sexual satisfaction for both women and men (p. 162). This became the model of heterosexuality in the 1920s and 1930s, although, as Simmons makes clear, it did not go uncontested by those, especially women, who felt that the new sexualized marriages diminished female power. In previous middle-class arrangements, women had held a moral power that enabled them to determine the shape of their sexual relationships. In companionate marriages, women's role became a responsive one. Women were counselled to follow men's sexual lead; to withdraw from sex was to threaten the marriage, to treat a husband unfairly. Sex was the glue that was to hold these marriages together. Gender-based roles under male control were the prescription for making sex work. Heterosexuality itself became synonymous with gender hierarchy.

By the 1940s, companionate forms of heterosexual marriage had achieved dominance as *the* way of organizing erotic, emotional, and reproductive life. The "revival of domesticity" after the war helped to entrench the strict gender dichotomies that held up these forms of marriage, while efforts to control extra-marital sex contributed to their sexualization, a process that was seen as one route to family harmony and domestic stability. The increasing influence of psychoanalytic theories in the postwar period also meant that heterosexuality was not simply a means of organizing relationships between women and men; rather, it came to be seen as essential to the expression of "maturity," and it determined one's ability to make claims on normality, that most important of postwar social classifications.

It was not until the postwar period that the process of developing a proper heterosexual identity came to be understood as something that took place before marriage. Not only was teenage sexuality acknowledged—in dozens of advice books and magazine articles on petting and necking—but it was watched and nurtured and guided in socially appropriate directions by sex educators, concerned parents, various civic bodies, and voluntary organizations. Following Freud, heterosexual development was seen as a fragile process, one open to corruption. Adult heterosexuality was not taken to be an inevitability; it was an achievement, a marker of safe passage through adolescence.

What I want to stress in sketching how the notion of heterosexuality developed is both its only recent emergence as an articulated concept and the fact that it has, over the last 100 years, changed considerably as an idea and a practice. As an important sexual category that is too often taken for granted, it requires historical and sociological investigation. Such scrutiny is especially important in light of present-day popular wisdom about so-called family values, in which nothing is seen as more natural and universal than heterosexuality and the nuclear families many people build around it.

To say that homo- and heterosexuality are only recent concepts is, of course, not to say that people in earlier eras did not engage in activities which today we would think of as homo- or heterosexual. Nor is it to suggest that forms of sexual expression were not, previously, subjected to processes and differentiation and regulation. The point is that over the course of several decades, sexual desire and behaviours came to be seen in a new light, as central to identity, as keys to the personality of the individual, and, most importantly for this study, to his or her claim on normality.

In this study, the trouble with normal is its taken-for-grantedness and its power as a regulatory sexual category. In the 1940s and 1950s, the difference between definitions of normal and abnormal sexuality operated as a profound space of social marginalization and exclusion. As a powerful organizer of everyday life, the imperative to be normal limited possibility in people's lives; certainly it limited the forms of sexual expression and identity available to them[....]

[....]To argue that sexuality is socially constructed, that it changes across time and place, is not to say that we experience it that way. Certainly, as Foucault and others have pointed out, people in western cultures have not done so over the last two centuries during which sexological, medical, and psychoanalytic discourses have all, in various ways, come to place sexuality at the centre of our personal identities. To say that sexuality is socially constructed is not to say that it is not real right now, in the late 1990s, that it is a trivial force in our lives, or that it is easily changed. Rather, it is to suggest the importance of questioning the way we think about sexuality, how it is organized and regulated. Why is it that we categorize ourselves and others by our sexual behaviours and identities? Why has sexuality come to be so "personal"? Why is it assumed to hold the key to our development as individuals?

For Foucault, sexual discourses are conduits through which power gains access to human bodies and where it is expressed by them at the most fundamental level: "When I think of the mechanics of power, I think of its capillary form of existence, of the extent to which power seeps into the very grain of individuals, reaches right into their bodies, permeates their gestures, their posture, what they say, how they learn to live and work with other people" (cited by Martin, 1988, p. 6). This particular understanding of the relationship between sexuality and power and the framing of power as something which operates within and through the individual is immensely important to contemporary notions of sexuality as one of the primary defining features of the individual[....]

As a concept, normalization draws our attention to discourses and practices that produce subjects who are "normal," who live "normality," and, most importantly, who find it hard to imagine anything different. These discourses and practices work to delineate possible forms of expression, sexual or otherwise, as legitimate, while others are left to exist beyond the limits of acceptability. As

Cathy Urwin describes it, normalization operates as a type of deviance-prevention mechanism (Steedman, Urwin & Walkerdine, 1985, p.165). Individuals are encouraged, through a variety of discursive and institutional practices, to meet normative standards, and they come to desire the rewards that meeting those standards makes possible. In this way individuals become self-regulating. While repressive mechanisms may be tied to this process, as in the criminalization of homosexual behaviours in the 1950s, their effects are far outweighed by the power of the original "encouragement."

What makes normalization such an effective exercise of power is the way it operates at the level of the individual, the way, as Foucault says, it uses its subjects. As a form of social regulation, normalization defines and limits the choices that are available to us. Julian Henriques and colleagues write that norms form the "conditions of [our] desire" (Henriques et al., 1984, p. 218). The point is not that we simply try to meet social norms, it's that we *want* to. In the 1950s, this tendency to conformity was lauded and derided by social critics; many thought it was one of the defining features of the period (See Reisman, 1961).

While there is definitely a relationship between social norms and various scientific and professional constructions of "normality," these two categories are not entirely synonymous. Norms are not always based on what's normal. Normal, as Ian Hacking points out, can refer simply to what's usual or typical, a definition which may approximate the norm or may not.[6] To simplify Hacking's argument, the notion of normal as what is usual comes from medicine where, in the 1820s, it evolved as an empirical category counterposed to be pathological. In this sense "normal" was descriptive; however, it also had a positive value, as in "healthy." This normal/pathological opposition eventually moved from medical fields to sociological and political ones. As social systems were perceived to be in an unhealthy state, normal conditions were what these systems had deviated from—normal conditions were seen as "the good ones." Here, normal does match "the norm" in the sense of how "things ought to be."[7]

Both of these senses of the word—normal as description, normal as desirable—differ from more recent connotations of normality as a statistical category. In this usage, normal is not necessarily desirable; it is "mediocre," as Hacking puts it, following Francis Galton. Normal is the point from which we deviate, for better or worse. It is perhaps not a coincidence that "the normal curve," the bell curve, was developed in 1893, at the same time that sexologists were detailing and defining the "normal" sexual type known as heterosexuality.[8] While these two modes of deter-

[6] Hacking, "Normal." Thanks to Ian Hacking for sharing his notes with me and thanks, too, to James Heap for bringing the paper to my attention.
[7] Ibid., 13.
[8] Thanks to James Heap for pointing this out to me.

mining normality were different, they both helped contribute to notions of its importance as a social marker, a means of measuring difference.

It is when this measure of difference goes to work through moral discourses that it becomes a norm, a regulatory standard of behaviour, an expression of disciplinary power. In detailing the competing means of defining normal, Hacking makes clear that this progression is not inevitable. Nevertheless, what I want to suggest here is that sexual and moral discourses were so tightly connected in the post-Second World War period that definitions of "normal sexuality"—as defined, for instance, in sex education manuals, in films for teenagers, or in magazine articles—and social/sexual norms and the moral discourses through which they are produced. It's for this reason that Alfred Kinsey, in his statistical studies of sexual behaviours, tried to avoid using "normal" as a category. In the present study, the relationship between definitions of normality and social norms is often a circular one.

Historical sociologists Philip Corrigan and Derek Sayer identify the power of the norm and the process of normalization as an important aspect of what they call moral regulation—the social and political project of rendering "natural" the perspectives and ideologies of hegemonic interests (Corrigan & Sayer, 1995, p. 4). Their idea of moral regulation shares certain features with the forms of disciplinary power, the self-regulatory processes described by Foucault in *The History of Sexuality* and elsewhere (Foucault, 1980, p. 116. See also Foucault, 1977). Like Foucault, Corrigan, and Sayer are concerned with the ways that discourses come to work through us so that we become not only easily regulated, but self-regulating. But Corrigan and Sayer, more than Foucault, tend to focus on the fact that only certain discourses seem to gain this power. There are powerful and less powerful discourses, a distinction that has much to do with the material relationships within which they are grounded. The effects of even the "positive," "productive" exercise of power are related to material circumstances through, for instance, the means by which discourses are circulated, whether that be printed materials, television and radio broadcasts, public school lessons, or any of a multitude of other means. Such attention to the inequities in the distribution of power is crucial to an analysis of sexuality, where the realities of subordination and domination are longstanding and impossible to ignore.

Corrigan and Sayer suggest that moral regulation works by limiting the forms of expression available to us—in part, by masking difference under an illusion of social unity. It homogenizes. What we take to be "normal" are, for the most part, representations of dominant interests. Moral regulation helps establish dominant modes of being as not only legitimate, but desirable. Thus, as individuals, we become embedded in and embrace the very processes which restrict possibility in our lives and which diminish our abilities to make sense of ourselves and the world around us. If, for instance, heterosexuality is revered and validated while same-sex sex is punishable by law, by social ostracism, or by its definition as abnormal, it can be difficult for young people who feel they are homosexual to reconcile their sexual and social desires. Fears of punishment, or of not fitting in, can inhibit their ability to express themselves in a manner of their own choosing. It's in this most insidious way that moral regulation limits the number of acceptable or possible social identities that we can take on, all the while making this situation of reduced opportunity appear natural.

It is because the various procedures and regulatory techniques of normalization are directed towards the formation of appropriate kinds of persons that discussions of moral regulation, and the normalization that accomplishes it, are by necessity discussions about subjectivity and about the construction of social subjects. Here, subjectivity is to be understood as both the conscious and unconscious aspects of the individual. It refers to the way we understand who we are in the world and how we take our place in it. We make this knowledge "ours," not through the revelations of our "true selves," but via our negotiations through and within discourse—regulated systems of what can be expressed or said. Our discursive attachments let us bring meaning to the world around us and to our place within it. They offer us subject positions through which we come to understand who and what we are. Our location at the confluence of a variety of discourses makes possible the range of ways we have of expressing ourselves, as well as the meanings we assign to our expressions. It makes it possible to resist what some have called "discourse-determinism."

The production of subjectivity is an ongoing and contested process, not something that occurs once and for all. In terms of the marginalization of homosexualities, for instance, we need to question how such a process of differentiation is accomplished, and how difference comes to be known (and respected or resisted) by people on either side of it. How is "queerness," for instance, positioned by the discourses and practices which contribute to dominant heterosexual norms? The point is, as Richard Johnston writes, that subjectivities—even the most normal and heterosexual ones—are "produced and not given and are therefore the objects of inquiry, not the premises or starting points" (Johnson, Winter 1986/1987, p. 23). [I explore] some of the conditions of possibility within postwar sexual subjectivities were produced. What were the systems of sexual meaning available to adults and teenagers, through which identity could be expressed and understood? While I talk very little about the subjectivities of specific individuals, I am interested in the different subject positions produced in and made available by various discursive formations, in the way discourses position both those who speak through them and those of whom they speak. It is through the negotiation of multiple, often contradictory subject positions that subjectivity is produced. In this light, it is the "preconditions" of subjectivity that I am concerned with here. How were specific subject positions—the juvenile delinquent, the pervert, the nice girl, the sissy, the promiscuous teen—organized through discourse? What was their relationship to the "normal heterosexual"?

In my research I looked at a variety of sites through which the postwar social-sexual order was constructed and maintained: schools, courtrooms, social-work agencies, municipal bureaucracies, popular advice literature, and mainstream social comment[....] As a concept, heterosexuality was not yet sixty years old as the Second World War ended. Still, it has already evolved considerably: from a category of deviant sexual behaviour, to a classification of sexual object choice, to the basis of successful marriages, to a marker of the maturity and ability to conform that were critical to social reckoning at mid-century. Moreover, between the 1920s and the 1940s, definitions of heterosexuality came to encompass notions about proper gender roles, about the nature of sexualized relationships between women and men, and about the emotional and psychic development of individuals. Indeed, by the late 1940s, the meanings of heterosexuality had expanded to such an extent that its hegemonic position in Canadian culture—as represented by the number of Canadians marrying and starting families—was read as a marker of national stability.

Clearly, heterosexuality is not reducible to any type of natural or biological essence. Neither is it a simple matter of sexual attraction between women and men, nor of the particular forms of sexual behaviour women and men might engage in with each other. Heterosexuality is a discursively constituted social category that organizes relations not only between women and men, but also between those who fit definitions of heterosexuality and those who do not, and between adults and youth. Heterosexuality also helps to constitute relations of class, ethnicity, and race. It is frequently made meaningful by way of non-sexual discourses, and, in turn, these discourses are themselves sexualized.

The ability to lay claim to a definition of normality was a crucial marker of postwar social belonging. To be marked as sexually "abnormal" in any way was to throw into question the possibility of achieving or maintaining status as an adult, as a "responsible citizen," as a valued contributor to the social whole. Normal sexuality, as constructed in postwar advice books, films, magazines, and sex-education curricula, in legal, medical, psychological, and popular discourses, was invariably the preserve of married, monogamous, adult heterosexual couples who produced children, and of the adolescent girls and boys who were preparing themselves to fit into that model. That young people could "prepare for" or be prepared for normal sexuality is a central aspect of postwar sexual discourses. With the rise of developmental psychology, so-called normal sexuality was understood to be an emotional and psychic achievement. While this process played itself out on biological terrain, biology alone was not enough to guarantee one's normalness. Hence the tremendous impulse, expressed by many adults, to intervene in teenage sexual development.

Teens were assumed, in many senses, to be works-in-progress, malleable and easily influenced—characteristics that many adults thought could facilitate their turning into either delinquents or model, sexually responsible citizens. As a group, therefore, teens were often the targets of an "ideal" sexual knowledge intended to guide them towards maturity. Youth were portrayed in popular media and sex education materials as the "parents of the future," a formulation which brought teen sexual development to social prominence and aligned it with the development of society as a whole. Given this, it is not surprising that teenagers were frequently the ground over which the boundaries of normative sexuality were negotiated and reinforced. But young people were not simply the targets of sexual knowledge. Notions about their moral and physical capacities also helped to constitute sexual discourse in a more general sense. The desire to "protect" youth and the future they were assumed to represent helped to constitute sexual discourse in a more general sense. The desire to "protect" youth and the future they were assumed to represent helped to motivate broad-ranging initiatives of moral and sexual regulation that took adults and young people as their objects. Common-sense ideas about the nature of adolescent sexual and moral development contributed to the setting of limits on how and where sexuality could be expressed or represented, and by whom. Some adults saw teenagers as being under the control of their blossoming sex drives. These adults wanted to set limits on public discussions of sexuality because they feared such discussions would set teens off in an orgy of experimentation. Other adults were less concerned about the impulses of puberty and the exigencies of hormones than they were about teenagers' moral immaturity. They worried that boys and girls faced with sexual information or images could be unable to distinguish right from wrong and thus, "innocently," might engage in questionable activities. In both perspectives, notions of sexuality as potentially dangerous, destabilizing, and morally charged combined with ideas about the nature of puberty and adolescent development to curtail public discussion of sex—as we saw in previous chapters in debates over both sex education and indecent literature.

As a concept, "youth" was part of what made postwar sexual discourses work. Regulatory efforts that were promised as a means of "protecting the children" carried a certain moral weight that both justified their existence and increased the likelihood of their success. In this framework, images and discussions of juvenile delinquency operated as the possible fate of young people who were left "unprotected." While delinquency had many social meanings in the postwar years, it was routinely invoked as a sexual category, as the consequence of the moral corruption of youth, or of youthful sexuality run amok. In either case, fears about delinquency contributed to calls for regulation that would control the sexual activities of young people and efforts that would steer teenage morality in the right direction.

The centrality of youth in postwar sexual discourses was a product of the particular social conditions of the era. After six years of war and the decade-long

Depression that had preceded them, Canadians were not always trusting of what the future might bring. They worried about the rise of the cold war and expressed fears about the fragility of the nascent peace and prosperity. At the same time, people revelled in the allied victory over fascism and demonstrated a heightened faith in democracy. Technological change and the increasing availability of consumer goods put "modern life" within the reach of large segments of the Canadian population. These contradictory aspects of postwar life combined to orient Canadians in a profound way towards home, family, and stability. Nuclear families would help protect Canadians against the insecurities of the age. They would also provide the base for the growing consumer economy and for the democracy that was promoted as the route to victory in the cold war. Families were understood to be the primary stabilizing influence on both individuals and the nation as a whole.

In this context, postwar youth, as the "parents of the future," would prove critical to Canada's success or failure in the modern age. As a collectivity, youth were represented in popular discourses as a product of both wartime disruptions and modern prosperity. The social progress of adolescents was read by many as an indication of the shape society would take in the future. While the "youth problem" was taken up as a sign of social disarray, the confidence of "modern" teens was seen as a sign of postwar progress. Issues of sexuality could determine which of these images was prominent or appropriate at any given time for particular groups of young people. Were they behaving "normally" or not? If teenagers were normal—that is, if they met the social norms through which sexual normality was constituted—popular discourses suggested that the future would be normal too.

CRITICAL THINKING QUESTIONS

1. In the context of sexuality, what does the author suggest is the trouble with normal?
2. What distinct meanings are embedded in the terms "teenager," "youth," and "delinquent"? What are the different discursive attachments of each term? How have these changed over the past few decades?
3. What subject positions do you occupy in your own life? Explain how these have shaped your subjectivity.
4. What is the relationship between the normalization of the heterosexual nuclear family and the marginalization of homosexuality?
5. Is hetersexual hegemony as solid today as it was in the 1950s?
6. Why is the growth and popularization of psychology so important to our understanding of sexuality?

7. How did sexuality come to be something that youth needed to protected from? Do you believe that young people need such protection?

SUGGESTED READINGS

Cohen, Stanley (1972). *Folk Devils and Moral Panics: The Creation of Mods and Rockers*. London: MacGibbon and Kee.
> This is a classic study of problem youth in Britain. Cohen shows the way that debates over young people draw on concerns about a whole range of social issues.

Foucault, Michel (1981). *The History of Sexuality. Volume I*. New York: Pelican.
> A key text in the study of sexuality, this book explicitly challenges the idea that the history of sexuality has been one long march from repression to liberation. The book outlines the author's understanding of sexual discourses as vehicles through which power gains access to human bodies. A challenging text that addresses the question of how sexuality has come to be one of the primary defining features of the individual in contemporary western cultures.

Friedenberg, Edgar (1959). *The Vanishing Adolescent*. New York: Dell, 1959.
> An important, radical discussion of teenagers written in the late 1950s: a counter to much of the anxious concern over youth culture at the time. Clearly on the side of young people, Friedenberg places the blame for the so-called youth problem on the shoulders of adults who care more about regulating youth than about nurturing them.

Katz, Jonathan Ned (1995). *The Invention of Heterosexuality*. New York: Dutton.
> This book, written by one of the first North American gay historians, presents historical evidence for the argument that heterosexuality is not an unchanging, natural part of life but is a socially constructed identity that came to prominence in the early twentieth century.

Kinsman, Gary (1996). *The Regulation of Desire*. Second edition. Montreal: Black Rose.
> An overview of the history of sexuality in Canada. The author is very attentive to the role of social movements in changing sexual values and norms.

Kinsey, Alfred et. al (1948). *Sexual Behaviour in the Human Male*. Philadelphia: W.B. Saunders.
> This important work is credited with changing sexual discourses in 1950s North America. It is a huge empirical study of sexual habits that the author hoped would challenge restrictive norms. His main findings were the huge gap between norms and actual behaviour. The follow-up study, *Sexual Behaviour in the Human Female*, published in 1953 was so explosive when it appeared that Kinsey subsequently lost his funding.

May, Elaine Tyler (1988). *Homeward Bound: American Families in the Cold War Era*. New York: Basic Books.
> A social history of the late 1940s and 1950s that relates broader issues like foreign policy to more personal issues like marriage and the family. May argues that it is impossible to understand the politics of the Cold War era without looking at the gender and sexual norms of the time.

WEB LINK

www.univie.ac.at/Wirtschaftsgeschichte/sexbibl/
> An online bibliography that contains about 16,600 titles addressing of the history of sexuality in Europe and Northern America from 1700 to 1945.

CHAPTER 6

Constructing "Normal": Psychology and the Canadian Family, 1945–1960[1]

BY MONA GLEASON

In the years following the Second World War, the mental health of Canadians, amongst various other aspects of life, attracted the attention of a variety of commentators. After years of fighting, separation, and death, citizens were told to prepare for a considerable amount of strain in their postwar relationships with family and friends. From family life, to the relationship between men and women, to the difficult process of growing up, a potent mixture of social scientists, journalists, and other commentators maintained that the experience of war had significantly challenged, and indeed even altered, the conventional meaning and character of family life in Canada. The assumption was that the long years of economic depression and war had left Canadian families shaken and in need of strengthening. Rising divorce rates, juvenile delinquency, increases in the number of married women in the workforce, and general anxiety about the threat of communism and nuclear annihilation as the Cold War loomed were highlighted as signposts of trouble.

This chapter explores how popular psychology constructed and regulated family life during this period. Psychologists achieved this by reinterpreting traditional civic qualities necessary to sustain the status quo, such as industriousness, obedience, and happiness, in "psychologized" terms. To the traditional dichotomies used to characterize families, such as bad or good, weak or strong, was added another binary opposition: normal or abnormal. I argue that psychologists' discussions of normal families and normal family members were shaped not by so-called objective, unchanging scientific "truths," but rather by the hegemonic values and priorities of white, middle-class Canadians. Cultural traditions regarding family life deemed "un-Canadian" were discouraged in popular psychological discourse on the grounds that they jeopardized children's

---

[1] Revised version of (1997 September) Psychology and the Construction of the "Normal" Family in Postwar Canada, 1945–1960. *Canadian Historical Review 78*, 442–477.

ability to adjust successfully to society. My focus is largely on English Canada since psychology in Quebec reflected and legitimized the theology of Roman Catholicism (Wright & Myers, 1982). Despite the special circumstances Quebec represented at this time, psychologists such as William Blatz and Samuel Laycock intended their message to be applicable to all Canadians.

Popular psychology's regulation of normalcy mattered to Canadians because it denied important differences between and across individuals, racial and ethnic groups, and classes. The normal child, teenager, and family were equated with the idealized, and more socially acceptable, Anglo-Celtic, middle-class child, teenager, and family. This normalized ideal consolidated the diversity of family life into the confines of an a priori model and had significant consequences in a number of areas, including the entrenchment of traditional gender roles for women and men. So-called normal mothers stayed at home and raised well-adjusted, bright, industrious children while normal fathers skilfully divided time between the office and home. An idealized "every family" became the standard against which the unique needs and circumstances of those outside the ideal, such as immigrant, working-class, non-nuclear, or female-headed families, were measured and judged.

Nevertheless, psychologists writing in the popular arena, predominately white, male, middle-class professionals such as Samuel Laycock, William Blatz, Karl Bernhardt, and David Ketchum, assumed that their audience either shared their social standing or aspired to it. William Blatz, founder of the Institute of Child Study in Toronto, introduced Canadian parents to the psychological tenets of childrearing in the late 1920s. He became one of the general public's main interpreters of child psychology for the next forty years (Raymond, 1991). Samuel Laycock, an educational psychologist at the University of Saskatchewan, was also a well-known promoter of mental health in the field of parenting, education, penal corrections, and medicine. According to Gordon A. McMurray, one of his successors at the University of Saskatchewan, Laycock was popularly known as "Mr. Psychology" in the province and beyond (McMurray, 1982; Richardson, 1989). Dr. Laycock dispensed a great deal of advice to Canadian parents before his death at age 89 in 1971. A year earlier, he received the Medal of Service Order of Canada for his contributions in the area of education and gifted children, and in clinical practice. He acted as godfather to some seventeen children "scattered across Canada and overseas" and was reportedly known as "Uncle Sam" to many others.

Karl Bernhardt also contributed substantially to the public dissemination of psychological advice regarding the family and parenting in postwar Canada. In 1938, Bernhardt became head of the Parent Education division at the Institute of Child Study and published many popular articles aimed at parents in the journal initiated under his direction, *Bulletin of the Institute of Child Study*. When William Blatz retired, Bernhardt temporarily took over directorship of the Institute until poor health forced him to step aside (Raymond, 1991). Bernhardt captured something of psychology's appeal for Canadian parents when he wrote in 1947: "Why study child development? Why construct more and more tests? There can be only one answer in terms of purpose; and that is so that more people can be more happy" (Bernhardt, 1947, p. 57). In the opinion of Bernhardt and others who shared his views, psychological knowledge promised to contribute to a secure and happy future. The horrors of the war encouraged human relations experts like psychologists to teach citizens the world over to more successfully manage problems in the "modern age." Canadians, experts such as Blatz, Laycock, and Bernhardt reasoned, needed new coping strategies to ensure a peaceful, contented, and normal future.

REGULATING "NORMAL": THEORETICAL PERSPECTIVES ON PSYCHOLOGY AND POWER

How and why did psychologists come to hold and exercise considerable social power and influence in postwar society? Part of the answer lies in the fact that they re-defined family problems using the language of psychology. Recasting problems plaguing the family in psychological terms, Canadian psychologists represented part of a process by which "a certain idea or model of man [sic] became normative, self-evident, and supposedly universal" (Martin, 1988, p. 15). In other words, by describing, defining, and diagnosing family problems in terms of "normal personality" and "behaviour adjustment," psychologists effectively "psychologized" family life. They became the logical experts in determining normalcy and deviance. Psychologists not only singled out and diagnosed deviance but also, as scholar Mariana Valverde argues, "proactively predicted and pre-empted its development." Valverde argues "social regulation is best understood not as the control of already distinct areas of social activity but rather as a process which first constitutes the object to be administered" (Valverde, 1992, pp. 19, 143). In other words, in order for social regulation to occur, a "problem," defined by a certain set of criteria and in need of intervention, control, and/or solution, has to first be imagined or invented.

How are we to recognize this normalizing power that postwar psychologists exercised? Theorist Michel Foucault has suggested a useful set of concepts that help unearth and make visible the otherwise taken for granted or transparent workings of power. He suggests five overlapping components or strategies that constitute normalizing power. According to him, normalizing power compares, differentiates, hierarchizes, homogenizes, and excludes—each of these strategies adds to its rhetorical and social power (Foucault, 1977). These components of normalizing power described by Foucault correspond with the very strategies employed by postwar psychology. It's normalizing relied on these strategies of comparing, differentiating, hierarchizing, homogenizing, and excluding to regulate families. Numerous examples of this power at work abound within psychological discourse: personality inventories compared and differentiated the proper adjustment of children; definitions of normalcy established static boundaries and homogenized differences amongst families; and the reinforcement of traditional gender roles protected the male-headed hierarchical marriage arrangement. I will argue here that Foucault's typology of normalizing power helps us to identify how and why psychologists attempted to shape the family in specific ways in postwar Canada.

I have chosen to focus on popularized psychology's contributions to the regulation of the normal family in the postwar years for two specific reasons. First, while it has not received much attention from historians in Canada, psychological advice aimed at the postwar family in magazines, newspapers, and over the radio was popular and plentiful and represented an important feature of the postwar cultural landscape. After 1945 and into the 1960s and beyond, psychologists solidified their place amongst the ranks of increasingly popular human relations experts, mostly social scientists like sociologists, marriage and family counsellors, probation officers, and social workers, whose advice and pronouncements appeared regularly in the popular press and in self-help manuals. Second, popular psychological discourse helped define both normal and deviant human relations and set social standards of propriety and acceptability. In an effort to sustain the professional momentum established through their work in the army, psychologists worked to bring their expertise out of the ivory tower and into the homes of ordinary Canadians. They recast private and individual experience like motherhood and parenthood into highly complicated undertakings "requiring the most specialized knowledge and training" (Abbott, 1988; Bailey, 1988; Chunn, 1992; May, 1988; Walker, 1991). Psychologists believed they had something uniquely valuable to offer Canadians: the expertise to understand themselves and the way their actions affected others.

TAMING THE FIFTIES FAMILY: MARRIAGE, DIVORCE, AND PSYCHOLOGY

The postwar debate on the emotional health of the family signified a reaction not against familial breakdown *per se*, but rather to the rapid changes and transformations which it represented and which social leaders found uncomfortable, improper, or threatening. Dorothy Chunn has pointed out that "crises of the family" seem to crop up whenever a gap between middle-class and non-middle-class conceptions of propriety became too wide. When this occurs, middle-class efforts aimed at "upgrading standards of family life" follow (Chunn, 1992, pp. 40–41). In fact, the recurring or cyclical incidence of crises of the family has been a feature of Canadian society since the nineteenth-century, fostering the emergence of the welfare state and shoring up the "ideology of familialism" that characterized the interwar period (Ursel, 1992). Family crisis rhetoric represented (and continues to represent) a powerful way to regulate definitions of acceptable families.

Historians in Canada have begun to tackle and dispel many myths surrounding family life after the war. The notion that the fifties marked a high point of social optimism, prosperity, naivety, conformity, and innocence obscures many of the era's complexities and says more about the tendency to look back at this period with nostalgic eyes than about the period itself.[2] Women, as workers, wives, and mothers, for example, received highly contradictory directives that betrayed a considerable degree of anxiety regarding their changing roles after the war. Popular stereotypes tended to paint all women, regardless of their unique circumstances, as quintessential "angels of the house," at the same time that growing numbers of them sought and found new opportunities for paid employment outside the home (Strong-Boag, 1974 Fall). Recent studies have also dispelled myths surrounding women's idyllic experiences in postwar suburbs, focusing instead on the strategies they forged to help cope with isolation and loneliness. The nostalgic image of the fifties as a time of willing conformity amongst all Canadians, often associated with suburban living, flies in the face of the findings of scholars such as Franca Iacovetta. In her important work on Italian immigrants in postwar Toronto, Iacovetta demonstrates that attempts to "Canadianize" newcomers, though often only partially successful, were grounded in a desire to assimilate cultural outsiders into a mainstream Anglo-Celtic and middle-class worldview that dominated postwar Canada. The Beat movement, which swept North America in the 1950s emphasizing a rejection of conventional society, also challenged the normalizing efforts of psychologists.

From the point of view of postwar psychology, the health of the Canadian family was determined by the emotional and behavioural maturity of its members. Journalists, social commentators, doctors, and governmental officials borrowed the language of psychology, a language imbued with the components of normalizing power identified by Foucault, to explain how the family has been dislocated during the war (Gölz, Strong-Boag, Kisker, *Maclean's Magazine*, p. 1947). A whole spectrum of familial pathologies was discussed using psychological jargon, from increasing unwed motherhood, unfulfilled housewives, absent fathers, increasing child abuse and family desertion, to the threat of the sexual deviant, often assumed to be homosexual, stalking young children. The causes of problems were described in various ways: poor parenting, the absence of the father as the traditional familial authority figure, the death of a relative or family-friend in the war; the increased bombardment in movies, radio, newspaper, and, later television, of

---

[2] Referring to women's experiences, for example, Joanne Meyerowitz points out that the tendency to view the postwar years in this way "flattens the history of women, reducing the multidimensional complexity of the past to a snapshot of middle-class women in suburban homes." Introduction—Women and Gender in Postwar America, 1945–1960 (1994). In Joanne Meyerowitz, (Ed.) *Not June Cleaver* (p. 2). Philadelphia: Temple University Press.

the horrors of battle; the absence of working mothers from the home; the increased freedom, and concurrent disobedience and rebelliousness of teenagers, and increasing urbanization. Speaking to his listening audience over the CBC in 1954, psychologist David Ketchum suggested "no Canadian institution, not even education, is viewed with more alarm today than the Canadian family."[3]

The divorce rate, cited as a symptom of the declining strength of the family, seemed to support the need for psychological expertise. In the province of Saskatchewan, for example, statistics gathered by the Department of Public Health and the Registrar General indicated the number of divorces and annulments granted in the province rose steadily from a total of 127 in 1940, to 285 in 1945. In 1946, this number rose dramatically to 518, peaking in 1947 with 520. By 1948, however, the total number of divorces or annulments granted dropped to 339. (Pitsula, 1982, p. 72) Saskatchewan was not a unique case. This general pattern of rising divorce rates following the end of the war was repeated throughout the country. At the end of the war, divorce rates nationally had tripled: in 1941, there were 2471 divorces granted in Canada and by 1946, 7683 divorces were granted (*Canadian Dominion Bureau of Statistics*, 1945; *CDBS*, 1950). By 1948, however, the number of divorces in Canada dropped to 6881 and, in 1949, dropped further to 5934 (*CDBS*, 1955). Between 1948 and 1958, despite population growth, the number of divorces in Canada did not rise above 6300 (*CDBS*, 1960).

Few commentators acknowledged the steady decline in divorce rates after the early postwar years. Nor did they acknowledge the same increases in divorce, and the same lamentations about the state of the family, which accompanied the end of the First World War. The same assumption that prolonged separation of spouses resulted in marital estrangement and increased extra-marital activity, underscored discussions of rising divorce and separation rates in both eras. Psychologists interpreted postwar marriage breakdown as symptomatic of improper emotional and behavioural adjustment. Divorce, as Samuel Laycock understood it, was the result of emotional immaturity on the part of one or both marriage partners. (Laycock, 1945) The fact that Laycock remained a bachelor didn't compromise his advice: psychologists believed that experience was an unnecessary hindrance. Superior spousal and familial interaction was learned, not gained through experience. In a course on marriage given to the Two-By-Two Club of the Metropolitan United Church of Saskatoon, for example, Laycock based his discussion on "several research studies" on the "psychological factors in marriage happiness" (Laycock, 1950). Among the factors which helped make a marriage successful (or, if absent, unsuccessful) Laycock included "a happy childhood, lack of conflict with the

---

[3] The next of the radio programme reappeared in J.D. Ketchum. (1961). The Family: Changing Patterns in an Industrial Society. In *Canadian Family Study, 1957–1960* (p. 16). Toronto: Canadian Home and School and Parent-Teacher Federation.

mother, home discipline that was firm but not harsh, strong attachment to the mother without being dependent on her, strong attachment to the father without being childishly dependent, parental frankness about sex, and a premarital attitude to sex which is free from disgust" (Laycock, pp. 12–13).

Despite concerns about healthy marriages, Canadians were marrying in greater numbers during the mid-1940s. Douglas Owram has suggested that in fact a "cult of marriage" characterized the era (Laycock, p. 9). During the early years of the Depression, the marriage rate had fallen below 65,000 per year or 5.9 marriages for every thousand people. In 1944, 104,000 couples were married, or 8.5 marriages per thousand people. By 1945, this number rose to 8.9 marriages per thousand people and by 1946, 10.9 marriages per thousand people took place (*CDBS*, 1950). The marriage rate was, by the end of the war, unprecedented. Between 1951 and 1952, however, marriage rates gradually declined from 9.2 to 8.9 per thousand population (*CDBS*, 1955). In 1958, statisticians pointed out that 7.7 marriages per thousand population took place, the lowest marriage rate in 20 years. This trend continued in 1960 with 7.0 marriages per thousand (*CDBS*, 1960). Although more Canadians were marrying than in the darkest days of the Depression, "marriage-mania" was cooling near the end of the 1950s. Those who did marry, however, did so at an increasingly younger age. Between 1941 and 1961, the average age of marriage dropped from 25.4 years to 22 years for women and from 26.4 years to 24.8 years for men (Prentice, et. al, 1988).

Psychologists, along with other social commentators, argued that just as the family had been democratized by the lessons of the war, so too had marriage become a more democratic institution. Ideally, modern marriage was no longer based on the sole authority of the husband, "For in making the authoritarian type of marriage structure obsolete," promised Toronto psychologist David Ketchum, "it will give us a chance to rear a generation free from many of our shortcomings" (Ketchum, 1961, p. 16). While Ketchum did not specify from which shortcomings he and his generation suffered, he played on postwar anxiety surrounding perceptions of increasing divorce and juvenile delinquency. The horrors and triumphs of the war opened the doors for a new articulation, a new ideal, in healthy martial relations. In turn, the reasoning went, healthy martial relations ensured healthy family life. The maintenance of traditional hierarchies, an important component of normalizing power, remained critical.

Democratic marriages, however, did not necessarily mean equality between the sexes. As part of a popular series of *Chatelaine* articles on the state of marriage in postwar Canada, William Blatz told his readers "in every human relationship there is a dominant and a submissive party" (Blatz, 1955, p. 17). In past marriage practices, he argued, the husband was always dominant and the wife always submissive. Blatz pointed out that with the lessons of the war and heightened awareness of psychology, husbands and wives learned to shift between dominant and submissive roles, depending on the situation at hand. Detailing the specific workings of such an agreement, Blatz suggested "...they could agree that the husband will dominate in certain fields such as the handling of the family's finances while the wife will dominate in the handling of the children. In other words they must assign spheres of influence to each other if this modern concept of partnership in marriage is going to work" (Blatz, 1955, p. 82). Blatz promoted the notion of the modern democratic marriage based on his idea of spousal cooperation, not equality. As the above quotation suggests, this negotiation between dominance and submission did not necessarily subvert traditional gender roles for men and women. In Blatz's conception, men still interacted with the public world of finance and breadwinning while the women looked after the children.

Blatz presented marital problems in terms of emotional weaknesses and inability to avoid conflict.[4] However, that he placed the main responsibility for the emotional climate in marriage on women, garnered mixed reactions from his readers. The targets of psychologists' advice, it is important to acknowledge, did not simply remain passive listeners. Madeline Mann from Toronto praised Blatz for a "very fine and understanding" article. Likewise, K. Waites from Woodbridge thanked Blatz for "helping us to solve the current problems of modern living." Some readers, sensitive to the plight of many unfulfilled women in the strictly gendered postwar society were less impressed. Responding to Blatz's article on wives who "bore" their husbands, E. Ross wrote: "So everybody is bored with the housewife, that poor unfortunate whose only excuse for existence is survival of the race. No wonder! Has it ever occurred to anyone that we, who may be handicapped by the possession of a few brains, are bored with ourselves and our boring jobs, from which there is no escape?" ("Letters to Chatelaine," 1956 May, p. 3) Mrs. E.B. from Ottawa maintained that quarrelling with her spouse actually improved her marriage. She confided that while she and her husband had had many quarrels over the years, "we can honestly say that there has grown a deep and sympathetic bond between us which would not necessarily have been had we not known the true feelings of each other" ("Letters to Chatelaine,"1957 January, p. 2). These varied responses to Blatz show that not all Canadian women accepted his version of their submissive role in marriage. E. Ross, in particular, recognized and disagreed with the political consequences of Blatz's support for breadwinning husbands and stay at home mothers. The contradiction inherent in the notion of democratic marriages built on traditional gender roles remained unexamined.

[4] Blatz's own forty-year marriage to Margery Rowland ended in 1960. Jocelyn Motyer Raymond suggests that the decision to do so had been made early in their married lives and was to take place after their daughter, Margery, nicknamed Gery, had grown. They were reportedly "devoted parents and each other's good friends, willingly taking the consequences of an earlier, younger decision in order to give their daughter a stable childhood…" in *The Nursery World of Dr. Blatz,* p. 197.

While marriage was characterized in psychological discourse as an important relational state sustained by the satisfaction of the "basic psychological needs" of both partners, its discussion reflected hegemonic social values rather than scientific certainty. The pronouncements of Samuel Laycock, while based on "the results of research studies and the best findings of clinicians," centred on the nature of martial qualities such as affection, belonging, independence, achievement, approval, and sense of worth (Samuel Laycock Papers, 1951). He warned of the psychological problems associated with interracial marriages, thereby cloaking the socially unacceptable in the guise of psychological pathology. Cultural differences between spouses in any or all areas of life, Laycock warned, were "apt to cause trouble." "Mixed marriages" were discouraged simply on the grounds that they too often ended in divorce.

REGULATING THE KIDS: JUVENILE DELINQUENCY AND THE PROMISE OF "NORMAL"

Children and teenagers were also identified as suffering from "crippled personalities" and this helped justify a great deal of discussion regarding their proper place in postwar society. Concern about the actions of teenagers signalled anxiety, based at least in part on generational differences, about the deterioration of the social status quo. During the war, for example, employment opportunities for teenagers provided financial rewards, freedom, and personal expression. These new opportunities, however, also created new tensions: "Many of these young people, with too much money to spend, were supposedly making a mockery of the taboos and standards that had hitherto governed their conduct. The war, in effect, was producing an unsavoury, and unstructured climate on the home front that threatened the health, education and morals of impressionable teenagers" (Johnson, 1988, p. 356). Social leaders, as these comments suggest, were concerned because young people were not acting as they were supposed to act. While they were perceived to be more independent, brash, and undisciplined, teenagers were also made to seem more vulnerable then they had been before the war.

Although the perception of a youth problem received substantial attention in the popular press at the time, historians have argued that the incidence of criminal activity on the part of the country's juveniles during the postwar years was not, in strict statistical terms, on the increase (Australian-Canadian Studies, 1985; Brannigan, 1986; Gleason, 1996; McGinnis, 1988). In the writings of psychologists, however, delinquency represented a threat to traditional qualities of compliance and obedience and was far from simply equated with crime statistics. For them, the term conjured up a much broader set of problems, combining truancy, anti-social behaviour, and habitual challenges to authority that subverted the acceptable paradigm of adult authority.

Rather than criminalizing suspect behaviour, psychologists were much more eager to reinterpret it using their terms—to focus on the emotional and behavioural pathology of juvenile delinquency. As was the case with the problems of marriage and divorce, psychologists portrayed juvenile delinquency as symptomatic of impaired psychological development. Moreover, they often traced this impaired psychological development back to the family: "Delinquency occurs when adults in home, school, and community fail to provide children with the environment they need in order to grow up straight and strong. Delinquency, then, is really an adult problem. In other words, it isn't a case of delinquent children; rather it is a case of delinquent adults" (Edmison, 1949; Laycock, 1945).

The failure on the part of parents to create a satisfactory environment, according to postwar psychologists, was more to blame for juvenile delinquency than bad children, or hard economic times, or inadequate social support. This line of reasoning, that parents and communities were to blame for the inadequacies of children, significantly widened the audience for psychologists' discourse. Not only did it provide a focused source of children's problems, it made possible a powerful preventive orientation. A "failed environment," for example, referred to a home in which children's psychological needs were unfulfilled, ignored, and/or frustrated by parents. Thus, psychological discourse did not focus simply on studying, describing, and administering to delinquent behaviour rather, its prime objective was to disseminate a new ideal regarding family life, thereby including parents under its professional gaze. Families could be judged acceptable or not acceptable according to psychological criteria and this helped open the door to the normalizing activities of any intervening helping professionals, such as public health nurses, social workers, or caseworkers from juvenile courts. Using the techniques of comparing, differentiating, hierarchizing, homogenizing, and excluding, psychologists hoped to shape young Canadians in their own image.

Teenagers were taught to evaluate and even improve their own psychological maturity. A high-school textbook used in Canadian classrooms, for example, instructed young readers to steer clear of immature personality traits, such as "irresponsibility, self-centredness, and blowing up easily." The mature alternatives to these undesirable traits included "responsibility, concern for others, controlling your emotions" (Clarke & Woodsworth, 1959, pp. 28–29). Psychological advice thereby bolstered the desirability of parental power over children. An obedient teenager or child was much more than simply good—he or she was normalized through this kind of rhetoric. It described how the ideal child, the ideal teenager, or the ideal family would or should cope rather than how the majority of children, teenagers, or families coped with life. Any kind of familial conflict, this kind of reasoning suggested, was a sign of abnormality and was best avoided. Of course, this kind of advice set up an unattainable ideal that no family could successfully hope to achieve.

BLAMING MOM: THE ROLE OF PARENTS IN "NORMAL" FAMILIES

In postwar psychological discourse, it was parents, ultimately, who determined whether children enjoyed normal personality development or had personality pathologies. Psychology's recognition of this important influence in children's lives, however, did not mean that parents were to be left to their own devices. On the contrary, the need for psychologists' guidance and advice was promoted more vigorously than ever before. Just as children and teenagers were susceptible to personality pathologies, adults too could fall away from the boundaries of normalcy. For adults, especially parents, the stakes were even higher. In a lecture entitled "Good Parents," psychologist Robert Jones told his audience: "The moral is plain—the best way to take advantage of a child's suggestibility and imitativeness is to put your own life in order so that you can set an example worthy of impressing the child. If you argue, pout, quarrel, cry, or course your child will pick up on these traits" (Jones, 1944 p. 2). Jones' comments suggested that the psychological mishandling of children eventually came back to haunt ill-prepared parents. It is significant to note that Jones represented reactions such as arguing, pouting, and crying as character "traits" and not as common reactions to disappointment or injury. The possibility of doing emotional damage to children, given that unpleasant yet common human emotions like anger, disappointment, and frustration were not to be openly displayed by adults, seemed inevitable. He suggested further than Canadians either were or were not good parents, depending on their knowledge of psychology and their willingness to put it into practice. Behaviour characterized by variety, individuality, and spontaneity, in light of Jones' position, could be considered suspect.

Undoubtedly, mothers were acknowledged as centrally important in the emotional lives of their children but the issues surrounding this were complex and often contradictory. Some psychologists turned to the physical fact of pregnancy as a logical explanation for their identification of mothers as the primary caregiver. Women, rather than men, the argument went, had a closer, more meaningful bond with their infants because mothers and babies shared the physiological process of pregnancy and birth. This perception was even more pronounced in Quebec where, combined with the Catholic belief that propagating children was a religious duty, "'maternal instinct' was invoked so frequently that the qualities associated with it seemed innate" (Lévesque, 1994, p. 24). The next logical assumption, that mothers naturally made gifted parents, was nevertheless denied in psychological discourse. Even before the war, psychologists were carving out a niche for their knowledge claims by asserting that the proper approach to mothering was learned from psychologists; it did not exist innately. William Blatz proclaimed in 1928 that while it was "formerly believed that mother instinct or mother love was a safe basis for the problems of training," scientific mothering—

mothering learned by following the strict advice of the experts—was the modern way (Blatz & Boot, 1928, p. viii). Similarly, Samuel Laycock, reacting in 1944 to an unfavourable Edmonton newspaper editorial regarding the necessity of parent education, stated that "one would think that this writer, if he goes about with his eyes open, must see that 'natural instinct' does not tell mothers how to look after their children either physically or psychologically" (Laycock, 1944, pp. 4–5).

These reactions against women's "instincts" for proper mothering did not mean that psychologists had an enlightened view of women's diverse roles or her power to choose her life course. By differentiating between psychological insight and "natural" ability, psychologists made their expertise in the area of parenting all the more palatable and possible. The techniques associated with normalizing power—comparing inferior motherly "instinct" with superior scientific or expert-driven mothering, placing the opinions of psychologists over that of women themselves, differentiating normal children from abnormal children—were clearly at work. A central tension in the psychological discourse concerning mothers could be easily reconciled: because mothers were the most important person in the child's life, they needed the most guidance from parenting experts to do their job well.

Instead of focusing on wider social problems as possible explanations for family troubles, psychologists suggested other remedies to an unhappy situation. The father figure was of particular interest. In keeping with the often-contradictory meanings attached to democratic marriages in psychological discourse, fathers were encouraged to use their positions of authority to ensure and protect children's sense of confidence and security. The psychologists' solution to the problem of "over mothering," for example, was simple: evoke the calming presence of the father (Drakich, 1989). A father who played with his children, read them stories, and took an interest in their lives, psychologists' counselled, helped counteract the dangers posed by an overly zealous mother: "The closeness with a father as well as a mother during early childhood is of great importance. It doubly enriches a child's life to know and love two people instead of one. Children whose fathers as well as their mothers take an active part in their lives need not feel that home is a woman-dominated place where a man is either too stupid or too aloof to find his way around" (Black, 1953, pp. 101–102).

Such commentary suggested that the "woman-dominated" home had inherent dangers for the normal upbringing of postwar children. It also exemplified the gendered thinking so prevalent in psychological discourse. The problem of over-mothering, women's supposed tendency to be prone to frustration and selfishness, and the loss of male dominance in the postwar home were recurrent themes in discussions of the importance of mothers and fathers. Children brought up by mothers alone, psychologists warned, ran the risk of developing abnormal attitudes towards the proper roles of the sexes. Psychologist Anna Wolf, frequently cited as a source of childrearing advice for Canadian parents, noted that children raised in "fatherless" homes grew up believing that "women are born to be the world's real bosses; such a belief tends to breed passive men and aggressive women" (Wolf, 1946, pp. 216–217). Psychologists were often blunt and homophobic in their condemnation of postwar women who refused the idealized, and therefore submissive (and normal) middle-class feminine role: "The man wants a partner in marriage, not a competitor. The woman, in her fight for her rights, has put herself too much into a competing position. She has tried to turn man instead of remaining woman. A man does not want to marry another man" (Baruch & Travis, 1944, p. 233).

In broader terms, this tendency to construct a hierarchy of parenting functions within psychological discourse worked to reproduce traditional attitudes towards gender and legitimized the belief that, although prone to "over parenting," women were best suited to look after very young children. Furthermore, it reinforced the idea that while a mother's attention was useful, it was a father's crowning guidance that made the real difference in a child's normal development.

ABNORMAL OTHERS: PSYCHOLOGY AND PROBLEMS OF RACE, CLASS, AND ETHNICITY

For many parents, the idealized vision of happy, affectionate families preoccupied with building normal personalities was hardly straightforward or relevant. The experience of new immigrant families to Canada in the postwar period highlighted the socially constructed nature of the psychologists' approach to parenting and family life. Handpicked by government officials for their potential to positively affect the postwar economic picture and for "congenial" (i.e., non-Communist) political views, Eastern European immigrants were expected to quickly conform to Canadian society. The very fact of being an immigrant, however, was interpreted as a parenting handicap. In her 1951 study of adolescent girls referred to the Mental Hygiene Institute in Montreal, Roberta Bruce seized on her subjects' immigrant parents as likely contributors to problems of juvenile delinquency: "Seventeen [out of the 23 studied] of their parents had been born in Continental Europe. This meant that for these 17, there had to be an adjustment between the cultural patterns of the old and the new worlds. In some cases, the parents were still experiencing a conflict between these two cultures, and this conflict was affecting their relationship to the girls" (Bruce, 1951, p. 80). In this condemnation of the unsuitability of old cultural ways on the part of European immigrants, Bruce's reasoning oscillated between class considerations and ethnicity. Girls turned to delinquent behaviour, Bruce argued, because they came from "small, overcrowded homes, situated in poor neighbourhoods." Others suffered in families plagued by "financial insecurity or severe financial deprivation'" where the majority of fathers and all of the mothers worked in semi-skilled or unskilled jobs (Bruce, p. 81). Overall, the parents in Bruce's study were "unable to give them [girls] the needed love and discipline necessary for the development of a normal personality" (Bruce, p. 81).

A different reading of Bruce's study suggests, however, these European immigrants were judged to be inadequate, or by extension abnormal, because they failed to adopt to and mimic the psychological definition of the normal family. Normal families were financially secure, comfortable, happy and had mothers who stayed at home and looked after the children. Franca Iacovetta argues that Italian families were encouraged to adopt Canadian standards of parenting as part of a larger commitment to "Canadianization" (Iacovetta, 1992). Italian women learned "Canadian techniques in everything from cooking to parenting…while in their public lecturing on childrearing, public health nurses encouraged immigrant women to adopt North American conventions" (Iacovetta, 1992, p. 126). Iacovetta found, however, that pursing "Canadianization" through new childrearing techniques caused apprehension and fear on the part of some Italian immigrants, mostly mothers. Postwar psychologists encouraged women who had small children to stay at home and be fulltime caregivers, a luxury recent immigrants who relied upon women as secondary breadwinners did not have. Moreover, Iacovetta suggests many Italian parents, especially mothers, were not willing to adopt wholesale the parenting advice of outsiders. In their refusal to abandon strong extended kinship ties in favour of the nuclear family ideal, for example, family life for many postwar immigrants proceeded outside the dominant discourse.

The experience of aboriginal peoples also suggests that attempts at "Canadianization" could be devastating. The priority on assimilation, combined with widespread abuse and lack of emotional support in residential schools, robbed many aboriginal parents of the entire experience of parenting and family living well into the postwar period. Moreover, far from preparing them to be good parents, the residential school experience left a generation of young aboriginals severely traumatized.

CONCLUSIONS

In these ways, psychological discourse shaped and regulated conceptions of normal family life in the postwar years. Psychologists, venturing to bring their knowledge claims to bear on the meaning of family, often "defined old problems in new ways" (Abbott, 1988, p. 30). They did so largely by exercising normalizing power, described by Michel Foucault as including comparing, hierarchizing, differentiating, excluding, and homogenizing. And they were in an advantageous position to do so. The presentation of the war as a watershed event threatening family breakdown and rapid social change enabled psychologists to construct problems best tackled with psychological know-how. The function of the family was presented as much more complex and delicate than had previously been the case. "Building personalities," parents were told, was their main responsibility and the failure to do so successfully could result in emotionally damaged children and teenagers. By "psychologizing" the family and family life, postwar psychologists attempted to create a demand for their regulating expertise.

The authority with which psychologists claimed to speak on the family betrays something of the cultural ideals of the socially powerful in postwar Canadian society. Their call for an approach to family life based on emotional and behavioural sensitivity was meant to appeal to postwar Canadians on a broad level. The contradictory nature of much of the psychologists' advice, however, had significant negative implications for all members of the family, but most particularly for women. From the role of the father, to the normal characteristics of childhood and adolescence, psychological discourse nonetheless promoted a plan for constructing happier children and happier families. This suggests that changes taking place on the home front, changes that were affecting how society understood the role of the family, were causing a great deal of anxiety on the part of middle-class professionals like psychologists. They offered new ways of thinking about the meaning of family life, new ways of measuring success within the family circle, and new ways of conceiving of the importance of mothers and fathers. The normalized familial ideal constructed and promoted in this psychological discourse, however, ultimately left Canadian families with contradictory directives and unattainable goals.

CRITICAL THINKING QUESTIONS

1. What are some contemporary examples of experts who shape notions of the "normal family?" What are some of the assumptions behind their attempts to do so? Are they justified?

2. Why were Canadian women the focus of psychologist's attempts at regulation?

3. Why was the promotion of a particular model of the "normal" family so important to Canadians after the war?

4. Look through two or three issues of *Chatelaine Magazine* from the 1950s. Who else besides psychologists attempted to regulate the Canadian family? How did they do this and why?

5. What is the relationship between the family and the state? Why is the family so important to the "health" of the country? Who determines this relationship?

6. In contemporary Canada, how supportive are we of the family's well being? Do some families continue to be more acceptable than others? Why might this be so?

7. Think back to your own childhood. Consider the ways in which you were learned what was and what was not "acceptable" behaviour. What messages did you receive about gender, sexuality, race, and class? Who taught you these particular values?

SUGGESTED READINGS

Adams, Mary Louise (1997). *The Trouble with Normal: Postwar Youth and the Making of Heterosexuality*. Toronto: University of Toronto Press.
    Adams takes on the notion that heterosexuality is "normal" while homosexuality is "abnormal." She considers history's role in constructing sexualities and traces attempts on the part of doctors, psychologists, and educators to convince Canadian youth to act accordingly.

Comacchio, Cynthia R. (1999). *The Infinite Bonds of Family: Domesticity in Canada, 1850-1940*. Toronto: University of Toronto Press.
    Comacchio provides an accessible survey of the history of the family in Canada from Confederation to the postwar period

Foucault, Michel (1977). *Discipline and Punish: The Birth of the Prison*. New York: Pantheon.
    Foucault is a leading theorist in the area of regulation studies. This particular book traces the evolution of disciplining power from external violence to internalized self-discipline. It has implications for the ways in which we can identify, critique, and deconstruct disciplining power.

Gleason, Mona (1999). *Normalizing the Ideal: Psychology, Schooling and the Family in Postwar Canada*. Toronto: University of Toronto Press.
    This work expands on my essay, giving more background detail of the evolution of psychology as a social science in Canada, the role of particular prominent psychologists, and the school's role in the dissemination of psychologized normalizing about acceptability.

Korinek, Valerie (2000). *Roughing in the Suburbs: Reading Chatelaine Magazine in the Fifties and Sixties*. Toronto: University of Toronto Press.
    As the major Canadian women's magazine, Chatelaine provides something of a bellwether for historians interested in Canadian women's history. It provides excellent context for the postwar years and for the rapidly changing roles of women after the war.

Strange, Carolyn & Loo, Tina (1977). *Making Good: Law and Moral Regulation in Canada, 1867-1939*. Toronto: University of Toronto Press.
    Focusing on the period from Confederation to the onset of World War II, Strange and Loo look at the relationship between law and morality in Canada. Over this period, numerous forms of law—municipal, civil, criminal, and constitutional—evolved and instituted particular forms of "immorality" as illegal. Much of the legal reform, they argue, was undertaken to make Canadians into "good" citizens.

Sutherland, Neil (1997). *Growing Up: Childhood in English Canada from the Great War to the Age of Television*. Toronto: University of Toronto Press.

Sutherland's work is unique in that he pays attention to children's perspectives on change over time. Tapping into this "culture of childhood" allows us to consider the work of parents, teachers, and even psychologists, from the viewpoint of the children they sought to mould and shape in the postwar years.

WEB LINKS

History of Education and Childhood
www.socsci.kun.nl/ped/whp/histeduc/
> Located at Nijmeger University, the Netherlands, this is a comprehensive site for a large variety of sources, primary and secondary, devoted to all aspects of the history of education and childhood. Of particular interest are sources highlighting expert advice to families throughout history.

History of Psychology – Journal of the American Psychological Association
www.apa.org/journals/hop.html
> Dedicated to the history of psychology, this site allows users to search the journal for relevant articles exploring the social and cultural impact of psychology on North American life.

CHAPTER 7

NATIONAL SECURITY AS MORAL REGULATION: MAKING THE NORMAL AND THE DEVIANT IN THE SECURITY CAMPAIGNS AGAINST GAY MEN AND LESBIANS

BY GARY KINSMAN

This chapter focuses on the moral regulation organized through the anti-homosexual national security campaigns in the 1950s and 1960s in Cold War Canada. Moral regulation can be seen as the social institutions, discourses, and practices making the normal, and the moral; normalizing and naturalizing only certain ways of living. A crucial part of the national security campaigns was the making of heterosexuality as the moral, national, safe, and normal sexuality while gay and lesbian sexualities were made into the "immoral," "risky," and "deviant" sexualities that were thrown outside the fabric of the "nation." This marking of queer sexualities as "suspect" and "risky" has a legacy in our historical present[1] continuing to shape social practices of discrimination against lesbians, gay men, bisexuals, and transgendered people who do not fit into the dominant two-gender system. I use queer to reclaim and neutralize a term of abuse directed against us, as a broader term than lesbian and gay, and as a place from which to challenge heterosexual hegemony—the social practices, discourses, and ideologies constructing heterosexuality as the only "natural," and "normal" sexuality.

During the 1950s and 1960s, hundreds if not thousands of homosexuals and suspected homosexuals lost their jobs in the public service and the military, as the RCMP collected the names of close to 9,000 suspected lesbians and gay men by 1967–1968 in the Ottawa area (Directorate of Security and Intelligence Annual Report, 1967–1968). Pressuring gay men to inform on other homosexuals, hundreds were interrogated, and many were followed, photographed, and spied upon. Later we will hear from some of these men. The Canadian government even funded research into the detection of

---

[1] This term is used by Jeffrey Weeks in *Sexuality and Its Discontents*, London: Routledge and Kegan Paul, pp. 5–10.

homosexuality known as the "fruit machine" for more than four years.[2] Homosexuals were portrayed in this Cold War national security discourse as suffering from a "character weakness" or "moral failing" that would make us vulnerable to blackmail and compromise by foreign agents and therefore into "security risks." Although these national security campaigns lessened in intensity in much of the public service in the 1970s and 1980s, they continued at a high rate of intensity in the RCMP and military into the late 1980s and for the military the early 1990s. To this day closeted homosexuals can be denied security clearances with the argument that they have something to hide and therefore are vulnerable to blackmail and are a "security risk."[3]

THE MORALIZATION AND NORMALIZATION OF SEXUALITY

Mary Douglas, in her anthropological work shows how social and moral notions of purity, pollution, and taboo have often been built on the social relations of physiological reproduction and erotic practices. These symbols have played an important part in organizing social boundaries and in providing a sense of social and moral order in an often chaotic and conflicted world, "Ideas about separating, purifying, demarcating, and punishing transgressions have as their main function to impose system on an inherently untidy experience. It is only be exaggerating the difference between within and without, above and below, male and female, that a semblance of order is created" (Douglas, 1979, p. 4).

Douglas argues that, "nothing is more essentially transmitted by a social process of learning than sexual behaviour and this of course is closely related to morality" (Douglas, 1973, p. 93). Reproductive and sexual norms and taboos produce a "natural" order around which life comes to be organized. This natural order depends on boundaries separating the normal from the ambiguous. Any challenge to these boundaries by "deviant" behaviour leads to the mobilization of social fear and anxiety.

---

[2] The label "fruit machine" came from RCMP officers who were to be members of the "normal" (read heterosexual) control group for this study. Such was the concern that psychology had the ability to reveal what one did not know about oneself, or that the investigative process was itself defective, these officers feared that even though they were recruited into the research as "normals" they would be found out to be "fruits." See John Sawatsky, (1980). *Men in the Shadows* (pp. 133–136), Toronto: Totem. Also see Gary Kinsman and Patrizia Gentile, with the assistance of Heidi McDonell and Mary Mahood-Greer, (1998). *In the Interests of the State: The Anti-Gay, Anti-Lesbian National Security Campaign in Canada*, (pp. 106–116). Laurentian University.

[3] A Canadian Security and Intelligence (CSIS) spokesperson reiterated this position in 1998. See Brian K. Smith, CBC Radio, 1998. Also see Jeff Sallot, 'The Spy Masters' Talent Hunt Goes Public, (1999, June 22). *The Globe and Mail*, pp. A1, A14.

This moral order therefore depends on the marginalization of anomalies and firm social boundaries demarcated by "natural" markers that are rigorously policed.

Moral regulation is made up of a broad range of social discourses, institutions, ideologies, and practices. Ideologies are the ruling ideas in a society that are usually just taken-for-granted as "common-sense."[4] Moral regulation covers a much broader terrain than that of "the sexual," including non-sexual practices such as alcohol, drug-use, gambling, and crime. At the same time eroticism and sexual activity has been a key area for moral regulation, often informing the moral regulation of seemingly non-sexual activities. Sexual regulation includes the various practices, ideologies, and institutions that define and regulate our sexual lives. More recently, as I mention later, there has been a limited moral de-regulation of queer sexualities as new less moral forms of sexual regulation have emerged to contain queer sexualities while at the same time buttressing heterosexual hegemony.

The making of the moral and the immoral—the right and wrong ways to live—which often in the west has its roots in absolutist church ideologies, has especially been applied to the body and its pleasures over the last two centuries. New secular, or non-church-based, disciplinary knowledges like medicine, psychiatry, and psychology, came to build on earlier church-based prohibitions and came to transform and shift moral/immoral distinctions on a new secular and "scientific" basis. The new terrain of sexuality came to be defined in the 19th century as an essential "instinct" or drive that defined people's activities and began to become the "truth" of people's beings. This new concept of sexuality emerged through the opening up of new social spaces outside the family realm and the household economy through the development of capitalist social relations. The new disciplinary knowledges and forms of sexual policing developed in response to the emergence of forms of "sexual deviance" in these social spaces. Sexual policing is the social policing of this new terrain of "sexuality," focusing on the regulation of "deviant" sexualities through the extension of the Criminal Code and police activity into new areas of sexual activity. It includes expansion of the policing of the "sexual" through growing police and criminal justice systems and other social agencies. Forms of sexual resistance were generated by groups of people actively seizing these new social spaces in order to meet their erotic needs. The response to these new forms of policing and new forms of "scientific" knowledge was the emergence of forms of sexual difference and oppositional erotic cultures that would eventually be called homosexual, gay, and lesbian.

Through this process of struggle and social transformation, the sexual became a highly moralized terrain. The Criminal Code sections referring to sex-related

---

[4] "Ideology refers to all forms of knowledge that are divorced from their conditions of production (their grounds)." Roslyn Wallach Bologh, (1979). *Dialectical Phenomenology: Marx's Method*, (p. 19). Boston: Northeastern University Press. On ideology also see the work of Dorothy E. Smith and Himani Bannerji.

offences in Canada were referred to as "offences against morality," until they were moved into a new section called "Sexual Offences" in the 1950s. This moralization of the "sexual" continued even after there was a shift away from moral conservatism—an approach that argues that there is only one "right" sexuality, that is often religiously based, and generally argues for a rather repressive approach to erotic activity outside marriage—towards a more liberal policy of sexual regulation focused on public/private distinctions in the 1960s. In this liberal strategy there was still a common public morality which prohibited the public affirmation of queer sexualities, and the limited private "moral" space provided for homosexual sex was clearly subordinated to this public morality. This was also the terrain of the making of heterosexuality as "normal" in the 1950s and 1960s. If we think of the struggles over the "moral" and the "normal" of the last forty years, key to this has been struggles over sex education; birth control, abortion and reproductive rights; lesbian and gay rights; prostitution; pornography; and AIDS/HIV.

In the late nineteenth and twentieth centuries heterosexuality was associated with the natural, the normal, the clean, the healthy, and the pure; homosexuality was in contrast the dangerous, the impure, the unnatural, the sick, and the abnormal.[5] In this chapter, I focus on how homosexuality was made into a moral problem through the national security campaigns. This was built on top of earlier moral constructions of homosexuality and heterosexuality. One extract from right-wing discourse shows this mobilization against queers because we were seen to transgress sexual, class, political, and other social boundaries. R.C. Waldeck in *The International Homosexual Conspiracy* published in 1960 gives us a taste of this discourse,

> Homosexual officials are a peril for us in the present struggle between West and East: members of one conspiracy are prone to join another…many homosexuals from being enemies of society in general become enemies of capitalism in particular. Without being necessarily Marxist they serve the ends of the Communist International in the name of their rebellion against the prejudices, standards, ideals of the "bourgeois" world. Another reason for the homosexual-Communist alliance is the instability and passion for intrigue for intrigue's sake, which is inherent in the homosexual personality. A third reason is the social promiscuity within the homosexual minority and the fusion of its effects between upper class and proletarian corruption. (1981, p. 13)

---

[5] For some similar analysis although developed in a sexual libertarian perspective see Gayle Rubin, (1984). Thinking Sex: Notes for Radical Theory of the Politics of Sexuality. In Carole S. Vance, (Ed.), *Pleasure and Danger: Exploring Female Sexuality*, (pp. 280–283). Boston and London: Routledge and Kegan Paul. On the historical and social construction of heterosexuality see Jonathan Ned Katz, (1995). *The Invention of Heterosexuality*, New York: Dutton and Mary Louise Adams, (1997). *The Trouble With Normal: Postwar Youth and the Making of Heterosexuality*, Toronto: University of Toronto Press.

We get a clear sense of the "homosexual personality" characteristics, which are perceived to be a problem, and also the association constructed with Marxism and its challenge to capitalism. The challenging of erotic and social boundaries is equated with challenging class and political boundaries. The construction of homosexuality as a moral and political problem has been closely related to its construction as a "deviant" sexuality. Deviance constructs groups like homosexuals as different, other, and "abnormal." A key strategy of disciplinary power and power/knowledge relations, as Michel Foucault has pointed out, is normalization. For Foucault forms of power are expressed through the claims to knowledge of doctors, psychiatrists and other "experts" and knowledge is always bound up with power relations. Normalization leads to the making normal of only some practices and ways of living and the making of others as pathological, abnormal, and deviant. The pathological strategy constructs some ways of living as physiological or mental sickness or illness. The normalization of sexuality has involved forms of policing and criminalization as well as psychiatric, psychological, and sociological forms of disciplinary knowledge. For instance, mainstream sociological notions of the "normal" and the "deviant," often resting on statistical regimes of the "norm," have played an important part in strategies of normalization. Even critical approaches to deviancy studies by not taking up the social standpoints of those labelled as "deviants" can end up participating in normalizing practices by suggesting there really is something that is "deviant" about these groups of people. Deviancy is an administrative collecting category grouping together different social practices with very different social characteristics so they can all be addressed together as "deviant."[6] Administrative knowledge is designed for state and professional agencies, and for corporations to rule over, classify, manage, and administer the lives of people in this society.

Central to this making of the normal and the deviant, as already suggested, have been questions of sexuality and sexual identification. The paradigmatic examples of "deviance" have been homosexuality and prostitution. This has been part of the relational normalization of heterosexuality and the "deviantization" of homosexuality. This historical and social process not only marginalizes the "deviant" homosexual on the social periphery it also places the "normal" heterosexual at the social centre. The national security campaigns against queers are a key part of this social and historical project.

[6] See my comments in Gary Kinsman, (1998). Constructing Sexual Problems: 'These Problems May Lead to the Tragedy of Our Species.' In Les Samuelson and Wayne Antony, (Eds.), *Power and Resistance: Critical Thinking About Canadian Social Issues*, (p. 265). Halifax: Fernwood Publishing. On administrative collecting categories which group together a series of social practices so that they can be dealt with through common ruling classifications see Philip Corrigan, (1981). On Moral Regulation, *Sociological Review*, V. 29, 313–316.

"I Have Undergone An Experience Which Has Destroyed The Efforts Of My Life To Date"

I begin exploring the moralization and normalization work of the national security campaigns against queers with a quote from a gay man whose life was very detrimentally affected by the campaigns. I contrast this with the national security campaign's ideology that mandated this campaign against queers.

The following quote from a first-hand account written by Harold in the early 1960s tells of his experiences of being purged from the Canadian Navy in the late 1950s and the impact of this in his life.[7]

> Until recently I was a trusted, respected citizen. I held a position of responsibility and had spent years working hard in what I believed—and still do—was a worthwhile, if not highly remunerative organization. Then one day, the culmination of months of severe mental stress, I was dismissed….Quite unnecessarily, I feel, I have undergone an experience which has destroyed the efforts of my life to date…I have been deprived of two basic human needs—a reason for living and a degree of self-confidence….At an age when I had commenced to reap the benefit of years of conscientious and highly commended effort I have been removed from my position and world because, very belatedly, it seems, my superiors discovered I am a homosexual. ("Harold, Case Study," 1960–1961)

This quote brings into view the rupture, or line of fault,[8] between Harold's lived social experiences and the security regime practices which made him into a security problem with the "solution" of forcing his resignation from the Navy. In starting here I start a critical investigation of the social organization of the national security campaign from the social standpoint of the oppressed in relation to national security. The world of national security looks very different if we start from the social experiences of those most detrimentally affected as opposed to the RCMP agents or state officials directly involved in organizing queers as a "national security threat." Harold's experiences were shaped both through security regime practices that defined homosexuals as threats to "national security" because of their "character weakness" and the policies of the Canadian military which called for the "disposal" of all "sex deviates" found in the military, which pre-dated and helped to shape these security campaigns.

---

[7] Throughout this chapter I use pseudonyms for the people I have interviewed to protect their anonymity. Square brackets at the end of interview extracts are the date the interview took place.

[8] On ruptures and lines of fault between ruling discourses and the social experiences of oppressed and marginalized people see Dorothy E. Smith, (1987). *The Everyday World as Problematic, A Feminist Sociology*, especially pp. 49–60. Toronto: University of Toronto Press.

I contrast this first-hand account of the destruction of Harold's career and life with the national security construction of the homosexual "problem." This construction of homosexuality made homosexuality into a moral/ethical problem as well as a security problem—and in some ways a security problem because of these "immoral" characteristics,

> …sexual abnormalities appear to be the favourite target of hostile intelligence agencies, and of these homosexuality is most often used.…The nature of homosexuality appears to adapt itself to this kind of exploitation. By exercising fairly simple precautions, homosexuals are usually able to keep their habits hidden from those who are not specifically seeking them out. Further, homosexuals often appear to believe that the accepted ethical code, which governs normal human relationships does not apply to them.…The case of the homosexual is particularly difficult for a number of reasons. From the small amount of information we have been able to obtain about homosexual behaviour generally, certain characteristics appear to stand out—instability, willing self-deceit, defiance towards society, a tendency to surround oneself with persons of similar propensities, regardless of other considerations—none of which inspire the confidence one would hope to have in persons required to fill positions of trust and responsibility. (Wall, 1959, pp. 12–13)

This quote comes from a 1959 Canadian Security Panel memorandum. The Security Panel was the inter-departmental committee that co-ordinated the national security efforts of various agencies and institutions within Canadian state formation. In this security text, homosexuals were constructed as a security problem because of their characteristics which included "weaknesses," "unreliability" and "unethical" and "immoral" characteristics. These constructions were built on psychiatric knowledge that regarded homosexuals as "psychopathic personalities" who were unable to tell the difference between right and wrong or to control their sexual impulses, and this linked to national security concerns regarding moral and character weakness. This conceptualization of the "deficiencies" of the homosexual character is one of the central ways that the practices of moral regulation enter into the national security campaigns against gay men and lesbians. While not always being overtly and explicitly moral in character, moral regulation is carried forward through the active work of the concept of "character weakness" in the discourse and practices of the national security regime. We also see here that homosexuals are constructed as distinct from the "normal." We begin to see that what led to the end of Harold's career was the mobilization of moral regulation through the national security campaigns.

CRITICALLY INTERROGATING NATIONAL SECURITY

To explore the social organization of this security campaign, I use two major theoretical/methodological approaches. The first is Dorothy Smith's marxist feminist sociological contributions of a sociology for women and the oppressed; text-mediated social organization; and her alternative way of doing sociology called institutional ethnography.[9] Dorothy Smith uses the social and historical materialist approach developed by Karl Marx, adapted for feminism, as a critical method of analysis to examine the relation between the oppression of women and the social relations of capitalism. Her method is to disclose the social practices of people, while resisting the profound social processes of reification that transform social relations between people into relations between things in a capitalist society.

I start this inquiry from the social standpoints of those who were most directly affected by these national security campaigns. From these standpoints we can critically interrogate and analyze the national security campaigns against queers and can disclose their social organization from a vantage point that allows us to move beyond the ideological limitations of national security discourse.

The social relations and practices of the national security campaigns are organized, mobilized, and mediated through the documents of the national security regime and other official texts. These texts are used by people in the national security regime to co-ordinate their work of defining and doing surveillance work on "national security risks." Using Smith's approach, I read the national security texts as active texts used to organize the campaigns against gay men and lesbians. These national security texts and their conceptual framings of queers as "national security risks" suffering from a "character weakness" were used to mandate and co-ordinate the purging of queers and spying upon gay men and lesbians.

Smith's alternative way of doing sociology—institutional ethnography—allows me to turn the insights of ethnographic analysis (how cultures and forms of social organization work) to critically interrogate the institutional relations of the national security regime from the standpoints of queers in order to explicate how they organized problems in the everyday/everynight lives of gay men and lesbians.

---

[9] See Dorothy E. Smith, (1987). *The Everyday World as Problematic*, Toronto: University of Toronto Press; "The Active Text" and "Textually Mediated Social Organization" in *Texts, Facts, and Femininity*, London and New York: Routledge, 1990, pp.120–158, 209–224 and her *Writing the Social*, (1999). Toronto: University of Toronto Press. On institutional ethnography also see Marjorie L. Devault, "Institutional Ethnography: A Strategy for Feminist Inquiry," in her *Liberating Method*, (2002). *Feminism and Social Research*, Philadelphia: Temple University Press, 1999, pp. 46–54 and Marie Campbell and Frances Gregor, (2002) *Mapping Social Relations: A Primer in Doing Institutional Ethnography*, Aurora: Garamond Press.

Institutional ethnography involves a critical analysis of the ideological organization of the national security campaigns including that of national security itself. This is a broader notion of work that allows us to grasp the concerted activities going into the social organization of the national security campaigns and the resistance and accommodation to it; and the ways in which the national security campaigns are hooked up to the broader social relations of the criminalization and social stigmatization of homosexuality and the national security policies of the USA, Canada, and England. The national security regime is accomplished by people active in a number of different institutional locations. This regime can be seen as being made up of a number of intersecting and coordinated social relations. First, this research is based on interviews with more than 30 people who were purged, transferred, or forced into informing on others. These interviews begin to interrogate the broader institutional relations through which this security campaign was organized as well as critical textual analysis of national security discourse from a grounded social analysis developed from the accounts of those most directly affected.

Second, I use analysis derived from the work of Michel Foucault to explore the organization of the security regime as a concrete and grounded form of power/knowledge relation based on social surveillance, normalization, and disciplinary power. While Foucault's work has major insights and is especially useful in critically addressing the technologies and strategies of social surveillance and normalization, it also has some significant limitations given its tendency towards discourse reductionism and determinism. While Foucault believes that power is everywhere, he never locates power as the social accomplishments of people in the historical and social contexts in which we live. In my use of Foucault's insights, I try to always read discourse and power as social accomplishments. What has been produced socially can also be transformed collectively by the people ourselves. Foucault's work on governmentality, which focuses on how power operates around and across public/private boundaries and on practices of self-formation, is also useful for this investigation. While national security has a lot to do with self-formation and self-surveillance and it involves the collaboration of groups outside state relations, it is also a very state-focused practice.

NATIONAL SECURITY AND MORAL REGULATION

The social organization of the security regime in Canada is an under-documented and under-theorized area in Canadian history and sociology, especially as it relates to sexual and moral regulation. Here I focus on the moral dimensions of the work of the security regime, while noting this work is only one of its central features. In specifying more precisely the moral character of national security we also begin to see the shifting strategies of moral regulation across time and space.

"National security" rests on the construction of the nation and the national interest. The very construction of the nation and its subjects, and state formation more generally, is an intensely moral project. It is a project of moral regulation and normalization—the construction of moral subjects and "citizens." The constructions of nation and national security are ideological productions and cannot be simply assumed or taken-for-granted. We always have to ask, which nation and whose security is being defined and defended? On the one hand, the unitary or totalizing construction of the "nation" of Canada codes Canadians with particular social characteristics, including racial characteristics painting Canada as "white" and in this context as "normally" and "morally" heterosexual. At the very same time, the very real social differences of sexuality, class, gender, race, ethnicity, age, ability, language, and nation, especially regarding Quebec and the First Nations which are subsumed under this "unitary" Canadianness, can also be polarized out, individualized, or otherized as "threats" to the nation, as homosexuals were in Canada in the 1950s, 1960s, and 1970s. There is a dialectic here between the unitary classification of "Canadian" and the very real social differences people live in their lives in relation to sexuality, class, race, gender, and other social relations.

The ideological construction of nation and national security includes some as being moral/normal Canadians, while at the every same time, excluding others like queers as immoral/deviants. The construction of national security is defined in particular by the "interests" of the "nation," including capitalist social relations, national defence concerns, and the inter-state alliances in which the Canadian state was involved. To define someone as a "national security risk" was also a moral evaluation, a way of denying them citizenship and civil rights and a way of "cutting" them out of "normal" social interaction. Homosexuals were thereby cut out of or excluded from the national social fabric, defined as breaking the boundaries of public morality, and therefore were able to be entered into the investigation and surveillance relations mandated in national security discourse.

"National security risks," especially those claimed to be suffering from a "character weakness" or moral failing, were constructed as immoral subjects that made them unreliable and suspect. They supposedly had something to hide and therefore were vulnerable to compromise and blackmail. The notion of "character" has been invested historically with important moral content, especially in the context of Canadian nation-building and state formation, where much work has been directed at producing the "proper" character among those claimed as Canadians. For instance, Bruce Curtis points out in his study of the educational state in 19th century Canada West, that the "central concern of governing classes in *state* education was the reconstruction of popular character and culture" (1988, p. 14). There was also a very immoral character associated with "risk" and with "national security risk."

One important aspect of the security campaign was an attempt to construct moral/normal subjects who would not jeopardize "national security." This was to be constructed in part, through actual social surveillance and perhaps more significantly as in the Foucaultian image of the Panopticon (Jeremy Bentham's ideal model for a prison in which prisoners could be under constant surveillance) through the constant threat or possibility of being watched and monitored by the security police.[10] This was a project of attempted self-surveillance and self-governance which had a certain effectiveness in forcing people into the living of a double life and the relations of the closet, but at the same time as we will see, this could not prevent non-cooperation and resistance to the national security campaigns. Living a double life is a survival strategy when a person performs themselves in the "public" world of work as heterosexual and is only "gay" or "lesbian" in more "private" gay or lesbian circles spaces. The social relations of the closet is produced through criminalization, social stigmatization, and the national security campaigns themselves which often forced people to live in the closet performing themselves as heterosexual in the work world and many other aspects of their lives as well. They were generally not visible as gay or lesbian to any other people around them.

The national security regime was organized through two key conceptual practices. First, it was organised and mandated through "national security" itself which defined this against the "other"—against socialists, trade unionists, immigrants, peace activists, gay men and lesbians, student activists, and the black community in Nova Scotia in the late 60s, among many others. Second, on top of this construction of national security, lesbians and gay men were inscribed into the conceptualization of "character weakness." The classification of "character weakness" was an administrative collecting category grouping together a series of unrelated practices that could include excessive drinking, gambling, adultery, and homosexuality. At the same time, this classification became increasingly homosexualized in Canadian national security discourse and practice by the late 1950s. Basically, character weakness came to equal homosexual.

I talked to Fred, who worked in the Character Weakness subdivision of the RCMP's Directorate of Security and Intelligence in Ottawa in the late 1960s. Close to 90 percent of his work, he said, was dealing with homosexuals [October 21, 1994]. The clear implication was that homosexuals raised moral, character, and security questions that most heterosexuals did not. This focus on homosexuals was not simply a mistake or an aberration as some have suggested, or the result of homophobic prejudices among some in the security regime. Nor is it to imply that homosexuals were not the real threat, while other people were. For this last formulation retains national security discourse. Rather I want to draw attention to

[10] On Foucault's use of the Panopticon, see *Discipline and Punish*, pp. 195–228.

a particular social construction of national security, which produces lesbians and gays as a threat to the "nation-state."

This chapter focuses mostly on the social experiences of gay men, since men were more present in security positions during these years and gay men were more visibly constructed as a social danger. However, it is important to also stress that these security campaigns did have major impacts in the lives of women and lesbians.[11] During these years, lesbians in the military were routinely purged from the ranks. At the same time, the RCMP encountered major problems in undertaking surveillance work on lesbians. Fred, reported that lesbians were hard to talk to and were sometimes hostile towards male RCMP officers [October 21, 1994].

By the late 1950s and early 1960s, more women were being employed in the public service and gender anxieties were managed to some extent as these women entered into a previously largely "masculine" areas of work through the organization of beauty contests such as Miss Civil Service, and the construction of the "proper" feminine women worker who did not challenge gender boundaries. Much of this focused on the presentation and development of "proper" feminine character.[12] Significant dress codes were also imposed on women in the military. Sue tells us a bit about this and also about resistance to these practices in the military when she was in the militia and at military camp in the late 1950s,

> We would be out with sergeants, staff sergeants, corporals, privates, lieutenants…no rank was untouched….So we would be running all over camp. And the deal was you weren't allowed to leave the premises, so of course, we wanted wine, women, and song. So in order to get wine, women and song you had to leave the base. So you had to go out. But you weren't allowed to wear butchy clothing. You had to wear a *dress* [her emphasis]. So what we used to do was pull our pant legs up and hide them with our skirt. And you'd go out and through the gates in your skirt right, lookin' all femmy and lovely. Well this one night we came home and we got a little too drunk. Well trust me that the pants were down. And we, we were up on charges the next day for being in some place we weren't supposed to be, improper attire, all kinds of things. So we learned that we shouldn't drink too much. [Feb. 23, 1996]

---

[11] At the same time this does not entail that lesbians were less oppressed than gay men. Lesbians were less visible than gay men and had less social space because of the general denial of the social and economic autonomy of women from men and the specific social denial of lesbianism in the construction of heterosexual hegemony.

[12] See Patrizia Gentile, "'Government Girls' and 'Ottawa Men': Cold War Management of Gender Relations in the Civil Service," *Whose National Security?*, 131–141. On the social construction of heterosexual femininity see Dorothy E. Smith, "Femininity as Discourse," in *Texts, Facts and Femininity*, London and New York: Routledge, 1990, pp. 159–208.

The Social Relations of Interrogation and Blackmail: "Which is the Greater Treason...Treason to Your Country or Treason to Your Friends?"

Once gay men and lesbians were designated as "national security risks" suffering from a "character weakness" and following security surveillance confirmation that they were a "confirmed homosexual" through a number of identifications from gay informants or surveillance work individual gay and lesbian members of the public service and the military could be held in the social relations of interrogation (Kinsman, 2000). In a 1994 interview, Harold, whom we have already met, told me that the RCMP was much more heavy-handed than Naval Intelligence during interrogations [February 21, 1994]. This was related to their different mandates and the division of labour developed between them. The RCMP bore major responsibility for the national security campaigns while the responsibility of Naval Intelligence was organized differently and related far more to the policies of the military including the "disposal" of homosexuals.

According to Harold the RCMP would ask over and over again for the names of homosexuals and they would tape the interrogations. Harold also said the two officers interrogating him would make statements like "'Look you've got to know something for gods sake tell us, tell us. We won't hurt anybody but tell us come on tell us.' [bangs on table] Boy you have no idea of how I hated them"[February 21, 1994].

In his written account written shortly after he was forced out of the Navy Harold described the interrogation.

> This particular agency [the RCMP] does not operate with kid gloves....It is true that to state the terms used by these agents were, mildly expressed, forceful but the method of attack was decidedly clever....I was told that persons of my calibre are so much easier to handle than "drug store cowboys." To my enquiry why, the answer was that I was an individual of responsibility, integrity, and background as could readily understand the terrible import of the question, "Which is the greater treason....treason to your country or treason to your friends?" Or, "A person like yourself must realize what a serious disservice you may do your country by withholding the names of people we must ensure are never exposed to treasonous blackmail."....All they wanted was that I should talk, give names and suspicions. ("Harold, Case Study," 1960–1961)

There is a construction here of a divergence of loyalty to gay friends versus loyalty to the country in which loyalty to the nation is constructed as the most significant and privileged. In contrast loyalty to his homosexual friends was constructed as disloyalty or risk to national security. Loyalty to his friends meant he was a traitor to Canada. This theme also cropped up in other interviews we have done. When

Peaches Latour, a French-Canadian performer and hair stylist, was being questioned by the RCMP in the late 1960s the RCMP officer called him in and,

> said it was my civic duty to tell on them [other gays]—and I mean being French-Canadian and not [well] educated I didn't have a clue what he meant....I said "well, explain it to me"...."well" he said, "it would be on your shoulders that [some gay acquaintance] would be a traitor to Canada." I said, "a traitor! All I do is shows!" [August 31, 1994]

INVERTING THE PROBLEM OF BLACKMAIL

The RCMP interrogations were oriented around "security" concerns and "blackmail," as Harold's text suggests,

> They were, of course, applying a form of blackmail very difficult to resist. It contained an appeal to patriotism and reason, the pseudo-flattery of apparent recognition of integrity and a thinly veiled threat..."we are not concerning ourselves, right now, with the criminal aspects of the situation."....To my sickened dismay, even the success I had achieved in keeping my professional and personal lives strictly separated was turned against me. I was told I MUST know quite a "ring" of homosexuals in professional circles and my statement that I did not was immediately and emphatically rejected as a lie.... ("Harold, Case Study," 1960–1961)

Harold made an important reversal here of the security argument that homosexuals were vulnerable to blackmail from Soviet agents to viewing the RCMP itself as trying to "blackmail" him. They used him being gay and living a "double life" to try to "blackmail" him into doing what he did not want to do. In response Harold attempted to develop an alternative ethical form of resistance that refused to allow his statements to be turned against his friends. Implicitly this begins to develop an ethical position that challenges national security by placing loyalty to one's friends and other gay men above the interests of "national security." There was also the threat from the RCMP officers that they might be able to lay criminal charges against him given that RCMP work is also organized through the Criminal Code and at this time all homosexual acts were criminalized.

This view of the RCMP, police or military authorities as the blackmailers resonates with other accounts we have heard and read from gay men and lesbians who had experienced surveillance and interrogation. Harold stated that he was "only ever blackmailed by the RCMP" [Feb. 20, 1995]. Axel Otto Olson, then living in Toronto, was one of the few "non-expert" witnesses to give testimony before the Commission investigating the criminal law relating to Criminal Sexual Psychopaths which led to the extension of the criminalization of homosexual acts and individuals (Kinsmen, 1996). Criminal Sexual Psychopath legislation, which I come back to later, had been expanded to include all homosexual activities as possible "triggering" offences which made it possible for conviction for a consensual homosexual offence to lead to an indefinite sentence. In his 1956 testimony to the Commission, Olson detailed a series of blackmail attempts against himself and other men which followed accusations of homosexuality that were carried out by "certain police officers, court officials, and members of religious youth organizations." Like other gay men during these years, he located the very real problems of blackmail that they faced in the laws criminalizing homosexuality, in police actions, and in social practices stigmatizing homosexuality. He described being falsely charged with having sex with boys and being dragged to the police station and through the courts in Montreal where he was kept in jail for several weeks. The government he said was investigating and blackmailing men in the civil service. It was "almost impossible to teach school," said Olson, "because if you are friendly with the pupils you run the risk of being accused of being homosexual or a sex deviate." As he stated, "I don't believe the sex deviate…is the main problem." In his view the blackmailers were the "most serious problem." This was also an important inversion of the hegemonic discourse, that permeated state policy and the social "common-sense" put in place through the criminalization of homosexuality, through the psychiatric/psychological construction of homosexuality as a mental illness, and the mainstream media coverage of "sex deviation" that then existed.

Harold and Olson were in different ways reversing the focus of the national security campaign, and turning back the accusation of "blackmail" against the RCMP and the police. This is part of the development of an ethics of resistance, which begins by turning the practices of ruling moral regulation on its head. The early gay rights position argued that it was only because of laws criminalizing homosexual sex that such blackmail was possible. Early gay activist Jim Egan felt that the security campaigns, ignored the fact that the only reason they were possibly subject to blackmail was because of the laws that made the whole thing illegal. And if they had issued a directive to every commanding officer [or person in charge of a government department] that he was to inform his men [sic] that if they were approached by a foreign agent that they could report the matter to their commanding officer who would guarantee them absolute immunity and they could have cooperated in trapping foreign agents. Instead of that they thought the solution was the wholesale firing of anyone who was or was suspected of being gay [Jan. 5, 1998]. Yvette, a woman who was purged from the military in the 1950s for being a lesbian stated that, "They say that being a lesbian or a homosexual puts you as a target for blackmail. Well, if it were legitimized, it would no longer be, there would be no blackmail."[13]

[13] This account comes from the preliminary research interviews conducted for the film *Forbidden Love* (NFB, 1993). I thank Lynne Fernie and Aerlyn Weissman for their permission to use this account for this research.

The national security campaigns against queers, along with the criminalization of homosexual sexual activities, were an important part of the putting in place of the social relations of the closet and living a double life, as mentioned earlier. The national security regime was both aware of the social relations of the closet and the consequent need for secrecy and invisibility on the part of gay men and lesbians as we saw earlier when a memo for the Security Panel read, "By exercising fairly simple precautions, homosexuals are usually able to keep their habits hidden from those who are not specifically seeking them out" (Wall, 1959, p. 12). The national security regime themselves made use of and intensified the social space of the closet to organize their national security campaigns. While the early gay movement was beginning to call for the repeal of anti-gay laws and social stigmas as a way of getting rid of blackmail concerns, the RCMP and national security discourse by simply accepting this as a "natural" and not a social and historical construction positioned the need for secrecy and invisibility as inherent in the homosexual character. They did not locate this as a response to specific social and historical conditions, including the national security campaigns themselves. Judging from the documents we have been able to read no one on the Security Panel suggested that there was a need to repeal the laws criminalizing homosexuality to begin to alleviate the problems of blackmail facing many gay men and lesbians.

THE MEDIATED CHARACTER OF NATIONAL SECURITY

The national security campaign against queers did not exist independently. It had a mediated or mutually constructed character also being organized and shaped through the criminalization of homosexuality. This was especially the case for the RCMP whose work was also organized through the Criminal Code that then mandated the criminalization of all homosexual sexual practices. But this also occurred through many other social practices and policies stigmatizing homosexuality and constructing heterosexual hegemony. The national security campaigns against queers were thereby tied into other regulatory strategies then being deployed against gay men and lesbians. In the 1950s and into the 1960s, homosexuality was being constructed as a social, sexual, national, and *moral* danger. The national security campaigns against queers were also organized in relation to the campaigns against the left and the various ways in which the national security campaigns impacted on race, gender, class, and other social relations. Lois, for instance, describes how she was caught up in the security campaigns in the 1950s because she had a sexual relationship with a left-wing woman who was married to a member of the Communist Party of the U.S. As a result, Lois' household in

Ottawa was placed under surveillance and her husband was forced to resign from a position with the Department of National Defence.[14] Here national security surveillance against leftists and against lesbians was brought together. Queers *and* heterosexuals never simply live their lives as queers or "straights" but always in relation to race, gender, class, ability, age, and other social relations. The oppression of queers is also organized through class, gender, and racial relations.

The 1950s and into the 1960s was a period of the extension of the criminalization of male homosexual activities with the incorporation of consensual homosexual offences (such as "gross indecency" and "buggery") as triggering offences into Criminal Sexual Psychopath and later Dangerous Sexual Offender sentencing procedures, as mentioned earlier. This rested on the linking together of criminal and psychiatric regulation, since psychiatric testimony was required to inscribe these individuals into these legal classifications. Once convicted of a homosexual offence a sentencing hearing could be held. If the psychiatric testimony confirmed the individual to be a sexual psychopath or dangerous sexual offender (for instance that he was likely to engage in further homosexual activity) then he could be sentenced under these provisions to indefinite detention. As George Smith pointed out, the organization of the sexual policing of gay men's lives has been textually mediated through the classifications of the Criminal Code, which mobilize the police to criminalize sexual activities between men (Smith, 1988).

There was also a prohibition on membership of lesbians and gay men in the military and the RCMP. In the military there had been prohibitions against those classified as having "psychopathic personalities with abnormal sexuality" during the years of World War II. There were military directives mandating the disposal of "sex deviates" (Kinsmen, 1996). In part, this was organized through the mobilization within military and para-military state institutions of the organizing ideology of the heterosexual masculinity, of "fighting men" and its integral relation to nation-state building and national security. Gay men were not seen as the disciplined fighting men who should be in these institutions and sex between men was seen as disruptive of military discipline and hierarchy. Lesbians were also seen as a particular threat to the "proper femininity" of women within the military (Berube & D'Emilio, 1994; Meyer, 1992, 1996). These strategies, along with the hegemony of psychological and psychiatric theories of homosexual causation, sociological theories of "deviance," and the unfounded association of gay men with "child molestation" were part of a broader construction of the normalization of heterosexuality during these years, which was constructed relationally in response to various queer "threats."

---

[14] The Lesbians Making History Collective, (1989 Spring). "People Think This Didn't Happen in Canada," *Fireweed*, No. 28, 84. I also interviewed Lois for this research on February 22, 1995. See Kinsman and Gentile, *"In the Interests of the State,"* pp. 50–51.

By the 1960s in Canada, there was an uneven shift in official regulatory strategy towards a liberal public/private strategy of sexual regulation. The 1957 British *Wolfenden Report* on homosexuality and prostitution articulated a new strategy of sexual and moral regulation oriented around public/private and adult/youth distinctions. This conceptual framework was developed at a level of abstraction that allowed it to be applied to a number of sexual and moral related terrains, especially female prostitution and male homosexuality. This established a limited realm of "private" morality (basically behind bedroom doors) which was not always to be directly regulated by the criminal law. In this narrow space, homosexual acts were to become a personal moral question and homosexual acts between two consenting adults were to be decriminalized. At the same time, a much more expansive terrain of "public" morality was to lead to a clamping down on "public" expressions of homosexual eroticism and female prostitution. In relation to homosexual acts, those in "private" and those involving two individuals aged 21 and over ("adults") were to be decriminalized. Those in "public" or those involving anyone under 21 ("youth") were to continue to be highly policed. A very strong heterosexist "public" morality continued. This Wolfenden approach, which was enacted in Canada in 1969, led to only a partial decriminalization of homosexual acts. Heterosexual hegemony was held in place while it was at the same time modified and shifted. This liberal strategy gained cogency, establishing a certain resiliency in the face of the growing inability of moral conservative strategies of regulation to handle sexual and moral contradictions in the face of dramatic transformations in sex and gender and other social relations in the postwar years. Early gay activists in Canada in the 1960s like the Association for Social Knowledge tried to use the Wolfenden approach to open up a space for criminal law reform and popular education. This space was narrowed when the 1969 reform took place which reduced the popular education around homosexuality these groups were undertaking to questions of whether homosexual sex was in "private" or in "public."

When implemented in Canada, the Wolfenden approach was linked to a sickness conceptualization of homosexuality. Supporters of this approach argued that homosexuals who engaged in acts with only one other consenting adult in "private" were no longer criminals but were sick. Rather than being locked away in jail they should be under a doctors or a therapists care (Kinsmen, 1996). The passage of the 1969 reform did nothing in the short term to lessen the national security campaigns against gay men and lesbians. Even though the national security campaign was shaped by the total criminalization of homosexual activity it was not dependent on it. Even when some homosexual acts were decriminalized these homosexuals could still be considered to be suffering from a "character weakness," which meant they had something to hide and therefore they were still vulnerable to compromise and were "risks" to national security.

RESISTANCE AND ETHICS

The security campaign encountered difficulties in the 1960s from the non-cooperation of the gay informants they relied on for information in identifying homosexuals. As we will see this resistance had a social and ethical basis to it. In 1962 to 1963 the RCMP reported that,

> During the past fiscal year the homosexual screening program…was hindered by the lack of cooperation on the part of homosexuals approached as sources. Persons of this type, who had hitherto been our most consistent and productive informers, have exhibited an increasing reluctance to identify their homosexual friends and associates… (Directorate of Security and Intelligence Annual Report, 1962–1963, p. 19)

These people began to engage in practices similar to that reported by Harold earlier in this chapter. They began to place loyalty to their gay friends and lovers above those of Canadian "security" interests and the RCMP. In 1963–64 the *Annual Report of the Security Service* reported,

> During the year the investigation to identify homosexuals employed in or by the Federal Government resulted in initial interviews with twenty-one homosexuals, four of whom proved to be uncooperative, and re-interviews with twenty-two previously cooperative homosexuals, seven of whom declined to extend further cooperation. (p. 30)

They seem rather frustrated at encountering this growing opposition. They constructed a distinction between "cooperative" and "un-cooperative" homosexuals to try to deal with this situation of growing non-cooperation. This was related to the process of constructing the RCMP/informant relation and the rating of the usefulness of homosexual informants. Clearly with the growth of forms of resistance and non-cooperation, previously cooperative homosexuals were moving into the uncooperative classification. This was an important dividing line for RCMP work and only those homosexuals designated to be "cooperative" would be helpful in producing the "confirmed" homosexuals the RCMP was after.

The other side of this "lack of cooperation" is in part described by David [May 12, 1994]. David was not a civil servant but was involved in gay networks in Ottawa in the 1960s. David's involvement in the security investigations began when a friend gave the RCMP his name during a park sweep. David was interrogated by the RCMP, he was followed, and his place was searched.

A gay RCMP officer who was later cashiered had earlier given David some advice on what to do if he was interrogated that he found quite useful. His account gives us a clear sense of awareness of the security campaign in the networks he participated in from about 1964 on. David describes two situations that I report here. The first regards men with cameras taking pictures of gay men in the

Lord Elgin Hotel, and the second the response of a group of young gays to being pulled in by the RCMP.

David reported that gay men who hung out in the tavern in the basement of the Lord Elgin, which had became a gay meeting spot before the early 1960s, encountered police-organized surveillance. As David described this situation,

> we even knew occasionally that there was somebody in some police force or some investigator who would be sitting in a bar....And you would see someone with a...newspaper held right up and if you...looked real closely you could find him holding behind the newspaper a camera and these people were photographing everyone in the bar. As a matter of fact, when my RCMP friend was about to be cashiered from the RCMP he was shown pictures that had been taken in the bar—that is the tavern downstairs in the Lord Elgin Hotel—of everybody and you could see the vantage point at which the person had been sitting behind a newspaper and taking pictures. He said there were pictures of everybody including myself sitting there having a drink....The thing is you could even tell where the person had been sitting from the views of the walls and the people who were there and he was asked to name all the people at the various tables.

This is one way the RCMP collected information on homosexuals and part of the relations of surveillance it organized. What is most remarkable, however, is how David then described the response of the men in the bar to this surveillance.

> We always said that when you saw someone with a newspaper held up in front of their face...that somebody would take out something like a wallet and do this sort of thing [like snapping a photo] and then of course everyone would then point over to the person you see and of course I'm sure that the person hiding behind the newspaper knew that he had been found out. But that was the thing. You would take out a wallet or a package of matches or something like that...—it was always sort of a joke. You would see somebody...and you would catch everyone's eye and you would go like this [snapping a photo]. And everyone knew watch out for this guy....But the thing is that we were often quite aware that there was somebody in there that was taking pictures.

David's account gives us a glimpse of non-cooperation and resistance to the security investigations as well as a resistance strategy of exposing and mocking the security campaign. During our discussion David also described a group of young gay men who were detained by the RCMP.

> One group of about seven friends all got pulled in....All were asked to give names. They all said "I know the following people" and gave the names of the other six. And the next person would give the names of the other six. All they [the RCMP] did was get that one circle of names.

David described how these young men thought they had outwitted the RCMP since they had only given information to them that they already had and had not revealed the names of any other gays. By giving them some names this also meant they would be released. We also get a clear sense from this story of how the "cooperation" that the RCMP did manage to get was sometimes produced.

Michael, a civilian employee of the military and then a non-civil servant who was interrogated by the RCMP in the 1960s, stated that the advice in the gay networks he was familiar with was to say nothing to the RCMP about people's names or identities and "if anybody did give anything they were ostracized." There was a clear ethical position of not giving names in the gay networks of which he was part. If this position was violated, a response was organized against the person who had violated the ethical code within the gay networks of the day. Michael also reported that when he was left alone in the interrogation room with one RCMP officer that officer said,

> "'is it true that you are a homosexual?" and I said "yes!" And he looked at me and I said, "is it true that you ride side saddle?" and he laughed and that almost ended the interview. I mean, my intent was there, don't bother me any more, because I began to get the impression that it was a witch hunt. It was a real witch hunt. [July 15, 1994]

These stories of elementary resistance are very informative in beginning to flesh out the social organization of the "non-cooperation" mentioned in the RCMP texts. The response in the Lord Elgin suggested that people went beyond exposing the officer; they were able to turn the tables on him so to speak. It also was a way of making fun of him and the security and police campaigns, using humour and camp as a way to survive. Camp sensibility and humour, which plays with elements of incongruity and theatricality and at times the glorification of female stars, is a cultural form produced by gay men to manage and negotiate the contradictions between our particular experiences of the world as gays and the institutionalized heterosexuality that hegemonizes social relations. It can provide a creative way of dealing with social stigma—a way of fully embracing it, thereby neutralizing it and making it laughable. A crucial part of this cultural formation is to denaturalize normality and heterosexuality by making fun of it. As David says "I think that the way people coped with the whole situation of surveillance and harassment and so on was basically to make the best of it. And turn it as much as possible into a humorous situation…" [May 12, 1994]. People had enough of a sense of themselves and the expanding queer networks and community formation they participated in to engage in these collective and individual acts of defiance. The social basis for this non-cooperation and resistance was the expanding social spaces queers came to occupy in the 1960s and the expansion of queer networks, community formation, solidarity, and queer talk, within and around these spaces.

In contrast to the attempt within ruling moral regulation to portray homosexuality as a moral problem and a national security risk, what we see here is that moral regulation becomes a contested terrain with some gay men and lesbians challenging the basis of this campaign by refusing to give the names of other homosexuals. In developing an ethics of resistance they placed their erotic, emotional, and social ties to their friends and other homosexuals, and their loyalty to other queers, above the interests of "national security." The ethics developed within these gay networks had a very different character to it than the moral regulation driving the national security campaigns. I choose the expression ethics of resistance deliberately here since ethics has a rather different connotation than morals and morality.

Ruling forms of moral regulation—or "morality from above"—tends to rely on moral rules that are portrayed ideologically as being absolute, law-like, and historical. The conceptualization of "character weakness" for instance views unreliability and subversion as inherent in the homosexual character. The ethics of resistance developed "from below" by Harold, David, and others in contrast has much more of an affective, erotic, contextual, social, and historical character, as well as being more clearly self-made by the oppressed themselves in resistance to ruling forms of regulation. Mariana Valverde once explored the important differences between morality and ethics in relation to the feminist sex debates of the early 1980s:

> It would be a contradiction in terms to develop a "feminist morality," a code of rights and wrongs based on some arbitrary notion of individual feminist virtue. But while the term "morality" suggests both rigidity and individualism, the term "ethics" is more suited to the kind of approach that feminists need. Ethics connotes reasoning about values and actions; it connotes discussion and community. Ethics also suggests the development of guidelines, and not so much the drawing up of a rigid code that would substitute for the process of reasoning and discussion. A feminist sexual ethics would be based on the recognition of sexual diversity… (1985, p. 203–204)

What we need is not a new morality or moral code but an ethics of resistance and social transformation that provides us with a basis for discussion and guidelines for practice that allows us to resist ruling forms of moral and social regulation and can clarify how we as individuals and as communities can make decisions that lead us towards more democratic control over our own lives, and which undermine oppression and inequality. In the early resistance to the national security campaigns by gay men and lesbians in Canada we see the generation of an ethics of resistance that allowed some gay men and lesbians to place their ties to other queers above the needs of "national security." This provided a basis for them to refuse to cooperate with the security police.

SUMMARY: NATIONAL SECURITY AS MORAL REGULATION AND NORMALIZATION AND ITS CURRENT RELEVANCE

In summing up this investigation, I draw some conclusions about the relation between national security and strategies of moral regulation and normalization. First of all from this investigation we can clearly see the "moral" character of the construction of the "nation" and state formation—of Canada and Canadianness. The conceptualizations of "national security," "security risk," and "character weakness" rely on notions of moral character that participate in constantly constructing the moral and the immoral and the normal/deviant. In this sense national security *is* moral regulation and national security *is* an important strategy of normalization. Second, the national security campaigns played an important part in constructing homosexuality as against the nation—as "immoral," "risky" and "abnormal" while at the very same time constructing heterosexuality as moral, safe and normal—as the national sexuality. This was a central aspect of the Canadian Cold war and the national security campaigns in Canadian state and social formation. National security was therefore an important part of sexual regulation more generally during these years and was also closely related to the management of gender relations.

These anti-queer national security practices have also shaped our historical present. They have had a lasting and active impact in constructing lesbians and gays as immoral, as deviant, as risks, as a danger, as being unreliable workers, and in the organization of employment discrimination and the construction of the social relations of the closet which still shape and constrain many of our lives in the present. The national security campaigns against queers are not yet over and other targets have also been selected for national security surveillance.

The moral regulation and normalization of the national security campaigns also became a contested terrain, with some gay men and lesbians able to engage in acts of non-cooperation and resistance. Even within major social constraints and prior to the development of gay and lesbian movements, some gay men and lesbians were able to engage in limited acts of resistance and were able to generate an ethics of resistance that disputed the logic of the national security campaigns. Viewing moral regulation as a contested terrain and seeing how resistance takes on ethical forms give us insights and resources for our continuing struggles against oppression in the present.

Most recently Canadian state agencies have produced the anti-capitalist globalization or global justice movement (Cockburn, St. Clair, & Seluka, 2000; Klein, 2000; McNally, 2002) from the protests against the Asia Pacific Economic Cooperation (APEC) meetings in Vancouver in 1997 to the protests against the Free Trade Area of the Americas (FTAA) in Quebec City in April 2001, to the protests against the meetings of the G8 countries in 2002, as threats to "national security." This has mandated forms of police repression and violence against protestors from pepper spray, tear gas, and plastic and rubber bullets. Here "national security" gets defined by the international trade and investment agreements into which the Canadian state enters. In relation to the protests against the FTAA, the focus has been especially against "anarchists" by the Canadian Security and Intelligence Service (CSIS—which took over security work from the discredited RCMP in the 1980s), state officials, and much of the mainstream media. In part this is done by associating the global justice movement with "violence" even though it is state agencies directing police repression against demonstrators and inflicting institutional and social violence against poor people around the world. In response, a new ethics of resistance based in civil disobedience and direct action that places responsibility to oppressed and poor people, people in "third world" countries, to the environment, and to more direct forms of democracy above those of loyalty to the Canadian state, has emerged. We have a lot to learn from the struggles of the past in dislodging these contemporary forms of national security and in challenging the moral regulation and normalization strategies that would read global justice protestors out of the national social fabric as "deviant" and "immoral."

Thanks to Lynne Dupuis for her assistance on this chapter and to Patrizia Gentile for her collaboration in the research on the Canadian national security campaigns against gay men and lesbians. Also, thanks to the reviewers and to Deborah Brock, for their comments.

CRITICAL THINKING QUESTIONS

1. Why is sexual regulation such a key terrain for moral regulation?
2. Who defines what national security is?
3. How does "national security" operate to deny, or cut some people off from their democratic rights?
4. Why and how were gay men and lesbians seen to be "a threat to national security"?
5. How did the national security campaigns strengthen the social relations of "the closet"?
6. What is the relation between notions of character and moral regulation?
7. What are the problems with labelling groups of people as "deviant"?
8. Why do we need to challenge the relations of "normality"?

SUGGESTED READINGS

Philip Corrigan and Derek Sayer (1985). *The Great Arch: English State Formation as Cultural Revolution*. Oxford: Basil Blackwell

An important exploration of state formation as cultural revolution. This focuses on the moral character of state regulation in the context of English state formation.

Foucault, Michel (1980). *The History of Sexuality, Volume One: An Introduction*. New York: Vintage.
A powerful analysis of the historical emergence of sexuality and the relations between social power and sexuality. A very useful critique of the hypothesis that our sexualities have been simply "repressed" by forms of social power.

Foucault, Michel (1979). *Discipline and Punish, The Birth of the Prison*. New York: Vintage Books/Random House.
In this insightful historical-social analysis of the emergence of the prison and contemporary notions of criminal justice, Foucault outlines the emergence of new forms of disciplinary power based on social surveillance, examination and normalization.

Kinsman, Gary (1996). *The Regulation of Desire: Homo and Hetero Sexualities*. Montreal: Black Rose.
A historical-sociological investigation of the relational emergence of homosexualities and heterosexualities in the Canadian context including some analysis of the national security campaigns against gay men and lesbians.

Kinsman, Gary, Dieter K. Buse and Mercedes Steedman, eds. (2000). *Whose National Security? Canadian State Surveillance and the Creation of Enemies*. Toronto: Between the Lines.
A collection that addresses many of the groups that have come under national security surveillance in Canada, including gay men and lesbians. This book tries to extend and broaden our analysis of the impact of national security and develops a profound challenge to the ideology and practice of national security.

Smith, Dorothy E. (1987). *The Everyday World as Problematic: A Feminist Sociology*. Toronto: University of Toronto Press.
In this book Dorothy Smith develops a sociology for women and her alternative way of doing sociology—called institutional ethnography.

Smith, Dorothy E. (1999). *Writing the Social, Critique, Theory, and Investigations*. Toronto: University of Toronto Press.
In this book Dorothy Smith investigates the text-mediated organization of social relations and moves further in getting us to see how we can write the social without reifying (or "thingifying") the social worlds around us.

WEB LINKS

muse.jhu.edu/journals/sex/
The Journal of the History of Sexuality, and its companion Web site, contains historical and cross-cultural articles, which are critical and theoretical. It is multidisciplinary in character, making it a useful resource for researchers across a range of fields.

muse.jhu.edu/journals/glq/
GLQ: A Journal of Lesbian and Gay Studies is an interdisciplinary journal that publishes scholarship, criticism, and commentary from a range of diverse areas, including literary studies, history, law, science, religion, and political studies.

CHAPTER 8

STRIPTEASE ON THE LINE: INVESTIGATING TRENDS IN FEMALE EROTIC ENTERTAINMENT

BY BECKI L. ROSS

THE COMMERCIAL SEX INDUSTRY[1]

Today, the **commercial sex industry** in North America openly flouts taboos in order to capitalize on an increasingly public appetite for erotic stimulation. More than ever, sex sells. The production and consumption of erotic goods and services generates billions of dollars in revenues, and reflects the slow liberalization of community standards. Sexual underworlds are mined in the Hollywood films *Leaving Las Vegas* (1995), *Striptease* (1996), *Boogie Nights* (1997), and *Eyes Wide Shut* (1999). The December 1998 issue of *Playboy* magazine featured a ten-page spread of Olympic champion figure skater Katarina Witt, tastefully nude. Women read the evening news on the Internet while gradually disrobing inside a downtown Toronto studio for four million viewers monthly (Hampson, 2001, pp. R1, R4). "Drive-through stripping" is sold to customers in cars at the Climax Gentlemen's club in Delmont, Pennsylvannia. The Dangerettes in Toronto and Fluffgirl and Empire Burlesque Productions in Vancouver recently launched their revival of the mystery and the magic of 1950s **burlesque** revues, complete with pasties, g-strings, and live orchestras (Izzo, 2000; Carlson, 2002; Gill, 2002; Ross 2002). And in California, a troupe of 70- and 80-year old women—the Fabulous Palm Springs Follies—parades around in little more than sequins, feathers, and stiletto heels, and charms audiences from around the world (Bramham, 2001, p. A16). While

---

[1] This research is generously supported by the Canadian government's Social Sciences and Humanities Research Council grant, 1999-2002. An earlier version of this chapter was published in *Labour/le travail* 46 (Fall 2000). I am pleased to acknowledge the excellent research assistance of Kim Greenwell and Michelle Swann, both of whom made a commitment to the "Striptease Project" well above and beyond the terms of their employment contract. My sincere thanks to all the women and men we've interviewed so far, whose plentiful stories impel me to keep going.

some condemn all varieties of sexual entertainment as a threat to family values, and others trumpet the end of sexual puritanism, the brisk sale and purchase of sex-related commodities is a cultural phenomenon that invites social scientific inquiry.

Given the scope and innovative nature of women's and men's employment in the commercial sex industry, it seems surprising that scholars have paid so little attention to studying "the business." In Canada, labour studies specialists have tended to focus on the injustices of structural unemployment, ugly conflicts between workers and management, the exploitation of non-Anglo immigrants, the consolidation of a gender-segmented labour force, declining rates of unionization, and deepening class schisms, as flagrant, wretched features of capitalist social formation (Palmer, 1983; Heron & Storey, 1986; Kealey, 1995; Bercuson & Bright, 1994; Iacovetta, 1994; Parr, 1990; Creese, 1999; Heron, 1998; Sangster, 1995; Smith & Wakewich, 1999). Contributors to the expanding field of sexuality studies have explored the histories of homosexuality, bisexuality, and heterosexuality, as well as the formation of sexual communities, and the emergence of state and extra-state campaigns to police the "sexually indecent" and the "sexually dangerous" (Kinsman, 1996, 2000; Maynard, 1997; Adams, 1997; Dubinsky, 1999; Chauncey, 1994; Kennedy & Davis, 1993; Chamberland, 1996). However, fruitful intercourse between the research fields of "labour" and "sexuality" remains under-developed.

What we know is that for centuries in North America, largely white, heterosexual, monied men have had the means to define what they want sexually, how, and when they've wanted it. Both married and unmarried, wealthy and working class, white and non-white, men have made payments for a variety of sex-related interactions with women.[2] It has been predominantly working-class white women and women of colour who have enabled the carnal appetites and fantasies of men, or lubricated them, through their paid labour.[3] Yet there is a dearth of substantive, in-depth analysis of women's complex, lived experiences as sex workers—prostitutes, escort service workers, peep show performers, massage parlour workers, pin-up/pornography models, telephone sex workers, burlesque dancers, and stripteasers (for exceptions see Walkowitz, 1980, 1992; Rotenberg, 1974; Rosen, 1982; Nilsen, 1980; Bell, 1994, 1995; Roberts, 1992; Riley, 1997; Kish, 1997; Scott, 1996; Brock, 1998; Pheterson, 1989, 1996; Dudash, 1997; Lewis, 1998; Liepe-Levinson, 2002; Wood, 1999; Burana, 2001; Ross, 2000).

---

[2] The act of men paying men/male youth for sexual services has a long, compelling history; due to constraints of time and money, it is not a topic of consideration here.

[3] This is not to discount the uneven and complex sexual exchanges between young, largely working-class boys and older men. On this subject, see the superb essay by Steven Maynard. (1997 June). "Horrible Temptations": Sex, Men and Working Class Male Youth in Urban Ontario, 1890-1935. *Canadian Historical Review 78*, 191-235.

Unveiling Striptease: The Past as a Window on the Present

This chapter unravels the complicated entanglements of sexuality, gender, race, labour, and social class in the history of twentieth century striptease, or erotic entertainment, in North America. A subset of the larger sex industry, striptease was, and is, a significant employment category for women, though absent from Canada Census data. Preliminary archival and ethnographic findings from my case study on burlesque and striptease culture in Vancouver, British Columbia, 1945–1980,[4] uncover the working conditions and artistic influences of former dancers, the racialized expectations of erotic spectacle, and the **queer** dimensions of strip culture. Anti-racist/post-colonial theorists such as Edward Said and Anne McClintock, and queer theorists such as Judith Butler, help me to scrutinize assumptions about striptease as a primarily white, heterosexual industry.

Some feminist theorists argue that the female sex worker symbolizes the quintessential victim of patriarchal coercion and control in a man's world: she's a degraded and exploited pawn (Millett, 1973; Wynter, 1987, Dolan, 1988, Mackinnon, 1993). In fact, over the past twenty years, the disappearance and presumed murder of at least sixty-eight women who lived and worked in Vancouver's downtown eastside—many of them working as prostitutes, and most of whom were First Nations, drug-users, and poor—graphically attests to sex workers' vulnerability to harm (see Wood, 1999). Yet while evidence of sometimes dangerous, oppressive working conditions exists, I maintain that the self-determined agency of female sex workers, specifically erotic dancers, has been largely overlooked. The voices of vendors (and buyers) of erotic services have been solicited only rarely; and recognition of sex-related work *as work* has eluded influential feminist scholars. So, in contrast to feminist research that judges female sex workers as disempowered dupes, I propose a competing feminist framework, following the lead of sociologist Dorothy E. Smith (1987), that places the everyday, local experiences of "business insiders" in burlesque/striptease—dancers, choreographers, club owners, booking agents, and musicians—at the centre of inquiry.

---

[4] There is an important sociological literature that focuses on the business of striptease or "exotic dancing" in the 1980s and 1990s, though much of the work is uncritically rooted in the tradition of the sociology of deviance. See Craig Forsyth & Tina Deshotels (1998). A Deviant Process: The Sojourn of the Stripper, *Sociological Spectrum*, 18, 77–92; William Thompson & Jackie Harred (1992). Topless Dancers: Managing Stigma in a Deviant Occupation, *Deviant Behaviour 13*, 291–311; Scott Reid, Jonathon Epstein, & D.E. Benson (1995). Does Exotic Dancing Pay Well But Cost Dearly? In A. Thio and T. Calhoun, (Eds.), *Readings in Deviant Behaviour.* (pp. 284–288). New York; and G.E. Enck and J.D. Preston (1988). Counterfeit Intimacy: A Dramaturgical Analysis of an Erotic Performance, *Deviant Behaviour, 9*, 360–381.

I am inspired by the contributions of activist female sex workers, primarily in the geo-political North, who have found resources to write their own illuminating tales of accommodation *and* resistance (Scott, Miller & Hotchkiss, 1987; St. James, 1987; Delacoste & Alexander, 1987; Pheterson, 1989, 1996; Highcrest, 1997; Nagle, 1997; Chapkis, 1997; Feindel, 1988; Dudash, 1997; Scott, 2001; Burana, 2001). Self-claimed feminists, they have begun to chronicle their challenges to grinding stereotypes, their efforts to combine sex-related labour with familial intimacy, their fights against "bad dates," their battles against the regulatory practices of police, politicians, and moral reformers, and their spirited bids to organize and unionize, among other measures of resistance. Their stories illuminate contradictions unique to the trade. For instance, unlike female cannery workers, fishers, bakers, stenographers, child-minders, and retail clerks, women who earned income performing striptease in the 1950s found themselves at once desired *and* criminalized, or at the very least, scorned and marginalized in disturbing ways.

Insiders in the business of burlesque/striptease have always been the "expert practitioners" of their own lives, hence probing the meanings they attach to their craft promises rich sociological insights (Smith, 1987, p. 154). Indeed, to grasp the complex social organization of institutions, i.e., policing, liquor licensing, mass media, and law-making, I begin from the standpoint of insiders whose lives were intimately enmeshed in what Smith terms extra-local relations of ruling (1987, pp. 107–111). Moral and social regulation theory developed by Michel Foucault (1980), Philip Corrigan & Derek Sayer (1981, 1985), Mariana Valverde (1988, 2000), Joan Sangster (1996), Carolyn Strange & Tina Loo (1997), Deborah Brock (1998), and others, also helps us to analyze why and how burlesque/striptease has been produced, at different times, as a social problem in need of state and extra-state supervision. Adapting Sangster (1996), moral regulation in the context of postwar striptease involved processes whereby some behaviours, ideals, and values were marginalized and proscribed, while others were legitimized and naturalized (p. 241). These processes were, explains Sangster, "central to social relations of power, reinforcing dominance and subjection" (pp. 241–242).

Because the business of striptease has changed so dramatically since the early 1980s, I elected to return to the postwar decades in order to shed light on the enduring appeal *and* the enduring stigmatization of "bump and grind." My entrée into the dynamics of striptease after World War II from a feminist, anti-racist perspective, wedges open a window onto deep-seated cultural anxieties about gender and sexual norms, popular amusements, and racial otherness. The chapter ends with comments about the intersection of sex and the Canadian nation in the history of erotic entertainment.

> ## "THE BUSINESS OF STRIPTEASE RE-INVENTS ITSELF FOR THE NEW MILLENNIUM"
>
> The business of burlesque/striptease has changed dramatically in the past twenty years. Reflecting on her exit from the business in 1980, Montreal-based dancer Lindalee Tracey (1997) observes, "Striptease fell from grace because the world stopped dreaming" (p. 210). After 1980 across North America, we see the move away from big, expensive production numbers, the introduction of "spreading," table dancing, lap dancing, private booths and, in several American cities, "stage fees" paid by dancers to work in nightclubs. Lap dancing was declared "indecent and illegal" in a Supreme Court of Canada ruling in 1997, however, municipalities have unevenly enforced the law (see Lewis, 1998, 2000). In the 1980s and 1990s the business of striptease stepped-up its marketing and merchandising through the sale of videos, the advent of contests such as the Miss Golden G-String (Las Vegas, 1983), and the emergence of magazines by and for erotic dancers such as Danzine (Portland, Oregon). Once absent from the club owners' circle, women like entrepreneur Brandi Sarionder are infiltrating the male-dominated world of strip bars. Sarionder opened Vancouver-based "Brandi's" in 2000, and has plans to expand her successful "exotic nightclub" to Palm Springs, California in 2002 (Chow, 2001, pp. B5, B10). Since 1980, there has been an explosion of Internet sites featuring live strip shows on-line. It wasn't until the early 1990s that we see the first successful effort to unionize—the Lusty Lady Theater in San Francisco. And over the past twenty years, a global migrant labour force has emerged: dancers from Canada, the U.S., Eastern Europe, Japan, Thailand, the Philippines, Australia, and Latin America criss-cross national borders, some with more employment options than others.

NICE GIRLS, SMART GIRLS, GOOD GIRLS DO NOT DISROBE IN PUBLIC

Female burlesque, go-go, and striptease have been perceived by religious, civic, and moral reformers as commercialized sexual vice that inflame men's passions (already fuelled by alcohol), propel them to seek adulterous liaisons, abandon their families, and jeopardize their workplace productivity (Corio, 1968; McCaghy & Skipper, 1972; Allen, 1991; Jarrett, 1997). For almost a century, popular conflations of striptease with nymphomania, illiteracy, drug addiction, prostitution, and disease labelled female erotic performers dangerous to the social order, the family, and nation-building (see Skipper & McCaghy, 1970, 1971).

In the 1920s and 1930s, striptease within the broad rubric of burlesque was a unique combination of sexual humour and female sexual display, with a focus on sexual suggestiveness aided by the "tease" factor (Allen, 1991, p. 244). Historian Andrea Friedman (1996) notes, "The key to the striptease was not how much a woman stripped, but how much the people in the audience thought she stripped, as well as how successfully she encouraged their desire that she strip" (p. 204). It was maintenance of the illusion of nudity that afforded the business some legal protection from obscenity laws. Italian American Ann Corio (1968), a stripteaser throughout the 1930s, remembers incidences of state power over sexual representation, and the tricks employed to safeguard illicit shows,

> [At the Howard Theatre in Boston], once the ticket-taker saw the censor coming up the stairs, he pressed his foot on a pedal. On stage, the show might be in full production. A stripper might be giving her all for mankind, shimmying and grinding. Clothes might be flying in all directions. The crowd would be yelling, "Take it off," and the music might be crashing to a crescendo. Suddenly a red light would start blinking in the footlights. A censor had arrived….Imagine Mickey Mantle trying to stop in the middle of his swing. That's what those stormy strippers would have to do….Red light! Hold it! The hips would stop as if paralyzed. Those clothes would come flying back from the wings. The perspiring musicians would dissolve to a waltz. And by the time the censor reached the top of the stairs and looked down on the stage he would see—not a hip-swinging, hair-tossing, half-naked tigress—but a nun on a casual stroll through a most unlikely convent. (p. 175)

Friedman (1996) shows how a decade-long campaign against burlesque waged in New York by religious, anti-vice, and municipal activists, including Mayor LaGuardia, resulted in a city-wide ban on burlesque entertainment in 1937. Friedman's research also suggests that anxieties about the disorderliness and immorality of the male burlesque audience were at the heart of contests to eradicate sexual entertainment in New York in the 1930s (p. 237). By 1942, every burlesque theatre licence in the Big Apple was revoked on the grounds that the shows promoted filth, vulgarity, immorality, and male sexual violence (pp. 235, 238). In effect, anti-burlesque initiatives were part of a larger set of strategies to regulate the sexual content of commercial culture, which included motion pictures, crime comics, and "smutty" magazines. Ironically, as Marilyn Hegarty (1998) notes, some mainstream American magazines during World War II featured "sizzling" female dancehall and canteen entertainers in g-strings as morale builders for the troops. For a brief moment, the nation's soldiers, and by extension the nation, depended on public displays of feminine (hetero) sexiness. However, the entertainers' patriotism remained suspect due to their "potential promiscuity" and "descent into prostitution" (p. 122).

STRIPTEASE AS A PUBLIC MORALITY PROBLEM

In the post World War II era, burlesque and striptease flourished in Canadian cities, especially Quebec's urban jewel, Montreal (Weintraub, 1996). On the west coast, in Vancouver, B.C., the subculture took root in blind pigs or afterhours booze cans, a handful of small nightclubs, and several mainstream theatres. Marketed as adult entertainment for locals and tourists in the port city, erotic performance was "most legal" and "most respectable" in large, soft-seat nightclubs such as the Cave Supper Club, the Penthouse Cabaret, and later, Isy's Supper Club in the affluent downtown core. Here, American swing bands, large-scale musicals, and big-name lounge acts routinely rehearsed in Vancouver before hitting the "big time" in Las Vegas. Another cluster of smaller Vancouver nightclubs (detailed below) also booked striptease in the postwar period in the working-class, ethnicized neighborhoods of Chinatown and Strathcona.

Clergy, public officials, women's groups, and police argued for the careful scrutiny of Vancouver's "low class" venues associated with the "criminal classes," and at different times mobilized a range of municipal by-laws, provincial liquor laws, and federal Criminal Code provisions to turn up the heat on unscrupulous hoteliers, nightclub owners, and dancers.[5]

Isy Walters outside his Vancouver supper club.

[5] Robert Campbell (1991). *Demon Rum or Easy Money: Government Control of Liquor in British Columbia from Prohibition to Privatization.* (pp. 50–55). Ottawa: Carleton University Press, argues that the B.C. Liquor Control Board enforced a "no food, no entertainment, no dancing" policy in Vancouver's beer parlours (in hotels), until 1954. Campbell points out that the Chief Inspector for the B.C. Liquor Board rejected applications for a liquor licence from Chinese in Vancouver, as it "has been found that Chinese are not able to handle this type of business" (p. 123).

The temperance-minded Vancouver Council of Women (VCW) actively endorsed the censorship of burlesque shows that promoted "looseness of thought" and "undermined the sacredness of home and marriage" ([1930], cited in Zumsteg, 1998, p.2). Indeed, striptease on the stages of quasi-legal, unlicensed **bottle clubs** (which themselves traded in the forbidden), and later, post-1970, when "bottomless" strip acts were legalized, contributed to the city's reputation as home to the hottest nightclubs north of San Francisco (Wasserman, 1971, p. A5).

In Vancouver in 1941, a special Police Delegation of religious and temperance leaders inspected the city's night spots: they were known as the "special constables," and were part of a long tradition of anthropological treatment of the city as, quoting Carolyn Strange (1995), "a laboratory full of troubling specimens of urban life" (p. 106). When they roamed city streets in search of flourishing vice both inside and adjacent to well-known red-light districts, they became social geographers, mapping the locations of moral evils. Upon visiting a local cabaret, Mrs. McKay of the Vancouver Local Council of Women, representing seventy-eight women's groups, told reporters for the *Vancouver News Herald,* "The floor show was objectionable, with girls naked except brassieres and loin clothes." Rev. Cook complained of "immoral conduct highly suggestive of Sodom and Gomorrah" (Anon., 1941, p. 10).

In 1951, the State Theatre, a popular burlesque hall in Vancouver's east end, had its licence suspended for presenting "an indecent strip act." Defending his decision, Licence Inspector Arthur Moore reminded the city council that members had agreed to ban all strip and burlesque shows in 1946. Moore reported that "a girl had taken off her clothing piece by piece until she was wearing semi-transparent brassiere and panties, and from the back rows, she appeared to be nude" (Anon., 1951, 19). Though the licence was quickly reissued by city councillors, the club was raided again in January 1952: two "exotic dancers" and a male comedian were arrested for "bumps and grinds and suggestive jokes" in "Holiday Spirits"—an "indecent show," and "cheesecake pictures were seized from the Theatre's marquee" (Anon., 1952, p. 1). Two weeks later, the three performers and two theatre owners were convicted in police court of "presenting an indecent vaudeville performance;" all five were fined and the Theatre's licence was revoked (Anon., 1952, p. 25).

In 1965, Tom Hazlitt of the *Vancouver Daily Province* commented, "The city's cabarets are crowded with bottle-packing juveniles. Drunkenness and fights are commonplace. So is drug addiction, prostitution, and erotic dancing of a bizarre nature. Some places are frequented by men who dress up as women and women who dress up as men" (p. A3). In 1966, reporter George Peloquin of the *Vancouver Sun* quoted the city's Chief Licence Inspector, Mitch Harrell, "Two cabarets were warned: the attire on their girls was too skimpy. One involved dancers with transparent, black chiffon blouses. The by-law forbids any person to produce in any building or place in the city any immoral or lewd theatrical performance of any kind" (p. A4). Ten years later, in 1976, the Attorney General's office instructed the B.C. Liquor Control Board to enforce a ban on "bare-breasted waitresses" in Vancouver nightclubs (p. A5). Well before 1980, striptease had emerged as a "sitting duck:" to quell fears of unchecked permissiveness, and to justify their own regulatory practices (and budgets), law enforcers and social reformers sought, through a variety of techniques, to administer burlesque/striptease as a social problem that called for normalizing interventions (see Foucault, 1980, p. 68).

THE PENTHOUSE CABARET: A FAVOURITE TARGET OF THE "BOYS IN BLUE"

The Penthouse Cabaret opened on Seymour St. in downtown Vancouver officially in 1951 (unofficially in 1947), and was owned and run by the Filippone brothers—Joe, Ross, Mickey, and Jimmy, and their sister Florence.[6] It started out as Joe's penthouse apartment where he privately entertained guests above the family's Diamond Cabs and Eagle Time Delivery service, and it was raided for liquor infractions the first night open. Still operating in 2002, and still run by members of the Filippone family, it is the longest-standing striptease venue in Canada. In 1968, reporter Alex MacGillivray wrote that The Penthouse was "a watering spot for bookies and brokers, doctors and dentists, guys and dolls, ladies and gentlemen, and just about anybody who could smell a good time" (p. A2). Show business celebrities such as Tony Bennett, Sophie Tucker, Sammy Davis Jr., Liberace, and Ella Fitzgerald entertained at the Penthouse, as did headlining stripteasers such as Sally Rand (the famous fan dancer), Evelyn West—the "Hubba Hubba Girl" (with breasts insured by Lloyds of London for $50,000), and the multi-talented Tempest Storm. Extravagant Las Vegas-style revues full of scantily-clad, plumed, and spangled showgirls were imported, and the burlesque acts were accompanied by live jazz and swing bands (Wiseman, 1982, p. 68). Until his death in 1983, Joe Filippone vowed that he never allowed total nudity on the stage at the Penthouse's Gold Room. All the dancers were cautioned to keep their g-strings firmly in place (Ibid., p. 27).

Between 1951 and 1968, nightspots like the Penthouse were strictly bottle clubs. Patrons brought bottled liquor to the club or purchased drinks from the illegal stash behind the bar, as well as a "set up"—a tray of mix and ice. In so doing, they made themselves vulnerable to police busts. According to Ross Filippone, his brother Joe arranged for a lookout on the roof who buzzed a waiter downstairs when he spotted the "Dry Squad." The waiter then warned patrons to hide their booze on built-in ledges under the tables, and to deny any wrong doing to the gun-and-holstered boys in blue. In 1968, after decades of lobbying by the

---

[6] Filippone is the anglicized version of the original Phillipponi, invented by a racist immigration officer when Joe (the eldest) and his parents arrived in British Columbia from San Nicola, Italy, in 1929.

West Coast Cabaret Owners Association, the Penthouse was finally awarded a liquor licence, which legalized liquor sales years after hotel parlours in the city had been granted the right to sell beer (by the glass).

Though the Filippone brothers prohibited full nudity on stage until the mid-1970s, the Penthouse quickly earned a reputation as the best place in the city to meet elite sex workers who frequented the club, bought food and drinks, and charmed a loyal clientele of tourists and locals (Wood, 1997, p. 104). In December 1975, after a five-month-long undercover operation, the Filippone brothers, a cashier, and a doorman were charged with living off the avails of prostitution and conspiring to corrupt public morals. According to a cover story in *Dick MacLean's Guide* (1978), "the full operation, which involved 12 officers, included surveillance by means of electronic eavesdropping devices, hidden cameras, motor vehicle surveillance, and male officers entering the club to pose as prostitutes' clients" (pp. 112–15). Finally, in 1978, after a forced, padlocked closure lasting two-and-a-half years, convictions, fines, appeals, and $1.5 million in litigation fees, all of the accused were acquitted, and the Penthouse reopened their doors (Didon, 1978, pp. 1–3, Mackie 2001, p. E5).[7]

Although Vancouver nightclubs were never closed down en masse à la New York City in 1942, hotspots like the State Theatre, Penthouse Cabaret, Smilin' Buddha, and Cafe Kobenhavn were consistently under the gaze of moral and legal authorities, scapegoated as dens of immorality, obscenity, and indecency. Dancers periodically suffered from lost access to performance venues when the State Theatre and the Penthouse were forced to shut down, and competition for jobs in the business stiffened. Stripteasers were commonly assumed to moonlight as prostitutes, and they were never exempted from the scrutiny of those who damned nightclubs as the playgrounds of gangsters, bootleggers, bookies, pimps, hookers, and sex fiends. Not surprisingly, dancers were vulnerable to charges of "gross indecency" when they staged acts in spaces already targeted by police for sales of illegal liquor and gambling. In the postwar era, the common-sense equation of "booze + nudity = immorality" afforded Vancouver law enforcers significant discretion and disciplinary power to patrol the city's nightclubs. Dancers' bodies, to apply Foucault (1980), were insistently observed, caressed, and contacted by powers vested with the authority to adjudicate "the healthy" vs. "the pathological" (p. 44). As a result, dancers were compelled to practice self-regulation and self-surveillance, at once balancing the threat of morality officers with, and against, club owners' expectations for displays of more and more flesh.

---

[7] John Lowman, (1986) in Street Prostitution in Vancouver: Some Notes on the Genesis of a Social Problem, *Canadian Journal of Criminology* 28, convincingly argues that the closure of the Penthouse Cabaret in 1975, combined with the closure of other off-street prostitution venues in Vancouver, played a decisive role in the spread of street prostitution, and hence the increased vulnerability of sex workers to violence and murder (pp. 1–16). Deborah Brock charts a similar process in Toronto in 1977 following the crackdown on Yonge Street massage parlours (1998).

WORKING CONDITIONS: THE GOOD, THE BAD, THE UGLY

Headliners Sally Rand, Gypsy Rose Lee, the "Glamazon" Ricki Covette, Lili St. Cyr: "Queen of the Strippers," and Tempest Storm, performed in Vancouver during the 1950s, 1960s, and 1970s. They each netted top price —upwards of $4,000 per week even when they were over forty, which was more than a woman earned in any other job category (Jarrett, 1997, p. 170). However, a handsome pay cheque did not necessarily translate into respect. In 1969, American sociologists Jesser and Donovan (1969) interviewed 155 university students and 122 parents of students, all of whom assigned stripteasers a lower occupational ranking than what were seen to be traditionally low-status jobs: janitor, artist's model, and professional gambler (p. 356). Interviews I conducted with fourteen former dancers in Vancouver, B.C., suggest that female erotic dancers who performed in Vancouver clubs such as the Penthouse and the Cave, and later, the Number 5 Orange Hotel, the Drake Hotel, and the Cecil Hotel, negotiated salary and working conditions in a stigmatized, male-controlled profession.[8]

Table 8.1 on the following page profiles fourteen former dancers I interviewed, though the data does not reflect a representative sample. Among these women, four of whom are women of colour, the youngest entered the business as early as 16 and the oldest at 26, with an average age of 20.1. Their careers as dancers averaged 9.5 years. Nine of the 14 women (64%) had no dance training: they learned on the job. A surprisingly high number—eight dancers (57%)—worked past the age of thirty, which is rare in today's youth-driven market. Only five of 14 (36%) raised children while working in striptease: almost two-thirds elected either to postpone or to forgo motherhood altogether. In **Table 8.2** on page 158, only four women

---

[8] For a selection of autobiographical writings on striptease from 1970 to 2002, see Misty, (1973). *Strip!* Toronto; Janet Feindel, (1988). *A Particular Class of Woman*, Vancouver; Margaret Dragu and A.S.A. Harrison, (1988). *Revelations: Essays on Striptease and Sexuality*, London; Annie Ample, (1988). *The Bare Facts: My Life as a Stripper*, Toronto; Lindalee Tracey, (1997). *Growing Up Naked: My Years in Bump and Grind*, Vancouver; Diana Atkinson, (1995). *Highways and Dancehalls*, Toronto; Shannon Bell, Ed.) (1995). *Whore Carnival*, New York; Gwendolyn, (1992). Nothing Butt: The Truth about the Sex Trade. *Toward the Slaughterhouse of History* (pp.16–23) Toronto; Chris Bearchell, (February 1986). No Apologies: Strippers as the Upfront Line in a Battle to Communicate. *The Body Politic*, 123, 26–29; Kim Derko, (Spring/Summer 1991). A High-Heeled Point of View. *Independent Eye*, 12, 1–8; Sasha, "Taking it Off is One Thing…," *The Globe and Mail* (January 22, 2000), A15; Merri Lisa Johnson, (1999). Pole Work: Autoethnography of a Strip Club. In Barry Dank and Roberto Refinetti, (Eds.), *Sex Work and Sex Workers*. (pp. 149–158). New Brunswick, New Jersey; Valerie Scott, "I Love Sex and I'm Good At It," *The Globe and Mail* (March 17, 2001), R14; Lily Burana. (2002). *Strip City: A Stripper's Farewell Journey Across America*. New York: Hyperion.

(28.5%) identify as working class, four women (28.5%) grew up in single-parent families, and eight (57%) are high school graduates, which combine to combat the stereotypes that erotic dancers are raised dysfunctionally by poor mothers, and are lazy, uneducated, and otherwise unemployable.

TABLE 8.1

DANCER PROFILES: RACE, SEXUALITY, DANCE TRAINING, STARTING AGE, CHILDREN, YEARS DANCED

Name	Racial/Ethnic Background	Sexual Identity	Formal Dance Classes?	Age When Started Dancing	Children While Dancing?	Number of Years Danced
Miss Lovie	African Canadian	Heterosexual	None	24	No	8
Roxanne	French, Russian & Cree	Lesbian	Some Celtic, tap & ballet	21	Yes	10
Bonnie Scott	First Nations	Heterosexual	None	14	No	15
Salem/Silver Fox	White	Heterosexual	None	24	No	12
Coco Fontaine	African Canadian	Heterosexual	Some jazz dance	18	Yes	14
Tarren Rae	White	Heterosexual	None	16	No	17
Virginia	White	Heterosexual	No dance; movement classes at SFU	24	Yes	3
Shelinda	White	Heterosexual	Some ballet & jazz	17	No	14
Cathy	White	Heterosexual	No dance; some gymnastics	19	No	4
April Paris	White	Heterosexual	None	26	No	10
Jasmine Tea	White	Heterosexual	Some ballet and modern	18	Yes	7
Flashdance	White	Lesbian	None	25	No	5
Shawna Black	White	Heterosexual	None	20	No	6
Shalimar	White	Heterosexual	Ballet	16	Yes	8

n = 14   Average age of entry in the business: 20.1   Average number of years danced: 9.5
Source: Interviews with Retired dancers in Vancouver, B.C., 1998-2002

TABLE 8.2

DANCER PROFILES: SOCIAL CLASS, SCHOOLING, FAMILY OF ORIGIN

Name	Social Class Background	Level of Formal Schooling While Dancing	Family of Origin
Miss Lovie	Working class	High school graduate, two years art college; nursing training	Single mother (until 14), eldest of three siblings
Roxanne	Working class	High school graduate	Single mother (at 5), sibling
Bonnie Scott	Working class	Dropped out of high school (after retired, earned B.A.)	Single mother, siblings
Salem/Silver Fox	Middle class	High school graduate, one year university	Two parent family, siblings
Coco Fontaine	Working class	Dropped out of high school	Two parent family, siblings
Tarren Rae	Middle class	Dropped out of high school	Two parent family, sibling
Virginia	Middle class	High school graduate, nursing training	Two parent family, only child
Shelinda	Middle class	Dropped out of high school; returned to get diploma while dancing	Two parent family, siblings
Cathy	Upper middle	High school graduate, some college	Two parent family, siblings
April Paris	Lower middle class	Dropped out of high school	Two parent family, siblings
Jasmine Tea	Upper class	High school graduate	Two parent family, siblings
Flashdance	Lower middle class	High school graduate, degree in horse training	Two parent family, sibling
Shawna Black	Middle class	Dropped out of high school	Single mother, sibling
Shalimar	Middle to upper middle class	High school graduate	Two parent family, adopted, only child

Source: Interviews with former dancers in Vancouver, B.C., 1998–2002.

Commonly perceived as sex deviants (alongside unwed mothers, homosexuals, prostitutes, and unattached wage-earning women), female erotic dancers were subjected to surveillance, police arrest, detention, extortion, violence, and rejection by family and friends. One fifty-year-old former dancer has never told her twenty-something children about her years in burlesque. At the same time, dancers like Virginia—middle class and British born—made more money, had more freedom, worked fewer hours, and had more control over her work than the waitresses, nurses, teachers, chambermaids, and secretaries she knew. Others like Shelinda and Flashdance told stories of long, twelve-hour days, split shifts "on an invisible leash," and six-day weeks cooped up in "ratty hotels with broken-down beds and cockroaches…in small towns with people who had more keys to your room than you did."

The amount of pay for dancing, the quality of dressing room and performance space, lighting and music, food services, accommodation, promotion, and treatment by management and staff, depended on the nightclub. Until the late 1970s, a dancer was contracted to perform a set of 20–22 minutes every hour over the course on an eight-hour shift. Vancouver-based "A" dancers or headliners worked six nights a week and earned an average of $1,000 to $1,800 per week, while "B" and "C" dancers averaged $500 to $1,000 per week. A-dancers with their enchanting, Vegas-style outfits, props and sets, were featured at high-end clubs such as the Cave, the Penthouse, and later Isy's Supper Club in Vancouver's affluent, predominantly white, west end. B-dancers and "novelty dancers"—predominantly dancers of colour—tended to work a tightly knit rotation of lower-end clubs which played up their "ethnic status" in the working-class, east-end neighbourhoods of Chinatown and Strathcona. The club names—Kublai Khan, Smilin' Buddha, New Delhi, and the Harlem Nocturne belie the myth of Chinatown's homogeneity and suggest that in the area's nightclubs, communities of colour converged to carve a space for themselves unavailable in other parts of the city. Chinatown's history as an ethnic neighbourhood was already synonymous in the white imagination with exotic romance, intrigue, vice, and immorality, and club owners traded in the allure of the racial and sexual "Other" to tantalize locals and uptown "slummers'" (see Anderson, 1991; Ross and Greenwell, 2002).

By the 1970s, categories of dancers had begun to blur as downtown hotels rushed to capitalize on a 1970 ruling that made pasties and g-strings optional (Wiseman 1982, p.33). Ironically, these were the same hotel beer parlours that had prohibited women's presence as "indecent and disorderly" in the 1920s (Campbell, 2001, p. 53). The mushrooming of "peeler pubs"—upwards of thirty-five locations by the mid-1970s—combined with the closures of "respectable, high-end" supper clubs, meant abundant work but uneven, less desirable conditions as dancers scaled down their acts to fit stages that were small, often dirty, roughly-assembled, and poorly lit.

Erotic dancers across British Columbia were customarily paid in cash; they earmarked a standard ten percent of their earnings for their booking agent, and on occasion, paid fines to club owners for minor infractions such as showing up late or skipping a gig without adequate notice. Dancers travelled around the province to small communities such as Nanaimo, Terrace, and Kamloops, and were paid more money on the circuit to compensate for being on the road. Some like

Virginia managed her earnings wisely: she saved, got investment advice, and left the striptease business after three years and later earned her real estate licence. Upon retiring from the scene in Vancouver in 1975, Virginia, who often felt like a counsellor and "the one bright thing" in her customers' lives, received a "solid silver tea service from the gentlemen, the skid row types," who were her regulars. Other former dancers like Flashdance had a tougher time, "I was raised Catholic, so it was like, you gotta have savings, but I had no money management skills whatsoever. When I retired, I pissed it all away on living for a year and a half, and on love. A dollar was like a penny to me. I could piss away money faster than anything…that career did not set me up for being good with money."

RISKY BUSINESS: DANGERS IN THE WORKPLACE

Some occupational hazards were unique to the striptease business, others were common to female-dominated service work. Choreographer Jack Card tells the story of Las Vegas show-girls in the 1950s running out at rehearsal breaks to get silicone injected directly into their breasts prior to the invention of implants. Diane Middlebrook (1998), author of *Suits Me: The Double Life of Billy Tipton*, quotes a male nightclub goer who recalls that in the 1960s across the U.S., "guys would try to scrub out cigarettes or cigars on a stripper. Entice her over, use a cigarette to burn her leg, sometimes try to light their silken gowns on fire. I know one girl was burned to death when that happened, and many strippers carried burns on their bodies" (p. 221). Former dancers complained of lewd comments and the frustration of competing with "Hockey Night in Canada" broadcasts that began to fill TV screens inside hotel pubs in the early 1970s.

Female factory employees have recalled suffering sexual harassment on the line, though clerical staff at Quaker Oats (in Ontario) in the 1940s tended to accept this behaviour as "part of the job" in an era that predated feminist analysis of unwanted, intrusive male advances (Sangster, pp. 98, 112). Though it's difficult to prove that female dancers were, in every instance, subject to greater frequency and/or intensity of sexual innuendo, harassment, and assault than other female workers, they worked in an explicitly sexualized environment where these kinds of intrusions came with the territory.

One male narrator who booked strippers for fraternity house parties on the campus of the University of British Columbia in the 1950s recalled that "college boys could be monsters." One evening, he escorted a dancer to a campus stag only to rescue her from "an ugly scene," and then "drove her home along back alleys, with the headlights out, in order to lose crazy kids who were following us." Two dancers told stories about club owners offering cocaine to underage prospects as a recruitment ploy, and all remember the fear of being mugged for cash (salary and tips) at the end of a night's shift. At the most extreme end of the spectrum, former booking agent Jeannie Runnalls was called

"Striptease and Unionization"

Exotic dancers picketing the Cecil Hotel in Vancouver. The strike began when club owners cut the dancers, pay citing reduced revenues due to a transit strike.

Since the 1960s, striptease dancers have made efforts in Vancouver and elsewhere to unionize in order to improve working conditions, including wages and benefits: the right to strike, workers' compensation, sick leave, vacation pay, and pensions. In 1981, Tarren Rae and others formed the Vancouver Exotic Dancers Alliance (VEDA). Tarren said, "We didn't form a union because unions scared the pants off of hotel owners. They would drum you out of the business if you even mentioned a union. The owners would say, 'Who do you think you are?' We're the people who give you bread and butter!" Over a six-year stretch, VEDA raised money for charities, supported dancers who were financially "in real trouble," and bought a van for the Variety Club, though Tarren ruefully remembers that club members permitted only the acronym, "VEDA" to appear on the van's side panel, and not the words "exotic dancers."

In 1997, erotic dancers at Lusty Lady, an adult theatre in San Francisco, organized a union drive, represented by the Service Employees International Union (SEIU), local 790. They wanted a first collective agreement, and with it, the right to health insurance, sick pay, an end to firings without just cause, and an end to scheduling practices based on "race" and breast size. (Dancers of colour were routinely allotted fewer shifts, and were never booked in the more lucrative "Private Pleasures" booth.) After five months of difficult negotiation and dissatisfying compromises, dancers ratified the first "strippers' union" in the United States. (For more on Lusty Lady, see Dudash, 1997; the documentary film, *Live Nude Girls Unite* directed by Julia Query and Vicky Funari (1999), distributed by Women Make Movies, New York).

to the Vancouver city morgue to identify the bodies of two striptease dancers who had been murdered in downtown Vancouver nightclubs in the 1960s.

Regardless of the venue, none of the former dancers had access to vacation pay, sick leave, extended health coverage, disability leave, or pension plans. On the unionization front, in Vancouver in 1967, three "topless dancers" staged a two-night picket at a local nightclub (Anon., 1967). They demanded higher wages, staff privileges, and a dressing room heater. They expressed the desire to organize dancers at six other nightclubs, though dancers never certified in Vancouver. In Toronto, the Canadian Association of Burlesque Entertainers (CABE) was a local of the Canadian Labour Congress in the 1970s, though it did not survive long, nor did the American Guild of Variety Artists which represented sex performers in central Canada until the early 1970s (Cooke, 1987; Johnson, 1987). Former dancer Tarren Rae noted that waves of union activity in Vancouver throughout the 1970s and 1980s often corresponded with times of economic affluence in the city, though club owners and booking agents consistently and fervently opposed the labour agitation. Additionally, Bonnie recalled the competitive conditions under which dancers secured paying gigs, the lack of pro-union consciousness among the women, and the need for dancers to tour, all of which impeded worker solidarity and thwarted unionization.

On occasion in postwar Vancouver, erotic dancers supplemented their nightclub earnings by modelling, movie work, all-male stag events (which date back to the late 1800s), magazine work, and legitimate dance in chorus lines and with jazz troupes. In the mid-1960s, a number of Vancouver-based erotic dancers performed fifteen-minute acts between pornography reels on the stage of the Chinese-owned Venus movie house on Main Street, on the edge of Chinatown. I suspect that a small percentage of former dancers combined striptease with prostitution, though no one I've interviewed has disclosed involvement in the exchange of sex for money. Instead, the majority of dancers emphasized their careers as artists, and set themselves apart from prostitutes who laboured under more severe criminal sanctions and stigma. As such, erotic dancers ranked themselves, and were ranked by others, according to a moral hierarchy with "no-talent hookers at the bottom," which made unity among women across occupational sites exceedingly difficult. Striptease dancers were much more likely to imagine solidarity with can can dancers and Vegas show queens than with prostitutes who were believed guilty of giving strippers a "bad name."

(UN)DRESSING FOR SUCCESS

Dancers and choreographers were influenced by numerous artistic, cultural, aesthetic, and musical traditions. According to former dancer Margaret Dragu (1988), "Burlesque queens of the 1920s through 1940s possessed trunkloads of vaudeville-style costumes replete with long gloves, stockings with garters, gowns with sequins, ostrich plumes, marabou trim, and rhinestone-studded chiffon. They were the last purveyors of the classic bump and grind" (p. 24). In the 1930s, some women disrobed on stage behind a screen or a white shadowgraph, while

> ## "Striptease in Hollywood Film"
>
> Most portrayals of erotic dancers on Hollywood's silver screen reinforce the age-old madonna/whore dichotomy: respectable, middle-class "good girls" vs. wayward, working-class "bad girls" (see the films, *Applause*, 1929; *The Trouble with Women*, 1947; *The Stripper*, 1963). In the Oscar-decorated blockbuster hit, *The Graduate* (1967), newly minted but aimless university graduate Benjamin Braddock (Dustin Hoffman) is pressured to escort Elaine Robinson (Katherine Ross), the daughter of his lover, Mrs. Robinson (Ann Bancroft), on a date. By insisting on accompanying Elaine to a downtown stripclub, Benjamin succeeds in publicly humiliating and punishing the white, upper-class, virgin by forcing her to witness the sullying debauchery of a stripteaser who twirls ornamental tassels from jewelled pasties (double-dutch style) for a living. Elaine is not supposed to aspire to the skills of the stage performer, or desire what she sees; she is expected to display her wounded femininity. Indeed, at the horrifying sight of Elaine's tears, Benjamin is jolted into class-conscious chivalry and proceeds to lunge angrily, violently at the dancer on stage. Pursuing a fleeing Elaine out of the club, he later comforts her with kisses and food in the safety and style of his red convertible sportscar.

others alternately covered and "flashed" their flesh by manipulating artful props or peekaboo devices: a sheer body leotard (with strategically-placed sequins), the panel dress, feathers, parasols, fans, banana skirts, Spanish shawls, pasties, netting, veils, smoke and bubble machines, body makeup, and g-strings (Corio, 1968, pp. 71–76). The g-string, Ann Corio observed, "was a tiny jewel-like bauble on a string around the waist covering up its specific subject" (Ibid., p. 76, and see Van Gelder, 1999). In Vancouver, as elsewhere, the A-dancers, or "top drawer" dancers, invested a considerable percentage of their earnings in costumes, props, expensive make-up, and, by the 1970s, taped music. They also combined elements of pantomime, magic, puppetry, theatre, gymnastics, comedy, and dance training.

In the 1962 film, *Gypsy*, starring Natalie Wood and Rosalynd Russell, an entire production number instructs "strippers" in the art of plying a gimmick. Jack Card, a well-known choreographer born in Vancouver, recalls that, "At Isy's Supper Club, strippers worked with live doves or did fire shows, Yvette Dare trained a "sacred" parrot, "Jeta," to pluck her clothes off, one stripper was a magician, and another sat on an electric trapeez and stripped while swinging." Stage names were invented by popular Vancouver headliners: Miss Lovie, Dee Dee Special, April Paris, Suzanne Vegas, Marilyn Marquis, Lilly Marlene, Tia Maria, Jasmine Tea, Silver Fox/Salem, Bonnie Scott, Coco Fontaine, Princess Lillian, Tarren Rae, and Lottie the Body.

Regardless of how much nudity was allowed, or required (by the early 1970s), female bodies were expected to conform to male-defined standards of female sexiness: pretty face, medium to large breasts, long, shapely legs, small waist, long hair. "Bombshells" like Annie Ample, Morganna, and Chesty Morgan had legendary breast sizes.[9] For nine years, Bonnie Scott perfected her show-stopping extravaganza,

> I had a champagne glass act. I started off in a beaded gown by Claude Dubois. Then I climbed an iron staircase that went up into the glass, and stripped inside it. I had a bubble machine, fog machine, and black lights. I had a matching pink plush bathmat, pink towel, and a little powder table. I used to buy my bubble bath from Avon because its bubbles lasted the longest....I had a fox stole and an ivory cigarette holder and I'd do Eartha Kitt: "My champagne case and your beer bottle bucket...." When I quit dancing, I had forty thousand dollars worth of equipment and costumes.

Lili St. Cyr took her trademark bubblebaths in a transparent glass tub, dried off with a tiny towel, and then slowly proceeded to get dresssed, a "striptease in reverse" (Sullivan, 1995, p. 274). African American ex-patriates Miss Lovie, Lawanda the Bronze Goddess, and Mitzi Dupré were marketed in racist terms as novelty acts. Mitzi sprayed pingpong balls and played a flute with her vagina; Lawanda lit her pasties' tassels on fire and spun them like propellors; and Miss Lovie perfected a dance on her buttocks on the floor, to the rhythm of conga drums.

Jack Card worked and travelled with headliner Gypsy Rose Lee who performed in Vancouver, and more regularly, in the extravagant Las Vegas revues where each of her costumes carried a $5,000 price tag. Underneath the sequined gowns and furs, in addition to jewelled pasties and g-strings (worn layered over one another), rhinestone clips were popular in the 1950s and 1960s: v-shaped and glittery, they fitted over the pubic area, were made of sprung steel, and inserted into the vagina. In Montreal in 1951, Lili St. Cyr was arrested and subjected to a trial for giving an obscene and immoral performance, and arrested again in 1967 before tourists arrived for Expo (Campbell, 1999, p. A3). Perhaps because of St. Cyr's brush with the law, dancers across Canada in the 1960s were known to wear merkins—patches of artificial pubic hair glued to the pubic region in order to avoid arrest for indecency while perpetuating the illusion of nudity.

---

[9] In a fascinating article, Kristina Zarlengo characterizes the "bombshell" as a "deeply desirable, unattainable woman with an inflated body and intense sexuality—a steadfast atomic age feminine ideal...who represented raw power of a kind frequently associated with the atom bomb." See Zarlengo, "Civilian Threat, the Suburban Citadel, and Atomic Age American Women", (Fall 1999). *Signs: Journal of Women in Culture and Society*, 25, 946.

THE COLONIAL CARNIVALESQUE UNDER THE BIG TENT

Lured by the promise of a twenty-week season and a steady pay cheque, many burlesque dancers packed their trunks and joined the summer exhibitions or carnivals, often in the twilight of their career. "Girlie Shows" had become staples of the touring carnival and circus across North America, beginning after the World's Columbia Exposition in Chicago in 1893 (Stencell, 1999, p. 4). Alongside the merry-go-rounds, arcades, shooting galleries and side-shows spotlighting bearded ladies, alligator-skinned boys, and "midgits," stripteasers were main features (Bogdan, 1988). Carnival showmen added "more spice and less wardrobe" to give their tent-shows more edge than downtown cabaret acts (Stencell, 1999, p. 13). While other showgirls paraded their (hetero)femininity by baking cakes in competition, or strutting their stuff as beauty pageant contestants vying for the crown of Miss Pacific National Exposition (P.N.E.), strippers on carnival stages sang, danced, told jokes, and shed their elaborate costumes.

In the 1950s in Vancouver, impresario Isy Walters, who owned the Cave Supper Club, and later, Isy's Supper Club, also booked strip acts at the P.N.E. Isy's Black Tent Show, which was next door to his White Tent Show, invited patrons to pass between the legs of a 50-foot plywood cut-out of a black burlesque dancer at the tent's entrance on the fairgrounds.[10] As Jack Card recalls, inside the neon-lit tent, the talker introduced, "'The African Queen, DIRECT from the jungles of Africa', and behind her there'd be Nubian slave girls in chains, a bumping and a thumping." Here, the colonial trope of **African primitivism**, bound up with the imperialist custom and fantasy of captivity, was remade as titillating foreignness at the same time, and in the same city, that African American singer Lena Horne was refused hotel accommodation for "being a Negro." A decade later in Vancouver, Hogan's Alley—the city's working-class African Canadian enclave—was bulldozed into the ground (Fatona & Wyngaarten, 1994). Significantly, the discourse of burlesque under the Big Tent was never about sex alone. It was tangled up with the economic, cultural, and political privileges of a white body politic.

The racist, colonial trappings of the business of striptease were no accident. In 1815, Sara Baartman, a West African woman was captured by Dutch colonizers and displayed, fully nude, across England and Europe, advertised as a "wanton, orangatan-like, freak of nature" (Gillman, 1985; Fausto-Sterling, 1995). In circuses and carnivals across North America throughout the 1900s, black performers who were paid consistently less than their white counterparts, were routinely consigned

---

[10] In the U.S., the "black show" was typically referred to as the "Nig Show." See C. Strange and T. Loo, (June 1996). "Spectacular Justice: The Circus on Trial and the Trial as Circus, Picton 1903, *Canadian Historical Review, 77*, 159–184.

to the role of cannibals, Zulu warriors, bushmen, and bear-women from the "darkest Africa" (Strange & Loo 1996, pp. 179–80). In addition, for more than a century, some white burlesque dancers disguised themselves as Algerian, Egyptian, Hawaiian, Asian, or Arabian in an effort to feed white appetites for the exotic by trading in **Orientalism**.

Gawking at dancers of colour and white women who impersonated the Other, white consumers were reassured of their own normality and cultural dominance; social boundaries between spectators and performers, the "civilized" and the "uncivilized", were conserved. Pre-existing racial and gender stereotypes were animated in the interests of carnies or showmen smartly fluent in the commonsense, naturalized precepts of mass entertainment. The speech of the talker, the colourful images on the bally front, and the handbills advertising the event, were embedded in a racial, gender, and class grammar that distinguished native instinct from white self-discipline, and native lust from white civility (see Stoler 1997, pp. 178–179).

Josephine Baker, an African American born poor in St. Louis in 1906, escaped in 1925 to work as a burlesque performer in France, and later performed in Vancouver in the 1950s. Cast in the show, "La Revue Negre" in Paris, and across Europe, as a "tribal, uncivilized savage" from a prehistoric era, hence consigned to **anachronistic space**, Baker was rendered intelligible and digestible to white voyeurs as an oversexed jezebel (see McClintock, 1995, p. 40; Hammonds, 1997). Narrating the fantasy of the jungle bunny—the oversexed object of white European fascination and repulsion, she danced in banana skirt and feathers. And in other shows, straight out of the racist minstrel tradition, "she was a ragamuffin in black face wearing bright cotton smocks and clown shoes" (Dalton and Gates, 1998, p. 911). Importantly, Baker also initiated desegregation in Las Vegas nightclubs in the 1950s by being the first dancer to refuse to perform for a white-only audience.

Racism in burlesque and striptease played out in myriad ways. In the U.S. in 1956, Princess Do May—the "Cherokee Half Breed," was photographed in full feather headdress, beaded headband, and a (sacred) drum, freeze-framed in time and space anachronistically as an Indian artefact displaced from community and territory, and repositioned against an untouched, untamed wilderness ripe for conquest. A picture of condensed and standardized symbols of Indianness, and of imperialism as commodity spectacle, she served to make invisible the multiple identities and multiple interests of diverse First Nations (McClintock, 1995, p. 56). All colonial histories of slaughter and subjugation are absented in this rendition of the myth of the noble savage. The Princess was employed in burlesque to excite the sexual imagination of white men who engineered Euro-Canadian and Euro-American expansion, settlement, and industry on the frontier (Furniss, 1997/98; Barman, 1997/98; Carter, 1996; Perry 2001).

Counterpose this image of Princess Do May against the seductive Lili St. Cyr. The American-born St. Cyr (born Marie Van Schaak in Minneapolis in 1918 of

Poster advertising the Revue Negre at the Music Hall des Champs-Elysees in Paris.

Josephine Baker in Paris in one of her well-known "exotic" costumes.

Swedish/Dutch heritage), spent many famous years in Montreal, beginning in 1944, and was well-known for her aforementioned bubble baths, her acts as a jungle goddess and a biblical temptress, and her penchant for eccentric storytelling on stage (Weintraub, 1996). It was widely reported that the highlight of her act came when an invisible fishing line tugged off her g-string over the heads of the audience while the house lights faded to darkness (Campbell 1999, p. A3). The Nordic, voluptuous cowgirl, replete with ten-gallon hat, holster and guns, leather boots and lariat, is equally burdened by a condensation of symbols and metaphors—in this case, those of the conquerors of aboriginal peoples, and the keepers of Euro-Canadian myths of colonial rule. Here, St. Cyr stands in for the brave, heroic, pioneering men and women who have been memorialized as the founding ancestors of the contemporary nation—emblems of national identity, pride, and prosperity. St. Cyr embodies the colonial myth of the rough and tumble Wild West, the promise of abundant resources free for the taking, and the danger of encountering Indians who had never seen a white man or woman (Furniss 1997/98, p. 29). Decked out in traditional rancher garb, St. Cyr fetishizes the triumph of European colonizers all the while reminding white men in the audience that force was at their disposal if they needed or wanted it. At the same time, paradoxically, she sends up the machismo of the Marlboro Man by appropriating cowboy kitsch to her own cheeky ends.

Lili St. Cyr performing orientalism.

HOOCHIE COOCHIE QUEERS?

In their 1965 study of women's prisons in the U.S., Ward and Kassebaum (1965) quote a traditional maxim of prison life, "strippers and models are likely to be homosexual" (p. 75). In 1969, American sociologists James Skipper and Charles McCaghy (1971) interviewed thirty-five "exotic dancers" who informed them that approximately 50 percent of their colleagues engaged in either prostitution or lesbian activities (p. 283). In 1971, Canadian journalist Marilyn Salutin (1971) stated that 75 percent of female strippers were gay (pp. 12–22). In his book *Girl Show: Into the Canvas World of Bump and Grind*, A.W. Stencell (1999) claims that, "Gays were often found in 10-in-1 side shows doing the half-man/half-woman act and working in drag on carnival girl shows. Many of the dancers who worked gay cabarets during the winter went with carnival shows in the summer…it was a safe world where you were judged only on the job you did" (p. 95).

In spite of flimsy social science data, there is no doubt that lesbian and gay dancers and choreographers, make-up artists, prop-makers, costume designers, wig-makers, and customers, found a home in the business of striptease. According to choreographer Jack Card, some of the most beautiful showgirls he knew were lesbians, and many of the dancing boys with their bare chests and false eyelashes were gay. Former erotic dancers Maud Allan, Josephine Baker, Gypsy Rose Lee, and Tempest Storm are rumoured to have had women lovers. In 1958, renowned lesbian historian Lillian Faderman began stripping in California clubs to defray the costs of attending college. In 1998, at a queer history conference in Tacoma, Washington, Faderman mused publicly about the shame that closeted her bumping and grinding for forty years.

If stripteasers identified as gay women, what relationship, if any, did they develop to Vancouver's **butch and femme** bar culture? (Cosco, 1997; Weissman & Fernie, 1992; Nestle, 1992; Munt, 1998; Ross, 1997). Kennedy and Davis (1993) in their book *Boots of Leather, Slippers of Gold: The History of a Lesbian Community*, note that in the 1940s and 1950s, femmes in Buffalo, New York typically had steady paid employment while their butch lovers struggled with long stretches of unsteady, sporadic labour and financial uncertainty as car jockeys, elevator operators, and couriers (pp. 278–322). So, did the wages of femmes in g-strings subsidize the earnings of their butch lovers? Historian Lisa Davis (1992) notes that in New York's Greenwich Village in the 1940s, nightclubs operating under protection of the mob employed "gorgeous femme" strippers who embodied showgirl glamour (p. 45). Given the tendency of butches to bind their breasts, wear men's clothing, and spurn feminine artifice, was stripteaser a primarily femme occupational category?

Almost twenty years before *Xena: Warrior Princess* on prime-time TV, *Klute*—a butch lesbian in disguise—successfully reworked themes from *Conan the Barbarian* as an s-and-m dominatrix, and played with the fantasies of men who longed to be topped. As she recalled, she never fit the "high femme, mega-feature look." Instead, she played with gender ambiguity on stage until she was ostracized for being "too dykey." Former headliner Tarren Rae recalls performing for spirited, appreciative crowds of whistling women at the Vanport and the New Fountain, two of Vancouver's renowned gay pubs. Indeed, some female spectators, whether or not they were openly lesbian or bisexual, nurtured same-sex erotic fantasies in the presence of super-sexy female stripteasers. In 1938, sexologist Alfred Kinsey and colleagues measured the sexual arousal levels of several thousand female spectators at burlesque/night club acts, and found that 25.7 percent of white college women disclosed feelings of arousal towards stripteasers that ranged from "little" to "much" as shown on the following page.

In 1962, American jazz musician Billy Tipton—a biological female who passed successfully as a man all his adult life—"married" Kitty Kelly, a striptease entertainer who was well-known to Vancouver audiences in the 1960s (Middlebrook, 1998, pp. 220–232). Because striptease demanded public display of exaggerated hetero-femininity, Kitty's occupation surely enhanced Billy's masquerade as a

TABLE 8.3

SEXUAL AROUSAL BY BURLESQUE OR NIGHT CLUB ACTS, KINSEY REPORTS, 1938.

Degree of Arousal	Male White College	Male White Non-college	Male Black College	Female White College	Female White Non-College	Female Black College
	%	%	%	%	%	%
None	31.7	45.5	36.5	69.0	70.1	88.2
None and offended	4.2	1.0	2.2	16.8	16.4	3.9
Little	13.4	8.4	15.3	6.2	4.3	1.3
Some	10.5	14.7	15.3	2.7	3.0	3.9
Much	28.3	19.0	20.4	3.9	5.7	2.6
None now, formerly more	11.3	10.9	8.8	1.6	0.5	0.0
Little now, formerly more	0.6	0.5	0.7	0.0	0.0	0.0
Some now, formerly much	0.1	0.0	0.7	0.0	0.0	0.0
Number of Viewers	3961	580	137	1849	562	76

Standard Question: "Are you sexually aroused by burlesque or night club acts? If affirmative reply: 'Much, some, or little.'"

Source: Table 406. *The Kinsey Data: Marginal Tabulations of the 1938-1963 Interviews Conducted by the Institute for Sex Research*. Paul H. Gebhard and Alan B. Johnson. Bloomington, Indiana: Indiana University Press, 1979, p. 455.

red-blooded heterosexual male. And what about male-to-female **transgenders** who successfully passed on stage in the 1950s and 1960s as ultra-feminine, sexy girls in full view of adoring (straight?) male fans? **Transsexual** burlesque stripper, Hedy Jo Star not only performed her own striptease act, but she owned carnival girl shows where she employed female impersonators in the 1950s (Stencell, 1999, p. 92). Jaydee Easton, a female impersonator in the 1950s, flashed in drag by looping her penis with an elastic band, attaching it to a small rubber ball, and inserting it into her anus (Ibid., p. 93). Other female impersonators such as Jackie Starr, most of whom were gay men, performed in straight nightclubs and gay cabarets such as Seattle's famous "Garden of Allah" until the 1970s when full nudity in stripclubs made drag virtually impossible (Paulson, 1996, pp. 127–134).

Jackie Starr replaced an ill Gypsy Rose Lee several times on music hall stages in New York in the 1940s, and was the top headliner at the Garden of Allah for ten years. At the same time, female "drag artistes"—singers and masters of ceremony—impersonated men on nightclub stages in New York's Greenwich Village, and dazzled female fans, both straight and lesbian (Davis, 1992, p. 45).

The presence of queers on and off striptease stages troubles the naturalized presumption that nightclubs and carnivals were undisputably heterosexual milieux. Acting out moments of what theorist Judith Butler (1997) calls "insurrectionary queerness" inside cabarets, stripclubs, and under big tents, queer performers, staff, and fans interrupted the **heteronormative** (p. 159). What is not yet apparent is the complexity of queer relationships to the closet, as well as to communities beyond the borders of the nightclub world. Given the criminalization of homosexuality prior to 1969, combined with the persistent stigmatization of striptease, I suspect that most lesbians and gay men in the business prior to gay liberation in the 1970s sought the same subterfuge that sheltered Hollywood he-man Rock Hudson for so long.

THE ROLE OF SEX IN BUILDING THE CANADIAN NATION

In the end, a fundamental paradox governed the business of erotic entertainment before 1980. On the one hand, stripteasers were well-paid, glamorous entertainers who, as working-class women with limited employment training, or as middle-class women with a thirst for rebellion, stripped first for the money. The women we've interviewed took pride in putting on a good show, they loved the applause, and the challenge of developing new routines, costumes, and props. On the other hand, they were subjected to criminal and social sanctions that pressured them to be ashamed of their work, to pretend that they did something else for a living, or to abandon their careers as dancers altogether. Their skills and expertise, dedication, flare, and originality as workers, were overshadowed, if not entirely discounted, by moral reformers, police, and civic officials who, at various times and for a variety of purposes, were in the business of scapegoating non-conformists. While professional female dancers in ballet, modern, and jazz increasingly inspired awe and veneration in the second half of the twentieth century, stripteasers were consigned to the interstices between acceptance and rejection.

Female erotic dancers did not qualify as full-fledged citizens dedicated to the ideal family, the social order, and the health of the Canadian nation. Perceived by many as no better than disgraced whores who haunted the quasi-legal underworld in postwar Vancouver, dancers were positioned outside of discourses that elaborated what it meant to be a normal, moral, and patriotic citizen. Lindalee Tracy, former dancer and author of *Growing Up Naked* (1997), reflects,

> It was always tricky explaining that I'd been a stripper once; it was startling to other sensibilities, as harsh a class distinction as one can make. People reacted with suspicion, pity or sometimes prurient fascination. They leaped into their assumptions, imagining me a whore, an idiot, a victim. I winced, not from my shame, because there really wasn't any, but from the shame people wanted to impose. (p. 209)

Like Tracey, dancers could never take for granted the fundamental constituents of substantive citizenship such as inclusion, belonging, equity, and justice (Weeks, 1998, pp. 35–39). Like other sex trade workers in an era of suburbanized, privatized domesticity, and marital nuclearity, erotic dancers were presumed to be devoid of real jobs, families, and meaningful, intimate relationships (see Korinek, 2000). No dancer raising children, especially if she was non-white, was ever honoured for her role as mother and moral guardian of the "race." Because strippers were commonly perceived as anti-family, they were presumed to possess no maternal honour worth protecting. Rather than being extended dignity, security, and safety, their family forms were stigmatized as a menace to the stability of the nation state (see Räthzel, 1995, p. 168). Two retired dancers I interviewed who balanced child-rearing and their careers as strippers recall the painful judgement of other parents, daycare workers, coaches, and teachers who disapproved of their chosen field of work. In her autobiography, Lindalee Tracey (1997) describes her desire to donate the proceeds from a large-scale strip-a-thon ("Tits for Tots") in Montreal to a charity for disabled kids, and the rejections she faced from agencies which explained they had "reputations" to uphold (p. 163).

THE FUTURE OF STRIPTEASE AS (UN)FREE ENTERPRISE

All across North America, the paradox persists. Today, more money is spent at stripclubs than at large-scale commercial theatres, regional and non-profit theatres, the opera, the ballet, jazz, and classical music performances—combined (Schlosser 1997, 44; Chow, 2001, B5). In the U.S., the number of strip clubs has doubled in the past decade, with the fastest growth in upscale Gentlemen's Clubs which have reframed striptease as adult entertainment that upholds the highest standards of the hospitality industry. Over the past decade, Canada's Immigration Department has granted thousands of temporary six-month work permits to women from Romania, the Czech Republic, Hungary, and Poland, to serve Canada's burgeoning stripclub business as "burlesque entertainers" (Oziewicz, 2000, A11). Capitalist globalization has spurred other migrant sex workers, including dancers, to travel to Canada, and once here, most face formidable barriers to labour and immigration rights, as well as the threat of deportation and criminal charges, particularly in Ontario if they are caught dancing without a licence (Brock et al.,

Track Star Forced off Her University's Team

In February 1999, Leilani Rios—a 21-year-old Latina track star for the University of California State, Fullerton—was purged from the track and field team. Several members of the male baseball team at Fullerton witnessed Rios's striptease act at the Anaheim Flamingo Theater, and reported her performance to authorities. Handed an ultimatum by her coach John Elders to choose between her sport and her job as an erotic dancer, Rios elected to keep dancing because as a non-scholarship athlete, she needed the money. In a written statement, Coach Elders said: "I determined that Ms. Rios's decision to remain an exotic dancer would detract from the image and accomplishments of her teammates, the athletics department, and the university" (cited in Lin, 2001, F4). The baseball players were neither reprimanded nor expelled—their consumption of striptease did not besmirch the university's reputation. Rather, the well-worn adage "boys will be boys" afforded them not only protection from rebuke, but in some quarters, authenticated their status as "real" men. Rios, by contrast, was reminded that good, (white), obedient girls who keep their noses clean, their shorts on, and their loyalties straight, get team membership, praise, and the promise of future dividends. Bad, (non-white), disloyal girls like Rios who embarrass and shame an entire school and a state, get purged as immoral trespassers and traitors.

2000, pp. 84–86). In the summer of 2001, the department of Human Resources and Development Canada (HRDC) used its Web site and federal job centres to post free job advertisements from a Toronto stripclub for female exotic dancers (Leblanc, 2001, p. A5). At the same time, striptease continues to be a lightning rod for cultural/legal and political conflicts all over North America (Hanna, 1998, p. 62). Unresolved debates swirl around the legal and moral character of lap dancing, peep shows, live sex acts on stage, the geographical location of "exotic dancing," and nightclubs as venues for prostitution.

Community groups and politicians have staged protests to keep stripclubs out of their lives and neighbourhoods. Susan Marshall, Executive Director of Safe Neighborhoods in Portland, Oregon, claims that, "Obscene speech, nude dancing, and hard-core violent pornography serve no social purpose" ("Gentlemen's Clubs," 1996). Residents all over North America have lobbied for stepped-up patrolling activities and surveillance. In a move that conjures up Michel Foucault's theory of the **panopticon**, police in the U.S. routinely install cameras in clubs and dressing rooms to record criminal activity—a move that engenders hyper self-consciousness and self-discipline among dancers (1980, pp. 195–227). At the same time, cameras positioned inside the performance space electronically transmit live strip shows to viewers via the Internet—a move that satisfies the needs of at-home consumers, blurs public and private boundaries, and deposits little or no extra cash in the hands of working women.

In 1996, New York Mayor, Rudy Guiliani called erotic dancing, "a dirty, vicious business...[where one] finds the exploitation of sex that has lead to the deterioration of New York and places throughout the U.S." ("Gentlemen's Clubs," 1996). Defending his clean-up campaign, Guiliani argued: "If people express themselves in ways that destroy property values, increase crime, bring in organized crime, and start to destroy a city, then you have to have the discretion to do something about it." Like Guiliani, Jerry Elsner, Executive Director of the Illinois Crime Centre, loathes the behaviour of stripclub patons: "A certain element of people go night after night after night, buy porn when they leave, then go home and hide in the basement and watch dirty movies all night. They're a threat to everybody in our community; they tend to congregate at watering holes—this is where the action is, where their friends and peers are at. One degenerate in the neighbourhood is bad; two hundred is real bad" ("Gentlemen's Clubs," 1996).

The combination of old-fashioned police pressure, residents' associations dedicated to protecting property and family values, media sensationalism, and the manipulation of zoning ordinances, has meant heated attacks on stripclub culture, with sobering results. Since 1993, striptease has been the number one topic of Free Speech litigation in the U.S (DeWitt, 1995, pp. 112–127). According to anthropologist Judith Lynne Hanna (1998), over sixty-two communities across North America have enacted laws to restrict striptease, including Seattle, Tacoma, Fort Lauderdale, Syracuse, and Phoenix (p. 40). New laws continually resurface. Only time will tell whether or not similar, discriminatory prohibitions will be invoked to control (or obliterate) erotic dancing in Vancouver, B.C., or in any other Canadian city. So long as stripper bodies conjure up popular associations of worthless, diseased, lazy, drug-addicted, oversexed, dangerous, and unCanadian bodies, the erotic labour performed by dancers, past and present, will never be appreciated *as labour;* it will be forever figured as something else. And age-old struggles by dancers for improved working conditions, union certification, and destigmatization of their artform, will continue in the absence of a titanic transformation in the cultural meanings attached to bump and grind.

CRITICAL THINKING QUESTIONS

1. In this chapter, what evidence is presented that female sex workers, including erotic dancers, have resisted both damaging stereotypes and difficult, sometimes dangerous working conditions?

2. How do we account for the discrepancy between the valued, celebrity status of professional figure skaters, golfers and hockey players, and the devalued, stigmatized status of professional erotic dancers?

> ## "STUDYING STRIPPERS? AN INTERNATIONAL NEWS STORY"
>
> In June 2000, articles in the *Vancouver Sun* and *The Globe and Mail* that publicized my SSHRC grant (1999–2002), catalyzed an international media feeding frenzy. Lurid headlines read: "Sociologist In Search of Naked Truth," and "Study Targets Ex-Strippers." *The Globe and Mail* article by Dene Moore at Canadian Press was printed in newspapers all across Canada, as well as in the *Bangkok Post* and the *Arab Times*. Radio, TV, and print journalists from England, Scotland, Australia, Germany, South Africa, the U.S., and Canada contacted me to justify my spending of "taxpayers' dollars" on "studying strippers." (Canadians were still reeling from news, in February 2000, of a $3 million "spending scandal" the federal ministry of Human Resources and Development. See John Geddes, "Saving Ms. Stewart," *Maclean's* (February 14, 2000, pp. 14–19.) On several talk-radio shows in Toronto, Calgary, and Vancouver, I was attacked by successive callers incensed that the government would " waste their money" on such a "useless, disgusting project." Several male callers barked that a history of logging or mining in the province of British Columbia was far more constructive. Though erotic dancers paid personal income tax and sales tax, and some bought Canada Savings Bonds, and later, RRSPs, they were automatically disqualified from national conversations about the allocation of state resources, which again underscores their lack of claim to substantive citizenship. Three months of media heat confirmed my suspicion that, in the eyes of the majority, the impressive, century-long contribution of erotic dancers to local economies and performance traditions is anything but deserving of state-supported inquiry.

3. Who is a "business insider" in the nightclub world of burlesque and striptease, and who is a "business outsider?"

4. How has the business of erotic dancing in Vancouver, and more broadly across North America, changed since 1980? What role has the advent of new technologies played?

5. How have colonial, racist stereotypes of women of colour operated in the world of striptease, both on nightclub stages, and at exhibition fairgrounds?

6. What does the author mean when she claims that investigation of striptease culture reveals valuable insights into the social construction of the Canadian nation?

7. Discuss the benefits of unionization for erotic dancers. Speculate on explanations for why they have been largely unsuccessful in their bids to organize and collectively bargain to improve working conditions.

SUGGESTED READINGS

Hanna, Judith Lynne (1998). Undressing the First Amendment and Corsetting the Striptease Dancer. *The Drama Review, 42*, 38-69.

> A former erotic dancer and practicing anthropologist, Hanna carefully and precisely details her role as an "expert witness" concerned to defend the rights of "exotic dancers" charged with unlawful behaviour in court cases across the U.S. since 1995. Based on interviews with dancers, customers, club owners, managers, staff and First Amendment lawyers, Hanna makes an argument for exotic dance as artistic conduct or "speech" deserving of constitutional protection under the First Amendment in the U.S. Hanna reviews the legal constraints on nude dancing, as well as the morality based campaigns by the Religious Right to "target the body as a surveillance zone central to the operation of power" (p. 54).

Jarrett, Robin (1997). *Stripping In Time: A History of Erotic Dancing*. London: HarperCollins Publishers.

> Jarrett's well-documented research chronicles the "art of stripping," beginning in the 1860s in the dance halls and music halls of London, England, and Paris, France. Using news clippings, Hollywood film, diaries, and records of court cases, she acknowledges the influence of the Ziegfeld Follies, and later, the open sexuality of American dancers Gypsy Rose Lee, Georgia Southern, Ann Corio, and Margie Hart.

Latham, Angela (2000). *Posing a Threat: Flappers, Chorus Girls, and Other Brazen Performers of the American 1920s*. Hanover and London: University Press of New England.

> Basing her analysis on a vast range of print media sources from the 1920s, Latham argues that this decade marks a pivotal period that expanded the "market" for sexually explicit displays by female performers in the U.S. The morality-based regulation of women's bodies, and women's nudity in particular, is explored, as are the ways in which women contested the censorship of their performances. The chapter, "The Right To Bare" supplies details of theatrical shows that emphasized women's sexual allure, and that prefigured the emergence of Burlesque Queens in the 1930s, and topless/bottomless "Exotic Dancers" in the 1970s.

Lewis, Jacqueline (2000). Controlling Lap Dancing: Law, Morality, and Sex Work. In R. Weitzer (Ed.), *Sex for Sale: Prostitution, Pornography and the Sex Industry* (pp. 203–216). New York: Routledge.

> Lewis focuses on debates re: lap dancing in Ontario between 1994 and 1997 and argues that two harm-based discourses dominated media coverage. One emphasized lap dancing as harmful to public morality, while another emphasized lap dancing as harmful to the health and well-being of dancers. Both converged to create a single dominant discourse: lap dancing is harmful and should be prohibited.

Skipper, James and Charles McCaghy (1970). Stripteasers: The Anatomy and Career Contingencies of a Deviant Occupation. *Social Problems* 17(3), 391-404.

> Contributors to the "deviance school" of sociology, Skipper and McCaghy conducted a field study in the late 1960s using observational and ethnographic techniques to collect data on 75 female stripteasers from 10 major U.S. cities. The focus of this paper concerns a description of the occupation; data pertaining to physical, psychological, and social characteristics of women stripping on the theatre circuit; and data on the situational factors surrounding their decision to

enter the profession. They conclude that 1) there is a tendency toward exhibitionistic behaviour for gain, 2) an opportunity structure making stripping an accessible occupational option, and 3) awareness by the girls [sic] of easy economic rewards derived from stripping.

Stencell, A.W. (1999). *Girl Show: Into the Canvas World of Bump and Grind*. Toronto: ECW Press.
In this beautifully illustrated text, Stencell tells the rich, multi-faceted story of "girlie shows"— the main adult entertainment on fairgrounds across Canada and the United States from the early 1900s to the mid-1970s.

Tracey, Lindalee (1997). *Growing Up Naked: My Years in Bump and Grind*. Vancouver and Toronto: Douglas and McIntyre.
In this memoir, Lindalee Tracey offers a moving portrait of the decade she worked as a striptease dancer in Montreal nightclubs: her struggles to define her art form, the lure of drugs, her friendships with other dancers, and critique of feminist filmmakers who wrongfully represented her in the National Film Board documentary, *Not A Love Story* (1982).

WEB LINKS

www.exoticworld.com
This site introduces the Exotic World Burlesque Museum in Helendale, California. Run by former dancer, Dixie Evans—a Marilyn Monroe impersonator—it's a non-profit "resting place" for sequinned and rhinestoned memorabilia from famous burlesque stars, exotic dancers, and go-go girls from around the world.

www.tempeststorm.com
This site details Tempest Storm's career as a top-billed striptease performer, movie star, and published author. The "stormy redheaded fireball" was a headlining dancer at the most prestigious venues, including Isy's Supper Club, and the Penthouse Cabaret in Vancouver, B.C. She is now in her early 80s, and is writing a second book.

www.danzine.org
Danzine is a collaboration of sex workers based in Portland, Oregon. Since 1995, this group of exotic dancers, escorts and lingerie models has published *Danzine*, an independent magazine by and for women in the business of erotic entertainment, and it runs two health programs.

www.streetswing.com/hismai2/d2gypsy1.htm
This site introduces Gypsy Rose Lee (1914-1970), an icon in the world of striptease history. Included is information about Gypsy's filmography, her authored texts and plays, and her sister, June Hovac.

www.karamae.com/lili/photo.html
Lili St. Cyr, was known as "queen of the strippers" in the 1950s and 1960s, and this site compiles photographs of her "in action," and information about her career, eight years of which she spent in Montreal.

Part Three

Bad Mothers and Endangered Children

As Dorothy Chunn finds in an earlier chapter, while families have long been considered the private sphere, this does not mean that they are outside of the realm of regulation. Rather, as the contributors to this section demonstrate, "families" and even "mothers" as we understand them are created through administrative procedures. Social and economic policy and law, as well as interests separate from the state (i.e., religious or private charity organizations) making potent moral claims about families shape our perceptions of what families should and should not be, as well as the rights and responsibilities of those who live within them.

As new forms of intervention (or what Foucauldian analysis would refer to as "techniques of governing") emerge, so too do new "experts" who themselves develop and administer these techniques. While administrators and professionals in psychology, social work, health, education, law, etc. intervene in both obvious and less apparent ways into *all* families, those which are considered to be *problem* families are particularly subject to surveillance and intervention. This intervention may be justified because children are perceived to be at **risk**. But how is risk understood? What constitutes risk? Xiaobei Chen addresses this question in her chapter.

When we read our daily newspaper or turn on the TV to watch the evening news, we might find ourselves faced with tragic narratives of severely abused children, some of whom die from their injuries. It is no wonder, then, that a public climate has developed which favours more stringent regulation of the abusers of children. Yet while our support for what Kirsten Johnson Kramar refers to as "vengeance for the innocents" is an understandable emotional response, we need to think about the implications of carte blanche support for new forms of regulation. Chen argues that tougher criminal sanctions against the perpetrators of abuse give a false sense of accomplishment, which does little to actually protect children.

Currently, there is significant concern about children who manage to "fall through the cracks of the system." Despite being already identified as children at risk, they die from abuse and neglect. However, Chen finds that children receiving the services of the Children's Aid Society in Ontario have a death rate that is actually lower than for the rest of the population. Among other intriguing findings, she notes that children are most at risk from accidents, particularly motor vehicle accidents. She wonders why there is so much attention to the child protection system and so little attention to means to prevent these much more numerous deaths. Moreover, Chen notes that children identified as in need of protection are most likely to fall into this category because of living circumstances related to poverty, rather than because they are deliberately neglected or abused.

Given that it is overwhelmingly women who have the primary responsibility for the care of children, it is perhaps not surprising that the administration of child protection should focus so much attention on mothers. Yet both Chen and Kramar find that a lot is going on behind this seemingly straightforward logic. Chen uses the governmentality approach to explore the constitution of mothers, particularly young single mothers, as dangerous for their children, and the techniques emerging to deal with them. She finds that governing technologies are producing a two pronged approach, the first comprised of risk management, and the second comprised of punishment.

Kristin Johnson Kramar is particularly concerned with the trend toward increasing punishment of mothers. One of the indications that this is occurring is the call for the elimination of the legal category of Infanticide in Canada, so that women who would previously have been so charged would now be charged with child abuse and other homicide offences. Infanticide has since the origins of the Canadian Criminal Code been a woman specific offence, designed to account for the circumstances in which desperate women give birth to unwanted babies, and attempt to immediately conceal the birth through actions which deliberately or unwittingly lead to the newborn's death. Compassion for the circumstances which these women face, lead to the suggestion that a distinct homicide provision was warranted. The charge of Infanticide has rarely been laid in recent decades, because the killing of babies by their mothers immediately after the birth is a rare event, and because it is indeed only applied in what are considered to be specific and special circumstances. Johnson Kramar explores how Infanticide is being reconceptualized as child abuse homicide, on the basis of cases which were unrelated to the legal definition of Infanticide. She addresses this within the context of an analysis of the ways in which child abuse came to be regarded as a significant social problem. Her analysis includes the development of medical and legal strategies for the regulation of child abuse.

Johnson Kramar, Chen, and Little draw our attention to the ways in which single mothers are automatically considered to be problem mothers, and subject to extra regulatory strategies. Margaret Little explains how single mothers who require social assistance in Ontario are required to prove themselves both financially and morally deserving of support, under an ever expanding set of rules, for a diminishing amount of financial assistance. Little examines how moral regulation occurs at the provincial and federal levels of the Canadian state,[1] as well as through a range of private organizations such as charities devoted to helping the poor. While Chen takes up a governmentality approach, Little's use of the concept of moral regulation is grounded in a materialist analysis of poverty. She explains how the welfare system benefits capitalism, and that welfare policy is not only an economic project but also a moral project. She demonstrates the on-going usefulness of the concept of moral regulation as a tool for social analysis.

All three contributors to this section make a link between the growing attention to bad mothers and endangered children and the expansion of anti-welfarist New Right political discourse and social policy in Ontario. This is not to imply that they think that all mothers really are "angels in the home" raising happy, well cared for children. Rather, they suggest that current directions in the administration of families are increasingly punitive toward those which are not considered to be normal families (those which do not measure up to the 1950s ideal discussed by Gleason in an earlier chapter). Technologies for the governance of families, which have been produced and deployed through the work of state agencies, private service organizations, and mainstream media, have been so successful that even persons who consider themselves worlds away from this ideal might enthusiastically consent to the discipline and punishment of those perceived as unworthy. After reading these chapters, we ask you to explore and compare events in your own province, and to think about the origins of your own beliefs about bad mothers and endangered children.

[1] The local level state is also implicated. She addresses this in other work, cited in her recommended readings.

CHAPTER 9

VENGEANCE FOR THE INNOCENTS: THE NEW MEDICO-LEGAL DESIGNATION OF "INFANTICIDE" AS "CHILD ABUSE HOMICIDE"

BY KIRSTEN JOHNSON KRAMAR

This essay examines cases of infant death investigated by the Ontario Office of the Coroner between 1980 and 1998 in order to analyze the medico-legal processes whereby many, if not most, infant deaths investigated by coroners have come to be regarded as undetected incidents of "child abuse homicide." This chapter will show that significant kinds of regulatory practices and categories of deviance emerge from certain historical events that are unrelated to the events or processes subsequently subject to regulation. One of the central organizing underlying messages of this essay is that critical criminologists and socio-legal theorists should not be too quick to describe the resultant patterns of regulation as inevitable outcomes of patriarchal capitalism or discourses. What this research will show is that these kinds of over-arching theoretical formulations are sometimes incorrect because the development of regulatory categories and criminal laws is open and contingent, with their outcomes often unpredictable. In the case of the development of the law of infanticide governing maternal neonaticide in the early 20th century in Canada and its current application by the courts, a very complex series of historical events with ironic outcomes and unintended consequences might be critically examined from a perspective that attends to the ways in which regulatory categories are operationalized by agents of the state.[1] And, they can be further analysed in terms of their effects on the women to whom the regulatory category or law applies. In other words, the *effects* of regulatory categories and laws should remain firmly in view, rather than the seemingly oppressive historical conditions from whence they came.

In the first section of this essay, I describe the discovery and medicalization of child abuse in North America and the United Kingdom in the broadest terms; the identification

---

[1] The term infanticide and maternal neonaticide are used throughout this essay to refer to the killing of unwanted babies by their biological mothers. However, readers should note that infanticide is a legal category while maternal neonaticide is a non-legal description of events.

of child abuse as a significant social problem and one which should be of special concern to forensic pathologists. In the second section, I describe the development of the medico-legal concept of "battered baby syndrome" and the implementation of "child death review teams" as a means of identifying and/or preventing "missed" incidents of the syndrome. According to Hacking (1995, p. 56) child abuse is always "discovered" after sensational (or sensationalized) incidents. In other words, while vile behaviour towards children is far from a new phenomenon it requires "inventing new descriptions [and] providing new ways to see old acts—and a great deal of social agitation" before it becomes an objective of investigation and social action (Hacking, 1995, p. 55). My research at the Office of the Chief Coroner illustrates how new descriptions or interpretations of maternal neonaticide has been invented by medico-legal authorities which are then publicised by the press, providing the public with "new ways of seeing old acts." In the third section, I provide a contemporary illustration of this process. Here, I discuss a press campaign mounted in the *Toronto Star* designed to highlight maternal neonaticide cases, which the newspaper considered to be examples of "women getting away with murder." I show how closely this campaign was linked to activities of the Office of the Chief Coroner, which I describe in the next section. These activities included the establishment of a number of inquests, as well as a broader campaign to influence the public and especially legislators and those responsible for child protection policy about undetected and under-prosecuted cases of "child abuse homicide." This campaign had its counterpart at the federal level in the establishment of a broader consultation process, which includes the consideration of amendments to the Criminal Code framework governing infant homicides, which is discussed in the final section of this essay.

"Vengeance for the Innocents" demonstrates how law and order advocates have misconstrued infanticide as a kind of "child abuse" and have consequently responded to the practice as "child abuse homicide," resulting in attempts to convict very vulnerable young women for first and second degree murder. This response to infanticide is largely justified in the name of the "innocent" baby who has emerged as the latest rights bearing victim in Canadian criminal and family law. The essay shows how heightened moral condemnation of "child abuse" resulted in augmented criminal law responses by coroners, police, and social workers to infanticide. These various agents rely on reports submitted by only a few forensic pathologists who specialise in the identification of child abuse homicide. Many of these reports actually defined "child abuse" as an official "cause of death" for infants who are killed or die shortly following unattended labour and delivery, despite the fact that the World Health Organization does not include this as an officially recognised cause of death category.[2] The essay demonstrates

[2] See infant mortality data, World Health Organization Statistical Information System: <www.who.int/whosis/>

how a kind of very public and sensationalised campaign unfolded in Ontario during the 1990s, largely in response to toddlers who died from serious neglect and abuse and which consequently drew attention to the fairly serious and ongoing social problem of child beating. However, the extension of the category of "child abuse homicide" from these kinds of cases to homicides involving newborns is problematic. The essay highlights the kinds of problems involving poorly thought out public policy recommendations that fail to distinguish between two very different phenomena: "child abuse" and "infanticide."

HISTORICAL BACKDROP: THE DEVELOPMENT OF IDEAS ABOUT "INFANTICIDE" AND "CHILD ABUSE"

During the nineteenth and early twentieth centuries, in Canada, maternal neonaticide, or infanticide, to use the legal term, was considered an immoral act generally committed by poor, unmarried, and socially isolated women. Most members of Canadian society could understand and excuse the women's actions as the unfortunate outcome of straightened social circumstances. Few of these women were ever subject to criminal law punishment, and if they were charged and convicted of murder, their sentences were invariably commuted (Kramar, 2000). Today, in the late twentieth and early twenty-first centuries, maternal neonaticide is re-cast in terms of criminal responsibility for a wholly wanted pregnancy that requires criminal law punishment. A variety of reforms in law and in public sensibility have resulted in the overall elevation of the status of the ex-nuptial infant and its unwilling mother. First, the reform of inheritance laws intended to prevent illegitimacy and its socially unacceptable counterpart single motherhood. Then decriminalization, and subsequent access to, contraception and abortion; the symbolic rise in the legal status of the infant, due in part to the political tactics of the anti-choice movement which has showed us pictures of a fetus in utero to garner sympathy and support of the idea that abortion is akin to killing a born-alive human being. Finally, media reports of maternal neonaticide now tend to refer to these incidents as "dumpster babies" implying that the women (and sometimes men) who put them there, think of these unwanted babies as *garbage* rather than accepting that they are plainly attempting to conceal their pregnancies and subsequent births.

In this context, official responses to maternal neonaticide using the infanticide provision have been broadened to include punishment using family law provisions and harsher criminal charges.[3] There has also been a significant scholarly critique from feminist perspectives of the infanticide provision itself, widely argued to be an instance of the patriarchal "medicalization of women's deviance" that fails to account for the very social conditions of unwanted, socially isolated motherhood, especially in the context of young women's limited access to contraception and abortion. There are those, too, who see the infanticide provision as an instance of "chivalry" in which violent women are given less punitive treatment than men by the criminal justice system. The more Foucauldian feminist approach would be to evaluate the infanticide provision in terms of its broader social impact including the positive and negative effects of law. This view argues that there is a difference between the law and practice. Here it is the practical effects of law in everyday practice as opposed to the wording of the legal text that is the central concern of critical scholars.

Within the context of these academic debates, my contribution will be to draw attention to the role played by medico-legal authorities, specifically coroners, whose authority to define or re-interpret a cause of death finding can influence police and crown attorneys in their decisions about whether or not to charge and prosecute persons (typically mothers) with a particular criminal offence like murder. My approach with this essay is closest to what I've described as the Foucaultian feminist approach. Here I want to draw attention to the consequences of law and order approaches that resort to criminal law as a means of solving what are essentially problems with broader social antecedents and defend the use of the infanticide provision despite its apparent medicalization of deviance.

Such an analysis of case files of Ontario coroners' investigations into infant deaths will show how coroners, police, and Crown Attorneys have come to

---

[3] In two cases that I know of, Children's Aid Societies in Ontario (1994 and 1995) have applied to the courts for Crown wardship on the grounds that a child was in need of protection on the basis of evidence of infanticide. In one case, the CAS sought wardship of an infant on the grounds that her mother, 41 years old at the time, described as developmentally handicapped and mentally ill, had been convicted of infanticide when she was 20 years old. According to the CAS rationale, this woman's choice to become a mother was forfeited when she was conviction for infanticide some 21 years earlier. The order was granted, mainly on the theory that the child was at serious risk of harm, and without any evidence that mothers who commit infanticide are likely to repeat the offence decades later. In fact, most infanticide sentencing dispositions highlight the fact that these women *do not* pose any future threat (*CAS of the Durham Region* v. *J.R.* [1995] O.J. No. 3419 online: QL). In the second case, CAS sought guardianship appointment of a 16-year-old girl who gave birth unassisted and put the dead baby in a dumpster. CAS argued that she was a child in need of protection who had suffered emotional harm from her *mother's* lack of knowledge of her pregnancy and failure to make legal arrangements for the daughter! This application was dismissed on the grounds that there was no evidence the teen's mother had failed in her duty as a parent (*CAS for the Districts of Sudbury and Manitoulin* v. *M.S.* [1994] O.J. No. 2902, online: QL). I could find no evidence of such applications being made in other jurisdictions or during an earlier period.

approach the prosecution of maternal neonaticide in the context of other kinds of homicide typically constructed as child abuse murder, and how, in light of a perceived failure of the criminal justice and child welfare systems to prevent these deaths and punish the perpetrators, "infanticide" cases are now responded to in a decidedly more punitive fashion than previously. In this broader socio-legal context, the Criminal Code infanticide provision has become academically unfashionable, as well as an only rarely preferred criminal charge. "Infanticide" is no longer a popular category since it is now only used to define a baby killed under the narrowest of circumstances. And, to complicate matters, "plea arrangements" from women charged with manslaughter are sometimes accepted by Crown Attorneys for the lesser charge of infanticide for cases of infant homicide which clearly do not conform to the aims of the Criminal Code infanticide provision.

In what follows, I also chart the rise of what is known as a child abuse discourse, from its emergence in the mid-twentieth century, when it was identified as a "new" phenomenon, to its contemporary position as the dominant paradigm through which virtually all childhood suffering, and certainly all child homicides, are apprehended. This essay thus explores a significant historical shift in the criminal justice regulation of maternal neonaticide. Canadian authorities historically constructed maternal neonaticide as a "device of last resort" for desperate young women but they now construct it as a wholly willed and wicked act of an abusive violent mother despite the fact that the some of the cultural conditions that prompt maternal neonaticide still persist. The regulation of maternal neonaticide as child abuse homicide has resulted in a flawed re-conceptualization of these kinds of deaths as "child abuse homicide." Infanticide-type deaths bear no social or legal connection to the professional designation "child abuse" which is generally understood by the child protection movement to be a dysfunctional social relation between a caregiver and a small child. Babies killed at birth have not yet had any social relation with their caregivers and generally live no more than a few seconds before they are killed or left to die. This event, defined as "infanticide" since the early seventeenth century in England and since the eighteen and nineteenth centuries in Canada and the United States has never been considered a form of "child abuse," until now. In fact, many infant deaths are difficult for authorities to figure out. They remain without clear causes and are typically classified as "unexplained" or "sudden infant deaths," but these designations are now often suspected to mask child abuse, warranting extensive investigation and surveillance of single women by social workers, police, and forensic pathologists, under the coordination of the Offices of the Coroners. Child abuse homicide is targeted for a punitive legal response in the form of a first or second degree murder charge with the mothers often as prime suspects despite the fact that from the point of view of criminal conviction, causes of death remain vague. The changes in the way in which cases of infant death are scrutinized by agents of the criminal justice system have had a significant impact on the eventual outcomes of a range of cases caught up in the web of fears about undetected child abuse in North America and elsewhere (Best, 1990; Jenks, 1996; Scheper-Hughes & Stein, 1987).

INFANTICIDE AND THE MEDICALIZATION OF CHILD ABUSE: THE "DISCOVERY" OF "CHILD ABUSE" IN CANADA, BRITAIN, AND THE UNITED STATES

The "discovery" of "child abuse" as a serious social problem and its subsequent definition as "deviance" requiring medical, legal, and social welfare intervention is identified by various authors as emerging between the 1940s and the 1960s in differing professional contexts mainly in the United States. This approach developed alongside a gradual disappearance of cultural attitudes sanctioning corporal punishment. Battering first became characterized as an illness and only subsequently became characterized as criminal deviance in the 1980s (Pfohl, 1977). Hacking (1995, p. 56) argues that the exact phrase "child abuse" seldom appeared before 1960, its predecessor being "cruelty to children."

The "discovery" of "child abuse" within the academic and professional disciplines is generally credited to J. Caffey, a forensic pathologist, who published his discovery of fractures in long bones of infants who had died from subdural hematoma in the *American Journal of Radiology* in 1946 (Caffey, 1946, pp. 163–173). Amongst forensic pathologists interested in child abuse, this is identified as the earliest discovery of what was then known as "Caffey's Syndrome." This was, however, not the first time that violence against children had been discovered. In the late nineteenth century, the people involved in the nascent social work industry had identified cruelty towards children as a significant social problem requiring drastic intervention (Pfohl, 1977). This "discovery" of child abuse by Caffey in 1946 led to a range of research studies by forensic pathologists in the U.S. who ventured to scientifically document and describe whether or not and how babies had died from a range of violent means (usually chronic subdural hematoma). In addition, they raised concerns about the designation of "sudden infant death syndrome" or "sudden unexplained death" as providing a tenuous category that potentially masked intentional homicides. Underlying the discovery of child abuse was the belief that known cases typically referred to as "fatal battered babies" represented only a tiny fraction of the actual occurrences.

In practical, or procedural, terms Caffey's "discovery" resulted in a range of forensic pathologists being trained to autopsy babies with a view towards determining if they had been the victims of child abuse. In 1960, Lester Adelson a forensic pathologist working in Cleveland, Ohio, published *Pathology of Homicide* and influenced subsequent generations of forensic pathologists in the

United States.[4] Those who trained under Adelson went on to initiate research which recognized "child abuse syndrome" and "shaken baby syndrome" as a *bona fide* causes of death in infants (see Helfer, Kempe, & Krugman, 1997).

Commenting on the British experience, Jenkins (1992, p. 104) argued that the discovery of child abuse was linked to professional aspirations mainly amongst groups such as pediatric radiologists and forensic pathologists who actively published in Britain on the subject. According to Jenkins, the *British Medical Journal* is widely credited with publishing the first discovery of the so-called battered baby syndrome in 1963. Scheper-Hughes and Stein (1987, p. 339) argue that child abuse and neglect, long grappled with as a vexing and chronic social problem by generations of child welfare and social workers, was suddenly "discovered" and expropriated by a more powerful profession: medicine. When C. Henry Kempe and his associates (1962) at Colorado General Hospital created a new diagnostic entity the "Battered Child Syndrome" the American public finally sat up and took notice.

This "discovery" of child abuse by the medical profession in the U.S. led to broader discoveries and increasing reports of child abuse. A range of national incidence studies, beginning in the 1970s, "reported sharp increases annually in the reports of maltreatment." According to Scheper-Hughes and Stein, this reported rise in incidents had a particular effect,

> Between 1976 and 1981, the total number of reports documented nationwide has more than doubled (the American Humane Association 1983). Social and behavioral scientists rushed in, often with premature causal explanations based on retrospective studies of poorly defined abusers and abused. Research instruments and procedures were designed and implemented for the early detection of "high risk" parents (i.e., *mothers*) at public hospitals. Welfare patients, especially single mothers, were observed throughout labor, delivery, and the hours postpartum for signs of inadequate attachment to their newborns (*see* Kempe & Kempe, 1978 pp. 62–63). Based on inferences from this brief period of observation, "problem" mothers were targeted for early intervention programs that included home visits by nurses, clinical social workers, and child welfare workers. (1987, p. 339)

It is, as Scheper-Hughes and Stein (1987, p. 339) note, unsurprising that the development of these interventionist strategies gave rise to the child abuse "expert" in a range of fields,

---

[4] Michael S. Pollanen, M.D., Ph.D., (Personal Communication) Department of Laboratory Medicine and Pathobiology, Office of the Chief Coroner for Ontario and Forensic Science Programme, University of Toronto. February 2000.

the discovery of child abuse and the consequent development of interventionist strategies also resulted in a proliferation of child abuse experts, researchers, educators, clinicians, therapists, and social workers occupying newly created positions as members of child trauma teams in hospitals, on child abuse "hot lines", as facilitators in self-help "parenting" and stress management groups, and in emergency shelters and treatment programs for the abused. Child Abuse Prevention (CAP) workers visited schools, clinics, and day care programs in order to alert teachers, doctors and child care professionals to the covert signs (i.e., distress and agitation) thought to be symptomatic of "sexually abused" children. In addition, they hold classes to educate even young toddlers, with the use of "anatomically correct" puppets and dolls, about the differences in "good: and "bad" touches by parents and other adult caretakers. This was said to be part of the process of "empowering" children. (Scheper-Hughes and Stein 1987. pp. 339–340)

And finally, the media played a role in buttressing the interventions of these experts by publicizing some of the most bizarre and sadistic examples of child abuse. According to Scheper-Hughes and Stein, these narratives played a significant role in justifying the new and unprecedented "public interventions into the private lives of citizens" (1987, p. 340).

One aspect of the definition of child abuse across the different professions that is clearly evident is that infanticide or maternal neonaticide is usually not included as part of the social relations of child abuse.[5] Infanticide has generally been viewed as a gender specific form of homicide within a framework that mitigates women's culpability on either a compassionate or a psychiatric basis. The diminished responsibility lens through which infanticide has been viewed stands in stark contrast to the law and order lens through which many now regulate child abuse and infant homicide as intentional lethal violence perpetrated by parents and caregivers. In the process, infanticide became almost obsolete, subsumed under the "child abuse homicide" concept, with its focus on intervention, detection, and punishment. This is not because the practice of infanticide has disappeared, but because these kinds of deaths have been swept up into another category entirely.

---

[5] See for example, Dorne (1989). There is a great deal of conceptual slippage between the use of the terms infanticide and child abuse. U.S. sociologists tend to keep the line fairly clear, however, they also attach the more severe descriptions of postpartum psychosis to the practice. Any maternal neonaticides that fall outside of the strong psychiatric paradigm tend to be viewed as something "other" than "infanticide." See for example Ewing (1997) on "dumpster babies" and for an overview of U.S. research on postpartum illness see Hamilton Harberger (Eds.) (1992).

"FATAL CHILD ABUSE SYNDROME" AND CHILD DEATH REVIEW TEAMS: THE INTERNATIONAL CONTEXT

By the mid-1980s a number of cases in Britain and the United States revealed that children had died who had been in the care of state child protection agencies and social workers. In Britain, there were numerous investigations following an inquiry into the death of seven-year-old Maria Colwell in 1973. Maria Colwell had been removed from her home to a foster home and then returned only to be starved and repeatedly beaten before eventually being murdered by her stepfather. The inquest into her death led to intense media scrutiny and criticism of individual social workers and the child protection agency (Jenkins 1992, pp. 104–105). According to Jenkins, the Colwell case galvanized a range of professional interests resulting in a range of social and political reactions. Most significantly, the concept of child abuse entered public consciousness in a new way and mobilized a range of experts who came to view child abuse as a problem of crime control rather than unmet social welfare needs. According to Jenkins (1992, p. 105),

> The consequences of the Colwell case have been described as a moral panic over the theme of physical abuse, a topic frequently addressed in book, documentaries, and fictional works during the next three years. In 1976, a Parliamentary Select Committee on Violence in the Family produced a report with a separate volume on violence perpetrated against children. *Child Abuse* entered public debate as a concept and a term. In 1970, the central problem was *battered babies*; *nonaccidental injury* came to the fore by 1974; by 1978 *child abuse* established itself as a dominant phrase. The usage was consolidated and popularized by the British publication during 1978 of *Child Abuse*, by R.S. and C. Henry Kempe.[6]

The Colwell inquiry led to a range of procedural amendments for the regulation and administration of the child protection system in the United Kingdom

---

[6] This book was first published in the United States in 1968 by R.E. Helfer and C. Henry Kempe with the University of Chicago Press. The fifth edition was recently published in paperback (1997) as *The Battered Child* but without the editorial assistance of C. Henry Kempe, who died in 1984, or Ray Helfer who died in 1992. This work was continued by M.E. Helfer and R.S. Kempe, the widows and colleagues of Ray Helfer and C. Henry Kempe respectively. As a student and later colleague of both R. Helfer and C. Henry Kempe, R.D. Krugman provided editorial assistance on the fifth edition. Kempe himself was *the* key figure in the child abuse and neglect studies movement. Born in Germany, he spent most of his professional life in the United States and founded the International Society for the Prevention of Child Abuse and Neglect and its journal *Child Abuse and Neglect.* According to Jenkins (1992, p. 111) "these institutions provided a forum for British specialists and activists and an opportunity to exchange ideas with their American and European counterparts."

with the underlying aim of detecting children "at risk" for child abuse to prevent possible murders. Interagency coordination was a key feature of this new protection system. Tracking suspected or known child abusers and providing education and training to social workers in order to identify the warning signs of child abuse were the focus of intervention and prevention. This focus on those "at risk" through the education of social workers and the development of centralized child abuser registries were the main policy solutions that developed during this period. The identification of risk factors for infant homicide soon became the Holy Grail of social workers, police, and investigating forensic pathologists. In addition, feminist movements pressed authorities to recognize and criminalize child sexual abuse.

The first child death review team in North American was established in the late 1970s in the U.S. Since that time, child death review teams have been established in most U.S. states and two Canadian provinces (Wilczynski, 1997, p. 186). The main objective of these teams has been to re-evaluate forensic medical evidence and provide amended "cause of death" designations in light of newly acquired knowledge about child abuse homicide. These teams have been established largely without public pressure or support and are the result of concerns by persons in certain professional sectors who have witnessed child deaths and felt powerless to either prevent them or participate actively in a punitive carceral response. However, the news media, alerted to the professional concerns, would do their best to generate public interest and concern about the issue. In Ontario, in the late 1990s, the *Toronto Star* threw its weight behind the campaign for criminal and civil law reform.

THE *TORONTO STAR* DISCOVERS CHILD BEATING

"They Died Despite Signs of Abuse"

(Walsh & Donovan, 1996, September 18, p. A1) In 1996 two staff reporters for the *Toronto Star* newspaper wrote that they approached the Ontario Coroner's Office and asked the coroner to review child deaths for a five-year time period which they had already researched to determine if the case files showed "trends similar" to those their researchers had observed, which included especially the overly lenient sanctions deployed against mothers, fathers, and parents together charged in the deaths of their children. Perhaps, not surprisingly, given that the Coroner's Office had already identified the problem and a number of inquests were pending, the Coroner's Office investigation following the *Star*'s prompt "discovered" the same thing.[7]

---

[7] Moira Welsh and Kevin Donovan, the *Toronto Star*, September 18, 1996, p. A1. This newspaper report is in fact not quite accurate. The Ontario Coroner's Office had been concerned about the deaths of children in the care of Child and Family Services for quite some time before the *Toronto Star* became involved and had identified the "trend" in the cases of infant deaths they had investigated over the years.

The newspaper report characterizes missed warning signs as a serious problem and a failure of the Children's Aid Societies. According to the *Star*'s "ongoing investigation of 77 child deaths in the past five years" it was discovered that "serious warning signs" existed prior to death in at least 23 cases.[8] According to the *Star* report: "Of the 23, children's aid societies were involved in hearing of abuse in 15 cases" (p. A6). This figure represents a total of 19.4 percent of all cases reviewed over a five-year period. The *Star* further reported that, "the coroner's review examined 135 homicide cases in the same time period. That review, which is also preliminary, showed that 22 of the 135 cases were known to an Ontario children's aid society prior to the homicide" (Ibid. p. A6).

According to the Coroner's study, there were slightly fewer children "known to" Children's Aid Societies (16.3%) in which the children may have died from parental violence than found in the study the *Star* claimed to have conducted. In other words, of all the cases reviewed those children "known to" Children's Aid Societies (CAS) were slightly better off than those not "known to." Nevertheless, the suspicion was that there were many more cases "known to" Children's Aid Societies that simply remained undocumented. Dr. Jim Cairns, Deputy Chief Coroner at the Toronto office, signalled the potential reality of many more "unknown" infant homicides when he noted that he would only be able to confirm if Children's Aid was involved if it was written in the coroner's file (Ibid. p. A6). However, the use of the category of "children known to" Children's Aid Societies is a poor category: these are not children who are actually under the care of Children's Aid Societies; they are simply "known to" the Societies for one reason or another. These are not children with whom social workers have any particularly regular contact and therefore the idea of social worker accountability in their deaths is usually misplaced.

The *Star* report was timed to coordinate with the announcement by Dr. Cairns that a joint task force with the Ontario Association of Children's Aid Societies would study the causes of child mortality in Ontario with a view towards prevention of future deaths and creating a system to evaluate the risk of serious injury or death in each case known to Child and Family Services (p. A1). According to Cairns, "his research found numerous cases where a young homicide victim was known to a Children's Aid Society prior to death, often because of abuse or neglect" (Ibid. p. A1). Both the proposed Inquest and the newly established Ontario Child Mortality Task Force targeted (or had already in mind) a range of "long overdue" administrative and criminal legal changes to remedy deficiencies of the child welfare system. These included the eventual implementation of a centralized

---

[8] Moira Welsh and Kevin Donovan, the *Toronto Star*, September 18, 1996, p. A1. This represents 30 percent of those cases in which the deaths of "children" under the age of 18 were investigated by the Ontario Coroner's Office over a five-year period.

interactive child abuse registry managed by the Ministry of Community and Social Services for tracking known and suspected child abusers which would be accessible to all provincial Children's Aid Societies, police, coroners and doctors who suspected abuse.[9] This centralized system would replace the poorly managed and ineffectual provincial child abuse registry.[10] In addition, the Office of the Coroner was committed to improving its own investigative procedures. Dr. Cairns noted that "we need to educate all professionals involved with high risk children with a view to learning how to prevent deaths" (Welsh & Donovan, 1996, September 18, p. A6).

The first story introduced the readers to one case, which involved a baby who had died where signs of abuse were missed by the pathologist who performed the initial autopsy and determined that the cause of death of the eight-month-old infant was sudden infant death syndrome. The body of this infant was exhumed three years later when it was discovered that a month old sibling was hospitalized with a broken leg, bruises and a bleeding nose (Ibid. p. A6). In yet another example, a six-month-old died following numerous contacts with health care professionals. A doctor failed to diagnose a broken arm as intentional child abuse and the abuse was also missed by child welfare workers who, according to the report,

> didn't investigate Sara's living conditions and accepted denials of abuse by her crack-addicted parents; a Canadian Mothercraft Society worker didn't investigate Sara's room for the obvious signs of neglect and abuse; and the children's aid society did not heed warnings from the parole officer of the baby's father, who had been jailed five years for assaulting his son, Mikey Junior, so viciously that he was left permanently disabled and blind. The parole officer had warned that the father was planning to move back with the family. (Ibid. p. A6)

The *Star* story attempted to make clear that there were instances in which serious questions were raised about the management of these cases. This case was included to highlight something that had been noticed by the Coroner's Office over the

---

[9] According to Cyril Greenland (1973, p. 27) the province's child abuse registry has been in operation since 1966 and in the first four years of its operation, over 1,600 cases were reported, with only 4 percent of those being cases of repeat battering. In these 4 years, 172 charges were laid with 42 convictions. Greenland's 1973 study identified many of the same problems with the registry identified in the 1990s by the Office of the Chief Coroner. One major problem identified by Greenland, but not the Office of the Chief Coroner is the registry's limited value for statistical purposes because of the lack of a standardized definition of "child abuse."

[10] At the same time, a "super inquest" into domestic violence was announced. This announcement came too after a so-called "groundbreaking investigation of domestic violence by the *Star*." Dr. Bonnie Porter, a deputy chief coroner for the Niagara region stated simply that: "The aim is to start a war against domestic abuse similar to the campaign now waged against drunk driving." "Super inquest to probe growing family violence" Canadian Press, the *Toronto Star*, September 18, 1996, p. A1

years, which was that the labelling of deaths as SIDS often disguised deaths from what they called "child abuse syndrome."

"Cry for the Children"

Following the high profile announcements about the Coroner's Inquests, and the Ontario Child Mortality Task Force Joint Task Force by Deputy Chief Coroner Dr. Jim Cairns, the *Star* ran a series titled "Cry for the Children" between April and June of 1997 in which they described the circumstances of a few especially shocking deaths of babies and toddlers "known to" Children's Aid Societies. In the first story of the series "Cry for the Children," which ran on the front page of Saturday, April 19's, paper, the *Star* described the infants as "victims of the system," which "put the rights of abusive parents over the safety of their children" (Welsh & Donovan,1997, April 19, p. A1). This story, along with others in the series, in fact highlighted the worst examples of child poverty, parental neglect, and abuse. In the discussion of these few cases, it was pointed out that signs of abuse were evident, yet further violence resulted in death. Sprinkled with photographs of abused and murdered babies and toddlers, the series described in intimate detail the injuries inflicted on the babies and toddlers, often by their mother's boyfriends and sometimes by the father, while pointing out the failures of both the Ontario provincial welfare and Canadian federal criminal justice systems and urging a range of policy changes to save the lives of children.

Following the story six months earlier which had described one or two cases in which infants and toddlers were the victims of domestic violence, this so-called "investigative report" was meant to draw out, for the public, the extent and nature of the problem of child abuse by presenting the material in an individualized and very personalized manner. It is evident from that first story in September 1996, and the ones which followed in the spring of 1997, that the media coverage was in some way aimed at educating the public about the nature and extent of the problem of child abuse homicides to prepare the public for the administrative and criminal law procedural changes that would reappear in 1998 as Inquest and Task Force recommendations. By the time these recommendations were announced, the readership of the *Star* was already intimately familiar with the kinds of injuries sustained by the few infants and toddlers who died from intentional violence and with the frustrations of police who thought they could have prevented their deaths had they been informed. The readership was also informed, through individual case narratives and the opinions advanced by the Office of the Coroner, that the criminal sentences given to perpetrators did not reflect the seriousness of the crime pointing to a need for more punitive sanctions. And finally, and perhaps most importantly of all, the readership was encouraged to see that something could be done about it if laws and attitudes were changed.

"A Cop's Crusade"

The second story, "A Cop's Crusade," which ran a week later, described the failures of the child protection system from the point of view of the Provincial Police Detective who investigated the death of Tiffani Coville. His personal account of his frustration with failures to protect the infant are used as a narrative device to highlight once again the failure of the child welfare and criminal justice systems from the vantage point of her posthumous "hero;" the police officer (Welsh & Donovan, 1997, April 26, p. A1). The story argues that Tiffani was failed in life and in death by doctors, nurses, and social workers who had not called the police, by a system that did not track known child abusers and by a coroner who listed her death as sudden infant death syndrome and allowed her burial even though x-rays would eventually suggest, when read a second time by a senior radiologist that there were healing fractured rib injuries, an unusual and suspicious finding in an infant so young. The police officer hero is credited with bringing a measure of "justice" to her death by uncovering the sequence of events that led to her death at the hands of her mother's common-law spouse. The story suggests that good police work along with certain procedural changes in reporting to police will lead to the detection and prosecution of many more cases of child abuse and murder.

"Getting Away with Murder"

The third story in the *Star* series presented the argument that "most parents who kill their children in Ontario receive little or no punishment for their crimes" (Welsh & Donovan, 1997, May 18, p. A1). Their claims are buttressed by quotes from homicide detectives interviewed for the story who supported the authors' dismay at the sentences. One officer is quoted as saying that "The life of a child is cheap, very cheap" (Ibid. p. A1).

According to the *Star,*

> Serious charges like second-degree murder are often plea bargained down because of poor medical and police investigations, the tendency of police, crown attorneys and judges to feel sympathy for the accused parent, and the simple fact that children are so easy to kill that little trace of the crime remains. As a result, parents charged in the death of a child typically receive no jail time or sentences of less than two years. And the younger the child killed, the lower the punishment. Jim Cairns, Ontario's deputy chief coroner, who is making it much of his life's work to change standards for child death investigations, agrees that sentences don't reflect the horror of the crime. (Ibid. p. A1)

This story frames the issue in terms of a failure of the criminal justice system to adequately address the seriousness of this sort of crime in much the same way as it had framed the earlier issues; in this article, individual cases are again personalized and highlighted for intense scrutiny. This decontextualized approach made it appear as though parents were and are in fact "getting away with murder." The story provides the reader with reporter produced information on sentencing practices in statistical form "proving" their claim is true. Just in case the point is missed by any of the readers, the authors provide a table of nine cases entitled "crime and little punishment" to illustrate their thesis that people are getting away with the murder of children. These cases are detailed in the report to educate the reader on the difficulties with gaining "appropriate" convictions, with the underlying message that "appropriate" means either first or second degree murder charges.

What is striking about the presentation of these materials (aside from the absolute failure to provide any kind of balanced assessment of the individual cases in the context of homicide more generally either by providing Canadian Criminal Justice Statistics on infant homicide or by interviewing sociologists and criminologists who might provide this contextual perspective) is the way in which their sample of 70 cases is presented as 70 cases of *actual* child abuse. They present these 70 cases as though there is no question that these are, in fact, purposeful child abuse cases in which an infant or toddler dies from repeated abuse and that the perpetrators are, in fact, guilty. It is important to note that the 70 cases in their sample, and even the 52 of the cases that went to court, are *not* all cases of child abuse, as the reporters claim. This story ignores the possibility that the reason many of these cases did not go to trial or were plea-bargained is because they were one-time-only events and/or accidental. Nevertheless, the story tells us that "71 percent got off with little or no punishment" and that "in return for a guilty plea, the charge was plea bargained down to a lesser charge in 51 percent of the 41 cases where a parent or caregiver was convicted" (Welsh & Donovan, 1997, May 18, p. A6). We are also told that less jail time is received for younger victims, again without any notion of the circumstances of the death, as though the criminal justice response in all homicide cases should simply result in convictions of second degree murder regardless of the circumstances of the individual deaths. Thus, not only does the story not provide the reader with information on how these charging and plea-bargaining practices compare with the homicides of adults, but it also fails to provide the reader a sense of the circumstances in each case that might actually warrant lesser charges and reduced penalties.

The cases, both in the table and the bold statistical figures, provide the reader with the impression that all of these infants were the victims of child abuse and that all of the perpetrators are guilty of the Criminal Code offence of murder. If one explores their data in more depth even using the numbers they provided, one discovers that in 29 percent of the cases that went to court, the accused received sentences of between two and seven years or life sentences. But of the 71 percent who supposedly "got off with little or no punishment," 30 percent (21 percent of those who went to court) were acquitted or determined to be not guilty, which means that of those who were found guilty (41 in all), 63 percent "got off with little or no punishment," as the *Star* puts it. We can separate "little" from "no." Twenty-four percent of those found guilty of a criminal offence, received no actual jail sentence (but were likely sentenced to years of probation and community service). Those in the "little" category amounted to 39 percent of those who were found guilty. 19.5 percent were sentenced to jail for one year or less and 19.5% were sentenced to one to two years in jail (Ibid. p. A6). While a number of those found guilty are certainly treated leniently, the suggestion that 71 percent of child murderers in the sample got off with little or no punishment is misleading at best, and a gross distortion at worst.

A similar kind of statistical evaluation is provided by the *Star* for those cases that are "plea bargained" down to a lesser charge to show the reader that 51 percent of the 41 cases where a parent or caregiver was charged, a plea bargain was accepted for a guilty plea. But this figure is practically meaningless without other data to compare it to, begging the question of whether or not *all* charges are to a certain extent subject to this level of reduction through special plea arrangements. If this were to be the case, not only would the plea arrangements in these cases seem more appropriate, but the suspicion that police and Crown attorneys may lay "inappropriately" serious charges in anticipation of this process would be bolstered.

And lastly, the *Star* reporters claim that their research discovered that the age of the victim was related to the jail term received and that less jail time was given when the victims were younger. Here, taking "average age" of victim as the category around which to make statements about jail terms is more than meaningless. Their presentation of the material as a bar chart in which a jail term of one year or less for a victim whose average age is fourteen months and a jail term of more than one year for a victim whose average is thirty-two months provides the reader with the impression that if you kill a younger infant, then regardless of the circumstances, you are unlikely to receive more than one year in jail. Their representation assumes that all the cases in their sample are "like" cases and ignores the likelihood that many victims died from differing, sometimes accidental, causes, or were cases in which the perpetrator was found not criminally responsible by reason of insanity or guilty of infanticide; that is, causes of death and social circumstances other than child abuse.

In the Coroner's database, used to collate and track all deaths by type, the Coroners list a "death factor." The death factor is not necessarily the technical "cause of death" which would be discovered if the file is examined. Causes of death are medical determinations that describe how a person died. Subdural hematoma, asphyxiation, burns, blunt trauma to the head, suffocation, drowning are all medical causes of death, some of which *are* listed in infanticide cases as "death factors." But "death factors" often describe a kind of "mediate cause of death" which alerts the Coroners to significant types of death which they may feel deserve special attention. As such, the "death factor" designation represents an almost textbook example of the kinds of professional classification which can be described as the social construction of a social problem (see Best, 1990; Pfohl, 1977; Scheper-Hughes & Stein, 1987). The actual causes of death in the *Star*'s sample were not necessarily the result of intentional and repeated violence, the kinds of violence usually associated by professionals with "child abuse." But the Office of the Chief Coroner for Ontario lists "child abuse" as a "death factor" in almost all infant deaths due to violence they investigate, regardless of whether or not there is evidence of old injuries to the infant. Some cases in which the proximate cause of death was that the babies were shaken are one time only events of violence not typically considered *bona fide* "child abuse" by experts in the field. In addition, there was a case of maternal neonaticide in the *Star*'s sample, again not conforming to the notion of "child abuse," (and in which, incidentally, the police report indicated that the baby had 20 stab wounds, as reported in the *Star*, when in fact, the autopsy listed the wounds as "multiple cuts" rather than "stab wounds.") (Welsh & Donovan, 1997, May 18, p. A6; Coroner's Case File No. 28183, 1993). This case in particular, illustrates how a failure to provide a social and historical context to criminal justice responses to homicide can provide a misleading picture of the nature of a social problem. The young single mother was initially charged with second degree murder and pled guilty to manslaughter, a much harsher disposition than those that have been handed out in almost all similar cases over the last 100 years.

In addition, there were two cases in which fathers are convicted of criminal negligence and manslaughter respectively when their infants were shaken to death. The report fails to inform the reader whether these events were one time only events, or even possibly unintentional deaths rather than actual "child abuse" in which the infants had old injuries. Cases of death from "shaken baby syndrome," as they are referred to by the Coroner's Office, can often involve infants who clearly suffered other kinds of violence, but they can also be one-time only events resulting in death. The difference in the criminal justice response might then reflect a difference in the circumstances of the death and therefore in the actual severity of the crime.

"How to Save the Children"

In the final story of the *Star* series, the readership was informed about "how to save the children." This final front-page story instructs the reader that "both laws and attitudes must be changed so that child safety becomes paramount over the rights of abusive parents" (Welsh & Donovan, 1997, June 21, p. A1). Seven individual changes are suggested:

1. Change the law so that children come first.
2. Give watchdog powers to the ministry that funds children's aid.

3. Institute province-wide investigative training of social workers.
4. Create a computer database linking all 55 Children's Aid Societies.
5. Initiate a public information campaign against child abuse.
6. Crack down on doctors and other professionals not reporting abuse.
7. Launch innovative prevention programs province-wide. (Ibid. p. A1)

The article then provides a detailed explanation of the need for each of these recommendations to solve "the problem" of child abuse. Their suggestions provide a sense that their recommendations are novel, and that, by implementing these improvements to the child welfare system, coupled with criminal justice responses to punish abusive parents, "society" can solve "the problem" of child abuse. The story provides no information about the success or failure of these kinds of initiatives in other jurisdictions and adds little new information to the broader debate about the root causes of child abuse *per se*.

Their discussion does highlight one longstanding anxiety about juvenile delinquency. Child psychiatrist, Dr. Steinhauer, provides the *biological* ideas necessary to logically justify administrative and criminal law intervention strategies in preventive terms. According to Dr. Steinhauer, "With brain development, the first three years are critical. We have huge numbers of children who live in chronic conflict and tension, and that impacts on the areas of the midbrain that cause rage, anxiety and a predisposition to violence (p. A1).

In addition, the story cites a U.S. study as authoritative evidence that child abuse leads eventually to juvenile delinquency, "A U.S. study published this week by the Child Welfare League shows abused and neglected children are 67 times more likely to become juvenile offenders than those who are not abused" (p. A1).

What the report fails to tell its readers is that this old idea has its roots in 19th century reform movements, which sought to save society from juvenile delinquency by removing children from "bad" homes. Rather than aim their responses "at ameliorating abuse or correcting abusive parents," the late nineteenth and early twentieth century reform movements sought to remove children from their corrupt environments and put them in institutions or "houses of refuge" on the grounds that "they could learn order, regularity and obedience" (Pfohl 1977, p. 311). Unlike the reform movement of the late nineteenth and early twentieth century, however, the *Star*'s suggestions included institutionalizing *both* child and parent. The solutions would institutionalize the suspected abused child under the care of Child and Family Services and the suspected abusers would be prosecuted more efficiently by the criminal justice system with the aim of incarcerating the abusers in jails and prisons. This new approach varies only slightly from the older one in that it seeks to focus more directly on the process by which perpetrators of abuse can be more efficiently prosecuted by the criminal justice system. However, like the earlier reform efforts the recommendations would have the effect of expanding the scope and intensity of professional interventions in the lives of identified "bad parents" and children deemed "at risk," and would correlatively require the expansion and enhanced training of a range of professional groups.

SPEAKING FOR THE DEAD: THE CORONER'S INQUESTS AND THE ONTARIO CHILD MORTALITY TASK FORCE

In April of 1998, the Ontario Child Mortality Task Force (OCMTF), working for the Ontario Association of Children's Aid Societies (OACAS), published a final progress report that assessed the implementation progress of the broad changes suggested by the Coroner's Juries, regarding child welfare agencies, the coroners office and the government. In addition, the OACAS prepared a collation of Coroner's Inquest Recommendations by Topic, released in February 1998. "Inquest Recommendations by Topic" is, for our purposes, the more important document because it addresses the prevention of, and response to, child abuse homicides in much greater detail, and includes careful consideration of the Criminal Code options. The Ontario Child Mortality Task Force Recommendations are consistent with the Coroner's Inquest Recommendations, but its focus is especially on the role of the Coroner's Office, establishment of a pediatric death review process, and the implementation of reforms in child welfare.

By the time these reports were issued, the *Toronto Star* had done its best to prepare the public to receive their recommendations as both reasonable and long overdue. Indeed, what is striking is the similarity between the framework for response developed in the *Star* series and that produced in an entirely different context, partly by experts on child abuse and child welfare, by the Coroner's Inquest jurors, the Ontario Child Mortality Task Force (as well as by those who contributed to a Federal Department of Justice consultation paper "Child Victims," produced years later). These reports are uniquely connected to the *Star* series because the cases upon which their argument for change was built came from the Ontario Chief Coroner's Office and the comments of the Deputy Chief Coroner, Dr. Jim Cairns, had been much in evidence in the *Star*'s reports. Dr. Cairns was professionally involved in both the Inquests and as member of the Ontario Child Mortality Task Force. The newspaper's recommendations and the similar technical professional recommendations that followed were, then, of a piece, and the problems of child abuse and child abuse homicide were already a part of the public consciousness, and were, in any event well established within the social work and criminal justice community well before they were announced as formal recommendations by the Inquest jurors and the Task Force members.

Coroner's Inquest Recommendations

In the fall of 1996 and winter of 1997, shortly after the announcements in he *Toronto Star*, the Office of the Chief Coroner of Ontario began its inquests into the deaths of eight "children"[11] "known to" Children's Aid Societies in Ontario. By February 1998 they had conducted and completed six inquests and the Ontario Association of Children's Aid Societies (OACAS) issued its report on their findings. The following is a summary of each inquest conducted:

- Shanay Johnson died at age two years of a head injury on October 6, 1993 in Toronto. The mother has been convicted in this death. The Metropolitan Toronto CAS was involved in providing services. One hundred and seven recommendations were made by the Coroner's jury.
- Wilson Kasonde died at age ten and Margaret Kasonde died at age eight in Ottawa as a result of gunshot wounds on May 25, 1995. Their father has been convicted in their deaths. Ottawa-Carleton CAS was involved at the time of their murders. Seventy-four recommendations were made by the Coroner's jury.
- David Dombroskie died at age four, Angela Dombroskie died at age eight; Devin Burns died at age three; and Jamie Lee Burns died at age four in a house fire in Kitchener on June 11, 1996. Waterloo F&CS was working with the mother and children at the time of their deaths. Forty-six recommendations were made by the Coroner's jury.
- Lisa Marie MacLean died at age 18 months in Sault Ste. Marie after being released from police custody. She was a Crown Ward of the Algoma CAS. Five recommendations were made by the Coroner's jury.
- Kasandra Shepherd died in 1991 at three years of age. Her stepmother has been convicted in this death. A physician was acquitted on appeal of obstructing justice in the investigation into Kasandra's death. Peel CAS was involved with the family at the time of the child's death. Seventy-three recommendations were made by the Coroner's jury.
- Jennifer Koval's'kyj-England died at age six as a result of injuries received during an attack by her father. The Metropolitan Toronto CAS was providing services at the time of Jennifer's death. One hundred and twenty-four recommendations were made by the Coroner's jury. (Ontario Association of Children's Aid Societies, 1998, February, p. 1)

The OACAS report groups all of these individual jury recommendations by topic and 58 individual recommendations are discussed in detail in this 71-page report. The jury's recommendations add technical detail onto the framework introduced in the *Star* series. In particular, the jury sets out in painstaking detail

---

[11] The definition of "children" includes anyone up to 18 years of age.

the ingredients of the "innovative prevention programs" the *Star* had demanded. All this added up to an enhancement of the investigation, monitoring, and reporting practices for children at risk; virtually, a new and very detailed blueprint for professional involvement in these cases.

While many of their recommendations had to do with amending practices, policies, and family law, there were certain recommendations with an impact on the disposition of instances of maternal neonaticide. Chief among these is the recommendation for the creation of criminal offences involving child abuse and neglect, and the specific recommendation that "infanticide" be removed from the Criminal Code to be replaced with an offence of Death by Child Abuse/Neglect that would not require proof of "intent" (Ontario Association CAS, 1998, February, p. 17). This recommendation came from the two inquests held in Toronto. The first was into the death of Shanay Johnson, aged two, whose mother was convicted of manslaughter and sentenced to four years in jail. The second inquest from which this recommendation came was into the death of six-year-old Jennifer Koval's'kyj-England who died after being attacked by her father. Therefore, the only case in which infanticide law might have appeared relevant was that of Shanay Johnson, although Shanay was in fact too old to be covered by the infanticide provision.[12]

According to a newspaper report at the time when the jury announced its recommendations, Shanay Johnson's mother, Patricia Johnson "had been beating Shanay, depriving her of food, burning her with scalding water and leaving her in a crib for hours unattended all while the family was under the [children's aid] society's supervision" (Toronto Star, 1998, May 8, p. A3). The details of the living conditions into which Shanay Johnson was born were horrific. In 1996, shortly before the inquest recommendations were made public, the *Toronto Star* reported the following details,

> Shanay Johnson's mother was a crack addict with four other children in a house that smelled of urine and feces. In 1991, the first of her two children were taken from her by the Metro Toronto Children's Aid Society, but returned a month later. After Shanay was born later that year, the society took the three children away. Then, in 1993, deciding again that she was now a fit mother, they returned them to her. Five months later, Shanay, 21 months old at the time, was dead. Her mother had whipped her with a belt or coat hangar; she was punched and kicked; three of her teeth were knocked out; her body was black and blue.

[12] A request for all inquests into the deaths of children (1980–1998) in Ontario revealed only one case of maternal neonaticide in which an inquest was held. The inquest into the death of baby W in February of 1981 made only vague recommendations about infanticide itself as opposed to the law of infanticide. This jury recommended that "information regarding infanticide should be made available to those agencies where it would be helpful for them to track those people who have had previous offences." Verdict of the Coroner's Jury, Office of the Chief Coroner for Ontario, Case File No. 12164, 1981.

Five days before Shanay's October, 1993 death, there was a final warning sign. Shanay's mother called 911 to say the child had scalded herself by turning on the hot water tap in the bath. She was allowed to keep her children and five days later Shanay was dead. The pathologist found that her tiny buttocks were dunked in scalding water. The mother, Patricia Johnson, was sentenced to four years in prison. (Welsh & Donovan, 1996, September 18, p. A6)

No doubt due to the severity of the abuse suffered by the deceased toddler, the fact that she had come into contact with Toronto Children's Aid Society and the high profile reports in the newspapers about this case, the Jury's response to her death was particularly fraught with emotion, resulting in a high pitched response couched in terms which, even in a case of this severity, appear melodramatic. The "Opening Statement" of the Verdict of the Coroner's Jury outlining the recommendations set the moral tone for the extensive recommendations,

> We the Jury on behalf of the citizens of Metropolitan Toronto wish to express our sympathy for the lost life of Shanay Jani Johnson.
>
> When we say the word mother we think of someone who provides unconditional love, keeps us safe, and provides a happy home. This didn't happen for you. For a part of your short span of life you were loved, safe, and happy with your Foster Family. Then you were returned to your birth family through a system that did not recognize your rights and needs as an individual and that failed to recognize your danger. Four short months later we lost you forever.
>
> Shanay, be assured, with these recommendations implemented, the large cracks in the child protection system will surely be filled by the people, Government of Ontario and agencies responsible for the safe keeping of our children.
>
> Shanay, the final chapter of your short life now comes to an end. Little one, you can now rest in peace knowing that society has benefited from your death even though it did not have the opportunity to benefit from your life and what you would have contributed. Your memory will never be lost to any of our hearts and minds. (Verdict of the Coroner's Jury, Shanay Johnson, May 1997)

The jurors made their recommendations to alter the policy and practices at the federal and provincial levels of government. They recommended amendments to the Criminal Code of Canada, the concept of "best interests of the child" in family law, and the Child and Family Services Act itself. Jurors recommended procedural and policy changes to the Ministry of Community and Social Services, Children's Aid Societies, and health professionals' reporting practices.

With respect to the Criminal Code, the jurors recommended both the repeal of the infanticide law and a new category of homicide, which would not require the

Crown to prove intent. This suggestion is based on the rationale that the "innocence" of a child deserves a stronger punitive response. Below are their recommendations and rationale for same:

1. We recommend the Federal Government of Canada amend the Criminal Code to include an offense of Death by Child Abuse/Neglect which does require specific intent to kill with a minimum term of imprisonment without eligibility for parole to be classed as second degree murder.
   Rationale: The death of one of society's most vulnerable members must be seen as being, at least, if not more than equal to the death of an adult as in their innocence they are unable to defend themselves or escape from danger.
2. We recommend removal of Infanticide from the Criminal Code.
   Rationale: It would be replaced with sections under Death by Child Abuse/Neglect. (Verdict of the Coroner's Jury, Shanay Johnson, Recommendations 1 and 2, 1997 May)

CHILD VICTIMS AND THE FEDERAL DEPARTMENT OF JUSTICE

The suggestion from the Toronto inquests that the federal government entertain the addition of a new form of homicide "Child Abuse/Neglect" to the homicide law of Canada and remove the infanticide law was taken up by the Family, Children and Youth Section of the Department of Justice as part of a broader consultative project addressing various questions about child victims and witnesses in a context of heightened recognition of "the true scope and extent of child abuse, neglect and exploitation and the harms they cause" (Canada, Department of Justice, 1999 November, p. 3). The paper describes recent events that have given rise to a range of recommendations aimed at protecting children from various kind of harm. According to the Background Paper:

> There have been a number of alarming incidents that have given rise to concern about the safety of children. Adults use various means to approach and have sex with children, as well as those fourteen years of age or older, who are over the general minimum age of consent to sexual activity. Adults have killed children in a number of jurisdictions by direct physical attacks and through the most horrendous forms of neglect. Children have also been the victims of severe, long-lasting, and often permanent physical and emotional harms and injuries. (Ibid. p. 5)

The Department of Justice notes in this paper that these events have given rise to a renewed interest in child protection and to a call from certain professional sectors for criminal law and child welfare reforms,

The issues and suggestions for reform come from a wide range of sources in response to reported cases of grievous injury and death of children. Those recommending greater protection for children include judges, Crown prosecutors, defence lawyers, police, health care workers (including those active in the mental health field), hospital child abuse teams, public health nurses, academics, social workers and others directly concerned with child protection. Suggestions also include recommendations from judicial inquiries, coroner's inquest juries, child fatality review committees, and other review bodies.[13]

The paper makes it clear that it only "focuses on extreme forms of conduct and injury that can never be justified or defended. Its object is to help ensure that there are child-specific criminal offences available which accurately reflect the horrendous types of conduct involved and make successful prosecutions possible" (Ibid. p. 5). In this context, the removal of infanticide is considered.

In light of the paper's careful definition of its purpose, the consideration of the removal of infanticide is awkwardly positioned. Infanticide has never been considered an extreme form of abuse or homicide, and it operates as a specific kind of defence to murder. Nevertheless, its removal is considered in the broader context of child-specific criminal offences, specifically, child homicide which includes the removal of "intent."

CONCLUSION

I have shown how concerns over the nature and extent of "child abuse" have become connected to the investigation and prosecution of maternal neonaticide, drawing authorities towards more intensive investigation, supervision, and prevention regimes. In this context, the Canadian infanticide law has been challenged on a number of troubling fronts, not just on the ground that it represents an inappropriate medicalization of the actions of rational women in difficult circumstances, but also because it provides insufficient retribution for heinous crimes committed by fully responsible and wicked individuals. This claim is grounded in the generalized concern about child abuse and neglect as serious, widespread, and even horrifying problems. In fact, the law and order advocates have been quick to appropriate the feminist critique of the medicalization of women's deviance seemingly represented by the infanticide provision for their own purposes (see, for instance, Bauman 1997, pp. 149–151; Pearson 1997, pp. 78–79).

Without in any way suggesting that the medico-legal category of infanticide is unproblematic or unconstituted, the extension of the category of child abuse/

---

[13] Child Victims and the Criminal Justice System, Technical Background Paper, November 1999, p. 6. Department of Justice, Canada. This comment is made in explanation of the Background Paper's non-consideration of the defence of reasonable force by way of correction toward a pupil or child.

neglect homicide to cover maternal neonaticides which conform to the established infanticide scenarios seems even less appropriate. Such a designation allows for little mitigation and indeed operates more as a flag that a particularly heinous and blameworthy crime has been committed. The suggestion that this new offence would not require intent to be proved is especially troubling and unlikely to survive Charter scrutiny. Whilst it might be argued that in cases of death following long-standing serious abuse the gross failure to fulfill parental responsibilities amounts to intent, where such a category is made to cover homicides in which there is no evidence of previous abuse and which were carried out in traumatic circumstances that give rise to the possibility of some level of diminished culpability, the removal of an intent requirement amounts to a rendering of crucial evidence as all but legally irrelevant. In such cases, evidence typically exists which is positively indicative of a partial absence of intent, with the mother often acting "on the sudden" at a moment of acute distress. To remove the intent requirement so that it is effectively "read in" would seem highly inappropriate. In short, the infanticide provision creates a framework for mitigation, which, despite the conceptual weaknesses of the category, is appropriate for the circumstances legislators described when the provision was passed. Simply repealing the infanticide law at a time when a new offence of child abuse/neglect homicide is enacted would remove the opportunity for mitigation in these cases and bring to bear a new kind of vengeance upon women who have not behaved aggressively or with evil intent towards their newly born babies.[14]

CRITICAL THINKING QUESTIONS

1. How was child abuse discovered? And, how did the child abuse discourse develop?
2. What are the main underlying assumptions of the "child abuse" discourse?
3. Caffey's Syndrome is considered the earliest modern medical definition of child abuse. How do you view the role played by the medical profession in sensationalizing child abuse and child abuse homicides?
4. What are the potential consequences of child death review teams re-interpreting causes of death in infants?
5. What has been the role of the media in the creation of a moral panic about child abuse and neglect?
6. Why infanticide crimes are now being prosecuted as child abuse crimes?

---

[14] This is quite different from "reading in" mental disturbance in the amended infanticide provision; in the former case, the defendant is denied the opportunity to make full answer and defence, in the latter case, the defendant was granted an unproven mitigation, albeit as a means of enabling conviction.

7. What are some of the potential problems with abolishing the Canadian Criminal Code infanticide provision?

SUGGESTED READINGS

Backhouse, Constance (1984). Desperate Women and Compassionate Courts: Infanticide in Nineteenth-Century Canada. *University of Toronto Law Journal 34*, 447–478.
> This essay analyzes the responses of the Canadian legal system in the nineteenth century to women accused of "infanticide." Continues to be one of the best Canadian sources of information on the various ways the Canadian legal system approached the prosecution of this crime. The author discusses the various ways in which judges, jurors, and legislators contemplated leniency towards women accused of murdering their unwanted babies.

Best, Joel (1990). *Threatened Children: Rhetoric and Concern about Child Victims*. Chicago: University of Chicago Press.
> This book takes a constructionist approach to investigating the rise of the concept of the "child-victim." Best discusses the importance of claims-makers and the media in this history.

Jenks, Chris (1996). *Childhood*. New York: Routledge.
> A sociological analysis of the historical development of the concept of childhood across various disciplines. The author illustrates the various intellectual processes that produce the modern image of childhood.

Laster, Kathy (1989). Infanticide: A litmus test for Feminist Criminological Theory. *Australian and New Zealand Journal of Criminology, 22*, 151–166.
> Applies two broad theoretical feminist criminological approaches (the androgynous and the social control perspectives) to infanticide. The author argues that the challenge for feminist criminology is to adequately account for infanticide, a quintessentially female crime, without ignoring the fact that it is, indeed, women who commit these crimes. At the same time feminist criminology must remain attentive to the fact that the cause of the crime has little to do with women's essential nature.

O'Donovan, Katherine (1984). The Medicalisation of Infanticide. *The Criminal Law Review*, 259-264.
> Provides the reader with a brief history of the crime of infanticide in England from the time the first statute was passed in 1623 and provides an analysis of the strengths and weaknesses of both the medical and socio-economic models of infanticide.

Osborne, Judith A. (1987). The Crime of Infanticide: Throwing Out the Baby with the Bathwater. *Canadian Journal of Family Law 6*, 47-59.
> Canadian criminologist Judith Osborne discusses the current Canadian laws governing infanticide and reviews the history of legal responses to the crime of infanticide. The author concludes that proposals to abolish the infanticide provision must be accompanied by changes in how society views female criminality.

Pfohl, Stephen (1977). The "Discovery" of Child Abuse. *Social Problems*, 24, 310-323.
> This essay provides a sociological analysis of the social forces that gave rise to the deviant labelling of child beating and the development of the various child protection movements which successfully lobbied for universal criminal legislation on child abuse.

WEB LINKS

The following is a list of governmental and non-governmental organizations that provide valuable information on infanticide. It is important for researchers to note that it is very difficult to find scholarly or educational information on maternal neonaticide using "infanticide" as a key word Internet search term. This difficulty is owing to the fact that much of the information displayed is non-scholarly right-wing Christian rhetoric that fails to differentiate between abortion, which is legal and infanticide, which is a crime.

www.who.int/whosis/
> Web site of the World Heath Organization Statistical Information System (WHOSIS) provides health and health-related statistical information from the WHO Global Programme on Evidence for Health Policy. Provides current infant morality data by cause of death, sex, and age.

www.statcan.ca
> The official source for Canadian social and economic statistics and products. Contains useful information on health and crime. Provides rates of infanticide per 100,000 population.

canada.justice.gc.ca/
> The official Web site of the Canadian Department of Justice. Provides many useful links to important Canadian criminal justice issues, social policy recommendations, programmes, news and events administered by the Department.

www.gendercide.org/
> Web site of the Gendercide Watch organization, a project of the Gender Issues Education Foundation (GIEF), a registered charitable foundation based in Edmonton, Alberta. According to the Gendercide Web site, Gendercide Watch: "seeks to confront acts of gender-selective mass killing around the world. We believe that such atrocities against ordinary men and women constitute one of humanity's worst blights, and one of its greatest challenges in the new millennium." Provides excellent link to information about female infanticide in China and India.

CHAPTER 10

Constituting "Dangerous Parents" Through the Spectre of Child Death: A Critique of Child Protection Restructuring in Ontario

by Xiaobei Chen, Ph.D.

On September 18, 1996, the headline pictures of two murdered babies hit readers of the *Toronto Star*. Two absolutely innocent and defenseless children were pictured; one baby's eyes were not even open and the other was shown sucking on his thumb. The caption provided their names and explained that Sara Podniewicz was six months old when she was murdered by her parents and Johnny James died from a severe blow to the lower abdomen when he was sixteen months old. This introduced readers to a full-page exclusive report of a *Toronto Star* investigation of some child deaths in the previous five years (1991–1995), particularly cases in which there were signs of abuse and neglect by parents prior to children's deaths and in which "the [child protection] system failed these kids."

The *Star* report began:

"Kasandra Shepherd. Tiffani Coville. Johnny James. Shanay Johnson. Paulo Trotta. Sara Podniewicz. All dead children. All showed signs of abuse or neglect prior to death.

All glaring examples of the failure of Ontario's child protection system—the children's aid workers, doctors and provincial officials who were supposed to be looking for them."

The list of names set the grim tone of the report. Every period following a child's name was distressing, apparently suggesting the cold and cruel end of the life of each child. The repetitive use of the word "all" left the impression that this was a dreadful pattern and there were many more similar dead children: a hidden epidemic of child killing. That report marked the beginning of an era of heightened public sensitivity to child deaths in Ontario. Now when we read newspaper or watch TV, we are often confronted with horrifying stories of child deaths. We wonder, how could these deaths happen? It seems only natural to question. The flood of public responses featured a few types of understandings. Almost all were convinced that these tragic deaths of children happened because their parents, often mothers, were evil—they were cold, selfish,

WHO PROVIDES CHILD PROTECTION?

The Canadian state is a federal state, whose constitution provides for the division of power between the federal government and the provinces. The general interpretation of the Canadian constitutions is that provinces have primary jurisdiction over social welfare functions (Armitage, 1996).

As for child protection, provinces and territories have authority in providing services. In Ontario, child protection activities is governed by the Child and Family Services Act. Child protection services are delivered by Children's Aid Societies, which are non-profit agencies incorporated under The Child and Family Services Act, and which are fully funded by the Ministry of Community and Social Services of the provincial government. Children's Aid Societies' main functions are legislated as follows:

- investigate allegations of abuse and neglect
- protect children where necessary provide guidance, counselling and other services to families for protecting children and for the prevention of circumstances requiring the protection of children
- provide care or supervision for children removed from their families
- place children for adoption

Recently, the federal government is actively considering its involvement in child protection from the angle of criminal justice. A federal consultation paper provides this following description of the division of power:

"Providing services to children in need of protection is the responsibility of the provinces and territories. Ensuring that appropriate [categories of criminal] offences and penalties [on parents] are available to protect children again grievous harms and injuries is the responsibility of the Government of Canada" (Canada, Department of Justice, 1999, p. 4).

Child protection services has been critiqued for being overly concerned with investigative and protective practices, but not with providing support to children and mothers (Wharf, 1993; Swift, 1995).

violent, dishonest, and often addicted to alcohol or drugs. Many questioned the competency of social workers. The *Toronto Star* report framed it; children died at the hands of their violent parent-murderers who were repetitively let go by the police, doctors, and social workers (see also Callahan & Callahan, 1997). Some saw it as a sign of the degeneracy of Canadian society. All agreed that something must be done. Subsequently, the Ontario Coroner's Office played a pivotal role in mobilizing pressure for reforming the child protection system. The Coroner's

Office, in particular Jim Cairns,[1] a deputy chief coroner, pressed for a review of child deaths through a task force on child mortality and convened a series of coroner's inquests into individual child deaths. The coroner's rationale for taking these actions was his office's mandate of preventing further deaths. As Cairns put it in the *Toronto Star*, September 18, 1996 edition: "We have to educate all professionals involved with high risk children with a view to learning how to prevent deaths". In the following years, six coroners' inquests were convened which, together with a Child Mortality Task Force, steered the Child Welfare Reform of Ontario's Ministry of Community and Social Services for the purpose of preventing child deaths. What kind of child deaths to prevent, however, turns out to be a question, and a complex one. I provide a detailed analysis of this question later, but would like to mention briefly here that there are conventionally seven kinds of child deaths by different causes—Natural Causes, SID (Sudden Infant Death Syndrome), Sudden Unexplained Death (SUD), Accidents, Suicide, Homicide, and Undetermined Causes. Child homicide cases tend to capture most publicity in media and coroners' inquests; however it was accidental deaths and ostensibly their prevention that became the rationale for the Child Welfare Reform.

The Child Welfare Reform resulted in a restructuring of the child protection system, which puts a stronger emphasis on neglect, prioritizes children's personal safety over the interests of family as a whole, applies stricter rules on professionals' duty to report suspected abuse and neglect, and requires the use of the "Risk Assessment Model" by all children's aid workers. The Task Force and coroner's inquests, together with similar activities in other provinces, also played a significant role in prompting reviews at the federal government level. In particular, the Department of Justice Canada is conducting a "Child Victims and the Criminal Justice System" consultation with a view to revise the Criminal Code so that more perpetrators of child abuse and neglect can be subjected to tougher criminal punishment.

Shouldn't we applaud these actions, since surely these measures will prevent further child deaths and improve the child protection system? My answer is no.

---

[1] Jim Cairns, who had previously been in charge of overseeing investigations of child deaths, was not unknown for his advocacy for policy changes from the viewpoint of preventing death. For example, he presided in over the 1993 coroner's inquest into the murder of Christopher Stephen. In 1994 he publicly took dramatic action of reconvening an inquest jury for an update on how inadequately government followed through with recommendations, which was a first for the province. According to the *Toronto Star* on February 25, 1994, Cairns warned the federal government of "murders of more innocent children unless repeat violent sex offenders [were] kept behind bars for good." The federal government decided against introducing a sexual offender registry. However, the Ontario government passed the Christopher's Law in March 2001.

A close look of patterns of child deaths in Ontario shows that the child protection-focused reforms actually will not do much to prevent most child deaths. In Ontario, as in other provinces, there are many more deaths in the general population of children who have never been abused or neglected (as in child protection terms). According to Ontario Child Mortality Task Force's survey of child deaths during the two years of 1994 and 1995, there were 3,199 child deaths across Ontario, among which only 100 were children known to Children's Aid Societies because of signs of abuse and neglect; in contrast 499 children died of accidents, most often motor vehicle accidents. Furthermore, the analysis of the figures shows that the death rate of children receiving services from Children's Aid Societies was lower than that of the general population of children (Ontario Child Mortality Task Force, 1997, p. 6). Given these facts, if the objective is to prevent child deaths, it does not seem an effective measure to scrutinize only the child protection system when it has nothing to do with the vast majority of deaths of children. In comparison, it seems more reasonable, for example, to reform the highway traffic regulation system to reduce preventable deaths of children by half.[2]

As for the question whether current reforms improve the child protection system, it is important to note that these reforms are driven by a few extreme cases which were quite isolated from the broader context. The vast majority of cases that the children's aid workers deal with everyday do not have dramatic endings. For example, in 1995 Ontario Children's Aid Societies provided service to 87,000 families, 150,000 children and youth and provided substitute care to 20,800 children. Among these children, only 57 died while receiving services from a Children's Aid Society (Ontario Child Mortality Task Force, 1997, p. 6). That is a percentage of 0.038. Thus these cases of child deaths hardly represent the reality of most situations in the child protection system.

In contrast to the 0.038 percent of cases ending with child deaths, more than 70 percent of children and families involved with the child protection system live in poverty (the Children's Aid Society of Toronto Web site, <www.casmt.on.ca>, cited April 23, 2001); 40 percent of cases are households headed by single-mothers; in 34 percent of cases "caregivers" have problems of alcohol or drug use; in 24 percent of cases "caregivers" have mental health problems (Trocmé et al., 2001). As other scholars point out, child protection cases are primarily the results of poverty and the effects of associated disadvantages such as single motherhood, lack of education, substance use, mental health problems, low-standard housing or no housing (Armitage, 1993; Swift, 1995a, 1999), and they do not arise from

---

[2] Of the 3,199 child deaths across Ontario during 1994 and 1995, 2,344 deaths were of natural causes. In general terms, one can say that the rest of the deaths, about 855, were preventable. Of the 855 preventable deaths, 499 occurred in motor vehicle accidents.

mothers' malicious intentions to harm or even to kill their children.[3] If we want to improve the child protection system, it certainly makes more sense to focus on the prevention of widespread, chronic poverty and other forms of marginalizations experienced by mothers and children, instead of the prevention of isolated extreme cases of child deaths and treating mothers as potential killers.

The emergence of the issue of child deaths is connected with the societal and political obsession with personal safety, which in recent post-deficit years is one of few viable objectives of public policy. I have discussed the preoccupation with safety and its ultimate antithesis, i.e., death, elsewhere (Chen, 2000). In this chapter I examine the effects of this preoccupation. The focus of the Child Welfare Reform is distorted when it is centred on the child protection system's failure to prevent tragic but proportionately a very small number of child deaths. To make child deaths and their prevention the theme of reforms is completely unwarranted, as I have shown above. To evaluate and then change the child protection system in ways that are dictated by the issue of child deaths is a grave injustice to most mothers involved with the system and to the Children's Aid workers. This is because in the vast majority of child protection cases mothers do not and will not likely kill their children. The focus on deaths diverts attention from issues of structural marginalizations such as resource deprivation, which are destructive, often chronic and complex, but not as sensational or dramatic as deaths of individual children. To shape the child protection system on a model of preventing and punishing personal crimes of killing children does not address complex structural problems, which make children vulnerable to abuse and neglect in the first place. Worse, it diverts precious resources from addressing these issues.

The restructuring of child protection will be analyzed in detail in the rest of the chapter. The analysis developed in this chapter loosely follows what is called the governmentality approach. "Governmentality" was first introduced by Michel Foucault (Foucault, 1979) and has since then stimulated a rich body of writing on alternative thinking about power in western liberal societies. Studies following the governmentality approach concern themselves with governance, or governmental activities, such as, activities undertaken by various authorities to shape conduct of individuals or groups in particular ways, using a variety of techniques and knowledge

[3] Although the child protection system uses a gender-neutral language, it is important to make it visible that child protection targets women. First, child protection focuses on the caring for children, which is mainly thought of as the women's responsibility in Canadian society. In all cases, women have always been identified as the adult clients of the system, thus objects of governance. Finally, the largest category of households dealt with by child protection agencies are headed by single mothers (for an excellent discussion of child protection as a women's issue, see Swift, 1995b). The newly invented category of "dangerous parents" continues the practice of obscuring the gendered nature of child protection. As an attempt to counter that, in the rest of the chapter I use a gender-explicit language and refer to adult clients of the child protection system as mothers.

> ## DEFINITION OF GOVERNMENT
>
> "Government is a more or less calculated and rational activity, undertaken by a multiplicity of authorities and agencies, employing a variety of techniques and forms of knowledge, that seeks to shape conduct by working through our desires, aspirations, interests and beliefs, for definite but shifting ends and with a diverse set of relatively unpredictable consequences, effects and outcomes."
>
> (Dean 1999, p. 11)

(Dean, 1999). Thus, governmentality and the more familiar sociological studies of social control or social regulation are somewhat alike in that they are interested in understanding the processes by which the behaviour of individuals or groups is formed, managed, and restricted. However, governmentality's underlying principles mark itself as a separate paradigm. Perhaps one of the most important differences between governmentality and conventional social regulation studies is the former's rejection of identifying governmental activities with the state. Governmentality extends its analytical gaze beyond the state to micro-settings, even those within the self, to understand how individuals or groups are guided, disciplined, and managed to think and act in certain ways. Another important characteristic of governmentality, which is reflected more prominently in this chapter, is that governmental activities are analyzed through examining "political rationalities" and "governing technologies." Briefly, political rationalities refer to relatively systematic thinking that are involved in governing action—definition of objectives, application of social or economic theories, and invention of categories; and governing technologies are the means to translate ideas into actual governing practices, such as programmes, techniques, and procedures. The influence of govermentality on this chapter—here, mainly the concern with "political rationalities" and "technologies"—is visible in the two issues that the following analysis focuses on: namely the constitution of mothers involved with the child protection system as "dangerous parents," and emerging technologies designed to deal with such "dangerous parents."

These will be addressed in two sections respectively. The first section examines the focus of deaths and its role in the constitution of the category of "dangerous parents." It lays out the problematic ways in which extreme cases of child abuse and neglect leading to child deaths were used to portray mothers who are involved with the child protection system as "dangerous parents," who are likely to harm or even kill their children through personal criminal acts. The second section provides an overview and a critique of changes to the child protection mechanism. It shows that the restructuring is transforming the system into one that emphasizes risk management on the one hand and punishment on the other. The analysis

> ## CHILD PROTECTION FACTS
>
> Currently there are 53 Children's Aid Societies in Ontario.
>
> According to the Ontario Association of Children's Aid Societies' figures, during the period between April 1, 1999 and March 31, 2000, Children's Aid Societies across the province received calls about and provided services to more than 204,487 children and families.
>
> During the same period, the annual expenditures of Children's Aid Societies was $638 million
>
> Source: Ontario Association of Children's Aid Societies Web site, <www.oacas.org>, cited April 23, 2001.

makes a two-folded argument. First, during the restructuring of the child protection system at the turn of this century, through the spectre of child death, mothers at the margins of society are construed as "dangerous parents" capable of killing their children, and as such they are made into a particular type of subjects to be regulated by risk management and supplementary criminal punishment. Second, these changes are connected with the New Right agendas. Governance in forms of risk management and criminal punishment assume the governed, many of whom are poor single mothers, as the evil and dangerous individuals, who no longer deserve considerations of circumstances. Risk assessment and criminal punishment do not seek to address complex structural problems which make children vulnerable to abuse and neglect in the first place, but instead put the burden of removing disadvantages on the shoulders of individual mothers.

A discussion of the Child Welfare Reform from the above angles is important for several reasons. Child protection is a system with extraordinary power over hundreds of thousands children and women every year in Ontario alone, many of whom are at the margins of society. Its sheer magnitude and pervasiveness make it a serious area for studies of governing activities. Furthermore, because changes taking place in the area of child protection have their echoes in many other areas, students of the broadly defined social regulation will find the discussion relevant to transformation of modes of governance in western liberal democracies at the turn of twenty-first century.

THE DISCOURSE OF CHILD DEATH AND THE INVENTION OF "DANGEROUS PARENTS"

All across Britain, North America, Europe, and Australia, child deaths have emerged as the entry point for public scrutiny of and political deliberation on child protection systems (Ontario Child Mortality Task Force, 1997, p. 2). In Canada in the 1990s, British Columbia's well-publicized Gove Inquiry on Child

Protection (1995) was the first example of effecting policy and service system restructuring through a massive inquiry into the tragic death of a child involved with the child protection system. In Ontario, the same year of 1995 marked the shifting of attention to the issue of child deaths in relation to child protection. This shift was evidenced by the fact that before then the issue of child deaths was not on the agenda of front-line workers, researchers, or even experts on deaths such as coroners. Similar to professionals, the media did not react to child deaths as anything extraordinary or to the scandals of the child protection system until 1995. Surely some children died in earlier years, even those involved with Children's Aid Societies, but I have yet to unearth any report linking child deaths to the failure of the child protection system in the years before 1995.

In April 1996, the Office of the Coroner for the Province of Ontario, and the Ontario Association of Children's Aid Societies, with support from the Ministry of Community and Social Services, established the Ontario Child Mortality Task Force with the purpose of addressing the "significant information and knowledge gap" on child deaths (Ontario Child Mortality Task Force, 1997, p. 2). In July 1997, the *Ontario Child Mortality Task Force Final Report* was released, which presented data on deaths of children involved with the child protection system in 1994 and 1995 and policy recommendations which were generated on the basis of the analysis of data. There are several problems with the Task Force's analysis of data and conclusions, all of which operated to portray mothers struggling with problems of poverty, single motherhood, domestic abuse, use of substance and alcohol, and mental health problems as "dangerous parents," who are probable killers of their own children. The following elaborates on these problems.

The Invention of "Dangerous Parents"

One conclusion that the Ontario Child Mortality Task Force reached is that we should *assume* that the death rate among children involved with the child protection system is higher than the general population of children (therefore certain actions ought to be taken to reduce the higher probability of death). This conclusion was not at all supported by the Task Force's own data. In the two years of 1994 and 1995, there were 3,199 child deaths across Ontario, among which 100 were children known to children's aid societies. The Task Force's analysis of death rates showed that the death rate for children receiving services from a CAS is lower than the general population: 0.038 per cent (or 3.8 deaths per 10,000 children) for those children known to a CAS, versus 0.055 per cent (or 5.5 deaths per 10,000 children) in general.

Then some curious steps were taken to reach the conclusion that is opposite to the above facts. In the survey, all child deaths were categorized into seven groups by cause of death: Natural Causes, SID (Sudden Infant Death Symdrome), Sudden Unexplained Death (SUD), Accidents, Suicide, Homicide, and Undetermined Causes. Without any explanation or apparent rationale, the Task Force chose to cluster together four categories of causes of deaths: Accident, Suicide, Homicide, and Undetermined Causes. It compared the death rate of this sub-group to the corresponding sub-group of the general population and concluded that the former was higher than the latter: 0.017 per cent (or 1.7 deaths per 10,000 children) for those known to a CAS, versus 0.012 per cent (or 1.2 deaths per 10,000 children in general), though the difference was not statistically significant.

Arguably, it is problematic to lump these four categories together, as I illustrate with Table 10.1, which is compiled drawing upon data provided by the report of the Child Mortality Task Force. First, of the four categories of death causes, accident deaths did not occur in disproportionately greater numbers among children

TABLE 10.1

PERCENTAGE OF CHILDREN KNOWN TO CASs AND PERCENTAGES OF DEATHS OF CHILDREN KNOWN TO CASs IN THE GENERAL POPULATION OF CHILDREN, ONTARIO

Years of 1994 and 1995	Children in Ontario	Children known to CASs	Percentages of children known to CASs in children in Ontario
No. of children (1995 only)	c. 2.8 million	150,000	5.0%
Total no. of child deaths	3,199	100	3.1%
categories of causes of deaths	Natural causes	2,344	381.6%
	Sudden Infant Death Syndrome (SIDS)	150	149.3%
	Sudden Unexplained Death (SUD)	41	921.9%
	Accidents	499	214.2%
	Suicide	79	67.6%
	Homicide	56	1119.6%
	Undetermined	30	13.3%

Compiled on the basis of data provided in the *Ontario Child Mortality Task Force Final Report*, 1997, published by the Ontario Association of Children's Aid Societies as a special edition of the Journal, July 1997.

involved with the child protection system. As a benchmark, during the two years under examination 5 percent of all children in Ontario were involved with the child protection system; in comparison, 4.2 percent of children who died of accident deaths were involved with the child protection. However, disproportionately high percentage of children who died of suicide (7.6 percent) and homicide (19.6 percent) were involved with the child protection system. Aggregation inevitably and mistakenly led to an impression of higher probability of the occurrence of accidental deaths. Second, these four causes of deaths are so different by nature that if deaths are preventable and are to be prevented, as is claimed to be the objective, they have to be tackled differently. For example, about 76 percent of accidental deaths (or 16 out of 21 cases) occurred in car accidents and house fires; in contrast, 83 percent suicide deaths (or 5 out of 6 cases) occurred to children in care of Children's Aid Societies: living in foster care, group care, or an institution at the time of committing suicide.

On top of these problems, the Task Force's subsequent analysis and interpretation of data is even more troubling. The difference between the death rate for children known to CASs who died from accident, suicide, homicide, and undetermined causes and the death rate for children who died of the same causes in general is "not statistically significant" (Ontario Child Mortality Task Force, 1997, p. 7). Nonetheless, the Task Force concluded, contrary to their own statistical analysis results, that children known to the child protection system have a higher probability of dying from abuse and neglect.

The Task Force explained that a higher death rate should be expected. It claimed,

"Although the difference in the death rates is not statistically significant, a difference *should be expected* considering the *special characteristics* of the families and vulnerability of the children known to Children's Aid Societies." [emphasis added]

- many families live below the poverty line
- many parents were victims of child abuse and neglect themselves
- many families are single parent families relying on social assistance
- women are subject to spousal violence
- there is frequent substance and alcohol dependency in this population
- many of the parents and the children have mental health problems
- all families have been referred to CASs because of difficulties in caring for their children and carrying out their parental responsibilities
(Ontario Child Mortality Task Force, 1997, pp. 6–7)

In that paragraph, the Task Force linked "special characteristics of the families," such as, poverty, history of child abuse and neglect, single motherhood, receipt of social welfare, with an imagined higher death rate of children in these families. Each of these two concepts established and reinforced the other. The dynamic began from the notion of "special characteristics," which rendered parents of these families, mainly mothers, as a separate category of people, as others who are different from the rest of us. It proceeded to use "special characteristics" to construct the "knowledge" that their otherness is likely to cause more deaths of their own children. Then, the probability of killing works to confirm that these "parents" are indeed dangerous others and thus warrant the New Right interventions of risk management and supplementary criminal punishment. It is important to highlight that this problematic notion of *expected higher death rate* was precisely the cornerstone for a series of recommendations made by the Task Force for reforming the child protection system.

THE SLIPPAGE FROM CHILD DEATHS BY HOMICIDE TO ACCIDENTAL DEATHS

Another issue with the Ontario Child Mortality Task Force's handling of statistics concerns the transformation of a panic about an epidemic of child deaths by homicide to a problem of accidental deaths "by neglect." It was clear that when the Child Mortality Task Force and six coroner's inquests were launched in 1996, deaths of children by homicide, or so-called "fatal child abuse," was the most gripping issue and thus the focus for investigation. The initial focus on child homicide is evident in the choices of cases for convening coroners' inquests.

The focus however shifted away from child deaths by homicide in the report delivered by the Child Mortality Task Force. To its credit, the Child Mortality Task Force noted the rarity of homicide cases and the difficulty of predicting child homicide because "factors associated with child maltreatment are not necessarily the same correlates associated with child fatality by homicide" (Ontario Child Mortality Task Force, p. 20, quoting Trocmé and Lindsey, 1996). By taking this stance, the Child Mortality Task Force essentially stated that the child protection did not fail in preventing child deaths by homicides, nor can it be expected to do any better.

However, the death of children by *accidents* was then portrayed as a major problem confronting society and the child protection system, *and* was linked to neglect. An examination of the section on "Accidents" in the Task Force Report reveals some of the problematic linkages made between accidental deaths and neglect. The section on "Accidents" in the Task Force Report was not just the longest, but also the only one immediately followed with an analysis titled "Relationship between neglect and child deaths."

One theme of the section on "Accidents" is that many accidental deaths are preventable. The Task Force cited a couple of studies on three forms of accidental deaths of children and how such death could be prevented:
Eighty-six percent of *motor vehicle fatalities*, according to an Arizona study, could be prevented through:

- use of safety measures such as seatbelts, child safety seats, bike helmets;
- non-usage of open-backed trucks for child transportation;
- proper conduct of such as abstinence from the use of alcohol or drugs.

Eighty-five percent of child deaths by *drowning*, according to the same Arizona study, could be prevented through

- supervision

Many *fire deaths*, according to a study by Squires and Busuttil in 1995, could be prevented through

- safety measures such as the safe storage of matches and lighters and the installation of functioning fire detectors;
- proper conduct of parents and caregivers, particularly with alcohol.

The study claims that "Alcohol played a significant role in the commencement of fires. In the majority of cases, an alcohol positive adult was the parent of the child" (Ontario Child Mortality Task Force, 1997, pp. 15–16).

In summarizing these two studies, the Task Force chose to focus only on the factor of supervision by stating that: "[m]any 'accidental' deaths could be prevented if greater attention was paid to supervision of young children (Ibid., p. 15)," even though one can argue that the availability of safety devices and the application of safe measures are probably the most effective in preventing most accidental deaths since most accidental deaths occurred in motor vehicle accidents and house fires. Nevertheless, through the summarizing statement, the Task Force laid the first step stone leading to child neglect, since lack of supervision is among the most common of neglect issues, as Swift showed in her study (Swift, 1995a).

Manufacturing the Relation Between Child Deaths and Neglect

An examination of the section on the "Relationship Between Neglect and Child Deaths" reveals even further slippage from accidental deaths to neglect, particularly neglect of children by single mothers. The Task Force rationalizes the analysis of the relationship between neglect and child deaths by stating that "[using a] broad definition of [neglect], it was found that neglect factors were cited on 79 occasions [of child deaths during 1994 and 1995] as the reason for the involvement of the children's aid society" (Ontario Child Mortality Task Force, 1997, p. 16). The flaw of this rationale lies with the fact that the sample was taken from the population of children involved with the child protection system, among whom neglect is one of the largest cause for involvement. Thus, a high percentage of neglect factors among children who died does not clearly suggest that there is a relationship between neglect and child deaths, since a high percentage of neglect factors is very likely to be also found among children who did not die.

In the rest of the same section, the Task Force cited a study on "fatal child neglect" or "neglect fatality" (Margolin 1990, cited in Ontario Child Mortality Task Force, 1997, p. 17). This study profiles the typical "neglect fatality" as "a male child, younger than three living with his mother and two or three siblings." The study was quoted as arguing that "[i]n the vast majority of fatalities from neglect, the parent was simply not there at a critical moment. The most common family structure for fatal neglect was a single-parent family in which the parent is the only adult in the household. Forty-four percent of the neglect fatalities came from a family of this type" (Ontario Child Mortality Task Force, 1997, p. 17, quoting Margolin, 1990). Whether that applies to Ontario families is not clear because the Task Force stopped short of reporting how many child deaths examined by itself actually occurred in single-parent households.

The section "Relationship Between Neglect and Child Deaths" thus purports the extremely misleading suggestion that child neglect, particularly neglect by single mothers, is a key cause of child deaths and therefore a major problem to be addressed. The following is a critique of this suggestion. First of all, the emphasis on accidental deaths among children known to Children's Aid Societies and then "neglect fatality" is unjustified, since accidental deaths to children known to a Children's Aid Society were in fact proportionately smaller in number than those to children in general, as I have discussed in detail in a previous section. Indeed, as figures in Table 10.1, on page 217 shows, from the perspective of numbers, if we want to prevent the largest category of child deaths in Ontario, we should work on preventing motor vehicle accidents. Motor vehicle accidents actually are more likely to happen to children who have never shown signs of abuse and neglect than to children known to Children's Aid Societies as a result of suspicion of abuse and neglect. From the perspective of proportions, if we want to prevent categories of deaths that seem to be particularly related to the child protection system as indicated by the disproportionate greater numbers, suicides of children who were in care of Children's Aid Societies (i.e. living in foster homes, group homes, or an institution at the time of committing suicide) are the category of deaths that we should take a hard look at. These children's suicides perhaps can tell us more about what is wrong with the child protection system than the false panic about "neglect fatality."

Second, the Task Force's report leads the reader to equate deaths of children who showed signs of being neglected with accidental deaths, when there is a significant discrepancy. In the earlier section on "Accidents," accidental deaths encompassed: motor vehicle accidents, drowning in the bathtub, and house fires. However, by "neglect fatality" the Task Force actually referred to death related to neglect in the sense of lack of supervision or care, usually involving drowning in the bathtub, house fires, substandard housing, and parents failing to follow medical instructions or delaying seeking medical attention (Ontario Child Mortality Task Force, 1997, p. 17). The omission of deaths by motor vehicle accidents was glaring, given that 43 percent (or 9 out of 21) accidental deaths of children known to children's aid occurred in motor vehicle accidents (Ontario Child Mortality Task Force, 1997, p. 14).

Third, the use of relatively new terms such as "fatal child neglect," "neglect fatality," and "death by neglect" is a linguistic device that attempts to link child neglect to child death. These terms produce the misimpression that neglect is a common cause of child deaths. They also insidiously change the way neglect as a problem is understood. Traditionally, knowledge of causes of deaths is in medical terms. For example, a pathologist's report would list "brain damage," "head injury," or "strangulation" as causes of particular deaths. Terms such as "death by neglect" in effect equate neglect, a problem with complex social and economic underpinning, to medical or biological conditions caused by personal acts. As such, these terms encourage people to think of neglect as caused by mothers personally, not as effects of poverty and other forms of marginalizations. This is another effect of the focus on child deaths—mothers deemed as being neglectful, most single mothers suffering from severe deprivation of resources, are being criminalized, or at least portrayed as "dangerous parents," through child deaths.

On the basis of the problematic presentation and interpretation of statistics, the Task Force put forward its recommendations for a "stronger focus on child neglect" and the targeting of single mothers, alcohol users, and drug users for more intrusive and intensive regulation. These recommendations bear little relevance to the initial concern with child homicide, or even child deaths in general. More than anything, they seem to be connected with the New Right political discourse of anti-welfarism; they reflect the rising of authoritarian approaches to "deviance" which subject categories of marginalized populations—here encapsulated as "dangerous parents"—to intensified coercive interventions and likely criminal punishment.

THE RESTRUCTURED CHILD PROTECTION SYSTEM: A CRITICAL ANALYSIS

Concurrent to the Child Mortality Task Force, juries of six coroner's inquests into deaths of children who died while receiving services from a Children's Aid Society also generated a large number of recommendations. Three broad themes pervade recommendations put forward by the Child Mortality Task Force and coroner's inquests. First, the courts, professionals other than social workers (e.g., medical doctors, school teachers, and lawyers), and the general public need to be more alerted to the harmful effects of child abuse and neglect. Second, principles of "family preservation" and the "least restrictive intervention," which underlined the law in the 1980s and 1990s, should come secondary to the protection of children. Third, the child welfare system needs more and stronger legal tools and system supports. Specifically, the recommended tools include adding neglect as a ground for child protection, standardized risk assessment tools, inter-linked data systems, increased funds and staff for Children's Aid Societies in the province of Ontario, and even creation of new child-specific criminal offences in the criminal code at the federal level (Ontario Child Mortality Task Force, 1997; Ontario Association of Children's Aid Societies, 1998a, 1998b; Canada Department of Justice, 1999a, 1999b).

At the provincial level, reforms of the child protection system were carried out notably in British Columbia and Ontario. In Ontario, the Ministry of Community and Social Services adopted a large number of the recommendations put forward by the Child Mortality Task Force and six coroner's inquests. From 1997 to 1999, the Ministry of Community and Social Services took these following actions:

- it put in place a standardized risk assessment system, mandated for all Children's Aid Societies across Ontario; (Ontario Ministry of Community and Social Services, 1998)
- it started setting up a new information database for tracking high risk families and linking all organizations involved in the child protection system;
- it appointed a Panel of Experts to review the Child and Family Services Act with particular attention to Part III on child protection;[4]
- it twice invested additional funding for hiring nearly 1,000 new front-line workers, training, and supporting the new database;
- it introduced a new funding formula, in which the province assumed 100 percent funding of the Children's Aid Societies[5] and which linked funding to actual caseloads, types of cases, and status of case in the work flow process;
- in collaboration with the Ministry of Health, it also established and expanded the Healthy Babies/ Healthy Children programme, a prevention and early intervention programme for high risk children under age six.

On top of these, in October 1998 Ontario's Community and Social Services, Minister, Janet Ecker, introduced the Child and Family Services Amendment Act (Child Welfare Reform), 1998. Due to unrelated legislative process delays, the Act had to be reintroduced in April 1999. It passed the Ontario Legislature in May 1999 and was proclaimed in March 2000. The major changes brought about by the Act include:

- the shifting of emphasis from considering the interests of families as a whole to privileging "children's best interests";
- recognizing "patterns of neglect" as a ground for mandatory protection services;

---

[4] Other parts of Ontario's Child and Family Services Act deal with issues such as young offenders, adoption, and Indian and Native child and family services for example.

[5] In the past the funding was shared between the provincial government and municipalities.

> ## Comparing the Declaration of Principles of the 1990 and 2000 Child and Family Services Act (major changes are highlighted in italics)
>
> | 1990 Act | 2000 Act |
> |---|---|
> | The purpose of this Act are:
• as a paramount objective, to promote the best interests, protection and well-being of children;
• to recognize that while *parents often need help* in caring for their children, that help should give support to the autonomy and integrity of the family unit and, wherever possible, be provided on the basis of mutual consent;
• to recognize that *the least restrictive or disruptive course of action* that is available and is appropriate in a particular case to help a child or family *should be followed;* | 1 (1) The paramount purpose of this Act is to promote the best interests, protection and well being of children.
(2) *The additional purposes of this Act, so long as they are consistent with the best interests, protection and well being of children,* are:
• To recognize that while *parents may need help* in caring for their children, that help should give support to the autonomy and integrity of the family unit and, wherever possible, be provided on the basis of mutual consent.
• To recognize that *the least disruptive course of action* that is available and is appropriate in a particular case to help a child *should be considered.* |

- stricter regulation of professionals' duty to report suspicions of child abuse and neglect;
- a shorter time frame for planning permanent arrangements; and
- more difficult access of family relatives or friends to children who have been made Crown Wards.

These changes encourage seeing children as separate component parts of the family, dichotomize children's interests and those of mothers, and endorse punitive approaches towards mothers whose "special characteristics"—notably poverty, history of abuse and neglect, single motherhood, receipt of welfare, substance use, and mental health problems—supposedly puts children under risk of harm or even death. Predictably, since the reform there is significant increase in the numbers of reports of child abuse and neglect, interventions, children removed from their families, and children who will not return to their families because of faster permanency planning for long-term care (See Table 10.2 on the following page).

At the federal level, the Department of Justice is also taking part in the rethinking and retooling of the child protection system. Specifically, it is conducting a "Child Victims and the Criminal Justice System" consultation which started in November 1999 and is still ongoing at the time of this writing. According to the Department of Justice, the consultation is conducted in response to suggestions of "judges, Crown prosecutors, defence lawyers, police, health care workers, hospital child abuse teams, public health nurses, academics, social workers and others directly concerned with child protection," and also recommendations from "judicial inquiries, coroner's inquests, child fatality review committees, and other review bodies" (Canada Department of Justice, 1999b, p. 6). The consultation paper is a curious synthesis of views on varied topics related to children. Of particular interest is the meshing of issues of sexual abuse of children with deaths of children. The discussion of what to do with sexual abuse of children draws on the 1984 report of the Committee on Sexual Offences Against

TABLE 10.2

STATISTICS ON CHILD PROTECTION SERVICES IN ONTARIO: 1997 – 2000

	1997	1998-1999	1999-2000	increase/ decrease since 1997
Net expenditures – annuals	$441,666,229	$540,978,097	$638,496,023	+ 44%
Total staff	4,273 (31/12/1997)	4,961 (1/4/1999)	5,396 (1/4/2000)	+26%
Reports/ Inquiries – annual	56,454	52,526	65,542	+16%
Open investigation, protection, and other child welfare cases	29,477 (31/12/1997)	29,408 (1/4/1999)	35,091 (1/4/2000)	+19%
Children in care	11,260 (31/12/1997)	12,911 (1/4/1999)	14,219 (1/4/2000)	+26%
Children served	21,328	23,682	25,586	+20%

Source: Adapted from Table "Provincial Statistics," on Ontario Association of Children's Aid Societies Web site, <www.oacas.org/content/about_child_welfare/index.html> (cited April 23, 2001)

Children and Youths (the Badgley Committee); while the discussion of what to do to prevent deaths and serious injuries of children as a result of physical abuse and neglect largely relies on recent provincial inquests and reviews on child deaths. Specifically, the consultation paper identified three areas of possible reform of the Criminal Code:

- creating more child-specific offences, such as, criminal physical abuse of a child, criminal neglect of a child, criminal emotional abuse of a child, child homicide (a child-specific form of manslaughter), and failing to report crimes involving child abuse or neglect;
- sentencing changes to improve protection for children from those who might re-offend, in other words, more severe sentences and longer terms of supervision and treatment;
- facilitating child victims' testimony and providing for assistance to child witnesses.
(Canada Department of Justice, 1999)

What follows is a detailed examination of two major instruments of regulating "dangerous parents" that are embodied in these initiatives: risk management and criminal punishment.

Risk Management

As some critics point out, child protection services are focusing more and more on investigation, assessment, analysis, and documenting of parental inadequacies, than meeting the needs of family in providing up-to-standard caring for children through direct support or help with accessing supplementary resources (Baines, 2000; Parton, 1998, 1999; Swift, 1999). This is particularly evident in the mandated professional protocol—the Risk Assessment Model.

The Risk Assessment Model is far more than a tool for assessing risk factors. It is a machinery of child protection work, which is designed to identify, document, classify, rate, and analyze risk factors related to the safety of a child in the context of abuse and neglect. Among the components of the Risk Assessment Model, Eligibility Assessment, Safety Assessment, and Risk Assessment are considered by the Ministry as "three important phases" incorporated in the Risk Assessment Model (Ontario Ministry of Community and Social Services, 1997, p. 1). Eligibility Assessment is conducted mainly through using the Eligibility Spectrum Tool at the time of referral. According to the Ministry, Eligibility Assessment accomplishes three things: (1) it helps ensure that all children and families who are eligible for child welfare services will actually receive those services; (2) it classifies "reasons for service" requests to enable better society planning; and (3) it records all intake activity so that society workloads can be better evaluated. The primary objective of conducting Eligibility Assessment is to make "consistent and accurate

> ## RISK ASSESSMENT MODEL FOR CHILD PROTECTION IN ONTARIO: SIX KEY COMPONENTS
>
> 1. Eleven risk decision points, which describe eleven decisions to be made (e.g., Risk Decision #3: Is child safe now?), and which structure the decision-making flow by defining the sequence of decisions;
> 2. Criteria to guide each decision point;
> 3. Eligibility Assessment;
> 4. Safety Assessment;
> 5. Risk Assessment;
> 6. Plan of Service connected to the Risk Assessment.
>
> (Ontario Ministry of Community and Social Services, 1997, p. 3)

decisions about eligibility for service" (Ministry of Community and Social Services, 1997, p. 1). The outcome in practice is the classification of protection investigation cases and non-protection investigation cases. Classification will likely lean towards more protection investigation cases, partly because it would be better to err on the safe side and partly because the funding formula favours protection investigation cases.

Safety Assessment is conducted at the time of the first face-to-face interview through the use of Safety Assessment Form, which guides workers in an analysis of selected safety factors and circumstances. The objective is to make a judgement about whether the child is safe or unsafe at that point in time. If the child is judged unsafe, immediate interventions will be implemented to "control the dangerous situation." The Safety Assessment may be conducted at any other point in the case to assist in assessing the impact on the child's safety by any change in the family's situation (Ontario Ministry of Community and Social Services, 1997, pp. 2, 7).

Risk Assessment is conducted when it is time to make a decision as to whether to provide service, what kind of service, or whether to continue providing service after a "child protection investigation," through the use of the Risk Assessment Form.

As the Ministry explains, Risk Assessment is an analysis of "risk related elements, the family's own perceptions, an identification and examination of a family's strengths, and any other significant case circumstances that may affect family functioning." Its primary objective is to help evaluate "the likelihood that a child may be abused or neglected in the future." Risk Assessment is different from Safety Assessment in that it is future-oriented and is to assist drawing up a Plan of Service, which aims at "long-term risk reduction" and "resolution of identified problems that create risk."

The Risk Assessment Form is the most comprehensive, complicated, and thus time-consuming of all the three tools. It is five pages long and organizes the assessment by looking into five categories of influences: Caregiver Influence, Child Influence, Family Influence, Intervention Influence, and Abuse/Neglect Influence. Under each category, there are five or six factors/topics, the extent of risk as related to each factor is to be rated at five possible levels. For example, under the category of Caregiver Influence, Alcohol or Drug Use is a factor, along with five other factors. Alcohol or Drug Use is then assessed or rated from level 0 to level 4, corresponding to "No misuse of alcohol or use of drugs" and "Substance use with severe social/ behavioural consequences" (Ontario Ministry of Community and Social Services, 2000).

The Risk Assessment Model regards mothers as a "bundle of risks" and who pose danger to their children's personal safety. It is conceived as an instrument to predict how safe/unsafe children are due to the absence/presence of a range of their mothers' "speciical characteristics," or risk factors. As such, it is likely to have the following effects:

First, the Risk Assessment Model structures practice in such a way that the reality of children's existence becomes intelligible only in terms of their individual safety. As one senior staff member of a Children's Aid Society shared with me optimistically: "[The Model] is helpful for making work easier because it organizes your thought and zeroes in on relevant information."[6] It structures not only the thinking but also action. Following the Model, child protection practices only concern children's needs and define their needs in terms of safety. The result is that for children to receive any professional help, they will have to be deemed as being in an unsafe situation, and mothers will have to be perceived, assessed, documented, and acted upon as potential perpetrators posing danger to children. History has provided ample examples of how a particular definition of need impacted on practice and clients' experiences. In the late nineteenth century, when services were devised for meeting the needs of delinquent children, some were sent to industrial schools by parents who wanted them to learn a trade and claimed that they were incorrigible. Later when services were devised for children with emotional problems, they would have to be categorized as suffering from emotional problems in order to access child welfare institutions, as illustrated by Carol Baines's study of Earlscourt (Baines, 1994). If children were given IQ tests in the past, today's children and mothers are subject to safety tests and risk of harm assessment. The thread running through this is the failure in recognizing and addressing the needs of children and mothers from their own perspective.

Second, risk assessment excludes considerations of the socio-economic and cultural-ethnic context in which the needs of children and families occur (Baines,

---

[6] Personal communication with the Children's Aid Society of Toronto Staff.

2000; Parton 1998, 1999; Swift, 1999). The Risk Assessment Model embodies the paradigm shift from considering certain aspects of reality as social problems to considering them risk factors. These include poverty, mental illness, single motherhood, substance use, poor housing, and domestic abuse. These issues have been refashioned from social problems into things that are distant, apolitical factors; things that can be taken for granted and dealt with indifferently without relating to collective responsibility; things that can be quantified and rated for their inherent danger to children.

Third, the reduction of risk seems to be the responsibility of mothers. The role of the social worker is not so much in solving these problems, but rating and analyzing them according to definite formula and taking children away if mothers have failed in reducing the magnitude of danger posed by their conduct to children's safety. Ironically, despite the reliance on service language such as "service eligibility" (for a "service" for which no one wants to be eligible), services in the sense of providing support to families have apparently been pushed to the very margins of social work activities.

Child-Specific Criminal Offences

If at the provincial and local level mothers are primarily governed through risk management in increasingly bureaucratized and "child-focused" child protection work, at the federal level they are the central objects of a consultative discussion initiated by the Department of Justice about toughening criminal punishment for perpetrators of child abuse and neglect. As the Department of Justice explained, "Providing services to children in need of protection is the responsibility of the provinces and territories; ensuring that appropriate offences and penalties are available is the responsibility of the Government of Canada" (Canada, Department of Justice, 1999a, p. 2). The following discussion addresses the criminal punishment side of current restructuring of the child protection system. Specifically I will discuss the proposed creation of child-specific criminal offences, which, I argue, is a technology for regulating individualized obligations owed by adults, particularly mothers, to children.

In its consultation paper *Child Victims and the Criminal Justice System*, the Department of Justice made substantive reference to recommendations from Ontario, particularly in relation to the creation of child-specific offences. Among the six coroner's inquests in Ontario, three recommended that the federal government amend the Criminal Code. All three recommended the inclusion of an offence of Death by Child Abuse/Neglect in the Criminal Code.[7] One inquest

---

[7] One of the six coroner's inquests in Ontario recommended the removal of infanticide from the Criminal Code, which, as a woman-specific offence and separate from murder and manslaughter, has historically embodies a theme of tragedy and sympathy

recommended at the same time the removal of infanticide from the Criminal Code, which, as a woman-specific offence and separate from murder and manslaughter, has historically embodied a theme of tragedy and sympathy, and hence lenient punishment (Backhouse, 1984, 1991). Another inquest proposed that the offence of Death by Child Abuse/Neglect not "require the specific intent to kill[,] with a minimum term of imprisonment[,] without eligibility for parole [and] to be classed as second degree murder" (Ontario Association of Children's Aid Society, 1998), not recognizing that the very definition of murder rests on the proof of intent to kill. The objective of creating such a new offence, as the Department of Justice duly noted, is to result in more convictions and lengthier sentences and to "focus attention on society's condemnation" of such conduct (Canada Department of Justice, 1999b, p. 19).

It seems obvious from the structure of the consultation paper that the Department of Justice considered the contemplated reform as an extension of legal reforms set in motion by the Badgley Committee. The main components of earlier reforms focusing on sexual offences were described in the introduction to the consultation paper as well as the background sections of all three subsequent parts. Throughout the consultation paper, slippages from sex to death, and then to physical and emotional harm, occurred consistently. For example, a statement on emotional harm caused by sexual abuse would slip to emotional harm in general without any explanation:

A National Population Survey, considering the experience of 7,000 sexually assaulted children and young people, disclosed that a larger proportion suffered more emotional harm than physical injury. Government at all levels and courts are increasingly recognizing the prevalence of severe emotional and psychological harms caused to children by all forms of abuse, and are seeking ways to protect children from such harm (Canada Department of Justice, 1999b, p. 13).

Similarly, in the discussion of options for toughening sentencing so as to correspond to perceived extra severity of offences against children, the Department of Justice reviewed several sentencing provisions for sexual offences against children. Then the discussion turned to ways for "Addressing the Needs and Interests of Children in Sentencing Policy." At this point, sexual offence suddenly disappeared from the narrative and the subject became child abuse (Canada Department of Justice, 1999b, pp. 24–26).

The principles concerning the special legal status of children laid down in the context of sexual offences by the Badgley Committee are now being expanded to all other forms of abuse, through the narrative technique of association or slippage, rather than logical arguments. In the current Criminal Code, most offences under the heading of "Sexual Offences" deal with those against children, with only a very few exceptions. It seems that these offences are set aside from sexual assault in general, and thus considered distinct and particularly punishable, because they involve sexual acts *and* children. If reforms are to be implemented following the direction laid out in the consultation paper, what will emerge is a child-specific territory on the map of criminal offences, subject to harsher criminal punishment. As Mariana Valverde has argued, the creation of distinct spaces is a crucial device for articulating and hence allowing unequal treatment in liberal governance (Valverde, 1996). The basis for creating more child-specific offenced (separated from other cases of assault, failing to perform the duty to provide necessaries, or homicide) is the adult-child relationship in general, and the mother-child relationship in particular.

Shelley Gavigan (1989–1990) has examined one historical example of relation-specific offences, namely petit treason in eighteenth-century England, which was limited to a particular class of murder: murder of a husband by his wife, or a master by a servant, or a religious superior by a religious inferior. We can draw some implications of creating child-specific offences from the example of petit treason. As Gavigan suggested, petit treason reflected the pre-capitalist social and economic relations in England, which were based on "obligations of duty, subjection, and allegiance." The murder of one's master was greater than murder; it was "the conscious and deliberate breach of one's duty" and "the abuse of a confidence." The murder of one's husband was also greater than murder, as it was the violation of subjection and obedience that was due (only) from the wife to the husband. Thus, murder in this class was a treachery exceeded only by disloyalty to the King, which was called high treason. In her article, Gavigan laid emphasis on petit treason cases in which wives were accused of murdering their husbands. Women who killed their husbands were burned at the stake as traitors if convicted. The exemplary penalties for women were considered necessary on the basis of their violation of the "most sacred obligation" (Gavigan, 1989–1990). Thus, the law of petit treason both reflected and reinforced social and economic relations of gender and class, which were anchored in feudal forms of obligations. Parental obligations of duty and trust is a central theme in child-specific offences and consequent "appropriately serious penalties" (Canada Department of Justice, 1999b, p. 15). Indeed, at the very beginning of the consultation paper, the Department of Justice laid out terms of parental duties, "The law has long recognized that parents have the primary role in supporting, protecting and educating their children, and has defined parental duties to take into account in the needs of children, as well as the fact that as children grow older, they become less dependent on their parents." (Canada Department of Justice, 1999a, p. 2; 1999b, p. 1).

According to the Department of Justice, one objective of the criminal law is punishing and deterring violations of parent-child relationship set above; penalty wise, violations of such code should be specified as aggravating factors in sentencing (Canada Department of Justice, 1999b, p. 8).

The restructuring child protection system, exemplified by the Risk Assessment Model and the proposed creation of child-specific criminal offences, regards mothers as "dangerous parents" who are likely to harm or even kill their children because of their "special characteristics" of poverty, single motherhood, substance use, mental health and so on. At the provincial level, the child protection system prioritizes tasks of investigation and information management at the expense of assisting and supporting mothers; at the federal level, the government seems preoccupied with designing punishment and deterrence mechanisms.

CONCLUSION

The restructuring of child protection was driven by a few high profile, tragic child deaths. These extreme cases became an entry point for public scrutiny of and political deliberation on the child protection system. In Ontario, the restructuring in child protection was largely steered by the Child Mortality Task Force and a series of coroner's inquests into several child deaths. These processes, which were connected to the New Right agendas of welfare-bashing and moral hyper-sensitivity, construed mothers, who were mostly poor and single, and involved with the child protection system as "dangerous parents," who are likely to harm or even kill their own children. This newly invented category directs attention to mothers' faults as individuals, when in fact most mothers get tangled in the child protection system as a result of structural inequalities and exclusions. Risk assessment and criminal punishment are instruments designed to regulate mothers as "dangerous parents," not as people in need of assistance and support. The restructuring dictated by the focus on child deaths can do little in preventing most deaths that occur in this province. It does not offer much help to the vast majority of children and their families who come to the attention of the child protection system; worse, it has made their lives more difficult.

CRITICAL THINKING QUESTIONS

1. Having read this chapter, if you encounter stories of child deaths in newspaper or on TV, would you react to the stories and think about solutions differently?

2. Extreme cases of child abuse and neglect leading to child deaths prompted and oriented the Child Welfare Reform in Ontario. How does this work against the majority of children and women involved with the child protection system?

3. What were the processes through which the category of "dangerous parents" was constituted during the Child Welfare Reform?

4. What are the effects of the production of the category of "dangerous parents" on child protection policy and practice?

5. What are the main components of the restructuring in child protection and do they help most children and mothers?

6. What do you think are societal problems that lead to child abuse and neglect? How are these societal problems related to the right wing reforms of the welfare system, housing provisions, etc.?

7. What would you suggest the child protection system do to address these societal problems?

SUGGESTED READINGS

Baines, C. (2000). Restructuring Services for Children: Lessons from the Past. In Shelia M. Neysmith (Ed.) *Restructuring Caring Labour: Discourse, State Practice, and Everyday Life.* Don Mills, Ontario: Oxford University Press.
> Provides historical analysis on the needs of children and families and then uses the analysis to effectively critique risk-assessment policies.

Callahan, M. and K. Callahan (1997). Victims and Villains: Scandals, the Press and Policy Making in Child Welfare. In Jane Pulkingham and Gordon Ternowetsky (Eds.), *Child and Family Policies: Struggles, Strategies and Options.* Halifax: Fernwood Publishing.
> Uses discourse analysis skills to examine press coverage of Gove Inquiry in B.C., demonstrates that the press was only interested in reporting personal defects of mothers and turned a blind eye to difficult issues of poverty, mental illness, and isolation.

Chen, X. (2000). Is It All Neo-Liberal? Some Reflections on Child Protection Policy and Neo-Conservatism in Ontario. *Canadian Review of Social Policy*, No. 45 & 46.
> Draws attention to the influence of neo-conservatism on the Child Welfare Reform in Ontario.

Parton, N. (1998). Risk, Advanced Liberalism and Child Welfare: The Need to Rediscover Uncertainty and Ambiguity. *British Journal of Social Work* 28, 5-27.
> Useful critical analysis of the emphasis on assessing and managing risk, influenced by the governmentality approach.

Schmidt, G. (1997). The Gove Report and First Nations Child Welfare. In Jane Pulkingham and Gordon Ternowetsky (Eds.), *Child and Family Polices: Struggles, Strategies and Options*. Halifax: Fernwood Publishing, 1997.
> Insightful analysis of the questionable impact of the Gove Report on the relatively new First Nations Child Welfare system.

Swift, K. (1995). *Manufacturing "Bad Mothers:" A Critical Perspective on Child Neglect.* Toronto: University of Toronto Press.
> A valuable reading on the complex and punitive child protection system, with critical analysis of embedded class, race, and gender relations.

Wharf, Brian (Ed.) (1993). *Rethinking Child Welfare in Canada*. Toronto: McClelland & Stewart.
   A useful text on child protection. Although many aspects of the system have changed after the publication of the book, most of the analysis and argument for the need of a comprehensively supportive system is still relevant.

WEB LINKS

www.oacas.org
   Web site of the Ontario Association of Children's Aid Societies, containing information on the child protection system and practice in Ontario. OACAS represents 51 quasi-government Children's Aid Societies which deliver child protection services in Ontario.

www.gov.on.ca/CSS
   Web site of Ontario government's Ministry of Community, Family and Children's Services. You can find information on child protection legislation and other policy statements here.

www.gov.bc.ca/mcf
   Web site of British Columbia government's Ministry of Children and Family Development, which provides child protection services directly through its 11 regional offices. Under the "child protection" link, you can find information on relevant legislation and services.

CHAPTER 11

THE LEANER, MEANER WELFARE MACHINE: THE ONTARIO CONSERVATIVE GOVERNMENT'S IDEOLOGICAL AND MATERIAL ATTACK ON SINGLE MOTHERS[1]

BY MARGARET HILLYARD LITTLE

Marcey is recently divorced and trying to raise her 10-year-old son on welfare.[2] She is anxious because the government has recently cut her welfare cheque by 22 percent. As a result more than one-fifth of her income has disappeared overnight. She pleads with her landlord to lower the rent because she knows that she cannot feed her child *and* pay her rent. He agrees to lower the rent—provided she has sex with him occasionally. Because she refuses she is forced to look for another place to rent, worrying about how she can pay first and last months' rent and move her belongings—all on a reduced welfare cheque (Interview 6, Kenora, February 25, 1999).

Katrina recently left her violent boyfriend when she was seven months pregnant. She applied for welfare and was told that she was eligible provided she went to three job sites per day looking for work. She traipsed up and down the streets of her small town with swollen ankles inquiring about employment when she was obviously very pregnant and traumatized by the recent violence in her life. She suspects that her baby was born a month early because of this stress. (Interview 4, Greater Toronto Area, May 1998) Belinda recently discovered that her welfare cheque was cancelled because they are investigating her for welfare fraud. Apparently someone has called the welfare fraud telephone line and reported that she is living with a spouse. She has no partner but she is becoming friendly with a co-worker at her part-time job at the donut shop. They just talk while they're working—she hasn't even gone on a date. She suspects her ex-boyfriend

---

[1] This article is dedicated to the memory of my mother, Lorna Margaret Hillyard Little, who was the first to teach me about poverty. I wish to thank my friends in the country for providing me with a hide-away and entertaining diversions: Jerry Browne and Barb Hunt, Marilyn Hood, Patty Kenny, Diane Kearnan, and especially Willy Kearnan for his constant doggy company.

[2] Please note that the names of all welfare recipients interviewed have been changed to a pseudonym to protect their identities. All anti-poverty activists and advocates agreed to the use of their real names.

of calling the welfare fraud line but she does not know because all fraud complaints are anonymous (Interview 3, North Bay, January 28, 1999).

These are all true accounts of the lives of single mothers that reflect the impact of three major changes to welfare under the Conservative government in Ontario. While single mothers have always been harassed, forced to prove themselves deserving in order to receive welfare, this chapter will demonstrate how this level of scrutiny or moral regulation has greatly intensified under the Ontario Conservative government. This research is based on one-on-one interviews I have conducted with more than 30 workfare recipients across the province, interviews with anti-poverty activists, and 200 focus group interviews conducted by members of Ontario Workfare Watch, a non-profit organization established to monitor welfare changes across Ontario.[3] I have conducted this type of research for more than a decade so I was surprised to find myself so overwhelmed by this recent trek across the province. Although I knew about the dismantling of our social programs, these interviews forced me to come face to face with the devastating results of these policy changes. You, too, will be shocked and alarmed when you read about the everyday struggles of single mothers who are simply trying to feed and care for their children as best they can.

THE HISTORICAL AND NATIONAL CONTEXT

The poor have always been condemned in our society. Since the creation of the Elizabethan Poor Laws in the 1700s, our governments have divided between the worthy and unworthy poor. The Poor Laws required the poor to complete a work test in order to be eligible for public charity. If you were strong enough to cut a cord of wood you were generally considered ineligible for government help and

---

[3] My interviews were conducted with workfare recipients in Kenora, North Bay, Kingston, the Greater Metro Toronto area, and Sudbury from May 1998 to December 2000. As a result, these workfare recipients lived in northern, southern, rural, and urban Ontario communities. The majority of my interviews were with single mothers but approximately 10 percent of my interviews were with men in an effort to begin a preliminary gender comparison. The majority of these interviews were tape recorded and the participants signed consent forms specifying precisely what information I was permitted to use. I conducted my interviews in consultation with Workfare Watch in an effort to enhance their study. Workfare Watch paid honoaria to the participants. Workfare Watch focus group interviews were conducted in Peterborough, Guelph, Niagara Region, Sudbury, Durham Region, Thunder Bay, London, and Windsor. See "Broken Promises: Welfare Reform in Ontario," Interim Report, Ontario Workfare Watch, Toronto, Ontario, April 30, 1999, <www.welfarewatch.toronto.on.ca/promises/report/htm> I have used this empirical research to make other theoretical claims about the nature of the neo-liberal welfare state. For example, see: Little, M. (Spring 1999). The Limits of Canadian Democracy: The Citizenship Rights of Poor Women. *Canadian Review of Social Policy, 43*, 59-76.

expected to find your own work despite of the massive unemployment and social upheaval which was occurring during the industrial revolution. If you were deemed worthy you were given a few scanty provisions such as food and coal or you were eligible to live in a poorhouse, a disease-infested public home for the old, the sick, and single mothers.

With the creation of the modern welfare state in the early 20th century we incorporated these same basic premises about poverty into our so-called modern welfare programs. Initially governments only helped poor widows and deserted mothers who proved to be both financially and morally deserving. These women would receive a penurious welfare cheque on which it was simply not enough to live. It was expected that these women would top-up their welfare cheques with some part-time work that would not interfere with the time needed to care for their children. Eventually, governments expanded their welfare programs to include other types of single parents, such as divorced, unwed, and even single fathers. But every single parent had to prove continuously that they were both financially and morally deserving in order to receive government aid. Welfare administrators would scrutinize the cleanliness of the homes, the sleeping arrangements, the number and types of visitors to the homes, the dress and manner of the parent, the school records of the children, and many other aspects of daily life. All of this intense scrutiny was conducted in order to determine an applicant's worthiness. And once the welfare cheque was granted, home visits by welfare administrators continued in order to ensure that the recipient maintained a frugal and moral life.

But this is all in the past, you say. What does this have to do with today's poor single mothers? Although the moral regulation of poor single mothers has changed over time, it has persisted in new forms throughout the history of welfare.[4] Today, single mothers still have to prove themselves both financially and morally deserving in order to receive welfare. And during the era of the Ontario Conservative government, there are more and more rules to determine just who is and who is not a worthy single mother.

The Ontario Conservative government is not the only guilty party when it comes to the moral regulation of poor single mothers. The federal government has made this possible when it dismantled the Canada Assistance Plan (CAP) and replaced it with the Canada Health and Social Transfer in 1996. The CAP established in 1966, provided unlimited cost-shared federal funding for welfare and promised to eradicate many of the punitive features of earlier welfare policies. In order to receive this federal grant, welfare programs had to meet three conditions, (1) benefits based solely on financial need; (2) all provincial residence requirements

---

[4] For a more detailed account of how single mothers have been regulated by welfare throughout the 20th century see Little, Margaret Hillyard (1998). *No Car, No Radio, No Liquor Permit: The Moral Regulation of Single Mothers in Ontario, 1920-1997.* Toronto: Oxford University Press.

eradicated; and (3) an appeal board established in each province to protect recipients' rights.

While these CAP conditions had a number of limitations they stilled helped to guarantee the poor a certain level of financial security (Little, 1999 Spring). The first condition is important to highlight for the purposes of this chapter. This stipulation prohibited workfare and other employment-tied welfare programs. Regardless of the reason for a citizen's impoverishment, regardless of the citizen's employment history, she or he was eligible for welfare simply because of poverty. Also, regardless of the moral character of an applicant she or he was eligible for welfare provided she or he could prove economic need.

Despite the limitations of the CAP, it provided much more support to the poor than the CHST. With the CHST there is no federal funding specifically designated for welfare programs. Instead, each province receives a lump sum to spend on education, health, and welfare; each province can choose just how much to spend in each of these three areas. Given the popularity of health and education, provincial governments have begun to concentrate spending in these areas at the expense of welfare programs.

Under the CHST the federal government has erased almost all national standards for welfare. Poor Canadians no longer have a right to welfare based on economic need. Now the provinces can establish their own eligibility requirements. This change permits not only workfare but also any other eligibility criteria that the provincial and municipal governments wish to implement. It also allows provincial and municipal governments to refuse to grant a person welfare for any reason deemed appropriate. This has opened the door for a number of employment-tied welfare programs. We have now returned to the work test of the Elizabethan Poor Laws. It is not enough to be poor. You now must also prove that you are deserving. The implication is that you are responsible for the fact that you do not have a job during a time of high unemployment.

THE IMPORTANCE OF MORAL REGULATION

To best understand how changes to Ontario welfare policy under the Ontario Conservative government have affected single mothers I use the moral regulation approach. Phillip Corrigan and Derek Sayer used this approach in their innovative book, *The Great Arch*, to examine how the English state was established. They explored in detail the many activities, forms, routines, rituals, and regulations of the English state which helped to establish the relationship between government and its citizens (Corrigan & Sayer, 1985). I explore the Ontario Conservative government welfare policy changes to better understand the type of relationship that this government is attempting to form between the state and poor single mothers.

There are five aspects of moral regulation, which makes it a useful concept for my own work on welfare. First, it highlights certain moral processes in society. The government, and various social organizations, are involved in processes to create and perpetuate certain power inequities, be they class, race, gender, sexual inequities, or others. But while these organizations are creating and maintaining these inequities they are also creating and maintaining a certain moral order—a certain set of rules and regulations which establish what is moral and immoral. Second, this process of moral regulation is not static, but rather continuous. Once the rules and regulations are established they need to be maintained. When these rules and regulations are challenged the government and social organizations will re-establish or modify them. Third, the public must accept this process of moral regulation. If the public does not agree with these moral codes they can challenge these rules—they can vote for a different political party, run for political office, participate in a political protest or even attempt to overthrow the government. Consequently the government needs legitimacy of the public to maintain its moral rules and regulations. Fourth, this process or moral regulation will meet resistance. These moral codes are usually not accepted by all. The government does not have absolute power to impose these moral codes. I want to highlight this aspect of moral regulation because it is sometimes confused with social control. Social control implies that those who make and administer the regulations are all-powerful and do not meet with resistance. Instead, moral regulation scholars insist that this set of moral rules and regulations can and will be challenged. Fifth, the relationship between the regulator and the regulated is beneficial to both. Even in the most unequal relationships created by moral codes, both parties have something to gain from this relationship. The regulated, or the weaker party, often needs the regulator, or the stronger party, for money, food, and shelter. But the regulator also needs the regulated to establish his or her status, to ensure his or her moral superiority. In the case of welfare, the poor need the welfare worker in order to receive their welfare cheque and survive. But at the same time, the welfare worker needs the poor in order to continue to have a job and status in society. Otherwise, the welfare worker will be without work and she or he will end up applying for welfare! (See Piven & Cloward, 1971)

I will utilize moral regulation by applying a "moral lens" on top of a materialist analysis. Therefore I begin by establishing how welfare benefits capitalism. Here it is clear that welfare helps to oppress the poor and yet keep the poor alive so they can compete with other workers for jobs and benefits. As Piven and Cloward and other Marxist welfare theorists have shown throughout the history of welfare in the industrialized world, this policy has two distinct characteristics,

> (1) the welfare rate must always remain below the lowest paid to workers. This ensures that welfare is never too popular and that people will be prepared to do demeaning, back-breaking, even dangerous jobs because it is more lucrative than a welfare cheque;

(2) welfare is established to ensure the survival of at least some of the poor. Previously, the Poor Laws we used to simply let the poor die. Why does capitalism want to keep the poor alive? The poor can be a "reserve army of labour" ready and eager to work at any time. This helps to ensure workers' wages and demands are dampened because the poor are always ready to take their jobs.

This Marxist analysis helps to explain both why welfare exists and its general characteristics.

But this Marxist analysis cannot explain the many details of welfare regulation that do much more than keep the poor alive and competing for jobs. The welfare policy is also an important moral project. This moral project takes two forms. First, it ensures that the poor are seen as immoral or morally dubious. Second, it instills the moral values of our society for all citizens

By doing so, it establishes who are those with superior moral clout. Therefore it creates an unequal relationship between those who are guardians of morality and those who are considered immoral.

Application of Moral Regulation to Ontario Welfare Policy

The current welfare policy of Ontario is an excellent example of moral regulation at work. There are three policy changes under the Conservative government which have helped to perpetuate the notion that poor single mothers are morally undeserving. Both the welfare rate cuts and the implementation of workfare ensures that welfare is extremely stingy and punitive to its recipients. These two measures help to ensure that the current welfare policy meets the needs of capitalists. Today capitalists in this increasingly globalized market economy are competing with companies all over the world. Local capitalists require workers that will work for lower wages and less benefits. When the local welfare policy is made more stingy and punitive, making it almost impossible to survive on welfare, it encourages the poor to compete with workers for any jobs available. This in turn allows local capitalists to reduce wages and benefits to workers because they know there is a desperate group of poor citizens who are willing to work for less. Whereas the first two policy changes meet the current needs of intensified capitalism, the third policy change reinforces certain moral codes of society. This third policy change, the heightened policing of welfare fraud blatantly encourages the public to believe that all the poor are immoral cheaters who must be constantly investigated.

These welfare changes have had a dramatic impact on single mothers' lives. Not only is it increasingly difficult for single mothers to feed, clothe, and shelter their children, but it is almost impossible for them to insist that they are morally deserving of all the respect and dignity other citizens enjoy.

Welfare Rate Cuts

One of the most dramatic changes to welfare policy in Ontario occurred in 1995 when all able-bodied welfare recipients had their cheques reduced by 21.6 percent. In the entire history of welfare this was an unprecedented cut. While all welfare recipients have found this extremely difficult, single mothers have been particularly hurt by the cuts. With child-care responsibilities these mothers have less opportunities to top-up their scanty welfare cheques by finding employment. Especially given that the Chrétien government has reneged on its Red Book electoral promise to establish a national childcare programme. The impact of these cuts is told through poverty statistics and personal one-on-one interviews. The National Council of Welfare reported that single mothers have fallen further and further below the poverty line as a result of the Ontario welfare rate cuts. In 1995 single mothers in Ontario were $8,488 below the poverty line. After the welfare rate cuts they were $9,852 below the poverty line. In fact, the number of single mothers living on incomes less than *one half* of the poverty line jumped from 10.2 percent to 12.2 percent as a result of the welfare rate cuts (National Council of Welfare, 1995, 1996).

The everyday lives of single mothers have dramatically worsened. Single mothers that I have interviewed told me that they have attempted suicide, reduced their food consumption to one meal a day, sold almost all their household furniture, moved in with abusive ex-partners—all in an attempt to survive the welfare rate cuts.

Given that food is one of the largest non-fixed items in many single mothers' budgets this is where women are making huge sacrifices. Two-thirds of food bank recipients on welfare report, going without food at least one day per month. Most of them report that they go without food one day a week or more. Twenty-one of the thirty single mothers that I have recently interviewed across Ontario admit that they are eating less than three meals a day. One aboriginal single mother said, "I always wondered how vegetarians survive—now I know. I never see meat anymore. Tonight's supper is popcorn and a stale muffin I got on sale" (Interview 1, Kenora, February 25, 1999).

For example, one single mother in Kingston has lost 87 pounds since the Ontario Conservative government welfare cut. She has sacrificed her own health and nutrition in an attempt to ensure that her five children do not go hungry (Interview, Kingston, March 1997).

Another woman in a rural community said she picked a dead deer off the road, took it home, gutted it and put it in the freezer to feed her children (*Workfare Watch Interim Report*, 1999).

These are only a few examples but they speak to the sacrifices single mothers are making in order to care for their children.

A study conducted by nutritionists at the University of Toronto Faculty of Medicine only confirms my interview findings. They interviewed single mothers who use food banks and found that 70 percent had gone moderately or severely hungry in the past year and 57 percent had done so within the past 30 days. More than 60 percent said they had cut the size of their own meals due to the lack of food. The study also found that these women were nutritionally malnourished (Tarasuk, 1997).

Many of the single mothers I interviewed were desperate to prove to me just how creative they were to provide food for their children. One mother opened up every kitchen cupboard at the beginning of the interview to show me that she had lots of food to feed her children, including food from the local foodbank (Interview 12, Greater Toronto Area, May 1998).

Another single mother confided that she has a vegetable garden at a friend's house and she cans, freezes, and hides this food at her parent's home (Interview 6, Kenora, February 25, 1999).

Another woman went immediately to the grocery store after I handed her the honorarium at the end of the interview, stating that she had not gone grocery shopping in two months (Interview 10, Kenora, February 24, 1999).

In more than a decade of conducting interviews with single mothers, I have never seen them so desperate to prove to me that they are deserving and faithfully feeding their children.

Some single mothers have given up every item that is not an absolute necessity. One interviewee in Kenora said that she gave up her beaten-up vehicle once the welfare rate cut came in, even though she lives 15 kilometres from town and the bus service does not run on the weekends or after 7 p.m. on weekdays (Interview 2, Kenora, February 25, 1999).

Another hides her piano, her only family treasure, at a friend's home (Interview 6, Kenora, February 25, 1999).

I interviewed one aboriginal woman in her living room which was entirely bare except for our two straight-back chairs. She explained, "When the [welfare rate] cuts came I decided what stuff in the house could go—cable went, TV went, I sold most of my furniture but I didn't tell welfare or they would have deducted it from my cheque" (Interview 12, Kenora, February 24, 1999).

Even a telephone becomes a luxury for poor single mothers in the aftermath of the welfare rate cut. A recent survey of single mothers in Toronto found that as many as 27 percent of them had went without telephone service some time during the last two years (Ontario Workfare Watch, "Broken Promises," 1999).

Telephones fulfill three very important functions for single mothers. First, they link a mother to emergency services, which are particularly important when you are raising children on your own. Second, they are essential for seeking employment opportunities, which is an obligation for many on welfare. Third, they link a single mother who is often isolated in her own home to family and friends.

Housing has become an enormous concern for single mothers since the welfare rate cuts. Without stable housing, life is thrown into a constant upheaval and is reduced to a desperate scramble to find shelter, temporary, permanent, good or bad. Health suffers and damages the ability to make any long-term plans. Changes to welfare and tenant protection laws in Ontario have resulted in many people hanging on to their housing precariously, being forced into sub-standard accommodation, or worse, losing their housing altogether. Welfare benefits are paid in two parts: a shelter allowance plus a basic needs benefit that is supposed to cover all non-shelter costs. Maximum shelter allowances are far below the median rents actually paid by tenant households across Ontario.[5]

While shelter allowances have been frozen, rents have continued to rise, shrinking the number of affordable units, putting thousands more people at risk of homelessness. These housing changes have dramatically affected single mothers. A number of single mothers interviewed had their electricity, gas, or telephones cut off. Others have been evicted and have moved themselves and their children into shelters. All of this has placed enormous stress upon poor single mothers, for once a single mother loses her housing she is reported to the Children's Aid Society and she lives in fear that she will lose her child or children.

Women have also experienced increasing amounts of violence and harassment in their lives as a result of the cuts. While we do not know the precise degree of violence or the number of single mothers who are experiencing it, we do know that women, and particularly vulnerable women, encounter high levels of violence in their lives. The *Violence Against Women Survey*, conducted by Statistics Canada in the early 1990s, found that one in three women had suffered acts of violence as defined by the Criminal Code by their partners (Rodgers, 1994). Studies show that low-income women experience even greater degrees of violence. A study of low-income young mothers found that 50 percent had lived with a partner who had physically assaulted them or had abused drugs or alcohol (*Falkiner et al. V Her Majesty the Queen*, October 25, 1995). American studies suggest that 50 to 80 percent of women on welfare have experienced abuse from a partner.[6]

Certainly my research supports the general belief that low-income women experience high degrees of violence and that this violence escalates when they become even more vulnerable. During my recent interviews, single mothers explained that they had experienced more difficulties with ex-partners, employers,

---

[5] For example, the maximum shelter allowance for a single mother with one child is $511 while the median rent in Ontario for a two-bedroom apartment is $696 a month. "Taking Responsibility for Homelessness," Report of the Mayor's Homelessness Action Task Force, City of Toronto, January 1999.

[6] For a compilation of many recent American findings on the relationship between poverty and violence see: Raphael, J. & Tolman, R.M., (Eds.), (1997). *Trapped by Poverty, Trapped by Abuse*, Taylor Institute and the University of Michigan Research Development Center on Poverty, Risk and Mental Health.

and landlords. The Ontario shelter movement has reported that since the welfare rate cut more women are returning to abusive partners in order to feed and clothe their children (Ontario Association of Interval and Transition Houses, 1997).

One aboriginal woman told about her difficult decision to permit her abusive ex-partner to rejoin her and her son in their home. "With him here this month it's been such a change for me. I eat more often—I only ate once a day since the welfare rate cuts. I sleep better, I worry less. I have support" (Interview 12, Kenora, February 24, 1999).

One anti-poverty activist explains the difficult choices single mothers are forced to make. "Since the cuts, economic security means food in your child's belly and a fist in yours…Ex-spouses make spiteful allegations of fraud. It is then the fraud investigators [start] hounding their neighbours and friends for information; stalking is contracted out with tax payers' dollars and made 'legal'" (Thompson, 1997).

Many women report that the level of harassment in their lives has escalated since the welfare rate cut. One woman said that since the welfare rate cut, her ex-partner said he would give her $5 for a hug and more for sex—if she needed the money.[7]

In more than one community, single mothers have complained that landlords have attempted to exchange sex for lower rents. "He [the landlord] told me that if I had sex with him he would take off $150 a month for rent," explained one single mother (Interview 6, Kenora, February 25, 1999).

Anti-poverty activists stated that the welfare workers are unsympathetic to women's experiences of violence. "We all know that women who are abused often get back together [with their partner], then not together, then together but the welfare department has no sympathy for this. They just expect it to be clear—either you are living with someone or you are not," explains one advocate in Kenora (Interview 5, Kenora, February 26, 1999).

In one single mother's case, her ex-partner claimed that she had received $2,000 in child support and immediately her welfare cheque was cut off. According to this mother, her ex-partner had threatened her with a knife and had previous charges including assaulting two police officers. "I don't want to have to deal with him at all. Yet, here I was—being faced with welfare problems when I was in a shelter because he claimed he had given me money I'd never seen.…I was pretty stressed about that; they were even talking about charging me with fraud." She is currently has $50 per month deducted from her cheque because of this support payment the welfare department claims she received. Once she charges her ex-partner with violence, the welfare department will stop deducting this money but for several months she has been both financially and emotionally distressed because of this situation (Interview 4, Greater Toronto Area, May 1998).

---

[7] This type of proposition was reported during my interviews in Kenora and North Bay.

Most welfare recipients are attempting to top-up their miserable welfare cheques in whatever way they can. Because of childcare responsibilities, few single moms are able to find work to top-up their welfare cheques. Only one single mother I interviewed reported any type of underground employment, which would have enhanced the welfare cheque. This woman, in a snow-bound northern Ontario town, shared one pair of boots between herself and her son as they delivered newspapers.[8]

Instead of doing underground employment, many women have increased the amount of caring work they do. Some women have moved in with their parent(s) and are caring for them in exchange for cheap rent. Others visit the home of their parent(s) or other family members and care for them in exchange for groceries or other necessities.

This welfare cut has severely reduced a single mother's economic independence. Where the welfare cheque in the past often meant a release from oppressive personal relationships, this is increasingly no longer the case. Instead, single mothers have had to once again rely upon abusive ex-partners, harassing landlords, or demanding family members—all in an effort to feed, clothe, and shelter their children.

WORKFARE

From the introduction of welfare for single mothers in 1920 up until the arrival of the Ontario Conservative government, single mothers were considered a distinct category of welfare recipients whose primary responsibility was the care of their children. As a result single mothers were not expected to look for fulltime work. Instead, they were only encouraged to take work that did not interfere with their primary duty as mothers of the next generation. With the introduction of workfare, the Ontario Conservative government has dramatically altered the nature of welfare for single mothers. Now, all single mothers with school-aged children are expected to be participating in the workforce to the same degree as single men and women. In other words, single mothers are no longer fully recognized for their childcare responsibilities. Instead, they are treated very similarly to all other welfare recipients.

Treating single mothers with school-aged children as if they were *single* with no dependants creates enormous hardship for these mothers. First, all workfare recipients must attend a workfare orientation workshop. One single mother who had completed her course work for a Ph.D. and had previously held a $52,000-a-year government job described in detail the workfare orientation workshop which every recipient must attend,

---

[8] Men reported such highly skilled jobs as plumbing, carpentry, drywalling, and gardening and less-skilled jobs such as collecting bottles, shoveling snow, and collecting scrap metal.

They are two hours long....Ours was a group of 25 people....It was conducted by the welfare fraud investigator. The room was very hot and stuffy, very small but he [the investigator] wouldn't let two women leave for a moment and get a breath of fresh air when they felt faint....He had a big authority attitude. He said you would be cut off welfare if you missed the session. He emphasized that the assistance was *temporary*....He talked at great length about fraud. (Interview 5, Kenora, February 26, 1999)

Another workfare orientation in Kingston was held in the gymnasium of a local school with the doors left open. "Everyone I go to school with could walk by and see me sitting in the meeting. There was no confidentiality. I was embarrassed," explained one single mother (AWARE, 1999). Single mothers are increasingly expected to conduct job searches. There appears to be a lot of discrepancy in the rules about job searches. Of those interviewed, some were required to do three searches a day whereas others were told to do as many as ten. For some, these searches involved making a phone call to a company and writing down the company's name, date of call, and the response. For others, they had to go door-to-door, making face-to-face contact with employers and requesting their signatures as proof that they had completed this job search. In one case, a young woman who was eight months pregnant was forced to conduct door-to-door job searches. Her baby was born three-and-a-half weeks early and she blames this early delivery on the stress caused by these job searches (Interview 4, Greater Toronto Area, May 1998).

Interviews with anti-poverty advocates revealed that "inadequate job searches" are the most common reasons given for cutting people off welfare. "I'm hearing about this all the time now. You can't appeal 'inadequate job searches' so it is an easy way to reduce the welfare case load," explains Lana Mitchell, a single mother and long-time coordinator of Low Income Peoples Involvement, an anti-poverty group in North Bay (Interview, North Bay, January 28, 1999). Consequently, welfare recipients feel enormous pressure to conduct these job searches despite how futile they know the search to be.

Retraining and educational upgrading has been severely restricted under workfare. Welfare support for post-secondary education was abolished in 1996. Now any education and training approved under Ontario Works must be short-term and directed only at the fastest possible entry to the labour market. This has frustrated many of the single mothers interviewed. Some of them have attempted to remain in university or college and scrape by on the Ontario Student Aid Program but this requires them to carry huge debts that are much larger than the average student loan. Others have had to drop out of post-secondary education as a result of this policy change.

It is the Community Participation component that is the new aspect of this policy. This is what is publicly understood as workfare, unpaid work in return for welfare. Workfare recipients in this stream can be required to work up to 70 hours per month in a not-for-profit or public sector workplace.

A number of single mothers work part-time but this only leads to further problems with the workfare administration. One mother's situation exemplified the difficulties of part-time employment, "I'll make too much money one month and they'll cut me off welfare and then the next month I'll make much less and I have to re-apply all over. I'm always running back and forth from the donut shop to the welfare office with these $90 pay stubs. They don't pay for the transportation to get down to the welfare office every two weeks."

This mother works at a donut shop, which is on the highway outside her northern Ontario town. Her shifts are from 3 p.m. to 11 p.m. and there is no bus service. "Sometimes I hitchhike 'cause it's the only way I can do it even though I know it isn't safe. Otherwise, I walk home after I get off my shift at 11 p.m. and I get here [home] at 1:30 a.m." (Interview 1, Kenora, February 25, 1999). Another single mother in Kenora told me that she was harassed by her workfare worker because she worked only part-time at the local women's centre. "They wanted me to work fulltime even though I have a three-year-old daughter. They humiliated me every time I walked into the workfare office. I will never allow that to happen to me again." As a result this single mother now works at *five* part-time jobs—all in an effort to guarantee that she no longer has to suffer the indignities of workfare. Her daughter is farmed out to various friends and family—a different person every day (Interview 5, Kenora, February 26, 1999). These are just some of the sacrifices and risks single mothers are experiencing as a result of the implementation of workfare.

For others, workfare activities have thwarted their abilities to complete education and training that would lead to more secure employment. One mother said that she was one course away from a healthcare aid certificate when she had to begin her community placement at the local hospital. "They're hiring healthcare aids at the hospital where I volunteer [as part of my workfare community placement] but I'm one course away. It is very frustrating" (Interview 1, GTA, May 12, 1998).

Community participants are not considered real workers. Although they are eligible for Workers' Compensation, the Employment Standards Act or Employment Insurance does not cover them. Also, it remains unclear whether workfare participants will be protected by the Ontario Human Rights Code, which protects workers against discrimination, including sexual and other harassment. There are now many examples of American workfare participants assigned to dangerous and unsanitary placements. American participants have been found to be working with infectious hospital laundry without gloves that are prescribed for the regular laundry staff. Others have had to do highway cleanup without access to a public washroom. And one worker died of a heart attack at his community placement when he said he was not feeling well and was told he must continue his work (ACORN, 1998). When welfare recipients, already desperate for money to feed and clothe their children, do not have the same rights as other workers this severely affects their ability to refuse unsafe or unsatisfactory work.

There is also considerable evidence in the U.S. that women experience an increase in violence in their lives when they undertake workfare placements. Poor women generally have experienced more violence in their lives and workfare increases the vulnerability of poor women for a number of reasons. Abusive partners have been known to be jealous of the woman going to her workfare placement. Other partners have been upset because the woman is unable to keep up with her domestic duties. Women say they feel vulnerable and exposed at workfare placements where ex-partners come and harass them (Allard et al., 1997; Raphael, 1997).

Workfare participants cannot simply quit a placement. If you refuse an offer of employment, a community placement, or if you refuse to look for work you are no longer eligible for welfare. If you are considered to not be making enough effort in this regard you receive a warning and your case is refused within 30 days. If after the first warning you are still considered to not be making enough effort, your cheque is suspended for three months. Three months is a very long time when you have no other source of income or assets. After suspension you must re-apply and meet the requirements all over again in order to attempt to receive welfare benefits (Ministry of Community and Social Services, 2000).

The entire premise of workfare is that welfare recipients are lazy and require a "push" or incentive in order for them to find work. Nothing could be further from the truth. The reality is that most welfare recipients are on welfare for a very short time. The average amount of time a single employable person is on welfare is approximately one year. Single mothers average approximately three years even though they have small children. The largest study of welfare recipients in Ontario found that excluding those who were already working, going to school, were ill or had a disability, or reported that they had unavoidable childcare responsibilities, *three quarters* of single mothers were already looking for work (Ornstein, 1995). According to another study, 15 percent of single mothers were already doing volunteer work before workfare was implemented ("Broken Promises," 1999). Research also reveals that single mothers are more likely to work when their children are school-aged and when quality childcare is available. For example, a national study reveals that 72 percent of single mothers with school-aged children are in the labour force, whereas 41 percent of single mothers with children under three years of age are in the labour force ("Lone Parent Families," 1992). All of this evidence suggests that single mothers were actively pursuing work *before* the implementation of workfare.

For the most part, these retraining and workfare schemes do not provide adequate childcare; it is up to the single mother to find her own childcare. One mother was granted childcare for only one of her three children. Another mother was told to find childcare for her three-month-old baby. Another mother had to pay $40 per week out of her welfare cheque to finance her own childcare while she participated in workfare ("Broken Promises," 1999).

All of these examples are against the stated regulations of workfare. They demonstrate that there is little recognition that parenting is the first concern of most single mothers. Instead, single mothers are blamed if they are not able to participate in retraining and workfare schemes. Money is deducted from their welfare cheques or they are told that they are ineligible for welfare at all—unless they participate in these programs. At the same time, single mothers are blamed if their children "act up at school" for lack of attention at home. This brings us back to a long history of contradictory expectations for single mothers on welfare. We have always expected single mothers on welfare to financially provide for their children. But at the same time we also expect these single mothers to adequately care for their children. Financial provision and mothering are contradictory expectations that are often impossible to meet. Workfare only exacerbates this contradiction, making women's unpaid caring work even more demanding and more invisible than it has been in the past.

WELFARE FRAUD

The Ontario Conservative government has established a number of mechanisms to "stamp out" fraud. Several anti-fraud measures will be examined below to explore how single mothers, in particular, have been constructed as morally suspicious.

A number of new verification procedures have been created. Today, welfare workers can demand literally hundreds of different pieces of information, depending on the circumstances of the case and they can refuse, delay, or cancel welfare payments if this information is not provided. People are often told to provide information that they cannot possibly obtain, or to provide it within impossibly short periods of time. This documentation includes their Social Insurance Number, OHIP number, proof of identity and birthdate, complete information on income and assets, medical reports, information on budgetary requirements (lease, rent receipts, etc.), school attendance, employment activities, and status in Canada. Other documentation can, and is, demanded of people regularly. The information requirements frequently go well beyond what is required to establish a person's eligibility suggesting that workers can use their discretion about what documentation must be provided.

Welfare recipients are often asked to provide such documentation within ten working days or less. This is often difficult for single mothers who have to find childcare arrangements and additional transportation money to provide this information. And sometimes the documentation is very costly. For example, one single mother from North Bay said that her welfare worker had demanded that she provide monthly statements of her bankbook and those of her four children for the last three years. When she went to the bank to get these necessary documents the bank official said it would cost $120 per hour to provide this documentation. Another single mother had to produce evidence that she had given up her car 15 years ago (Interview 1, Kingston, May 1999). Many women stated that they have been forced to locate violent ex-partners in order to obtain some of the necessary documentation ("Workfare or WorkFair," p. 5). These are extremely intensive measures, which stigmatize those on welfare, encouraging the belief that welfare recipients are often thieves who must be caught. Women, because of their relationship to others, are generally required to provide more information than men on welfare. For example, a woman with a child must provide proof of the age and custody of the child, proof of her status in relation to any man, and proof of any payments from the father of the child. As one woman said, "It's harder to be honest with welfare—it takes so much time and so much paper" (Interview 3, Kenora, February 26, 1999).

Immigrant and aboriginal women have more difficulty obtaining the necessary documents for their welfare workers. Aboriginal women have to appeal to the Department of Indian and Northern Development to receive sworn documents. Birth certificates are not always available for aboriginal or immigrant women and the substitute documents require lengthy processing time. Also, people in smaller reserve communities tend not to have bank accounts therefore they are unable to provide the required bank statements. All of these exceptions require extra negotiation with the welfare caseworker (Interview 5, Kenora, February 26, 1999). Biometric fingerscanning has also been implemented to deter fraud. According to the government's rationale, fingerscanning has been established to stop "double-dipping", but there is no evidence that this is a major problem in welfare programs. Ian Morrison, one of Canada's leading poverty law experts states, "The claim that fingerscanning deters fraud is difficult to test, to say the least. Independent studies of some programs have found no savings whatever in light of the costs of the technology" (Morrison, 1999 May). Nevertheless, fingerscanning is a further step to encourage the belief that poverty is a crime.

In 1995 the Ontario Conservative government opened its provincial welfare fraud telephone. Granting anonymity to the person who calls to report welfare fraud raises some interesting questions. If someone calls the police department to report noise or other bylaw violations, your name, address, and telephone number must be given. As a rule these identification details are given to the person you have complained about. In the case of welfare fraud, the caller does not have to take any responsibility for his or her actions due to the cloak of anonymity. The recipient will never be told who provoked an investigation into her case. It is also interesting to note who takes advantage of and who is most often the scapegoat of these circumstances. According to welfare fraud evidence, single mothers are most often the targets of those who call the welfare office to report fraud. In the Ontario 1999 welfare fraud report, spouse-in-the-house issues were the second most common reason for people to call the welfare fraud telephone line. Also, according to interviews I conducted with anti-poverty advocates and community legal workers it is generally believed that ex-partners are amongst the most likely people to call the welfare fraud line to report on single mothers' activities (Ministry of Community and Social Services, 1998).

The Ontario Conservative government has also dramatically changed its position on single mothers' spousal relationship. From 1987 until 1995, Ontario had the most progressive legislation in Canada regarding spousal relations. During this period, single mothers were permitted to live with a partner for up to three years before the government considered the couple common-law and deducted the financial resources of the spouse from the welfare cheque. In August 1995 as part of an "anti-fraud" initiative, the Ontario Conservative government announced that single mothers would no longer be permitted to live with a spouse.

The impact of the Ontario Conservative government's anti-fraud campaign against single mothers in spousal relationships has been devastating. During the first eight months of this new amendment, more than 10,000 recipients were deemed ineligible under the new definition and cut off welfare, 89 percent of who were women (*Falkiner et al., v. Her Majesty the Queen*). A number of women have been falsely accused of cohabiting with former spouses when these men have relocated in other countries, are dead, or are imprisoned. Some have been cut off assistance without a hearing, which would have demonstrated their innocence. In all cases, a single mother is considered guilty until she proves herself innocent—until she demonstrates that she is not in a spousal relationship. As many single mothers have realized, providing evidence that you are not in a spousal relationship is, indeed, a challenge (Little & Morrison, 1999).

Those single mothers who have remained on welfare have experienced more extensive and intrusive investigation into their lives. When a man moves into their home they must fill out a questionnaire to determine whether the man is a boarder or a spouse. The 11-page questionnaire reveals that the definition of spouse is broad encompassing an economic, social, and familial relationship. The questionnaire includes the following questions:

> 14) Do you and your co-resident have common friends?
> 15b) Do other people invite the two of you over together?
> 18) Do you and your co-resident spend spare time at home together?
> 24b) Does your co-resident ever do your laundry (or the children's)?
> 27) Who takes care of you and your co-resident when either of you are ill?
> 35a) Does your co-resident attend your children's birthday parties?

(Ministry of Community and Social Services, 1995 October)

Such a questionnaire could hardly be more intrusive. And what makes it particularly insidious is that there is no rule regarding how many questions need to be answered in the affirmative in order to be declared in a spousal relationship. Even if the recipient succeeds in persuading the welfare worker that her co-resident is not a spouse her status remains in question. According to the Ontario regulations the same investigation will be carried out annually as long as the living arrangement continues.

This obsession with the spousal status of a single mother ignores the reality of poor women's lives. The combination of low welfare rates and widespread discrimination from landlords makes it extremely difficult for a single mother to find decent and affordable accommodation. Consequently many single mothers have a male friend or even an ex-partner view apartments with them and even co-sign leases or rental agreements. Also, some men agree to financially help a single mother meet the last month's rental deposit. Other single mothers continue to communicate with her ex-partner in order that her children can maintain a relationship with their father. Still others who have been abused sometimes seek out male boarders to act as protection against the abusive former partner and to be a good role model for their children. All of this, however, becomes evidence that a single mother is living with a spouse.

Community legal workers and welfare recipients spoke at length about how this change in spousal definition has deeply affected the lives of single mothers. In North Bay one mother was accused of being in a spousal relationship because her boarder drove her children to school. In another case, the mother and father had never lived together but the son was 18 years old and physically disabled. The father came over to help shower the child because the petite-framed mother could no longer do this on her own. This sharing of parental responsibility was considered evidence of a spousal relationship (Interview 3, North Bay, January 28, 1999). Another woman hides her engagement ring from her welfare worker because she is afraid this will be considered evidence that she is in a spousal relationship (Interview 5, North Bay, January 1999). The welfare department called one woman's house in Kenora and accused her of hanging men's clothes on her clothesline. "This was true, they were my son's and they were only out there for a couple hours," she explained (Interview 10, Kenora, February 1999). In Northern communities, single mothers have often rented trailers from men who live in the bush. This works well for both parties. The women have a cheap and secure place to live and the men receive rental income and do not have to worry that their pipes will freeze over the winter. But this arrangement can be accused of being in a spousal relationship as a result of this rental agreement. In one case in Ear Falls, a single mother had her cheque cut off when she was accused of have a spouse-in-the-house even though she had not even been asked to fill out a spousal questionnaire (Interview 4, Kenora Community Legal Clinic, January 1999). In another case a woman wept when she explained to me that she had lost a lifetime friend because she had rented his trailer. "I had phoned welfare and cleared it with them before I moved in," she explained. The owner came to town once a month to cash his employment cheque. He had his own large room with a special key, which just opened that room. She, similarly, had a special key for her bedroom. "He was harassed by the welfare worker. I was accused of being in a spousal relationship even though I've never had a relationship since my abusive husband. Now I've lost my childhood friend—he won't even look at me when we meet in the street" (Interview 10, Kenora, February 1999).

As well as implementing more mechanisms to "catch" welfare cheaters, the Ontario government has also dramatically increased the severity of the punishments. The Ontario Works Act permits recipients to be fined a maximum of $5,000 or six months imprisonment if someone receives workfare payments that they are not entitled to. The new legislation punishes those who obstruct or knowingly give false information to a welfare worker. Recently the Ontario government announced that it will ban for life anyone who is accused of any of these versions of welfare fraud (Ontario Government, 2000). This lifetime ban will increase the fear and suspicion which all welfare recipients breathe every day and it will financially devastate those who are charged. As Reverend Susan Eagle, co-chair of the Ontario Social Safety NetWork, explained, "It won't matter if this is a first time offence, whether the individual is destitute, desperate, or didn't understand the rules and regulations of the system. It's a no tolerance policy which flies in the face of established principles of justice" (Eagle, 2000).

The impact of being accused of welfare fraud is incredibly damaging. One single mother in North Bay wept when she recounted her story of being wrongly charged with welfare fraud. She was charged for "undeclared income" and explained that she had received a welfare cheque when she had obtained full-time employment (ironically her job was at the local welfare office). "I didn't even open up the cheque, I sent it right back and I kept telling them to cancel my benefits," she explained. Then one day the police came to the welfare office where she was working and charged her with welfare fraud. The next day she woke up to find her name, address, and the fact that she had been charged with welfare fraud in the local newspaper and on the local radio station every half an hour for a whole day. "North Bay is a small community. My kids didn't want to go to school because they were bothered by other kids about it." Even though the charges were eventually dropped, this woman fears that she will never find employment again in North Bay. "How can one person [the welfare worker] have the power to destroy someone's life? When your name has been slopped through the mud—how do you ever get your good name back?" This woman was proud of her accomplishments. As well as raising her three children on her own, she had completed a B.A. at the local university, published an article in an academic journal, and purchased a home (Interview 2, North Bay, January 1999).

The impact of welfare fraud charges is even more disturbing when one realizes that there is no evidence to support the government's obsession with welfare fraud. According to the most recent Ontario government welfare fraud report, there were 747 welfare fraud convictions of a 238,042 case load in 1998 to 1999, which means a welfare fraud rate of 0.3 per cent. Of the more than 49,000 recipients suspected of fraud (as a result of complaints from fraud line, information from welfare staff, information sharing with other governmental departments) more than two thirds were found to have no fraud or error. So the vast majority of those suspected of fraud are not cheating the system.[9]

It is important to remember that welfare recipients, who violate technical rules, knowingly or otherwise, remain very poor as very few such cases involve significant amounts of money. Because the rules are many, complicated, and largely unknown to recipients it is very possible for the most scrupulous person to break a regulation. Given that welfare payments are so inadequate an important study from the U.S. suggests that most people on welfare supplement their welfare incomes in some manner (Edin & Lein, 1997). In my interviews all of the men admitted to receiving either gifts in-kind or cash under the table to supplement their welfare cheques. The women interviewed did not have the same access to cash for work under the table but they spoke instead of ways they hid additional food or resources from welfare workers. As one woman explained during my first interviews with single mothers more than a decade ago, "That's called abuse, but we call it survival" (Little, 1998).

Despite all the evidence to the contrary, provincial governments are increasing their expenditures in the area of welfare fraud. All of these procedures are increasingly more punitive, intrusive, and degrading. Also, these anti-fraud campaigns are gendered and part of an ideological or moral battle. Poor women have always been more morally suspect. Although low-income women were early recipients of welfare,

---

[9] While it is generally very difficult to obtain any information about welfare cases, the Ontario government does provide annual welfare fraud reports and occasionally prints press releases boasting about the number of people who have left welfare. The latter reports give the current number of cases *on* welfare which is helpful information in an effort to calculate exactly what percentage of those on welfare are convicted of fraud. "Welfare Fraud Control Report 1998-99," Ministry of Community and Social Services, January 2000; "Nearly A Half a Million People Move Off Welfare in Ontario," Ministry of Community and Social Services, Press Release, May 5, 2000. These findings support earlier welfare fraud reports. The 1997-98 percentage of welfare fraud was .2 percent. "Welfare Fraud Control Report," Ministry of Community and Social Services, Toronto, November 1998; and "Government Anti-Fraud Initiatives Save $100 Million," Ministry of Community and Social Services News Release, Toronto, November 13, 1998. An Ontario welfare fraud study in 1994 examined 18,655 fraud allegations and found that a total of 92 were referred to police for further investigation, *and only 18 resulted in charges.* "Welfare Reform and Welfare Fraud: The Real Issues," Ontario Social Safety NetWork Backgrounder, Toronto, Fall 1997, pp. 5–6.

there was always considerable public debate about just which women were morally deserving and which ones were not. Such divisions between worthy and unworthy poor women have increased recently. And welfare fraud measures have legitimized the public's perception that welfare recipients, and particularly single mothers, are not automatically deserving of state aid.

Throughout the years welfare policies have denied certain poor women public assistance because they were divorced, deserted, unwed, teenage mothers, or otherwise considered unworthy of support. Such divisions between worthy and unworthy poor women have increased under the Ontario Conservative government.

CONCLUSION

These dramatic changes to the Ontario welfare policy have devastated the lives of poor single mothers. Because they are assumed to be undeserving, their benefits and other support services have been slashed. Because they are assumed to be lazy, there are coercive measures enforced to make sure that they are constantly looking for employment or participating in job-related activities. And because they are assumed to be cheaters, single mothers are constantly scrutinized by government workers, neighbours, landlords, teachers, and family. This is a highly intrusive, punitive welfare state, which does not begin to treat its citizens with dignity or recognize their real needs. This results in a loss of both material and moral power for poor single mothers. Single mothers have lost material resources—now many of them are constantly anxious about their ability to provide food, shelter, and clothing for their children. But as well, single mothers have lost moral ground. The government has convinced the public that many single mothers are not deserving of public help. As a result, there is little public outcry about the many mean-spirited investigative procedures which the government now uses to determine who is and who is not deserving of welfare. These material and ideological changes not only affect single mothers—they affect all women. When welfare programs are miserly, punitive, and demeaning in nature, it affects the choices all women can make about their lives. It discourages women from leaving abusive partners and harassing employers in an attempt to create a new and brighter future. We must all open our eyes and take stock of what our welfare policies are doing to single mothers and their children for the results will have a lasting impact on the next generation.

CRITICAL THINKING QUESTIONS

1. What are the five characteristics of moral regulation that the author finds useful for her work?
2. How does welfare benefit capitalist interests? Name two criteria that all welfare policies meet which aids capitalism.

3. Why are women experiencing more violence under the Ontario Conservative government welfare changes?
4. What are some of the ways that single mothers have attempted to make ends meet since the welfare rate cut occurred?
5. How has workfare made women's caring work more invisible?
6. List the anti-fraud measures that the Ontario Conservative government has implemented. Have they been effective in diminishing welfare fraud? Is welfare fraud a real problem?

SUGGESTED READINGS

Corrigan, Phillip & Sayer, Derek (1985). *The Great Arch: English State Formation as Cultural Revolution*. Oxford: Basil Blackwell.
    This book provides the theoretical groundwork for this article. While demonstrating how the English state was formed, with all of its particular rules and regulations, the authors explore the concept of moral regulation. They argue that all these rules and regulations were established to ensure that English workers and citizens were obedient to the state

Evans, Patricia and Swift, Karen (2000). Single Mothers and the Press: Rising Tides, Moral Panic, and Restructuring Discourses. In Sheila M. Neysmith (Ed.), *Restructuring Caring Labour: Discourse, State Practice, and Everyday Life* (pp. 93-116). Toronto: Oxford University Press. See entry under Sheila M. Neysmith.

Gordon, Linda (1994). *Pitied But Not Entitled: Single Mothers and the History of Welfare*. New York: Free Press.
    The author explores the history of the treatment of poor single mothers in the United States. She argues that while single mothers have often been pitied because of their struggles to raise children in impoverished conditions, the state has not provided them with adequate welfare payments that would solve their problems.

Little, Margaret Hillyard (1998). *No Car, No Radio, No Liquor Permit: The Moral Regulation of Single Mothers in Ontario, 1920-1997*. Toronto: Oxford University Press.
    This book details the history of the Ontario welfare policy created specifically for single mothers. The author begins with the lobby effort that led to the creation of welfare for single mothers in 1920 and follows the policy to its demise under the Ontario Conservative government in 1997. The book illustrates how single mothers, throughout this entire history, have always been forced to prove that they are both financially and morally deserving of welfare.

Little, Margaret and Morrison, Ian (1999). The "Pecker Detectors" Are Back: Regulation of the Family Form in Ontario Welfare Policy. *Journal of Canadian Studies*, 34, No. 2, 110-136.
    This article explores the impact of the reinstatement of the spouse-in-the-house rule for single mothers on welfare in Ontario in 1995. Since 1995, single mothers cannot receive welfare if they are living with a male spouse. As a result of this policy change many single mothers were

removed from the welfare rolls because they were suspected (often falsely) of living with a male spouse. The authors also illustrate that welfare administrators, neighbours, and family increasingly police single mothers in order to assess whether they are or are not living with a male spouse.

Mayson, Melodie. Ontario Works and Single Mothers: Redefining "Deservedness" and the Social Contract. *Journal of Canadian Studies*, 34, 2, 89-109.
This article details how the implementation of workfare in Ontario will make it more difficult for poor single mothers. The author argues that many single mothers already are working, that workfare placements rarely lead to fulltime jobs, and that the government does not provide enough support to permit single mothers to find fulltime employment.

Mosher, Janet (2000). Managing the Disentitlement of Women: Glorified Markets, the Idealized Family, and the Undeserving Other. In Sheila M. Neysmith (Ed.), *Restructuring Caring Labour: Discourse, State Practice, and Everyday Life* (pp. 30-51). Toronto: Oxford University Press. See entry under Sheila M. Neysmith.

National Council of Welfare. (1998 Spring). Profiles of Welfare: Welfare Myths and Realities.
This publication challenges many of the commonly believed myths about the poor. With statistical evidence it proves that the poor are not lazy, with an easy, comfortable life on welfare. Instead, this publication shows that many of the poor are working and that their jobs do not provide them with enough money to provide food and shelter for their families.

Neysmith, Sheila M. (Ed.), (2000). *Restructuring Caring Labour: Discourse, State Practice, and Everyday Life* (pp. 93-116). Toronto: Oxford University Press.
This collection provides a number of articles about how women continue to do the majority of caring work in Canadian society. The articles by Janet Mosher, Patricia Evans and Karen Swift. Karen Swift and Michael Birmingham are particularly relevant to this chapter for they discuss how single mothers are treated as Canadian social programs are restricted.

Pateman, Carole (1989). *The Disorder of Women: Democracy, Feminism, and Political Theory*. Stanford: Stanford University Press.
The author explores a variety of feminist theoretical questions but one of her main arguments is that women have been theorized differently than men and therefore have been incorporated into the state in different ways. For example, she argues that men have been understood by the state as soldiers and workers and because of their war and work sacrifices have had rights to certain social programs. Women, on the other hand, have been viewed as mothers and dependent caregivers. Women's dedicated caring activities have not been considered work and so they have not had the same rights to social programs that men have enjoyed.

Piven, Frances Fox & Cloward, Richard A. (1971). *Regulating the Poor: The Functions of Public Welfare*. New York: Pantheon Books.
This book details the history of welfare in the United States. The authors argue that welfare is provided, not because governments care about the poor, but because they want to ensure that the poor do not collectively organize and overthrow the state. The authors also explore under what conditions the poor are able to organize to demand better welfare conditions. While this is an American book the theme is relevant to welfare in Canada.

Swanson, Jean (2001). *Poor-Bashing: The Politics of Exclusion*. Toronto: Between the Lines. This author is the former president of the National Anti-Poverty Organization. She interviews poor people across the country and illustrates the many ways that they are harassed, ignored, and even murdered because they are poor. This book dispels many of the myths about the poor and shows how we, as a society, have promoted hatred of the poor.

WEB LINKS

www.welfarewatch.toronto.on.ca
This is the site of Workfare Watch and is a useful site to find a number of reports about the impact of the latest changes to welfare in Ontario.

www.policyalternatives.ca
The Web site of the Canadian Centre for Policy Alternatives, a national think tank which provides important information and analysis about Canadian public policies.

www.ccsd.ca
The site of a national think tank on social policy. Particularly interesting is their "*Canadian Fact Book on Poverty 2000*."

Part Four

Contemporary Controversies

It appears that nothing these days is more controversial than sex. That is why sex-related issues have received considerable attention in this collection, and why sex is the central topic for investigation in this final section addressing contemporary controversies. In the introduction to this book, I noted that new forms of knowledge were produced through the development of psychological discourse. This knowledge named sexuality as a source of truth about the individual and as central to our constitution as normal or abnormal subjects. Studies of sexuality have emerged precisely to focus on the social meanings given to sex, meanings which vary temporally and cross-culturally.

In his second contribution to this volume, Gary Kinsman reviews recent developments in the literature about sexuality, particularly the ways in which sexuality has been constituted in relation to gender and the body. He focuses on social constructionist challenges to biological determinist theories of sexualities (which is often pluralized in order to convey the complexity and diversity of sexuality). Kinsman contributes a social and historical materialist approach to the interpretation of this literature. It is an approach which he says learns from post-structuralist and post-modernist approaches to sexualities, but which attempts to move beyond what historical materialists regard as their limitations. Kinsman draws attention to the "socially made" character of scientific research. He regards "truths" as not simply produced through discourse, but as "the products of political, social, and moral struggles." For example, he agrees that science and psychology have played a key role in shaping what is understood as normal and abnormal, but he believes that our focus should be on situating the development of these discourses firmly within their material contexts. He asks questions such as, why are the causes of heterosexuality not investigated through scientific research? The answer to this question is of course that the presumed normative and natural character of heterosexuality pre-determines the directions that scientific research takes. Therefore, we need to account for the historically specific and materially grounded social relations that make this happen. Maintaining this recognition of social and political struggle remains crucial for the contemporary period, given the resurgence of biological determinist theories making claims not only about sexuality, but also about gender and race. Kinsman addresses the ramifications of queer people accepting biological determinist arguments about our sexuality. His work is a powerful reminder that abandoning a broader vision for social liberation and change in favour of a much narrower demand for civil and legal rights for a discriminated against minority group is a perilous course of action. While maintaining this broader vision, we must of course continue to analyse critically forms of regulation which the very social movements that we participate in may have a hand in creating.

Laws make moral claims about the sexual activities in which people engage. The need to critique how law might be used to further marginalize already stigmatized populations, such as prostitutes, "exotic" dancers, and gay men and lesbians is gaining acceptance (see Chunn, Ross, and Kinsman in this volume). It remains challenging to critique law and strategies of moral regulation when they address matters that disturb us. For example, few would argue that there is no need for sexual assault legislation or for legislation targeting the sexual and/or physical abuse of children. However, it is important that we pause and investigate the context for the creation of particular legal policies, as well as their organization and implications. Both Chen and Johnson Kramar challenged us to undertake this difficult task in the previous section. Now Doyle and Lacombe, and Valverde and Moore push us further still.

Kegan Doyle and Dany Lacombe analyse the now infamous case of Robin Sharpe, a Vancouver man who was charged in 1995 with the possession of child pornography. The Sharpe case made its way to the Supreme Court of British Columbia, which acquitted him of the charge in 1999. In making the acquittal, the province's highest court overturned the possession of child pornography provision in the Criminal Code of Canada. This decision was subsequently challenged by the Supreme Court of Canada. Doyle and Lacombe provide a more detailed account of the legal decision-making processes. The main focus of their research, however, addresses how they believe Sharpe came to be a scapegoat through the development of a moral panic about child sexual abuse, paedophilia, and child pornography. This panic, they find, was organized through the mainstream media, psychological discourse, and Canada's legal structure. Moreover, it was linked to "the iconic status of the child within late modern society," which occurs in contrast to "the paedophilia of everyday life."

Doyle and Lacombe regard moral panics as "an instance of moral regulation" which in this case is also linked to a more generalized fear of crime. They explore the origins and implications of a growing fear of crime in Canada and the U.S., and warn that only draconian laws can be produced in a climate of panic. Their analysis, then, requires us to recognize a complex web of social, political, and legal processes at work in the making of a moral panic.

The **risk society** is also implicated in Doyle and Lacombe's analysis. The concept of risk society attempts to capture emerging regimes of social protection in a variety of areas, from crime control to insurance rationalities. Risk society theorists (the theorists who investigate how this conceptualization is supported and put into practice) find that the risk society entails identifying and containing risks before unwanted actions occur. This requires more careful surveillance and management of social relations and containment of what is perceived to be dangerous or costly.

Risk society theorists associate the emergence of the risk society with the belief that models of crime control which have dominated social and penal policy in the post WWII period have been unsuccessful in reducing or eliminating crime. They therefore must be replaced with models of protection that more effectively identify, target, and punish the individuals who are perceived to be responsible for crime. Not surprisingly, the emergence of risk technologies accompanied the shift to the political and economic right in western capitalist countries.

In the final chapter in this collection, Valverde and Moore also link moral panics to moral regulation, and contextualize the fear of "date rape drugs" within the emergence of the risk society. Like Doyle and Lacombe, they believe that it is simplistic to claim that moral panics are produced through people's irrational psychological fears. Their purpose here is not to convince readers that the fear over date rape drugs is unfounded by replacing one set of "facts" with an alternative, more valid set of "facts." While they do note that they cannot find evidence supporting claims that date rape drugs are in circulation, the real focus of their research is on how certain claims come to be made. Moreover, they explore how "club drugs" and "date rape drugs" came to be associated with one another, and the governance effects over youth which were produced through this association. Youth are constituted and governed through formulations of what they refer to as **chronotypes**. They suggest that "governing through chronotypes" is increasing in popularity as scapegoating categories of people as responsible for "social evils" becomes less acceptable.

Their research should not be taken to suggest that women's concerns generally about sexual assault are based on exaggerated fears. It does suggest that women are made responsible for managing their own risk by campaigns like the anti-date-rape drug campaign, and required to engage in a lengthening list of self-governance practices. Their research provides you with an example of how to read advice to youth analytically, by moving beyond an analysis of the content to focus on the "format" of the advice.

CHAPTER 12

QUEERNESS IS NOT IN OUR GENES:[1] BIOLOGICAL DETERMINISM VERSUS SOCIAL LIBERATION

BY GARY KINSMAN

THE BIOLOGICAL AND THE SOCIAL

Since the early 1990s a vigorous reassertion of biological theories of the cause of homosexuality within scientific journals, the mainstream media, and much of the gay media has taken place (Bailey & Pillard, 1993; Harner et al., 1993; LeVay, 1991, 1993). In 1991 Simon LeVay, a gay neuroscientist, reported that the brain structures (specifically the hypothalamus) of gay and heterosexual men differed and that this mirrored the gender difference between heterosexual men and women (LeVay, 1991). In 1993 Dean Hamer and others reported that there may be a genetic basis and marker for homosexuality based on their twin studies (Hamer et al., 1993). Since then other tentative studies have received major media play as a new "commonsense" has been created that homosexuality is biological in character. "Commonsense" is a crucial part of the social construction of hegemony, the social practices of consent and coercion through which ruling in our society is organized.

This new "commonsense" has been used to undermine social construction-oriented perspectives on sexual politics and queer liberation which argue that sexualities are socially and historically made and are not determined by our hormones or genes. I use

---

[1] This title is derived from R.C. Lewontin, S. Rose, and L. Kamin, (1984). *Not In Our Genes.* New York: Pantheon, also published as Steven Rose, Leon J. Kiamin, and R.C. Lewontin, (1984). *Not In Our Genes, Biology, Ideology and Human Nature*, Penguin: Harmondsworth. General inspiration for this chapter was also provided by the late Stephen Jay Gould and especially his (1981) *The Mismeasure of Man.* New York: W.W. Norton. This chapter is based upon revising and expanding Gary Kinsman, (1994). Queerness Is Not In Our Genes: Against Biological Determinism—For Social Liberation. *Border/Lines*, No. 33, pp. 27–30. Also see Gary Kinsman (1993, Fall). Not In Our Genes: Against Biological and Genetic Determinism. *Sociologists' Lesbian and Gay Caucus Newsletter*, No. 76, pp. 4–6.

queer in this chapter first to reclaim a term of abuse that has been used against gay men, lesbians, bisexuals, transgendered people, two-spirited people, and others so it can no longer be used against us; second as a term that is broader than homosexual, lesbian or gay; and third as a place from which to challenge heterosexual hegemony.

Within the gay, and to a lesser extent, the lesbian communities this new popularity for biological theories has been used to undermine support for those of us who do not agree that we are simply born queer, and who wish to continue to challenge heterosexual hegemony, the social practices constructing heterosexuality as the only "normal" and "natural" sexuality. In this chapter I highlight the political stakes in this debate.

While there are many currents within biological research, including those that see an important interaction between the physiological and the social, these studies and the related media coverage focus on biological determinist theories. Biological determinist approaches are those that view aspects of the biological realm (such as hormones or genes) as determining social practices such as homosexuality and lesbianism. The biological in this view determines the social. These approaches are also reductionist in claiming that the complex physiological, social, historical, cultural, and psychological making of gender and sexuality are an aspect of the biological.

Social constructionism, which covers a broad range of approaches that emphasize that the social, cultural, and the historical, is crucial to the making of our genders, sexualities, and sexual identifications. Social constructionism includes the social and historical materialist approach I adopt as well as those identified with post-modernism and post-structuralism, which can reduce the social to the linguistic (the realm of language) or the discursive (Kinsman, 1993). This can at times replace a biological determinism with a discursive determinism. Discourse can be seen as the authorized social languages that tell us how we can speak about particular topics, including sexuality.

Post-structuralism is a theoretical approach that rejects the structuralist perspective that the social is determined through social structures. Rather than focusing on structures, post-structuralism focuses on fragmentation and difference. I view "post-modernism" as a general space or mood that has a number of common themes. On the social and political terrains, there is a general assumption that we are in a new period and are moving beyond "modernity," and perhaps even capitalism itself. There is an emphasis on language and discourse, where the individual subject is seen as being constituted through discourse. These approaches can be seen as a form of discourse determinism. Part of my project is to develop an historical-materialist alternative that learns from the acquisitions of post-modernism and post-structuralism but also moves beyond their limitations.

My perspective on social constructionism is that the social is far more than simply the discursive, and has a material basis. The material realm cannot be reduced to the "economic" or to "things" and "objects." The material world must also be seen as having a constantly changing and not a static character and must centrally include human sensuous social practices, including consciousness and eroticism, through which the social world is created and transformed. In Marx's historical materialism, philosophical idealism and more vulgar forms of materialism are synthesized to produce a new social and historical materialism.

An adequate social constructionism must therefore be fully historical, and must include an active sense of people's agency. It must not be a form of society determinism, in other words, a reification of the social (the "society says" approach I often encounter in popularized sociology), which converts the social into an external thing-like object or structure. "Society" is not a unitary, monolithic thing with agency, that determines or causes our behaviour. The absurdity of the excuse that "society made me do it" exposes the problems with society determinism. Reification is the social process through which social relations between people get converted into relations between things. It is all pervasive in a capitalist society.[2] We need to avoid reification in developing critical social analysis.

Social constructionism must also move beyond the stifling polarities of the "nature versus nurture" debate to see how our physiological potentialities get built upon, organized, and developed as they become part of our social bodies and worlds. To be socially made in this sense is not to be any "less real" than the physiological or the "natural" and the social is very deeply rooted in our bodies and lives. This way of developing social constructionism allows us to see the interactions and transformations between the physiological and the social, historical or cultural—which cannot be reduced to "nurture" or to notions of the "external environment." This is not in any way a rejection of physiology but always places the brain and body in a social and historical context. The body is always a social and historical body and the brain develops as part of broader social relations and interactions. The raw materials, so to speak, of our physiologies are not enough to establish our genders and sexualities. Instead these "raw materials" are built upon, made sense of, and transformed *in* society and history. As Anne Fausto-Sterling puts it, "As we grow and develop, we literally, not just 'discursively' (that is, through language and cultural practices), construct our bodies, incorporating experience into our very flesh. To understand this claim, we must erode the distinctions between the physical and the social body" (Fausto-Sterling, 2000, p. 20).

An analogy with language is useful here. Most of us (but not all of us) are born with the physiological capacities for speech. But this does not mean we will learn

---

[2] See commodity fetishism in Karl Marx (1977). The Fetishism of the Commodity and Its Secret. *Capital, A Critique of Political Economy, Volume One* (pp. 163–177). New York: Vintage/Random House. George Lukacs, (1968). Reification and the Class Consciousness of the Proletariat. *History and Class Consciousness, Studies in Marxist Dialectics,* (pp. 83–222). London: Merlin.

how to speak since this is a social process building on these physiological capacities. A child isolated from human culture will not learn a language. The physiological capacity for speech also does not determine in any way what language we will speak or how good we will be in speaking it. In a similar fashion most of us are born with the physiological capacities or potentialities to derive erotic pleasures from our bodies and our interactions with the bodies of others but this does not pre-determine what forms this eroticism will take. Eroticism is our capacity to derive erotic pleasure from our own bodies and the bodies of others. Social sexual practices are built on these erotic capacities and potentialities. The formation of our capacities for language and our capacities for eroticism and sexual practices are made as a very embodied social and historical process. They are social and relational and not simply individual or physiological.

My objective is not so much to dispute the "science" of this resurgent biological determinism, although I draw on the work of progressive biologists who critique it. Instead I write as someone who studies the social regulation of sexuality and the social organization of sexual and gender knowledge. All knowledge is produced in a social context and is socially organized in the context of social relations of power. I focus on how this research and the media amplification of it is part of a broader social organization of knowledge regarding queerness that has disturbing characteristics.

The Social And Political Character of Science and Biology

All scientific research is socially made and this includes biological research. It is never simply neutral or objective but is shaped and influenced by social power. In the 19th century it was reigning scientific "truth" that black people were less intelligent than white people. This "science" was defined by the social relations of racism.[3] Women's attempts to enter higher education were challenged through the ruling scientific "truth" that this would lead to the nervous degeneration of women's reproductive capacities. Biology, which was formed as a distinct disciplinary "science" at the start of the 19th century in Europe and the U.S., has been bound up since its formation with gender, sexual, racial, and national politics. The biological "truths" about sexuality and gender are the products of political, social, and moral struggles. As Fausto-Sterling argues "scientists do not simply read nature to find truths to apply in the social world. Instead, they use truths taken from our social relationships to structure, read, and interpret the natural" (2000, pp.115–116).

---

[3] On this see Stephen Jay Gould (1981). *The Mismeasure of Man.* New York and London: W.W. Norton and Company.

Biological and medical knowledges are produced in the context of class, gender, sexual, racial, and other struggles. Biological determinism and reductionism have developed in response to social struggles for equality and liberation. As Fausto-Sterling, building on the work of feminist Donna Haraway, has put it,

> biology is politics by other means...We will, I am sure, continue to fight our politics through arguments about biology. I want us never, in the process, to lose sight of the fact that our debates about the body's biology are always simultaneously moral, ethical and political debates about social and political equality and the possibilities for change. Nothing less is at stake. (2000, p. 255)

Biological knowledge is an integral part of the disciplinary and "bio-power" power/knowledge relations that Michel Foucault wrote about. Bio-power is a term used by Foucault to describe knowledge and strategies used to exercise power over and through bodies and to harness reproductive and sexual capacities for social power. These scientific knowledges were centrally implicated in making the "normal," the "natural, " the "pathological," and the "deviant" and were a form of "expert" knowledge from above. The pathological strategy of regulation is one that focuses on constructing forms of "deviance" as resulting from physiological or mental illness and sickness. "Deviance" constructs groups like homosexuals as different from the "norm," as "other" and as "abnormal." The other side of the construction of "deviance" is the making of the "normal." Deviance is a collecting category bringing together a series of groups with different social characteristics as "deviant" so they can be addressed through common administrative practices.

Biological knowledge plays a key part in ruling strategies for the normalization and naturalization of only some ways of life, and the making of others as pathological and deviant. Much of this was based on the new statistical regimes of "truth" collection that became integral to the emergence of the bureaucratic state and its disciplinary power relations. It is the rise of statistics that created the possibility for 20th century scientists to begin to make claims about sex and gender differences in the brain. These statistical regimes established "norms" and "averages" and did not focus on the vast variations and diversity within the categories like male and female that they used. This inability to account for the vast diversity of human relations and practices within "biological" groupings is one major area of weakness with these approaches.

Biological determinist knowledges also became a major default or fallback form of knowledge. As Jeffrey Weeks (1986, p. 51) points out "If all else fails to explain human phenomona, then a biological explanation *must* exist." These new biological-based forms of knowledge were able to claim jurisdiction over the classification and interpretation of bodies.

The everyday work of biological researchers is often defined by the "common-sense" of the day so that the major assumptions that underlie their work become invisible to them. At the same time, biological knowledge has been constructed as being the most "natural" or closest to the "truth" of the disciplinary forms of knowledge. This helps to establish a particular hegemony for forms of biological knowledge. As David Fernbach points out, the sense of social difference, of not fitting in experienced many gay men since the time that we were very young leads some of us to a vague and diffuse sense that we were "born different." It is this vague sense of early difference that provides part of the social basis for the popularity of biological determinist theories among some gay men (Fernbach, 1998, p. 47–66).

Why is Queerness In Need of Explanation?

For more than 150 years, homosexuality and lesbianism have been actively made into social problems by dominant social institutions and professions. This has included medical, biological, psychiatric, psychological, sociological, sexological, and other forms of scientific research. This research has often been based on answering the question of what "causes" the deviant/abnormal" sexuality—homosexuality. We need to ask why this is such an important question? And why are the "causes" of "normal" heterosexuality never probed in a similar fashion?

Before research even gets started, homosexuality has already been pre-packaged as the "deviance" that stands in need of explanation. It is already assumed that heterosexuality is the "normal" majority sexuality and that homosexuality is the "deviant" minority sexuality needing to be explained. These research questions have been shaped within dominant social power/knowledge relations that problematize homosexuality but not heterosexuality. This is why when I am asked the question "what causes homosexuality?" (as I am over and over again) I try to reverse the question and get the person thinking about how and why they are asking it. I try to get them thinking about why they are not asking what causes heterosexuality.

Challenging Ideological Assumptions

As suggested above biological determinism rests on taken-for-granted ideological assumptions about gender and sexuality. Ideologies are the ruling ideas in society and are usually ungrounded from the social practices through which they themselves are produced. For instance, gender and sexuality appear as natural and as pre-social when they are actually historically and socially made building on physiological potentials. Ideologies attend to ruling and managing people's lives, rather than producing knowledge that allows people to grasp the social organization of their lives or to transform their lives. A series of unexamined assumptions regarding gender and sexuality permeate biological determinist work. In many ways in this society sexual assumptions are built on gender ones. For instance, feminist biologist Fausto-Sterling points out that while some gay men and much of the gay media hailed Simon LeVay as a hero: "Feminists such as myself disliked his unquestioning use of gender dichotomies, which have in the past never worked to further equality for women" (2000, p. 26). Within some of this biological determinist theorizing, gender-inversion theories of male homosexuality (that male homosexuals express "female" attributes) are alive and well along with major assumptions about the dichotomous (or "opposite") two-gender system which is just assumed to be "natural."

Gender

As Kessler and McKenna pointed out in their ground-breaking research on gender as an everyday social accomplishment scientists and biologists have often started off their work from within the "natural attitude" assumptions of the hegemonic way of doing gender.[4] The assumption is that there are two dichotomous genders based on biological sex difference—male and female. This is never investigated or proven, it is simply accepted as "commonsense." However as Fausto-Sterling puts it,

> labelling someone a man or a woman is a social decision. We may use scientific knowledge to help us make this decision, but only our beliefs about gender—not science—can define our sex. Furthermore, our beliefs about gender affect what kinds of knowledge scientists produce about sex in the first place. (2000, p. 3)

As can be seen here both "biological sex" and "social gender" are social constructions. Imposing a gender label on people is therefore socially and not "scientifically" driven. There are a number of ways in which ideological assumptions are made in biological determinist theories of gender.

First, gender has not been done in universal ways. If we look at how gender has been done throughout history and across cultures we discover that the current hegemonic way of doing gender is only one of the many social ways in which gender has been accomplished. Among some First Nations' cultures, before the coming of "white civilization," there were up to four different gender groupings and gender was attributed to people on the basis not only of their anatomy but also on the basis of their social and work interests. These "two-spirited" peoples, shared the spirits of both genders (although French Colonialists problematically referred to them as the "berdache," derived from the word for male prostitute. In

---

[4] Their research develops new directions in ethnomethodology. Ethnomethodology is the study of the methods people use to produce and account for the social world. The founder of ethnomethodology is Harold Garfinkel. Kessler and McKenna take the insights in Garfinkel's work much further in elaborating a social theory of the accomplishment of gender. See Suzanne J. Kessler and Wendy McKenna. (1978). *Gender: An Ethnomethodological Approach.* Chicago: University of Chicago Press.

some cultures there have co-existed with more typically general gendered men and women third and fourth gender groupings. These were physiological males who participated in some "female" activities within the social division of labour, and physiological females who participated in some "male" activities within the social division of labour (Blackwood, 1984; Lang, 1999; Roscoe, 1988, 1991, 1996, 1998; Williams, 1986). In some African cultures ways of doing gender made it possible for there to be boy-wives and female husbands. A person's gender could be transferred from one social gender to the other (Amadiume, 1987; Kendall, 1999; Mburu, 2000; Murray & Roscoe, 1998). These different ways of doing gender created contexts for different ways of doing eroticism as well. In the face of this gender diversity our current ideological assumptions about there being only two dichotomous genders collapses.

Second, even in our culture we do not usually rely on presumed biological markers (genitals, hormones, genes) when we attribute gender to the people with which we come into contact. We don't ask people to drop their pants or pull up their skirts so we can examine their genitals before we attribute a gender to them. We also don't take specimens of their hormones or genetic material back to the lab for examination before we attribute them gender. Instead we rely on various social cues and indicators (clothing, hair, talk, way of walking and taking up space, jewellery, perfume, occupation, etc.) to make a gender attribution. The practices of gender attribution are the socially shared methods we use in our everyday lives to transform a social world of vast gender diversity and variation into a world where we assign people into "female" and "male" classifications and create a "natural" world defined by only two "opposite" genders.

Third, in our own society the experiences of transsexuals challenge the "natural attitude" towards gender by demonstrating that a person can shift from one gender to another. Transsexuals are those who feel that their actual gender conflicts with their physiological anatomy and therefore with the gender assigned to them at birth. This can lead to gender re-assignment surgery where anatomy is altered to coincide with the perceived gender. Ethnomethodologists have been especially interested in learning from pre-operative transsexuals about how they perform their gender prior to re-assignment surgery since pre-operative transsexuals usually have to live as the gender they wish to be attributed for a period of six months to two years before getting approval for the surgery as part of the medical regulation of this transition. Many pre-operative transsexuals are remarkably successful in performing their gender so that they get the gender attributions they wish from others through learning the social methods through which we all perform and attribute gender. The experiences of pre-operative transsexuals demonstrates that a person can live and perform oneself and be socially attributed the gender one wishes to be prior to any anatomical changes (Kessler & McKenna, 1978).

At the same time the medical regulation of transsexuals attempts to re-incorporate transsexuals back within the two-gender system. The medical profession manages this challenge to the "naturalness" of gender relations by constructing an essential "core gender identity" that is seen in some situations to be in conflict with a person's physiological anatomy. The medical solution to this dilemma is to "fix" the anatomy to match the gender identification and to try to integrate the transsexual back within the two-gender system. The new transgendered movement, made up of people who do not fit into the two-gender system, including cross-dressers, transvestites, and transsexuals, has challenged gender naturalism and has begun to undermine the current ways of doing gender in a far more profound fashion, as well as making visible how many of us don't really fit into this way of doing gender.

Finally, Kessler's work on the medical management of "intersexed" infants demonstrates that doctors rely on social and not "biological" ways of doing gender. The minority of infants who are born with anomalous genitalia and physical attributes and get labelled as "intersexed" by the medical profession, present a problem for the standard social practices of gender assignment in a medical context based on a quick genital inspection. They present a "natural" challenge to the two-gender system by demonstrating the variation among human bodies. In contrast to earlier notions of the hermaphrodite who combined physiological aspects of both sexes and was often seen as part of a gender/sexual continuum, the "intersexed" label is intended to be a temporary one until the medical professionals have determined which gender will be assigned to the infant. The conceptualization of "intersexed" in its medical form is a way of fitting these anomalies back into the two-gender system.

In order to maintain the hegemonic dichotomous two-gender system, these "intersexed" infants have to be assigned to one gender or the other. Anomalies have to be marginalized and eliminated. As Fausto-Sterling puts it: "To maintain gender divisions, we must control those bodies that are so unruly as to blur the borders" (2000, p. 8). Again challenges to the hegemonic way of doing gender must be neutralized, and re-assigned within the two-gender system.

Medical professionals use a number of tests to determine what gender to assign the infant and then will alter the "natural" anatomy to fit with the choice made. In her research, Kessler discovered that often the assumption that guided this medical work was the formulation "good penis equals male; absence of good penis equals female" (Kessler, 1995 p. 19). This reveals not only sexist assumptions but also a notion that the size of the penis and heterosexist assumptions made about its later adequacy for heterosexual penis/vagina intercourse are what are key in this decision-making process. These are clearly social evaluations shaped by social discourses and gender and sexual practices. As Fausto-Sterling points out this illustrates how in this case biological sex and gender is "literally, constructed. Surgeons remove parts and use plastic to create 'appropriate' genitals for body parts that are not easily identifiable as male or female" (2000, p. 27). As Kessler argues through these practices: "The belief that gender consists of two exclusive types is maintained and perpetuated by the medical community in the face of incontrovertible physical evidence that this is not mandated by biology" (1995, p, 22). Biological determinist approaches are therefore actually social practices. These ideological assumptions also invade biological determinist approaches to homosexuality.

Homosexuality

Advocates of the biological causation of homosexuality also start within ideological "commonsense" by simply assuming two rigidly dichotomous, biologically based heterosexual and homosexual sexualities that have always been around. Rather than beginning with the actual complexities of people's lived erotic and gender experiences, they begin with a simplistic assertion of hegemonic "commonsense." They simply assert that the vast majority of people are and always have been heterosexual, with sexual feelings only toward the "opposite sex," and that only a small homosexual minority prefer their own gender. Rather than demonstrating this, advocates of biological causation simply claim this as "fact." Of course all "facts" are socially made and are claims to knowledge and authority. Scientific knowledge that claims to be "factual" often becomes just taken-for-granted, preventing us from seeing how these "facts" have been produced within particular power/knowledge relations. By accepting hegemonic notions of sexuality rather than critically interrogating them, and by not starting with people's contradictory lived experiences of erotic and gender life, advocates of the biological causation approach fail to challenge their own ideological assumptions. They unquestionably accept the classifications of the ruling regime of sexual regulation.

Critical research on sexuality shows that eroticism and sexual practice are far from being simply biologically determined. This work has often been informed by early social constructionist approaches that emerged out of the feminist, lesbian, and gay liberation revolts that challenged the assumption that our oppression, rather than being rooted in social power relations, was rooted in "nature" or in biology and therefore could not be changed.

A number of these social constructionist insights are useful to examine here. Although many of these insights are shared by more materialist and post-structuralist social constructionist approaches I emphasize their social and material character. "Heterosexuality" and "homosexuality" are not nearly as sharply dichotomous as biological determinism contends. For instance, far more men engage in sex with other men at various times in their lives than would ever define themselves as homosexual or bisexual. In the context of the AIDS crisis it has been re-discovered that many men who engage in sex with other men do not identify themselves as homosexual, gay, bisexual, or queer and will not be reached by AIDS education that addresses them as such. This is why the expression "men who have sex with men" has been used in safer sex and AIDS work (Patton, 1985, 1989, 1990,

1996). Many studies—from the Alfred Kinsey studies (which talked both about a continuum of sexual activity between complete heterosexual and complete homosexual activity and also pointed out that a very large minority of men engaged in some same-gender erotic activities) to more recent studies—demonstrate that many people who define themselves as heterosexual have engaged in sex with members of the same gender. Fifty percent of the white males interviewed for the Kinsey report on men, admitted erotic responses to other males, and thirty-seven percent of all men in all occupational groups reported at least one homosexual experience to the point of orgasm between adolescence and old age (Kinsey et al., 1948, 1953). The notion of a sexual continuum is used by a number of theorists to point to the flux and variation in people's sexual practices and identifications throughout their lives.

People's sexual practices can also shift throughout their life history and can be more fluid than fixed. For instance, there are many men who lived their lives quite happily as heterosexual until their 30s or later when they then began to feel that their sexual interests were shifting to men and then came out. Similar situations have occurred in many women's lives. Biological determinist approaches cannot account for this erotic flux.

Usually biological determinist approaches ignore bisexual experience. When they do acknowledge bisexuals, they suggest that bisexuals are a microscopic proportion of the population. However, as recent bisexual organizing has demonstrated, this is not the case. The experiences of bisexuals sharply undermine the notion of there being two dichotomous sexualities rooted in biological difference.

Just as with gender relations there is also no universal way in which sexual practices have been organized throughout human history. This again undermines the validity and adequacy of biological determinist approaches. While there have been same and different gender erotic activities throughout human history, the ways in which these have been organized and understood has varied dramatically. There has been no stable "heterosexual" majority or "homosexual" minority.

In many cultures there has been no dichotomy between participating in sex with a member of the same gender and participating in sex with a member of the other gender. For example, prior to the imposition of colonial rule and western beliefs and practices, the Sambia in Papua made same-gender "erotic" activity for males between seven and nineteen mandatory. Boys fellated men on a daily basis, so they would grow into masculine adults. In this patriarchal culture they believed males cannot produce sperm on their own; they can only recycle it from one generation to the next. In their adult lives these men also engage in sex with women.[5] One cannot make sense of this very different cultural context for eroticism through our contemporary lens of the heterosexual/homosexual dichotomy.

---

[5] On the Sambia see sources cited in Joseph Harry (1982). *Gay Children Grown Up: Gender Culture and Gender Deviance* (p. 3). New York: Praeger.

In Ancient Greece erotic activity was organized not through the distinction between homosexual and heterosexual desires but was organized through an age and status organization of sexual activity. While male-male erotic relations were seen as being an important part of the pedagogical relations between a boy and a male citizen of the Greek city-state, once the younger male became a citizen he had to stop participating in "passive" positions in erotic activities. The male citizen could only participate in what were viewed as "active" forms of erotic practice. Women, slaves, and boys only were to take up "passive" positions. There was no contradiction in this social context for the male citizen to engage in "active" sex with a woman or with other males (See Dover, 1980; Foucault, 1985; Halperin, 1990). Again the contemporary dichotomy of heterosexual/homosexual does not allow us to grasp what was going on in this society.

In some cultures there were more than two genders, creating a very different terrain for erotic possibilities, as mentioned earlier. It was possible in these contexts for erotic relationships between individuals with the same genitals (say between a more typically gendered male and a physiologically male two-spirited individual who in our society would most often be interpreted as homosexual) to be considered to be an erotic relation between members of different genders (having therefore some similarities with what is often understood to be heterosexuality in our society). Biological determinism cannot account for these experiences of gender and erotic life.

Biological determinism does not look at and learn from the extensive research that has been done that challenges biologically reductionist assumptions. What we find is that all too often these studies are based on a simple acceptance of the ruling ideologies regarding sex and gender and not on learning from and addressing the rich sociological, historical, social-psychological, anthropological, social/biological, and other research that now exists on the social and cultural dimensions of eroticism and gender.

Rather than trying to account for sexual diversity, these studies focus on trying to find what is "different" about those labelled homosexual—thus already assuming a biological difference between heterosexuals and homosexuals. These studies basically set out to demonstrate what they have already assumed. Instead it is these very assumptions that need to be questioned.

Little of this recent biologically determinist research has been able to find a possible biological cause for lesbianism. Most of the research has focused on male homosexuality, which has at times been more socially visible and been constructed as more of a "social danger." While this continues the sexism of biological research, this inability to account for lesbianism also undermines the validity of this research.

Homo and Hetero as Historical and Social Terms

The terms "homosexual" and "heterosexual" themselves were not coined until the later 19th century in the context of profound social, economic, and sexual changes with the formation of industrial capitalism and bureaucratic ruling regimes of state and professional agencies. The emergence of new same-gender based erotic cultures in these social contexts, which had roots in the development of same-gender erotic networks over the previous few centuries, were met by new forms of sexual policing and professional disciplines that produced classifications of "normal" hetero and "deviant" queer sexualities (D'Emilio, 1983; Foucault, 1980; Jagose, 1996; Kinsmen, 1996).

"Heterosexual" entered into popular usage in the English language during this time to describe a new form of "necessary" erotic attraction between men and women. This new heterosexuality, which was different from previous forms of social organization of different-gender sex, was defined as an essential erotic orientation, not simply as an engagement in reproductive sex or participation in a gendered familial division of labour. The way heterosexuality is practiced in our society is not at all "natural" if we look at the incredible diversity of different-gender sexual practices that exist in cross-cultural and historical studies.

Sexual dichotomies like heterosexual/homosexual that are often taken for granted today as having always been around are themselves historically and socially made. Projecting them into the past, and rooting them in biology not only distorts our understanding of the past, but also our ability to understand our present sexual and gender lives and possibilities for future transformations.

Cure or Elimination: From Biology to Psychology and Back

The implication of much of this research is that if the "cause" of homosexuality can be identified then it can be "cured" or "eliminated" altogether. This has been a crucial part of the medicalization of homosexuality. Research on the "causes" of homosexuality has ranged from a focus on physiological degeneration in the later part of the 19th century and early 20th century to psychiatric and psychological disorders in much of the 20th century. Psychological approaches have included crude versions of Freudianism, like the mythology of the over-bearing mother and/or absent father, both of whom were the supposed "cause" of homosexuality in boys. When I came out to my mother in the early 1970s she first responded by mouthing this psychological discourse. Blaming herself for my sexuality she said, "was your father not around enough when you were young?" More recently, these psychiatric and psychological theories have proven inadequate to account for queerness as lesbians and gay men have challenged the medicalization of homosexuality and have overthrown definitions of mental illness applied to queers.

In the face of this challenge from queer movements, some researchers have now reverted back towards biologically based explanations that were in vogue at the end of the 19th century, when homosexuality was classified as a "congenital inversion" rooted in biological degeneration or anomaly. The current development and refinement of technology means that researchers are now able to discover hormonal and genetic materials that could never have been identified in the past, and can impute causative powers to them. For example, the different cell groupings in the hypothalamus that LeVay studied can only be identified through the use of new technology.

This resurgence of biological determinism ranges from those who stress the influence of hormones (including the theory that stress for the mother during pregnancy leads to homosexuality in the male fetus she is carrying) to genetic arguments.[6] There are major methodological and theoretical problems with hormonal determinist and then genetic determinist approaches.

Do Hormones Rule Our Lives?

As Fausto-Sterling describes, the development of biological science led to the identification and the gendered labelling of the hormones,

> In a period from 1900 to 1940 scientists carved up nature in a particular fashion, creating the categories of sex hormones. The hormones themselves became markers of sexual difference....But if one looks, as I do, historically, one can see that steroid hormones need not have been divided into sex and non-sex categories. They could, for example, have been considered to be growth hormones affecting a wide swath of tissues, including reproductive organs. (2000, p. 28)

These are not actually "sex" hormones and it might be better to see them as growth regulators that have different impacts in different parts of the body. At the same time, the gendered construction of knowledge about hormones can be very hard to resist. Testosterone has been so gendered as "male" that it just becomes taken for granted as "commonsense" rather than recognizing that both male and female bodies produce this hormone. An assumption gets made, especially again in popularized biology, that hormones cause certain types of actions or behaviours. For instance, it is assumed that testosterone causes aggression and violence despite the studies that show us that practices of aggression, like fighting lead to the release of testosterone. There is no established causal relation of a hormone influencing behaviour. There is more convincing evidence that social experiences also lead to the release of hormones. It may be that hormones and social experience co-produce behaviour patterns.

The hormonal determinist theories of homosexual causation usually refer to the impact of hormones on the fetus developing in the womb. This assumes our

---

[6] This theory is put forward in "Brain Sex" which was shown on *Witness*, CBC TV, 1992.

brains are wired for gender and sexuality at birth. At the same time other biological research, which is more open to the impact of the social on the physiological and in interaction with the physiological, points out that much critical brain development in human beings occurs after birth and that differences in brain anatomy may have been produced by social processes. For instance, differences in sexual practices could cause rather then be caused by differences in the brain structure.

As Fausto-Sterling points out, we are made up of many complex cells and each cell has its own history. When we look at cells and organs within the body we begin to see how events outside the body "become incorporated into our very flesh." As she puts it, our "brains and nervous systems are plastic. Overall anatomy—as well as the less visible physical connections among nerve cells…organs, and the brain—change not only just after birth but even into the adult years" (2000, p. 239). She continues that "Examples abound in which a social interaction causes a physical change in the nervous system….These examples show how nervous systems develop as part of social systems" (Ibid., p. 239). Describing some of the ways that social constructions of gender and sexuality enter the body, she tells us that sensations, thoughts, feelings, movements, and social interaction can change the structure of the brain.

Much hormonal research is based on animal studies, which have major flaws when applied to human beings. Human brings are not the same as rats, other rodents, or even monkeys.

As Rose *et al.* in *Not In Our Genes* (1984, p. 158) have put it,

Again and again, in order to support their claims to the inevitability of a given feature of the human order, biological determinists seek to imply the universality of their claims. If male dominance exists in humans, it is because it exists also in baboons, in lions, in ducks, or whatever. The ethological literature is replete with accounts of 'harem-keeping' by baboons, the male lion's dominance of 'his' pride, 'gang-rape' in mallard ducks, 'prostitution' in humming-birds.

As Jeffrey Weeks (1986, p.51) adds,

It should hardly need saying that what is happening here is the attribution of highly coloured social explanations to animal behaviour. Why should groupings of female animals be seen as harems? They could equally well be seen, for all the counter-evidence available, as prototypes of women's consciousness raising groups. To say that perhaps evokes a smile. But so should the circular argument by which explanations drawn from human experience are attributed to animals and then used to justify social divisions in the present.

Socially constructed assumptions enter into the hormonal determinist research in a number of ways. For instance, mounting behaviours among rodents in many of these studies are coded as "male" even though there are many circumstances in which female rodents engage in mounting activities. The attempt to apply "masculine" and "feminine" and "heterosexual" and "homosexual" to rats just does not work. The theories derived from these experiments on rodents "are inadequate even for rodents" (Fausto-Sterling, 2000 p. 232).

Is It All In Our Genes?

Genes have now replaced hormones at the centre of much biological determinist research. Again an assumption is made that the gene, or genetic material, causes particular forms of behaviours, including homosexuality. Some of the earlier genetic research was of course tied up with and influenced by eugenic concerns (Allen, 1997). Eugenics, in the context of concerns mobilized against the breeding of the "unfit" and the corresponding fears of race and class suicide of the white ruling and middle class, led to proposals in Canada in the early twentieth century for the improvement of the "quality" of the "race" through selective breeding, including the segregation and sterilization of "inferior" immigrants to Canada so that "Canada could remain forever white, Anglo-Saxon and Protestant" (Chapman, 1977 p. 9; McLaren, 1990). The consequences in Germany, of course, were to be far worse.

This biological determinism is especially clear with popularizations of this research in the mainstream media, which usually gives all power to the gene. This can lead to a genetic reductionism whereby genes are seen to cause human sexuality reducing the complex social and human processes through which sexuality is formed to genetics.

As Jennifer Terry argues, the implication regarding social inequality and oppression is that "If it is all in the genes, then there is no use in trying to solve people's problems by ameliorating the conditions in which they live" (1999, p. 396). The Nazis, firm believers in biological determinism and eugenics, subscribed to the view that homosexuality was genetic in origin and used this as an argument for the extermination of homosexuals.

Despite the assertion of genetic determinists that genes are all powerful, they can only be understood in the context of the developmental system that we call a cell and the organism more generally. The overused shorthand that genes make proteins gets us into trouble since genes also need other molecules. As Richard C. Lewontin explains, "genes can make *nothing*" on their own, they are not the uniquely determining units of biological and especially social life (2001, p.83). There is a complex interaction between different parts of the organism that can not be reduced to one of its elements—the genes. "If anything in the world can be said to be self-replicating," explains Lewontin, "it is not the gene, but the entire organism as a complex system" (Ibid.).

Seen in this light, I have suggested that a much better approach to gays and genes would be the slogan seen on a T-shirt in the U.S.—"My gay genes are 501's." This more clearly captures the social and cultural construction of one presentation of contemporary queerness. At the same time it also makes clear how socially constructed gay cultural/erotic presentation has gotten tied up with and organized through consumer capitalist relations.

SOCIAL CONTEXT: THE SOCIAL ORGANIZATION OF "BACKLASH" TO LIBERATION

It is always necessary to look at the social and historical context of the social organization of knowledge. The new resurgence of biological determinist explanations of homosexuality is occurring in the broader context of a new popularity for biological determinist explanations of human behaviour—strongly reflected in and promoted in much of the mainstream media and in popularized notions of "science." This is also related to a broader resurgence of biological explanations of gender and gender inequality, in some circles of race and racial inequality, and of explanations of other social differences. For instance, some researchers now argue that women's mathematical and spatial skills are really not the biological equal of men's. Therefore the social equality that feminism seeks is seen to go against "nature." Many white gay men seem to be unaware that every time they support biological determinism in relation to homosexual causation they also buttress it in relation to gender and racial inequality. This helps to break the solidarities that have been built through past struggles among and between gays, lesbians, feminists, and anti-racist activists.

This social organization of knowledge is part of a broader social organization of a "backlash"[7] against feminism and racial equality—a backlash against women's and people of colour's struggles for social and economic equality with white men. It must also be remembered that this is not the first time that biological science has been invoked to justify social inequality. "Biology" has long been invoked to justify the social subordination of blacks, women, and other groups.

"WE CAN'T HELP BEING THE WAY WE ARE"

There was a significant shift from a critique of biological determinism in gay liberation and lesbian feminism of the 1970s to an increasing adoption of it by middle-class white gay men in particular in the later 1980s, 1990s, and into the 2000s. The rather different but parallel form of feminist essentialism among some forms

---

[7] On some of the problems with the use of "backlash" see Janice Newson (1991, Fall/Winter). "Backlash" against Feminism: A Disempowering Metaphor. *Resources for Feminist Research, 20,* No. 3/4, pp. 93–97.

of radical and lesbian feminism that argues that the differences between men and women are "natural" and implicitly rooted in biology is not being specifically addressed here. Many "liberal" heterosexuals, some gay men, and fewer lesbians now argue that it will be easier for us to be accepted in a hostile society if it is argued that "we were born this way and therefore cannot help being the way we are." I find this a naive approach, which is unfamiliar with previous historical uses of this line of argument. It is also not a good basis for building proud liberation movements. Our own agency as queers, how we participate in making ourselves, our sexualities, our communities, our cultures, and our movements, is entirely removed—we become simply biological anomalies who should be tolerated. We come to fetishize or to reify (thingify) our sexuality as some sort of intrinsic biological essence or "thing" that is removed from the social and the historical worlds of which we are part. This undermines any commitment to the agency or the oppressed and the social and historical character of gender and sexuality that is, in my view, at the very heart of queer liberationist politics.

Although some hope that biological determinist arguments which attempt to avoid the messy right-wing accusations of homosexual "recruitment" and "seduction" will create greater tolerance, historical experience teaches us otherwise. The assumption of biological causation of sexual "deviance" has led to horrific operations and experiments on the bodies of people in the past who were seen as suffering from gender and sexual "disorders." In Nazi Germany a commitment to eugenics, racial purity, and to a biological basis for homosexuality led to horrific experiments on the bodies of gay men, the working to death of thousands of homosexual men in the concentration camps, as well as the incarceration of lesbians as "anti-socials" (Haeberle, 1980; Lautman, 1980; Plant, 1986). In the 1960s and 1970s aversion therapy, directed at creating an aversive response, including physical pain and vomiting, to homosexual images as part of an attempt to "cure" homosexual men and lesbians, was being used against homosexuals in North America. At the same time, a number of men in Germany had parts of their hypothalamus surgically destroyed to try to extinguish their homosexual desires.

We can also look at how the social construction of race as a "biological" difference with which people are born has done nothing to end the widespread and institutionalized racism that people of colour continue to face. Appeals to "nature" do not get rid of social discrimination and oppression.

There is also little evidence that acceptance of homosexuality as "biological" in character will lead to significantly greater support for the social equality of lesbians and gay men. In response to LeVay's tentative research suggesting a different structure in the hypothalamus in gay and heterosexual men, extensive media coverage sparked calls to health clinics from heterosexual parents-to-be. They wanted to know if, in light of this study, their fetus could be "tested" for gayness and aborted solely for that reason (Diaz, 1992). People are also speculated that if there is a gene that causes homosexuality perhaps it could be eliminated so that the homosexual "problem" could be "solved" once and for all. Even the authors of the gay gene study recognized this in their warnings against this interpretation of their research. As Jennifer Terry insightfully points out, "But regardless of LeVay and Hamer's attempts to control the implications of their research, there is a growing popular trend toward regarding biological evidence for things like homosexuality as a possible means for targeting "carriers" and removing them from the gene pool" (1999, p. 396).

In one area of widely recognized and continuing trouble—the difficulties young gay men, lesbians, bisexuals, two-spirited, and transgendered people have in coming to terms with their sexualities in the often very hostile worlds they face in families, schools, churches, youth cultures, and on the streets, this position also does not seem to help. As Jennifer Terry reports,

> A social worker who works with gay suicidal teens recently remarked that the biology is destiny line can be deadly. Thinking they are "afflicted" with homosexual desire as a kind of disease or biological defect rather than thinking of it as a desire they somehow choose is, for many gay teenagers, one more reason to commit suicide rather than to live in a world so hostile to their desires. (Ibid., p. 396)

RELATION TO QUEER COMMUNITY AND CLASS FORMATION

How then with all these problems and contradictions has the new "commonsense" of biological determinism achieved such staying power in much gay men's media, within gay community formation and among mainstream gay political formations? To begin with, the social impact of the AIDS crisis since the early 1980s played a part in altering the orientation of some gay men towards medical and biological science. From an inital position of hostility towards medical, biological, and psychological "science" for participation in the stigmatization of homosexuality, a shift occurred with the development of AIDS. The scientific establishment (including medicine and biological research) developed some forms of treatment under pressure from AIDS activists and People Living With AIDS, leading to much more of a "pro-science" orientation among many gay men.

This new form of biological determinism has also become one of the underlying assumptions behind the social construction of gays and lesbians as an ethnic-type minority community in the 1980s and 1990s. Even though those supporting social construction approaches were very active in the early gay and lesbian-feminist revolts, these approaches often became eclipsed in the later 1980s and in the 1990s. The dominant male, middle-class and white "liberal" current in the gay "community," has come to rely on the biological model as one of the assumptions buttressing its construction of the gay community as a legitimate and "natural" minority group. However, queers are regulated not as an ethnic group but as an oppressed and marginalized erotic minority and oppressed sexuality.

This biological assumption has provided some basis for asserting a narrow gay pride and a limited notion of an often adult-defined gay "community" (most often coded as male, white and middle class) in a social and legal context where "rights" are often only seen to be justified when derived from "natural," immutable differences. These "rights" only allow for access to and integration within existing social and political forms based on capitalist, patriarchal, and racist social relations. At the very same time, the hegemony of biological determinism has also been part of blunting the subversion of institutionalized heterosexuality that our movements initiated. This biological assumption has provided a limited basis for expanding the ghettoes and limited social spaces we have won through our diverse struggles. However, it also participates in marginalizing and ghettoizing our impact on broader social relations and struggles, moves us away from building alliances with other groups facing oppression, and from challenging heterosexual hegemony and oppressive sexual regulations more generally. It can also blind us to see the serious problems facing queer youth and even to abandon the needs and concerns of young people through its focus on a "natural," but ironically "adult" community.

The social layers that have now gained social and political hegemony in much gay community formation are precisely those professional, managerial, and business layers (what I sometimes refer to as the gay professional, managerial strata) who no longer wish to challenge capitalist relations or to build alliances for social transformation with other oppressed and marginalized groups. Through this process of class formation within gay community formation, a new largely white and male middle-class elite has come to stand over and against the rest of the community and is able to speak for the "community" to and within ruling relations. This class strata is also committed to displaying and performing their social respectability and responsibility so they can be granted access to the existing social order (Kinsman, 1996; Sears, 2000). For some this is expressed through the position that winning the right to marry is the end point for the struggle for social respectability and responsibility, even though major forms of discrimination and oppression will continue to exist (Sears, 2001; Warner, 1999). This hegemony of biological determinism therefore fits into a process of class formation and hegemony within gay communities that moves us away from challenging fundamental characteristics of heterosexual hegemony and capitalist, patriarchal, and racist social relations in an accommodation with the existing order.

This conceptualization of a natural, biological gay minority also makes it more difficult to address the many social differences among and between those of us who practice same-gender erotic delights. It separates the "queer" aspects of our experiences away from other aspects of our lives. Even through queer is always lived in and through relations of class, gender, race, ability, age, health, language, culture, and other social relations this biological determinist approach allows for us only to see "gay" and "queer" unencumbered with connections with class exploitation and racial oppression. This is part of how the universal "gay" or "queer" who gets constructed in mainstream gay discourse is coded as white, middle-class and usually male.

In this way, the hegemony of biological determinism within queer communities and movements can also become a site of class and social struggle within queer community formation. The self-organization of lesbians and gays of colour, of working-class lesbians and gays and queers in the union movement, of two-spirited people, and queers living with disabilities has shattered the mythology of a unitary gayness or "queerness." Queerness is always mediated or mutually constructed (Bannerji, 1995). It is lived and organized through social relations of class, race, gender, and other social relations. We are never simply queer. Our desires, pleasures, and oppressions are lived very differently on the basis of race, class, gender, ability, sexual practices, HIV status, and this has to be addressed in queer liberationist politics.

Queerness is not some biological essence, but is socially made through our own activities in contestation with heterosexual hegemony. The physiological is transformed in a social context—it becomes part of the historical and the social. Queerness has to do not with our genes, but with our socially made desires, lusts and pleasures, and the social and political choices, alliances, connections, and solidarities we make and build based on these. It is only an approach that nurtures our capacities for resistance and transformation that can move us beyond the "natural" appearance of heterosexual hegemony that surrounds us and move us beyond the reification of our genders and sexualities as "things" we have no control over. Biological determinism instead emphasizes a "natural" commonality among gays which does not facilitate dealing with social power differences among and between queers, and obscures the class and social struggles that need to be engaged in within queer communities. Instead we need to deal with our many social differences. But while celebrating and recognizing our differences we also need to avoid a type of "multicultural" form of tolerance for those with "differences" which maintains white middle-class hegemony at the centre and does not get at the social roots of oppression. We have to engage actively in the breaking down of social power relations and inequalities within our movements, communities, and societies.

SOCIAL ANALYSIS AND LIBERATION, NOT "BIOLOGICAL" ACCOMMODATION WITH HETEROSEXUAL HEGEMONY

In these biologically determinist approaches, homosexuality is seen as the problem needing to be explained. Heterosexuality is in contrast taken for granted, as "normal" and "natural." To accept that homosexuality is simply a biologically based, minority sexuality is not only to accept hegemonic ideological assumptions that cannot account for people's present erotic and gender lives, but is, more importantly, to close off the important challenges feminism and queer liberation presents to heterosexual hegemonic relations. It is to leave heterosexuality intact as the "natural" majority sexuality for all time. And it is these very same relations of heterosexual hegemony that organize the oppression that we continue to live in our everyday lives. Biological determinism is therefore not a useful approach for critical social analysis or for moving towards lesbians, gay, bisexual, transgendered, or queer liberation. It leads to accepting the small social spaces we have already won as all we will ever get, and does not provide a strategy for expanding and radicalizing our diverse struggles.

It is much better, in my view, to rely on the broader notion of the social making of genders and sexualities rooted in people's bodies, needs, cultures, and histories. This allows us to start from people's lived experiences and erotic practices in all their diversities to clarify how genders and sexualities are made as historical and social practices. It provides a much firmer social and historical grounding and basis for our claims for liberation and for de-stabilizing and transforming heterosexual hegemony.

Social construction approaches not only make much better sense of the available information we have on gender and sexuality and of our experiences of them, they also can provide grounds for optimism and hope. While biological determinism would suggest we cannot do that much to transform the oppression we currently face except to expand our ghettoes and liberal tolerance towards us, this kind of social constructionist approach suggests that if heterosexual hegemony is socially made it can be collectively remade and transformed. The terrain for queer liberation is thereby immensely expanded.

Thanks to Kaili Beck for her assistance on this chapter. Thanks also to the reviewers and Deborah Brock.

CRITICAL THINKING QUESTIONS

1. Why is the question asked always "what causes homosexuality?" and never "what causes heterosexuality?"
2. What is the relation between the social and the biological?
3. How is biological knowledge socially constructed?
4. What can we learn from the experiences of transsexuals and the "intersexed"?
5. Does the acceptance of homosexuality as having a biological cause lead to any diminishing of heterosexism?
6. How is the current popularity of biological explanations of homosexuality among some gay men linked to questions of class, gender, and race?

SUGGESTED READINGS

Bornstein, Kate (1994). *Gender Outlaw: On Men, Women and the Rest of Us.* New York: Vintage/Random House.
   In this insightful book Kate Bornstein both reflects on her own experiences of moving from one gender to another and develops a powerful transgendered critique of the current gender system.

Fausto-Sterling, Anne (2000). *Sexing the Body, Gender Politics and the Construction of Sexuality.* New York: Basic Books.
   This book is a comprehensive critical examination of biological determinist research and the outlining of erspective of social and physiological synthesis that provides a very useful basis for a social and historical approach to gender and sexuality.

Foucault, Michel (1980). *The History of Sexuality, Volume One: An Introduction.* New York: Vintage.
   A powerful analysis of the historical emergence of sexuality and the relations between disciplinary social power, bio-power and sexuality. A very useful critique of the hypothesis that our sexualities have been simply 'repressed' by forms of social power.

Kessler, Suzanne J. and Wendy McKenna (1978). *Gender: An Ethnomethodological Approach.* Chicago: University of Chicago Press.
   An early and powerful outlining of gender as an everyday social accomplishment based on gender attribution that learns from cross-cultural accounts of gender, the experiences of pre-operative transsexuals, and a critical analysis of biological and psychological accounts of gender.

Kessler, Suzanne J. (1998). *Lessons from the Intersexed.* New Brunswick, N.J.: Rutgers University Press.
   A powerful book examining what can be learned from the experiences of those defined as "intersexed" – those who are unable to be easily assigned a gender at birth because of anomalous genitalia – and how they are managed by the medical profession in particular. Kessler learns a great deal from the emerging intersexed liberation movement.

Kinsman, Gary (1996). *The Regulation of Desire: Homo and Hetero Sexualities.* Montreal: Black Rose.
   An historical-sociological investigation of the relational emergence of homosexualities and heterosexualities in the Canadian context. This includes how homosexuality has been constructed as a social problem and how heterosexuality has been normalized and naturalized.

Terry, Jennifer (1999). *An American Obsession, Science, Medicine, and Homosexuality in Modern Society.* Chicago and London: The University of Chicago Press.
   A critical historical and social examination of the focus in US science, medicine and culture on the "problem" and the "causes" of homosexuality and lesbianism.

WEB LINKS

rmc.library.cornell.edu/HSC
   Resources for researching sexuality can be located through The Human Sexuality Collection at Cornell University Library.

eserver.org/marx/
   Many of Karl Marx's writings are now available on the Internet. For example see, Marx and Engels' Writings

www.appstate.edu/~stanovskydj/marxfiles/html
   The MarX-Files

www.philosophypages.com/ph/marx/htm
   Karl Marx (1818-1883)

CHAPTER 13

MORAL PANIC AND CHILD PORNOGRAPHY: THE CASE OF ROBIN SHARPE

BY KEGAN DOYLE AND DANY LACOMBE[1]

On January 16, 1999, Justice Shaw of the Supreme Court of British Columbia (heretofore B.C.), Canada struck down the possession provision of the child pornography law, stating that it was a profound invasion of freedom of expression and privacy. While it was still an offence to produce, make, or distribute child pornography, or to possess child pornography for the purpose of distribution, it became no longer illegal to possess it for private use.

The decision shocked and outraged the community. "The bonehead should be removed from the bench," a Vancouver talk-show host fumed during a discussion (Culbert & Hall, 1999, p. A3). In a letter to the *Vancouver Sun* editors, (1999, January 21) a citizen demanded: "What's next? Necrophiliacs being granted access to funeral parlors?" Public anger was not expressed through the media alone. After the ruling, the B.C. Law Courts were swamped with furious callers asking for Justice Shaw's removal from the bench. Lloyd McKenzie, a retired B.C. Supreme Court judge now serving as an information officer for the courts, claims he never saw anything as emotional in his forty-year career: "The level of hate that has been directed at [Justice Shaw] is remarkable. People are phoning me and phoning a number of other people at the Law Courts, including the judge's secretary just heaping invective upon the judge." (Hall, 1999, p. A1) Public anger with the judge culminated in a death-threat. While the Attorney General of B.C., government officials, and journalists quickly condemned the death-threat on Justice Shaw as a grave attack on one of our democratic institutions, few tried to pacify the people by clarifying the judgement. Instead, they too participated in the creation of a moral panic by asserting judicial error and urging an expedient appeal of the judgement for the sake of children's safety. As one Member of Parliament

---

[1] This research was funded by a Social Sciences and Humanities Research Counsel of Canada. The authors would like to thank Don Ray for his research assistance. Please send your comments to lacombe@sfu.ca

> **WARNING!!**
>
> **ROBIN JOHN SHARPE**
> THE MAN ABOVE WAS RECENTLY QUOTED IN A NATIONAL NEWSPAPER STATING THAT SEX WITH <u>CHILDREN</u> IS ACCEPTABLE "..IF THERE IS CONSENT"! WHEN ASKED IF HE HAS EVER HARMED A CHILD HE REPLIED "I DON'T KNOW"!
>
> HE IS ACTIVE IN YOUR COMMUNITY AND LIVES AT ▇▇▇▇▇▇▇▇▇▇▇▇▇ HE SHOPS, EATS, WALKS, AND LIVES WHERE YOU AND YOUR CHILDREN DO AND HE <u>PROUDLY</u> ADVOCATES SEX WITH <u>CHILDREN</u>.
>
> FOR THE SAKE OF YOUR FAMILY AND YOUR COMMUNITY, WATCH FOR HIM.......
> BECAUSE YOU HAVE TO KNOW
> HE'S WATCHING YOU

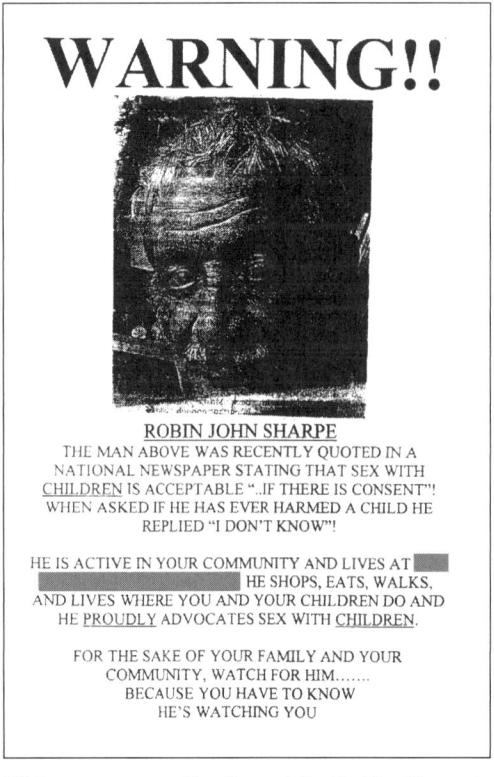

This poster was distributed in Robin Sharpe's Kitsilano neighbourhood, sparking a public outcry. Sharpe has since moved from the neighbourhood.

declared: "The decision gives pedophiles the right to abuse children" (Gray, 1999, p. J2). Or as the B.C. Teacher's Federation president stated: "This outrageous ruling…places children—the most vulnerable members of society—at the mercy of pedophiles and those who would profit from pedophilia" (Culbert, 1999, p. B1).

The connection between child pornography, pedophilia and child sexual abuse was confirmed when journalists reported on the man at the centre of the controversy, Robin J. Sharpe. Sharpe's media portrayal was narrow, focusing almost exclusively on his sexual orientation and his age—he is gay and was 65 at the time—his sexual preference for "boys" and the voluminous child pornographic material—computer disks, books, stories, and photographs—Canadian Customs officials and Vancouver police seized from him. Only one title of the seized written material was mentioned, a title which unequivocally linked him with child sexual abuse: *Flogging, Fun and Fortitude: A Collection of Kiddie Kink Classics*, by Sam Paloc.

Sharpe's sex life was what mattered the most for journalists who relentlessly questioned him on his sexual adventures with children. Among other things, journalists asked him the age of the "youngest" person he has had sex with, whether it would be acceptable to have sex with an 11-year-old, and if he had ever harmed a child. Sharpe provided elusive answers to these questions, preferring to address the larger issue of youth-adult sex in terms of the context in which it takes place. The following illustrates the answers he gave journalists: "This is not a confession. But inter-generational sex, particularly involving adolescent boys, is a practice of long standing in society" (*National Post*, 1999, January 16, p. A2). With these answers Sharpe became in the eyes of the community not just a child pornographer, but a pedophile and a freak—someone to be policed. A poster campaign soon appeared in Kitsilano, the gentrified beach area where Mr. Sharpe lived.

In this poster, Sharpe came across as something larger than life—as pedophiles so often do. He is presented as deceiving, manipulative, and cunning or as equipped with a dangerous capacity for behavioral transformation, since "he shops, eats, walks and lives where you and your children do" without you ever noticing him. The warning "watch for him…because you have to know he's watching you" represents him as having something akin to panoptic power—he has an "evil eye."

The media construction of Robin J. Sharpe relied upon the omission of key aspects of his life story. No journalist attempted to go beyond the legal charges to describe the content of the material seized, and this despite the fact that Mr. Sharpe had openly invited the media in his home to discuss the ruling and his passion for kiddie kink. Had journalists reported on the content of the 10 photographs that led to the initial charges, they would have found out that they were of two hustler friends of Mr. Sharpe's, alleged to be 16 and 17 years old, who continue many years later to visit their old companion for the occasional game of backgammon. They would also have had to report that Sam Paloc, the author of *A Collection of Kiddie Kink Classics*, was Mr. Sharpe's *nom de plume.* All the seized written material, which were eventually returned to him because it could not be charged, consisted mainly of poetry chap books, semi-biographical novellas, travelogues, and short stories authored by Sharpe, as Mr. Sharpe is an aspiring literary writer (Cholmondeley, 1997; Sharpe, 1994, 1997; Watmough, 1994). Regardless of the literary merit of Sharpe's work, what is astonishing about the media frenzy is that almost no mention of Sharpe's literary ambitions or frail success was ever presented. Indeed, Sharpe was presented as scarcely human.

The evidence given above indicates that Sharpe has become not just a freak or a deviant, but a scapegoat. This paper examines why. To do so, we situate his treatment in relation to an endemic moral panic over child abuse, pedophilia, and child pornography. We examine how this panic has expressed itself in the Canadian media, in the Canadian and American psychiatric institutions and discourse, and, finally, in Canada's legal structure. We conclude by arguing that this panic is a product of the iconic status of the child within late-modern society and of what scholars have identified as "the pedophilia of everyday life."

DEFINITION OF MORAL PANIC

Before proceeding, we should clarify the term "moral panic." *Folk Devils and Moral Panics* (1972), Stanley Cohen's seminal study of the demonization of English youth groups, provides the clearest definition of the term,

> Societies appear to be subject, every now and then, to periods of moral panic. A condition, episode, person or group of persons emerges to become defined as threat to the societal values and interests; its nature is presented in a stylized and stereotypical

fashion by the mass media; the moral barricades are manned by editors, bishops, politicians and other right-thinking people; socially accredited experts pronounce their diagnoses and solutions; ways of coping are evolved or (more often) resorted to; the condition then disappears, submerges or deteriorates and becomes more visible. Sometimes the object of the panic is quite novel and at other times it is something which has been in existence long enough, but suddenly appears in the limelight. Sometimes the panic passes over and is forgotten, except in folklore and collective memory; at other times it has more serious and long-lasting repercussions and might produce such changes as those in legal and social policy or even in the way the society conceives itself. (1972, p. 9)

Moral panic is a useful paradigm for understanding the current hysteria over child safety; however, it is highly schematic. Jeffrey Weeks (1991), for example, criticizes this moral panic for its inability to explain why symbolic agents become the target of social anxieties. Yet he finds moral panic a "valuable framework for describing the course of events" leading to the scapegoating of deviants. Alan Hunt (1999) on the other hand, finds the concept too conspiratorial and suggests abandoning it altogether.

Hunt argues that moral panic implies a top-down process whereby the state, through its agencies such as the police and the courts, manufactures a crisis to re-establish a conservative social order. In place of the concept of moral panic, Hunt and others (Brock, 2000; Valverde & Weir, 1988) offer the concept of moral regulation, which explains the complex strategies involved in the construction and control of deviants. Moral regulation, they say, is not the preserve of the state alone; rather it is exercised by a variety of organizations and professionals located in civil society, such as medical experts, psychologists, victims' groups, and university professors. Moral regulation involves complex interactions between the state and civil society and between public and private sectors. It is through these interactions that deviance is produced and specific populations are controlled.

We find Hunt's critique of moral panic too strong. There is nothing in Cohen's definition of moral panic that suggests the uni-dimensional, state-centred, top-down process criticized by Hunt. While Cohen's concept of "moral panic" highlights the centrality of the media in the production of social anxieties leading to the scapegoating of certain individuals, it also points to the role that various other institutions, agencies, and actors play in this process. Moral panic is best described as an instance of moral regulation, albeit an extreme one. It is a short-lived but heightened moment in the construction of social anxieties. In a moral panic, both the quality and quantity of deviance is exaggerated, as particular events and/or individuals become the cause of a moral breakdown. As we show in this paper, various institutions (state and non-state) helped create widespread social anxiety over the safety of children. The concept of moral panic helps us describe the course of events leading to this anxiety and its transfer to specific scapegoats. Why such panics occur and why certain groups and not others are singled out as symbols of breakdown, however, is not adequately explained by either the concept of moral panic or moral regulation—a point we shall return to in the second half of the paper.

Before we proceed, we should also point out that the current panic over child abuse is inseparable from a more generalized panic about crime. In our society, there has been a quantifiable increase in fear over the last two decades. Despite the disappearance of most pre-modern and early modern dangers and risks, our society, Pratt argues, continues to perceive the world as a "scary place" (1996, p. 71). Thanks to the proliferation of news media and information services in the last two decades of the 20th century, the world "seems to be getting scarier all the time" (Ibid., p. 71). People feel threatened by an ever-growing number of dangers; some of which they can control; some they cannot control. Crime is at the top of most people's list of dangers. Why? Partly because of the new "regimes of truth"—or sources of information—about crime dangers. As Pratt explains: "[t]hese new sources include university-organized crime surveys, independent victim surveys, self-report studies, surveys conducted by phone, those organized by sections of the media and so on—all of which claim to represent the reality of crime" (1996, p. 72). These new sources of risks, coupled with more traditional sources of information such as the news media not only provide us with more information about crime and criminals, they "enhance fear" by creating the feeling that there is a crime epidemic.

According to Kathlyn Taylor Gaubatz, in *Crime and the Public Mind*, Americans "have placed criminal offenders *beyond the pale*. They are not imputing to them good intentions; they are not looking upon them as really just like us. Forgiveness and the avoidance of vengeance may be important standards for the commerce of everyday life—with family, friends, schoolmates, and business associates—but the treatment of criminals is not a part of everyday life" (1995, p.165). This othering of criminal offenders is in part a consequence of the recent inclusion of so many "others" in mainstream American life, others whose behaviour is not necessarily accepted by mainstream Americans. As Taylor Gaubatz puts it, "our already strong tendency to place criminal offenders beyond the pale…[is] a natural reaction to our having moved to take so many others *in*, in recent years" (1995, p.168). As a result of so often "opening the boundaries of acceptance, of forgiveness, of understanding" to include those who have been historically marginalized, America has grown exhausted—"We are a tired nation" exclaims Taylor Gaubatz (1995, p.171). Because of this exhaustion, Americans have decided to close the door on criminal offenders. "[C]riminal offenders are the last frontier" (1995, p.171). Criminal offenders thus play a crucial role in the formation of emotional solidarity as they are the "not-us" of a highly heterogeneous, unsettled society. Not surprisingly in this context, criminals become the object of deep-seated and pandemic social antipathy.

Regardless of whether this attitude towards crime and criminals is the product of new technologies or of the increased heterogeneity of modern society or both, it has produced what has become known as "the risk society" (Beck, 1992; Ericson & Haggerty, 1997; Feeley & Simon, 1992; O'Malley, 1992; Simon, 1987). According to risk-society theorists, risk rationality and the emergent regime of social protection it assumes, are predicated on identifying "future" criminals and penalizing them for "who they are" not for "what" they have done (Foucault, 1988; Pratt, 1995, 1996). For example, since the 1990s, most English-speaking countries have enacted "dangerous offenders" legislation allowing the courts to sentence those identified as "dangerous" to indeterminate terms of imprisonment and to impose special restrictions on those offenders upon their release into the community. Risk rationality involves creating types, a taxonomy of the dangerous, on the basis of actuarial predictions. Thus legal "guarantees" against future crimes by "dangerous or potentially dangerous" individuals are sought and justified no longer on the basis of legal criteria, such as whether the person committed an offence, but on the threat these individuals are for others. A dialectic is at work between risk rationality and the demonization of specific criminals—the more the dangerous criminal is singled out as something monstrous and ungovernable, the more risk rationality is able to function and police the community. Similarly, the more risk rationality infiltrates society to protect the community of law abiding citizens—the more its gaze spreads through society—the more likely it is that dangerous criminals will be demonized.

The panic around child abuse thus must be understood within the context of a culture that has become more hostile to criminals in general. However, the child molester often stands out as a sort of meta-criminal, the worst among various evils. In much popular culture, for instance, child molesters appear to be the most heinous of criminals; their crime is not only vile in itself but is seen as the origin of uncontrolled violence and the cause of societal breakdown. The mystery at the heart of the hugely successful series *Twin Peaks* in the early nineties was the molestation and murder of Laura Palmer by her father. Similarly, the killers in so-called serial killer movies such as *Natural Born Killers* were abused children. These films imply that the true evil behind evil is child molestation.

THE PANIC AROUND CHILD ABUSE
Changing Definitions

As stated at the outset, Sharpe's harsh treatment must be understood as part of a larger moral panic around child abuse, pedophilia, and child pornography. This panic is both a cause and effect of a drastic reconsideration of our everyday interactions with children and of the institutions and public spaces within which they move, including schools, athletic organizations, churches, and malls. According to official reports, there has been an unprecedented increase in cases of child abuse in western societies over the last three decades, an increase perceived as a sign that children are at ever-increasing risk of abuse (*Report of the Committee*, 1984). While child abuse is real and serious, the recent increase in cases should not be interpreted to mean that children are abused more frequently than before. On the contrary, historians of childhood show that, from a broad historical perspective, cases of child abuse are becoming increasingly rare. The apparent increase in child abuse reflects not an increase in abuse itself rather an increase in *reported* cases, an increase which suggests a willingness on people's part to go to the police and a dramatic change in people's perception of what constitutes child abuse. For example, what a few decades ago was advocated as normal discipline—spanking or giving the strap—today is often perceived and reported as abuse. Child abuse, Jenks contends, has become more common because we live in an increasingly panoptic society: it has "clearly 'increased' through the magnification and breadth of our gaze" (1997 p. 108). One extreme example of this heightened sensitivity towards child abuse is the case of Denise Perrigo. Perrigo was giving suck to her baby. Surprised at and ashamed of the pleasure she felt, she phoned the rape crisis centre for advice. Rather than counselling her, the worker at the centre phoned the police, who promptly arrested Perrigo. Eighteen months later her baby was still in custody (*Nude and Natural, 12*, 1993, p. 2).

THE ROLE OF THE MEDIA

This change in the perception of abuse is related partly to the proliferation of media stories about imperiled children. Every week, the public encounters tales of unsuspecting children snatched from the playground by perverts, of toddlers abused at their daycare, school, or church, of parents practicing satanic rituals on their own sons and daughters. In one week in 1997, for example, Canadians read the following: "Parents in fear as girl escapes in 7th abduction bid" (*Toronto Star*, 1997, February 12); "Paedophile alert issued by schools" (*The Globe and Mail*, 1997, February 11); and "ARE YOUR KIDS SAFE? From hockey to schools to scouting, the hunt is on for sexual predators" (*Maclean's*, 1997, February 10).

Several of the major news stories in Canada between 1989 and 1999 involved cases of child abuse. In 1991, Linda Sterling, who ran a daycare centre out of her home in Martensville, Saskatchewan, was accused, along with her husband Ron and son Travis, of practicing satanic rituals involving children (Harris 1998). Five police officers were also alleged to have participated in the abuse. Linda and Ron Sterling were exonerated; the charges against the police officers stayed; and Travis Sterling was convicted of sexual assault. The case attracted national attention and is alleged to have cost the province of Saskatchewan $1 million (*Alberta Report*, 1994, April 25, p. 43; *Maclean's*, 1994, February 21, p. 21).

Other highly publicized cases of abuse involved the Catholic Church. In 1989, multiple charges of physical and sexual abuse were levelled against the Christian

Brothers at Mount Cashel Orphanage in St. John's, Newfoundland (Jenkins, 1996). Thirty-one victims and more than 250 witnesses told stories of beatings, fondling, and sodomy. By the time the trials ended in 1992, the Brothers had closed the orphanage and sold the land to provide the $36 million in compensation awarded to victims in lawsuits. Meanwhile, hundreds of lawsuits have been filed by First Nations people against the Catholic, Anglican, and United Churches for cases of abuse. Three hundred people assigned to Catholic orphanages in Quebec in the 1940s and 1950s have also sought an apology and monetary compensation for the physical and sexual abuse they experienced. On March 4, 1999, *then* Quebec Premier Lucien Bouchard offered an apology and U.S. $2 million in compensation. The point, of course, is not the veracity of these claims, but the fact that these stories have dominated the media.[2]

One of the most widely covered cases of child sexual abuse in the past decade involved Canada's national sport, hockey. In 1996, Sheldon Kennedy, a player with the Boston Bruins, publicly claimed to have been sexually assaulted hundreds of times between the ages of 15 and 20 by Graham James, his coach while he played junior hockey with the Swift Current Broncos. In 1997, James was sentenced to three years and six months imprisonment after pleading guilty to two counts of sexual assault on Kennedy and another player. This incident was quickly followed by the revelation of a "pedophile ring" at the famous Maple Leaf Gardens hockey arena in Toronto. Thirty-four-year-old Martin Kruze accused maintenance workers of having abused him while he was a junior hockey player. His accusations led to the arrest of maintenance workers Gordon Stuckless, 47, and John Paul Roby, 54. After the initial arrest, the police were inundated with a deluge of allegations of abuse at the hockey shrine. Kruze and those who alleged abuse claimed that their abusers would offer them jobs at Maple Leaf Gardens in exchange for sex. Aside from jobs, the teenagers were also "lured with free tickets" to hockey games and rock concerts, as well as expensive dinners. John McCarthy recalls that the abuse lasted 10 years: "It happened hundred of times....And a lot of people working there knew about it" (Deacon & Nemeth, 1997, p. 54; *Maclean's*, 1997, March 10; McLean, 1998, p. 26).

The Kennedy and Kruze stories have been followed by numerous reports of sexual abuse in junior hockey and other sports. Dozens of coaches in Canada and the United States have been accused of abuse and the whole relationship between coaches and young athletes has become an object of intense public scrutiny (Nack

---

[2] D.W. Hendon, D.D. Allman, and D.E. Greco, (1999, Summer). *Journal of Church and States 41* (3), 628. The Mount Cashel case of child abuse was the subject of a three-hour made-for-television Canadian movie *The Boys of St. Vincent* (1994), which was a huge critical and popular success. Carla Yu. (1998, November 30). But a corrupt tree bringeth forth evil fruit: still plagued by sex scandal, churches struggle to restore clerical credibility. *Alberta Report. 25* (50), 34.

& Yaeger, 1999). Yet the mainstream media failed to report on important aspects of both the Kennedy and Kruze cases. According to Rachel Giese, from *Xtra*, Toronto's gay newspaper, the media ignored the fact that the maintenance workers at Maple Leaf Gardens "were not in a position of power over the teenagers. The teenagers didn't have to go to the Gardens, accept gifts, or return after the first sexual advance." Moreover, she points out that none of the alleged victims said they were threatened, coerced, or physically intimidated. Giese claims that "The real bogeyman [in the story] is homosexuality, not sexual abuse" (1997, February 17). On the other hand, journalist Max Allen revealed that the abuse suffered by Kennedy involved neither physical penetration nor oral sex. According to the sentencing transcripts Allen examined, only acts of mutual masturbation were involved in the Kennedy case against James (Allen, 1997). Allen's revelation has led some to question whether or not what Kennedy experienced was abuse. Finally, the Sharpe case was preceded in the media by the story of William Bennest, principal of Clinton Elementary School in Burnaby, B.C. Bennest was initially arrested on charges of possessing child pornography. The case intensified as four more charges were added: making child pornography, sexual touching of a boy under the age of 14, sexually assaulting the same boy, and procuring the sexual services of a minor. The situation was perceived as so catastrophic that "five trauma counsellors" were needed to help "teachers, parents, and students at Clinton elementary deal with the shocking news about their respected principal" (*Province*, 1996, p. A4). Local newspapers published Bennest's home address forcing him to go into hiding. Eventually, most charges fell. The charges of sexual touching and assaulting were dropped, and the charges of making child porn and procuring from a minor were stayed, leaving Bennest to plead guilty to possessing child porn. Most of the evidence gathered by the police consisted of commercial gay pornography (video and print), and six homemade movies featuring men identified by the police as "young males." Bennest had spliced nonsexual images of one of his former students, a 12-year-old boy, in his homemade video collection. Bennest also pasted the student's face onto bodies of gay men engaged in sex. Bennest received a two-year suspended sentence. The public was outraged, demanding a custodial sentence. Journalist Tom Yeung notes that although the Bennest story made front page of the local newspapers when he was first arrested, his sentence, and the dropped and stayed charges "merited merely five column inches in the bottom left hand corner of the [*Sun*'s] B-section on October 8" (Lang, 1997, January 23, p. 9; Yeung, 1997, October 16, p. 7).

When the Sharpe story exploded in the Canadian media, it did not do so in a vacuum. As we have seen media stories about pedophiles and child porn rings have been hugely popular for the past decade. As with the Sharpe case, what stands out in the reporting of such cases is the limited and heavily stylized portrayal of the abuser.

THE LAW'S RESPONSE

Partially in response to such stories, a whole new industry specializing in helping parents protect their children through practicing good security and streetproofing children has emerged. Police stations and community outreach organizations abound with literature on child safety. Canadian video stores are likely to carry *Never be a Victim* (1996), a four-part video series produced by an ex-officer of the Toronto Police force, to provide—free of charge—"invaluable" guidelines for streetproofing children. In the mid-1990s, *Oprah*, the most watched talk-show on television, aired a two-part *Child Alert Mission* series, to provide kids with the safety tips and skills they need to beat "sex predators" (Lacombe, <www.tryoung.com/journal-grad.html/4Shon /index4. html>).

In Canada since 1988, four new laws were enacted and nine laws were reformed as a result of calls to protect children. These laws cover sexual assault, sexual interference, invitation to sexual touching, sexual exploitation, indecent acts and indecent exposure, incest, anal intercourse, bestiality, parent or guardian procuring sexual activity, householders permitting sexual activity, living on avails of a prostitute under 18, obtaining a person under 18 for sexual purpose, and child pornography. Indeed, over the last two decades, in both Canada and the United States, there has been a series of calls for tougher legislation to help control child abuse. These calls have led to, among other things, the creation of community notification programmes, sex offenders' registries, and to the implementation of longer prison sentences for some offenders and chemical castration for others. Many U.S. states have implemented community notification programmes whereby communities notify residents and schools of the presence of high-risk sex offenders. In some states, the released sex offender must go from door to door to warn his neighbours that he lives in their community. Some notification programmes post warnings about the new resident on telephone poles. In Louisiana, released sex offenders were required until recently to wear special clothing and indicate their status on their house or by putting bumper stickers on their cars (Jenkins, 1998, p. 200). Some states prefer exile, requiring that the released offender leave the state in which he lives. In California, a CD-Rom database, available to the public, identifies with photographs and zip code locations approximately 57,000 former sex offenders. Some of these offenders were charged as long as 50 years ago with offences such as "lewd conduct" that no longer exist (Ricardi & Leeds, 1997). The Web site <www.childmolester.com> not only lists offenders by state and country, but also gives offenders' biographies and photographs.

Many U.S. states have inaugurated programmes whereby a released sex offender is required to register with a police department. He (or sometimes she) is required to provide photographs and information about his (or her) past and current residence and employment. The Massachusetts Sex Offender Registry is one of the most stringent in the U.S. It lists virtually all categories of persons found guilty of felonies or misdemeanours involving sex except for people who have committed prostitution-related offences. Offenders remain on the list for 20 years; if the offender is considered high-risk, he remains on the list for life. Any Massachusetts citizen can access names, photographs, and information about a sex offender living within a mile of their home. Organizations concerned with the welfare of women, children, and youth can get the information on all sex offenders in the registry and are not limited by the one-mile radius.

Another treatment for sexual offenders that is becoming increasingly popular in the United States is chemical castration. In September 1996, California instituted a mandatory program of chemical castration for high-risk sex offenders. Repeat child molesters are given weekly injections of Depo-Provera, the castration drug, as are first-time offenders if so ordered by the judge (Kincaid, 1998, p. 90). This programme has proven overwhelmingly popular, although some leading Democrats in California have asked that the program's name "chemical castration" be changed to "hormonal suppression treatment" (Ibid., p 90). In the United Kingdom, meanwhile, some have called for an entirely new institution with which to deal with sex offenders. The London Home Office has proposed "a new 'third system'—outside of prison and health systems—" to lock up pedophiles "for life even if they have not been convicted of a violent offence" (Bradley, 1999, p. 19).

Although the more extreme cases come from elsewhere, Canada has also adopted harsh techniques for dealing with sex offenders and pedophiles. In Canada, when a high-risk sex offender is about to be released, the police can require that conditions be placed on him. Some offenders, for instance, are not allowed in certain parks, to touch alcohol, or to be in the presence of a child without an adult. Much of the concern about child sexual abuse, however, has focused on the circulation of child pornography. As stated above, child pornography is now perceived in Canada and elsewhere as part of the overall menace to children's safety and as the outrage at Mr. Sharpe indicates child pornography has become not just linked to, but symbolic of, the sexual abuse of children.

Canada's current legal problems with pornography date back to the early 1980s when the government, inspired by public outcry, created two commissions of inquiry, commissions that produced the *Badgley Report* on sexual offences against children (1984) and the *Fraser Report* on pornography and prostitution (1985). These reports contained much controversial data, including the finding that "about one in two females and one in three males had been victims of sexual abuse" (1984, p.193). The reports also linked child sexual abuse, prostitution and pornography, by showing how abusers used pornography,

> Pornographic depictions were not infrequently shown to children by abusers to reduce the child's inhibitions and to school the child in the acts to be performed. *The linkage is clear.* Again, it has been found that many juvenile prostitutes have

run away from home following incidents of sexual abuse; such may well be the prior history of many adult prostitutes. Finally, completing the vicious circle, the empirical studies show that those who abuse children sexually were frequently themselves the victims of just such abuse. (Canada, Department of Justice, 1985 p. 4, emphasis added)

While several attempts to reform legislation against adult pornography failed, the government did succeed in enacting child pornography legislation in 1993. Section 163(1) of the Criminal Code defines child pornography as any visual representation of a child engaged in sexually explicit activity or any visual depiction "for a sexual purpose" of the genital or anal area of a child. Child pornography also covers written material which "advocates or counsels" sexual activity with a child. Remarkably, a child is defined as any person under 18 years old. The law also makes it an illegal offence punishable by 10 years imprisonment to make, print, distribute, or possess for the purpose of distribution child pornography, and it makes simple possession of child pornography an offence punishable by five years imprisonment.

It is in many ways a Draconian law that could only have come out of a climate of panic. Many hypothetical situations highlighting the law's profound invasion of privacy and freedom of expression were eventually presented in the two Appeal hearings following Justice Shaw's decision in *Sharpe*. Two examples serve to illustrate the problems with the legislation. Example 1: In Canada, the age of sexual consent is 14. While two 16 year olds can engage in lawful sexual activities with each other, they are prevented from visually representing their activities; if they do they would be in possession of child pornography. Example 2: Youth-adult sex is legal in Canada as long as it neither involves the exchange of money or goods nor violates a relation of authority or trust. It is a criminal offence for a professor to have sex with her student if she/he is under 18. If the professor were to fantasize about having sex with her 17-year-old student and decide to record her thoughts in a diary, she would be in possession of child pornography.

Realizing the problematic applications of the law, the Supreme Court of Canada decided to find a "remedy" by "reading into" the prohibition against child pornography two exceptions. First, the prohibition does not apply in the case of self-created (written or visual) material, provided the material is kept by the creator "for his or her eyes alone" (para. 116). Second, the prohibition does not apply in the case of private visual recordings of lawful sexual activity provided they are kept in "strict privacy" and "intended exclusively for private use by the creator and the persons depicted therein" (para. 116).

The Supreme Court of Canada recognized those problematic applications of the law when it heard the appeal of the Sharpe case, but instead of finding the child pornography law unconstitutional as did the B.C. Supreme Court and the B.C. Appeal Court, it found a "remedy" by "reading into" the prohibition two exceptions.[3] In March 2002, Sharpe was eventually found guilty of possessing child pornography only in respect to his photographs. Justice Shaw found that Sharpe's written materials, described as "morally repugnant," do not fall within the category of child pornography (para. 35). Moreover, he asserted that: "[The materials] are properly termed transgressive literature, Mr Sharpe show skills in the literary quality of his work and the literary devices he uses, although not to the level of most established writers *R. v. Sharpe* 2002 BCSC 423 at para. 109).

Sharpe's initial attempt to challenge the child pornography law could have been construed as a rational attempt to challenge a problematic law. Instead, as the examples given at the outset of this paper indicate his challenge has led to a terrible recrudescence of the very anxiety and hatred that helped create the law in the first place.

The Role of Experts

According to Cohen, "socially accredited experts" play a crucial role in diagnosing and finding a cure for the object of a moral panic. While the work done by experts seems "neutral" and "objective" because it takes place within "legitimate" institutions, it nonetheless serves to augment social anxiety and hostility.

The moral panic around child abuse is both a cause and effect of changes in the therapeutic institution. The last two decades have witnessed a prodigious outflow of discourse of the subject of abuse. As of 1977, there still had been relatively few books published by professionals and activists on the subject of abuse. Between 1978 and 1981, however, a series of pivotal works appeared, including *The Sexual Assault of Children and Adolescents* (Burgess et al. 1978), *Sexually Victimized Children* (Finkelhor, 1979), *Betrayal of Innocence* (Forward & Buck, 1979), *The Best-Kept Secret* (Rush, 1980) and *Father-Daughter Incest* (Herman & Hirschman, 1981). By the mid-1980s, Jenkins (1998) notes, a large literature on the effects of abuse and the treatment and rehabilitation of abuse victims had appeared.

Along with these texts came a new species of therapeutic professional: the child-abuse specialist. The child-abuse specialist is expert at detecting signs of abuse and eliciting memories of abuse from victims. These experts have played a vital role in helping thousands of victims of abuse uncover repressed memories and in helping children confess to abuses that hitherto would have remained ignored. Their work has led to a number of celebrated cases against abusive parents and other adult authority figures. Yet because the specialists have adopted a

---

[3] *R. v. Sharpe* [2001] 1 S.C.R. 45 an appeal from a judgement of the British Columbia Court of Appeal (1999), 136 C.C.C. (3d) 97, from a decision of the British Columbia Supreme Court [1999], B.C.J. No 54 (QL).

highly subjective definition of abuse—what feels like abuse is abuse—they have come under fire. Recent studies such as *Victims of Memory* (Pendergrast, 1995) and *Satan's Silence* (Nathan & Snedeker, 1995) have shown how much of the work done by therapists who specialize in false memories is based on a highly spurious set of assumptions.

While experts have been redefining abuse, they have also been redefining the abuser. Since the 1980s a new type of child molester has emerged. Habitual in his crime, he is virtually unstoppable and totally untreatable. Referred to as a "serial pedophile" or "serial molester," this new type of criminal is among the most heinous of deviants. His crimes not only damage children, they also perpetuate the cycle of abuse: the abused will grow up to become abusers. Since the mid-1990s, an even more severe vocabulary has been applied to child molesters, who are now routinely referred to as "predators" (Jenkins, 1997 pp. 191–196).

Psychiatric expertise has played a crucial role in the case against Robin Sharpe, and it is worth examining it in greater detail. The Crown in Mr. Sharpe's trial tendered Dr. Collins, the darling forensic psychiatrist of the Canadian court circuit, as expert witness on sexual deviance to provide evidence of the link between pedophilia, child pornography, and harm to children. Dr. Collins claims to have "appeared as an expert witness probably over 400 times."[4] His expertise in sexual deviance is based on his clinical practice, which prior to 1993 was exclusively devoted to the "assessment and treatment of pedophiles, as well as other sex offenders: rapists, exhibitionists, voyeurs, frotteurs, the whole gamut." Compounded with his clinical experience is Dr. Collins' expertise in profiling the sex offender. Since 1993, Dr. Collins has been working closely with law enforcement agencies in Canada, the U.S., and Europe as consultant in the area of "criminal investigative analysis work." While Dr. Collins is affiliated with the Clark Institute in Toronto, he is also the manager of the Forensic Psychiatry Unit of the Investigation Support Bureau of the Ontario Provincial Police and a consultant to the respective Profiling Units of the Royal Mounted Police and the FBI.

Dr. Collins defines pedophilia as a form of paraphilia, that is to say sexual deviance. While pedophilia refers exclusively to the erotic attraction to pre-pubescent children, Dr. Collins uses the term to cover all erotic attractions to minors. Moreover, following the latest trend in Canadian research on the sex offender, he equates sexual attraction to minors to "child molestation." Dr. Collins' description of pedophilia serves to erase the category hebephilia. This erasure is not uncommon. In their analysis of another recent moral panic over a so-called child porn ring in London, Ontario, Bell and Couture (2000, p. 40) show how the category

---

[4] All the quotes from Dr. Collins are taken from the court transcript of *R. v. Sharpe* [1999] B.C.J. No. 54 (B.C.S.C.).

"pedophile" [was] extended to include sex between adults and youth 15, 16, and 17 years old. The very category *hebephilia* [was] erased. "It means love for hebos…by which [is] understood a young man who ha[s] passed the age of puberty" (Brandt, 1932, p. 414); this is the love of many of the men for the male teenagers in London.

Hebephilia becomes pedophilia, which becomes child molestation: an acceptable sexual practice, in other words, becomes a pathology.

In spite of the fact that he is uncertain of the origin of the "disease" of pedophilia and of the fact that he lacks a clear psychological profile of the pedophile, Dr. Collins asserts that there exists a large gulf separating the pedophile from us. A true pedophile, according to Collins, can be discovered through phallometric testing. Dr. Collins is aware that phallometric testing shows that most "normal" individuals respond positively to images of youth.[5] Yet he is adamant that pedophiles are different. Ironically, one thing that makes them different is their ability to fake test results. Only pedophiles seem to "fake the test" and produce "false negative results." Such faking, Dr. Collins suggests, reveals the manipulative and cunning nature of the pedophile.

The other characteristic setting the pedophile apart from the rest of us is his appalling fantasy life. "Pedophiles are notorious collectors" of what is known in forensic language as "collateral material." "Erotic collateral material" is "anything which serves a sexual purpose." "Anything" is the key word here for virtually any depictions of children will "fuel [the pedophile's] fantasies." For example, Dr. Collins identifies the following as "erotic collateral material:" photographs of fully clothed and partially clothed children, nudist camp brochures depicting nude children, parental and teen magazines, the underwear section of the Sears catalogue, Internet kiddie porn, "writings which have pedophilic themes," "letters [pedophiles] write to other pedophiles," "television shows that [pedophiles] videotape that have child stars," and "movies which [pedophiles] will misinterpret as having pedophilic themes." Erotic collateral material, which the pedophile secretly collects in scrapbooks, is highly valued because aside from arousing him and being used in the "grooming" of children, it also reinforces his "cognitive distortions." The pedophile's two chief cognitive distortions are his belief that children *want* sex with adults and *benefit* from such sex. Dr. Collins deems cognitive distortions,

---

[5] Researchers on sexual behaviour believe that sexual attraction for adolescents is so common in "normal" adults that it should be considered the norm rather than an aberration. See Kilpatrick, (1987). Childhood Sexual Experiences: Problems and Issues in Studying Long-Range Effects, 23 *J. Sex Res.* 173. ; Freund, (1972). The Female Child as a Surrogate Object, 2 *Archives of Sexual Behav.* 119–30; Taylor B. (Ed.) (1981). *Perspectives on Pedophilia*, London: Batsford Academic and Educational; Stanley, Lawrence A. (1989). The Child Porn Myth, *Cardozo Arts and Entertainment* 7, pp. 295-358.

"offence-facilitating beliefs." This expression captures the essence of the danger posed by child pornography: child porn leads to child sexual abuse. Or, as it was dramatically expressed at the Appeal trial, "Child pornography is not only 'crime scene photos' of child sexual abuse and exploitation, but also a criminal tool for such abuse and exploitation. It is a tool of incitement for paedophiles and child molesters, and a tool of seduction for child victims."

Pornography has long been considered to have special power; child pornography, however, seems to have an awesome power at least in the eyes of experts. This is because those who consume child porn are pedophiles. According to Dr. Collins, pedophiles "are driven by fantasies." The danger of child pornography, or for that matter the child underwear section of the Sears catalogue, according to Collins, is that it fuels pedophiles' fantasies and leads to their arousal which in turn creates "the risk that they'll go on and actually carry out their fantasies." The reason why this is the case Dr. Collins explains is that fantasy, the driving force of "sexually deviant acting out…is based on behaviour and we know that behaviour is based on fantasy." Because pedophiles' fantasies lead to acting out, Dr. Collins is adamant that such fantasies stop: "when we, in clinical medicine, treat pedophiles…we don't want them to fantasize at all because those who still fantasize are at risk for sexually assaulting children."

This argument assumes that those who read pornography automatically act on their fantasies. During his cross-examination by Mr. Sharpe, Dr. Collins acknowledges that not all pedophiles aroused by their fantasies will go on acting out:

> **Dr. Collins:** The problem is you have a group who will masturbate and not offend but you have the group who will masturbate, get aroused and then will offend.
>
> **Sharpe:** Well, do they offend after masturbation or do they offend as an alternative or substitute for masturbating?
>
> **Dr. Collins:** There's good research that says that some will do it as an alternative. However, the problem is the ones who masturbate as an alternative to offending sometimes may go on to offend. As I mentioned before in examination in chief, there are probably pedophiles out there who have never offended.

Dr. Collins' admission is crucial, because it shows that there is nothing intrinsically dangerous about child pornography, or nothing more intrinsically dangerous than other types of pornography. From where then does this argument derive that child porn makes one act? It is in part a strange conflation of reader with subject matter. The person reading about childhood becomes a child himself: he cannot distinguish fantasy from reality.

We will return to the question of the pedophile's subjectivity below. Suffice it to say for now that Dr. Collins' definition of the pedophile is typical of how the therapeutic institution approaches this new category of deviant. The pedophile is pathology incarnate, at once invisible and monstrous, child-like and omnipotent. The pedophile not only collects and consumes pornography, he lives it—for he is unable to tell the difference between pornography and life.

As we have shown above, the psychiatric establishment's construction of the pedophile is part of a larger moral panic around pedophilia—a panic that has manifested in the media and in legislation and public policy. In the remainder of this paper, we will examine some reasons why this panic has occurred.

Causes of the Panic

The panic over child sexual abuse is in large part due to the fact that the child has become an icon, one that represents society itself. Jenks suggests that in a present characterized by rapid social transformations, the decline of collective aspirations, and "disenchantment with the sense of purpose previously exercised by the concept of 'progress'" (1997, p.106), people's need for coherence and continuity is heightened. But the traditional sources of identity and integration have lost their ground. People experience the fleeting quality of social relationships, such as marriage, friendship, and class solidarity, which were once meant to bring security, interdependency and trust. Thus they find in the child the last repository of their identity, their last attachment to collective life. Ulrich Beck (1992, p. 118) claims that the child has become the centre of our identity,

> The child is the source of the last remaining, irrevocable, unexchangeable primary relationship. Partners come and go. The child stays. Everything that is desired, but not realizable in the relationship, is directed to the child. With the increasing fragility of the relationship between the sexes, the child acquires a monopoly on practical companionship, on an expression of feelings in a biological give and take that otherwise is becoming increasingly uncommon and doubtful. Here an anachronistic social experience is celebrated and cultivated which has become improbable and longed for precisely because of the individualization process. The excessive affection for children, the 'staging of childhood' which is granted to them—the poor overloved creatures—and the nasty struggle for the children during and after divorces are some symptoms of this. (Quoted in Jenks 1997, p.107)

It follows from this that anything that threatens the child threatens society itself. Child abuse becomes not just one crime among many, but the most grave of transgressions, a threat to what remains of the sacred.

While the current moral panic is due in part to the iconic status of the child, it is also due to our ambivalent attitude towards child sexuality. Children have a sexuality. We have all heard or read the popularized rendition of Freud's thesis about children's libido; we have been informed about Kinsey's finding that children can have orgasms, and many of us have observed first-hand how children are sexually curious and playful. But child sexuality stops where adult sexuality begins. Child sexuality, we have decided, is radically different from the adult's and not to be interfered with. The reason is obvious to us all: children, like their sexuality, are innocent and pure.

Children's innocence and purity, cultural theorist James Kincaid (1992, 1998) reminds us, is a fairly recent invention. In fact, the contemporary idea of the child as a separate conceptual and biological category from the adult, is a product of the nineteenth century. Before the Victorian era, the child was viewed simply as a little adult, a little bit shorter but an adult nonetheless. The writings of Jean Jacques Rousseau and others gave birth to the modern idea of childhood as distinct from and in opposition to adulthood. Rousseau turned the Christian idea of Original sin on its head and proposed in its stead an idealized universe where children were the vessels of purity and truth and only later would become corrupted by society. Following Rousseau's insight Victorian society defined the child in opposition to the corrupted—and obviously sexual—nature of the adult. Purged from all adult characteristics, childhood became an emptiness, an absence or incapacity. So it remains today. "Childhood in our culture" Kincaid tells us, "has come to be largely a coordinate set of *have nots*: the child is that which *does not have*. Its liberty, however much prized, is a negative attribute, as is its innocence and purity" (1998, p. 211). Kincaid further argues that the same characteristics defining the child—innocence and purity—also became firmly attached to the erotic in the nineteenth century, so as to produce the "erotic child,"

> We see children as, among other things, sweet, innocent, vacant, smooth-skinned, spontaneous, and mischievous. We construct the desirable as, among other things, sweet, innocent, vacant, smooth-skinned, spontaneous, and mischievous. There's more to how we see the child, and more to how we construct what is sexually desirable—but not much more. To the extent that we learn to see "the child" and "the erotic" as coincident, we are in trouble. So are the children. (1998, p. 14)

For the last two hundred years, our cultural factories have confused us by instructing us to find sexually desirable that which we do not have, and might even think we have lost, but in fact never had: innocence and purity. The overlap between the child and the erotic has thus turned the precious child into an object of allure and herein lies the danger, for we lust for the child.

The paradoxical eroticization of innocence is something with deep roots in our culture, one that has created a kind of pathogenic double bind. Drawing on Freudian and post-Freudian theory, Kendrick (1995), Mohr (1996) and Kincaid (1992, 1998) identify a "pedophilia of everyday life." They show how various ads such as those of Calvin Klein, the Partnership For A Drug-Free America, Tommy Hilfiger, and Havana Joe Boots among others, and films such as *Kids* by Larry Clark or *Lolita* by Adrian Lyne employ the semiotics of pornography to encourage the pedophilic gaze—thus allowing viewers to indulge in suppressed pedophilic fantasy. While at the same time, they argue, those texts encode signs indicating that such a gaze, such a subject position is the unthinkable itself. Such duplicity, where matters of libido and morality are concerned, these critics argue, is itself akin to a psychopathology and creates a climate in which those explicitly linked to the eroticization of children, such as Sharpe, are doomed to demonization. To acknowledge Sharpe—the pedophile without—to grant him humanity, subjectivity would be to acknowledge the pedophile within. Mohr (1996) explains why pedophiles provoke such terror in us,

> [T]oday's hysteria springs mainly from adults' fear of themselves, but this fear issues from their half-recognition that to admit explicitly, as pornography does, that children are sexy would mean that virtually everyone is a pedophile. In light of the current cultural view that sexual interest in children flows only from, is contingent solely on, the mind of the pedophile, for anyone to admit that he or she has any *frisson* at all from looking at children is necessarily to be branded as deviant. Were society to allow itself to articulate that it does have sexual interests in children...society would have met the enemy and seen that it is us.

CONCLUSION

Sexuality has played a significant role in moral panics in the west, partly because, as Gayle Rubin explains, "sexuality in western societies is so mystified" (1984, p. 297). A growing scholarship has documented how widespread fears and anxieties have often been associated or displaced onto a sexual activity or a sexual minority and quickly channelled into conservative political action and social change. The white slavery hysteria of the 1880s in England led to social purity campaigns that identified the prostitute as the source of vice. This hysteria resulted in legislation that raised the age of consent from 13 to 16, and proscribed prostitution, indecent acts between consenting adult males, and indecent literature and performances (Walkowitz, 1980). The hysteria over sex offenders from the 1930s to the 1950s in the United States led to the passage of sexual psychopath legislation in 29 states, which sought to regulate actions ranging from rape, child molestation, and sex murder through sodomy and indecent exposure (exhibitionism). While the law was rarely used, it created the unfortunate identification between homosexuals and pedophiles (Freedman, 1987; Jenkins, 1998; Sutherland, 1950). According to Rubin, the term "sex offender" eventually became "a code for homosexuals" (1984, p. 269). As we have seen, the hysteria over violence against women and child sexual abuse in the 1980s in Canada led to anti-pornography campaigns. These campaigns resulted, in the case of adult pornography, with the censoring of gay and lesbian sado-masochistic images, and, in the case of child pornography, with the classification of adolescents as "children."[8] Currently, in Canada, we are engulfed in a moral panic around pedophiles.

A stream of melodramatic media stories has fuelled this panic. It has led to the creation of a small industry of surveillance and technology devoted to the protection of children. In the United States, and to a lesser extend in Canada, it has resulted in extremely harsh policies towards dangerous sex offenders. A new genre of expert has been born at the centre of this panic, one who has deemed that the pedophile is many things, just most definitely not one of us.

Finally, this panic has led to threats on the life of Robin Sharpe. Like so many moral panics before it, this one will neither improve society nor alleviate any social ill; like other such panics, it has and will continue to lead to the needless suffering of innocent minorities. It is difficult to see an easy way out of such a situation, but a good place to start would be with a free and open discussion of sexuality, and of children.

CRITICAL THINKING QUESTIONS

1. What are some other issues/people that have become involved in moral panic?
2. What role do such panics play in the functioning of society?
3. The moral panic about child abuse assumes that child pornography is one of the causes of abuse. Discuss the disadvantages of the current law against child pornography. How might the law be modified?
4. Discuss the difficulties involved in defining child abuse. How might child abuse best be defined?
5. Think of several examples of highly visible children or child-like adults in popular culture (from movies and television, for example). Does our society eroticize the child? If so, when and how?
6. Explain how criminal offenders, such as pedophiles, play a crucial role in the formation of emotional solidarity?
7. We end our chapter by calling for a frank discussion of child and teen sexuality. How and where might such a discussion proceed? What would be the obstacles to such a discussion?

---

[8] For an analysis of the public campaigns to criminalize pornography and their effects on sexual minorities see Lacombe, D. (1994). *Blue Politics: Pornography and the Law in the Age of Feminism.* Toronto: University of Toronto Press; Cossman, B. et al. (1997). *Bad Attitude/s on Trial: Pornography, Feminism and the Butler Decision.* Toronto: University of Toronto Press; Blackey, S. & Fuller, J. (1995). *Restricted Entry: Censorship on Trial.* Vancouver: Press Gang Publishers.

SUGGESTED READINGS

Cohen, Stanley (1972). *Folk Devils and Moral Panics: The Creation of the Mods and Rockers*. London: MacGibbon and Kee.

Foucault, Michel (1988). The Dangerous Individual. In Lawrence D. Kritzman (Ed.), *Michel Foucault: Politics, Philosophy, Culture. Interviews and Other Writings 1977-1984.* (pp. 125–151). New York: Routledge.

Jenkins, Philip (1997). *Moral Panic: Changing Concepts of the Child Molester in Modern America*. New Haven: Yale University Press.

Jenks, Chris (1997). *Childhood*. London: Routledge

Kincaid, James (1998). *Erotic Innocence: The Culture of Child Molesting*. Durham: Duke University Press.

Rubin, Gayle (1984). Thinking Sex: Notes for a Radical Theory of the Politics of Sexuality. In Florence Rush, (1980). *The Best Kept Secret: Sexual Abuse of Children*. Englewood N.J.: Prentice-Hall

Simon, Jonathan (1998). *Managing the Monstrous: Sex Offenders and the New Penology Psychology, Public Policy, and Law*. 4 (1/2), 452–467.

WEB LINKS

www.robinsharpe.ca/rvss.htm
> This is Mr. Robin Sharpe's Web site. You will find his own personal account of his journey through the courts, as well as newspaper articles on his case.

www.walnet.org/csis/index.html#top
> This is the Commercial Sex Information Service (CSIS) Web site. It provides analyses, legal cases, government reports and newspaper articles on various aspects concerning commercial sex. You will find articles on the Sharpe case, as well as the first judgement of Justice Shaw from the British Columbia Supreme Court.

CHAPTER 14

Party Girls and Predators: "Date Rape Drugs" and Chronotopes of Gendered Risk

BY DAWN MOORE AND MARIANA VALVERDE

TOOLS FOR STUDYING "MORAL PANICS"

Critical analyses of moral regulation campaigns have usually emphasized the irrational character of the fears tapped into and amplified by these campaigns. Typically, these studies show that there is little or no empirical basis for the fears spread by media and rumours. Being mugged in the street by black youth (Hall et al., 1978), becoming the victim of a psycho serial killer (Jenkins, 1994), having one's child die after eating a Halloween apple with a razor in it (Best & Horiuchi, 1985)—these and other popular sources of worry have been analyzed by "rational" critical sociologists as highly unusual, statistically unlikely events around which moral panics can be successfully constructed insofar as people are in the grip of deep irrational anxieties that can be activated through myth-laden images.

In our study, we want to question the rational/irrational dichotomy that underlies many previous studies of moral regulation, especially studies of moral panics. We do not deny that unconscious, almost primal fears do play some role in the construction and management of social issues. But we argue that it's high time to move beyond the usual "irrationality" explanations of moral campaigns and moral regulation strategies. First of all, there's something that is all too convenient about claiming the irrational fears and unconscious drives of the populace that can only be dispelled by enlightened critical sociologists. Explaining moral panics by reference to the unconscious fears of the populace has the effect of making it seem as if ordinary people—those who read the *Toronto Sun* or watch commercial TV—are more irrational, and thus more primitive, than we cool critical sociologists who study moral panics. This is an elitist and self-serving assumption.

Second, there is a marked weakness in the logic of most such analyses. In studies conducted by such classic "moral panics" writers as Philip Jenkins (1994, 1999), irrational fears are presented not only as emotional fuel for regulatory projects but as actually *explaining* various regimes of moral regulation. This is problematic, in that documenting the presence of "primal" fears does not suffice to prove that the fears *explain* the particular character of the specific social phenomenon being analyzed. Women have often been afraid of walking on their own in urban spaces late at night for fear of being assaulted by unknown men. However, as Judith Walkowitz's analysis of the "Jack the Ripper" case shows, this general fear resulted, in the context of late Victorian London, in specific claims about Jews and/or about corrupt aristocrats (Walkowitz, 1992, chap. 7). Panics about stranger child abduction, to give another example, have occurred in many places. But the "primal" parental fears about such an event that may well be the common denominator among various child-murder panics don't explain why in medieval Europe such fears gave rise to anti-Semitic pogroms, whereas in the 1950s they led to campaigns to stigmatize homosexuals as psychopaths. Particular regimes of moral regulation do not arise out of the primal unconscious of the populace. They are constituted through the coming together of historically specific cultural, political, and legal tools. As Alan Hunt concludes from his overview of various European and North American moral reform projects (Hunt, 1999, pp. 10–14), moral regulation projects are sometimes top-down, social-control projects by which the upper classes seek to regulate the lower, but in our time moral concerns are often strongest in working-class populist circles. Furthermore, although there is an affinity between conservative politics and moral reform campaigns, some progressive movements, mainly feminism, have sometimes used moral-reform discourses to convey their goals. Additionally, while moral panics have sometimes featured law reform as a key objective, in other situations, movements have been based on the view that the state cannot enforce morality through law, and have even denounced compulsory legal measures to enforce morals (as was the case in the British late-nineteenth century campaign against the Contagious Diseases Acts). Analyses of moral panics, we argue, do not greatly advance our understanding of social change when they merely point out that X or Y fear is not justified by crime statistics. Instead, it is more productive to show that anxieties about danger and chaos can be linked to very different political aims and regulatory strategies, depending on the political, cultural, and legal context in which they occur.

Third, emphasizing the "irrational" character of moral panics has the effect of suggesting that solid information and rational analysis are the best, indeed the only remedy, to cure the panics. Studies of public opinion on crime by critical criminologists unfortunately tell us, however, that better statistics and more reliable information do not suffice to alter people's perceptions about the crime rate or about the likelihood of certain crimes. Rational information and aggregate data don't necessarily counteract moral panics. If they did, the American war on drugs would have been over long ago, since there's a mountain of information showing that the harms caused by legal substances (alcohol and cigarettes, mainly) far surpass the harms of illegal drugs. Campaigns to stamp out this or that moral evil, we argue, aren't reducible to or completely explained by popular ignorance and unconscious fears, and will not disappear with the application of solid information. No doubt ignorance and unconscious motives are present in popular discourses; but we believe it is high time to get away from the notion that the populace is in the grip of irrational myths and that only the enlightened philosophers (or critical sociologists) can save the world through Reason and accurate facts.

The case study presented here shows that while the particular object of a campaign—in this case, the "date rape drugs" supposedly used by young men intent on drugging women so as to more easily rape them—may be somewhat fantastical, nevertheless the campaign built around this perhaps questionable object has many real social effects. It allows young people, especially women but also men, to acknowledge, to think through, and to learn to manage risks that are very real, in this case, the gendered risk of sexual assault by men one knows. Telling people that the category "date rape drugs" has no scientific validity (as a traditional "social construction of social problems" approach would do) may be helpful in some contexts.[1] But since this article is meant to sharpen our analytic skills, not to serve as an alternative educational vehicle, our aim here is not to replace one set of factual claims by another. Rather than try to counter one set of facts (the dangers of "date rape drugs") by another set of facts (solid scientific information about drugs and about sexual assault), we turn our attention here to the *format* of the claims made, leaving aside the issue of whether the claims are scientifically valid.

The main analytical innovation that we bring to the study of what could be seen as a classic moral panic—the fears about "date rape drugs" that circulated on university campuses and other youth circles in the last couple of years of the 20th century—is the decision to focus more on the *format* than on the *content* of the claims made by various information providers. Exaggerated or mythical risks are not necessarily presented in anti-scientific sensationalist formats. In paying close attention to "knowledge formats," a concept we adapt from Richard Ericson's "information formats" (Ericson & Haggerty, 1997) we have found that information aimed at youth about the risks of such drugs as Ecstasy and Rohypnol is usually presented in a mixed format that includes scientific data presented in charts and graphics alongside personal stories and moralizing melodramatic narratives. The mixed or hybrid knowledge formats that we document in one area, and that exist in other areas as well, require a mixed analysis, we suggest, and thus a combination of analytical tools from diverse traditions. We have thus here borrowed from the Foucaultian sociologists who study risk management (Castel, 1991;

---

[1] The key study of "club drugs" from the critical sociology, "social construction of social problems" approach is Philip Jenkins' book on designer drugs (Jenkins, 1999).

O'Malley, 1993; O'Malley, 2000; Rose, 1999). We have also borrowed one particular tool from the Russian cultural theorist Mikhail Bakhtin (the notion of "the chronotope"), and a few other techniques from cultural studies and semiotics that can serve to analyze the formatting of communications about risk.

SETTING THE SCENE: THE Y2K RAPE DRUG ALERT

The fears and frissons experienced around the world on New Year's Eve, 1999 were in Toronto exacerbated by the spectre of "date rape drugs". The popular tabloid the *Toronto Sun* featured a front-page headline in 72-point bold type: WOMEN WARNED OF DRUGGED BOOZE, with a subtitle reading: "Coroner, cops tell revellers to beware of date-rape drinks spiked with Ecstasy." Inside the paper, there were two anxiety-producing stories: "Y2K rape drug alert: Women told to watch drinks at New Year bashes" and "Ecstasy kills 8 this year: deadly designer drug popular with rave goers" (1999, December 30, *Toronto Sun*, pp. 1, 5).

Little corroboration for these fears about Ecstasy was available. First of all, Ecstasy (MDMA) is an "upper" and does not put potential rape victims to sleep: indeed, one of the reasons why "ravers" take it is to help them to stay awake while dancing through the night. In addition, consumption of this substance is generally associated with feelings of empathy and love for everyone, not sexual aggression (Eisner, 1994; Jenkins, 1999, chap. 4; Reynolds, 1999). The *Sun*'s claims (and those of Ontario coroner Dr. Jim Cairns, the social crusader-cum-pathologist who was the main source of the news) thus lacked corroboration from other sources, but they gained some credibility indirectly, by their similarity and proximity to other stories about other drugs. Ecstasy is often mentioned in the same breath as Rohypnol and GHB, since they are supposedly consumed by middle-class white youth at dance parties. And these latter drugs can indeed produce stupor or intoxication. The specifics of Ecstasy thus disappeared into the confused grab-bag category of drugs used by youth at clubs.

Stories about "date rape drugs"—plot-driven tales often lacking in scientific information about the particular pharmacological effects of the specific substance consumed—had been circulating, since 1996,[2] in a wide range of educational material on drugs, alcohol, and "party safety" aimed at youth. These include educational pamphlets made and distributed by universities, Web-based information distributed by American drug "education" agencies and by sexual assault centres, and posters and workshops developed by campus safety and alcohol-and-drug

---

[2] The emergence of Rohypnol as a social problem can be dated to a spate of newspaper stories, many in campus papers, about the dangers of the Rohypnol pills being brought back to the U.S. by university students vacationing in Mexico over the March break of 1996.

education officers.[3] These materials will be examined shortly, but it is likely that their combined influence was less than that of an episode of the soap opera aimed at teenagers and undergraduates, *Beverly Hills 90210* and aired to celebrate Valentine's day, 1998.

In the episode, aptly entitled "Cupid's Arrow," Valerie, a not entirely likeable party girl who is known for taking sexual risks, is shown at a nightclub with two men that she knows. One, Noah, plays the trusted friend role and exudes an air of benevolence and protection. The other, Noah's brother, plays the villain role. When Valerie's attention is distracted, Noah's brother slips some white powder into her drink. Much to his chagrin, however, she ends up leaving the club with Noah—who proceeds to have sex with her while she is under the effects of the drug. The next morning, Valerie, obviously educated about "date rape drugs," quickly removes herself to the hospital, where tests reveal the presence of Rohypnol in her blood.

The story's plot is virtually identical to the turn-of-the-century "white slavery" narratives about innocent maidens moving to the city and being inveigled into a life of prostitution through "knock-out drops" or chloroform-containing chocolates (Walkowitz, 1992; Valverde, 1991). But this old plot is here given timeliness as well as plausibility through the fact that the substance featured is a trendy new object classified as a youth "designer" drug (Jenkins, 1999). Perhaps more importantly, the old plot takes place in the trendy, contemporary space of the nightclub. What exactly counts as a club, or as a rave, is never made clear. In the materials produced by educational and law enforcement authorities, the youth dance club merges with raves, frat parties, and other leisure-time spaces inhabited by youth late at night. Party-oriented spaces are often under suspicion, whoever is using them, while nighttime is always associated with heightened safety risks. Thus, the combination of the place (club) and the time (late at night) involved in clubbing and raving is experienced as fraught with both sexual and pharmacological risks.

The Russian cultural theorist Bakhtin's term "chronotope"—the experience of space and time that defines and is constituted by each major literary genre, such as the epic or the novel (Bakhtin, 1981), can be borrowed here to understand how dancing, regarded as totally harmless in some contexts (wedding receptions, say) could suddenly become infused with danger when transplanted into the youth club or rave. An everyday event like finding a ring will, if inserted into the plot of

---

[3] At Canada's largest university, the University of Toronto, safety officers and campus police conducted "date rape drug" workshops for students who live in residence from 1996 to 1999. When asked why this was not being repeated in the 1999–2000 school year, one of the safety educators told us that there had been no reported cases of "date rape drug" use on campus. The educational efforts continue, however: posters about Rohypnol are prominently displayed in many female public bathrooms on campus.

an epic, immediately suggest adventure and battles between good and evil. Similarly, dancing changes in character depending on the chronotope within which it occurs. While the wedding reception is a "chronotope" of family and respectability, the youth party is another kettle of fish altogether—another chronotope. The club/rave choronotope is supercharged with risk because it combines the sexual danger of late night partying and the chemical dangers of "designer drugs".

The literature that informs youth about the risks of partying doesn't really differentiate between expensive, licenced clubs, on the one hand, and the informal raves that sometimes go on in parking lots, abandoned warehouses, or other much less formally organized spaces, on the other, despite the very sharp differences in safety and security between these two kinds of events. Toronto newspaper accounts of the evils of raves and Ecstasy published during 1999 did not point out that most clubs have been and still are heavily regulated through the complex legal machinery of liquor licensing, through which management can be compelled to limit the numbers of patrons, hire private security, provide a certain range of drinks, and so on. Raves that are held in alcohol-free spaces, however, are much more difficult to regulate. A police officer attending a meeting of the Toronto Dance Safety Committee lamented that "those people" (meaning rave promoters) don't bother to ask for a liquor licence, and thus deny police the automatic right of entry granted to them under liquor laws.[4] The lack of regulatory structures for raves could thus be seen as due to the young people's lack of interest in the traditional drug of Saturday night in Canada, namely alcohol. But instead of asking how young people manage to have a good time without drinking, the media focused obsessively on the consumption of new risky substances, mainly Ecstasy, GHB, and Rohypnol.

Instead of looking at how different kinds of spaces can be regulated so as to minimize certain kinds of risks, the voyeuristic accounts found in the media and in the statements of older adults such as Dr. Jim Cairns construct a single chronotope associated with the combination of "date rape drugs" and "raving." Certain sets of events that do not seem threatening most of the time are regarded as probable in that particular chronotope; among them, women are thought to be at great risk of being drugged and raped even by their good friends. This logic is chronotope-specific: the use of drugs for rape purposes is never portrayed as happening in the daytime in coffee shops or in doctor's offices—even though most of the few Canadian reported cases involving sexual assaults of drugged women that have been documented feature doctors and dentists as "the bad guys."[5]

[4] Personal observation, TDSC meeting, Queen West Community Health Centre, March 2000.
[5] A search of relevant cases using Quicklaw came up with four cases, two of which featured physicians, with one featuring a dentist who assaulted a patient after drugging her with anaesthetic.

In the time-space unit created by the silent merging of fears about a time of day (late night), a kind of space (the dance club), and a type of person (youth), all men are constantly suspect. On the Beverly Hills TV show, even the good-guy Noah, who is presented earlier counselling Valerie on relationship issues, can't help himself when he sees her succumbing to the soporific effects of the evil potion: he just has to have sex with/rape her. In this as in virtually every other source of information for youth on "date rape drugs," male sexual aggression is naturalized and taken for granted. Despite everything that is now known about gender role socialization, the date-rape-drugs discourse generally repeats the Ann-Landers-type advice given to young women in the 1950s: women have to protect themselves at all times and take evasive measures because "men just can't help it, dear, remember that."

It thus might seem as if this TV episode is simply a Victorian "maidens in distress" melodrama re-shot in the "cool" setting of electronically created music. But there is a striking difference. Victorian melodrama, and for that matter many popular tales of the 1950s, featured a "white knight" appearing just in the nick of time to save the maiden in question—a gallant gentleman, a police officer, perhaps, or a family member. In the TV show, by contrast, and in all of the educational materials on the gendered risks of club and party going examined for this article, no white knights are portrayed. No irate fathers or wise police officers are shown appearing just in time to rescue the girl. And there are no chaperones, either. The club or rave is an all-youth space. The maidens in distress of the campus scene, therefore, cannot rely on anyone to save them. In line with the safety advice now handed out by authorities from baby furniture manufacturers to police departments, the consumers are presented as totally responsible for ensuring their own security; they must save themselves through constant risk-monitoring and risk reduction.

The particular features of the drugs in question make it difficult, however, to argue that eternal vigilance is the best remedy. The drugs in question are presented as dangerous precisely because they make one feel sleepy or intoxicated: in other words, they impair the ability to calculate and manage risks that is the essential tool of contemporary programmes to "responsibilize" citizens for their own safety. Thus, much is made of the need to mobilize others as protectors. These others are not white knights, however. They are (female) friends. It was of course feminism that first mobilized groups of women against the risks of male violence and made masculine sexual threats calculable (Stanko, 1999). But the students and other young people to which these materials are addressed are never told this, and indeed are never provided with any explicitly feminist images, or feminist risk analysis. So feminist practices—women watching out for one another, phoning one another when they get home, giving rides to other women, and making sure that the friend is actually in the house before driving off—are borrowed, but in such a way as to suppress the feminist origin of this kind of practice. This is a classic instance of "recuperation"—that is, borrowing an idea devised by radical movements to challenge the status quo for the purposes of upholding that very status quo.

The Chronotope of "Club Drugs/Date Rape Drugs"

There are some scientific studies of Ecstasy and its effects, particularly its effects on memory; but it is doubtful that any drug authority except Ontario deputy coroner Dr. Jim Cairns thinks of Ecstasy as a "date rape drug". Searching for information on "date rape drugs" using Internet search engines produces a mix of medical and popular facts and tales mainly featuring two drugs: Rohypnol, a sleeping pill manufactured by the giant Swiss firm Hoffman-La Roche and still legal in places like Mexico and Switzerland, and GHB, an ambiguous non-industrially produced substance that used to be sold in North American health food stores as a body-building and feel-good supplement. Both of these are, in the U.S. and Canada and in many other countries, legally controlled that even medical prescription is forbidden. Although there are no figures on the number of sexual assaults in which these drugs have been used, these two substances are enveloped in tales such as the ones just described. They are thus "date rape drugs" in the North American imagination, though not in many other countries.

Just how a substance gets classified as a date rape drug is not clear. A few American Web sites recognize that alcohol is the original date rape drug: but this insight remains very marginal. This is probably because it is in conflict with North American "war on drugs" priorities, and also because focusing on alcohol would mean that the middle-age adults might have to question their own leisure time pursuits. How does law identify "date rape drugs"? The 1996 American federal Drug Induced Rape Prevention and Punishment Act criminalizes "giving a controlled substance to anyone without their knowledge with the intent of committing a violent crime."[6] Legal tranquilizers, and for that matter alcohol, are controlled, but all the discussions around this Act and around "date rape drug" issues in the U.S. have highlighted illegal drugs only.

A couple of years after this U.S. federal law was passed, around 1998–99, the term "club drugs" suddenly became popular, and to some extent merged with "date rape drugs." The obvious difficulties of legally or chemically identifying

---

[6] A search of American newspapers to ascertain how the public was informed about "date rape drugs" through coverage of this Act's passage revealed that few sources acknowledged that statutes already existed under which one could have prosecuted sexual assaults facilitated by administering a noxious substance. The *LA Daily News* is typical: "For the first time, using a drug as a weapon is illegal under the new law. Supporters argue that dropping a pill in someone's drink is just as nefarious as putting a knife to her throat." *(LA Daily News,* 1996, October 14, p. N12.)

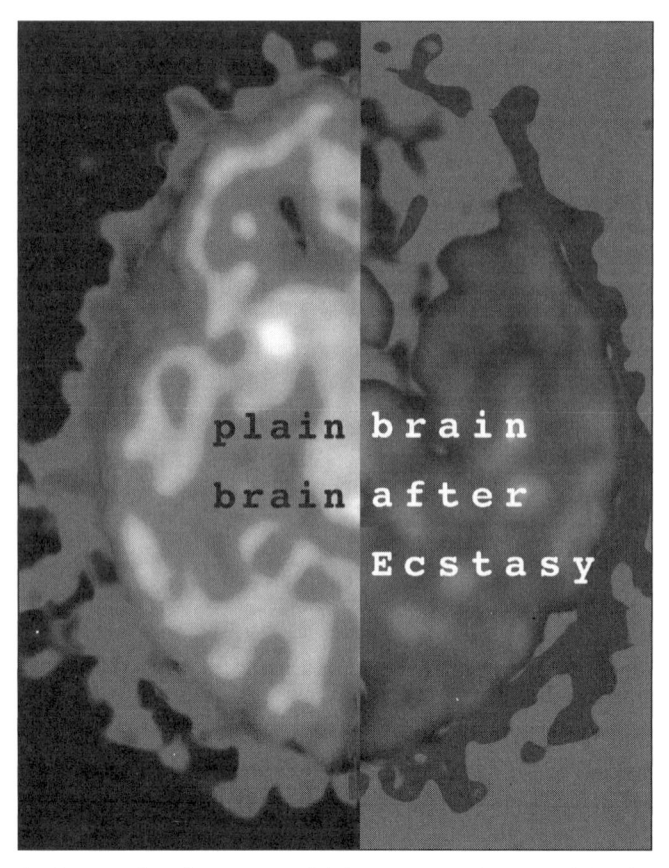

An image taken from <www.clubdrugs.org>, a site created by the U.S. National Institute on Drug Abuse in order to educate users to the dangers of drug abuse.

"date rape drugs" were circumvented by the simple technique of proceeding instead to talk about "club drugs"—a slippage between substances facilitated by the fact that these ill-defined pills and liquids are thought to pervade the same sort of chronotope, namely the weekend youth party. The club was tainted with the bad pre-existing reputation of "date rape drugs," and the hard to pin down "date rape drugs" were in turn given some kind of empirical status by being said to be those that circulate in clubs and raves.

More specifically, Rohypnol and GHB, the main "date rape drugs" discussed in news stories in 1996, became the headliners in the new classification—disseminated around the world by the large, powerful, and multiply linked Web sites of the Drug Enforcement Administration (DEA) and the National Institute for Drug Abuse (NIDA)—of "club drugs." NIDA recently designed a separate Web page entitled "Clubdrugs.org," whose URL, as often happens with drug-education material aimed at American youth, does not reveal its official provenance. This Web site, though fairly new, already has links to many non-government sites. The Web page attempts to fix the meaning of several substances (including Ecstasy, GHB, and Rohypnol) through such techniques as a lurid-colour picture of a "plain brain" compared to an apparently rotting "brain after Ecstasy" <www.clubdrugs.org>.

The first thing to note about these pictures is that we don't actually see brains. We see pictures of brain sections examined through a microscope whose photographic images have been taken after some kind of dye has been injected so as to make certain regions of the brain more visible. If we were to look directly at a brain (say, in an autopsy) we would not see bright red and yellow patches. Second, the average person cannot tell just what is significant about the differences between the two sets of coloured patches. It's like looking at a sonogram of a ten-week fetus: we have to take the technician's word for it that "this" is the baby's head while "that" is an insignificant dark patch. Most of us don't know whether the brain of "drug-free" people is always identical to what we are being shown here under the label "plain." We have to trust experts that the differences between the two pictures amount to drug-induced brain damage.

Pictures, however, carry the implicit promise that we are seeing the scientific truth with our own eyes, unaided by expert interpretations. As Bruno Latour has explained in his analysis of the rhetoric of science, even when we don't know what the squiggles or dark patches or coloured patches or graph lines mean, we all somehow find it more convincing to be shown a picture than to be told that something is true (Latour, 1987, p. 48 ff). The scientist can say to the skeptical lay person, "here, if you don't believe me, look with your own eyes." We all tend to find images more persuasive than words—even when we know or suspect that the images have been digitally or chemically "enhanced." And in the case of the "plain brain," the Web designers know very well that we will (a) think that we are actually seeing the truth, rather than being told something by an expert; and that (b) we will automatically assume that any difference from the picture labelled "plain brain" will be read as "brain damage."

This is the effect of the formats used to teach us science in textbooks as well as in the sort of drawings found inside tampon packages: we are all trained to see pictures of bodies that represent not particular individuals but the "ideal" body—or the "plain" brain. Looking at the picture, we will thus assume that any deviation from the "plain" norm amounts to abnormality—even though all we really see are bits of colour whose meaning and significance is quite beyond us. Scientifically produced images—photos taken through a microscope of brain tissue sections with dye injected in them—are thus here used in such a way that we go away from our computer thinking that we have seen the risks of Ecstasy for ourselves, with our own eyes. Scientific formats can thus be used very effectively to reinforce and yet conceal the American law enforcement authorities that run the "clubdrugs" Web site. Science, far from being the cure for moral panics, is often the chosen vehicle of today's moral panics.[7]

---

[7] A relevant example is one of the new illustrations on Canadian cigarette packages. While some of the compulsorily printed pictures use dramatic, non-scientific formats (a column of ash drooping off a lit cigarette represents impotence, for instance), one of the pictures simply shows a graph comparing how many people die from smoking each year compared to the size of various towns in Canada.

In sharp contrast to the amorphous catch-all category of "club drugs" found in official sources, the Web sites, magazines, and books for and by drug users tend to be quite specific. Commonly, authors denigrate certain substances as "truly addictive", while praising their favourite poison as a source of inner growth and enlightenment that the wise consumer can use without harm.[8] Given that "club drugs" does not function as a common term for drug connoisseurs, then, what are the governance effects of this new category? The governance effects of "club drugs" could be regarded as illustrating some features of what we might call, after Jonathan Simon's "governing through crime" (Simon, 1997), governing through chronotope (Bakhtin, 1981).

Governing through chronotope works as follows. First, a space/time unit (the club, the campus party) is used to unify and give an identity to otherwise heterogeneous and/or ill-defined risks, including pharmacological risks. But then (as municipal authorities seeking to govern raves know) it turns out to be as difficult to legally define a mini-chronotope like a "rave" as it is to differentiate "club drugs" from other drugs. In Toronto, the authorities represented on the "Toronto Dance Safety Committee" active in 1998–99 operated with a negative definition of a rave: a large party that does not hold a liquor licence, and hence is not subject to closing hours or other regulatory powers granted to police and liquor inspectors by licencing laws.[9]

Similarly, an earlier British attempt to govern raves by specifying the particular beat of the music played in them was quickly defeated through the proliferation of somewhat different beats and kinds of music. Trying to define a kind of music is not a common strategy, however, probably because police officers and municipal politicians are not, as a group, consumers of contemporary music. The elusive rave is more often defined, in journalistic as well as in official discourse, by reference to a supposed group preference for Ecstasy—hence the title of Simon Reynolds' thoughtful account of the rise and fall of British and U.S. raves, *Generation Ecstasy*. But the social and even the chemical meaning of Ecstasy is in turn often defined by the space of its consumption (its chronotope), not by its pharmacology. A lengthy, multi-illustrated feature article in Canada's largest circulation daily, the *Toronto Star* (1999, November 20, pp. A1, A30) entitled "Agonizing Ecstasy" purported to be "about" the pleasures and dangers of Ecstasy the drug, but was in fact a journalistic account of raves and rave culture, as if the drug had no history or no current use outside of youthful raves.

The circular argument is as follows, then. The space/time is assumed to define the substances consumed in it, but simultaneously, substances define the chronotope.

---

[8] See Lenson 1995, which denounces heroin and cocaine while singing the praises of marihuana, and more generally, Jay 1998.

[9] Personal observation, meeting of the Toronto Dance Safety Committee, February 19, 2000.

The problem chronotope of the rave/club/campus party, while obviously full of pleasures, is thought to be simultaneously occupied by the risks of Rohypnol and GHB. Ecstasy—which used to be consumed primarily in psychotherapy sessions (Eisen, 1994)—has somehow become wholly embedded, culturally if not in fact, in the club. Thus, it has become a "date rape drug," despite its unsuitable chemical properties. The American war-on-drugs agency, National Institute on Drug Abuse, puts Ecstasy in the same category as Rohypnol—in the same social space (the club) and in the same quasi-medical space (the list of club drugs).

Club drugs are being used by young adults at all-night dance parties such as "raves" or "trances," dance clubs, and bars. MDMA (Ecstasy), GHB, Rohypnol, ketamin, methamphetamine, and LSD are some of the club or party drugs gaining popularity. NIDA-supported research has shown that use of club drugs can cause serious health problems and, in some cases, even death….No club drug is benign <www.clubdrugs.org>.

The much-publicized public-order risks of all-night raves are thus seamlessly merged with the physiological risks associated with old-fashioned psychedelics such as LSD, and the harms caused by substances that were the subjects of earlier panics, such as amphetamines. Ecstasy becomes guilty by association through the construction of a hybrid risk amalgam whose features are circularly defined. The *Toronto Sun* Y2K stories referred to above did not claim to have uncovered any rapes facilitated by Ecstasy, but somehow, from a story about some overzealous ravers dehydrating after taking Ecstasy, either the Ontario coroner Dr. Jim Cairns or the *Sun's* headline writer (it is unclear) concluded that the eight or nine deaths attributed to Ecstasy[10] warranted a warning about "drugged booze" at New Year's eve parties.[11] Thus, starting with a highly indeterminate space/time unit (the rave, or even vaguer, the party) and with an amorphous set of substances (date rape drugs, club drugs), and placing them in a circular relationship to one another, we end up with a conglomerate of risks of truly frightening proportions.

---

[10] Epidemiological practice allows coroners and other medical personnel investigating "cause of death" to inflate the risk of drugs by allowing them to put down as "drug *related* deaths" any deaths in which, say, someone consumed a drug and then drove into a tree, regardless of whether the drug actually caused them to lose control of the car. News reports about drugs regularly speak about drug *related* deaths as "deaths *caused* by drugs".

[11] As this article went to press (May 2000), Dr Cairns presided over a much-publicized inquest into an Ecstasy death that has become a sort of royal commission into raves. The Toronto Dance Safety Committee's counsel argued (through cross-examination of witnesses) that many drug-related deaths do not take place at raves, thus trying to break the circular relation between chronotopes and risks that we document here—not very successfully, since Toronto City Council voted to ban raves from city-owned spaces.

Studies, for example, by radical geographers, have investigated how youth are constituted and governed through the stigmatization of certain *spaces*: but we would argue that the club of "clubdrug.org" is best regarded not as a space but as a chronotope, since these deviant spaces would not be considered drug ridden or risky if visited at lunchtime. It is the combination of the space (club rather than restaurant) and time (after licencing hours) that creates the risky chronotope of the club/rave—which is then used to define and give content to the otherwise terminally vague phrase "club drugs."

It is crucial to our argument to note that virtually all the educational pamphlets and Web sites examined for this article featured *both* melodramatic tales *and* information derived from scientific sources and/or put in scientific-looking formats such as bar graphs. Most Web sites concerning "club drugs" aimed at youth, generated primarily by universities and, in the U.S., by drug-education agencies, contain a photograph of a "typical," anonymous scene—often featuring a glass of beer being prospectively gazed at by a dark (but always white) male while the woman whose glass it is talks or dances.[12] They also contain medical information, typically something along these lines:

Rohypnol (flunitrazepam) is a drug that is approved or sold in other countries as a sleeping aid...sedative effects are felt within 20 to 30 minutes....When mixed with alcohol, narcotics, or other central nervous system depressants, abuse can be lethal ("Rohypnol update," <www.connsacs.org/rohypnol.html>).

Borrowing the War on Drugs visual technique of presenting images of genuine drugs and accompanying paraphernalia (photos of needles and spoons accompanying anti-heroin materials or representations of cannabis plants accompanying anti-marijuana texts), Web sites also feature photographs of the actual pill. It is common to find pictures of "fake" Rohypnol (street name, Roofies) as well as images of the original legal drug in its bubble package, a wrapping that makes it look like an antihistamine or headache pill.[13] To complement the images and stories,

---

[12] A white short-haired man wearing a tie is portrayed dropping a pill into a woman's beer while she plays billiards in a picture reproduced in a number of Web sites, for instance <www.canoe.ca/CNEWSLifeArchive/981119_daterape.html>. The "nice well-dressed guy' image is in keeping with educational programs around "date rape", which teach women to beware of the very men who are considered socially acceptable "dates".

[13] A photo of a pile of white pills is accompanied by the following text: "To the eye they look as innocent as aspirin, but this drug has all the power of a knock-out punch. This is Rohypnol, or roofies..." This was the beginning of a news story about two teenage Virginia girls who went to a party and woke up at 5 a.m. the next morning not knowing what had happened the night before. The girls claimed to not have consumed alcohol, and the police concluded that Rohypnol had been slipped into their soft drinks though no tests were done to confirm this. The strong cultural stigma attached to girls drinking alcohol in the Southern United States might be thought to provide a major incentive to blame "date rape drugs" for unconsciousness, but this hypothesis is never explored in any of the dozens of news reports consulted.

the leaflets and the Web pages generally have some quantified information, usually in a graph form, such as "numbers of pills seized by U.S. Customs at the border."[14] Finally, most of the pamphlets and Web sites end with a list of "safety tips" (called "risk reduction measures" only in the most highbrow of Web sites).

The chronotope of "date rape drugs," then, is characterized by a highly mixed knowledge format.[15] Medical information; Victorian melodrama; girls-just-wanna-have-fun female group hedonism; War-on-Drugs, "scared straight" images of the nasty tools of a nasty business (used needles, etc.); posed photographs with professional models; graphs providing quantitative information; and community-police-type lists of "safety tips." When combined, these constitute a powerful risk information hybrid, which appeals simultaneously to virtually every dimension of a female student's experience and desire—appealing as much to her scientific curiosity as to her irrational fears.

Something that was not mentioned in any of the information sources we examined is the fact that the one Toronto rapist who did go around drugging and raping hundreds of victims in recent years used the legal tranquilizer Halcion, not one of the "club drugs". This massive crime against women received very little news coverage, and is not mentioned in any of the flyers and Web pages we examined. This corroborates our analysis of "date rape drugs": the Halcion rapist's activities could not be incorporated into any currently circulating risk narrative because there was no "War" on legal tranquillizers prescribed to adults, so they remained unique tales without broader cultural resonance.[16]

The date rape drug chronotope is filled with urban legends about unnamed women being raped somewhere else by unnamed men.[17] But it is not a strictly populist, "folk" space: it is a hybrid space of governance, in which not always exaggerated medical and social information about risks circulates alongside many other bits of texts, from feminist advice on sexual assault to lurid tales of sexual risk. The analysis

---

[14] The same combination of formats was employed in a lengthy feature piece, "Agonizing over Ecstasy", in Canada's largest circulation paper, the *Toronto Star* (1999, November 20, pp. A1 & A30). A colour photograph of three different versions of Ecstasy pills available locally was featured in the front page, while the back-page continuation featured both a scientific-looking graph showing a marked increase in "numbers of hits" and two psychedelic-looking colour photographs.

[15] We owe the phrase "knowledge formats" to Ericson & Haggerty, 1997.

[16] Interview with a Toronto Police sergeant from the sexual assault squad (1999, December); D. Brazao, "Man gets 16 years for forcing sex on drugged women" (*Toronto Star,* 1992, December 22, p. A1); D. Brazao, "Man serving jail term faces 274 new charges: victims assaulted by man posing as talent scout, police say" (*Toronto Star*, 1994, March 1, p. A2).

[17] A presentation on this topic by both authors in an undergraduate criminology class elicited tales about women students, always at some other university, who were victims of date rape drugs. At the same time, interviews with five well-placed safety, health, and student-service personnel at our own (very large) university failed to uncover a single documented case of "date rape drug" use.

presented here of how a particular danger is constructed through the simultaneous use of scientific and melodramatic information formats may be of wider significance.

"The Perfect Crime in a Pill": De-Gendering Sexual Assault By Personifying Drugs

The rave space, the space of after-hours dancing and "club drugs," is not presented as gendered either in the War on Drugs literature or in pro-drug or pro-rave writings. The accounts consulted present it as a post-feminist space in which "youth" is the main demographic factor, with "race" a distant second; the ravers argue about whether London's raves achieved a racial integration not found in football clubs, for instance (Reynolds, 1999, p. 170). Gender is largely, even wholly, invisible. But gender is nevertheless present, particularly when "date rape drugs" rather than "club drugs" are the discursive object at hand. The disjunction between text and photographs is telling. While the text rarely mentions gender or even "women," preferring to speak about "students," "partying," "youth," etc., the photographs are perfect pictures of traditional heterosexuality, featuring a young, pretty, always white woman engaged in hedonistic activity while an equally young and white male lurks menacingly in the background. Some photographs have no visible male, showing only a hand throwing something into a drink, thus completely degendering the assailant: but this is not a counter-example, since the visual context necessitates reading the detached hand as male.

A good example of this odd combination of highly gendered images and degendered texts is the educational video entitled "Rohypnol," made by the Niagara Region Police and shown on Canadian campuses in 1998–99. This shows stereotypically gendered students (all the women have long hair, all the men have short hair) while the script studiously avoids uttering the word "women," much less "gender." At one point in the video, the pretty long-haired female narrator turns to the camera with a sudden warning: "This means you too, guys!"[18] an attempt to address and include male viewers that only manages to reveal that the video is indeed aimed at women only, for if it were aimed at both sexes and concerned with potential homosexual as well as heterosexual rape one would hardly need to add the special warning for men. A university official in charge of student services corroborated this analysis, admitting in an interview that although the educational materials are aimed at "students" in general, the real target audience is women only, and the only risk that is being managed is that of heterosexual rape.[19]

[18] "Rohypnol" video available from the Brock University campus police (St. Catharines, Ont.)
[19] Interviews with a college dean of students, the campus safety officer, a campus community health educator, and two members of the city police's sexual assault squad were carried out to determine how these deliverers of risk information thought about their work. The interviews were granted on condition of anonymity.

The Rohypnol video and similar materials manage to address sexual violence without mentioning gender inequality through a curious technique: the intention to commit the crime is displaced from the man to the drug. The personification of problem substances is not unusual: a noted example of this is Jack London's famous memoir of alcohol and working-class masculinity, *John Barleycorn* (London, 1913), in which whisky ("John Barleycorn") is one of the two main characters, along with Jack London. But in the "club drugs" context, the personification of a chemical has the specific effect of degendering not only the specific criminal act but even the very desire to assault women. The criminal and sexist intent is not in the man, it is in the pill. A victim who testified before the U.S. Congress hearings on the date-rape-drug bill of 1996 stated that "the drug [not the criminal] destroyed my life," adding "it's the perfect crime in a pill."[20] This exact phrasing was reproduced in the show about date rape drugs put on by Oprah Winfrey: Oprah herself said that GHB was "the perfect crime in a pill" (cited in Jenkins, 1999, p. 167).

The displacement of moral properties from assailants to problem substances—from people to objects—is also achieved through the constant use of adjectives such as "odourless," "colourless," "tasteless," and "deceptive" to describe the drugs. It is as if the substances are themselves devious. In fact, Hoffman-LaRoche added a blue dye to Rohypnol in response to the fears about the invisibility and deviousness of the pill; but this seems to have had no effect on the way in which the drugs are described.[21]

The relocation of violent desires to the pill effects a recuperation of feminist activities around sexual assault that acknowledges rape but diverts attention away from gender: it is the pill, after all, that is criminal, not men. This displacement had the effect of pleasing feminists and law-and-order constituencies simultaneously—a task that the Clinton re-election campaign, during which the 1996 Act was passed, was keen to achieve, since it was necessary to consolidate the feminist support that has traditionally gone to the Democrats while reassuring middle America that Clinton was not soft on crime. While official acts such as the 1996 federal U.S. "date rape drug" act could be electorally "sold" to women voters as overdue recognitions of the longstanding feminist point that most abuse of women is committed by partners and acquaintances, the educational materials provided by official government sources all reproduce Victorian-melodrama pictures of pretty maidens and lecherous men. And in keeping with the gothic-novel myth of free-floating male evil, nobody thinks of addressing men in the educational

---

[20] Lisa Celestin, quoted in "Legislation targets drug used in date rapes", (*LA Times*, 1996, July 17, p. 14).
[21] Admittedly, much of what gets sold in North America as "Roofies" is not Swiss-made Rohypnol but rather domestically produced facsimiles, and it seems that these knock-offs are still white and leave little or no residue when dissolved in drinks.

materials and telling them to watch what their male friends do when out for the evening. Men are presented as immovable objects, as perpetual sources of risk. On their part, the youthful maidens are wholly "responsibilized" (O'Malley, 1996) for their own risks. The information disseminated by sexual assault centres does mention the broader issues of gender power, and, tellingly, it tends to eschew posed photographs in favour of "rational" picture-less texts: but we have thus far found no explicit feminist critique of the U.S. government's discourse on "date rape drugs."

"TRUSTED FRIENDS": MOBILIZING THE (HETEROSEXUAL) FEMALE COLLECTIVITY TO MONITOR RISKS

The pictures of threatening pills surreptitiously placed into drinks by de-gendered hands are, as one would expect, always followed by advice on how to prevent the risk just pictured. The advice given is quite diverse: police sources tend to be more pessimistic about all pleasure seeking, seeing criminogenic opportunities everywhere, while university and sexual assault-centre based sources tend to take a harm reduction approach. Instead of telling women to not go out, they tend to say, "this is what you should do when you go to a party." The information with which young women are to arm themselves when going out to the field of the club or the date is generally presented in a format that is ubiquitous these days: the "list of handy tips."

The risk management techniques presented to teenagers and undergraduates in the low-tech, folksy format of "tips" are unusual in that they rely on and construct a collective. Since date rape drugs are regarded as impairing and even abolishing the young women's ability to calculate, individual responsibilization and risk management is in this case of limited utility. Instead, a collective of "trusted friends" (who are rarely explicitly feminized, but whose gender is necessarily, structurally feminine) needs to be mobilized. Such mobilization of female networks is a plausible strategy because it can draw on existing relations of teenage and undergraduate female friendship. But the gendered nature of these existing friendship networks is rarely, if ever, explicitly acknowledged, as if for fear of appearing to sound feminist. The University of Alberta Web site encourages partiers to "stay in large groups of people," a piece of advice that, given the surrounding description of male lechery, seems to presuppose that the "people" who provide safety are mainly or wholly female. The University of Toronto's campus police "Rohypnol" pamphlet, on its part, ends with a section entitled "Protect yourself and your friends" which typically addresses an obviously female reader without actually naming her gender.

Invoking "trusted friends" as the solution was not invented in the context of date-rape-drugs. Alcohol education seminars for undergraduates often advise women to make pacts with each other before they go out to the effect that they will not leave the bar with anyone except the friends with whom they went there (Moore, 2000). This advice underlines the persistence of old-fashioned gender dangers, since one can hardly imagine male undergraduates being addressed in that way. But there are reasons why the "date rape drug/ club drug" chronotope is a fertile ground for the sort of female network envisaged by the educational projects examined here, reasons rooted in the nature of the (perceived) risks of these particular substances/ behaviours.

The tales about Rohypnol and GHB told in the literature emphasize the grave risks of losing both one's ability to plan and calculate *and* one's ability to remember events. Nowhere is there an explanation of why exactly it is so much worse to be raped and not remember it than to be raped while fully conscious: it is simply assumed, in all the sources examined, that this is indeed the case. This is not new: one finds this assumption in the trite Victorian plot device of having a villain slip opium into someone's drink, as well as in the anxieties generated by "multiple personality disorder" (Hacking, 1995). There are no doubt psychoanalytic explanations of the great fear that seems to attach to doing something, or having something done to one, without remembering afterwards or without willing it. But, to pursue a more sociological line of inquiry, fears of memory and consciousness loss called up by "date rape drugs"—whatever they might have meant in earlier panics about opiates, about "knock out drops" or about "Mickey Finns"—have a particular significance in our own day because they represent the worst possible risk, the risk of losing the calculating ability that is necessary for governing oneself autonomously and monitoring one's own risks. We are constantly told to watch our for our own investments because we can't trust governments to provide old age pensions; we are exhorted by police to burglar-proof our houses and street-proof our kids because we can't rely on police to save us from crime; everywhere we look, we are told that we are responsible for ensuring our own safety. It is thus a shock to the system to be also told that a particular substance will render us incapable of exercising vigilance.

The collective risk-monitoring strategies suggested for addressing this problem of loss of individual capacity to reason and calculate, while highly dependent on actually existing gender relations, are presented in genderless language. Here's one very typical list of "what to do" tips,

> When going to a bar, party, or social event, never go alone. Be with a friend whom you trust.
>
> Watch for unusual behaviour in your friends. If you suspect they are not acting like themselves, INTERVENE! Protect your friends from harm. The risks of having your friends angry with you are minimal compared to the harm they may be facing.

> Never accept a drink from anyone except the bartender or a trusted friend. If someone you don't trust offers to buy you a drink, have someone you do trust accompany them...
>
> Never leave your drink unattended.
>
> Never leave a bar or club with someone you have just met, especially if you are feeling intoxicated."[22]

That the "trusted friends" are always and necessarily female seems to go without saying. That these trusted friends are heterosexual as well as female is also assumed. Women are never suspected of wanting to seduce other women—while men are universally portrayed as posing a sexual risk to women. Thus, compulsory heterosexuality is reinscribed even as the stories and pictures tell tales, which one would think, would make young women eschew all heterosexual contact, for no man is truly safe. Similarly, the "trusted friends" technologies for collective risk management, while drawing on feminist techniques for "taking back the night" and protecting one another so as to be able to circulate through public space without the aid of a male knight, nevertheless suppresses the feminist source of this type of technology for collectively managing risks.

While the objective of the old feminist techniques of watching out for one's sisters was to constitute something like "a women's community," in which women would be free to choose heterosexuality precisely because they no longer needed men to escort them or to provide for them, the pamphlets in question never utter the word "community," despite the obvious similarities between the "tips" provided to women partiers and those given to home owners in community-policing literature. Young women are supposed to be "trusted friends"—but only for the purposes of heterosexual flirting and partying. They are not presented as spending their non-party time with other women, building community: they are, after all, universally heterosexual, however fraught the path to Mr. Right might be. The women's safety network is thus presented as specific to the chronotope of partying—not surprisingly, perhaps, since the risks of drugs and sexual assault are also presented as contained within the club/rave/frat party chronotope. Thus, both the risks and the measures to monitor and minimize risks reinscribe conventional heterosexuality even while acknowledging—through tales about nice guys slipping pills into girls' drinks—that perhaps it is the chronotope of conventional heterosexuality, not that of the club, that is truly risky.

---

[22] Pamphlet entitled "Rohypnol", produced by the University of Toronto campus police. The McMaster University Web site contains many of the same tips: "never go to a bar alone but with a [female] friend you trust"; "never leave your drink unattended"; "be suspicious of people who handle your drink or insist you accept a drink from them", and, somewhat contradictorily, "if YOU feel intoxicated with your first drink, ask for help."

CONCLUSIONS

The analysis of the knowledge formats employed to "educate" young people about "club drugs" and "date rape drugs" demonstrates that the fears attaching to substances such as Rohypnol are not mere eruptions of irrational primal anxieties. The current campaigns around youth party drugs, especially "date rape drugs" enable both authorities and ordinary people to think through important issues: sexual assault, especially at the hands of people one knows, and the potential harm of ingesting substances that, unlike alcohol, are unfamiliar to most Canadians. Both of these are by no means fictional dangers. Rape exists; overdoses exist. But it was not the purpose of this article to give empirical evidence to show that being drugged and raped is more likely to happen at home or in the doctor's office than at a rave, although such empirical evidence is probably available. Unlike many other critical analyses debunking moral panics, our analysis does not seek to replace one set of factual claims by another (more "rational") set of claims. We simply want to invite readers to sharpen their analytical skills so that, when confronted with educational materials about any kind of risk, they can critically analyze not only what is being said (the content or message) but also the significance of the "medium," particularly the format or formats chosen.

Sources of risk information available to youth often use "mixed" formats: a graph showing numerical information printed in a box beside a true-confessions personal tale, in turn juxtaposed with a scientific-looking picture and an anonymously authored list of "handy tips" to avoid the danger in question. Now that the Internet and other technological developments have made fancy visual presentations easily available, we have to have particularly sharp decoding skills if we want to be informed consumers of risk information. Examining both the format and the content, we have seen here that the date-rape-drugs materials made available to Canadian youth are neither all scientific nor consistently moralistic. Rather, they deploy both melodramatic, journalistic-style tales and scientific pictures and facts. The scientific pictures, however, do not always succeed in rationally persuading the viewer through scientific reasoning (as we saw in the example of the "plain brain" image). And the old-fashioned melodramatic tales are also deployed in unpredictable ways. A melodramatic tale can be used to convey a scientific message, just as a scientific-looking picture can be used to convey a moral tale about male sexual evil. And both the old risks of sexual victimization and the new risks attaching to particular kinds of drugs are presented not individually but as features of a homogeneous chronotope—the rave/club. We end here with the suggestion that now that it is no longer considered appropriate to target particular kinds of people as scapegoats for this or that social evil, as it was in the past, "governing through chronotope" may become more popular.

ACKNOWLEDGEMENTS

This essay is a revised version of an earlier published paper, "Maidens at risk: date rape drugs and hybrid risk knowledges," in *Economy and Society* Vol. 29 No. 4 (November 2000). We thank the journal editors for permission to use some of that text.

In addition, we acknowledge the advice and support given by our colleagues in and around the Centre of Criminology, University of Toronto, especially Kelly Hannah-Moffatt, Joe Hermer, Rosemary Gartner, Ron Levi, Paddy Stamp, and Maximo Sozzo, and by the Toronto History of the Present Network. Special thanks to Pat O'Malley.

CRITICAL THINKING QUESTIONS

1. Do you think there is evidence to suggest that the dangers to individuals and to the community of illegal drugs are greater than the dangers of legal drugs (nicotine, caffeine, alcohol)?
2. How do educational efforts around youth-oriented illegal drugs compare to educational efforts around legal drugs consumed by adults?
3. Can you think of other campaigns or moral panics in which young men's sexuality has been targeted?
4. How do different information formats [see glossary] shape the message of a news story or an educational Web page?
5. Surf the Net and collect some urban legends (that is, non-official and usually anonymous tales about mishaps and risks that circulate by word of mouth or by forwarding emails). If you can't find many, ask your friends and relatives to tell you their favourite urban legend. Think about how such stories differ from official accounts (e.g., scientific articles, textbooks, serious media stories), in both format and content.
6. Having collected some urban legends, from the Internet or from your friends, count to see how many of them involve innocent young women in sexually compromising situations. Count to see how many of them involve invisible powders or innocuous-looking pills whose dangers are not immediately apparent. What do you make of your results?
7. Do you think that people actually believe urban legends that they recount or reproduce? If not, why do you think they pass them on?

SUGGESTED READINGS

Best, J. & Horiuchi, G.T. (1985) The razor blade in the apple: the social construction of an urban legend. In R. Ericson, (Ed.) (1995) *Crime and the Media*. Dartmouth: Aldershot.

A pioneering analysis of one of the most persistent urban legends of North American life, this article shows that it was not the media but rather word-of-mouth communication that has kept the fear of razor blades in Halloween apples alive.

Douglas, M. (1992) *Risk and blame: essays in cultural theory*. New York: Routledge.
A broad-ranging account of the ways in which modern-day "risk" analysis is permeated by cultural values and myths, by one of the world's most influential cultural anthropologists.

Ericson, R., & Haggerty, K. (1997). *Policing the risk society*. Toronto: University of Toronto Press.
Richard Ericson, one of Canada's top criminologists, presents a thoroughly documented argument about the way in which police forces today are less concerned to police individual deviants, devoting their time instead to generating information for other institutions and producing risk analyses.

Jenkins, P. (1999). *Synthetic panics: the symbolic politics of designer drugs*. New York: New York University Press.
A study firmly located in the "moral panics" tradition, of the emergence of "designer drugs" as a subject for concern in the United States. Includes a chapter on Ecstasy.

O'Malley, P. (1996). Risk and responsibility. In A. Barry, T. Osborne & N. Rose, (Eds.) *Foucault and political reason*. London: California: UCL Press & Chicago: University of Chicago Press.
A leading criminological theorist analyzes the growing importance of risk management [see glossary] strategies along with what he calls strategies to "responsibilize" homeowners and other respectable citizens and get them to take responsibility for ensuring their own security.

Reynolds, S. (1999) *Generation Ecstasy*.
The author, a music critic, presents a thorough account of the emergence of "raves" in both the US and the UK. Covers the issue of drug use as well as looking at police and legal measures to regulate or ban "raves." Will be of particular interest to those who appreciate techno music.

Valverde, M. (1991). *The age of light, soap and water: moral reform in English Canada 1880s–1920s*. Toronto: McClelland and Stewart [Oxford].
An account of several interrelated moral reform campaigns that took place in Canada about 100 years ago; some of these are similar in both format and content to current-day fears about "date rape drugs."

WEB LINKS

www.clubdrugs.org
This multiply linked Web site is part of the U.S. government's war on drugs. It is part of the National Institute for Drug Abuse, although this is concealed in the URL address. Like other U.S. government Web sites, this site is built on the assumption that any use of illicit drugs is extremely harmful and leads to "addiction."

www.ecstasy.org
: An interesting contrast to the U.S. official view of Ecstasy is provided in this user-run, pro-Ecstasy Web site. Similar pro-use Web sites exist for marijuana and other "soft" drugs, but not for heroin or cocaine.

www.dancesafe.org
: This Web site is devoted to providing information to young people involved in the rave and club scenes so that they can make their own choices around drug use and minimize risks if they choose to use drugs. An excellent example of the "harm reduction" approach, which characterizes public health work on drugs in northern Europe, in Australia, and to some extent in Canada too. Note the conflicts between the approach taken in this Web site and that promoted in the U.S. government's Web sites.

Glossary Terms

1874 Industrial School Act: Ontario provincial legislation, which called for the formation of industrial schools to replace reformatory institutions for juvenile delinquents. Industrial schools were to be more like schools than prisons. The Act also empowered the courts to incarcerate juveniles not only on the basis of criminal transgressions, but also on the perceived delinquent potential of a child.

1908 Juvenile Delinquents Act (JDA): Federal legislation enacted to regulate juvenile delinquents between the ages of 7 and 17 (although this varied by province). It was replaced with the *Young Offenders Act* in 1984. The JDA legislated the distinction between adult and young offenders. It also called for the formation of separate juvenile courts and probation services.

African primitivism: Racist, sexist stereotypes of African/Black women as possessing a "primitive" sexual appetite and "primitive" genitalia that rendered them hypersexual and animalistic.

Agency: In an individual sense, agency refers to a capacity to act with some sense of consciousness and self-knowledge. In a collective sense, it refers to how social groups or classes participate in shaping human history. Some theorists regard agency as a foundational capacity of human beings; as a pre-given, fixed, and universal attribute. Others regard it as a social and relational process, shaped in social, historical and discursive conditions, and thus open to change; agency is always contingent.

Anachronistic space: Defined by Anne McClintock (1995, p. 41) as an administrative and regulatory practice whereby women, the colonized, and the industrial working classes were classified as prehistoric, atavistic, and irrational—out of place in modernity. She continues: "In the late Victorian era ... Africa came to be seen as the colonial paradigm of anachronistic space, a land perpetually out of time in modernity, marooned and historically abandoned".

Biological determinism/reductionism: The position that features of social organization are directly attributable to factors like physiology, genetics, population shifts, etc. This perspective is often applied to sexuality. Biological reductionism is a critical view of biological determinism, one, which asserts that we must examine history, culture, etc. for the sources of human conduct. It holds that biological determinism reduces features of social organization (like gender and sexuality) to a very narrow set of variables.

Bottle clubs: Nightclubs that permitted customers to bring alcohol into the premises in brown bags that would be stored under the table on a special, built-in shelf. These clubs were common in many English Canadian cities until the late 1960s, and flourished in spite of restrictive liquor licensing practices.

Burlesque (or burlycue): A form of entertainment that began in the United States in the 1860s. It was a combination of minstrel show and vaudeville performed on public stages. Favourite subjects of burlesque were politics, domestic relations, and all aspects of sex. It was predominantly satirical. While a wide variety of performances constituted burlesque, from comedians to chorus lines, at the centre of popular memory of burlesque is the stripper—a female performer who removed clothing and teased her audience as she moved about the stage "bumping and grinding" to live music.

Butch and femme: The cultural and erotic identities of some lesbians. Butch women transgress expected gender appearances and norms for women. While femme women adopt more typical gender appearances, these also counteract gender stereotypes; they are strong, earn wages, and take responsibility for actively seeking sexual and social partners.

Caffey's Syndrome: The name first given to "child abuse homicide" when Caffey (1946) published his discovery of long-bone fractures in infants who had died from subdural hematoma.

Canada Assistance Plan (CAP): A federal-provincial agreement established in 1966 which provided unlimited funding from the federal government for welfare provided the provincial government agreed:
- to match this funding, dollar-for-dollar
- to provide welfare to all those in financial need
- to provide welfare for those who came from a different province

- to not establish any retraining or work requirements to welfare recipients

This agreement lasted until 1996 when it was replaced by another federal-provincial agreement called the Canada Health and Social Transfer (CHST).

Canada Health and Social Transfer (CHST): This is a federal-provincial agreement established in 1996. As a block grant, the federal government established a lump sum of money provided for the provincial governments. The provincial governments do not have to provide matching funds. This federal money is provided for health, education, and welfare and it is up to each province to decide the amount from this block fund that they wish to spend on each of these three areas. The only stipulation is that the provinces must provide health, education, and welfare to citizens who arrive from a different province. Unlike the CAP, the CHST permits provinces to establish workfare, drug tests, literacy tests, and other requirements for recipients of these social programs.

Child abuse and neglect: Refers to forms of harm that a child suffers, or is likely to suffer. They include physical harm, sexual harm (molestation or exploitation), unmet medical needs, emotional harm, unmet needs related to a mental, emotional, or development condition, and abandonment. Child abuse refers to explicit acts that inflict harm on children. Child neglect, in comparison, is more complex and ambiguous, because it is mainly defined by lack of action. It refers to the failure of a person to care for, provide for, supervise, or protect a child. The definitions of child abuse and neglect may on the surface appear to be straightforward, but there is often lack of agreement about what is meant by these terms. As well, the definition of what constitutes child abuse and neglect vary culturally and change over time.

Child pornography: A representation that sexualizes a child. The Canadian Criminal Code, in Section 163.1, defines child pornography as:
(a) a photographic, film, video, or other visual representation, whether or not it was made by electronic or mechanical means,
(i) that shows a person who is or is depicted as being under the age of eighteen years and is engaged in or is depicted as engaged in explicit sexual activity, or
(ii) the dominant characteristic of which is the depiction, for a sexual purpose, of a sexual organ or the anal region of a person under the age of eighteen years; or
(b) any written material or visual representation that advocates or counsels sexual activity with a person under the age of eighteen years that would be an offence under this Act.

Child protection: Child protection refers to legal policies and actions that seek to protect children from harm caused by abuse and neglect. Unlike many other social services, such as daycare or settlement services to new immigrants, where clients are free to choose to access to services, child protection services are compulsory. Child protection services are similar to correctional services and certain aspects of mental illness services.

Children's Aid Society: The first Canadian Children's Aid Society was incorporated in Toronto, Ontario in 1891 to provide child protection services. The Society was recognized in child protection legislation but was supported by philanthropic funding, and voluntary work. Similar Children's Aid Societies were gradually formed in urban centres in other provinces across Canada. The twentieth century saw the steady increase of provincial government support to Children's Aid Societies and the concurrent replacement of Children's Aid Societies with government child and family services delivering child protection services in most provinces. Children's Aid Societies, or their government counterparts, provide child protection services and also adoption services.

Commercial sex industry: Refers to a range of practices involving the exchange of sex and/or sex-related goods or services for money. This includes prostitution, striptease, telephone sex, Internet sex, peep shows, lap and couch dancing, and pornography. The industry yields billions of dollars in profits annually.

Contagious Diseases Acts: In the 1860s, the British government decided to lower the risks of military personnel contracting sexually transmitted infections by establishing a rigorous programme for testing prostitutes and putting them away in "lock hospitals" if found to be infected. Early feminist groups fought successfully to overturn these acts on the basis that they were sexist and that they ignored the important role of men in the spread of such diseases.

Coroner's inquest: An inquest ordered by the Chief Coroner's Office, a coroner's inquest is a provincial form of public inquiry into deaths. There are two categories of inquests: mandatory inquests (e.g., inquests of deaths that occur in judicial custody, or in relation to an industrial site) and discretionary inquests (e.g., inquests deaths of children when abuse is suspected).

Criminogenic: An environment or a peer group is said to be "criminogenic" if it is thought to increase the likelihood of crimes being committed. From the Greek word "genesis", meaning "origin". Scholars and practitioners engaged in "risk management" often use the term.

Cultural capital: Pierre Bourdieu developed this concept to compliment the Marxist concept of economic capital. Where economic capital refers to the access one has to economic resources in a class society, cultural capital refers to the cultural resources to which one has access. From the moment that we begin to learn, the skills and information that are provided in the context of one's family will shape the educational opportunities and outcomes that one has. The criteria for judging what is to be valued and rewarded reflects what the dominant class already possesses, so is weighted in the interests of the children of the dominant class.

Cultural studies: A trend within sociology that focuses on the study of popular culture, often using semiotics and concepts borrowed from film or literary studies.

Deviant: Activities and people differing from the perceived norm. By defining individuals and activities as deviant, societal norms are created and reinforced.

Discipline/Disciplinary power: Foucault believed that modern societies are disciplinary societies, but where power is mainly exercised through knowledge rather than coercion. Disciplinary power is particularly concerned with practices that administer to individuals and populations according to categories developed in the social and psychological sciences. Foucault believes that this represents a break from earlier societies that relied on sovereign and external forms of power.

Discourses: Organized systems of knowledge, produced through cultural and institutional practices, that make possible what can be spoken about and how one may speak about it. Discourses produce social meanings that can have material effects in the world.

Empiricism: A commitment to and quest for knowledge based on observation and experiment. Empiricism is the basis of the scientific method of research.

Ethnocentrism: The belief that one's own nation and culture are superior to those of others, and the judgement of other nations and cultures against the presumed superiority of one's own.

Essentialism: A theoretical perspective that understands human qualities, such as gender and sexuality and race, as being natural and directly related to biology.

Ethics: The moral principles that are established for people, the moral choices that people make, and the values that inform these principles and choices.

Ethnomethodology: "The People's methods." Ethnomethodology is the study of how people use their social interaction to produce and account for the social world. Ethnomethodology was first described in the early 1960s by American sociologist Harold Garfinkel.

Formats (information formats, knowledge formats): Refers to methods used to deliver information and knowledge, such as electronically, in print, etc. The study of media and popular culture often includes both content analysis and the analysis of formats. This kind of study was popularized by the work of Marshall McLuhan—and encapsulated in his famous insight that "the medium is the message"—that how information is delivered is as meaningful and purposeful as the information itself.

Gender Attribution: The practices of gender attribution are the socially shared methods we use in our everyday lives to assign gender to the people we come into contact with. Through the practices of gender attribution we transform a social world of vast gender diversity and variation into a world where we can assign people into "female" and "male" classifications, creating a "natural" world defined by only two genders.

Genealogy: Rather than undertaking a general theory of history and society, Michel Foucault proposed that we should focus on undertaking focused, localized projects. This genealogical approach should focus on exploring histories of discourses and knowledge production, in order to generate specific histories of power and its effects.

Governance/Governing: Governing requires the use of people's capacity for action, in contrast to the concept of domination, which emphasizes repression. Administration, therapy, education, guidance, etc. are examples of how governing takes place.

Governing technologies: The programmes, techniques, and procedures of government. Foucault believed that governance occurs through governing technologies and political rationalities.

Government: Foucault describes government most famously as 'the conduct of conduct.' Foucault rejects the idea that government is synonymous with state power, in favour of the perspective that government is everywhere. It is found in attempts to guide or advise a person or persons, and in our relation to ourselves. People are governed not only by institutions, laws, norms, and in their interpersonal relations, but by their own ethical values and choices. For researchers, therefore, government becomes a problematic to be investigated.

Governmentality: Gradually, from the late eighteenth century, European rulers, statesmen, and political figures embraced the belief that attending to their subjects occurred more effectively through administering to the security, prosperity, and health of individuals and populations. Ruling occurred more effectively through government. Government in modern societies is, however, not restricted to the activities of rulers and political representatives.

Governmentalization of the state: Term developed by Foucault to describe what we know as "the state" (which he regarded as an abstraction, not a source of monolithic power) that carries on within contemporary power relations. The state is located within a vast network of technologies and strategies which are mobilized for the management of individuals and populations, including their economic life, their health and habits, and their civility. In this sense, he also de-centres the state's importance.

Hegemony: A concept which suggests that dominant ideologies are not simply imposed upon the less powerful people in society, rather they achieve their dominance through a process of building consent to them, often through cultural practices. While on the one hand, this makes dominant ideology far more effective, the consensus-building leaves them open to contestation and change.

Heteronormative: Describes the way in which heterosexual identity is privileged as the only normal and natural expression of human sexuality to the exclusion of all non-heterosexual identities.

Heterosexual hegemony: An application of the concept of hegemony in order to explain the manner in which heterosexuality comes to be understood as the dominant, normal, and natural sexuality.

History of the Present: Michel Foucault challenged the belief that history can be understood and documented as a process of steady advancement toward the present. Rather, he finds that history is discontinuous and fractured, and that it is the stories that we tell about history which make it appear to be otherwise. Foucault advocated a geneological approach to exploring the history of the present.

Homicide: The killing of one human being by another whether accidentally or deliberately.

Ideal family: In the context of post-World War II Canada, the ideal family consisted of a father, stay-at-home mother, and children. Other models of family life certainly existed in these years, such as single mothers and childless couples, but were portrayed as imperfect, incomplete, or deficient.

Ideology of familialism: A set of ideas and beliefs that triumph the traditional nuclear family as the only acceptable model for proper socialization.

Ideology: There is a range of approaches to defining ideology. In this book it is generally referred to as a set of doctrines or beliefs that provide the basis for a political or economic system. Ideologies express the ruling ideas in a society and they represent the world to subordinate groups in ways that support the values and interests of ruling groups.

Incorrigible: A term once officially used to identify those youth who were in institutions not because they had broken any federal, provincial, or municipal legislation, but rather because of their disruptive or violent behaviour.

Infanticide: The homicide of a newly born baby (up to and including 12 months) committed by its biological mother.

Intelligent motherhood: In the late nineteenth and early twentieth century, middle-class European women began to organize socially and politically to intervene in the public sphere. In fields such as health and education, these groups often claimed to speak on behalf of all women. They supported this stance by appealing to their presumption of superior reason as well-educated women, and to their claim to superior morality as mothers. The mantle of intelligent motherhood became an effective political slogan in these women's arguments for citizenship and rights, and for state support for social, health, and educational programs targeted for less fortunate women.

Juridical power: Foucault used this concept to refer to power that operates through control, coercion, and repression. This includes the use of military might, policing, the courts, etc. Foucault believed that this form of power is less effective than power circulating through practices of normalization. He believed that normalizing power is far more pervasive and persuasive in the contemporary period. He suggested that even what we think of as juridical power now functions largely through normalizing power.

Juvenile delinquent: A term developed in the nineteenth century to distinguish youthful offenders from adult criminals. Juvenile delinquents were to be treated in a fashion that promoted their welfare, as reflected in the Juvenile Delinquents Act. However, the term also came to be used more generally to describe young people who acted against the expected norms for their age.

Liberal reform: An approach that contends social change can be made through the formal provision of equal opportunities to individuals. This position contrasts with the view that inequalities are systemic, and so broader models of social change that target the whole of society must be implemented.

Marginalization: A process by which a group is denied access to important positions of social and political power, and economic resources within a society.

Master narratives: Universalizing explanations of social life and historical change.

Maternal neonaticide: A non-legal category or term used to describe the killing of a newborn baby by its biological mother.

Medicalization: A term that describes the process by which a physiological phenomenon, state of mind or pattern of behaviour is subject to medical interpretation. When child abuse was medicalized, perpetrators were described as ill, requiring therapeutic and legal intervention. This can be contrasted with a sociological approach, which seeks broader social meanings and solutions for child abuse.

Medico-legal: A term used to describe the issues that exist on the boundary of medicine and law (e.g., Medico-legal concepts, medico-legal issues, medico-legal dilemmas).

Mode of production: In Marxist thought, the way in which social and economic life is organized and reproduced is known as a mode of production.

Modernism: An approach to theory and research which developed with the Enlightenment. It is premised on the belief that we must use human reason and science to explore social and physical life in order to improve the human condition and implement social progress. Modernist thought informed virtually all social analysis until the development of postmodern theory in the 1970's.

Moral: Accepted rules and standards for character and conduct, which makes distinctions between right and wrong, goodness and badness.

Moral capital: Mariana Valverde developed this concept in order to extend Pierre Bourdieu's concept of cultural capital.

Moral panic: A term originally developed by British criminologists in the 1960s to refer to sudden campaigns, usually combining both popular fears and expert information, around some new and very imminent danger to the nation or the community. A moral panic is characterized by an overreaction to an act, event, or issue by media, police, courts, governments, and members of the public. Non-white immigration, the threat of communism, and AIDS are only a few of the things that have been the subject of moral panics in North America. Moral panics have often led to rushed repressive legislation.

Moral regulation: First, moral regulation establishes what is "right and proper." Second, it encourages certain forms of conduct and expression, while discouraging others. Third, it establishes disciplinary regimes (including a system of rewards and punishments) at the symbolic and institutional levels (Corrigan, 1980). Moral regulation need not entail coercive measures such as the use of direct physical contact or threats, nor the use of authority. Rather, moral regulation is part of what makes the person who she or he is; what he believes to be true; how she conducts herself. It shapes our identities, our conduct and our conscience "through self-appropriation of morals and beliefs about what is right and wrong, possible and impossible, normal and pathological" (Rousmaniere, Dehli, & de Coninck-Smith, 1997, p. 3).

Murder: The unlawful, premeditated killing of one human being by another. Murder may be qualified as either first or second degree. The term describes more serious kinds of criminal culpable killings.

New Right, the: Broadly speaking, the New Right consists of two distinct and in some ways competing and even contradictory trends of thought: neo-conservatism, committed to claiming social authority, and neo-liberalism, committed to the free market. What they have in common is the hostility towards the welfare state and associated modes of governance. Since the 1980s, the New Right has dominated the rethinking and restructuring of social welfare.

Normal/normalizing: The process by which a particular set of behaviours and values are considered acceptable, right, and good. The term normal is often used in a common-sense way to make distinctions between reason and madness, between what is good and proper, on one hand, and what is deviant and pathological, on the other. Critical research into normalization questions these commonly held beliefs to consider how views of what is normal are created and supported within society.

Normalizing power: Michel Foucault developed this concept in order to describe how discourses like psychology managed to shape notions of acceptability. Normalizing power compares, differentiates, hierarchizes, homogenizes, and excludes those who are non-compliant.

Norms: These are social rules and expectations that govern our behaviour in particular groups or situations; they tend to reflect and serve the interests of the dominant members of the groups in which they operate. Norms are produced and maintained by the actions of people so they can change over time.

Panoptic power: A type of power that is diffuse and omnipresent and which does not originate in a person or institution. Michel Foucault, who likens modern power to that of the panopticon (see Panopticon), first used the expression.

Panopticon, or Inspection House: An observation tower at the centre of a prison. Jeremy Bentham coined the term in 1787 as a solution to "discipline problems" within prisons, factories, workhouses, and schools. The tower would allow guards to monitor the prisoners and also provide a constant symbol of the guard's authority. Because all prisoners would be in constant view of the tower, they would eventually learn to discipline themselves according to the rules of the prison in order to avoid punishment. Over time, the panopticon would produce effects of discipline whether or not there was a guard inside it. Moreover, even the watchers were subject to this invisible surveillance.

Pastoral power: In his historical research on forms of power, Michel Foucault identified the dissemination of pastoral power, originally from the church throughout society, as a particularly modern phenomenon in Western Europe. First elaborated through the technology of confession, pastoral power functions by gaining knowledge of the 'inside' of people's minds, inviting individuals to 'tell the truth' about themselves. Such knowledge—of individual conscience, doubts, fears, the soul—can then be directed towards 'good,' 'normal' and 'moral' choices. Pastoral power does not command, exclude or prohibit conduct, rather it is normative and works through strategies of improvement and by supporting the capacity of individuals to make responsible choices. Thus, pastoral power is concerned with the exercise of freedom, rather than with domination.

Pedophilia: The Diagnostic and Statistical Manual of Mental Disorders defines pedophilia as paraphilia, a form of sexual deviance characterized by sexual attraction for pre-pubescent children.

Phallometric Testing: A procedure to determine sexual arousal by measuring changes in penile volume in subjects exposed to a variety of sexual and non-sexual stimuli. The procedure, which is believed to be able to identify a man's preferred object of sexual attraction, is used intermittently by Corrections Canada for the assessment of sex offenders.

Pluralism: The belief that modern democratic societies are characterized by a consideration of a diversity of opinions, values, theories, and political beliefs, and where power is shared.

Political rationalities: The naming of objectives, application of theories, and invention of categories which occurs in governmental activities. Foucault believed that governance occurs through political rationalities and governing technologies.

Postmodernism: Postmodernists reject master narratives, and instead approach social life and history as fragmented and discontinuous. Beyond this, postmodernism has a diversity of meanings which are specific to the areas of art, culture and theory to which it is applied. Moreover, postmodernism is also used as a term to describe the present condition of what were formerly modern capitalist societies. It expresses a social condition of fragmentation and incoherence which make it impossible to attribute larger meaning and purpose to social life.

Post-structuralism: Post-structuralists reject structuralist principles, which they believe do not allow for human agency or for open-ended social processes—in other words, the structures determine what people will do. They argue that meaning is always unstable and plural, and that people occupy a number of **subject positions** which can situate people so as to have conflicting interests and alliances.

Power: This is a concept with a broad range of definitions and applications. A basic definition, however, reveals that power usually involves, first, the ability of a person, group, organization, discourse, etc., to put into place a definition of a situation, to establish the terms through which what happens will be understood, and to establish the terms in which one can discuss the issues at hand. Second, power also involves the formulation of ideals which people and organizations should strive to achieve. Third, power entails the ability to define morality. Power is being exercised when we are so located within a particular vision or way of seeing that we cannot imagine alternatives to it; it shapes our thoughts, preferences, and acceptance of ourselves within the existing order of things. We may think that this "way" has been designed by God or by the natural order, and is thus unchangeable.

Power-knowledge: For Foucault, power and knowledge are inseparable, and are linked together in a circular manner so that they are both cause and effect of one another. Discourses are saturated with power-knowledge relations.

Queer: Is often used as an umbrella term to include lesbians, gays, bisexuals, and transgendered people. It is also used to convey the belief that sexual identities are not determined by nature, and are therefore not fixed. Rather, they are fluid, and the boundaries between these categories are often blurred.

Regulation: All of the ways in which certain attitudes and behaviours are accepted as "normal" or punished as "abnormal." Regulation can take place discursively—in language, dictums, advice, and advertising, and physically—or officially through incarceration, violence, and persuasion.

Reification: Occurs when a society is presented as if it has needs and intentions.

Restructuring: Generally refers to the massive economic and social policy changes in Western liberal democracies since the 1980s. The changes were intended as a means to fight the deficit and debt and the competition in the global market, such as reducing taxes, decentralizing responsibility for social programmes, cutting welfare benefits, and reforming social services. Although the specific content of restructuring policies varies by situation, the overall effect has been the deepening of social inequalities.

Risk: Risk is the probability of the occurrence of harm as a result of a set of conditions, or risk factors (e.g., history of abuse/neglect, substance use, ability to cope with stress, living conditions and so on).

Risk management: Governing a problem or a group of people through risk management techniques involves focusing on "risk factors" rather than on individual sins or deviant tendencies. For example, if drug users go to Narcotics Anonymous, they are supposed to be changing their inner selves, but if they go to a risk-management programme such as a needle exchange programme, they are merely trying to lower the risks associated with drug use. Similarly, homeowners can govern the risks of break-ins through measures such as alarm systems, measures that do not involve trying to change the souls or even the behaviour of burglars.

Risk Society: This concept attempts to capture emerging regimes of social protection in a variety of areas, from crime control to insurance rationalities. The identification and containment of risks is pursued before unwanted actions occur. This is premised on the belief that previous methods of reducing or eliminating harms such as crime have failed, and more effective models of identifying, targeting and punishing individuals who cause harm must be developed.

Scientific mothering: In response to a high rate of infant mortality in the late 1920s, experts admonished women to treat their babies like "little machines" and to keep to a rigid schedule of feeding, toileting, bathing, and sleeping. Everything a mother did, the experts, reasoned, was to be by the clock, measured, and scientific. Such scientific mothering, however, was difficult for many women to adhere to and was poorly suited to the needs of most babies. As a reaction to the rigidity of scientific mothering, the "permissive era" in childrearing, most notably represented by the advice of the American pediatrician, Benjamin Spock, came into vogue in the late 1940s and early 1950s.

Semiotics: Borrowing tools developed by European linguistics scholars in the 1920s and 1930s, semiotics is the study of the social meaning of all kinds of signs. It extends the insights gained by grammarians and linguists into how words are imbued with meaning and used to communicate to realms outside of linguistic signs. One can therefore do semiotic analyses of urban architecture, of dress codes, of department store layouts, and of police uniforms, to name only a few possibilities. In semiotic analyses, one always asks how meaning is constructed and how it is conveyed, regardless of the medium used.

Social construction: Social construction covers a broad range of approaches that point out that social, cultural, and historical perspectives are crucial to the making of gender, sexuality, and sexual identification. Social constructionism developed to challenge biological determinism.

Social constructionism: A theoretical perspective that understands human qualities such as gender, sexuality, and race as being products of social relations.

Social Darwinism: Herbert Spencer (1820-1903), rather than Darwin himself, developed social Darwinist thought. He problematically applied Darwin's conceptualization of 'survival of the fittest' to human social life in order to explain differences among human groups.

Social identity: This term is often used in sociological writing to indicate the location of individuals or groups in terms of social categories such as class, gender, sexuality, race, ethnicity and religion. Much social research makes assumptions about the connection between people's social identity and how they think and behave. Public institutions also organize and categorize people in terms of social identity in order to predict, plan, and intervene in society. For nation-states, political and social movements, the idea of social identity is often used to define the terms and limits of social membership, a sense of belonging and identification, as well as a demarcation of us and them.

Social regulation: The ways in which the beliefs and practices of people, individually and as members of specific populations, are infused with power relations which shape our will, our interests—in a word, our subjectivity—as well as our actions.

Status Offence: An offence that is a crime only for a person under a particular age, i.e., a person having a particular status as a child or juvenile. Under the JDA, juvenile delinquents could be institutionalized not only for criminal but also for status offences such as "sexual immorality" and "incorrigibility." Status offences, other than truancy, were eliminated under the Young Offenders Act.

Structuralism: The belief that there are underlying 'structures' shaping social life and shaping language, and that can be studied in an objective, scientific manner. The reference to 'structures' is made to signal the belief that there are underlying features or elements to particular phenomenon (such as systems of language or class) which are linked together in a way to produce that particular phenomenon. Once these elements are discovered, one can then undertake a full explanation of the phenomenon.

Subdural Hematoma: A description, used by forensic pathologists, of an injury causing bruising below the skin. A baby who suffers a fall or is struck by an object might sustain this kind of injury.

Subjectivity: In some approaches, subjectivity is seen as a complex and incomplete process of making sense of who we are and our experience, a process that involves both conscious and unconscious dimensions. Others view subjectivity as a contingent and situated effect of, or response to, discourses and contexts that vary over time and across cultures. Two related concepts are subjection (being subjected to forms of power) and subject position (discursive categories with which we are invited to identify).

Subject positions: Individual subjectivity is constituted by a range of social, economic, and political forces and relationships, or by discourses (depending on your theoretical starting point). These are conflicting and contestable, meaning that the subject is never fixed, but continually in a process of negotiation and change. Post-structuralists developed the concept because they rejected the humanist belief in a unified self with a core identity. (Also see subjectivity.)

Sudden Infant Death Syndrome/Sudden Unexplained Death: A residual cause of death category used by forensic pathologists when all other causes of death have been excluded or eliminated or in cases when there is no cause of death.

Taxonomy: A system of classification.

Techniques of power: Foucault directed us to explore the technology, or techniques, of power. This operates through the administration of 'life'; for example in discourses about mental illness, disease, sexuality, penology, immigration, and so on. These produce the disciplinary society, with new techniques for the surveillance and regulation of populations.

Technologies of governance: The programmes, techniques, procedures, calculations, etc. of government.

Teleological: The assumption that events occur in a particular way because there is a larger purpose, goal, or end point that must be achieved.

Training school: The type of institution used to confine those accused of being juvenile delinquents under the Juvenile Delinquents Act. These were secure facilities and, prior to the 1930s, were referred to as industrial schools.

Transgender: An umbrella term used to describe the various groups of people who do not fit into the dominant two-gender system. This includes crossdressers, transvestites, female and male impersonators, drag kings, drag queens, non-, pre-, and post-operative transsexuals, and those whose perceived gender or anatomic sex may conflict with their gender expression.

Transsexual: Transsexuals are those people who feel that their gender conflicts with the physiological anatomy. This group includes individuals who seek to have, or have had, sex reassignment surgery (SRS). Some transsexuals seek a combination of surgical and hormonal treatment to correct their false or incorrect anatomical sex. The most common complaint made by pre-operative transsexuals is that their anatomical sex is incongruent with their desired sexual or gender identity.

Trope: Most often used in studies of literature, this term can refer to a figure of speech, a metaphor, or a narrative theme. Tropes are highly effective in framing what can and cannot be said, and in suggesting the kinds of words that ought to be used to describe and analyze experiences or events.

Truancy: A juvenile who fails to attend school could be sentenced to a youth facility for truancy.

Urban legends: In contrast to official accounts of danger and risk (e.g. public health department warnings), urban legends communicate information about all manner of dangers by informal, unscientific means. Urban legends are usually anonymous. In the past they circulated by word of mouth (e.g. "my cousin said that she heard that some maniac is handing out Halloween candies with anthrax dust..."), but now they also circulate through the Internet. Urban legends often fuel conspiracy theories.

Author Profiles

Mary Louise Adams teaches in the School of Physical and Health Education and the Department of Sociology at Queen's University. She is the author of *The Trouble with Normal: Postwar Youth and the Construction of Heterosexuality* (University of Toronto Press, 1997).

Deborah Brock is on faculty in the Department of Sociology at York University. She is also author of *Making Work, Making Trouble: Prostitution as a Social Problem*, which was published by the University of Toronto Press in 1998.

Xiaobei Chen is an Assistant Professor at the school of Social Work at the University of Victoria. She has published articles in referred journals, has contributed to a few titles, and is a co-editor of a book on social work and women in China. Her current research and writing focuses on international adoptions, globalization, citizenship, and the Foucaultian governmentality approach.

Dorothy E. Chunn teaches in the School of Criminology and is co-director of the Feminist Institute for Studies on Law and Society at SFU. Among her recent publications are two co-edited collections: *Law as a Gendering Practice* (with Dany Lacombe) and *Regulating Lives: Historical Essays on the State, Society, the Individual and the Law* (with John McLaren and Robert Menzies). Current research projects focus on the historical regulation of sex in the Canadian welfare state; feminism, law, and social change in Canada since the 1960s; and, poor women's experiences of health and housing.

Kari Dehli is Associate Professor in the Department of Sociology and Equity Studies in Education, Ontario Institute for Studies in Education, University of Toronto, where she teaches courses in feminist and social theory, cultural studies and education policy. Her major research interests are in the politics of education and practices of representation.

Enakshi Dua is an Associate Professor in the School of Women's Studies at York University. She teaches anti-racist feminist theory, post colonial studies, development studies, and globalization. She is the co-editor of *Scratching the Surface: Canadian Anti-Racist Feminist Thought*. She is currently working on several research projects. One focuses on the historical construction of the categories of nation, race, and gender in Canada. Her other research includes immigration processes, women and health, equity policies, the ways in which the criminalization of Afro-Caribbean men shapes Afro-Caribbean women's experiences with gender, globalization, and biodiversity. She has almost 20 years of experience in anti-racist feminist organising at the community level, and has held administrative positions that deal with feminist, anti-racist, and equity issues within the academy.

Kegan Doyle teaches English Literature and Foundations at the University of British Columbia.

Mona Gleason is an Assistant Professor in the Department of Educational Studies at the University of British Columbia. Her current research project traces the construction of "healthy" children in medical and educational discourses in Canada between 1850 and 1960.

Gary Kinsman is an Associate Professor in the Sociology Department at Laurentian University in Sudbury, Ontario. He is the author of *The Regulation of Desire: Homo and Hetero Sexualities* and co-editor along with Dieter Buse and Mercedes Steedman of *Whose National Security? Canadian State Surveillance and the Creation of Enemies* as well as numerous book chapters, and articles on sexual and gender politics. With Patrizia Gentile he is the co-author of the forthcoming *The Canadian War on "Queers": National Security as Sexual Regulation*. He is a gay liberation, global justice and socialist activist.

Kirsten Kramar is a sociologist of law and crime. Her courses are cross-listed between Sociology and Women's Studies and Criminology. Prof. Kramar received her Ph.D. in Criminology from the University of Toronto in 2000. Her dissertation is entitled: "Unwilling Mothers and Unwanted Babies: 'Infanticide' and Medico-legal Responsibility in 20th Century Canadian Legal Discourse." She is the author of *Undressing the Canadian State:*

The Politics of Porn from Hicklin to Butler (Fernwood Books, 1995) and co-editor of *Wife Assault and the Criminal Justice System: Issues and Policies* (Centre of Criminology, 1995). Her current research and writing interests include examinations of the relationship between law and medicine and especially the decline in use of special psychiatric defences for women charged with criminal offences and the Canadian criminal justice system's treatment of mothers whose babies have died from unexplained causes or suspected child abuse.

Dany Lacombe teaches Sociology and Criminology at Simon Fraser University.

Margaret Little is a long-time antipoverty activist. She teaches Women's Studies and Political Studies at Queen's University in Kingston. Her book, *"No Car, No Radio, No Liquor Permit": The Moral Regulation of Single Mothers in Ontario, 1920-1997* was published by Oxford University Press in 1998.

Paula Maurutto teaches in the Department of Sociology at the University of Toronto. Her forthcoming book *Governing Charities* with McGill-Queen's University Press examines the interrelations between voluntary organizations and the state. It specifically focuses on the regulation of Catholic charities and juvenile institutions in Ontario.

Dawn Moore is a Ph.D. candidate at the Centre of Criminology at the University of Toronto, and the author of several journal articles on the governance of youth alcohol and drug use. Her dissertation research is on drug treatment programs for prisoners and probationers in Ontario.

Becki L. Ross teaches in Sociology and Women's Studies at the University of British Columbia. She is the author of *The House That Jill Built: A Lesbian Nation in Formation* (1995) and a co-author of *Bad Attitude/s on Trial: Pornography, Feminism and the Butler Decision* (1997). She has published in *Atlantis: A Women's Studies Journal*, *Labour/le travail*, *The Journal of the History of Sexuality, Society and Space*, and *The Journal of Canadian Studies*. In 2001–2002, she was a monthly columnist for *Xtra West* magazine. Her research interests include gender/sexual politics, popular culture, social movements, and athletics. She is completing a book on the history of erotic entertainment in postwar Vancouver, British Columbia.

Mariana Valverde's most recent book is *Diseases of the Will: Alcohol and the Dilemmas of Freedom* (Cambridge). She is currently working on a book entitled *Common Knowledge*, to be published by Princeton University Press. She is a Professor at the Centre of Criminology at the University of Toronto.

REFERENCES

Abbott, A. (1988). *The systems of professions: An essay on the division of expert labor* (p. 30). Chicago: University of Chicago Press.

Abrams, P. (1982). *Historical sociology.* London: Open Books.

ACORN speaker. (1998, October 12-13). *Can Workfare be fair? Presented at conference.* Toronto, Ontario.

Agonizing ecstacy. (1999, November 20). *Toronto Star*, pp. A1, A3.

Allard, M. et al. (1997). In harm's way? Domestic violence, AFDC receipt and welfare reform in Massachussetts. Boston: University of Massachussetts.

Aldridge, A. O. (1971). American burlesque at home and abroad: Together with the etymology of go-go girl. *Journal of Popular Culture, 5* (3), 565-575.

Allen, G. E. (1997). The double-edged sword of genetic determinism, social and political agendas in genetic studies of homosexuality, 1940-1994. In V. A. Rosario (Ed.), *Science and homosexualities* (pp. 242-270). New York and London: Routledge Press.

Allen, M. (1997). CBC Ideas: *Sex Machines*

Allen, R. (1991). *Horrible prettiness: Burlesque and American culture.* Chapel Hill, NC: University of North Carolina Press.

Amadiume, I. (1987). *Male daughters, female husbands: Gender and sex in an African society.* London: Zed Press.

Ames, H. B. (1972). *The city below the hill.* Toronto: University of Toronto Press. (Original work published in 1897).

Anderson, B. (1983). *Imagined communities: Reflections on the origins and spread of nationalism.* London: Verso.

Archbishop denounces new B.C. marriage law. (1939, January 9). *Vancouver Sun.*

Archbishop Neil McNeil Papers (1925, September 26). *Charity Bulletin*, file MNWL04.214.

Arie, M. (1996, October 8). Protecting yourself from evil e-mail. *PC Magazine, 15*, 192.

Aries, P. (1962). *Centuries of childhood.* London: Cape.

Armitage, A. (1993). The policy and legislative context. In B. Wharf (Ed.), *Rethinking child welfare.* Toronto: McClelland & Stewart.

Arnup, K. (1994). *Education for motherhood: Advice for mothers in twentieth-century Canada.* Toronto: University of Toronto Press.

Arnup, K., Levesque, A., & Pierson, R. R. (Eds.) (1990). *Delivering motherhood: Maternal ideologies and practices in the 19th and 20th centuries.* London: Routledge Press.

Ask Principal's Removal (1921, October 28). *Telegram.*

AWARE & Single Mothers Support Network. (1999, November). *Workfare or WorkFair: Perspectives on Ontario works from single mothers, a report to Workfare Watch.* Kingston, 6.

Baber, M. (1937, December 1). Weir plans premarriage health certificate probe to sit during year. *Vancouver Province*, p. 1.

Baber, V. (Ed.) (1997). *Citizenship and exclusion.* Amsterdam: University of Amsterdam Press.

Bacchi, C. L. (1983). *Liberation deferred? The ideas of the English-Canadian suffragists, 1877-1918.* Toronto: University of Toronto Press.

Backhouse, C. (1984). Desperate women and compassionate courts: Infanticide in nineteenth-century Canada. *University of Toronto Law Journal 34*, 447-478.

Backhouse, C. (1985). Nineteenth-century Canadian prostitution law. *Histoire sociale/Social History 18*, 36, 387-423.

Backhouse, C. (1991). *Petticoats and prejudice: Women and law in nineteenth-century Canada.* Toronto: Women's Press.

Bailey, B. L. (1988). *From porch to back seat: Courtship in twentieth-century America* (pp. 119-125). Baltimore: John Hopkins University Press.

Bailey, J. M. & Pillard, R. C. (1993). A genetic study of male sexual orientation. *General Psychiatry, 50*, 217-223.

Baines, C. (1994). The children of Earlscourt, 1915-1948: All in the same boat: Except we were in a better boat. *Canadian Social Work Review 11*, 2, 184-200.

Baines, C. (2000). Restructuring services for children: Lessons from the past. In S. M. Neysmith (Ed.), *Restructuring caring labour: Discourse, state practice, and everyday life.* Don Mills, ON: Oxford University Press.

Bakhtin, M. (1981). Forms of time and of the chronotope in the novel. In M. Bakhtin (Ed.), *The dialogic imagination.* Austin: University of Texas Press.

Balibar, E. (1991). The nation form: History and ideology. In E. Balibar & I. Wallerstein (Eds.), *Race, nation, class.* London: Verso.

Bannerji, H. (1995). *Thinking through: Essays on feminism, marxism and anti-racism.* Toronto: Women's Press.

Bannerji, H. (2000). *The dark side of the nation, essays on multiculturalism, nationalism and gender.* Toronto: Canadian Scholar's Press.

Barman, J. (1996). *The West beyond the West: A history of British Columbia* (2nd ed.). Toronto: University of Toronto Press.

Barman, J. (1997/98). Taming aboriginal sexuality: Gender, power, and race in British Columbia, 1850-1900. *B.C. Studies, 115*/116, 237-266.

Barrett, M. & McIntosh, M. (1990). *The anti-social family* (2nd ed.). London: Verso.

Bauman, C. (1997). Rethinking the unthinkable: A study of child homicides. *Criminal Reports 8* C.R. 8, 1, 139-149.

Bayly, C. A. (1989). *Imperial meridan: The British empire and the world, 1780-1830.* London: Longman.

Beck, U. (1992). *Risk society: Towards a new modernity.* London: Sage Publications.

Bell, S. (1994). *Reading, writing and rewriting the prostitute body.* Bloomington, IN: Indiana University Press.

Bell, S. (1995). *Whore carnival.* New York: Automedia.

Bell, M. & Gardiner, M. (1998). *Bakhtin and the human sciences.* London: Sage.

Bell, S. & Couture, J. (2000). Justice and law: Passion, power, prejudice and so-called pedophilia. In D. Chunn & D. Lacombe, (Eds.), *Law as a gendering practice* (pp. 40-59). Toronto: Oxford University Press.

Bennest gets suspended sentence. (1997, October 16). *Xtra West!*, 109, 7.

Bennett, P. W. (1988, May). Taming "bad boys," of the "dangerous class": Child rescue and restraint at the Victorian Industrial School 1887-1935. *Social History 21*, 82, 86.

Bercuson, D., & Bright, D. (Eds.) (1994). *Canadian labour history: Selected readings*, (2nd ed.). Toronto: Copp Clark Pitman.

Bernhardt, K. (1947, June). Canadian psychology: Past, present and future. *Canadian Journal of Psychology 1*, 2, 57.

Berube, A., & D'Emilio, J. (1984). The military and lesbians during the McCarthy years. *Signs 9*, 4.

Best, J. (1990). *Threatened children: Rhetoric and concern about child-victims.* Chicago: University of Chicago Press.

Best, J. & Horiuchi, G.T. (1995). The razor blade in the apple: the social construction of an urban legend. *Social Problems* (1985). Reprinted in R. Ericson, (Ed.), *Crime and the media.* Aldershot: Dartmouth.

Black, I. S. (1953). *Off to a good start: A handbook for parents* (pp. 101-102). New York: Harcourt Brace and Company.

Blackwood, E. (1984). Sexuality and gender in certain North American tribes: The case of cross-gender females. *Signs, 10*, 27-42.

Bland, L. (1995). *Banishing the beast: English feminism and sexual morality, 1885-1914.* London: Penguin Books.

Blatz, W. (1955, November). Why husbands and wives nag each other. *Chatelaine 27*, 11, 17, 82.

Blatz, W., & Bott, H. (1928). *Parents and the pre-school child*, (p. viii). Toronto: Dent.

Bliss, M. (1981). Pure books on avoided subjects: Pre-Freudian sexual ideas in Canada. In S.E.D. Shortt, (Ed.), *Medicine in Canadian society: Historical perspectives.* Montreal: McGill-Queen's University Press.

Bogdan, R. (1988). *Freak show: Presenting human oddities for amusement and profit.* Chicago: University of Chicago Press.

Bolaria, S., & Li, P. (1988). *Racial oppression in Canada*, (2nd ed.). Toronto: Garamond Press.

Bolshevism in schools? Idea riles trustees (1919, January 9). *Telegram.*

Bornstein, K. (1994*). Gender outlaw: On men, women, and the rest of us.* New York and London: Routledge Press.

Boswell, J. (1988). *The kindness of strangers: The abandonment of children in Western Europe from late antiquity to the renaissance.* Harmondsworth: Penguin.

REFERENCES

Bourgeault, R. (1988). Race and class under mercantilism: Indigenous people in nineteenth-century Canada. In S. Bolaria & P. Li (Eds.), *Racial oppression in Canada.* Toronto: Garamond Press.

Boyd, S. B. (1989). Child custody, ideologies and employment. *Canadian Journal of Women and the Law 3*, 1, 111-133.

Boyd, S. B. (1997). Challenging the public/private divide: An overview. In S.B. Boyd, (Ed.), *Challenging the public/private divide: Feminism, law, and public policy.* Toronto: University of Toronto Press.

Bradley, A. (1999, April). The end of innocence. *Living Marxism*, 119.

Bramham, D. (2001, February 10). Long-stemmed lovelies play on. *Vancouver Sun*, p. A16.

Brandt, A. M. (1985). *No magic bullet: A social history of venereal disease in the United States since 1880.* Oxford: Oxford University Press.

Brannigan, C. (1985). Delinquency, comic and legislative reform in postwar Canada and Victoria. *Australian-Canadian Studies 3*, 53-69.

Brannigan, C. (1986). Mystification of the innocents: Crime comics and delinquency in Canada, 1931-1949. *Criminal Justice History VII*, 110-144.

British Columbia Conference. (1941, May) Evangelism and social service report. United Church of Canada. Dobson Papers, Box 13, File 9, United Church of Canada Archives.

British Columbia Law Reports (1911). *Re: Rahim, vol. xvi.*

British Columbia Law Reports (1912). *Re: Rahim, vol. xvii.*

British Columbia Law Reports (1914). *Re: Munshi Singh, vol. xx.*

British Columbia leads in venereal disease education: Authorities of Canada and United States recognize pioneer work of division. (1942, March 3). *Vancouver News-Herald*, p. 8.

British Columbia Premier. (1938) Summary of Legislation, GR1222 Box 154, File 4, Provincial Archives of British Columbia.

British Columbia Premier. (1942, October 7) G. E. Simms, Hon. Corresp. Secty, VLCW to Premier John Hart, GR1222 Box 43, File 7, Provincial Archives of British Columbia.

British Columbia Premier. (1943, December 22). E D. Hunt, Secty, Cobble Hill WI to Hart. GR1222, Box 54, File 5, Provincial Archives of British Columbia.

British Columbia Premier. (1944, January 14). R. Miller, Pres. Somanos WI to Hart. GR1222, Box 175, File 1, Provincial Archives of British Columbia.

British Columbia Premier. (1944, January 17). M. F. Maitland, Secty, Shawnigan Lake WI to Hart. GR1222, Box 175, File 2. Provincial Archives of British Columbia.

British Columbia Premier. (1944, January 28). E. M. Millwad, Secty, Langford WI to Hart. GR1222, Box 175, File 2. Provincial Archives of British Columbia.

British Columbia Premier. (1944, March 6). F. Barr, Secty, CSA Greater Victoria to Hart. GR1222 Box 175, File 1, Provincial Archives of British Columbia.

British Columbia Premier. (1944, April 4). M. Bradford, Executive director, VCSA to Hart. GR1222 Box 54, File 5, Provincial Archives of British Columbia.

British Columbia Premier. (1944, April 17). Amyot to Hart. GR1222 Box 54, File 5, Provincial Archives of British Columbia.

British Columbia Premier. (1944, April 18). M. Bradford, Executive director, VCSA to Hart. GR1222 Box 54, File 5, Provincial Archives of British Columbia.

British Columbia Premier. (1944, April 27). R. C. Weldon, Secty, Vancouver District WCTU to Hart. GR1222, Box 54, File 5, Provincial Archives of British Columbia.

British Columbia Premier. (1944, May 12). E. D. Fletcher, Secty, Fairview Baptist Church Women's Auxiliary to Hart. GR1222, Box 54, File 5, Provincial Archives of British Columbia.

British Columbia Premier. (1944, June 6). M. Reed, Secty, St. Margaret's Women Auxiliary (Vancouver) to Hart. GR1222, Box 54, File 5, Provincial Archives of British Columbia.

British Columbia Provincial Board of Health. (1937). The record system as set up for the division of VD control. Bulletin, Vol. 7, No.11, August Supplement. United Church Archives.

British Columbia Provincial Board of Health, Division of VD Control. (1938, May). Monthly Bulletin, Vol. 2, No.3. Dobson Papers, Box B13, File 9.

British Columbia Provincial Board of Health, Division of VD Control. (1939). Annual report for the year 1938. Bulletin of the B.C. Board of Health, Vol. 9, No. 3.

British Columbia Provincial Board of Health, Division of VD Control. (1941). Annual report for the year 1940. Bulletin of the B.C. Board of Health, Vol. 11, No. 2, pp.20-21, 22-23.

British Columbia Provincial Board of Health. (1946). *Report of the division of venereal disease control for 1945.* (No. C-86). Victoria: King's Printer.

British Columbia Provincial Secretary. (1937, March 2). P. Walker, Deputy PS to Warden, Provincial Goal, Oakalla; Principal, School for the Deaf and Blind, Vancouver; Medical Supt., Provincial Mental Hospital, Essondale; Supt., Prov. Industrial Home for Girls, Vancouver; Principal, Prov. Industrial School for Boys, Port Coquitlam; Medical Supt., Prov. Home for Incurables, Vancouver. GR496 Box, Box 41, File 18, Provincial Archives of British Columbia.

British Columbia Provincial Secretary. (1937, March 8). A. Westman to P. Walker, Deputy PS. GR496 Box, Box 41, File 18, Provincial Archives of British Columbia.

British Columbia Provincial Secretary. (1937, March 24). Goal Surgeon to Warden, Oakalla Prison Farm. GR496 Box, Box 41, File 18, Provincial Archives of British Columbia.

British Columbia Provincial Secretary. (1937, March 24). Warden, Oakalla Prison Farm to J. H. McMullin, Inspector of Gaols. GR496 Box, Box 41, File 18, Provincial Archives of British Columbia.

British Columbia Provincial Secretary. (1937, March 25). J. H. McMullin to Attorney General. GR496 Box, Box 41, File 18, Provincial Archives of British Columbia.

British Columbia Provincial Secretary. (1941, August 19). Provincial Secretary to H. P. Cain, Mayor, city of Tacoma. GR496 Box, Box 37, File 1, Provincial Archives of British Columbia.

British Columbia Provincial Secretary. (1942, January 14). Pearson to G. E. Simms, VLCW. GR1222, Box 43, File 7, Provincial Archives of British Columbia.

British Columbia Provincial Secretary. (1942, January 27). Amyot to Pearson. GR496, Box 37, File 20, Provincial Archives of British Columbia.

British Columbia Provincial Secretary. (1942, January 28). Pearson to Private Secretary of Lt. Governor. GR496, Box 37, File 1, Provincial Archives of British Columbia.

British Columbia Provincial Secretary. (1942, January 30). Pearson to Amyot. GR496, Box 37, File 1, Provincial Archives of British Columbia.

British Columbia Provincial Secretary. (1944, April 17). Amyot to Hart. GR1222, Box 54, File 5, Provincial Archives of British Columbia.

Brock, D. (1998). *Making work, making trouble: Prostitution as a social problem.* Toronto: University of Toronto Press.

Brock, D. (2000). Victim, nuisance, fallen women, outlaw, worker? Making the identity "prostitute" in Canadian criminal law." In D. E. Chunn & D. Lacombe (Eds.), *Law as a gendering practice.* Toronto: Oxford University Press.

Brock, D., Gillies, K., Oliver, C., & Sutdhibhasilp, M., (2000). Migrant sex work: A roundtable analysis. *Canadian Woman Studies Journal, 20,* 2, 84-91.

Brodie, J. G., Shelley, A.M., & Jenson, J. (1992). *The politics of abortion.* Toronto: Oxford University Press.

Brodie, J., (1995). *Politics on the margins: Restructuring and the Canadian women's movement.* Halifax: Fernwood Publishing.

Brown, E. N., & Williams, D. H. (1941, May 31). A word to the wise. *Boom, Voice of the Squadron 5.*

Bruce, R. M. (1951). *Parent-child relationships of 23 delinquent adolescent girls*, 80. Master of Social Work thesis, McGill University, Montreal, PQ.

Buckley, S., & McGinnis, J. D. (1982). Venereal disease and public health reform in Canada. *Canadian Historical Review 63,* 3, 337-354.

Burana, L. (2001). *Strip city: A stripper's farewell journey across America.* New York: Hyperion.

Burchell, G., Gordon, C., & Miller, P. (1991). *The Foucault effect: Studies in governmentality.* Chicago: University of Chicago Press.

Bureau of Municipal Research (1920, March). *Biographies of Individual Schools under the Toronto Board of Education 1, York Street School* (pp. 8, 19). Toronto: Bureau of Municipal Research.

Burgess, A., Groth, N., Holstrom, L., & Sgroi, S. (1978). *The sexual assault of children and adolescents.* New York: Lexington Books

Burgoyne, L. (1935). *A history of the home and school movement in Ontario.* Toronto: Charters Publishing.

Burnham, C. W. with Diewold, P. (1994). *Gender change employability issues: Including transitional employment survey results.* Vancouver: Perceptions Press.

Butler, J. (1997). *Excitable speech.* New York: Routledge Press.

Caffey, J. (1946). Multiple fractures in the long bones of infants suffering from chronic subdural hematoma. *American Journal of Radiology 56,* 163-173.

Callahan, M., & Callahan, K. (1997). Victims and villains: Scandals, the press and policy making in child welfare. In J. Pulkingham, & G. Ternowetsky (Eds.), *Child and family policies: Struggles, strategies and options.* Halifax: Fernwood Publishing.

Campbell, M. (1999, February 3). Memories of Montreal's skin queen. *The Globe and Mail,* p. A3.

Campbell, R. (1991). *Demon rum or easy money: Government control of liquor in British Columbia from prohibition to privatization.* Ottawa: Carleton University Press.

Campbell, R. (2001). *Sit down and drink your beer: Regulating Vancouver's beer parlours, 1925-1954.* Toronto: University of Toronto Press.

Canada, Acts and Statutes (1867). *The British North American Act.*

Canada, Acts and Statutes (1867). *The Constitution.*

Canada, Acts and Statutes (1876). *The Indian Act.*

Canada, Acts and Statutes (1881, 1886, 1906). *The Natualization Act.*

Canada, Acts and Statutes (1885). *An Act to Restrict and Regulate Chinese Immigration into Canada.*

Canada, Acts and Statutes (1886). *An Act Respecting Immigration and Immigrants.*

Canada, House of Commons Debates, (1880, March 11). *Commons Debates,* p. 1340).

Canada, House of Commons Debates, (1883). *Commons Debates,* p. 3010.

Canada. Department of Justice. (1985). *General summary of the discussions during the National Consultation with non-governmental organizations on the recommendations of the Badgley and Fraser Committees.* Prepared by Neville H. Avison. Ottawa: Ministry of Supply and Services.

Canada. Department of Justice, Family, Children and Youth Division. (1999, November). *Child Victims: Technical Background Paper.* Ottawa.

Canada. Department of Justice (1999a November). *Child victims and the criminal justice system: A consultation paper.* <canada.justice.gc.ca/en/cons/child/toc.html> (cited on February 18, 2000)

Canada. Department of Justice (1999b, November). *Child victims and the criminal justice system: Technical background paper.* p. 3.

Canadian Dominion Bureau of Statistics (1945). *The Canada Year Book, 1945* (pp. 150-151). Ottawa: King's Printer.

Canadian Dominion Bureau of Statistics (1950). *The Canada Year Book, 1950* (pp. 227-229, 232). Ottawa: King's Printer.

Canadian Dominion Bureau of Statistics. (1955). *The Canada Year Book, 1955* (pp. 220-221, 224). Ottawa: King's Printer.

Canadian Dominion Bureau of Statistics. (1960). *The Canada Year Book, 1960* (pp. 254, 261). Ottawa: King's Printer.

Carlson, T. (2002, January 10-17). Ready for take off. *Vancouver Sun, Queue Magazine,* pp. C6, C7.

Carter, S. (1996). First Nations' women of prairie Canada in the early reserve years, the 1870s to 1920s: a preliminary inquiry. In C. Miller & P. Churchryk, (Eds.), *Women of the First Nations: Power, wisdom, and strength* (pp. 51-76). Winnipeg: University of Manitoba Press.

Cassel, J. (1987). *The secret plague: Venereal disease in Canada, 1838-1939.* Toronto: University of Toronto Press.

Cassidy, H.M. (1936, May 19). *The problem of VD control in British Columbia: A report with recommendations* (unpublished) (pp. 18, 19). Public Archives of B.C.

Castel, R. (1991). From dangerousness to risk. In G. Burchell, C. Gordon, & P. Miller, (Eds.), *The Foucault effect: Studies in governmentality* (pp. 281-298). Chicago: Univ. of Chicago Press.

Catholic Big Brothers (1927, November 7). Better books for boys. *Catholic Register.*

Catholic Big Brothers (1930, June 3). Protecting the mind of childhood. *Catholic Register.*

Catholic Big Brothers (1930, June 5). The thoughtless and untidy child. *Catholic Register.*

Catholic Big Brothers (1930, December 25). Habits. *Catholic Register.*

Catholic Big Brothers (1931, March 19). The parent. *Catholic Register.*

Catholic Big Brothers (1932, June 12). How to keep our children happy during the long vacation. *Catholic Register.*

Catholic Welfare Bureau (1928, April 5). When children find good behaviour as interesting as bad. *Catholic Register.*

Catholic Welfare Bureau (1929, November 14). Responsibility to be placed on parents for juvenile crime. *Catholic Register.*

Chamberland, L. (1996). *Mémoires lesbiennes: le lesbianisme á Montreal entre 1950 et 1972.* Montreal: Editions du Remue-ménage.

Chapkis, W. (1997). *Live sex acts: Women performing erotic labour.* New York: Routledge Press.

Chapman, T. (1977). The early Eugenics movement in Western Canada. *Alberta History* 25: 9-17.

Chauncey, G. (1994). *Gay New York: Gender, urban culture and the making of the gay male world, 1890-1940.* New York: Basic Books.

Chauncey G. (2000). *Homosexuality in the city: A century of research at the University of Chicago* (pp. 3-8). Chicago: University of Chicago.

Chen, X. Is it all neo-liberal? Some reflections on child protection policy and neo-Conservatism in Ontario. *Canadian Review of Social Policy* 45-46: 237-246.

Child pornography: A victim on every page (letter to the editor). (1999, January 21). *Vancouver Sun.*

Cholmondeley, P. (1997, September 2). Beggar's tale not so Sharpe (Review of the book *Life on the corner: The moon eyed beggar's tale*). *The Ubyssey*, 13.

Chomsky, A. (1996). *West Indian workers and the United Fruit Company in Costa Rica, 1870-1940.* Baton Rouge, LA: Louisiana State University Press.

Chow, W. (2001, July 7). Owner of exotic nightclub plans upscale outlet in U. S. *Vancouver Sun,* pp. B5, B10.

Chunn, D. E. (1992). *From punishment to doing good: Family courts and socialized justice in Ontario, 1880-1940* (pp. 20-21, 37-39, 40-41, 167). Toronto: University of Toronto Press.

Clarke, S. C. T., & Woodsworth, J. G. (1959). *Youth and tomorrow* (pp. 28-29). Toronto: McClelland & Stewart.

Cleric urges archbishop to review stand: Marriage act discussed anew in city pulpit (1939, January 16). *Vancouver Sun.*

Cleveland, D. E. H., (1942). Summary report of the division of venereal disease control for 1942. *Annual report of the Provincial Board of Health,* CC 59.

Cohen, S. (1972). *Folk devils and moral panics.* London: MacGibbon and Kee.

Cooke, A. (1987). Stripping: Who calls the tune? In L. Bell (Ed.), *Good girls/bad girls: Sex trade workers and feminists face to face* (pp. 92-99). Toronto: Women's Press.

Corio, A. with DiMona, J. (1968). *This was burlesque.* New York: Madison Square Press.

Coroner's Investigation Case File No. 11148 and 26504, Office of the Chief Coroner for Ontario, Toronto, Ontario, 1990.

Coroner's Investigation Case File No. 12612, Office of the Chief Coroner for Ontario, Toronto, Ontario, 1991.

Coroner's Investigation Case File No. 19733 (6920), Office of the Chief Coroner for Ontario, Toronto, Ontario, 1987.

Coroner's Investigation Case File No. 2439, Office of the Chief Coroner for Ontario, Toronto, Ontario, 1996.

Coroner's Investigation Case File No. 3416 (4288), Office of the Chief Coroner for Ontario, Toronto, Ontario, 1988.

Coroner's Investigation Case File No. 3533 and 6615, Office of the Chief Coroner for Ontario, Toronto, Ontario, 1994.

Coroner's Investigation Case File No. 5451 and 28183, Office of the Chief Coroner for Ontario, Toronto, Ontario, 1993.

Coroner's Investigation Case File No. 925, Office of the Chief Coroner for Ontario, Toronto, Ontario, 1995.

Coroner's Investigation Case File No.14938, Office of the Chief Coroner for Ontario, Toronto, Ontario, 1996/1997.

Coroner's Investigation Case File No.30254 and 54, Office of the Chief Coroner for Ontario, Toronto, Ontario, 1992.

Corrigan, P. (1990). On moral regulation: Some preliminary remarks. In P. Corrigan (Ed.), *Social forms, human capacities.* London: Routledge Press.

Corrigan, P. (1994). Undoing the overdone state. In M. Valverde (Ed.), *Studies in moral regulation* (pp. 249-255). Toronto: Centre of Criminology, University of Toronto.

Corrigan, P. & Sayer, D. (1985). *The great arch: English state formation as cultural revolution.* Oxford: Basil Blackwell.

Cosco, V. (1997). *Obviously then I'm not hetersexual: Lesbian identities, discretion, and communities.* Master's thesis, Department of History, University of British Columbia, Canada.

Courtice, A. (1918). *The value of Home and School clubs* (p. 166). Ontario Education Association (OEA), Proceedings 1918.

Cover up, says A-G. (1976, August 31). *Vancouver Sun,* p. A5.

Creese, G. (1999). *Contracting masculinity: Gender, class, and race in a white-collar union, 1944-1994.* Don Mill, ON: Oxford University Press.

Cromwell, P. F., Olson, J. N., & Avary, D. A. W. (1991). *Breaking and entering: An ethnographic analysis of burglary (Vol. 8).* Newbury Park: Sage.

Crowley, T. (1980). Ada Mary Brown Courtice: Pacifist, feminist and educational reformer in early twentieth-century Canada. *Studies in History and Politics*, 75-114.

Culbert, L. (1999, January 20). Educators, youth workers back quick appeal in child-porn case, as quoted by Kit Krieger. *Vancouver Sun*, p. B1.

Curtis, B. (1998). *Building the educational state: Canada West, 1836-1871* (pp. 14, 145). London: Falmer Press/Althouse Press.

D'Emilio, J. (1983). Capitalism and gay identity. In Snitow, A., Stansell, C., & Thompson, S. (Eds.), *Powers of desire: The politics of sexuality* (pp. 100-113). New York: Monthly Review Press.

Dalton, K., & Gates, H. L., Jr. (1998). Josephine Baker and Paul Colin: African American dance seen through Parisian eyes. *Critical Inquiry, 24*, 903-934.

Dancers end picket at club: Deal reached. (1967, October 19). *Vancouver Sun*.

Davidson, A. (1997). *From subject to citizen: Australian citizenship in the twentieth century.* Cambridge, MA: Cambridge University Press.

Davis, L. (1992). The butch as drag artiste: Greenwich Village in the roaring forties. In J. Nestle (Ed.), *The persistent desire: A femme/butch reader* (pp. 45-53). Boston: Alyson Publications.

Dean, M. (1991). *The constitution of poverty: A genealogy of Liberal governance.* London: Routledge Press.

Dean, M. (1994). A social structure of many souls: Moral regulation, government, and self-formation. In M. Valverde (Ed.), *Studies in moral regulation* (pp. 145-168). Toronto: Centre of Criminology, University of Toronto.

Dean, M. (1999). *Governmentality: Power and rule in modern society.* London and Thousand Oaks, CA.: Sage Publications.

Deacon, J. & Nemeth, M. (1997, January 20). Darkening the hockey dream. *Maclean's, 110* (3), 54.

Dchli, K. (1993). Women and early kindergartens in North America: Uses and limitations of post-structuralism for feminist history. *Curriculum Studies 1*, 1, 11-33.

Dehli, K. (1996, September). Love and knowledge: Adult education in the Toronto Home and School Council, 1916-1940. *Ontario History 88*, 3, 207-228.

Delacoste, F., & Alexander, P. (Eds.) (1987). *Sex work: Writings by women in the sex industry.* Pittsburgh, PA: Cleis Press.

DeMause, L. (Ed.). (1976). *The history of childhood.* London: Souvenir.

DeWitt, C. (1995) Legal commentary. *Adult Video News*, 112-117.

Diaz, K. (1992, December). Are gay men born that way? *Z Magazine, 5*, 12, 42-46.

Dickason, O. (1992). *Canada's First Nations.* Toronto: McClelland & Stewart, Inc.

Dickenson, H. & Wotherspoon, T. (1992). From assimilation to self-government: Towards a political economy of Canada's Aboriginal policies. In V. Satzewich, (Ed.), *Deconstructing a nation: Immigration, multiculturalism and racism in 90s Canada.* Halifax, NS: Fernwood Publishing House.

Dickinson, H. D. (1993). Scientific parenthood: The mental hygiene movement and the reform of Canadian families, 1925-1950. *Journal of Comparative Family Studies 24*, 3, 387-402.

Didon, P. (1978, January 20). A candid interview: Phillipponi disapproves of nudity. *L'Eco D'Italia*, 1-3, 8.

Dobash, R. E., & Dobash, R. P. (1979). *Violence against wives.* New York: The Free Press.

Dobson, H. (1941, May; 1941, June 10; 1943, September 2). Correspondence with D. H. Williams. Dobson Papers, Box 13, File 9, United Church Archives.

Dolan, J. (1988). *The feminist spectator as critic.* Ann Arbor, MI: University of Michigan Research Press.

Donzelot, J. (1980). *The policing of families.* New York: Pantheon.

Dorne, C. (1989). *Crimes against children.* New York: Harrow and Heston Publishers.

Douglas, M. (1973). *Natural symbols* (p. 93). New York: Penguin.

Douglas, M. (1979). *Purity and danger* (p. 4). London: Routledge Press and Kegan Paul.

Dover, K. J. (1980). *Greek homosexuality.* New York: Vintage.

Dragu, M, & Harrison, A. S. A. (1988). *Revelations: Essays on striptease and sexuality.* London: Nightwood Editions.

Drakich, J. (1989). In search of the better parent: The social construction of ideologies of fatherhood. *Canadian Journal of Women and the Law 3*, 1, 73.

Drastic drive against VD here. (1939, January 13). *Vancouver Sun*, p. 14.

Drive launched against syphilis. (1942, February 2). *Victoria Daily Times*, p. 9.

Drunken, immoral conduct in cabarets: Church, temperance heads related visits to nightspots. (1941, December 13). *Vancouver News Herald*.

Dua, E. (1999). Racialising Imperial Canada: Indian Women and the Making of Ethnic Communities. In A. Burton (Ed.), *Unfinished business: gender, sexuality and colonial modernities*. New York: Routledge Press.

Dua, E. (2000). The Hindu woman's question: Canadian nation-building and the social construction of gender for south Asian-Canadian women. In G. Dei and A. Calliste (Eds.) *Anti-racist feminism*. Halifax: Fernwood Press.

Dubinsky, K. (1999). *The second greatest disappointment: Honeymooning and tourism at Niagara Falls*. Toronto: Between the Lines.

Dubois, E. C., & Gordon, L. (1984). Seeking ecstasy on the battlefield: Danger and pleasure in nineteenth-century feminist sexual thought. In C.S. Vance, (Ed.), *Pleasure and danger: exploring female sexuality*. London: Routledge Press & Kegan Paul.

Duckworth, J.C., Jr., & Levitt, E. E. (1984). Minnesota multiphasic personality inventory-2. In D. J. Keyser & R. C. Sweetland (Eds.), *Test critiques* (pp. 424-428). Austin, TX: Pro-Ed.

Dudash, T. (1997). Peepshow feminism. In J. Nagle (Ed.), *Whores and other feminists* (pp. 98-118.) New York: Routledge Press.

Eagle, S. (2000, February). Life sentence for welfare fraud. *Social Safety News, 24*, 1.

Ecstacy kills 8 this year: deadly designer drug popular with rave goers. (1999, December 30). *Toronto Sun*, p. 5.

Edin K., & Lein, L. (1997). *Making ends meet: How single mothers survive welfare and low-wage work*. New York: Russell-Sage Foundation.

Edmison, J. A. (1949, April). Gang delinquency. *The Canadian Forum XXIX*, 339, 7.

Eisner, B. (1994). *Ecstasy: the MDMA story*. Berkeley: Cronin.

Elkind, D. (1978). *The child's reality: Three development themes* (3rd ed.). New Jersey: Lawrence Erlbaum Associates.

End of sex scandal. (1994, February 21). *Maclean's*, 107 (8), 21.

Endorsation "prevention of prenatal syphilis week". (1942, January 31). *Vancouver Sun*.

"English only" is rule for students. (1919, January 17). *Toronto Daily Star*.

Epstein, S. (1996). *Impure science: AIDS, activism and the politics of knowledge*. Berkeley and Los Angeles: University of California Press.

Ericson, R. & Haggerty, K. (1997). *Policing the risk society*. Toronto: University of Toronto Press.

Eugenic law is defended as effort to halt social vice. (1939, January 16). *Vancouver News-Herald*.

Evans, M. (1922, December). The Home and School Club (pp. 262-263). *The School, Vol. 11*, no. 4.

Ewing, C. P. (1997). *Fatal families: The dynamics of intrafamilial homicide*. London: Sage Publications.

Exotics dancers to give free show Tuesday night. (1952, January 5). *Vancouver Sun*.

Falkiner et al. v. Her Majesty the Queen in Right of Ontario as Represented by the, Ministry of Community and Social Services, Court File No. 810/95 (Ontario Court [General Division] Divisional Court), Affidavit of Robert Fulton, October 25, 1995 as cited in Mosher, "Managing the Disentitlement of Women," p. 34.

Fathers settle it. Mothers keep silent. More or less. Humour in meeting of dads of J. R. Roberston school pupils. Approve principal. "The female of the species is more deadly than the male. (1921, November 2). *Toronto Daily Star*.

Fatona, A., & Wyngarten, C. (1994). *Hogan's Alley*. (Video) Vancouver, BC: Distributed by Video Out.

Fausto-Sterling, A. (1992). *Myths of gender: Biological theories about women and men*. New York: Basic Books.

Fausto-Sterling, A. (1995). Gender, race and nation: The comparative anatomy of "Hottentot" women in Europe, 1815-1817. In J. Terry & J. Urla (Eds.), *Deviant bodies* (pp. 10-48). Bloomington, IN: Indiana University Press.

Fausto-Sterling, A. (2000). *Sexing the body, gender politics and the construction of sexuality*. New York: Basic Books.

Featherstone, M. (1990). *Global culture: Nationalism, globalization and modernity*. London: Sage Press.

Feeley, M. M. & Simon, J. (1992). The new penology: Notes on the emerging strategy of corrections and its implications. *Criminology 4*, 449-474

Fernbach, D. (1998, March/April). Biology and gay identity. *New Left Review*, 228, 47-66.

Finch, L. (1993). *The classing gaze: Sexuality, class and surveillance*. Sydney: Allen & Unwin.

Finkelhor, D. (1981). *Sexually victimized children*. New York: Free Press.

Fitzgerald, T. (1996). *The face of the nation: Immigration, the state and the national identity*. Stanford: Stanford University Press.

Forcese, D. (1986). *The Canadian class structure* (3rd ed.). Toronto: McGraw-Hill Ryerson.

Foucault, M. (1977). *Discipline and punish: The birth of the prison* (pp. 177-184). New York: Pantheon.

Foucault, M. (1979). *Discipline and punish: The birth of the prison.* New York: Pantheon.

Foucault, M. (1980). *Power/Knowledge.* In C. Gordon (Ed.). New York: Pantheon.

Foucault, M. (1980). *The history of sexuality, volume one: An introduction.* New York: Vintage, 1980.

Foucault, M. (1985). *The history of sexuality, volume two: The use of pleasure.* New York: Pantheon.

Foucault, M. (1988). The dangerous individual. In L. D. Kritzman (Ed.), *M. Foucault: Politics, philosophy, culture. Interviews and other writings 1977-1984* (pp. 125-151). New York: Routledge.

Foucault, M. (1991). Governmentality. In G. Burchell, C. Gordon, & P. Miller, (Eds.), *The Foucault effect: Studies in governmentality.* Chicago: University of Chicago Press.

Foucault, M. (2000). *Power: Essential works of Foucault, Volume Three.* Faubion, New York: The New Press.

Friedman, A. (1996). The habitats of sex-crazed perverts: Campaigns against burlesque in Depression-era New York City. *Journal of the History of Sexuality, 7,* 2, 203-238.

Furniss, E. (1997/98). Pioneers, progress and the myth of the frontier: The landscape of public history in rural B.C. *B.C. Studies, 115/116,* 7-44.

The game of sex politics is already played out in the educational civic affairs of this city (1925, January 2). Editorial. *Toronto Daily Star.*

Gangulee, N. (1947). *Indians in the empire overseas.* London: The New India Publishing House.

Garland, D. (1985). *Punishment and modern society: A history of penal strategies* (p. 134). Aldershot: Gower Publishing Company.

Gaubatz, K. T. (1995). *Crime and the public mind.* Ann Arbor, MI: The University of Michigan Press.

Gavigan, S. A. M. (1989-1990). Petit treason in eighteenth-century England: Women's inequality before the law. *Canada Journal of Women and the Law 3,* 335-374.

Gavigan, S. A.M. (1993). Paradise lost, paradox revisited: The implications of familial ideology for feminist, lesbian, and gay engagement to law. *Osgoode Hall Law Journal 31,* 3, 589-624.

Gebhard, P. H., & Johnson, A. B. (1979). *The Kinsey data: Marginal tabulations of the 1938-1963 interviews conducted by the Institute for Sex Research.* Philadelphia: Saunders.

Gellner, E. (1983). *Nations and nationalism.* Oxford: Basil and Blackwell.

Giese, R. (1997, February 27). Pedophile night in Canada. *Xtra.*

Gill, A. (2002, February 12). The art of the tease. *The Globe and Mail,* pp. R1, R7.

Gilman, S. (1985). *Difference and pathology: Stereotypes of sexuality, race and madness.* Ithaca, NY: Cornell University Press.

Gilroy, P. (1991). *There ain't no black in the Union Jack: The cultural politics of race and nation.* Chicago: University of Chicago Press.

Gleason, M. (1996, May). Disciplining children, disciplining parents: The nature and meaning of psychological advice to Canadian parents, 1948-1955. *Historie Sociale/Social History 29,* 57, 187-210.

Gölz, A. (1947, August 1). Family matters. *Maclean's Magazine 60,* 1, 24-26.

Gölz, A. (1993, Fall). Family matters: The Canadian family and the state in the postwar period. *Left History 1,* 2, 9-50.

Gordon, L. (1977). *Woman's body, woman's right: A social history of birth control in America.* Harmondsworth: Penguin Books.

Gordon, L. (1988). *Heroes of their own lives: The politics and history of family violence.* Harmondsworth: Penguin Books.

Gove Inquiry into Child Protection (British Columbia, Canada. 1995). *Report of the Gove Inquiry into child protection in British Columbia: A commission of inquiry into the adequacy of the services, policies and practices of the Ministry of Social Services as they relate to the apparent neglect, abuse and death of Matthew John Vaudreuill.* Thomas J. Gove, the Commissioner. The Commission, 1995.

Government of Canada. (1984). *The report of the committee on sexual offences against children and youths.* Robin F. Badgley, chair. Ottawa: Ministry of Supply and Services.

Gray, J. M. (1999, February 6). Justice Shaw deserves better than a hit-and-run bandwagon as quoted by Members of Parliament, John Reynolds *Vancouver Sun.*

Greenland, Cyril. (1973). *Child abuse in Ontario.* Toronto: Ministry of Community and Social Services.

Grim tales from the Gardens: the sex scandal at the hockey mecca keeps growing. (1997, March 10) *Toronto Star*

Hacking, I. (1995). *Rewriting the soul: multiple personality and the sciences of memory.* Princeton University Press.

Haeberle, E. J. (1980-1981 Fall/Winter). Stigmata of degeneration, prisoner markings in Nazi concentration camps. In S. J. Licata & R. P. Peterson, (Ed.), *Historical perspectives on homosexuality*, special issue of *Journal of Homosexuality, 6,1/2*; co-published by the Haworth Press, Inc., pp. 135-139; Stein and Day, New York, 1981, pp. 141-160.

Hall, N. (1999, January 21). Child-porn judge gets death threat. *Vancouver Sun*, p. A1.

Hall, N. & Culbert, L. (1999, January 19). Surrey judge dismisses new child porn charges. *Vancouver Sun*, p. A3.

Hall, S., Critcher, C., Jefferson, T., Clarke, J. & Roberts, B. (1978). *Policing the crisis: mugging, the state, and law and order*. London: Macmillan.

Hall, S. (1997) Representation and the Media. Open University lecture on video.

Hall, S. (1980). Reformism and the legislation of consent. In National Deviancy Conference, (Ed.), *Permissiveness and control: The fate of the sixties legislation*. London: Macmillan.

Hall, S. (1997) (Ed.). *Representation: Cultural representations and signifying practices*. London: Sage.

Halperin, D. (1990). *One hundred years of homosexuality*. New York and London: Routledge Press.

Hamer, D. H. et al. (1993, July 16). A linkage between DNA markers on the X chromosone and male sexual orientation. *Science*, 261.

Hamilton, J. A., & Harberger, P. N. (Eds.) (1992). *Postpartum psychiatric illness: A picture puzzle*. Philadelphia: University of Pennsylvania Press.

Hammonds, E. (1997). Toward a genealogy of black female sexuality: The problematic of silence. In M. J. Alexander & C. Mohanty (Eds.), *Feminist genealogies, colonial legacies, democratic futures* (pp. 170-192). New York: Routledge Press.

Hampson, S. (2001, January 25). And now, the nudes. *The Globe and Mail*, pp. R1, R4.

Haney-Lopez, I. (1996). *White by law: The legal construction of race*. New York: University of New York.

Hanna, J. L. (1998). Undressing the first admendment and corsetting the striptease dancer. *The Drama Review, 42*, 38-69.

Hannah-Moffat, K. (1997). *From Christian maternalism to risk technologies: Penal powers and women's knowledges in the governance of female prisoners*. Ph.D. dissertation, Toronto, University of Toronto.

Harris, F. (1997). *Martensville—Truth or justice? The story of the Martensville daycare trials*. Toronto: Dundurn Press.

Havelock, E. (1912). *The task of social hygiene*. London: Constable.

Hazlitt, T. (1965, January 9). Legal or illegal: City's night spots roar wide open. *Vancouver Daily Province*, p. A3.

Health league hits pasteurization "buck passing": New president Dr. D. H. Williams plans "vitamin racket" campaign. (1941, March 29). *Vancouver News-Herald*.

Hegarty, M. (1998). Patriot or prostitute: Sexual discourses, print media, and American women during World War II. *Journal of Women's History, 10*, 2, 112-136.

Helfer, M. E., Kempe, R. S., & Krugman, R. D. (Eds.) (1997). *The battered child* (7th ed.) Chicago: University of Chicago Press.

Henriques, J., Urwin, C., Venn, C., & Walkerdine, V. (1984). *Changing the subject: Psychology social regulation and subjectivity*. London: Methuen.

Herman, J.L. (1981). *Father-daughter incest*. Cambridge: Harvard University Press.

Heron, C., & Storey, B. (1986). *On the job: Confronting the labour process in Canada*. Montreal and Kingston: McGill Queens University Press.

Highcrest, A. (1997). *At home on the stroll: My twenty years as a prostitute in Canada*. Toronto: Knopf.

Hindmarch, I. & Brinkman, R. (1999). Trends in the use of alcohol and other drugs in cases of sexual assault. *Human psychopharmacology 14* (4), 225-231.

Hobsbawm, E. (1990). *Nations and nationalism since 1780*. Cambridge, MA: Cambridge University Press.

Home and school club tries to be dictator. Interview with Trustee Wanless. (1922, January 24). *Toronto Daily Star*.

hooks, b. (1990). Homeplace. *In Yearning*. Toronto: Between the Lines.

Hunt, A. (1993). *Explorations in law and society: Toward a constitutive theory of law*. London: Routledge Press.

Hunt, A. (1999) *Governing morals: a social history of moral regulation*. New York: Cambridge University Press.

Hunt, A., & Wickham, G. (1994). *Foucault and law: Towards a sociology of law as governance*. Cambridge: Cambridge University Press.

Huttenback, R. (1976). *Racism and empire*. Ithaca: Cornell University Press.

Iacovetta, F. (1992). Such hardworking people: Italian immigrants in postwar Toronto. In

Remaking their lives: Women immigrants, survivors, and refugees (pp. 126, 135-167). Montreal & Kingston: McGill Queens University Press.

Iacovetta, F. (1992). Making "new Canadians": Social workers, women, and reshaping of immigrant families. In F. Iacovetta & M. Valverde (Eds.), *Gender conflicts: New essays in women's history* (p. 263). Toronto: University of Toronto Press.

Iacovetta, F., & Mitchinson, W. (1998). Social history and case files research. In F. Iacovetta & W. Mitchinson (Eds.), *On the case: Explorations in social history* (p. 21). Toronto: University of Toronto Press.

Ida Siegel, Taped Interview by Don Nethery, 31 May 1976, TBEA, Vertical Files.

International social hygiene day being observed here today: Health league plans special program for city. (1939, January 30). *Vancouver News-Herald*.

Izzo, K. (2001, May). Shake, rattle and roll. *Fashion* (Vancouver edition), 86-90.

Jacobson, D. (1996). *Rights across the border: Immigration and the decline of citizenship*. Baltimore: John Hopkins University Press.

Jagose, A. M. (1996). *Queer theory: An introduction* (pp. 7-21). New York: New York University Press.

Jarett, L. (1997). *Stripping in time: A history of erotic dancing*. London: HarperCollins.

Jateau, D. (1995) Theorizing from the margins: Ethnic communalizations in the world systems. *Nations and Nationalism 2*, 1, 45-65.

Jateau, D. (1997). Beyond multicultural citizenship: The challenge of pluralism in Canada. In V. Bader (Ed.), *Citizenship and exclusion*. Amsterdam: University of Amsterdam Press.

Jay, M. (1998). *Artificial paradises: a drugs reader*. Harmondsworth: Penguin.

Jealousy the cause of big school row (1921, October 28). *Toronto Daily Star*.

Jenkins, P. (1992). *Intimate enemies: moral panics in contemporary Great Britain*. New York: Aldine de Gruyter.

Jenkins, P. (1994). *Using murder: the social construction of serial homicide*. New York: Aldine De Gruyter.

Jenkins, P. (1996). *Pedophiles and priests: Anatomy of a contemporary crisis*. New York: Oxford University Press.

Jenkins, P. (1997). *Moral panic: Changing concepts of the child molester in modern America*. New Haven: Yale University Press.

Jenkins, P. (1999). *Synthetic panics: the symbolic politics of designer drugs*. New York: New York University Press.

Jenks, C. (1997). *Childhood*. New York: Routledge Press.

Jesser, C., & Donovan, L. (1969). Nudity in the art training process. *Sociological Quarterly, 10*, 355 371.

Johnson, A. G. (1995). *The Blackwell dictionary of sociology*. Cambridge: Blackwell.

Johnson, C. (1988). The children's war: The mobilization of Ontario youth during the Second World War. In R. Hall, W. Westfall, & L. S. McDowell (Eds.), *Patterns of the past. Interpreting Ontario's history*. Toronto: Dundern Press.

Johnson, M. (1987). CABE and strippers: A delicate union. In L. Bell (Ed.), *Good girls/bad girls: Sex trade workers and feminists face to face* (pp. 109-113). Toronto: Women's Press.

Johnson, R. (1986/87, Winter). What is Cultural Studies Anyway? *Social Text: Theory/Culture/Ideology 16*, 38-80

Johnston, H. (1989). *The voyage of the Komagata Maru: The Sikh challenge to Canada's colour bar*. Vancouver: University of British Columbia Press.

Jones, R. O. (1944). *Good parents*. School for parents: A series of talks given on the National Network of the CBC. Toronto: National Committee for Mental Hygiene (Canada).

Joppke, C. (Ed.) (1998). *Challenges to the nation-state*. London: Oxford University Press.

Juss, S. (1993). *Immigration, nationality and citizenship*. London: Mansell.

Kealey, G. (1995). *Workers and Canadian history*. Montreal and Kingston: McGill Queens University Press.

Kelly, J. (1991). *A politics of virtue: Hinduism, sexuality, and countercolonial discourse in Fiji*. Chicago: University of Chicago Press.

Kelso, J. J. (1905, April). The modern conception of a probation officer is not that he should exercise constabulary powers. *The Globe and Mail*, p. 116.

Kendall. (1999). Women in lesotho and the (Western) construction of homophobia. In E. Blackwood & Wieringa, S. E. (Eds.), *Female desires, same-sex relations and transgender practices across cultures* (pp. 157-178). New York: Columbia University Press.

Kendrick, W. (1993, January). Book Review of child loving: The erotic child and Victorian culture, by J. R. Kincaid. *The New York Times Book Review 24*, 5.

Kendrick, W. (1995, October). From Huck Finn to Calvin Klein's billboard nymphets. *New York Times Magazine 8*, 84-87.

Kennedy, E. L., & Davis, M. (1993). *Boots of leather, slippers of gold: The history of a lesbian community.* New York: Routledge Press.

Kessler, S. J. (1990). *Women in culture and society* (Report no. 81-502). Austin, TX: Pro-Ed.

Kessler, S.J. (1995). The medical construction of gender: Case management of intersexes infants. In E. D. Nelson & B. W. Robinson (Eds.), *Gender in the 1990s, images, realities and issues* (pp. 8-28). Toronto: Nelson Canada/ITP.

Kessler, S.J. (1998). *Lessons from the intersexed.* New Burnswick, N.J.: Rutgers University Press.

Kessler, S.J. & McKenna, W. (1978). *Gender: An enthnomethodological approach* (pp.112-141). Chicago: University of Chicago Press.

Ketchum, J.D. (1961). The family: Changing patterns in an industrial society. In *Canadian family study, 1957-1960* (pp.16, 19). Toronto: Canadian Home and School and Parent-Teacher Federation.

Kincaid, J. R. (1992). *Child-loving: The erotic child and Victorian culture.* New York: Routledge.

Kincaid, J. (1998). *Erotic innocence: The culture of child molesting.* Durham: Duke University Press.

Kinsey, A. C. et al. (1948). *Sexual behaviour in the human male.* Philadelphia and London: W.B. Saunders.

Kinsey, A. C. et al. (1953). *Sexual behaviour in the human female.* Philadelphia and London: W.B. Saunders.

Kinsman, G. (1996). *The regulation of desire: Homo and hetero sexualities* (2nd ed.) Montreal: Black Rose Books.

Kinsman, G. (1996, August). "Responsibility" as a strategy of governance: regulating people living with AIDS and lesbians and gay men in Ontario. *Economy and Society, 25*, 3, 393-409.

Kinsman, G. (2000). Constructing gay men and lesbians as national security *risks, 1950-9170*. In G. Kinsman, D. Buse, & M. Stedman (Eds.), *Whose national security? Canadian state surveillance and the creation of enemies* (pp. 143-153). Toronto: Between the Lines.

Kish, C. (1997). *A knee joint is not entertainment: The moral regulation of burlesque in early twentieth-century Toronto.* Unpublished master's thesis, Department of History, York University, Toronto, Ontario.

Kisker, G. (1947, August 1). Why you fight with your wife/husband. *Maclean's Magazine 60*, 1, 36-37.

Knock insane ideas out of the children's heads (1921, November 24). *Telegram.*

Kondapi, C. (1951). *Indians overseas, 1838-1949.* London: Oxford University Press.

Korinek, V. (2000). *Roughing it in the suburbs: Reading Chatelaine Magazine in the fifties and sixties.* Toronto: University of Toronto Press.

Kramar, K. J. (2000). *Unwilling mothers and unwanted babies: Infanticide and medico-legal responsibility in 20th century Canadian legal discourse.* Unpublished doctoral dissertation, Centre of Criminology, University of Toronto, Toronto, Ontario, Canada.

Kramarae, C., & Treichler, P., with Russo A. (1985). *A feminist dictionary.* Boston: Pandora Press.

Kuhn, A. (1988). *Cinema, censorship and sexuality, 1909-1925.* London: Routledge Press.

Kymilica, W. (1995). *Multicultural citizenship: A liberal theory of minority rights.* Oxford: Claredon Press.

Lancombe, D. (2001, Spring). The social construction of child safety: Oprah and the child abductor. *Red Feather Journal of Postmodern Criminology,* Article 003. Retrieved October 5, 2002, <www.tryoung.com/journal-grad.html/4Shon/index4.html>.

Lang, P. (1997, January 23). Bennest charges dropped: principal's reputation ruined despite withdrawl of two most serious charges. *Xtra West!*, p. 9.

Lang, S. (1999). Lesbians, men-women, and two-spirits: Homosexuality and gender in Native American cultures. In E. Blackwood & Wieringa, S. E. (Eds.), *Female desires, same-sex relations and transgender practices across cultures* (pp. 91-116). New York: Columbia University Press.

Lareau, A. (1989). *Home advantage: Social class and parental intervention in elementary education.* London: Falmer Press.

Latour, B. (1987). *Science in action.* Cambridge, MA: Harvard University Press.

Lautman, R. (1980-1981 Fall/ Winter). The pink triangle, the persecution of homosexual males in Nazi Germany. In S. J. Licata & R. P. Peterson, (Ed.), *Historical perspectives on homosexuality,* special issue of *Journal of Homosexuality,* 6,1/2; co-published by the Haworth Press, Inc., pp. 135-139; Stein and Day, New York, 1981, pp. 141-160.

LeVay, S. (1991, August). A difference in hypothalmic structure between heterosexual and homosexual men. *Science 253*, 30.

LeVay, S. (1993). *The sexual brain.* Cambridge, MA: MIT Press.

Laycock, S. R. (1944, December). Parent education is adult education. *Food for Thought 5*, 3, 4-5.

Laycock, S.R. (1945, December). New approaches to sex education. *The School*, 312.

Laycock, S. R. (1950, January). Psychological factors in marriage. *The Prairie Messenger*, 9, 12.

Leblanc, D. (2001, August 22). Ottawa gives free ad space to strip club. *The Globe and Mail*, p. A5.

Lenson, D. (1995). *On drugs.* Minneapolis: University of Minnesota.

Leroux, J. A. (1939, November 28). Blasted marriages and tragic babies mean social waste: Prudery and taboo stand in way of venereal disease control. *Vancouver Province.* Reprinted from Bulletin of the Provincial Board of Health.

Letters to Chatelaine. (1956, May). *Chatelaine 28*, 3

Lévesque, A. (1994). *Making and breaking the rules: Women in Quebec, 1919-1939* (Y. M Klein, Trans.) (p. 24). Toronto: McClelland & Stewart.

Levin, B. (2001). *Reforming education: From origins to outcomes.* London: Routledge Press Falmer.

Lewis, J. (1998). Lap dancing: Personal and legal implications for exotic dancers. In J. E. Elias, V.L. Bullough, et al. (Eds.), *Prostitution: Whores, hustlers, and johns* (pp. 376-389). Amherst: Prometheus.

Lewontin, R. C., (2001). Quoted by D. McNally in *Bodies of meaning, studies on language, labor, and liberation* (p. 83). Albany, NY: State University of New York Press.

Liazos, A. (1999) The poverty of the sociology of deviance: Nuts, sluts and preverts. In H. Pontell, (Ed.), *Social deviance* (3rd ed.) (pp. 117-130). New Jersey: Prentice Hall.

Liepe-Levinson, K. (2002). *Strip show: Performances of gender and desire.* London and New York: Routledge Press.

Lin, J. (2000, March 30). Three strips and she's out of here. *Vancouver Sun*, p. F4.

Little, M. (1998). *No car, no radio, no liquor permit: The moral regulation of single mothers in Ontario, 1920-1997.* Toronto: Oxford University Press.

Little, M. (1999, Spring). The limits of Canadian democracy: The citizenship rights of poor women. *Canadian Review of Social Policy*, 43, 59-76.

Little, M., & Morrison, I. (1999). The pecker detectors are back: Changes to the spousal definition in Ontario welfare policy. *Journal of Canadian Studies*, 34, 2, 110-136.

London, J. (1913). *John Barleycorn.* New York: The Century Co.

Loo, T., & Strange, C. (1997). *Making good: Law and moral regulation in Canada.* Toronto: University of Toronto Press.

MacGillivray, A. (1968, December 20). Column. *Vancouver Sun*, p. A2.

Mackie, J. (2001, March 10). Set'em up, Ross. *Vancouver Sun*, p. E5.

MacKinnon, C. (1983). The male ideology of privacy. *Radical America 17*, 4, 23-35.

MacKinnon, C. (1993). *Only words.* Cambridge, MA: Harvard University Press.

MacLean, D. (1978, October 4-18). *Dick MacLean's Guide: The Fortnightly Restaurant Magazine.*

Marshall, F. J. (Ed.) (1996). *Common ground.* Atlanta: Make Believe Publications.

Martin, R. (1988). Truth, power, self: An interview with Michel Foucault. In M. H. Luther, H. Gutman, & P. Hutton, (Eds.), *Technologies of the self: A seminar with Michel Foucault* (p. 15). Amherst, MA: University of Massachusetts Press.

Matters, I. (1984). Sinners or sinned against? Historical aspects of female juvenile delinquency in British Columbia. In B. K. Latham & R. J. Pazdro, (Eds.), *Not just pin money: Selected essays on the history of women's work in British Columbia.* Victoria: Camosun College.

Mawani, R. (2002). Regulating the "respectable" classes: Venereal disease, gender, and public health initiatives in Canada, 1914-1935. In J. P. S. McLaren, R. Menzies, & D.E. Chunn, (Eds.), *Regulating lives.* Vancouver: UBC Press.

May, E. T. (1988). *Homeword bound: The American family in the Cold War Era* (pp. 27-28, 187). New York: Basic Books.

Maynard, S. (1997). Horrible temptations: Sex, men, and working-class male youth in urban Ontario, 1890-1935. *Canadian Historical Review*, 78, 2, 191-235.

Mayor endorses health campaign. (1942, February). *Vancouver Sun*, p. 3.

Mburu, J. (2000). Awakenings: dreams and delusions of an incipient lesbian and gay movement in Kenya. In P. Drucker (Ed.), *Different rainbows* (pp. 179-182). London: Gay Men's Press.

McCaghy, C. & Skipper, J. (1970). Stripping: Anatomy of a deviant life style. In Feldman, S. & Theilbar, G. (Eds.), *Lifestyles: Diversity in American society.* Boston: Little Brown.

McClintock, A. (1995). *Imperial Leather: Race, gender and sexuality in the colonial contest.* New York: Routledge Press.

McDowell, L. & Sharp, J. (1999). *A feminist glossary of human geography.* New York: Oxford.

McGinnis, J. D. (1988). Bogeymen and the law: The crime comic and pornography. *Ottawa Law Review 20,* 1, 3-25.

McGinnis, J. D. (1988). From salvarsan to penicillin: Medical science and venereal disease control in Canada. In W. Mitchinson & J.D. McGinnis (Eds.), *Essays in the history of Canadian medicine.* Toronto: McClelland & Stewart.

McGinnis, J. D. (1990). Law and the leprosies of lust: Regulating syphilis and AIDS. *Ottawa Law Review 22,* 1, 49-75.

McLaren, A. (1990). *Our own master race: Eugenics in Canada, 1885-1945.* Toronto: McClelland & Stewart.

McLaren, A., & McLaren, A. T. (1998). *The bedroom and the state: The changing practices and politics of contraception and abortion in Canada, 1880-1980* (2nd ed.). Toronto: McClelland & Stewart.

McLaren, J. P. S. (1988). The Canadian magistracy and the anti-white slavery campaign, 1900-1920. In W. Pue & B. Wright, (Eds.), *Canadian perspectives on law & society: Issues in legal history.* Ottawa: Carleton University Press.

McLean, C. (1998, September 14). How a predator can gain family's trust. *Alberta Report, 25,* (39), 26.

McMurray, G. A. (1982). Psychology at Saskatchewan. In M. J. Wright & C. R. Myers (Eds.), *History of academic psychology in Canada* (pp. 181-182). Toronto: C.J. Hofrefe.

McNally, D. (2002). *Another world is possible: globalization and anti-capitalism.* Winnipeg: Arbeiter Ring Publishing.

Menzies, R. (2002). "Unfit" citizens and the B.C. Royal Commission on mental hygiene, 1925-1928. In R. Adamoski, D. E. Chunn, & R. Menzies, (Eds.), *Contesting Canadian citizenship: Historical readings.* Peterborough, ON: Broadview Press.

Middlebrook, D. W. (1998). *Suits me: The double life of Billy Tipton.* Boston and New York: Houghton and Mifflin Company.

Miles, R. (1989). *Racism.* London: Routledge.

Miller, J. R. (1996). *Shingwauk's vision: A history of native residential schooling.* Toronto: University of Toronto Press.

Miller, R. (1944, January 14). Pres. Somanos WI to Hart. GR1222, Box 175, File 1, Provincial Archives of British Columbia.

Millett, K. (1973). *The prostitution papers.* New York: Avon Books.

The $1 million Martensville trial. (1994, April 25). *Alberta Report, 21* (8), 43.

Dian M. (2000, Summer). Telling secrets: Sex, power and narratives in Indian residential school histories. *Canadian Woman Studies/les cahiers de la femme 20,* 2, 92-107.

Ministry of Community and Social Servies, Ontario. (1995, October). *Residing with a spouse.* Family benefits policy guidelines 0203-05.

Ministry of Community and Social Services, Ontario. (1998, November). *Welfare fraud control report.* News release.

Ministry of Community and Social Services, Ontario. (1998, November 13). *Government anti-fraud initiatives saves $100 million.* News release.

Ministry of Community and Social Services, Ontario. (2000, April 1). Press release, <www.gov.on.ca/CSS/page/news/news2000/apr1000.html>

Mohr, R. D. (1996, March/April). The pedophilia of everyday life. *Art Issues, 42.*

Moore, D. (2000). Risking Saturday night: regulating student alcohol use through commonsense. *Theoretical Criminology 4* (4), 411-428.

Munt, S. (1998). *Butch/femme: Inside lesbian gender.* New York: Routledge Press.

Murray, S. O. & Roscoe, W. (Eds.) (1998). *Boy-wives and female husbands: Studies of African homosexualities.* New York: St. Martin's Press.

Must use English tongue (1918, December 21). *Telegram.*

Nack, W. & Yaeger, D. (1999, September 13). Who's coaching your kid? The frightening truth about child molestation in youth sports. *Sports Illustrated,* 91 (10), 40-53.

Nagle, J. (Ed.) (1997). *Whores and other feminists.* New York: Routledge Press.

Nathan, D. & Snedeker, M. (1995). *Ritual abuse and the making of a modern American witch hunt.* New York: Basic Books.

National Council of Welfare (1995, 1996). *Poverty profile.* Ottawa: National Council of Welfare.

National Post, 1999, January 1999, p. A2.

Nestle, J. (Ed.) (1992). *Persistent desire: A femmebutch reader.* Boston: Alyson Publications, Inc.

Nilsen, D. (1980). The "social evil": Prostitution in Vancouver, 1900-1920. In B. Latham & C. Less

(Eds.), *Selected essays on women's history in B.C.* (pp. 205-228). Victoria: Camosun College.

No French in Brown School, board refuse permit to club (1922, February 3). *Telegram.*

Norris, K. (1938, July 30). Heart to heart: This girl's life need not have been destroyed; parents should take responsibility. *Vancouver Province.*

O'Malley, P. (1992). Risk, power, and crime prevention. *Economy and Society 21,* 252-275.

O'Malley, P. (1993) Risk and responsibility. *Economy and Society 21,* 3, 252-275.

O'Malley, P. (1996). Risk and responsibility. In A. Barry, T. Osborne, & N. Rose, (Eds.), *Foucault and political reason.* London: UCL Press.

O'Malley, P. (1999). Consuming risks: harm minimization and the government of drug "users". In R. Smandych, (Ed.), *Governable places: readings on governmentality and crime control.* Ashgate: Dartmouth.

O'Malley, P., Weir, L., & Shearing, C. (1997, November). Governmentality, criticism, politics. *Economy and Society 26,* 4, 501-517.

O'Donovan, K. (1985). *Sexual divisions in law.* London: Weidenfeld and Nicholson.

Ontario Association of Children's Aid Societies. (1998a, February). *Inquest Recommendations by Topic,* (pp. 1, 17). Toronto, ON.

Ontario Association of Children's Aid Societies. (1998b). *Ontario Child Mortality Task Force Recommendations: A Progress Report.*

Ontario Association of Interval and Transition Houses. (1997). *Some impacts of the Ontario Works Act on survivors of violence against women.*

Ontario Child Mortality Task Force. (1997). *Ontario Child Mortality Task Force—Final Report.* Ontario Association of Children's Aid Societies and the Office of the Chief Coroner of Ontario.

Ontario Department of the Provincial Secretary, (1917, February 7). J.J. Kelso, Superintendent, Neglected and dependent children, to honourable W. D. McPherson, Provincial Secretary. St. Mary's Industrial School Papers, RG 8, Archives of Ontario.

Ontario Department of the Provincial Secretary, (1937, March 8). Mental health director's report. St. Mary's Industrial School Papers, RG 60-11, MS 1124-MS 1127, Archives of Ontario.

Ontario Department of the Provincial Secretary, (1919-1937, passim). School attendance report, Placement Officer's report, Inspection of home for parole. St. Mary's Industrial School Papers, RG 60-11, MS 1124-MS 1127 and RG-60-9, MS 1097, Archives of Ontario.

Ontario Department of Public Welfare. (1931/32). Annual report of the minister of public welfare, p. 39. Ontario Archives.

Ontario Department of Public Welfare. (1932/33). Annual report of the minister of public welfare, p. 8. Ontario Archives.

Ontario Department of Public Welfare. (1933/34). Annual report of the minister of public welfare, pp. 23, 31, 33. Ontario Archives.

Ontario Department of Public Welfare. (1934/35). Annual report of the minister of public welfare, pp. 12-13, 17. Ontario Archives.

Ontario Department of Public Welfare. (1936/37). Annual report of the minister of public welfare, pp. 26, 28, 29. Ontario Archives.

Ontario Department of Public Welfare. (1957). A historical review of Ontario legislation on child welfare (p. 31). RG29-138-0-18. Ontario Archives.

Ontario Industrial School Advisory Board. (1935). Report of Committee Appointed to Investigate the Present Juvenile Reformatory Schools

Ontario Law Reform Commission. (1995). Report on the Law of Coroners.

Ontario Ministry of Community and Social Services. "Government's Step by Step Reform of the Child Welfare System," News release October 18, 1998. <www.gov.on.ca:80/CSS/page/news/nr97-98/oct2898fs.html>. (cited January 31, 2000).

Ontario Workfare Watch, Interim Report. (1999, April 30). *Broken promises: Welfare reform in Ontario.* Retrieved October 5, 2002, from <www.welfarewatch.toronto.on.ca/promises/report.htm>.

Ontario Workfare Watch, Interim Report. (1999, April 30). *Life on welfare in 1999. Broken promises: Welfare reform in Ontario.* Retrieved October 5, 2002, from <www.welfarewatch.toronto.on.ca/promises/life.htm>.

Ontario Workfare Watch, Interim Report. (1999, April 30). *Ontario works, on paper and on the ground. Broken promises: Welfare reform in Ontario.* Retrieved October 5, 2002, from <www.welfarewatch.toronto.on.ca/promises/paper.htm>.

Ornstein, M. (1995). *A profile of social assistance recipients in Ontario.* Toronto: Institute for Social Research, York University.

Ottawa, E. B. (1957, January). Quarrels beat the "road blocks". (Letter to the editor). *Chatelaine 29,* 1, 2.

Oziewicz, E. (2000, February 19). Canada's bare essentials. *The Globe and Mail,* p. A11.

Paedophile alert issued by schools. (1997, February 11). *The Globe and Mail.*

Palmer, B. (1983). *Working class experience: The rise and reconstitution of Canadian labour, 1800-1980.* Toronto and Vancouver: Butterworth & Co.

Parents in fear as girl escapes in 7th abduction bid. (1997, February 12*) Toronto Star.*

Parr, J. (1990). *The gender of breadwinners: Women, men and change in two industrial towns.* Toronto: University of Toronto Press.

Parton, N. (1998). Risk, advanced Liberalism and child welfare: The need to rediscover uncertainty and ambiguity. *British Journal of Social Work 28,* 5-27.

Parton, N. (1999). Reconfiguring child welfare practices: Risk, advanced Liberalism, and the government of freedom. In A. Chambon, A. Irving, & L. Epstein (Eds.), *Reading Foucault for social work.* New York: Columbia University Press.

Pateman, C. (1989). Feminist critiques of the public/private dichotomy." In C. Pateman (Ed.), *The disorder of women: Democracy, feminism and political theory.* Stanford: Stanford University Press.

Patton, C. (1985). *Sex and germs.* Montreal: Black Rose Books.

Patton, C. (1989). Resistance and the erotic reclaiming history, setting strategy as we face AIDS. In P. Aggleton, G. Hart, & P. Davies, (Eds.), *AIDS: Social representations, social practices* (pp. 237-251). London: Falmer Press.

Patton, C. (1990). *Inventing AIDS.* New York and London: Routledge Press.

Patton, C. (1996). *Fatal advice: How safe sex education went wrong.* Durham, N.C.: Duke University.

Paulson, D. with Simpson, R. (1996). *An evening at the garden of Allah: Seattle's gay cabaret.* New York: New York University Press.

Payne, M. (Ed.) (1996). *A dictionary of cultural and critical theory.* Oxford: Blackwell.

Pearson, P. (1997). *When she was bad: Violent women and the myth of innocence.* Toronto: Random House of Canada.

Peloquin, G. (1966, September 19). Go-Go cabarets can't go topless. *Vancouver Sun,* p. A4.

Pendergrast, M. (1995). *Victims of memory: Incest accusations and shattered lives.* Hinesburg: Upper Access Books.

Pennacchio, L. G. (1985, Spring). In defence of identity: Ida Siegel and the Jews of Toronto versus the assimilation attempts of the public school and its allies, 1900-1920. *Canadian Jewish Historical Society Journal 9,* 41-60.

Perry, A. (2001). *On the edge of empire: The making of British Columbia, 1849-1871.* Toronto: University of Toronto Press.

Pheterson, G. (1989). *A vindication of the rights of whores.* Seattle: Seal Press.

Pheterson, G. (1996). *The prostitution prism.* Amsterdam: University of Amsterdam Press.

Pfohl, S. (1977). The "discovery" of child abuse. *Social Problems 24,* 310-322.

Picket still on—Three dancers. (1967, October 18). *Vancouver Sun.*

Piven, F. F., & Cloward, R. A. (1971). *Regulating the poor: The functions of public welfare.* New York: Pantheon Books.

Pitsula, J. M. (1982). *Let the family flourish: A history of the Family Service Bureau of Regina, 1913-1982* (p. 72). Regina: Family Service Bureau of Regina.

Plant, R. (1986). *The pink triangle, the Nazi war against homosexuals.* New York: An Owl Book, A New Republic Book, Henry Holt and Company.

Police revert to one o'clock cabaret closing. (1941, December 13). *Vancouver News Herald.*

Poovey, M. (1998). *A history of the modern fact: problems of knowledge in the sciences of wealth and society.* Chicago: University of Chicago Press.

Portes, A. (Ed.) (1995). *The economic sociology of immigration.* New York: The Russell Sage Foundation.

Pratt, J. (1995). Dangerousness, risk and technologies of power. *The Australian and New Zealand Journal of Criminology 28,* 3-31.

Pratt, J. (1996). Criminology and history: Understanding the present. *Criminology and History 8* (1), 60-76

Prentice, A. (1985). Themes in the early history of the Women's Teachers' Association of Toronto. In P. Bourne (Ed.), *Women's paid and unpaid work: Historical and contemporary perspectives* (pp. 97-121, especially pp. 107-110). Toronto: New Hogtown Press.

Prentice, A., Bourne, P., Cuthbert, C. B., Light, B., Mitchinson, W. & Black, N. (1988). *Canadian women: A history* (p. 311). Toronto: Harcourt Brace Jovanovich.

Prentice, A. & Theobald, M. R. (1994). The historiography of women teachers: A retrospect. In A. Prentice & M. R. Theobald (Eds.), *Women who taught: Perspectives on the history of women and teaching* (p. 6). Toronto: University of Toronto Press.

Proper function of correctional institutions (1929, December 6). *Catholic Register*.

Province of British Columbia, Statutes, (1875). *An Act to Make Better for the Qualifications and Registration of Voters*.

Public information. (editorial) (1941, June 14). *Vancouver Herald*.

Raphael, J., & Tolman, R. M. (Eds.) (1997). *Trapped by poverty, trapped by abuse: New evidence documenting the relationship between domestic violence and welfare*. Taylor Institute and the University of Michigan Research Development Center on Poverty, Risk and Mental Health.

Räthzel, N. (1995). Nationalism and gender in West Europe: The German case. In H. Lutz, A. Phoenix, & N. Yuval-Davis, (Eds.), *Crossfires: Nationalism, racism and gender in Europe*. London: Pluto Press.

Ravinow, P. (Ed.) (1984). *The Foucault reader*. New York: Pantheon.

Raymond, J. C. (1991). *The nursery world of Dr. Blatz* (pp. 3-24, 144, 200). Toronto: University of Toronto.

RCMP, Directorate of Security and Intelligence (DSI), *Annual Report*, Ottawa, 1962-1963.

RCMP, Directorate of Security and Intelligence (DSI), *Annual Report*, Ottawa, 1963-1964.

RCMP, Directorate of Security and Intelligence (DSI), *Annual Report*, Ottawa, 1967-1968.

Reeves, M. (1929). *Training schools for delinquent girls* (pp. 337-338). New York: Russell Sage Foundation.

Reisman, D. (1961). *The lonely crowd: A study of the changing American character*. New Haven: Yale University Press.

Report shows big drop in venereal disease here: Syphilis infections down 53 percent in four years. (1942, December 8). *Vancouver News-Herald*.

Reynolds, S. (1999). *Generation ecstasy*. New York: Routledge Press.

Ricardi, N. & Leeds, J. (1997, February 24). Megan's Law calling up old, minor offences. Los Angeles Times. In M. Allen, CBC Ideas series, *Sex Machines*, 1997.

Richardson, T. R. (1989). *The century of the child: The mental hygiene movement and social policy in the United States and Canada* (p. 156). New York: State University of New York Press.

Rigid rules to govern the use of the schools (1921, December 17). *Toronto Daily Star*.

Riley, B. (1997). *Gold diggers of the Klondike: Prostitutes in Dawson City, Yukon, 1898-1908*. Toronto: Watson Dwyer.

Roberts, B. (1988). *Whence they came: Deportation from Canada, 1900-1835*. Ottawa: University of Ottawa Press.

Roberts, D. E. (1993). Racism and patriarchy in the meaning of motherhood. *American University Journal of Gender and the Law 1*, 1-38.

Roberts, N. (1992). *Whores in history: Prostitution in Western society*. London: HarperCollins.

Robin Sharpe. (1997, Winter). (Review of the book *Life on the corner*). Broken Pencil 4.

Rodgers, K. (1994). Wife assault: The findings of national survey, Juristat 14, 9, pp. 1-22 as cited in Mosher, *Managing the Disentitlement of Women*, p. 33.

Roscoe, W. (Ed.) (1988). Gay American Indians. In *Living the spirit, a gay American Indian anthology*. New York: St. Martin's Press.

Roscoe, W. (1996). How to become a berdache: Towards a unified analysis of gender diversity. In G. Herdt, (Ed.), *Third sex, third gender: Beyond sexual dimorphism in culture and history* (pp. 329-372). New York: Zone Books.

Roscoe, W. (1998). *Changing ones, third and fourth genders in Native North America*. New York: St. Martin's Griffin.

Rose, N. (1985). *The psychological complex: Psychology, politics and society in England, 1869-1939*. London: Routledge Press and Kegan Paul.

Rose, N. (1990). *Governing the soul: The shaping of the private self*. London: Routledge Press, 1990.

Rose, N. & Miller, P. (1992). Political power beyond the state: Problematics of government. *British Journal of Sociology 43*, 2,. 172-205.

Rose, S., Kiamin, L. J., & Lewontin, R. C. (1984). *Not in out genes, biology, ideology and human nature*. Harmondsworth: Penguin.

Rosen, R. (1982). *The lost sisterhood: Prostitution in America, 1900-1918*. Baltimore and London: John Hopkins University Press.

Ross, B. (1997). Destaining the (tattooed) delinquent body: Moral regulatory practices at Toronto's Street Haven, 1965-1969. *Journal of the History of Sexuality 8*, 1, 561-595.

Ross, B. (2000, Fall). Bumping and grinding on the line: Making nudity pay. *Labour/le travail 46*, 221-250.

Ross, B. (2002, February 7). Shake, shimmy, and flash that thing. *Xtra West!*, 12.

Ross, B., & Greenwell, K. (2002) *Spectacular striptease: Performing the racial and sexual other in postwar Vancouver.* Unpublished paper, University of British Columbia.

Rotenberg, L. (1974). The wayward worker: Toronto's prostitutes at the turn of the century. In J. Acton, P. Goldsmith, B. Shephard, (Eds.), *Women at work 1850-1930* (pp. 33-70). Toronto: Canadian Women's Educational Press.

Rothe, L. (1997). *The queens of burlesque: Vintage photographs from the 1940s and 1950s.* Atglen, PA: Schiffer Publishing Ltd.

Rothman, D. J. (1980). *Conscience and convenience: The asylum and its alternatives in progressive America.* (pp.252-253, 264). Glenview, IL: Scott, Foresman and Company.

Rush, F. (1980). *The best kept secret: Sexual abuse of children.* Englewood, NJ: Prentice-Hall

Said, D. (1979). *Orientalism.* New York: Vintage Books.

Salutin, M. (1971). Stripper Morality. *Trans-Action, 8,* 8, 12-23.

Samuel Laycock Papers. (1951). *Psychological factors in marriage,* 4.

Sangster, J. (1995). *Earning respect: The lives of working women in small town Ontario, 1920-1960.* Toronto: University of Toronto Press.

Sangster, J. (1996). Incarcerating "bad girls": The regulation of sexuality through the female refuges act in Ontario, 1920-1945. *Journal of the History of Sexuality 7,* 2, 239-275.

Sassen, S. (Ed.) (1996). *Globalization and its discontent.* New York: The New Press.

Scheper-Hughes, N., & Stein, H. F. (1987). Child abuse and the unconscious in American popular culture. In *Child survival: Anthropological perspectives on the treatment and maltreatment of children.* Berkeley: University of California Press.

Schlosser, E. (1997, February). The business of pornography. *U.S. News and World Report,* 10, 44.

Schlossman, S. (1998). Delinquent children: The juvenile reform school. In N. Morris & D. J. Rothman (Eds.), *The Oxford history of the prison* (pp. 330-331, 334-335). Oxford: Oxford University Press.

Scott, D. (1996). *Behind the G-string.* Jefferson, NC: McFarland & Company, Inc. Publishers.

Scott, V. (2001, March 17). I love sex and I'm good at it. *The Globe and Mail,* p. R14.

Scott, V., Miller, P., & Hotchkiss, R. (1987). Realistic feminists. In L.Bell (Ed.), *Good girls/bad girls: Sex trade workers and feminists face to face* (pp. 204-217). Toronto: Women's Press.

Sears, A. (1995). Before the welfare state: Public health and social policy. *Canadian Review of Sociology and Anthropology 32,*2, 169-88.

Sears, A. (2000, November/December). The opening and commodification of gay space, queer in a lean world. *Against the Current,* 89.

Sears, A. (2001, March/April). Can marriage be queer. *New Socialist, 29,* 31-33.

Seidman, S., & Alexander, J. C. (Eds.) (2001). Introduction. *The new social theory reader.* New York: Routledge Press.

Sex education in B.C. schools accomplished fact, says Weir. (1939, June 9). *Vancouver Province,* p. 32.

Sharpe, R. (1994). Manilla letter # 17. *Sodomite Invasion Review,* 6.

Showalter, E. (1990). *Sexual anarchy: Gender and culture at the Fin de Siecle.* Harmondsworth: Penguin Books.

Simmons, C. (1989) Modern sexuality and the myth of Victorian repression. In K. Reiss & C. Simmons, with R. Padgug (Eds.), *Passion and power: Sexuality and history* (pp. 157-177). Philadelphia: Temple University Press.

Simon, J. (1987). The emergence of a risk society: Insurance law and the state. *Socialist Review 95,* 61-89.

Simon, J. (1997). Governing through crime. In L. Friedman & G. Fisher, (Eds.), *The crime conundrum: essays on criminal justice.* New York: Westview Press.

Singer, L. (1993). *Erotic welfare: Sexual theory and politics in the age of epidemic.* London: Routledge Press.

Sissons, C. B. (1922). Little men and big issues. *The Canadian Forum 2,* 522-524.

Skipper, J., & McCaghy, C. (1970). Stripteasers: The anatomy and career contingencies of a deviant occupation. *Social Problems 17,* 3, 391-404.

Skipper, J., & McCaghy, C. (1971). Stripteasing: A sex-oriented occupation. In J. Henslin, (Ed.), *Studies in the sociology of sex* (pp. 275-296). New York: Meredith and Co.

Smart, C. (1989). *Feminism and the power of law.* New York: Routledge Press.

Smith, D. E. (1987). *The everyday world as problematic: Toward a feminist sociology.* Toronto: University of Toronto Press.

Smith, D. E. (1990). K is mentally ill. In D. E. Smith (Ed.), *Texts, facts, and femininity, exploring the relations of ruling.* London and New York: Routledge Press.

Smith, G. (1988). Policing the gay community: An inquiry into textually mediated social relations. *International Journal of the Sociology of Law 16,* 163-183.

Smith, H., & Wakewich, P. (1999). Beauty and the helldivers: Representing women's work and identities in a warplant newspaper. *Labour/le travail, 44,* 71-107.

Snell, J. G. (1983). "The white life for two": The defence of marriage and sexual morality in Canada, 1890-1914. *Histoire sociale/Social History 31,* 111-129.

Snell, J. G. & Abeele, C. C. (1988). Regulating nuptiality: Restricting access to marriage in early twentieth-century English-speaking Canada. *Canadian Historical Review 64/4:* 466-89.

Snell, J.G. *In the shadow of the law,* 9-10.

Sonne, J. L., & Pope, K. S. (1991). Treating victims of therapist-patient involvement. *Psychology, 28,* 174-187.

Spinner, J. (1994). *The boundaries of citizenship: Race, ethnicity and nationality in the liberal state.* Baltimore: John Hopkins University Press.

St. James, M. (1987). The reclamation of whores. In L. Bell (Ed.), *Good girls/bad girls: Sex trade workers and feminists face to face* (pp. 81-87). Toronto: Women's Press.

St. Mary's Training School Ward Files, RG 60-11, MS1124-MS1127; St. John's Training School Ward Files, RG 60-9, MS1090-MS1097, "Committal Reports;" "School Attendance Reports," 1919-1939, passim.

St. Mary's Training School Ward Files, RG 60-11, MS1125, Mental Health Director's Report, 8 March 1937.

Stanko, B. (1997). Safety talk: conceptualizing women's risk assessment as a "technology of the soul". *Theoretical criminology 1* (4), 479-499.

Statistics Canada. (1992). *Lone parent families in Canada* (p.22). Ottawa.

Steedman, C., Uriwn, C., Walkerdine, V., (Eds.) (1985). *Language, gender and childhood.* London: Routledge Press and Kegan Paul.

Stencell, A. W. (1999). *Girl show: Into the canvas world of bump and grind.* Toronto: ECW Press.

Stephen, J. (1995). "The "incorrigible," the "bad" and the "immoral": Toronto's "factory girls" and the work of the Toronto psychiatric clinic. In L. A. Knafla & S.W.S. Binnie, (Eds.*), Law, society and the state: Essays in modern legal history.* Toronto: University of Toronto Press.

Stolcke, V. (1997). The "name" of nationality. In V. Bader (Ed.), *Citizenship and exclusion.* Amsterdam: University of Amsterdam.

Stoler, A. L. (1995). *Race and the education of desire: Foucault's history of sexuality and the colonial order of things.* Durham and London: Duke University Press.

Stoler, A. L. (1997). *Race and the education of desire: Foucault's history of sexuality and the colonial order of things.* Durham and London: Duke University Press.

Stone, L. (1977). *The family, sex and marriage in England, 1500-1800.* London: Weidenfeld & Nicolson.

Strange, C. (1995). Report of the committee appointed to investigate the present juvenile reformatory schools system of Ontario. In *Toronto's girl problem: The perils and pleasure of the city, 1880-1930.* Toronto: University of Toronto Press.

Strange, C., & Loo, T. (1996). Spectacular justice: The circus and trial, and the trial as circus, Picton, 1903. *Canadian Historical Review 77,* 2, 159-184.

Strange C., & Loo, T. (1997). *Making good: Law and moral regulation in Canada.* Toronto: University of Toronto Press.

Strong-Boag, V. (1974, Fall). Canada's wage earning wives and the construction of the middle class, 1945-1960. *Journal of Canadian Studies 29,* 3, 5-25.

Strong-Boag, V. (1991). Home dreams: Women and the suburban experience in Canada, 1945-1960. *Canadian Historical Review, LXXII* 4, 471-504;

Strong-Board, V. (1995). Their side of the story: Women's voices from Ontario's suburbs, 1945-1960. In J. Parr (Ed.), *A diversity of women* (pp. 46-74). Toronto: University of Toronto Press.

Study Finds Free Care Used More. (1982, April). *Toronto Star,* p.14.

Sullivan, S. (1998). *Bombshells: Glamour girls of a lifetime.* New York: St. Martin's Griffin.

Super inquest to probe growing family violence. (1996, September 18). *Toronto Star,* p. A1.

Sutherland, E. (1950). The diffusion of sex psychopath laws. *American Journal of Sociology 56,* 142-148

Sutherland, E. (1950). The sexual psychopath laws. *Journal of Criminal Law and Criminology 40,* 534-554

Swift, K. (1995a). *Manufacturing "bad mothers": A critical perspective on child neglect.* Toronto: University of Toronto Press.

Swift, K. (1995b). Missing persons: Women in child welfare. *Child Welfare LXXIV 3*: 486-502.

Swift, K. (1999). *Failure to protect.* Presentation at the Annual Conference of the Canadian Association of Schools of Social Work. Université de Sherbrooke and Bishops University, Québec, Canada, June 1999.

Syphilis toll: useless tragedy. (1942, February 2). *Vancouver News-Herald*, p. 5.

Tacoma's mayor praises work of doctor in venereal control: Tribute to Dr. D. H. Williams. (1941, December 1). *Vancouver Sun.*

Tarasuk, V. (1997). *A nutrition study of women in families using food banks in Metropolitan Toronto.* Toronto: Department of Nutritional Sciences, Faculty of medicine, University of Toronto.

Teri, L. (1982). Depression in adolescence: Its relationship to assertion and various aspects of self-image. *Journal of Clinical Child Psychology, 11*, 3, 101-106.

Terry, J. (1999). *An American obsession, science, medicine, and homosexuality in modern society* (p. 396). Chicago and London: University of Chicago Press.

Terry, J. (1995). Anxious slippages between "us" and "them": A brief history of the scientific search for homosexual bodies. In J. Terry & J. Urla, (Eds.), *Deviant bodies: Critical perspectives on difference in science and popular culture* (pp. 129-169). Bloomington, IN: Indiana University Press.

Terry, J. (1999). The seductive power of science in the making of deviant subjectivity. In J. Terry (Ed.), *An American obsession, science, medicine, and homosexuality in modern society.* Chicago and London: University of Chicago Press.

Thompson, J. (1997, Fall). Ontario works legislation—Bill 142 legislated poverty for Women. *Lifespin*, cited in Mosher, *Managing the Disentitlement of Women*, p. 46.

Tinker, H. (1976). *Separate and unequal.* Vancouver: University of British Columbia Press.

Toronto Board of Education (1918, December 19). *Minutes* (p. 246).

Toronto Board of Education (1919, January 8). *Minutes*, Management Committee.

Toronto Board of Education (1921, December 8). *Come to defence of lady principals.* Newsclippings, microfilm reel 2, 1916-1921.

Toronto Daily Star, October 9, 1925.

Toronto Home and School Council (1916, February 12). *Minutes.* C7-4, 375 (Box 1 of 9). Toronto Board of Education Archives.

Toronto Home and School Council (1917, April 10). *Minutes.* C7-4, 375 (Box 1 of 9). Toronto Board of Education Archives.

Toronto Home and School Council (1917, June 11). *Minutes.* C7-4, 375 (Box 1 of 9). Toronto Board of Education Archives.

Toronto Home and School Council (1919, November 17). *Minutes.* C7-4, 375 (Box 1 of 9). Toronto Board of Education Archives.

Toronto Home and School Council (1922, January 10). *Minutes.* C7-4, 375 (Box 1 of 9). Toronto Board of Education Archives.

Toronto Home and School Council (1928, September 19). *Minutes.* C7-4, 375 (Box 1 of 9). Toronto Board of Education Archives.

Toronto Home and School Council (1936). *The story of the Toronto Home and School Council through the years 1918-1936* (pp. 20, 44-46). Toronto: the Council.

Tracey, L. (1997). *Growing up naked: My years in bump and grind.* Vancouver and Toronto: Douglas & McIntyre.

Trauma team called to help. (1996, September 6). *Vancouver Province*, p. A4.

Travis, L. E. & Baruch, D. W. (1944). *Problems of everyday life: Practical aspects of mental hygiene* (pp. 66-68, 233). New York: D. Appleton-Century.

Trocmé, N. et al. (2001). *Canadian incidence study of reported child abuse and neglect:* Final report. Health Canada.

Trustee Berlis, quoted in Trustees vote 9 to 7. (1922, February 3). *Toronto Daily Star.*

Turner, B. (Ed.) (1993). *Citizenship and social theory.* London: Sage Publisher.

Trustee Wanless. Home and School Club tries to be dictator.

University Health week (editorial). (1929, February 2). *Vancouver Province.*

Ursel, J. (1992). *Private lives, public policy: 100 years of state intervention in the family* (pp. 205-206). Toronto: Women's Press.

Valverde, M. (1985). *Sex, power and pleasure* (pp. 203-204). Toronto: Women's Press.

Valverde, M. (1991). *The age of light, soap and water: Moral reform in English Canada 1885-1925.* Toronto: McClelland and Stewart/Oxford.

Valverde, M. (1992). When the mother of the race is free. In F. Iaccovetta & M. Valverde (Eds.), *Gender Conflicts.* Toronto: University of Toronto Press.

Valverde, M. (1992). Representing childhood: The multiple fathers of the Dionne Quintuplets. In C. Smart, (Ed.), *Regulating womanhood: Historical essays on marriage, motherhood and sexuality* (pp. 19, 143). London: Routledge Press Press.

Valverde, M. (1994). Introduction. *The Canadian journal of sociology, special issue on moral regulation*, 19, 2 vi-xi.

Valverde, M. (1995). Building anti-delinquent communities: Morality, dender, and generation in the city. In J. Parr (Ed.), *A diversity of women: Ontario, 1945-1980* (pp. 32-34). Toronto: University of Toronto Press.

Valverde, M. (1995, Summer). The mixed social economy as a Canadian tradition. *Studies in political economy, 47*, pp. 33-60.

Valverde, M. (1996). "Despotism" and ethical liberal governance. *Economy and Society 25*, 3, 357-372.

Valverde, M. (1998). *Diseases of the will: Alcohol and the dilemmas of freedom.* Cambridge: Cambridge University Press.

Valverde, M. (Ed.) (1994). *Studies in moral regulation.* Toronto: Centre of Criminology, University of Toronto, 1994. Also published as a special issue of the *Canadian Journal of Sociology 19* (2), 1994.

Valverde, M., & Weir, L. (1988, September). The struggles of the immoral: Preliminary remarks on moral regulation. *Resources for Feminist Research 17*, 3, 31-34.

Vaiverde, Mariana, "When the Mother of the Race is Free" in Franca Iaccovetta and Mariana Valverde (eds) Gender Conflicts, University of Toronto Press, 1992.

Vancouver leads Canada in VD drop. (1941, September 17). *Vancouver News-Herald.*

Vancouver Medical Association (1941, July) (editorial) Bulletin of VMA.

Vancouver Medical Association (1942, February 26). Good pre-natal care for all mothers, rich and poor. *Vancouver Sun.* United Church Archives.

Van Gelder, L. (1999, March 9). Ann Corio, a burlesque queen on broadway is dead. *New York Times*, p. C27.

Venereal disease cases five times as numerous as T.B. in province Dr. Williams states: Prudery, big vested interests delay fight, education is crux campaign. (1939, April 21). *Nelson Daily News.*

Verdict of the Coroner's Jury, (Angela Dombroskie; David Dombroskie; Jamie Lee Burns; Devon Burns) Office of the Chief Coroner for Ontario, Case File No. n/a (1997).

Verdict of the Coroner's Jury, (Baby Girl Waldron), Office of the Chief Coroner for Ontario, Case File No. 12164. 1981.

Verdict of the Coroner's Jury, (Edward Maglicic), Office of the Chief Coroner for Ontario, Case File No. 12803, 1984.

Verdict of the Coroner's Jury, (Jennifer Koval's`kyj-England and Marion Johnson) Office of the Chief Coroner for Ontario, Case File No.n/a (1998).

Verdict of the Coroner's Jury, (Kasandra Hislop (aka) Shepherd), Office of the Chief Coroner for Ontario, Case File No. 14952 (1997).

Verdict of the Coroner's Jury, (Malcolm Bruce McArthur and Jody Lynn McArthur), Office of the Chief Coroner for Ontario, Case File No. 13440 (1986).

Verdict of the Coroner's Jury, (Margret Kasonde), Office of the Chief Coroner for Ontario, Case File No. n/a (1997).

Verdict of the Coroner's Jury, (Shanay Johnson), Office of the Chief Coroner for Ontario, Case File No. 14936, 1997.

Verdict of the Coroner's Jury, (Thomas Michael Davies), Office of the Chief Coroner for Ontario, Case File No. 13221 (1985).

Vice clean-up ordered in Vancouver, VD situation serious. (1939, January 14). *Calgary Daily Herald*, p. 3.

Victorians support anti-vice device. (1941, May 15). *Victoria Times.*

Vincenzi, C. (1998). *Crown powers, subjects and citizens.* London: Pinter.

Waldeck, R.C. (1960, September 29). *The international homosexual conspiracy.* Human Events, reprinted in New York Native, (1981, September 21/October 4), 13.

Walker, J. (1991). Intervention in families. In D. Clarke (Ed.) *Marriage, domestic life and social change: Writings for Jacqueline Burgoyne, 1944-1988.* New York: Routledge Press Press.

Walkowitz, J. (1980). *Prostitution and Victorian society: women, class, and the state.* Cambridge: Cambridge University Press

Walkowitz, J. (1992). *City of dreadful delight: narratives of sexual danger in late Victorian London.* Chicago: University of Chicago Press.

Walker, J. (1997). *"Race," rights and the law in the Supreme Court of Canada.* Toronto: Osgoode Law Society.

Wall, D.F. (1959, May 12). *Security cases involving character weaknesses, with special reference to the problem of homosexuality*. Memorandum to the Security Panel, p. 12.

Ward, D., & Kassebaum, G. (1965). *Women's prison : Sex and social structure*. Chicago : Aldine Publishing Co.

Warner, M. (1999). Beyond gay marriage. In M. Warner (Ed.), *The trouble with normal, sex, politics, and the ethics of queer life* (pp. 81-147). Cambridge, MA: Harvard University Press.

Wasserman, J. (1971, October 19). Jack Wasserman. *Vancouver Sun*, p. A5.

Watmough, D. (1994, May 6). Pro-paedophilia chapbook lacks social analysis. (Review of the book Manila Manic : Vignettes, Vice & Verse). *Xtra West!*, 19, 23.

Weaver, J. C. (1979). The modern city realized: Toronto civic affairs, 1880-1915. In A. Artbise & G. A. Stelter, (Eds.), *Planning and politics in the modern Canadian city* (p. 45). Toronto: MacMillan.

Weeks, J. (1981). *Sex, politics and society*. London: Longman.

Weeks, J. (1985). *Sexuality and its discontents*. London: Routledge Press and Kegan Paul.

Weeks, J. (1986). *Sexuality* (pp. 50-51). Cichester, London, and New York: Ellis Horwood and Tavistock Publications.

Weeks, J. (1991). *Against nature: Essays on history, sexuality and identity*. London: Rivers Oram Press ; Concord, MA: Paul and Co.

Weeks, J. (1995). *Invented moralities, sexual values in an age of uncertainty*. New York: Columbia University Press.

Weeks, J. (1998). The sexual citizen. *Theory, Culture and Society 15*, 3 /4 35-52.

Weintraub, W. (1996). Show business: Lili St. Cyr's town—and Al's and Oscar's. In W. Weintraub (Ed.), *City unique: Montreal days and nights in the 1940s and 50s*. Toronto: McClelland & Stewart Inc.

Weisman, R. (1993, June). *Reflections on the Oak Ridge experiment with psychiatric offenders, 1965-1968*. Paper presented at the annual meeting on the Canadian Sociology and Anthropology Association, Ottawa, ON.

Weissman, A., & Fernie, L. (Producers) (1992). *Forbidden love: the unashamed stories of Canadian lesbians*. [Motion picture]. National Film Board of Canada

Welsh, M., & Donovan, K. (1996, September 18). How the system failed these kids: They died despite signs of abuse. *Toronto Star*, p. A1, A6

Welsh, M., & Donovan, K. (1997, April 19). Cry for the children. *Toronto Star*, Serial Report, p. A1.

Welsh, M., & Donovan, K. (1997, April 26). A cop's crusade. *Toronto Star*, Serial Report, p. A1.

Welsh, M., & Donovan, K. (1997, May 18). Getting away with murder—of children. *Toronto Star*, Serial Report, p. A1, A6.

Welsh, M. & Donovan, K. (1997, June 21). How to save the children. *Toronto Star*, Serial Report, p. A1.

Welsh, M. & Donovan, K. (1998, May 8). *Toronto Star*, p. A3.

Western Weekly Reports (1914). *Re: The Immigration Act and Munshi Singh, vol. vi.*

White, K. (1993). *The first sexual revolution: The emergence of male heterosexuality in modern America*. New York: New York University Press.

Wilczynksi, A. (1997). *Child homicide*. London: Greenwich Medical Media Ltd.

Williams, D. H., M.D., director, division of VD control, British Columbia Board of Health. (1940, February 19). Our health authorities fight venereal disease: Their aim is to add this social plague to the growing list of foes of health vanquished by modern medical science. *Vancouver News-Herald*.

Williams, D. H. (1938, April 14). School, church, home must aid war on venereal disease: High standards of morality must be maintained—education vital. *Vancouver News-Herald*.

Williams, D. H. (1940). Summary report for the year 1940. British Columbia Provincial Board of Health, Division of VD Control. No. 4 (p. E38). Victoria: King's Printer, 1940.

Williams, D. H. (1943, September). Commercialized prostitution and venereal disease control: the results of the suppression of commercialized prostitution on venereal disease in the city of Vancouver. *Canadian Journal of Public Health* 34:8 461-472.

Williams, W. (1986). *The spirit and the flesh: sexual diversity in American Indian culture*. Boston: Beacon Press.

Wiseman, L. (1982, March). Young, sexy, and well-heeled. *Vancouver Magazine*, 29-35, 145.

Wiseman, L. (1982, April). Not your average Joe. *Vancouver Magazine*, 60-64, 68, 84

Wood, D. (1997, December). The naked and the dead: Truth isn't the only victim in the 50-year Penthouse saga. *Vancouver Magazine*, 102-115, 122, 145-146.

Wood, D. (1999). Missing. *Elmstreet Magazine* 4, 2, 96-98.

Woodward backs "prevention week". (1942, January 31). *Vancouver Sun.*

Wolf, A.W. M. (1946). *The parent's manual: A guide to the emotional development of young children* (pp. 216-217). New York: Simon & Schuster.

Wright, M. & Myers, C.R. (Eds.), (1982). *History of academic psychology in Canada* (pp. 145-146). Toronto: C.J. Hofrefe.

Wynter, S. (1987). WHISPER: Women hurt in systems of prostitution engaged in revolt. In F. Delacoste & P. Alexander (Eds.), *Sex work: Writings by women in* the sex industry (pp. 66-70). Pittsburgh, PA: Cleis Press.

Y2K rape drug alert: Women told to watch drinks at New Year bashes. (1999, December 30). *Toronto Sun*, p. 1.

Yeung, T. (1997, October 16). Bennest gets suspended sentence. *Xtra West!*, 7.

Young, R. J. C. (1995). *Colonial desire: Hybridity in theory, culture and race.* London: Routledge Press.

Zumsteg, B. (1998). *Promoting censorship in the name of youth: The Council of Women's Activism against vaudeville in the 1920s and 1930s in Vancouver.* Unpublished paper, University of British Columbia.

CREDITS

This page constitutes an extension of the copyright page. We have made every effort to trace the ownership of all copyrighted material and to secure permission from copyright holders. In the event of any question arising as to the use of any material, we will be pleased to make the necessary corrections in future printings. Thanks are due to the following authors, publishers, and agents for permission to use the material indicated.

TEXT

Chapter 1: **p. 4-16**: Reprinted by permission of Dr. Paula Maurutto; **Chapter 2**: **p. 18-37**: Copyright (1997) From *Discipline, Moral Regulation, and Schooling: A Social History* by Kate Rousmaniere, Kari Dehli and Ning De Coninck-Smith. Reproduced by permission of Routledge, Inc., part of The Taylor & Francis Group; **Chapter 3**: **p. 53-54**: Reproduced from, Western Weekly Report, Vol. V with permission of Carswell Publishing, through the Canadian Copyright Licensing Agency (CANCOPY); **p. 55-56**: Reproduced from, British Columbia Law Reports, Vol. XX with permission of Carswell Publishing, through the Canadian Copyright Licensing Agency (CANCOPY); **p. 56-57**: Reproduced from, British Columbia Law Reports, Vol. XX with permission of Carswell Publishing, through the Canadian Copyright Licensing Agency (CANCOPY); Chapter 4: **p. 63-84**: Reprinted by permission of University of Toronto Press; Chapter 5: **p. 90-101**: Reprinted by permission of University of Toronto Press; Chapter 6: **p. 104-118**: Reprinted by permission of Dr. Mona Gleason; **Chapter 7**: **p. 126**: Reprinted with permission; **p. 132**: Reprinted by permission of Dr. Gary Kinsman; **p. 133**: Reprinted with permission; **p. 140**: Reprinted by permission of Dr. Gary Kinsman; **Chapter 8**: **p. 170**: Reprinted by permission of The Kinsey Institute for Research in Sex. Gender, and Reproduction, Inc.; **Chapter 9**: **p. 201**: Reprinted by permission of Ontario Association of Children's Aid Societies; **Chapter 10**: **p. 217**: Reprinted by permission of Ontario Association of Children's Aid Societies; **Chapter 13**: **p. 301**: Reprinted with permission. 287-288: Copyright © Stanley Cohen, From: *Folk Devils and Moral Panic* by: Stanley Cohen. Reprinted with permission of Palgrave.

PHOTO

Chapter 8: **p.152**: Ross Kenward/Province; **p. 161**: Les Bazso/Province; **p. 167** (right): Bettmann/CORBIS/MAGMA; **p. 167** (left): Bettmann/CORBIS/MAGMA; **p. 168**: Hulton|Archive/Getty Images; **Chapter 14**: **p. 314**: Reprinted by permission of the National Institute on Drug Abuse.

Index

A

Aboriginal peoples
    "Canadianization" attempts, 117
    enfranchisement, 46
    single mothers and welfare anti-fraud measures, 250
    "two-spirited" peoples, 268
Abrams, Philip, 1
Act for the Prevention of Cruelty to, and Better Protection of Children (1892), 13
Adams, Mary Louise, 88–90, 90–101, xiv, xxix
Asian immigrants, 46–48

B

Bakhtin, Mikhail, 309, 310
Becker, Howard S., xii
bell curve, 96–97
Bernhardt, Karl, 105–106
Bernstein, Basil, xxvi
biological determinism
    biological knowledge, 266
    and bisexual experiences, 272
    gender, assumptions of, 268–271
    gendered labelling of hormones, 275–277
    and genes, focus on, 277–278
    and homosexuality, 262–283
    ideological assumptions, 267–268, 273
    inappropriateness of, 283
    and lesbianism, 273
    new "commonsense," 262, 280
    relation to gay community and class formation, 280–281
    and social organization of "backlash" against liberation, 278–280
Blatz, William, 105, 110–111, 114
bottle clubs, 153, 154
British North America Act, 44
Bruce, Roberta, 116–117
burlesque revues, 146

C

casework, 9
Chauncey, George, 93
Chen, Xiaobei, 179, 180, 181, 209–232, 260, xxx
child abuse
    "Caffey's Syndrome," 187
    child abuse homicide, development of, 186–187
    child death review teams, 190–200
    coroners' inquests, 200–204
    Department of Justice (federal), 204–205
    development of ideas about, 184–189
    discourse, rise of, 186
    "discovery" of, 187–189
    "fatal child abuse syndrome," 190–200
    increase in cases, interpretation of, 291
    international context, 190–200
    and juvenile delinquency, 199
    medicalization of, 187–189
    as official cause of death, 183
    Ontario Child Mortality Task Force, 200
    sentences for child abuse homicide, 197–198
    sexual abuse. *See* child sexual abuse
child deaths
    and child protection-focused reforms, 212
    Criminal Code, potential reform of, 226, 229–230
    Death by Child Abuse/Neglect, proposal for, 229–230
    discourse of, 215–216
    homicide, shift away from, 219–220
    and neglect, manufacture of relationship between, 220–222
    preoccupation with safety, 213
child pornography
    Canada's current legal problems with, 295–296
    exceptions, 296–297
    experts, role of, 299–300
    Justice Shaw's decision, 285–286
    law's response to, 294–297
    moral panic and, 290–303
child protection
    child-specific criminal offences, 229–232
    critical analysis of restructuring, 222–232
    "dangerous parents," invention of, 216–219
    facts, 215
    poverty and, 212–213
    provision of, 210
    restructuring of, 211
    Risk Assessment Model, 226–229
child sexual abuse
    causes of panic, 301–303
    experts, role of, 297–301
    law's response, 294–297
    media, role of, 291–293
    moral panic and, 289, 290–303
    special legal status of children, 230–231
Child Welfare Reform, 211

children at risk, 179
Children's Aid Societies, 13
chronotypes, 261, 309, 310–311, 313–320, 324
Chunn, Dorothy, 3, 63–84, 107, 179, xxix
citizenship
    Asian immigrants, 46–48
    and Imperial policies, 41
    imperialism and, 59
    Indian immigrants, 48–58
    ius suli, principle of, 43
    Komagata Maru case, 40–41
    Munshi Singh, 51–58
    Natal formula, 50–51
    nineteenth-century practices, 42–43
    race and, 58–60
    racialization of citizenship rights, 45–48
    subject and citizen notions in Canada, 43–45
class, and psychology, 116–117
club drugs, 314, 316, 317, 318
Cohen, Stanley, 287–288
commercial sex industry, 146–151
corporal punishment, 5
Corrigan, Philip, 21, 97, 238, xxix, xxvi–xxviii
Courtice, Ada, 22, 23–24, 27, 34
Curtis, Bruce, 19

D

date rape drugs
    chronotypes, 310–311, 313–320
    classification as, 313–314
    de-gendering sexual assault, 320–322
    highly mixed knowledge format, 319
    personification of, 320–322
    raves, 311, 316–317, 320
    "recuperation" of feminist practices as remedies, 312–313, 322–324
    stories about, 309–310
    "trusted friends" collective, 322–324
Davies, Lisa, 169
Dean, Mitchell, xxix
Dehli, Kari, 2, 18–37
delinquents. *See* juvenile delinquents
deviance
    constructing forms of, 266
    introduction, ix–xiv
    mainstream notions of, 125
disciplinary society, 2
discipline, 2
Discipline and Punish: The Birth of the Prison (Foucault), 5
discourse, xxii
Douglas, Mary, 122
Doyle, Kegan, 260–261, 285–303
Dua, Ena, 2, xxix, xxvii
Dua, Enkashi, 40–60
Dubois, W.E.B., xiv
Durkheim, Émile, xi, xxvi

E

Ecstasy, 309, 311, 315, 316
essentialist interpretation of sexuality, xxiii
ethnicity, and psychology, 116–117
ethnocentrism, xvi
experts' role in governance of delinquents, 9–11

F

fact, xxvii
family
    children, regulation of, 112–113
    dislocation, explanations for, 108
    divorce rate, 109–110
    emotional health of, 107
    family crisis rhetoric, 107
    parents, role of, 114–116
    postwar family life myths, 108
    propriety, gap in conceptions of, 107
    psychological construction of ideal family, 89, 104–118
female principals, 32–35
feminist analysis, relevance of, 83–84
the fifties. *See* family
Forcese, Dennis, xvi
Foucault, Michel
    "bio-power," 266
    bourgeois order, framing of, 58
    disciplinary society, 5
    discourses, 91, 97
    governing, concept of, xxxi
    governmentality, 213
    History of the Present approach, 1
    limitations of work, 129
    modern state power, context of, 58
    normalization as key power strategy, 125
    panopticon, theory of, 173
    power, approach to, xx, xxi
    power, normalization of, 106
    power, techniques of, xxiv
    sexual discourses, 95
    sexuality as social and historical construction, xxiii
Friedman, Andrea, 151

G

Gavigan, Shelley, 231
gender
    de-gendering sexual assault, 320–322
    "natural attitude" assumptions of, 268–271
genealogy, 2
GHB, 313, 314, 317, 321
Gleason, Mona, 87, 89, 104–118, xxix
Goffman, Erving, xii
gonorrhea, 70
    see also venereal disease
governance
    experts' role, and delinquents, 9–11
    probation, 13–15

G

governing technologies, xxx
governmentality
    citizenship and race, 58–60
    concept of, xxx–xxxi
    underlying principles, 214
Gramsci, Antonio, xix
The Great Arch (Corrigan and Sayer), xxvi

H

Hacking, Ian, 96
Hanna, Judith Lynne, 174
hebephilia, 298–299
Hegarty, Marilyn, 151
hegemony, xix
Henriques, Julian, 96
heteronormative, 171
heterosexual hegemony, xxvii
heterosexuality
    binary model of, 93
    development of, 94–95, 99
    dichotomization of, 92
    as discursively constituted social category, 99
    and gender hierarchy, 94
    as historical and social term, 274
    normative, model of, 88
    recent emergence as articulated concept, 94
    and reorganization of gender relations, 93
    sexualized marriages, 94
    social construction of, xiii–xiv
    as subject of investigation, 91–101
History of Sexuality (Foucault), xxiii
The History of Sexuality (Foucault), 97
History of the Present approach, 1
Home and School clubs. *See* Toronto Home and School Council
homosexuality
    biological determinism *vs.* social constructionism, 262–283
    "causes" of and relevance, 267
    community and class formation, 280–281
    criminalization of, 138
    cultural sexual practices, 272–273
    dichotomization of, 92
    diversity of experience and allegiance, 92
    equation with perversion, 92–93
    genes and, 277–278
    hegemonic "commonsense," assertions of, 271
    as historical and social term, 274
    lesbians in the military, 132
    medicalization of, 274–275
    national security as moral regulation, 121–144
    national security construction of, 127
    public/private distinctions, 138
    and striptease, 168–171
    Wolfenden approach, 138
Howell, Alfred, 45
humanist thought, xx
Hunt, Alan, 288, xxix, xxxi

I

Iacovetta, Franca, 108
immigrants
    Asian immigrants, 46–48
    Elizabeth Street/Hester Howe school controversy, 25–27
    Indian immigrants, 48–58
    Munshi Singh, 51–58
    parents, and juvenile delinquency, 116
    sex workers, 172–173
indentured labour, 49
Indian Act, 46
Indian immigrants, 48–58
industrial schools, 6–8, 80
infanticide
    as "child abuse homicide," 183, 184, 186, 205–206
    development of ideas about, 184–189
    repeal of, recommendations for, 202, 203–204, 205
    traditional view of, 189
institutional ethnography, 128–129
"intersexed" infants, 270

J

Jenkins, Philip, 306–307
Johnson Kramar, Kirsten, 179, 180, 182–206, 260, xxix
Johnston, Richard, 98
Jones, Robert, 114
juridical power, xxiv
juvenile delinquents
    casework, 9
    and child abuse, 199
    and discipline, 4–15
    experts, role of, 9–11
    historical perspective, 5–6
    and immigrant parents, 116
    industrial schools, 6–8
    moral regulation and, 4–15
    normalization of, 112–113
    parents, blame on, 113
    parole, 11–12
    in postwar years, 112–113
    probation, 13–15
    standardized reports, 9–10
Juvenile Delinquents Act (1908), 13

K

Katz, Jonathan Ned, 92
Kelso, J.J., 13
Ketchum, David, 105, 109, 110
Kincaid, James, 302
Kinsey, Alfred, 97, 169
Kinsman, Gary, 87, 89, 121–144, 259–260, 262–283, xiv, xxiv, xxvii
Komagata Maru, 40–41

L

Lacombe, Dany, 260–261, 285–303
Laycock, Samuel, 105, 109–110, 112, 115
Lewontin, Richard C., 277
Liazos, Alexander, xii–xiii
Little, Margaret Hillyard, 180–181, 235–255, xxvii

M

marriages
    democratization, 110–111
    in 1940s, 110
    sexualized marriages, 94
Maurutto, Paula, 2, 4–16
Marxist political theory, xvii–xix, xxii, xxiv
master narratives, xx
maternal neonaticide. *See* infanticide
McCaghy, Charles, 168
medical examinations, and moral judgment, 10–11
migration, 42–43, 58–60
Moore, Dawn, 261, 306–325, xxxi
moral panics
    child abuse, 289, 290–303
    child pornography, 290–303
    and child pornography, 285–303
    definition of, 287–290
    experts, role of, 297–301
    as moral regulation, 260
    pedophilia, 290–303
    risk society, 261, 290
    risk society and, xxx
    tools for study of, 306–309
moral regulation
    of entire families, 12
    forms of expression, limit on, 97–98
    introduction, xxvi–xxix, xxxi
    and juvenile delinquents, 4–15
    makeup of, 123
    medical examinations, 10–11
    of mothers, 20, 21–22
    national security as, 129–136
    Ontario welfare policy, 240
    and power of normalization, 97
    probation and, 13–15
    ruling forms of, 142
    and schools, 21–22
    of sexuality, 122–127
    single mothers, 237, 238–245
    subjectivity and construction of social subjects, 98
morality, definition of, xv
mothers
    see also Toronto Home and School Council
    blame on, 114–116
    conflict with principal, 32–35
    "good mother," notion of, 25–27, 36
    immigrant mothers, 25–27
    increasing punishment of, 180
    infanticide and child abuse homicide, 182–206
    moral regulation and, 21–22
    and school system, 18–37
    single mothers. *See* single mothers
    subordinate "insider" position, 20–21

N

Natal formula, 50–51
national security
    and anti-capitalist globalization movement, 143–144
    "character weakness," conceptualization of, 131–132
    construction of homosexuality, 127
    Foucault, analysis derived from, 129
    ideological construction of, 130–131
    interrogation and blackmail, 133–136
    lesbians, 132
    Marxist feminist sociological approach, 128
    mediated character of, 136–138
    and moral regulation, 129–136, 143–144
    resistance, 139–143
naturalisation laws, 43–45
normalization
    as deviance-prevention mechanism, 96
    discourses and practices, 95–96
    effective exercise of power, 96
    introduction, ix, xxiv
    juvenile delinquents, 112–113
    medical assessments on delinquents, 11
    and power, 125
    power of, and moral regulation, 97
    of sexuality, 122–127
    and social norms, 96
    subjectivity and construction of social subjects, 98
norms, 96

O

Ontario Industrial School Advisory Board, 12
Owram, Douglas, 110

P

parental rights, displacement of, 12
parents
    see also mothers
    "dangerous parents," invention of, 216–219
    and juvenile delinquency, 113
    moral regulation of, 21–22
    role of, in "normal" families, 114–116
    sentences for child abuse homicide, 197–198
    as social accomplishment, 19
parole, regulatory processes of, 11–12
Parsons, Talcott, xi
pedophilia
    hebephilia, erasure of, 298–299
    moral panic around, 290–303
    "of everyday life," 302–303
    redefinition of abuser, 298
    treatment of, 294–295

pluralist state, xvii
political rationalities, xxx
post-modernism, xx–xxi
post-structuralism, xxi
The Poverty of the Sociology of Deviance: Nuts, Sluts, and Preverts (Liazos), xii
power
    approaches to, xiv–xxv
    deviancy research and, xiii
    and normalization, 125
    psychology, 106–107
    techniques of, xxiv
probation, 13–15
prostitution, suppression of, 81–82
psychology
    class and, 116–117
    construction of family, 89, 104–118
    divorce rate, 109–110
    and ethnicity, 116–117
    gendered thinking, 115–116
    homosexuality, "cure" for, 274–275
    normalcy, regulation of, 105
    parental power over children, 113
    power and influence in postwar society, 106–107
    race and, 116–117
    theoretical perspectives on, 106–107
public/private distinction, 64–66, 138

R

race
    and citizenship, 42–43, 45–48, 58–60
    and migration, 42–43, 58–60
    "mothers of the race," sex regulation of, 73–78
    psychology and, 116–117
    social construction of, 279
    whiteness, as social location, xiv
racialization of citizenship rights, 45–48
racism
    focus on, xiv
    in striptease, 165–166
raves, 311, 316–317, 320
reification, xix–xx
reproduction, regulation of, 66–70, 73–78
resistance, 87, 139–143
risk management through governance, xxx
risk society, 261, 290, xxx
Rohypnol, 313, 314, 317, 318–319, 320–321
Ross, Becki, 87, 146–175, xxix

S

Salutin, Marilyn, 168
Sayer, Derek, 97, 238, xxvi–xxviii
school systems
    guidelines, 35–36
    moral regulation, 21–22
    parents, complaints about, 19–20
    restrictive language policy, 26–27

science, social and political character of, 265–267
sex and sexuality
    see also heterosexuality; homosexuality
    and the Canadian nation, 171–172
    moralization of, 122–127
    mores of the 50s, 90–91
    "mothers of the race," 73–78
    "normal sexuality," 97, 99
    normalization, 122–127
    regulation of, 63–84
    sexualized marriages, 94
    social and historical construction, xxiii
    social regulation and, 88
    state-sanctioned "experts," 67, 68
    teenaged sexuality, 94, 99–100
    transformation of place of sex in North America, 93–94
    "undeserving" women, regulation of, 78–82
sex offenders, 294–295
sex-related offences, 123–124
sex workers
    feminist viewpoint, 148
    lives of, 147
    migrant, 172–173
    self-determination, 148
    stories of, 149
sexual discourses, 95
Sharpe, Robin, 285–303
Siegel, Ida, 25–27
Simmons, Christina, 93–94
Singh, Gurdit, 40, 54
Singh, Munshi, 55–58
single mothers
    housing concerns, 243
    moral regulation of, 237, 238–245
    spousal relationships, 251–252
    telephones and, 242
    violence against, 243–244
    and welfare anti-fraud measures, 249–255
    welfare changes, impact of, 236
    and welfare rate cuts, 241–245
    workfare, 245–249
Skipper, James, 168
slut, xi
Smith, Dorothy E., 88, 128–129, 148
the social, 88
social construction, 88, 263–264
Social Darwinists, xvi
social hygiene, 66–70
social organization of "backlash" against liberation, 278–280
social regulation
    forms of, xxv
    public/private distinction, 64–66, 82
    and sexuality, 88
    women, impact on, 83
The Souls of Black Folk (Dubois), xiv
Spencer, Herbert, xvi
Stencell, A.W., 168

368   INDEX

striptease
    African primitivism, 165
    anachronistic space, 166
    business of, 150
    and butch and femme bar culture, 169
    carnivals, 165–167
    dancer profiles, 157–158
    future of, 172–174
    history of, 148–149
    Hollywood and, 163
    homosexuality and, 168–171
    influences on, 162–164
    and moral reformers, 150–151
    occupational hazards, 160–162
    Orientalism, 166
    paradox, 171–172
    Penthouse Cabaret, 154–155
    as public morality problem, 152–155
    queer dimensions of, 148
    racism, 165–166
    transgenders, 170
    transsexual, 170
    unionization, 161, 162
    working conditions, 156–162
subject, 3, 88
subject positions, xxi
subjectivity, 98
Suicide (Durkheim), xxvi
syphilis, 70, 73–75
    see also venereal disease

T

Taylor Gaubatz, Kathlyn, 289
techniques of power, xxiv
teenaged sexuality, 94, 99–100
teleological, xi
Terry, Jennifer, 277, 280
Toronto Home and School Council
    boundaries, arguments over, 35–36
    Brown Home and School Club controversy, 29–32
    central premise of, 20
    conflict with principal, 32–35
    Duke Street School, 29
    Elizabeth Street/Hester Howe school controversy, 25–27
    "foreign" and working-class districts, 25–29
    formation of, 22
    French-language instruction, 29–32
    functions, 23–24
    historical context, 24
    John Ross Robertson School controversy, 32–35
    leadership, 22–23
Tracey, Lindalee, 171–172
transsexuals, 269–270
The Trouble with Normal (Adams), 89, 90–101

U

Urwin, Cathy, 96

V

Valverde, Mariana, 14, 106, 261, 306–325, xxix, xxxi
venereal disease
    in British Columbia, 70–73
    compulsory testing, 75–78
    gendered nature of anti-VD educational initiatives, 69–70
    historical case study, 63–84
    legal coercion, 78–82
    "mothers of the race," 73–78
    prostitution, suppression of, 81–82
    public/private distinction, 64–66
    reconceptualization of, 71–72
    scientific/medical model, 69
    shifting perspectives on, 67
    state intervention, changes in degree of, 68
    sterilization, 80
    "undeserving" women, regulation of, 78–82
von Krafft-Ebing, Richard, 93

W

Waldeck, R.C., 124
Walkowitz, Judith, 307
Weeks, Jeffrey, 276, 288
Weir, Lorna, 15
welfare system
    and capitalism, 239–240
    historical and national context, 236–238
    moral regulation, application of, 240
    welfare fraud, 249–255
    welfare rate cuts, 241–245
    workfare, 245–249
whiteness, as social location, xiv
Wolf, Anna, 115–116
women
    and anti-VD educational initiatives, 69–70, 72
    appearance, emphasis on, 8
    "deserving" *vs.* "undeserving," 72
    female principals, 32–35
    lesbians in the military, 132
    mothers. *See* mothers
    postwar stereotypes and myths, 108
    prenatal syphilis, 73–75
    reproduction, regulation of, 66–70, 73–78
    sex workers, lives as, 147
    "undeserving" women, regulation of, 78–82
    venereal diseases, 10–11
    violence against, 243–244
    violence and workfare placements, 248

Y

young offenders. *See* juvenile delinquents
Youthful Offenders Act (1894), 13